D0508342

NETSCAPE & HTML
eXPLORER

Urban A. LeJeune

with Jeff Duntemann

Publisher	*Keith Weiskamp*
Editor	*Jeff Duntemann*
Proofreader	*Diane Green Cook*
Cover Design	*Gary Smith*
Interior Design	*Bradley Grannis*
Layout Production	*Jenni Aloi and Michelle Stroup*
Publicist	*Shannon Bounds*
Indexer	*Diane Green Cook*

Distributed to the book trade by IDG Books Worldwide, Inc.

Library of Congress Cataloging-in-Publication Data

LeJeune, Urban A.
Netscape & HTML Explorer / Urban A. LeJeune with Jeff Duntemann
p. cm.
Includes Index
ISBN 1-883577-57-8 : $39.99

Printed in the United States of America

10 9 8 7 6 5 4 3 2

CONTENTS

Introduction

I guess I got lucky. My introduction to the Internet came at the hands of Bob Smith, founder and president of Qualitas, Inc., and one of the most brilliant men currently active in our industry. Bob may have been borderline annoyed at me for not getting on the Internet sooner—or maybe he just wanted to be able to send me e-mail without having to go through CompuServe. Regardless, Bob came visiting one night with his beautiful wife Mary, and while the ladies were chatting after supper he hauled me back to my office and insisted that he dump some stuff on my hard disk. When the dust settled, I was several megabytes poorer in disk space, and staring at a raft of icons with peculiar names like Eudora, Trumpet, and...Netscape.

Then he logged into his account, and for the next hour I was dumbstruck at the wonders that came down the wire. Everything from FAQs to dissected frogs to pictures of comets striking Jupiter and Mick Jagger's lips. (The comet missed Mick's lips, fortunately for Stones fans.) Here was an entire universe displayable in real-time, the ridiculous and the sublime in one rowdy, effervescent mishmash that spanned the planet. I was hooked—and over the few months that followed, the Internet literally changed the way I did my research and my work in general.

Almost immediately we here at The Coriolis Group began a book/software project to bring this universe to our readers. It's taken a little longer than we'd hoped because, alas, this Internet stuff is a difficult business. It's not so difficult that it requires somebody with the brains of Bob Smith to pull it off—but it presents a very high "first rung" on the ladder. Anyone who's spent any time at all on the Internet can probably get a newcomer going in very little time—but a newcomer on his or her own is in an unenviable position. There are so many variables—different software, different modems, different providers—that it's virtually impossible to lay down a straightforward set of instructions and say, "This is your path to getting onto the Internet and the World Wide Web."

The World Wide Web isn't just another Internet-based information service. It's the first truly general effort to pull together all of the Internet into one unified, integrated whole. It's the fastest-growing aspect of the Internet, for the excellent reason that it provides a single place to stand, from which all of the rest of the Internet is easily accessible. And the best part about the Web is that it is a great universe for electronic publishing.

WHAT WE'RE TRYING TO DO

With that in mind, I'll spill the five goals for this book:

- To get you on the Internet as easily as possible
- To get you familiar with the Web and Netscape
- To show you how to use Netscape to access as much of the Internet as possible, including services like Gopher, FTP, and Usenet newsgroups
- To help you get published on the Web and create Web documents using HTML and incorporate text, images, sound, and even movies
- To teach you how to find things on the Web, including great publishing resources, and how to use Netscape and powerful search engines like Harvest

PUBLISHING MADE EASY

Of these five goals, the fourth and fifth are quite possibly the most exciting. Getting your "stuff" published on the Web is an exciting proposition, and the ease with which you can do so startles even an old computer hand like myself. Let me just point out a few facts about Web publishing. One of the easiest ways to make my point is by way of a comparison or two to print publishing, a trade that of course is near and dear to me. But it's also darned expensive. And hard work. And tough, slow going, especially for lengthy book projects like *Netscape & HTML Explorer.*

Case in point: We here at the Coriolis Group fret and haggle over where, when, and how much color to use in our magazine, *PC TECHNIQUES,* and in our books. The reason? Adding color to a publication is expensive. That's why, until *USA Today* broke ground, you rarely saw color in newspapers except for the Sunday comics and in ads. But when you publish on the Web, color costs nothing. Simply create or scan a color image so that you've got a good, high-resolution piece of artwork, then add the file to your Web page. It really is that simple. In fact, regardless of what you decide to publish on the Web, you can probably accomplish your publishing feats with little if any out-of-pocket costs to you. You don't have to buy paper, you don't have to pay typesetters, and you don't have to pay for any of the dozens of categories of overhead that we incur in the fun, but costly business of print publishing.

Another "problem" with print publishing is that the production process itself is lengthy—getting material from the manuscript stage to the bound book stage involves dozens of detailed steps in between—and when we've shipped cartons of a new book title to the bookstores, the book's content might as well be cast in stone. If we find errors or new, exciting material that we *really* want to add...well, we're out of luck—at least until the next printing or revision, which is often six months or longer following the first printing.

But when you publish on the Web, you've genuinely got an evolving, ongoing concern. At any time, you can make corrections, change the appearance of a Web page by adding artwork or rearranging the elements of the page, add new pages, add new links, update existing material.... The potential is almost limitless. And making changes can often be accomplished within minutes or hours.

And perhaps the most exciting part of Web publishing is the vast audience you gain with little or no marketing effort. What you publish today can be read tomorrow by a Web surfer in Russia or Finland or Japan or France or by anybody anywhere who has a Web browser and enough free time to go exploring.

The excitement for Web surfing and publishing is growing around the world, and we think that this book will give you the tools you need to "work the Web" like a pro. But I don't expect that you'll ever be really "satisfied" with what you find or with what you do on the Web. The Web is a lot like space in its vastness, and you'll always find some new region that you've yet to explore. Had Columbus set out on the Web in 1492, he'd still be sailing, because the ocean of knowledge, unlike something as trivial as the Atlantic, has no other side.

Jeff Duntemann

Acknowledgments

I would like to thank all who provided support, encouragement, and guidance during the course of this book's preparation. This list includes the legion of unknowing Internauts who provided information and training.

My deepest appreciation goes to my wife Pat. She provided invaluable support, encouragement, ideas, proofreading, and lots of coffee. This book wouldn't have happened without her love and effort.

Domenic Fuccillo, fuccillo@comp.uark.edu, sent for a copy of my newsletter *Artificial Stupidity* and replied with a list of things needing corrections. In quick succession he became my proofreader and friend. Thanks, Domenic.

Deep appreciation to Susan Karpati for her friendship, legal counseling, and all around sagacious advice.

Jon Lewis, jlewis@inorganic5.chem.ufl.edu, furnished Unix expertise by the gallon. He was of incredible help with CGI scripts and co-authored the CGI chapter. Maybe in the next edition we'll have an expanded CGI section with many of Jon's great scripts. Not only did Jon help, he did so with wit and charm.

Speaking of charm—net that is—my deepest thanks go to Craig Nordin, cnordin@charm.net. Craig told me at a Baltimore Internet Users group meeting, "I can have you up and running with a PPP account in an hour," and did it in a half-hour. Craig also bent a few rules to help me get going with CGI scripts. Charm Net remains one of the great Internet providers.

Thanks to Kathy Weldon, kweldon@acy.digex.net, for her help with many things.

To the gang at Corolis, what can I say? Jeff Duntemann, jeffd@coriolis.com—the Wizard of Scottsdale—stuck with me even after the original book grew into the 700+ page behometh you now hold in your hands. Marianne Krcma, surfer extraordinaire, found dozens of great resources regarding Web publishing and made numerous other contributions to the content and quality of this book. And a special thanks to publisher Keith Weiskamp, keithw@coriolis.com, who taught me that sleep isn't really all *that* important. Keith's never-ending suggestions and contributions have been a source of inspiration, as well as guidance along the path from project conceptualization to book reality. Thanks a million.

Thanks to the members of the South Jersey Internet Users Group for just "being there." Special thanks to members Ed Roworth, eroworth@acy.digex.net, who "walked me through many early HTML sessions, and Paula Jerome, pjerome@acy.digex.net, who was (and is) always willing to share a good idea and keep me honest with great questions.

Most of all I would like to thank each and every one of you who reads this book.

Tuckerton, NJ
May 1995

PART 1

Getting Started with the Web and Netscape

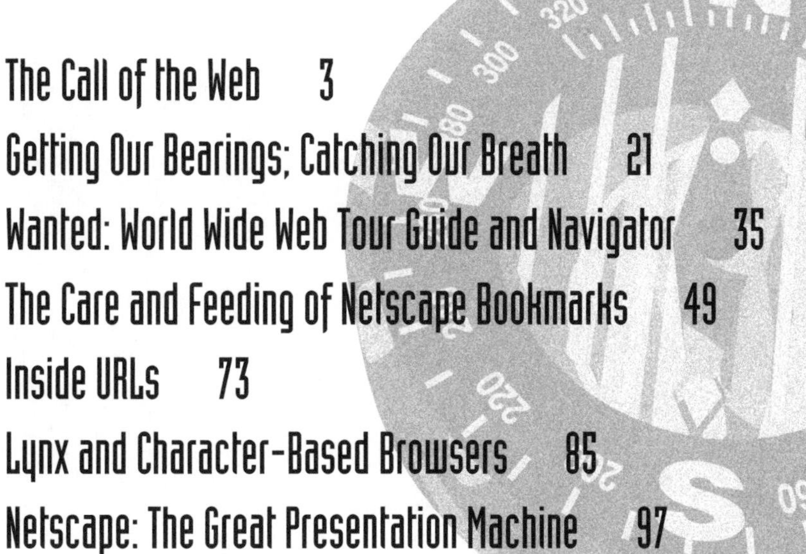

The Call of the Web

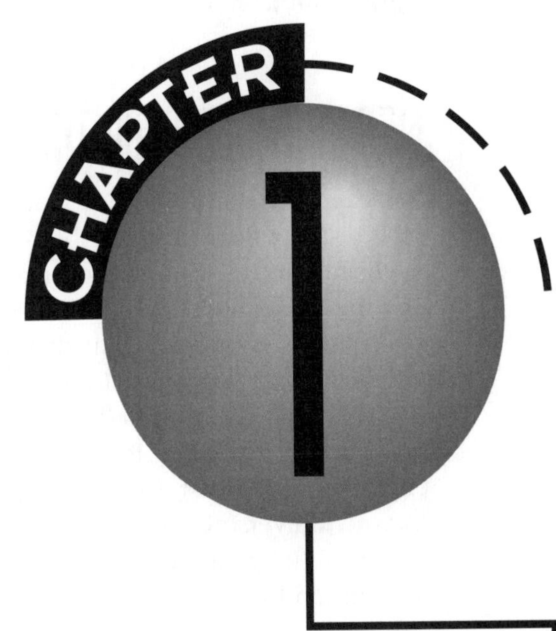

The World Wide Web—the great electronic publishing center of cyberspace—is waiting for you. All you need is a little knowledge and your powerful Web browser to explore its potential.

It's Saturday night. The dinner leftovers are stashed away and the Whirlpool is performing its magic on the dishes. The conversation turns to evening activities. We could go to one of several malls and drop a few bucks, or we could browse a mammoth bookstore containing a great technical section. If late-night hunger pangs strike, we could order a pizza from Pizza Hut. If we feel artistic, we could view artwork from the Louvre or the Vatican Exhibit at the Library of Congress. In a scientific vein, there is a movie of a frog dissection or one on collecting rocks. If we're feeling bizarre, there's always a stroll through "Bianca Troll's Smut Shack." Or we could forego any Internet adventures and go out! Naw.... Fire up your computer—World Wide Web, here we come!

WEB BROWSERS FOR THE REAL WORLD

Netscape and its siblings (Mosaic, Cello, WinWeb, InternetWorks, and many others) are called *browsers* because one of their main jobs is to help you navigate through the dizzying maze of information that we call the Internet and the World Wide Web. In fact, a key reason for the rapid rise in popularity of all these programs is that they helped tame the Internet by providing an interactive visual interface to the World Wide Web and other Internet services. The simple idea of a unified visual platform to be used in surfing all of Internet brought a lot of order to a world that was getting pretty chaotic, even for experienced Internet users. Trying to find specific information in the far-flung Internet universe is often an exercise in frustration. The Internet sometimes seems as though it were designed for a closed club of researchers and academicians, and in some ways, it was.

The visual Internet browser concept helped reorganize the Internet for the masses, largely by including a graphical user interface (GUI) that mere mortals could understand and use quickly and simply. Netscape and the other browsers are, for the most part, easy to use and increasingly easy to configure. And that's one of the goals of this book. I'll show you how to make the most of your Internet and World Wide Web travels using the powerful Netscape, and when the software bogs down in technical arcana, we'll help bring it back to a more real-world level—a level where most Internet users live (or at least would prefer to live).

This is an interesting time in the history of both the Internet and the Web. Usage is growing exponentially—new Web browsers are appearing (it seems) almost weekly, and new Web pages are being published daily. What was once a small club consisting of Mosaic and Cello (which appeared at almost the same time) is now a throng of competing products, some freeware, some shareware, some commercial. Each one is a little bit different, but from ten steps back they all have the same mission and they all operate in very much the same way.

Therefore, when I say "Netscape" in this book, I'm speaking primarily of the Web's most popular browser—but be aware that much of what can be said about Netscape can be said about the other browsers as well, including the original Mosaic. So if you're a Mosaic user (or you're using any of the more than two dozen browser choices now available), most of the same principles apply, and if the screens look a little different, I don't think that the differences will be too tough to figure out and place in context. In some cases, I'll actually show you a similar screen viewed on a different browser.

A year from now, who knows? Netscape may cease to be the King Browser, although I doubt it. But if you learn Netscape as a Web tool (and focus on how the Web works and how you can publish on the Web), you'll be building skills that will enable you to deal with any browser that may eventually come down the information pike.

USING THIS BOOK

This book is divided into four parts. The first part provides you with a hands-on exploration of the World Wide Web through Netscape. In the second part, you'll learn all about the techniques for publishing home pages and other Web pages with HTML. The third part covers a number of useful tips and techniques for gettting more done on the Web, including finding and retrieving files, searching for the best information, and customizing Netscape. The fourth part shows you how to install and configure the essential TCP/IP software through which Netscape (or any other browser) can access the Internet or the Web.

Explorations and Base Camp Briefings

You'll find two types of chapters along the way. The first (of which this chapter is one) I call an *exploration*—because that is simply what it is: A get-out-there-and-run Web surf-session that goes somewhere in Webspace and does something interesting. Each exploration, or small group of explorations, is followed by what I call a *base camp briefing*. Just like the explorers of old, we'll consolidate our gains periodically and talk about what we've seen so that we can put it all into context and (with some luck) keep it all straight in our heads.

There is, after all, a time for practice, and a time for theory—though we differ with history somewhat in thinking that practice comes first. Hey, when do you think you'll better appreciate the power of ancient technology: before you've ever seen the Great Pyramid of Cheops, or after you've journeyed to Egypt and climbed all the way to the top? It will be within the base camp briefings that the technical details encountered during the explorations are explained.

Each exploration in this book has a two-fold purpose: To take an interesting journey somewhere in the Internet universe, and in doing so illustrate a particular set of concepts and features of Netscape, HTML, and other Internet publishing tools. We have to warn you up front that the Internet changes hour by hour, and there's no guarantee that any particular journey we take will still be available by the time you read this. Internet sites come and go like TV series, except that how popular they are doesn't seem to have much connection with how long they live. (Some Internet sites, in fact, have proven so popular that their hosts have had to shut them down—but that's another story altogether.) Still, the techniques I demonstrate will be just as valid, and if you have to type a different URL (more on those later) and confront a different set of words and images, well, are you an explorer or what?

The first mission of this book is to *make* you an explorer, so that you can head out into the weird, wired wilderness solo and bring back the biggest game cyberspace has to offer. This will help you learn enough so that you can become your own Web publisher if you desire.

Waxing Your Web Surfboard

The fourth part of this book presents the details required to install Netscape and associated programs on your PC. Although it might seem strange to explain installation procedures later in the book rather than up front, there's a method behind this apparent madness: *You might never have to do the dirty work of installing Netscape or another Web browser from scratch.* More and more Internet service providers are simply handing their subscribers pre-configured diskettes full of Internet utilities, which need no more configuration than a simple Windows install. In fact, the fourth part provides information on how to install the Instant Internet software included on the companion CD-ROM so that you can get connected to the Internet in just a few minutes.

If you are one of those lucky subscribers, or if you're one of the many other fortunate users who are in a business or university setting with a system administrator who handles these details for you, your major interest will probably be to learn what you can do out on the Web rather than how to install Internet and Web browser software.

Connecting to the Internet

In any event, using a Windows-based Web browser requires that you connect directly to the Internet. However, the type of connection required to run a browser may not be as complex and costly as you've heard. If you have a conventional Unix shell account, a SLIP or PPP account might *not* be required to run your Web browser. The majority of people connected to the Internet through an account they purchase from a service provider are using a Unix shell account. Most students having dial-up Internet access also connect to a Unix host. If you have a Unix shell account, that's good news. If you also have some experience installing Windows software, you could have Netscape or something similar up and running in an hour or less, assuming you start from scratch, actually a few minutes if you use the software supplied on the companion CD-ROM. Again, if you want or need to install Netscape or Mosaic on your system before we start our explorations, you can skip to the last part of this book right now.

What You Should Know before We Begin

This book assumes that you understand the basics of using Windows applications as well as DOS directory structures. Great depth of knowledge is not required, but it would be helpful for you to understand basic Windows terminology, such as double-clicking, the desktop, menu bars, and the like. Understanding DOS path names, directories, and the wicked command-line prompt are desirable, as is the ability to use some form of plain text editor, such as DOS EDIT. (A great Window's Notepad replacement editor is supplied on the CD-ROM.) But you don't really need to have any great knowledge of the Internet or communications technology. Any Internet, Web, or Netscape-specific terms that we use will be defined on their first appearance in the book.

Starting Your Web Browser

It's time to get out and see the world via the World Wide Web. To do so, you'll need to start up your Web browser. Running your Windows-based Web browser is as simple as double-clicking on its icon, wherever it might be from Windows.

To start Netscape, click on the icon that looks something like this:

Note: For most of our explorations in this chapter, we'll be using the Netscape Web browser. If you have a different Web browser installed, such as Mosaic, you shouldn't have too much trouble following along.

The catch: Running your browser requires that your computer have the ability to "speak" *Transmission Control Protocol/Internet Protocol* (TCP/IP). TCP/IP is the language used when computer networks speak to each other. TCP/IP is in a very real sense the universal language of cyberspace. The Instant Internet software (also known as Chameleon) supplied on the companion CD-ROM speaks TCP/IP, so that with this software installed, your PC can be directly connected to the Internet and speak to the world's multitude of networks on their own terms. I'll explain in detail how this software is installed in the fourth part of this book.

To run any of the Windows-based Web browsers, you first must run Chameleon, Trumpet Winsock, or some other TCP/IP software (often called a *TCP/IP stack*), and use it to connect to your Internet provider. Exactly how this is done will vary depending on whom your provider is and what TCP/IP stack you're using. Your provider will have to tell you precisely how to log into their host system. It usually involves a password (or sometimes two passwords) and may also involve one or more numeric addresses that will need to be entered into one of the Chameleon configuration fields. I'll have more to say about this later in the book. In fact, I'll show you how to install the Instant Internet software so that you can easily get connected to the Internet and the World Wide Web. It's not really all that difficult—and once done, it doesn't have to be done again.

Running your browser will initiate some disk activity. With Netscape, you'll see continuous action within the Netscape logo in the upper-right corner of the Netscape window. If you haven't changed the default Netscape configuration, you will soon see the Netscape home page on your screen, as shown in Figure 1.1. If you are running Netscape through an Internet provider having its own home page (and assuming you received your copy of Netscape from them), you will most likely see your local home page when you run Netscape. (Figure 1.2 shows the NCSA Mosaic home page that is displayed if your browser is set to point to this popular home page.)

Starting Netscape at the Netscape Communications home page is not without its drawbacks. With hundreds of thousands of users downloading Netscape and accessing their home page all the time, the site is frequently too busy to accept additional connections. Strange error messages frequently appear when you try to bring back documents and images from Netscape. Although you might see a certain sentimental value in letting Netscape return to its birthplace, practicality should prevail. Another startup location may make a lot more sense, and I'll show you how to change your startup Web location in a little while.

A Client and a Browser

Netscape, shown displaying the Netscape Communications home page in Figure 1.1, is an Internet information browser and World Wide Web (or simply Web) client. A *client* is a program that receives information from another program

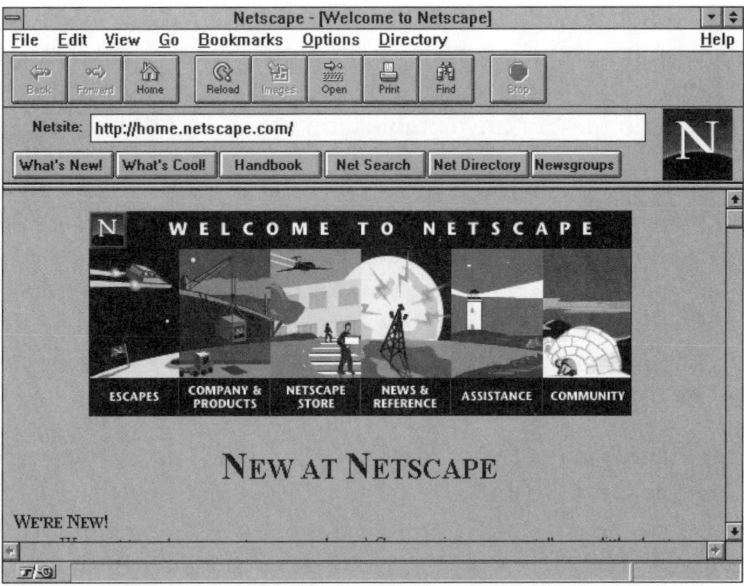

Figure 1.1 *Displaying Netscape Communication's home page with Netscape.*

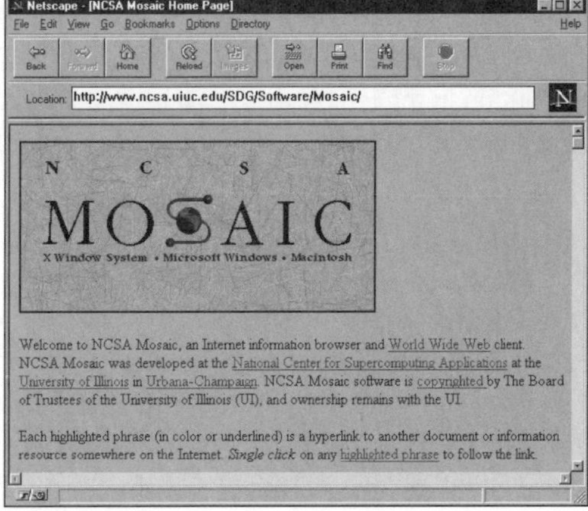

Figure 1.2 *The NCSA Mosaic home page.*

called a *server*, located somewhere else on a network. Documents readable from your browser may be located anywhere in the world. Assuming that there is in fact a connection between the client and the server, how far apart they are really doesn't make much difference.

Much as a word processor lets you view a document having special formatting features, such as boldface and underlining, Web browsers let you view

Internet-based documents having similar special formatting. Web documents may contain plain text, such as the text below the navigation image in the Netscape home page. The document may also contain other graphic images, video clips, sound files, or any combination of these and other goodies.

If graphic images do not display when you run Netscape, there is no need for concern. Someone may have set the Netscape menu item Options | Auto Load Images to off. Image display is frequently turned off to accelerate Netscape performance. Graphics take a long time to bring over your modem line, as you'll discover very early in your career as a Web explorer. Options | Auto Load Images is a *toggle;* that is, you click on it to change it to its alternate state much like the ON/OFF button on your TV set.

Turning off inline image display will result in a little "Image" icon appearing where a graphic image would normally be displayed. (Another likely reason that images may not display is that Netscape may not be able to locate a particular image. I'll tell you how to handle this in a later exploration.)

EXPLORER TIP

Manually Loading Images

If the Auto Load Images option is turned off and you want to display a specific image without turning the option back on, click on the Images button in the toolbar. Next, click on the Reload button from the toolbar in case the image doesn't appear.

The Netscape Desktop

If you're familiar with Windows applications, you will recognize most of the features of Netscape as shown in Figure 1.3. The top line, called the *title bar,* contains the title "Netscape - " plus the title contained in the viewed document enclosed within the "[ ]" bracket pair. The title of the application used in Figure 1.1 is "Welcome to Netscape," therefore the entire title is Netscape - [Welcome to Netscape]. The standard Windows control menu box appears on the left side of the title bar and the maximize and minimize buttons appear on the right side of the title bar.

The second line from the top contains the Netscape *menu bar.* The third line is the *toolbar,* which contains a series of icons that initiate specific commonly used features. Immediately below the toolbar is the *Uniform Resource Locator (URL)* area. A URL is a pointer to a Web document or service. I'll tell you everything you need to know about URLs in Chapter 3. The big "N" Netscape logo appears to the right of the combined toolbar and URL display area. When Netscape is doing anything requiring communication over the Internet, the logo becomes animated with the "N" icon flashing and changing shades of blue.

The bottom line is the *status line.* The status line gives us progress reports when information is being transferred, and it will also give us valuable information while reading a displayed page. In Netscape parlance, the *document viewing area* is the portion of the screen between the URL display area and the status line. Figure 1.3 shows a portion of the Netscape home page with the "Welcome" anchor underlined. If you select this anchor by pointing to it with your mouse, the URL for the selection will be displayed on the status line as shown in Figure 1.3. (More on anchors later.)

The right side of the document viewing area, and occasionally the bottom of the document viewing area, contains the familiar Windows scroll bars. A vertical scroll bar is included if the displayed document is longer than a single screen page. Likewise, a horizontal scroll bar is included only if the document is wider than a single screen. The displays of the toolbar, URL area, and status bar are user configurable and may not be displayed on your screen.

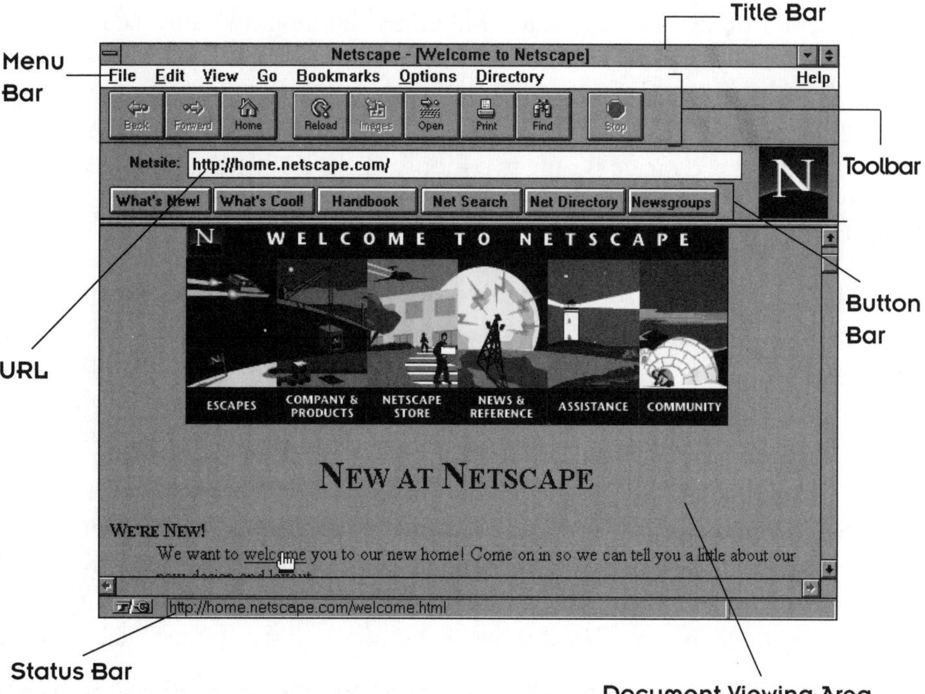

Figure 1.3 *Selecting an anchor on the Netscape home page.*

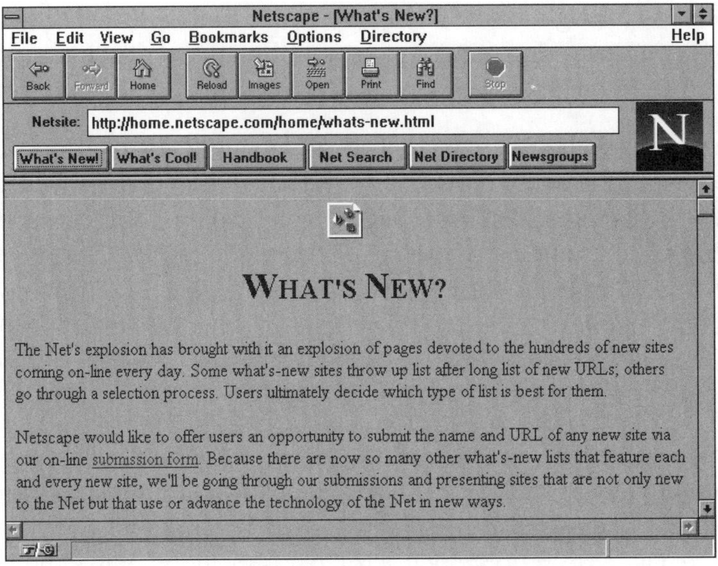

***Figure 1.4** The Netscape home page displayed with inline images turned off.*

Figure 1.4 shows another view of the Netscape home page. The graphic icon in the top center of the page indicates that either the Options | Auto Load Images option has been turned off (unchecked), or that the image was not received. Although the non-image mode of Netscape is not as pretty or as fun as Netscape displaying brightly colored graphical images, it is substantially faster. Additionally, a non-displayed image is only two mouse clicks away from being displayed.

Web Pages

Netscape is a Web browser designed to display hypermedia documents more commonly called *pages*. Hypermedia pages are created and stored in a format called *Hyper Text Markup Language (HTML)*. Netscape, and other Web browsers, may also display Gopher menus and documents, FTP directories and files, and many other formats. Netscape also has built-in support for newsgroups and other Internet services such as sending e-mail.

The choice of the term "page" for a Web document was unfortunate. Most computer users associate a page with what they see on the screen. Such is not the case with most web "pages," which may be quite long. Substitute the word "document" in your head when you see the term "page," at least until the whole Web world begins to make sense. You may move through the page, as you would with any other Windows document, by moving the scroll bar pointer with the mouse or by pressing the Page Up or Page Down keys, depending upon which direction you wish to travel.

Taking Your Browser for a Spin

In this project, we'll start Netscape and test some hyperlinks. Using links, we'll take you to a popular Web site called Yahoo.

Depending upon the version of Netscape that you're using, and the settings of your configuration file (netscape.ini), you'll see that certain areas of the text in the document view area are underlined, have a different color, or both. These items are *links* (technically, *hyperlinks*) to other resources. These other resources may be textual or they may contain multimedia information. The purpose of these document links is to provide a non-linear way for you to access information. Gone are the days of sequential processing and presentation. Now you can go where your interests lead you.

A hyperlink has two components: an *anchor* and a *reference*. The anchor is the displayed screen presence of the link (which may be either text or graphics) whereas the reference is the full network URL of the document or service. You see the anchor whenever the page is displayed, but the reference remains hidden. When the cursor strays over an anchor, its reference can be read in the status line at the bottom of the screen. When you click on a displayed anchor, Netscape will go out on the Web, fetch, and automatically display the document, play the audio, show the movie, or display the graphic, depending on the type of file fetched from the remote source.

Testing a Link

The row just under the Netsite: field (see Figure 1.3) contains a series of Directory buttons. Click on the button labeled Net Directory. Use your mouse to move the pointer across the screen. Notice that the shape of the pointer changes from an arrowhead to a pointing hand as you move to an anchor link area. To see how the hand works, place the cursor in the Yahoo area of the Net Directory page. As you move the mouse pointer into the anchor area, notice that the status line will show the complete URL link information—the reference portion—of the anchor to which the mouse is pointing. Activate the link with a single click on the underlined anchor area. Clicking on the anchor will start the process of retrieving the remote document and displaying it on

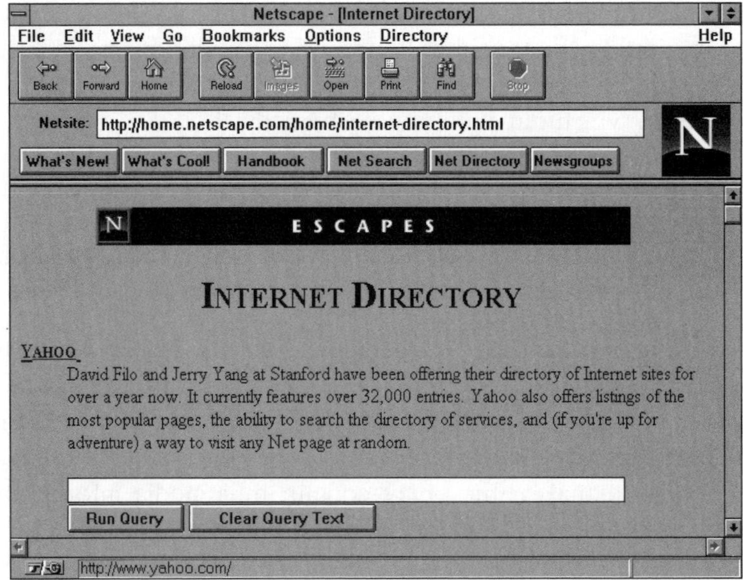

***Figure 1.5** Selecting the Yahoo anchor to select the Yahoo Web site.*

your monitor. Figure 1.5 shows the Netscape display after moving to the Yahoo anchor. Click on the anchor. The big "N" will start to flash, the Stop button will turn red, and away we go.

With a single mouse click we have connected to another Web site and transferred the hypermedia document that was located in California and displayed it on the screen. The document could have been located anywhere in the world. Figure 1.6 shows the Yahoo document entitled "Yahoo."

The Yahoo page is the greatest resource on the Web. It contains pointers to almost 40,000 sites, and seemingly grows by the minute. As you can see from Figure 1.6, the Web pointers are arranged by category. Additionally, this massive database can be searched. We'll spend a lot more time with our friend Yahoo in later explorations.

You may, of course, start to follow the links that appear on the Yahoo page. You might undertake a little side-exploration of your own and do just that. Again notice that the "Computers" anchor has been selected and its URL is displayed on the status line.

Long distance communication is thrilling. I've been a ham radio operator (W2DEC) since high school, and I have talked to hams in every country of the world, including some that I'd be hard pressed to justify as countries to non-

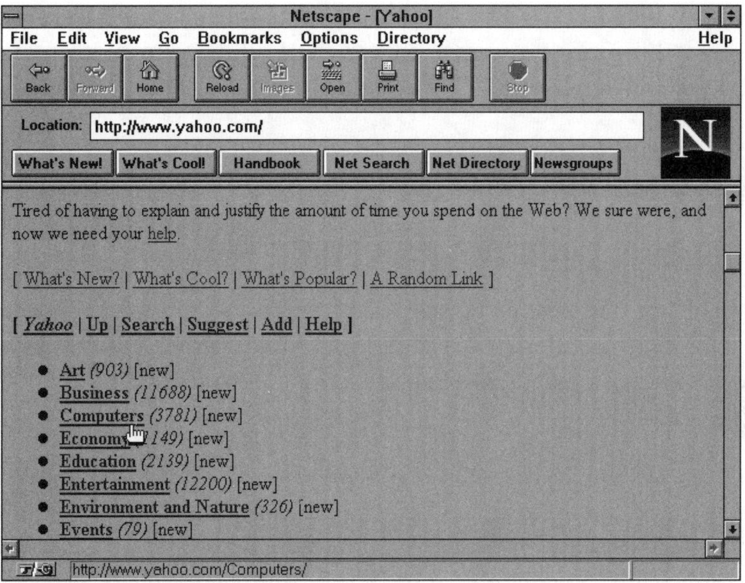

***Figure 1.6** Exploring the Yahoo home page.*

hams. For me, the thrill of communications has never waned. I now get excited when I connect to a web site in some exotic corner of the earth like mainland China. I also collect e-mail messages addressed to me from different countries, and I become borderline ecstatic when I get a message from a new country. I currently have personal messages from almost 100 different countries, which gives you some idea of Internet's scope.

Heading Home

Upon finishing an exploration, we typically want to return to our starting point and brag a little about our recent discoveries. Netscape makes it easy. The icon bar has a little stick house icon that, when clicked, returns us to the home page, the first location visited when we started the current session of Netscape. As you might expect, we could also go directly to any intermediate stop in one step. We will explore pointing Netscape to a specific location and using "bookmarks" in Chapter 3, *Wanted: World Wide Web Navigator and Tour Guide.*

We could also backtrack one step at a time, because Netscape has left a trail of invisible bread crumbs for us to follow. Clicking on the left pointer icon in the toolbar will take us back to the document that immediately preceded the document currently being displayed. Once we have moved backward, we may click the right pointer icon to move forward again by one document. Keep in mind that the two arrow icons can only be used to navigate along a trail you've already blazed; if you're at either end of the trail, the arrow pointing beyond trail's end will not work! Figure 1.7 shows the Back, Forward, and Home icons.

NETSCAPE CONFIGURATION

Netscape is highly configurable and customizable. But note that, in this context, we're talking about simple customization to satisfy your personal preferences regarding the way Netscape appears and services your requests. The more technical installation and configuration material (along with information on how to configure other browsers such as Mosaic) will be left for the last part of this book.

Frequently changed user preferences may be modified using the Options menu. (I'll have much more to say on the Options menu in later explorations.) Most of Netscape's run-time parameters are contained in a file named netscape.ini that is most likely stored in your c:\windows directory.

netscape.ini is a simple text file, albeit a pretty big one. You can inspect and edit it with any text editor, including Windows Notepad or DOS EDIT. Most of what it contains is of little interest to you, the user. For the most part, netscape.ini

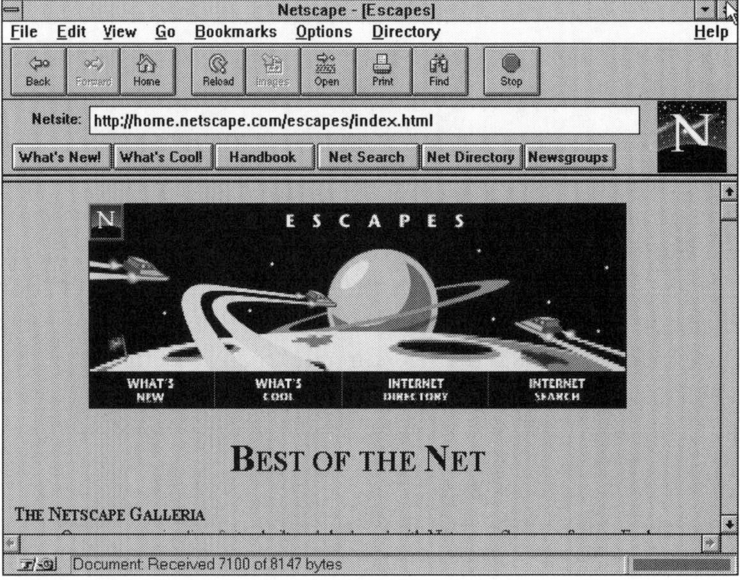

***Figure 1.7** Using the Netscape navigation buttons.*

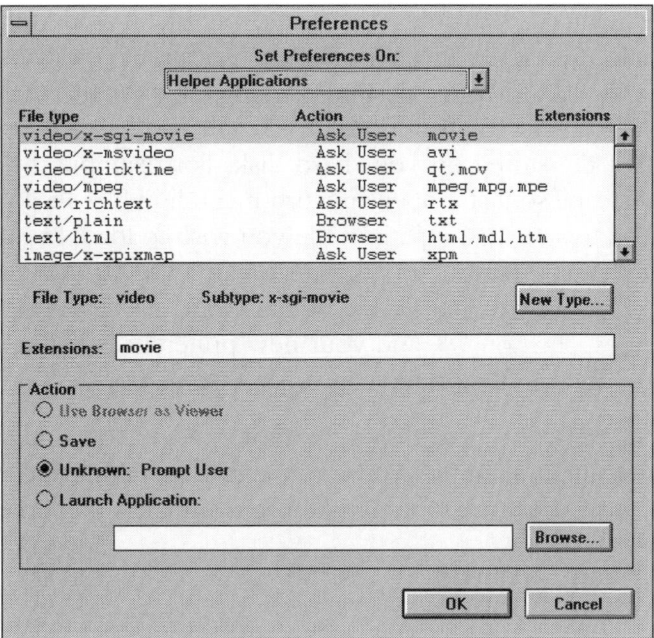

***Figure 1.8** Using Netscape's Preferences dialog to customize Netscape.*

can be transparently modified by executing the Options | Preferences menu sequence. Take a look at Figure 1.8 and you'll get a better idea of some of the information that is changeable from the Preferences dialog box.

As initially received from Netscape, the browser is configured to display the Netscape home page at the start of every session. After using Netscape a few times, you may want to have the program start without displaying any home page. Netscape will load much more quickly if it doesn't have to go out into cyberspace and fetch a home page. I prefer to load my own menu for my local hard disk when Netscape starts. My menu, urb-menu.htm, is contained on the enclosed CD-ROM. Directions on how to install the menu, or any other HTML document for your local hard drive, will be covered in a later exploration.

As I've already indicated, Netscape's home page is one of the busiest sites on the Internet. Let's look at two alternative possibilities: Not displaying a home page, or displaying a home page other than the Netscape's.

Activate the sequence Options | Preferences. If you do not have "Styles" displayed in the top text field, click on the down-pointing arrow and click on the "Styles" selection. If you would like to have Netscape start with a blank page, click on the "Start With Blank Page" radio button. If you want to start at another location, click on the "Home Page Location:" radio button. Then, simply enter the URL for the desired site. (Remember that the URL is the address of the location you want to go.) You can also set up Netscape so that it first opens a file stored on your hard disk. For example, I've set up my version of Netscape so that it opens my urb-menu.htm file. To do this on your own, you need to specify the path of file you wish to load. In doing this you must include three "/" slashes, not the customary two. Also note that they are Unix-like forward slashes, not DOS-type backward slashes. After making any desired changes, click on OK and your new preferences will take effect the next time you click on the home icon or start Netscape.

When started, Netscape may display graphic images, depending upon the setting of the configuration file. You can toggle this option from the Netscape menu at any time using the Options | Auto Load Images menu item.

A PEEK AT THE FUTURE

Many people have predicted that Web browsers like Netscape will change the way we use the Internet. Of that there can be no question. Taking the prognostication just a bit further, I believe that the World Wide Web will change the very way people live. Our society, and our educational system, has in the past highly rewarded people who could perform repetitive tasks. The economy of the United States, as well as that of most other industrialized countries, has switched from being chiefly product-based to being service-based. In other words, many of us no longer make things so much as we *do* things. Service, in the final analysis, is information—and the amount of available information is doubling every two years.

Gone are the days of high marks for memorizing a bunch of factual information or techniques and spitting them out on command. Adaptability to emerging technology and informational sources will be the new hallmark. Creative problem solvers will be a highly sought-after commodity. I hope our educational system recognizes skills are being taught that, increasingly, no one wants.

I think history will confirm my conviction that the World Wide Web is the future of the Internet, and that browsers like Netscape will become required applications of the Internet-based Information Superhighway. The emergence of the Web has already ushered in the era of online information for the masses.

LET'S REVIEW

Time for a quick review.

Netscape and other programs, such as Mosaic, are Web browsers designed to display the hyper text documents that comprise the Web. Web browsers and the Web itself are often confused as being the same thing—which they are not. Think of the Web as a conceptual world-spanning hyper text document, and Netscape and other Web browsers are tools for viewing and navigating that document. A hyper text document consists of multiple text files connected by hyperlinks (generally shortened to "links") that are pointers to other documents stored elsewhere on the Internet. The Web may be read non-sequentially by following links as need or interest requires.

Your Web browser can be launched by double-clicking on its icon. If you are running Netscape, you'll automatically see the Netscape Communication's home page when Netscape starts (unless you have modified your Preferences).

Links consist of a visible anchor, which is a text string or an image, and a reference, which is the actual pointer to another component of the larger hyper text document. The shape of the mouse pointer will change from an arrowhead to a pointing hand as it moves over an anchor. The URL of the link under the pointer will simultaneously be displayed by your Web browser. In Netscape, the URL is displayed in the status line. Clicking once on the anchor will cause your browser to load and display the file pointed to by the link reference.

Movement within a document can be accomplished a line at a time using the up or down arrow keys, or a page at a time using the Page Up and Page Down keys. Alternatively, the scroll bars will navigate through the document as well.

Clicking on the home page icon (the "stick house") will re-display the home page that started the session. Unless Netscape was modified by you, another user, or by your Internet provider, the defined home page will be the Netscape Communication's Welcome home page. The left and right arrow icons allow navigation over a hyper text path that has been traveled at least once.

Getting Our Bearings; Catching Our Breath

Before making any further explorations on the Web, you'll want to read this chapter to understand where Netscape and the Web have come from and where they are headed.

Now that you've seen Netscape in action and had a little taste test of the Web, you're probably anxious to spend the rest of the day surfing the Web. Once you get started, you'll get so consumed by the seductive power of the Web that you won't want to return to the day to day world of spreadsheets or tax programs. But before we get into the fun explorations such as searching the Web, creating home pages with HTML, and creating multimedia publishing projects, we need to get some concepts and terminology under our belts.

Many book authors like to tell you a lot more than you want (or need) to know about a particular topic. I'll try not to be guilty of this sin. However, one lingering fact remains: We are dealing with a sometimes highly technical topic—to wit, computer networks and very sophisticated software. When you run Netscape, it sometimes seems to have a mind of its own. How much detail do you need to become a Netscape user who is able to surf the Web with ease and eventually learn the art of Web publishing?

Which technical details of Internet do we cover and which do we leave out? Well, the answer lies somewhere between what I know and what you need to know to become a contented Web surfer and publisher. I promise to find the right mix. If it's really important, I'll include it in one of our base camp briefings, of which this is the first. If it's nice to know, but not a matter of urgent need, I'll place it someplace else, probably in an appendix.

Now that the campfire is ablaze and I've struck a jargon deal with you, let's get down to business.

A BRIEF HISTORY OF NETSCAPE AND THE WORLD WIDE WEB

Every age has a major development that ushers in a new way of living and thinking. The invention of the printing press, the commercialization of electricity, and the introduction of the automobile come to mind as such landmark developments. I believe future historians will record that the introduction of the World Wide Web and browsers like Netscape and Mosaic were the seminal developments ushering in the age of near-instantaneous information search and delivery for the masses.

Netscape, and its predecessor Mosaic, were designed to satisfy the need to provide a friendly interface for accessing organized information on the Internet. The Internet has always contained an incredible amount of information. However, it was almost impossible to find anything of value except by word of mouth. Before the advent of the Web and Gopher (a menu-oriented information finding utility), the organization of information on the Internet might charitably be described as chaotic. There were few real lists of information, and organization was a concept that didn't seem to apply. Someone would send you an e-mail message extolling the features of a new program, or a new source of data, and away you'd go to find it. Sometimes you would be successful, but other times the object of the quest had vanished in cyberspace before you reached it. As a result, frustration was the order of the day.

It's been a long road from there to here. Let's take a look at the route.

In the Beginning: FTP

The Internet has always been a vast depository of information, assistance, and software. The problem, until a few years ago, was that people couldn't find what they wanted. Although no one person knows where everything is, the gap between knowing something might be "out there" and actually finding where it is has narrowed considerably.

Almost from the beginning, a person using the Internet could transfer files between networks. Cooperating networks would agree upon a protocol allowing file transfer; this protocol eventually came to be called *FTP (File Transfer Protocol)*. Internet insiders often user lowercase for the FTP acronym, so if you see "ftp" in the literature (this book and others) it's not a typo—just a holdover from Unix, where somebody once decided that capital letters were declassé. A *protocol* is simply a set of rules governing digital communication, specifying certain commands, appropriate responses, and what these commands and their responses mean in different contexts. Most human interaction involves protocols of one sort or another. An auction is a fairly simple protocol for both establishing a market price and making a sale, all at the same time. You might even say that the protocol for this book is the English language. The Internet is really a catalog of protocols governing how various sorts of client programs interact with their appropriate server programs in the cause of orderly location and retrieval of data.

You may have already used FTP to get a file, or program, from a distant site. If you haven't, don't worry. You can use Netscape or another browser to retrieve files from FTP servers, even if you don't know a thing about FTP. (That's one of the seriously cool things about Netscape.) But one problem that occurs frequently is that you know file abc.xyz is exactly what you need—but you don't know where it resides. How can you find it?

Hello, Archie

Archie was the first major attempt to organize Internet information that was otherwise scattered with no apparent pattern. If there was an organizational model in the storage of files reachable via FTP, it certainly escaped most mere mortals. A group of dedicated people at McGill University in Canada designed Archie, and the transition from Internet chaos to organization was launched.

An Archie server periodically searches about 1,300 FTP server sites and builds a database of over 3 million records containing file names and other information associated with these files, such as the home of the FTP server and the directory in which the file resides. You can then use an Archie client program to query the Archie database about the location of file abc.xyz. We will use Netscape to find and then retrieve a remote file through FTP in a later exploration.

While Archie was a big step forward, it didn't fully solve the problem. If you knew the name of the file, you were home free, but if you didn't know the name, you were out of luck, since Archie doesn't know about file contents, only file *names*. If you don't know that file n16e11b3.exe is the latest Windows version of Netscape and its associated support files, you're clueless as to Netscape's whereabouts.

Giving Teeth to the Internet: Gopher

About three years ago (a lifetime in Internet terms), two ambitious attempts to organize Internet information were independently initiated. One, called Gopher, began its life at the University of Minnesota. The second, called the World Wide Web (or simply the Web), emerged from the European Laboratory for Particle Physics (CERN, the French acronym) in Geneva, Switzerland.

Both Gopher and the Web (in fact, most Internet services of any kind) are *client/server* systems requiring a client program on the user side, and a server program somewhere on a "big" system where the "served" information actually resides. The client and server programs engage in a dialog over the Net, usually defining what information the client's user wants. The server then serves up the requested information in a form that the client can in turn present to its user.

Gopher is a hierarchical menu-structured organizational technique, defined in a set of protocols for client and server software. Cooperating Gopher sites organize their information in the format defined by the Gopher protocols and supported by Gopher server software. The result is an intuitive interface that yields as much information and detail as the organizers desired. The first Gopher site was brought online in 1992.

Most Web browsers (including Netscape and Mosaic) understand the Gopher data protocols, and Gopher sites can be accessed effectively from those browsers. Gopher is thus extremely useful and will be the subject of several future explorations.

The World Wide Web

Now, the biggie. The Web is a system for organizing, transmitting, and retrieving information of all types. As mentioned earlier, the Web was originally conceived and developed at the CERN laboratory in Switzerland.

Central to the idea and organization of the Web are *hypermedia documents*. A hypermedia document is one that may be traversed in a non-linear fashion, via links from one place in a document to another, or between entirely separate document files. A hypermedia document may contain pointers to another hypermedia document, which also may contain a pointer to another document, and so on. Another hallmark of hypermedia documents is that they may contain non-textual material as well as plain text. An example of non-textual material could be a graphic image, a sound file, or a video clip.

So seamless are the links between different hypermedia documents that users literally follow these pathways all over the world without ever knowing the actual location of the information—unless choosing to stop to ask. Although these documents are truly hypermedia, since they may contain various information, they are almost always called hyper text documents in the literature. In this book, I will use the term "hyper text." But remember that Web-based documents are always hypermedia in nature.

We saw an example of non-linear reading of a hyper text document in the first exploration in Chapter 1. When we clicked on the Net Directory button we arrived at Netscape's "Escapes" page. The first selection was the "Yahoo" link. If we select that link, we are connected to the great Yahoo database. This site has almost 40,000 Web links arranged by categories. An added bonus is that the database is searchable. (There is an entire future exploration devoted to searching.) If we see something we like, we just click on the anchor link to retrieve the information. Think what a breakthrough this concept represents! If we are reading a book and find a topic on which we need additional information, we must first mark our current spot, then go to the index and find the location within the book of the desired information. Next we must go to the selected supportive information, and finally, go back to our original starting point. The search process is even more difficult if the desired level of detail is not contained in the same book.

Now look at the wonderful capability provided by Netscape: When we desire additional information on a topic, we click on the link that points to the supplemental knowledge, read the more detailed information, maybe even going down multiple levels for progressively more detailed information, and then automatically return to the original starting point. The additional information may reside halfway around the world or in the next room. Where it actually exists simply doesn't matter.

The Web, along with hypermedia servers and clients, predates Netscape and even Mosaic. The first browser developed at CERN was a character-based (that is, non-graphic) implementation, and in fact we'll be examining that browser shortly during an exploration. CERN wasn't being lazy for doing text-only processing. Virtually all Internet-related programs were character-based until very recently. The reasoning was strictly practical because almost everyone accessing the Internet was using a non-graphical (text-based) terminal over a relatively slow serial line.

That character-based Web browser from CERN was not a lot of fun to use and tended to be cryptic in operation. As a consequence, few network administrators put their information into Web-browsable format until the official introduction of Mosaic in early 1993. Upon Mosaic's release, there were perhaps 100 Web servers in the world. Since that day, there has been an explosion in the number of Web server sites and in the volume of information contained on those sites. Web-related Internet traffic has been growing at a rate of 25 to 35 percent per month! To put these percentages into perspective, Web traffic is doubling every three months or less. Talk about a growth industry! Based upon a recent article in *The New York Times*, it's interesting to note, despite Mosaic's early start, Netscape is now the browser of choice for about 75 percent of all Internet browser users.

Birth of a Browser

Development of Mosaic took place at the National Center for Supercomputing Applications (NCSA) located at the University of Illinois, Urbana-Champaign. Federal grants were the primary source of Mosaic project funding. As a tip of the hat to this government largess, NCSA Mosaic, while copyrighted by the university, is distributed without cost. Almost twenty companies have licensed Mosaic's underlying technology and source code, and derivative commercial versions are already appearing.

In addition to the development and enhancement of Mosaic, NCSA also maintains an up-to-date group of documents. The "NCSA What's New" page is one of the most frequently accessed pages in all Web-land. We will be showing you how to load a URL (Web document address) shortly, but in case you already know the technique, the URL for NCSA's "What's New" page is:

```
http://www.ncsa.uiuc.edu/SDG/Software/Mosaic/Docs/whats-new.html
```

The URL for the NCSA home page is:

```
http://www.ncsa.uiuc.edu/General/NCSAHome.html
```

Most Netscape sessions start at the Netscape home page, as we explained in Chapter 1. Any location that you desire may become your starting point by changing one field in your Netscape preference menu. Changing the starting location is actually a good idea since it can be difficult connecting to Netscape because of the high demands placed upon their computer. If you get strange error messages when starting your Netscape session, it may be the system's convoluted way of telling you that you are receiving a Netscape busy signal. In addition, it seems a terrible waste of network resources to see the same page every time you start a session.

Both Netscape and Gopher are frequently touted as do-all to end-all data management clients. In actuality, they are just the glamorous and highly visible pointers to information resources stored on the Internet. The genuinely incredible part of the Web and *gopherspace* (the system of menus that the Gopher client understands) is the underlying organization of the information. In less than two years, informational structure has replaced chaos. Geometric user growth has been the result of information organization coupled with user-friendly access, making access easy and the results worth the (minimal) effort.

The astonishing growth also reflects the evolving profile of the average Internet user. Three years ago, it was almost impossible for someone who was not an academic, corporate researcher, or government contractor to get an Internet account. Indeed, as recently as the summer of 1992, I taught at a college that would not generally give its own students Internet accounts. The new wave of Internet users tend to be less sophisticated in use of the arcane ways of the old guard and their beloved Unix command-line prompts. Mastering the difficulty of information access used to be a badge of honor. The new breed of user has demanded the same ease of Internet accessibility and user friendliness that they have come to expect from their windowed Mac and PC environments. When time is at a premium, the value of information becomes a function of the ease with which it may be obtained. Long live the new breed!

Not only has the number of Web and Gopher servers increased geometrically, the amount of information stored on most of these servers has also increased as fast or faster. To give you some idea of the rapid growth of graphical Web browsers, virtually all Internet books bearing a 1993 copyright don't even mention Mosaic! Another amazing piece of information (at least to an old-timer like me) is that anyone on the Internet for more than two years has been on the Net longer than 95 percent of the people currently using it.

An Explosion of Browsers

Although Netscape and Mosaic get most of the Web browser glory, it's only fair to point out that the first release of Mosaic and the first release of Cello (a browser from Cornell University) were very nearly simultaneous. Cello was a more modest effort, but it does many of the same things that Mosaic does.

After those two browsers proved the concept, the deluge began. NCSA licensed the Mosaic source code through a company called Spyglass, and several firms began developing commercial offshoots of Mosaic. The best-known of these is AirMosaic, which became part of a suite of Internet client utilities offered as a commercial product from Spry, Inc.

Both Netscape and Mosaic require a fair amount of memory (ideally, at least 8MB) to function well. To cater to people whose machines have only 4MB of memory, the WinWeb browser was released in mid-1994. Both Cello and WinWeb were created to be tight with system resources, although they lack some of the functionality of "bigger" browsers like Netscape and Mosaic.

Mark Andreesen, the NCSA lead programmer who created the original Mosaic program, left the University of Illinois in the spring of 1994 and helped to start a firm, Netscape Communications, to capitalize on the emerging market for Web servers and browsers. In a remarkably short period of time, the Netscape browser appeared, with more speed and more features than recent versions of Mosaic while requiring neither more memory nor the awkward Win32s subsystem. Nicknamed "Mozilla" (after Netscape's cartoon dinosaur mascot), the browser is distributed free (to employees of academic institutions, non-profit organizations, and for evaluation purposes) from Netscape's Web site. According to current reports, Netscape's main product line will be a number of Web servers with necessary commerce-oriented features like encrypted credit card transfer and digital cash transfer. With features like secure credit card shopping built into the Netscape Web browser, Andreesen and Co. (frequently called NCSA West on the Web) are hoping that broad free distribution of the browser will generate demand for their big-money Web server line.

A recent player is InternetWorks, a $99 Web browser designed from the outset as a one-stop entry point for all Internet services, including NetNews, e-mail, Gopher, ftp, chat, and (of course) the World Wide Web. InternetWorks is also available in free form with some of its features disabled. More and more products that began simply as Web browsers will doubtless add more features until they all begin to converge on the InternetWorks ideal of *one place to stand for all Internet access.* That is, one program to run, not a dozen.

Prodigy is already offering a Web browser as we go to press. America Online and CompuServe should have their Web browsers available by the time you are reading this chapter.

And at the heart of it, whatever its name may be, that one program will be a Web browser.

Where in the World Are We Going?

The past has shown us a world of explosive growth for the Web and interactive browsers. So what's in store for the future? New operating systems like Windows 95 are being designed to have Web browsers built right in. Even popular Windows programs like Word for Windows are being updated to support Web browsing.

New software applications like the Coriolis Group's NetSeeker™ are designed to give you another glimpse of the future. These applications, called *intelligent agents*, are designed to sneak out to the Web as you are performing other tasks and locate software and other goodies for you. Then, they bring located software back to your computer and install it. As the Web grows in complexity and the day to day traffic increases, these types of intelligent agents will certainty become much more valuable.

UNIFORM RESOURCE LOCATORS

When viewing a web document with Netscape or any other Web browser, the links (displayed underlined and in blue under Windows) contain hidden information pointing to the actual location and type of data at the far end of the link. This information is contained in something called a *Uniform Resource Locator*, or URL. I showed the Netscape home page in Chapter 1 (see Figure 1.1). The figure has the URL for this document displayed in the URL viewing area, which is below the line containing the toolbar with the Netscape icons. We will shortly be exploring how to enter URLs so that we can retrieve and read a specific hyper text document. By entering the following URL

```
http://home.netscape.com/home/welcome.html
```

we would bring back the Netscape home page. We will be dealing with URLs in detail during a subsequent exploration, but for now let's look at a few fundamentals.

A URL has several components. The first part tells the browser what type of document is being requested. This is the "http://" prefix in the URL shown above. The acronym "http" stands for *hyper text transmission protocol.* It tells your client what type of document to expect and how to interpret the data that comes back. Other common prefixes include "gopher://" and "ftp://", which represent Gopher locations and FTP sites.

The second part of the URL ("home.netscape.com" in this example) is the Internet address. This address contains several levels. The "com" part in this example is called the *top-level domain* and indicates that the site is a commercial organization. The "netscape" portion is commonly called the *domain*, and indicates that this site is Netscape Communications located in California. The "home" portion indicates a specific network at the Netscape domain, the Web network at Netscape Communications.

The next portion of the URL, "/home" in this example, is the *directory structure* on which the target file resides. Last, but certainly not least, is the actual file name of the target file, in our example, "welcome.html". (Note that this is not always an 8-character DOS file name with a 3-character extension but may be a Unix file name, which can pretty much be as long as it pleases.) The "html" extension is the convention for a file that is in Web standard hyper text. The acronym *HTML* stands for *Hyper Text Markup Language*, and it is a document standard allowing fancy formatted hypermedia text to be expressed in plain text characters.

We will be exploring URLs throughout this book as Netscape leads us into various type of documents and Internet services. Some of these services are FTP and Telnet. For now, let's digest this introduction to URLs.

HYPER TEXT MARKUP LANGUAGE (HTML)

Although it will be a good while before we start to develop our own hyper text documents, let's take a peek ahead. By doing so, you'll have a much better idea how hyper text links work. Hypertext might seem like magic, but it's really little more than some carefully placed formatting and linking codes within an ordinary text document—nothing mysterious at all.

We'll examine a portion of the Netscape home page, which is stored as the file welcome.html on the Netscape Web server. In future explorations, we'll actually bring some of these documents home to roost on our PCs. We'll change some of the reference pointers so that frequently accessed documents can reside on our PCs. If we load these documents from copies stored locally on our own hard disks, rather than fetching them from their remote home, we'll save both network bandwidth and the amount of time it takes Netscape to display them.

Let's get a taste of HTML documents by looking at a small portion of the Netscape home page file. Have Netscape display its home page, or look back to Chapter 1's Figure 1.1, as you examine the following HTML fragments.

Click on the View menu item on Netscape's menu bar. Next, click on the last item on the drop-down menu named, Source... In the future we will indicate this sequence as View | Source (first click on the View menu and then select the Source option).

Figure 2.1 shows a portion of the Netscape home page source document. This is the WELCOME.HTML file as seen by your browser.

HTML commands, usually called *tags*, are typically paired and enclosed between < and > characters. The second tag of a pair contains a forward slash /

***Figure 2.1** Viewing the HTML source of Netscape's Welcome page.*

and closes the sense of the tag pair. Often a pair of tags acts on the text that falls between them. The first line indicates that "Welcome to Netscape" should be displayed in the title area. The second line in the HTML file is

```
<CENTER>
```

indicating that everything until the closing **</CENTER>** tag is designed to be centered on the page. Centering is a Netscape enhancement to HTML; the effect will not be reproduced on most other browsers. If you are using a non-Netscape browser to follow this exploration, don't think something is wrong when items do not appear centered on your browser's desktop. The next three lines are used to display information for a file named home_igloo.gif, which is the graphic displayed as the first item in the document viewing area. The **<P>** command indicates that a new paragraph is to be started following the displayed graphic.

Moving down toward the bottom of the page, the items under **<DD>** represent plain text with two Web links thrown in for good measure. The greater part of most Web documents is plain text.

At the heart of most hyper text documents is the link, which is the mechanism by which a browser moves to another document or another place within the same document. As explained earlier, an HTML hyperlink has two components, the anchor and the reference. Look at the next to last line displayed in Figure 2.1. The portion of the line containing

```
<A HREF="/toc.html">new design and layout</A>
```

illustrates the practical application of these two components. The **<A>** and **</A>** pair encloses the two components. The 'HREF="/toc.html">' portion is the reference and the 'new design and layout' portion is the anchor, which is displayed as underlined text on the screen.

There is certainly much more, but let's hold off on the inner workings of HTML for a full-blown exploration that we can work through after you've gained more experience on the Web. Don't be concerned if this HTML business seems a little fuzzy at this point. The confounded documents actually start to make sense after you've read a few and gained a little more Netscape experience on the Web.

TIME TO PREPARE FOR ANOTHER EXPLORATION

Well, the glow of the campfire embers is starting to dim. It's time to wind up this briefing and get some rest so that we can journey into the Internet for another Netscape exploration.

LET'S REVIEW

The Internet coalesced as a group of linked networks at large corporations, universities, and especially government installations. All parties agreed to pass traffic through their systems on the way to other systems, taking off the stream only what applied to them.

The File Transfer Protocol (FTP) was implemented very early, allowing people to transfer files over the Internet from other systems on the Internet. The main problem was finding files. The Archie utility was the first general means of searching for material on the Internet. Later, the much more ambitious Gopher protocol was designed, which treated Internet files as hierarchical menus.

The most recent advance in Internet navigation was the World Wide Web, a new protocol treating material on the Internet as linked hyper text—and as a bonus, adding standard support for multimedia data like sound and video. The Web was mostly a curiosity until the University of Illinois released Mosaic, a graphical browser allowing easy "surfing" of the Internet, including services like FTP and Gopher. A special document format, the Hypertext Markup Language (HTML) was adapted from an earlier markup spec (SGML) for use in formatting Web documents.

Behind the general usefulness of Netscape, Mosaic, and other Web browsers is the idea of the Universal Resource Locator (URL), a standardized addressing scheme for all types of Internet data and services.

Chapter 3

Wanted: World Wide Web Tour Guide and Navigator

Now that you've seen Netscape and the Web, it's time to learn how you can make your own trail in Web cyberspace.

Do you remember the early worldwide navigators Christopher Columbus, Lewis and Clark, and other brave explorers? When they set out on their travels, they didn't know exactly where they were going and they certainly didn't expect to follow someone else's signs along someone else's trail. They made their own trails, even in the face of hazards. But as they traveled, they were wise enough to take the time to develop their own navigational tools and master the tools that were available to them in their day.

As you start exploring the Web on your own, you'll need to learn how to use the powerful navigational tools that Netscape offers. The more you know about URLs, bookmarks, hot spots, and Netscape's Go menu and History box, the better you'll be at getting around on the Web. In this chapter I'll introduce you to the basic Netscape navigational tools and then in Chapter 4, *The Care and Feeding of Netscape's Bookmarks,* we'll explore bookmark lists in much more detail.

TEACHING NETSCAPE TO POINT

Since you don't always want to be following someone else's links, you must be able to steer your Netscape navigational system on your own. An amazing number of Web sites await exploration, once you know how to get around. The trick is knowing how to find these sites, and once you find them, you need to know how to keep track of them. The Web is tremendously dynamic. New sites are being added at a rate of about 200 per week and increasing. The contents of existing sites are also being constantly improved and expanded.

Making a Stop at Baltimore's Charm Net

Baltimore's Charm Net has a great home page. This unique Web site, which is the pride of Maryland, also has a wonderful assortment of HTML document information and pointers to all types of interesting places. Enough said; let's go explore.

You can easily get to any Web site with Netscape once you know its location or URL. Recall from Chapter 1 that the URL is the Uniform Resource Locator. The URL serves as kind of a special Internet address for a Web page. Every Web resource, such as a document or graphic image, has its own unique Internet address (URL). Let's start our first exploration with a visit to Baltimore's Charm Net. This will show you how to use URLs to navigate the Internet seas. Fortunately, a net-surfer acquaintance supplied the URL for the Charm Net home page, which is:

```
http://www.charm.net/
```

Note the "/" at the end of this URL. Technically speaking, the "/" is a required URL terminator. However, most browsers, including Netscape, allow you to specify a URL without using the / terminator. Some browsers, notably NetCruiser, require the terminator.

Using Netscape, there are a few ways you can get to Charm Net. I'll show you all of them so that you can quickly learn different ways to navigate. One simple way to enter a URL and travel to a new Web site is to use the File menu. Open this menu by clicking on the File item in the menu bar and select the Open Location command from the File menu. When I present menu commands throughout this book, I'll use the notation File | Open Location to indicate that you need to open a menu (File, in this case) and then select a command (Open Location) from the menu. Figure 3.1 shows the Open Location dialog box that appears.

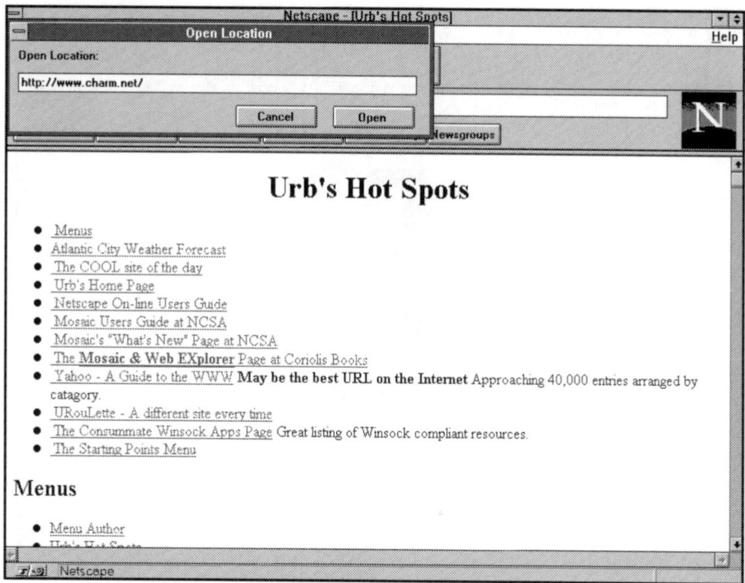

Figure 3.1 Using the Open Location dialog box.

An alternative to using the File menu to enter a URL is to click on the toolbar's Open folder icon. (Look for the icon displayed to the left of the Print icon on the toolbar.) A third method is to press Ctrl+L. (Hold down the Ctrl key while you press the L key.)

A fourth method, which is my personal favorite, is to delete the current URL in the Location text box (just under the toolbar), type in a new URL, and press Enter to activate the link. To delete the current URL, you can select it with the mouse (highlight it) and enter a new URL. Your new text will replace the highlighted URL. Or, you can click at the end of the URL and press the Backspace key to delete it.

You might want to use a portion of the current URL. For example, the characters "http://www" might begin both the existing URL and the URL you want to enter. In this case, simply position the cursor at the point you wish to start editing, press Ctrl+Delete, and everything to the right of the cursor will be deleted. This editing feature can come in handy if much of the current URL is usable.

Whichever method you have selected, enter the Charm Net URL (http://www.charm.net) in the URL field. Then, click the OK button or press Enter, and away we go to Charm Net.

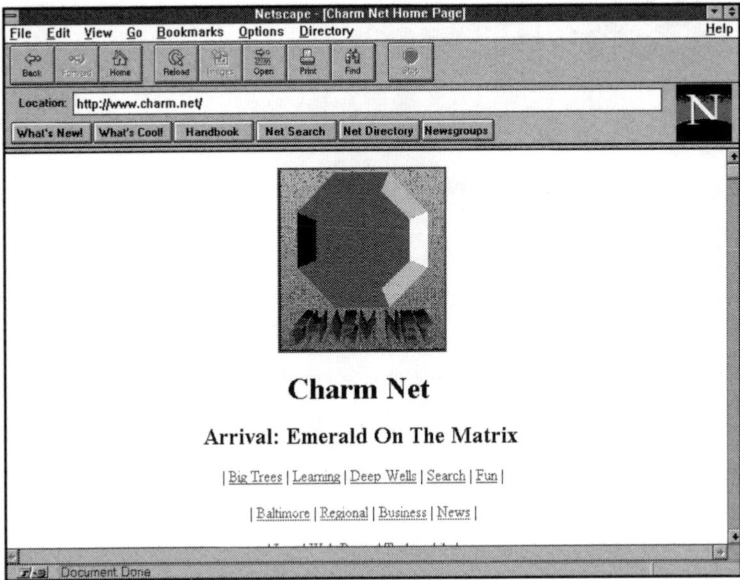

***Figure 3.2** Our first exploration—Charm Net's home page.*

The opening display includes a giant emerald, as shown in Figure 3.2. The Charm Net "Emerald on the Matrix" symbolically represents the city of Baltimore. If you like the Charm Net home page as much as I do (it has great lists of links to other places on the Web), you may want to make it easy to return for later explorations. Netscape makes return trips easy, and I'll show you how after a little background information.

Watch Your Case

A URL may have several components. Entering them can be a source of potential error, especially for DOS users, when typing the portion of a URL referencing the path on a remote server. A pathname contains the directories, subdirectories, and a file name. A DOS pathname might be

```
C:\WINDOWS\NETSCAPE.INI
```

which points to the file NETSCAPE.INI in the directory \WINDOWS on drive C:. DOS commands are not case sensitive, so you may type the above path as:

```
c:\windows\netscape.ini
```

A lowercase pathname may *not* work, however, if the Web server is running the Unix operating system, as most of them do. Unlike DOS, Unix is case-sensitive. Although we will have future explorations on URLs, let's do a short side trip to demonstrate how we can avoid this potential error. The URL

```
http://home.netscape.com/escapes/index.html
```

has three basic components. The first component shows the type of information being requested (in this case "http://"). The next component is the domain name (in this case, "home.netscape.com"). The part following the domain name is the path statement. "/escapes" is a subdirectory of the top level, or root, directory. The last part ("index.html") is the file name that contains the desired HTML document.

The domain name is not case sensitive; that means you can use uppercase or lowercase letters. However, the path name must be entered exactly as shown. To a Unix-based computer, "ESCAPES" and "escapes" are not the same thing. If you receive some type of error message after manually entering a URL, check your entered case very carefully.

BOOKMARKS: EXTRAORDINARY TOUR GUIDES

A good Internet navigational system is similar to a vacation tour guide. The guide is there 24 hours a day to help with suggestions when you need to do things. In addition, the guide should also hand you directions back to previously visited Web locations when you forget them but want to go back. Netscape does all of this and more. We have already seen that Netscape permits us to navigate the Web, either by following links provided in a home page, or by manually entering locations where the good stuff resides.

When I go on vacation, I like to get off the beaten track and find obscure things and visit out-of-the-way places. This is also how I like to explore the Web. Netscape can be extraordinarily helpful in this regard. Netscape provides a handy feature called *bookmarks* that let you easily keep track of the places you've been so that you quickly can go there again.

A bookmark has two components, a URL and a descriptive title. Look at the Charm Net page in Figure 3.2. Its bookmark is the URL shown in the Location: text box. Its title—Charm Net Home Page—is displayed on the top title line, just after "Netscape -" and it is enclosed by the "[ ]" bracket pair. The title is supplied by the document's creator.

Netscape provides two navigational tools utilizing bookmarks. First, it keeps a list of locations (history list) visited during the current session. The first two icons on the toolbar make use of the history list. The Back arrow button, the left arrow icon that is the first icon on the left of the toolbar, will take us back to the immediately visited site. (Provided we are not at the very first stop on our tour.) The Forward button, the right arrow icon just to the right of the back arrow icon, will take us forward, provided we have backed up at least once.

The second navigational tool is the Go menu. This menu allows us to jump over multiple sites. First, let's set the stage. My Netscape is configured to initially load a menu that I have created. This menu is my home page, or starting point, for the current session. (Much more about this in a later chapter.) Let's assume I click on a link, such as the entry for Charm Net's home page, and then I click on the News anchor in Charm Net's page, and then from the News page I click on What's New on Yahoo. (Yahoo is an incredible site; we'll talk about it shortly.) If I then open the Go menu, it will appear as shown in Figure 3.3.

The lowest portion of the Go drop-down menu is the history of our current session. This list is in the form of a stack, or what accountants call "last in first

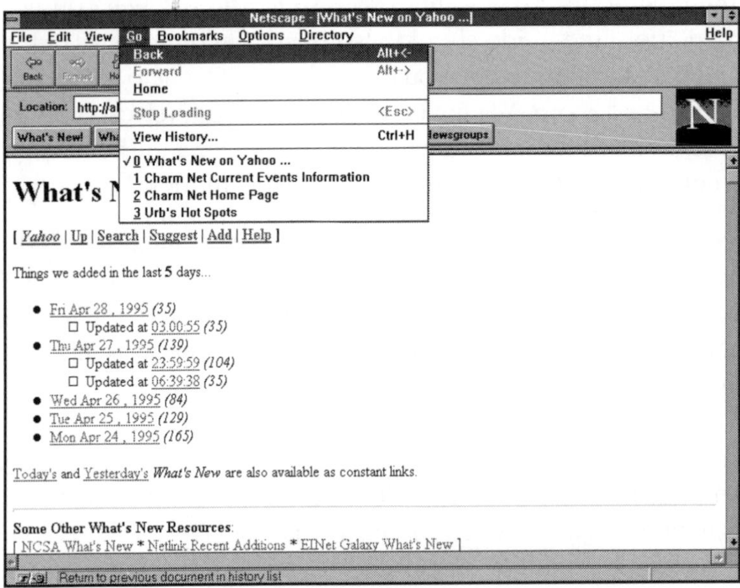

Figure 3.3 *The Go drop-down menu showing visited sites.*

out." The most recently visited site, in this case What's New on Yahoo, is at the top of the list. The check mark to the left of the name indicates it's the currently displayed document. Charm Net Current Events Information is the site visited immediately before the current site. If we press the left arrow, we would go to the item under the current site. Last on the list, Urb's Hot Spots, is where it all started. Like Superman, we can leap many bookmarks in a single bound, click on the desired site or press the number associated with the site to return to a previously viewed site.

In this example, we've been viewing the title portion of the history bookmarks. After opening the Go menu, you can select the View History command (or simply press V) to show the entire set of history bookmarks. This feature is shown in Figure 3.4. (You can also get there in one step at any time by pressing the shortcut keys Ctrl+H.) The history shows both the titles and their associated URLs. You can scroll to the right to see more of the URLs. You can also activate the highlighted bookmark by clicking on either the Go to button or any bookmark.

The history list is only maintained for the "most recent" descent from your home page. Let's assume we travel from Urb's Home Page, to United States, to New Jersey, and to Tuckerton. All the items are in the history list. Now, if we return to Urb's Home Page, to California, and then to San Diego, only the Urb to San Diego trip appears in the history list.

So we can jump around and return to sites previously visited during the current session at will. "Big deal," you might reply, "how about tomorrow?" Enter permanent bookmark files.

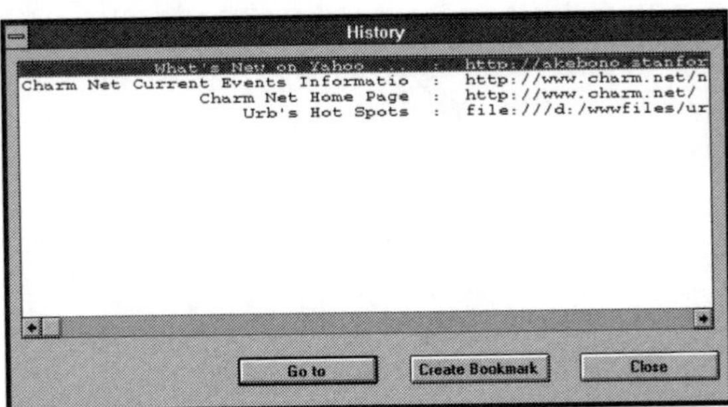

***Figure 3.4** Netscape's History of the current session.*

Send Pointers, Not Documents!

An excellent way to share information with friends or colleagues is to send them one of your favorite bookmark files or a subject portion of the file. A group of bookmarks is better than sending the actual documents, since a file contains pointers to the documents as they are maintained by their owners. (This also eliminates any possible copyright violations inherent in copying someone else's documents.) A mailed document may be older than the version of the document available on the server where it resides, and thus may be obsolete before the recipient even gets it. Finally, sending a bookmark list, or a portion of a list, as opposed to sending the entire document, is a far more efficient use of network resources.

The Care and Feeding of Bookmark Lists

A Netscape *bookmark list* is a file of stored Web sites. A URL link and its description are stored for each bookmark entry. A Netscape bookmark file also maintains the date the bookmark was initially added to the list and the most recent date the site was visited. A bookmark entry may also contain an optional user-defined description. Bookmark files may contain headers that are used to create submenus. Functionally, the bookmark organization can be used to create a hierarchical menu system.

The name of Netscape's initial bookmark file is bookmark.htm. It is a text file. Actually, it is an HTML file that uses Netscape HTML enhancements. Unfortunately, Netscape does not supply an initial bookmark file to help with the navigational process. I've corrected that oversight by supplying a bookmark file containing over 300 sites for you to visit. The bookmark file is organized by category and is contained on the enclosed CD-ROM. The name of the file is urbsbook.htm and it's in directory urbsstuf. More on Urb's Hot Spots in the next chapter.

There are a few different ways that you can use bookmark lists with Netscape:

- Just start exploring with an empty bookmark list.
- Organize a bookmark menu into a hierarchy of menus.
- Use an existing menu of bookmarks such as Urb's Hot Spots.
- Convert the menu portion of mosaic.ini to a Netscape bookmark file.
- Don't use the bookmark system at all.

With the exception of the last option, these approaches are not mutually exclusive. Let's explore the first option to get us started.

For the remainder of this chapter we'll go out to the Web and set our trail of "navigational crumbs." In the next chapter I'll show you how to update and manage bookmark lists. If you're the type of person who keeps a desk where one can actually see the surface, you may want to put a 3×5 file card in this page and skip to Chapter 4 so you can start this exploration in an organized fashion. If you're like me (I cannot remember the last time I saw the surface of my computer desk, or the rug on the side of my bed), you'll want to jump in head first.

ADDING YOUR OWN LINKS

Although serendipity may rule the day while exploring the Web, it can be difficult to make serendipity happen twice in a row. When you find something really interesting on the Web, you certainly don't want to depend upon your memory to get you back to it.

Navigating the Web is like navigating a maze—actually, it's worse, since there may be many paths for getting to any Web site. I don't know about you, but I have a hard time remembering where I put my car keys 15 minutes ago, much less where on the Web I found that great location for brownie recipes. What we need to accomplish symbolically is to sprinkle some crumbs in the snow along our path so that we can find our way back. (It's our problem if we don't make it back before spring and the newly arriving birds have eaten all our crumbs.)

Adding a New Link to a Bookmark List

New links may be added to an existing bookmark list at any time. For this project, let's go visit Yahoo, which is one of the great Web Sites. Yahoo is a database of almost 40,000 searchable net resources. We'll add its link to our bookmark list.

Using one of the techniques described earlier in this chapter, enter the URL:

```
http://www.yahoo.com
```

Once the document is displayed, its URL and title can be added to a bookmark list. Click on the Bookmark's entry on the menu bar or press Ctrl+B. Notice that the bookmark drop-down menu, as shown in Figure 3.5, only has the two items, Add Bookmark and View Bookmarks, at this point since we

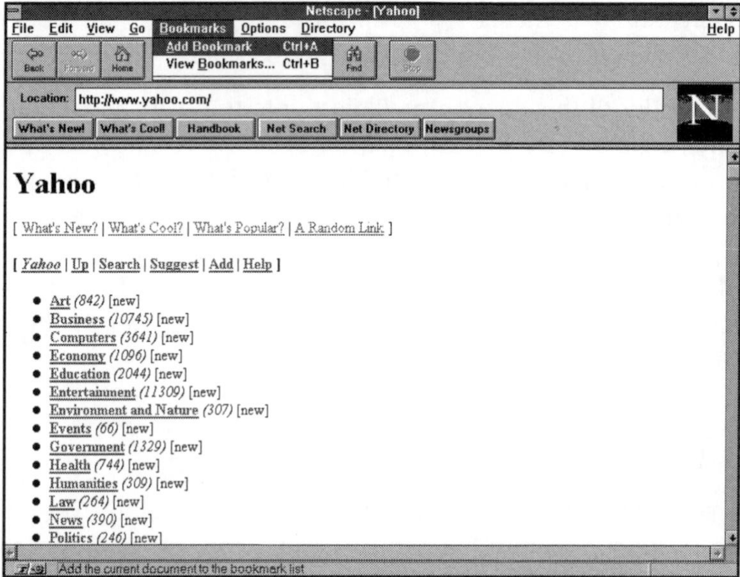

Figure 3.5 *The Bookmarks drop-down menu.*

are starting with an empty bookmark list. Clicking on the Add Bookmark item will add the title and URL of the currently viewed document to the bookmark list. We could also press Ctrl+A to add the current document to the bookmark list. Figure 3.6 shows the results of opening the Bookmarks menu after Ya-

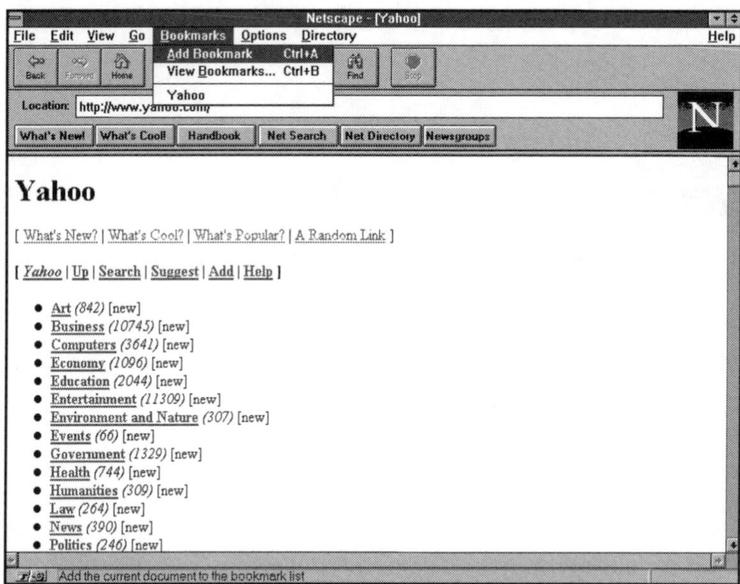

Figure 3.6 *Yahoo has been added as our first bookmark.*

hoo has been added. We may return to visit Yahoo at any time by opening the Bookmarks menu and clicking on Yahoo. Congratulations, we've just placed our first navigational crumb.

Let's enter the URL for my home page at Charm Net; it's:

```
http://www.charm.net/~lejeune
```

Notice the little character between the "/" and "lejeune". It's called a tilde and it's usually on the key just to the left of the 1 key. After displaying my home page, execute the sequence Go | Show History, which brings up the History dialog box as shown in Figure 3.7. Any item in the history can be turned into a bookmark. Highlight Urb's Home Page by clicking once on any part of the title or URL; next click on the Create Bookmark button. Finally, click on the Close button to exit the History dialog.

Open the Bookmarks menu again and—presto!—you'll have two bookmarks, as shown in Figure 3.8. You can bring back good old Yahoo or Urb at any time by opening the bookmark menu and clicking on your choice. When you exit Netscape, your bookmarks wait patiently for your next exploration. You can continue in this fashion to add interesting sites to your bookmark file until you fill up the screen with entries. When you see a note at the bottom of the screen stating "more bookmarks," it indicates you're ready for a little more sophistication in the management of your bookmarks.

Adding an Item to a Bookmark List

As you wander about cyberspace, you will undoubtedly find places of interest or valuable services that you would like to easily return to. The History box will help you return to a site visited during the current session—but how about tomorrow or next week? You begin with a fresh, empty History box

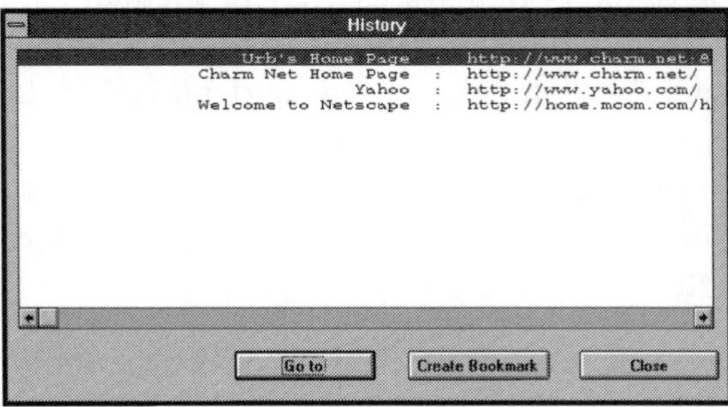

Figure 3.7 *Setting up the History dialog box to save a bookmark.*

***Figure 3.8** There are now two bookmarks available for instant recall.*

each time you launch Netscape and set out on the Web. An important Netscape feature is the ability to add your own links to existing, or new, bookmark files stored on disk. These lists remain between Netscape explorations. The creation and management of bookmark lists is the topic of the next chapter.

LET'S REVIEW

A Netscape bookmark list is functionally a folder containing pointers to Web sites or other Internet services. Bookmark lists are completely user configurable. Netscape's initial default bookmark list is named bookmark.htm and is found in the same directory with all the other Netscape files. The name and location of the bookmark list may be changed at any time. Bookmark lists can be created, deleted, and renamed. Individual bookmark items can likewise be added, deleted, copied, and moved. Selecting the menu sequence File|Open Location or clicking on the Open icon are common routes to the Open URL dialog box. Another method of activating a URL is to edit it directly in the Location text box. The dialog box is the mechanism for activating a URL.

The sequence in which you visited Web sites during the current Netscape session is displayed in the History box. Select the menu item Go|View History. Highlight the desired item and click on the Go to button to return to a previously visited site. You can also double-click on any history item to return to the document or service it describes.

The currently displayed document or service can be added to your bookmark list by executing the sequence Bookmarks | Add Bookmark. You can also use the shortcut Ctrl+A.

AND ONWARD!

Bookmark navigation is one of the most powerful features of Netscape. Take some time to get comfortable with the concepts behind bookmarks. Just because Christopher Columbus didn't know where he was going is no reason for us to assume that good things will automatically happen if we just wander out on the open sea. Not all explorers are as lucky as Chris.

In Chapter 4 we'll explore bookmark menu maintenance. This will be a big step in fine-tuning Netscape to our personal preferences.

EXPLORER TIP

Converting a Mosaic Menu List

If you have been using Mosaic and have built a substantial menu list, there is a cool utility that will convert the menu portion of mosaic.ini to a Netscape bookmark.htm style bookmark file. The enclosed CD-ROM contains the program CONVERT.EXE created by Martin Towner, phmct@siva.bris.ac.uk, for converting menu lists to bookmarks. The program also attempts to maintain the menu structure that you've lovingly assembled in your mosaic.ini file. Your mosaic.ini hotlist (if present) is added as a top-level menu.

To use the program, copy it to your hard drive. From the Windows' Program Manager enter File|Run. Enter c:\netscape\convert in the Command Line text box. Figure 3.9 shows the Mosaic-to-Netscape converter dialog box. CONVERT is designed to be run

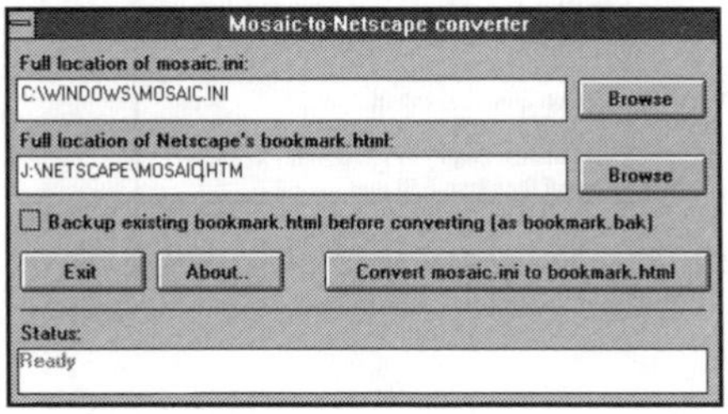

Figure 3.9 *The Mosaic- to-Netscape converter dialog box.*

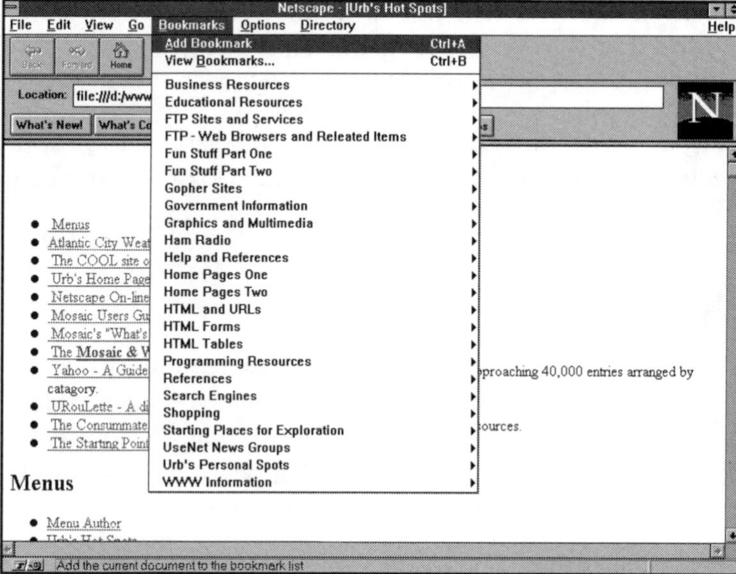

Figure 3.10 *Netscape displaying the converted mosaic.ini file as a bookmark list.*

immediately after installing Netscape. If you are going to use bookmark.htm as a file name, make sure you check the Backup box. Figure 3.10 shows the results of my Mosaic conversion. The right arrow on each line indicates the entry is a menu. Figure 3.11 shows the contents of the Search Engine menu.

This conversion program is only concerned with the menu aspect of mosaic.ini. The file associations stored in mosaic.ini are not converted.

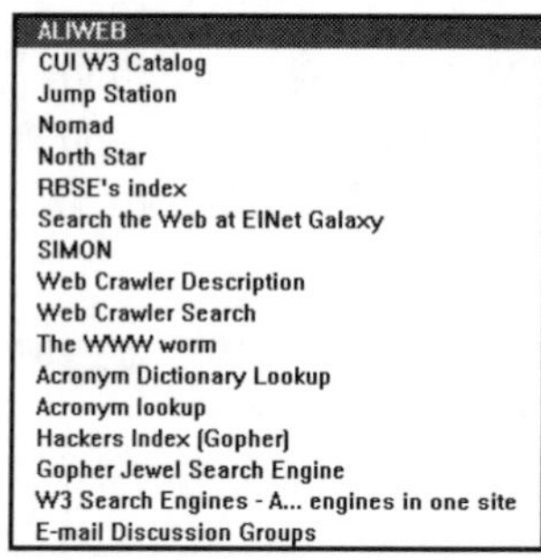

Figure 3.11 *The Search Engine's submenu portion of the bookmark file.*

Chapter 4

The Care and Feeding of Netscape Bookmarks

The story of bookmarks continues as we explore ways to customize Netscape's menu system and add new hotlists.

Popular folklore has it that very few people over the age of 35 can do anything creative. Being well over 35, I tend to think this observation is true simply because very few people ever do anything creative, period. Creativity is that most wonderful human characteristic that cries out, Find a *better way to do this!* At its highest level, creativity dares suggest: "Do this thing that has never before been done." Creativity is as much a mental attitude as it is a divine gift. Train yourself to use it.

After having used Netscape for a period of time, I'm inclined to paraphrase Pope Alfonso X's famous jibe and say, "Had I been present at the creation of Netscape, I would have proposed some improvements." One area that I would *not* change, however, is the organization of Netscape's bookmark menu system. Few things are more humanly intuitive than a hierarchical structure such as Netscape's menus of URLs—a perfect way to represent hotlists. However, I would have changed their methods of creating and maintaining a bookmark list. It's a great conceptual idea, just poorly implemented.

In this chapter we'll explore the techniques of supporting topical menus by creating and maintaining Netscape bookmark files—that's the easy part. The hard part is working out the details of the menu structures you wish to create, but that's where your creativity comes in. After you've been using Netscape for a while, you'll come up with all kinds of unique ways for arranging your menus and customizing the Netscape interface. To help you with the mechanics, this chapter will tell you everything you need to know about Netscape's bookmark system, from how bookmark files are organized and maintained to how you can create new ones on your own

USING NETSCAPE'S FLEXIBLE MENU SYSTEM

A Netscape bookmark file, as we learned in Chapter 3, is a menu of links to Web sites. A bookmark list provides a mouse-clickable selection of important documents around the world. Without menus and links, our computer work areas would look like a sea of yellow sticky notes containing all those great URLs. Half of them would have fallen behind the monitor at any given time, or else be stuck to the bottoms of your shoes.

Apart from bookmark lists, the only other structure that holds Web links is a "list of links" in a Web page somewhere. Many people build such lists of links into their own personal home pages so that others can profit from their Web explorations. We will create a home page in Chapter 9. This home page will incorporate personally chosen links into a nice-looking document. However, for general ease of use, nothing beats Netscape's built-in menu system, which we'll be exploring in this chapter.

Netscape's menu organization is hierarchical in nature. URLs and their titles are stored in a bookmark file. You can create multiple bookmark files, but only one may be the designated bookmark file at any one time. Since bookmark files are standard HTML files, you can have a bookmark link pointing to another bookmark file. Each bookmark menu can have any number of submenus—the only limitation is that all the submenus will be displayed at one time. Submenus in turn can have their own submenus going to almost any depth.

THE BASICS OF MODIFYING MENUS

Netscape provides three different techniques for modifying bookmarks and adding menu and submenu items. Here they are in ease-of-use order:

- Click on the Bookmarks | Add Bookmark option, or press Ctrl+A, to add the currently viewed document's URL and title to a previously selected menu group. If no group has been selected, the item will be added to the "top level" group.
- Use Netscape's bookmark editor by clicking on the Bookmarks | View Bookmarks option, or press Ctrl+B.
- Modify the file bookmark.htm, or any other bookmark file, using an editor.

The first option simply lets you add the URL and title of the currently displayed document to a bookmark file. The information is appended to the currently specified menu group. If no group has been specified, the item is added as a top-level entry. I'll show you how easy this is to do in our first project. The second option, using Netscape's bookmark editor, by contrast, lets you add, delete, and edit bookmarks as well as add, delete, move, and edit URL links and their titles.

The third option requires a little bit of manual work but it gives you the most control. A Netscape bookmark file is actually stored as a standard HTML file—with a few wrinkles. (As you will soon realize, Netscape doesn't do anything without a few wrinkles.) To change a bookmark file with an editor, you'll need to understand some of the basics of HTML. Therefore, we'll hold off the discussion of manually editing bookmark files until Chapter 19, *Advanced Browser Features.*

Keeping Abreast of Net Happenings

There is a Usenet newsgroup called comp.internet.net-happenings, and, as the name implies, it is a gold mine of new and interesting things happening on the Internet. Gleason Sackman, the moderator of the list, seems to be posting new and exciting things 24 hours a day. (I wonder if he ever sleeps.) The list is a great source of new URLs waiting to be explored.

If you don't have access to a Usenet newsreader, there is also a listserv list called net-happenings that distributes the same information. To subscribe to the list, send an e-mail message to:

```
majordomo@is.internic.org
```

In the body of the message place the following one line of text:

```
subscribe net-happenings <your-first-name> <your-last-name>
```

Shortly, you will receive a message proclaiming your acceptance to the inner circle. Read the message carefully because it tells you how to get off the list. This may become important if you have trouble keeping up with your daily flow of e-mail!

STARTING A NEW BOOKMARK FILE

The best way to see how bookmarks are created is to build and change a Netscape bookmark file. To create a new file, click on the Options | Preferences option, which will present a choice of eight different preference dialogs. We'll use the Applications and Directories preference. If another preference dialog is displayed, click on the down arrow just to the right of the top text box. When the menu opens, click on Applications and Directories.

Toward the bottom of the dialog box is an item named Bookmark File. The default entry is x:\netscape-path\bookmark.htm, where *x* is the drive holding Netscape and *netscape-path* is the path on your system that Netscape calls home. I'm going to select:

```
J:\NETSCAPE\my-menu.htm
```

You should select your Netscape path and enter a file name you want to use for your new bookmark list. Next, you must exit and restart Netscape for the change to become effective. After restarting Netscape, click on the Bookmarks menu item and you'll see the two drop-down menu items, Add Bookmark and View Bookmarks.

Adding Menu Entries

Now that we have a new bookmark file, let's start building a hierarchical system with a three-topic menu. We'll include these three items at the top level:

- Business
- Computers
- Resources

Then we'll add some other items to these top-level menus. To start, click on the Bookmarks | View Bookmarks option. This command displays the Book-

***Figure 4.1** The Bookmark List dialog box with an empty bookmark file.*

mark List dialog box, shown in Figure 4.1. Click on the Edit button located in the bottom-right corner of the dialog box to display the extended Bookmark List dialog box, as shown in Figure 4.2. Don't be overwhelmed by all the empty spaces and buttons—Rome wasn't built in a day.

The important items for us right now are the three buttons in the right middle of the screen. New Bookmark allows you to manually add a bookmark. As we discovered in the previous chapter, a bookmark consists of a URL and its associated title. The New Header button is used to create a menu or submenu title, and the New Separator button is used to insert a line to separate two logical groups of information.

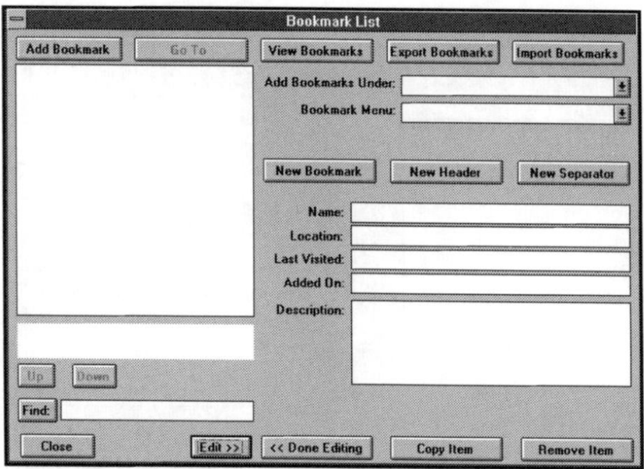

***Figure 4.2** The Bookmark List dialog box with the Edit portion opened.*

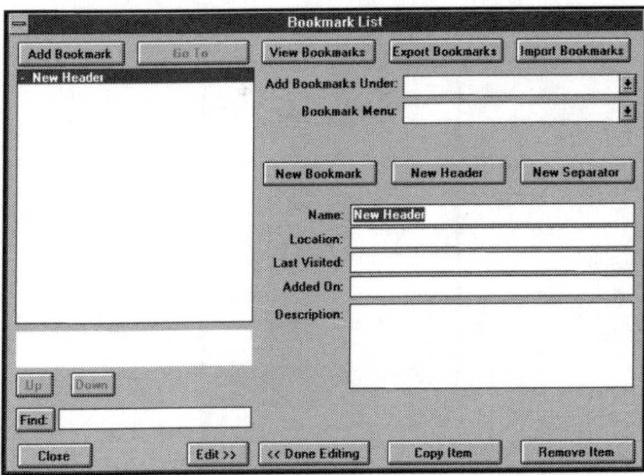

***Figure 4.3** The emerging bookmark list with a new header being created.*

Now let's create our three main menus. Click on New Header and the words "New Header" will appear both in the bookmark window on the left of the screen and in the Name: text box, as shown in Figure 4.3. Go to the Name: text box and enter "Computers". Notice that as you type, the header title in the main bookmark window changes, as well.

Click on New Header again and the title "New Header" appears in the Name text box, as well as in the bookmark window. Clicking on any of the "New" buttons causes an item to be inserted immediately under the currently highlighted item in the bookmark window. This time, enter "Business" as the header. With Business highlighted, click on New Header again and enter "Resources". Your screen should now look like the one shown in Figure 4.4.

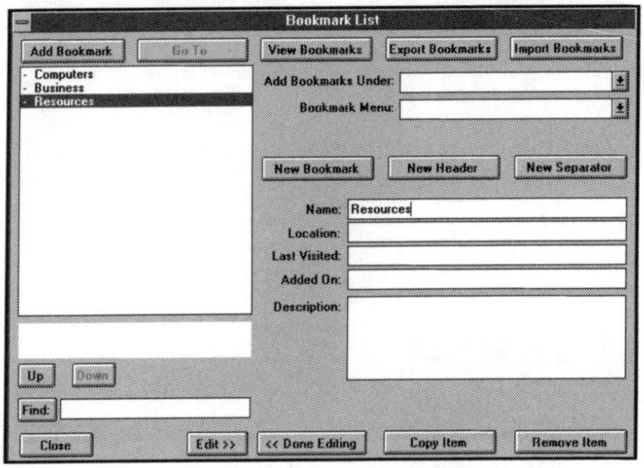

***Figure 4.4** Moving the "Business" menu item up in the hierarchy.*

Here's one little problem: Business is number two on the list, but we want it to be the first item, to keep alphabetic order. Click on Computers to highlight it, and then click once on the Down button. Notice that Computers won't go down to the same level as the other items, it went both down and to the right, as shown in Figure 4.5. Now it is a submenu of Business as opposed to being on the same level as Business. If a menu header is on the same level and we move it down, it first becomes a submenu. Clicking on Down once again will bring the menu to the desired level. The reverse is also true; clicking on Up will first move the menu item to a submenu level of the menu immediately above the highlighted item. Clicking on Up again will move it to the desired position.

Click on Close to finish the editing session and return to Netscape's browsing screen. Click on the Bookmarks menu. The drop-down menu now shows our menu handiwork (see Figure 4.6). The arrows to the right of each entry indicate a clickable menu. Clicking on a menu item at this point will have no effect, since the menus are empty. A common mistake at this point is to have a listing without the right arrow. If you clicked on New Bookmark while editing, as opposed to New Header, you would have added a bookmark rather than a menu item.

Let's continue the hierarchical construction process. We can fill a screen of Business or Computer bookmarks in short order. These submenus allow us to break down the categories to a more detailed level. Let's add Accounting,

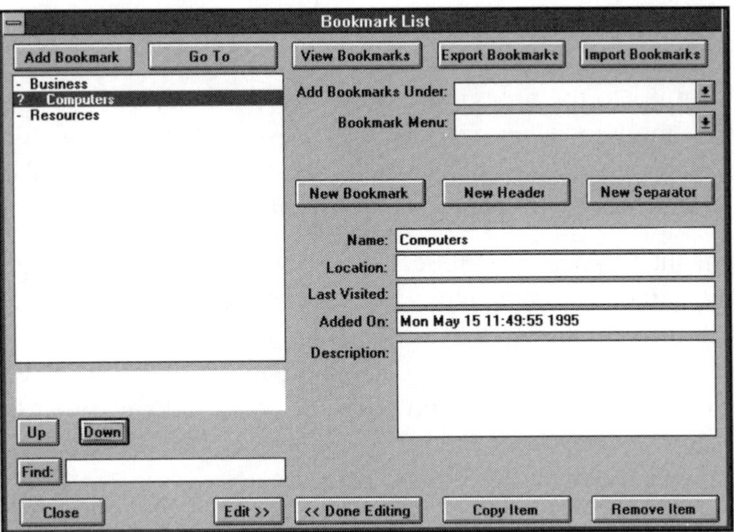

Figure 4.5 *Moving "Computers" down in the menu structure.*

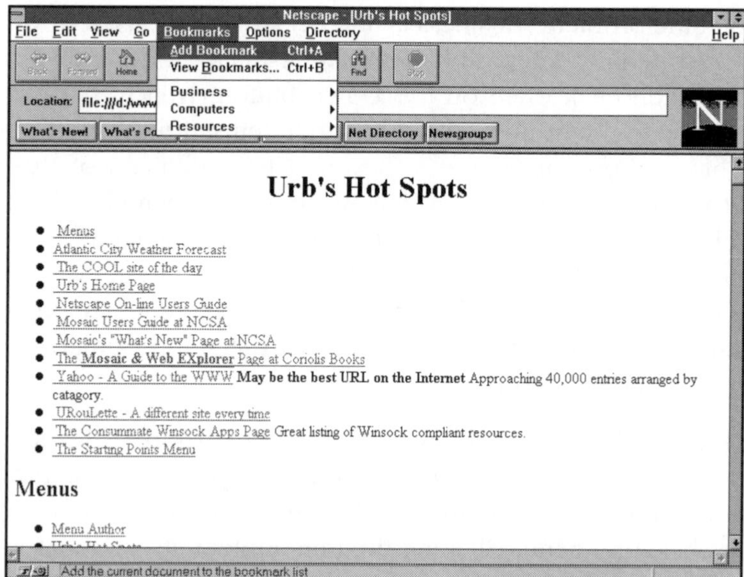

***Figure 4.6** The newly created menu items are now reachable from the Bookmarks drop-down menu.*

Finance, and Marketing as submenus below the Business menu, and add PC, Mac, and Unix as submenus under the Computers menu.

Click on the Bookmarks|View Bookmarks option and then, in the Book marks List dialog box, click on the Edit button to display the extended Bookmark List dialog box. Highlight the Computers menu header and click on New Header. Enter PC as the header item. PC is now the highlighted item, and is at the same level as the Computers menu item. Click once on Up and notice PC moves to the right, indicating it is now a submenu of Computers. Highlight Computers again and click on New Header, but this time enter Mac. Repeat the process for Unix. Move the items as necessary to make all three newly added items on the same level, below and to the right of Computers.

Next, highlight Business and repeat the above process for Accounting, Finance, and Marketing. Again, move the items to make them submenus below Business. Figure 4.7 shows the Bookmark List dialog box with three main menu items and the six newly added submenu items. Click on Close to return to the main Netscape screen, then click on Bookmarks to open the menu showing our three top-level menus. Clicking on Computers will cause the three submenus to appear, as shown in Figure 4.8.

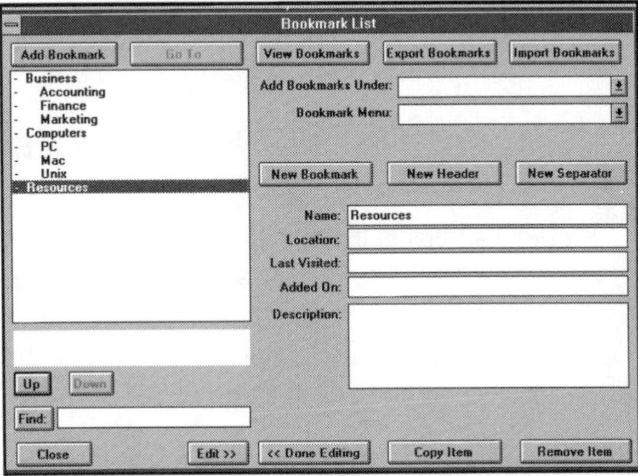

Figure 4.7 *The complete menu structure with both top-level menus and submenus.*

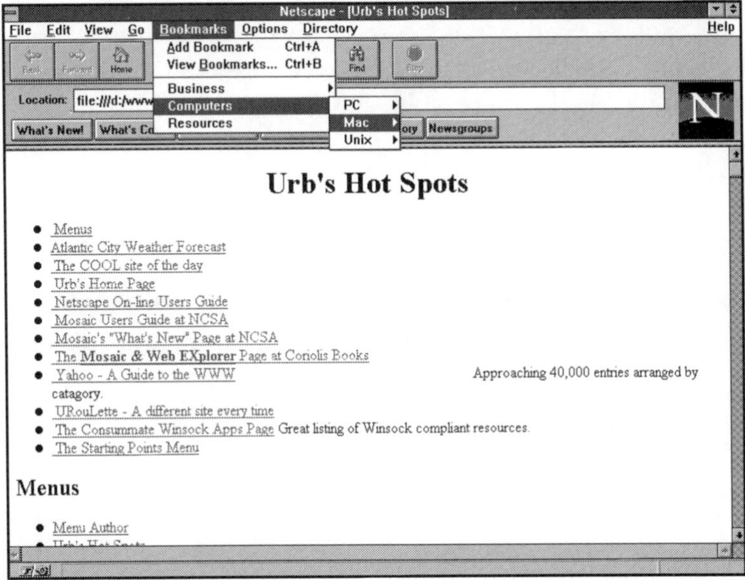

Figure 4.8 *The drop-down Bookmarks menu showing the Computers main menu selected which displays the three submenus.*

You now know more about Netscape's bookmark structure than 80 percent of the people using Netscape. On the Netscape discussion list there are more questions asked about bookmarks than any other subject. A frequent answer is, "Bookmarks are too complicated, go with regular menus."

With our newfound expertise, let's go forth and multiply. What good is a menu hierarchy if the structure doesn't contain anything of interest?

Snagging a Useful URL with Windows

For this project, we'll use the Windows clipboard to copy and paste a URL that points to an interesting Web site for Internet training material. This technique will illustrate how easy it is to use Windows to try out a new Internet resource and add it to a Netscape hotlist. We'll add the URL for this site to a menu by using the first and simplest technique for modifying menus and adding the hotlist items I described earlier.

One morning, my perennially overflowing electronic mailbox contained a message about a Web site with an interesting-sounding document called "Internet Training Resources." Figure 4.9 shows the e-mail message I received, displayed from within a Telnet session using Chameleon's Telnet client. (Telnet, which we'll explore later in this book, allows you to connect to a remote Internet network.) Notice that the message contains the URL of the site, which is exactly what we need to access the site. The URL is:

```
http://www.brandonu.ca/~ennsnr/Resources/Welcome.html
```
or
```
http://www.brandonu.ca/~ennsnr/resources.html
```

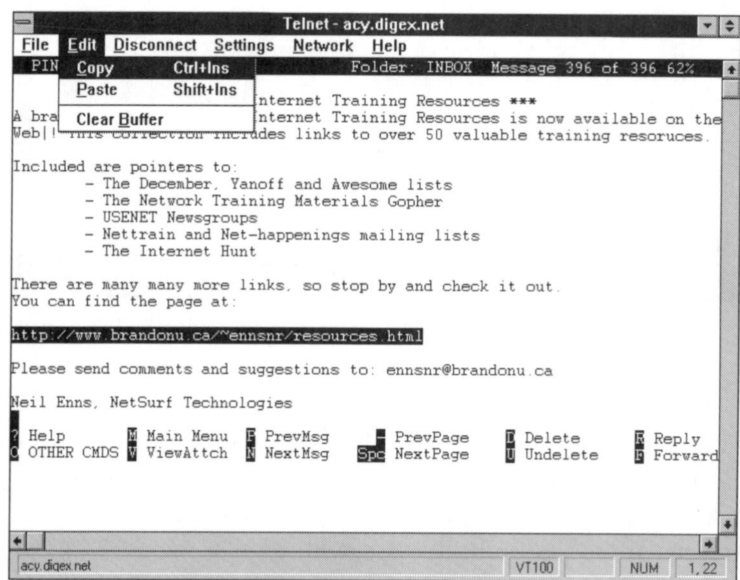

Figure 4.9 A message obtained through Telnet about the Internet Training Resources document.

Now let's see how the Windows clipboard can be used to help us transfer the URL from the e-mail message to Netscape. This technique can save you a lot of keystrokes and keep you from making typing mistakes as you transfer cumbersome URLs from an e-mail message to Netscape.

First, use your mouse to highlight the URL in the e-mail message, as shown in Figure 4.9. Then, you can copy the URL to the clipboard by using the Copy command with your e-mail program. (Virtually all Windows applications have an Edit menu that contains Copy and Paste commands.) As an example, Figure 4.9 demonstrates Chameleon's Telnet Edit drop-down menu. Keep in mind that this Edit menu may look a little different from the one you'll see in your own e-mail application. With Telnet, you can copy the URL to the Windows clipboard by clicking on the Copy item or by pressing Ctrl+Ins.

After copying the URL to the clipboard, you'll need to get into Netscape. If Netscape is already running as a Windows task, make it active by pressing Ctrl+Esc to go to the Windows Task List and then click on Netscape. If Netscape is not running, launch it from the Program Manager.

From within Netscape, highlight the URL in the Location: text box by dragging the cursor across the URL. (The Location: text box is the one normally displaying the current document's URL.) Press Ctrl+V to copy the contents of the clipboard into the URL field. Then, press enter to activate the URL. Figure 4.10

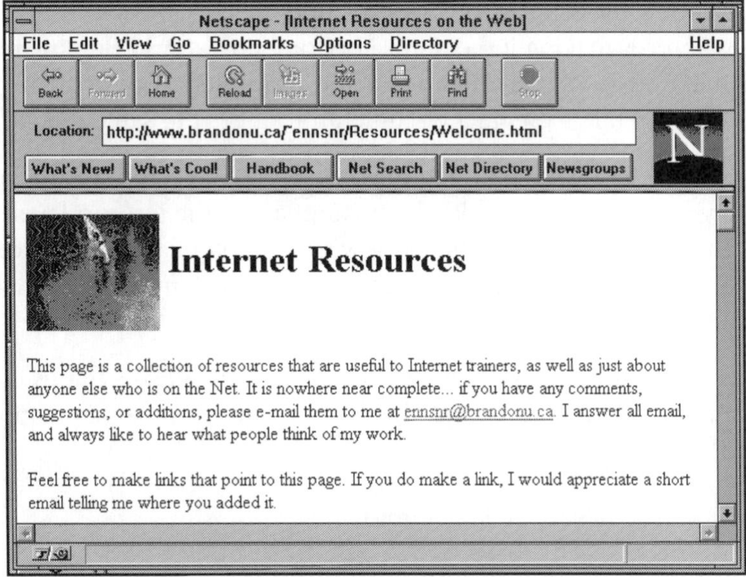

***Figure 4.10** Brandon University's Internet Resources home page.*

shows Brandon University's Internet Resources home page. It's a great resource if you're relatively new to Web surfing.

The contents of the "Internet Training Resources" are indeed impressive with pointers to over 75 different documents. We could print a copy of this document for future reference. However, there are two disadvantages to creating a hard copy version of this document: it will quickly become outdated, and—totally abhorrent to a lazy guy like me—you still must manually enter the URLs. The maintainer of the list, Neil Enns of NetSurf Technologies, keeps the list current by adding new information and changing existing information as needed. Simply saving the pointer to the list instead of just printing it will provide us continual access to the latest version.

Let's save it as a bookmark. Click on the Bookmarks|Add Bookmark option to add the information as a top-level menu item. This is just what the doctor ordered if you feel this URL is important enough to warrant top-level status. However, we're talking about a menu subsystem and top-level items defeat the structured concept. Let's pick a category and place the item in the corresponding menu level.

In this case the menu item Resources would certainly fit the bill. Click on Bookmarks|View Bookmarks|Edit. (From now on I'll just call this selection, "go to bookmark editing.") In the top of the upper-right corner is an item named Add Bookmarks Under: list box. Click on the down arrow to display a menu of choices showing all our menu categories, as shown in Figure 4.11. Click on Resources making it the depository of the next Add Bookmark action. Click on the Add Bookmark button in the upper-left corner of the screen. (Pressing Ctrl+A while viewing a document produces the same effect.)

We are now facing a Netscape bug head on. If the selected Add Bookmarks Under category is empty, the added item appears as the last top-level item. In this case, the fix is easy. Highlight the newly added item and click once on the Up button. Notice the item moves to the right without moving up. Life is not always so easy.

If you're into investing or finance, the SEC now maintains its filings online so that you can search them. They call the system EDGAR. A search engine I find very useful is at:

```
http://www.town.hall.org/cgi-bin/srch-edgar
```

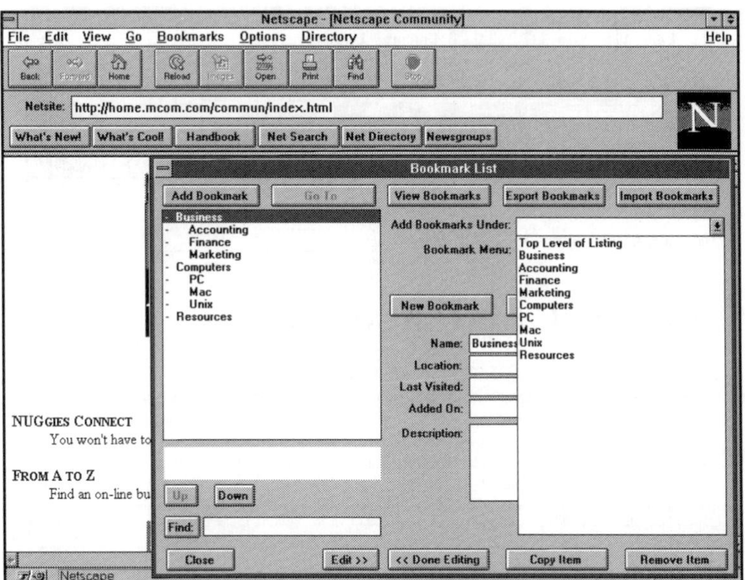

***Figure 4.11** Viewing the menu categories.*

Enter the URL into Netscape's Location: text box and press enter to activate it. Search using the name of your favorite company to see what they've been telling the SEC lately. This site is a for-sure site to come back to, so let's save it as a bookmark. Go to bookmark editing, display the Add Bookmarks Under menu, and select Finance. Bummer, poor EDGAR was added as the last top-level menu item. Of course, we could start moving it up, but this gets really tiring when there are several hundred bookmarks and you want the thing on the bottom close to the top.

This bug manifests itself only if the target menu is empty. A work around is to put a dummy item in each newly added menu item. While the newly added EDGAR item is still highlighted, click on the Remove Item button at the lower-right corner of the dialog box. Highlight the target menu item, Finance in this case. Click on New Bookmark and then click on Up to make the new bookmark subordinate to Finance. Notice that the new bookmark item starts with a "?" so it's distinguishable from a header item. Next, open the Add Bookmarks Under menu and again select Finance.

Now click on Add Bookmark—and there's EDGAR just under our dummy bookmark. New items are always added as the last entry in the particular menu structure. Highlight New Item and click on Remove Item; we no longer need the dummy field since Finance in no longer empty. Figure 4.12 shows the result of clicking on the Bookmarks | Business | Finance option.

***Figure 4.12** Selecting the newly added bookmark.*

What we have just performed is known as a "Kluge" in computer circles—we made something work despite a bug. Of course, the definition of a bug is a matter of where you happen to be sitting. Netscape has a listing on their home page called "Bug Like Features." I'll let that one pass without comment. If a Kluge is especially clever it can be elevated to the ranking of a Hack (sometimes called a Hax). Originally, someone performing these genuinely creative tasks on a regular basis was reverently called a "hacker." Unfortunately, the popular press has given hacking a very pejorative connotation.

Moving URLs between Menus

To keep your URLs organized, you'll often need to move them from one menu location to another. Fortunately, Netscape does provide a built-in operation for moving menu entries. Go to the bookmark list editing and highlight the item you wish to move. Click on Up or Down repeatedly to place the bookmark where you would like it to reside. Unfortunately, there is no drag and drop mechanism to allow jumping large menus in a single bound. (Are you listening Netscape?) Netscape also has no means by which you can move a group, such as a submenu, from one place to another. Don't despair, help is on the way.

Menu Overflow

Sooner or later it happens. You add a new item to a menu and the menu gets too darn big! When you open the menu, you'll see the item More Bookmarks.

If you press M, you're placed in the Bookmark List dialog box and you have to start scrolling through the available lists. This is not productive. When this happens, it's time to reorganize the menu.

I'm going to switch bookmark files to show you the nature of this problem and how to solve it. I bet it will come as no shock to discover my biggest menu category is Fun Stuff, shown in Figure 4.13. Right there under NetBoy Comic is the dreaded More Bookmarks message. The Bookmark List dialog box reveals 28 listings under Fun Stuff. There are two approaches to splitting the list. Put a new top-level header at the half way point and rename the first menu title, "Part One" or something like that. The second is to add the second part as a submenu under the main menu. Let's do both.

Notice that Lawyer Jokes is item 14 on my list. Let's put a new menu item immediately under this item. This will require a few steps. First, highlight the menu heading Fun Stuff. Then, change this title to Fun Stuff, Part One. Next, click on New Header and enter the title "Fun Stuff, Part Two". The new entry is added as the last item in the Fun Stuff group. If you try to move the Part Two menu title up in position, it will only move at the same level as the other menu items. The individual bookmark items in the Part One group must be moved. Highlight the item immediately above the new Part Two header. Click on Down twice; the first click promotes the level and the second click drops it to where we want it. Click on the item just above the Part Two header again

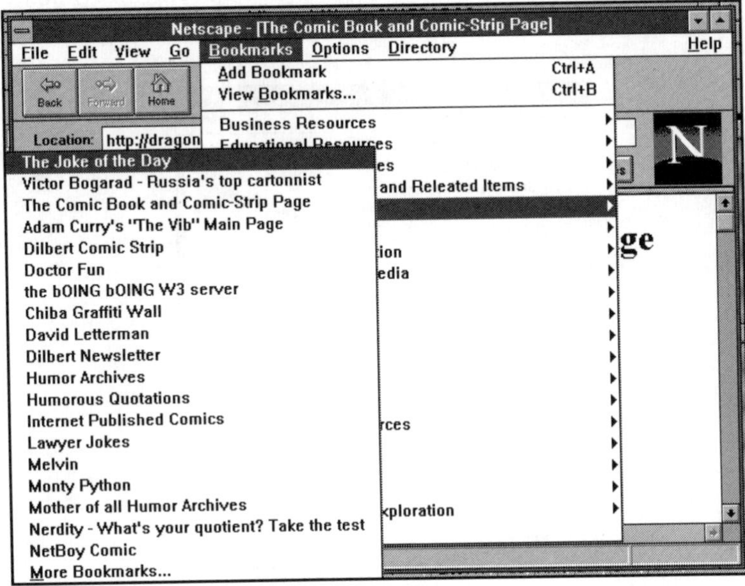

Figure 14.13 Viewing the menu items for Fun Stuff.

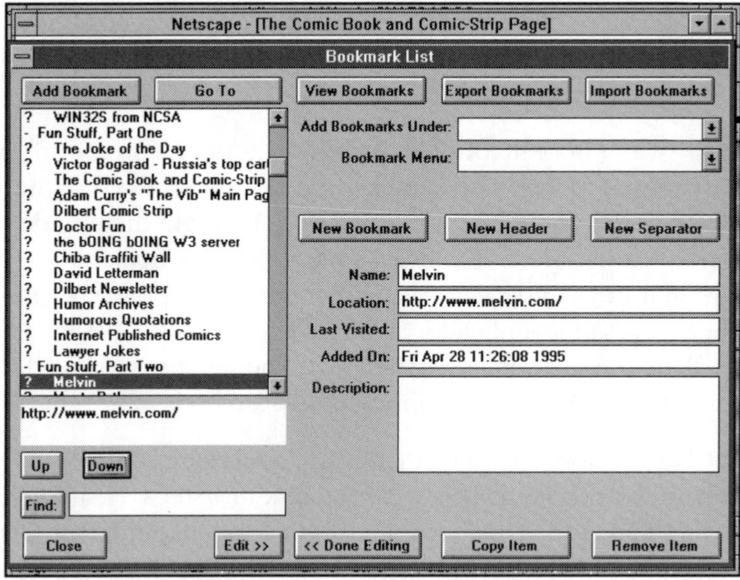

***Figure 4.14** The Fun Stuff entries now have two headers at the same level.*

and repeat the process until you've moved all the Part One entries. Figure 4.14 shows the new heading in its final resting place. Figure 4.15 shows the Bookmark's drop-down menu with the two Fun Stuff entries.

The problem with this approach is that the main menu becomes crowded with another item. The alternative is to make the second grouping of Fun

Add Bookmark	Ctrl+A
View Bookmarks...	Ctrl+B
Business Resources	▸
Educational Resources	▸
FTP Sites and Services	▸
FTP - Web Browsers and Releated Items	▸
Fun Stuff, Part One	▸
Fun Stuff, Part Two	▸
Gopher Sites	▸
Government Information	▸
Graphics and Multimedia	▸
Ham Radio	▸
Help and References	▸
Home Pages One	▸
HTML and URLs	▸
HTML Forms	▸
HTML Tables	▸
Programming Resources	▸
References	▸
Search Engines	▸
Shopping	▸
More Bookmarks...	

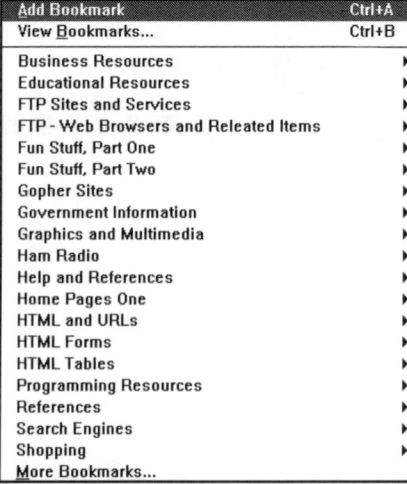

***Figure 4.15** The Bookmarks drop down menu showing both Fund Stuff top-level menu items.*

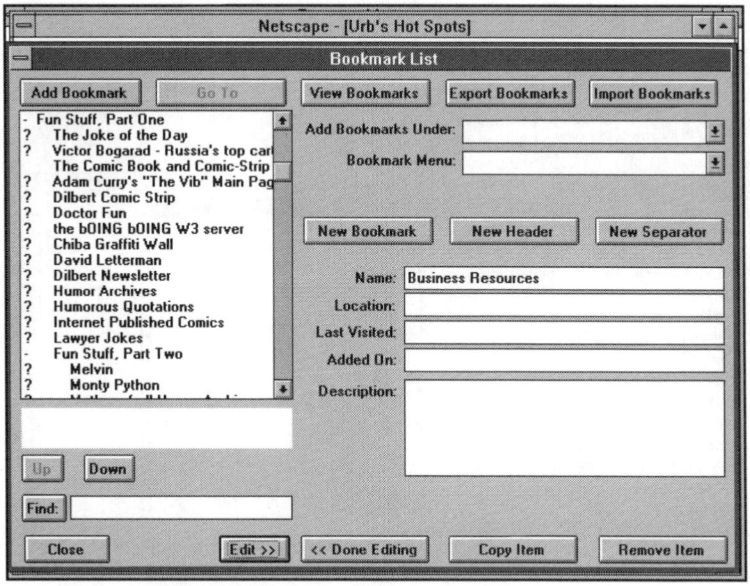

Figure 4.16 The multilevel Fun Stuff menu structure.

Stuff items a subgroup. This operation is easy. Highlight the Part Two header and click on Up. Fun Stuff, Part Two becomes a submenu of Fun Stuff, Part One and all of Part Two's items are dropped one level so they stay subordinate to the same menu. Figure 4.16 shows the subordinate ordering within the Bookmark List dialog box. The part that doesn't make sense to me is that you have to click on Up to demote a menu one level. As I said at the start of this chapter, "Had I been present at Netscape's creation, things would be different."

Figure 4.17 shows the main drop-down menu with Fun Stuff, Part One selected. As you can see, the last menu item—Fun Stuff, Part Two—is a pointer to a menu since there is an arrow on the right side of the window.

EXPLORER TIP

The Easiest (and Quickest) Way to Move a Menu Item

Here's a kluge that can help you get around Netscape's awkward menu editing system. The simplest way to move an entry over a great distance is to first activate the entry. After connecting, delete the item. Then select the new level and add the bookmark. Using this kluge you only have to move the item within its own group.

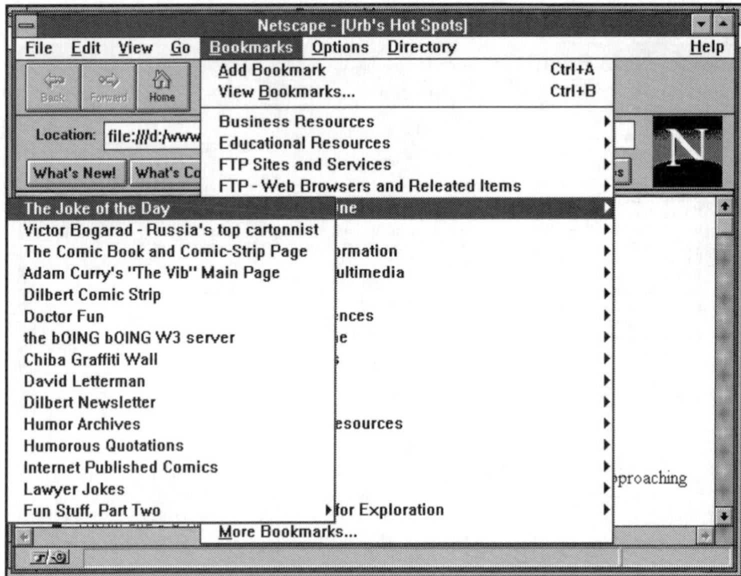

Figure 4.17 The multilevel Fun Stuff menu. The list item is a pointer to a submenu.

DELETING MENUS

Deleting a menu from within Netscape is easy, provided you want to delete all bookmarks associated with a particular menu. While in the Bookmark List dialog box, highlight the menu header you want to delete, then click on Delete Item. Unless the item is a header to an empty group, you will receive a message like:

```
Remove category "category-name"
And its X entries?
```

Click on OK to delete the header and all subordinate entries. Click on Cancel to abort the deletion. There is no way to delete a header without deleting all it's items. If you want to functionally delete a header without the items, you must first move the items.

USING ITEM SEPARATORS

A plain line may be inserted between two entries to create emphasis or make logical separations. To do this, go to bookmark editing and highlight the item you want to appear just *above* the separator. Click on New Separator and a blank line will appear. (The separator contains no text.)

Creating a Separator That Has a Label

If you want a logical separator to contain a title, create a bookmark entry without a URL. You'll get a lookup error if you click on it by mistake, but no harm is done.

STARTING FROM A SUBMENU

Often, there are times when you would like a submenu to become the temporary top-level menu. Maybe you are going to do some serious searching and need a submenu to store some of your findings. (Web surfing is not all fun and games.) Go to bookmark editing and click on the arrow to the right of the the Bookmark Menu: list box to display the menu. Select Search Engines from the choices. When you next click on the Bookmarks menu in Netscape's main window, Search Engines becomes the main menu, as shown in Figure 4.18. You can change the default menu for the current Netscape session.

IMPORTING AND EXPORTING MENUS

Other disappointments in Netscape's Bookmark List dialog box are the Import Bookmarks and Export Bookmark buttons. The Export Bookmarks but-

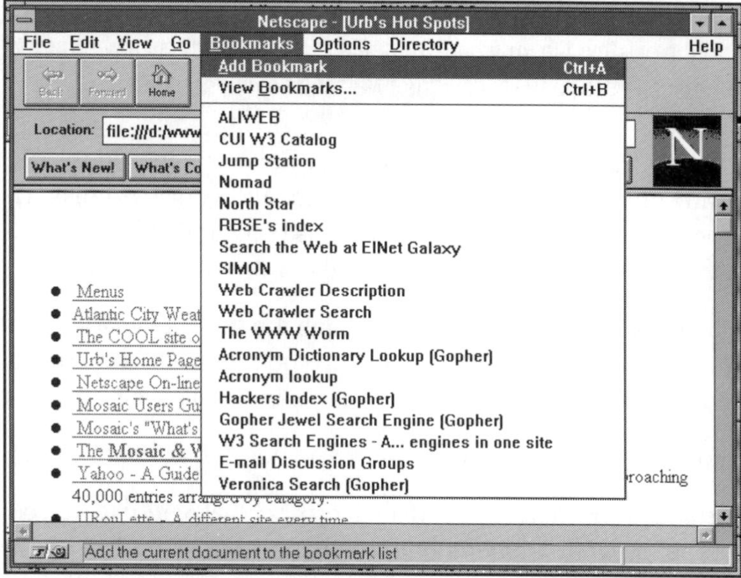

Figure 4.18 Changing the default menu to Search Engines.

ton simply copies the currently specified bookmark file. This is a feature I don't think is as useful as it could be. I wish you could select a portion of a menu structure to export. I often send a portion of my main menu to someone.

The Import Bookmarks button, on the other hand, is quite useful. To use it, go to editing bookmarks and click on Import Bookmarks. Select an HTML file and Netscape will do a great job of extracting the URLs and titles from within the document and importing them as a group at the bottom of the currently specified bookmark file. The heading from the copied document becomes the title of the newly created menu item.

NSMEDIT to the Rescue

As I mentioned earlier, Netscape bookmark files are great features that are poorly executed. Fortunately, Scott Chapman, schapman@ior.com, created a program called NSMEDIT to perform bookmark file maintenance tasks that Netscape left out. This program is available on the companion CD-ROM in the directory \tools\nsmedit.

> EXPLORER TIP
>
> ### Be Careful when You Edit Bookmark Files
>
> You shouldn't use NSMEDIT to edit a bookmark file that is currently in use by Netscape. Netscape reads the user-specified bookmark file (bookmark.htm if no file is specified) only once at the start of a session. Netscape also writes back the bookmark file when the program is closed, overwriting the existing file. Any bookmark file changes made by any program during an active Netscape session are lost when Netscape overwrites the file.

NSMEDIT installs easily. Go to the directory \tools\nsmedit on the companion CD-ROM and copy the program file nsmedit.exe to your hard disk. (I put it in my netscape directory.) If you plan to use this program a lot, you may want to use the Windows Program Manager to make a program item for it.

The program is well designed. Initially I though the documentation sparse. However, most operations are standard Windows type actions. If you use it a lot, you should send in $15 to register it. I'm a menu junkie so it's well worth it to me.

Before making any changes to your Netscape bookmark file, make a backup.

NSMEDIT starts with a File Open dialog box so that you can select a bookmark file. The program remembers which file you edited in the previous session and it lists the file as the default. Figure 4.19 shows the program's

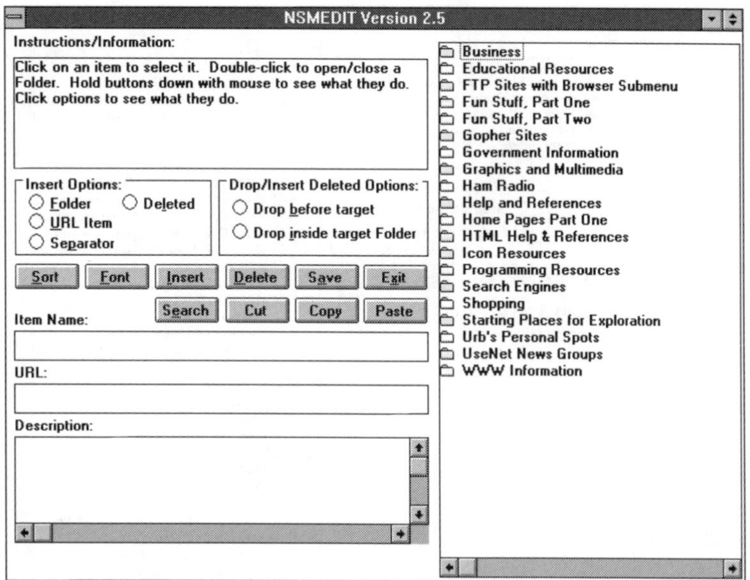

***Figure 4.19** The NSMEDIT dialog box.*

dialog. The window on the right initially displays only the top-level items. Top-level items are the entries displayed from within Netscape after clicking on the menu bar's Bookmarks item. This is already a big improvement over Netscape. I like the collapsed menus since they present an overview of the top-level hierarchy.

Highlight an item by clicking on it. The text boxes on the bottom-left side of the main window are for editing. I like to keep my bookmarks in alphabetic order. To do this, click on the Sort button, or press Ctrl+S, to sort the main menu structure. If you select a menu grou, and click on Sort, only the entries in the selected group will be sorted.

Double-click on a menu item to display its contents. Once expanded, double-clicking on a menu item will collapse the display of its components. Figure 4.20 shows the FTP-Web Browsers and Related Items, as well as the Ham Radio menus expanded.

This program's big selling point is its ability to move items using normal Windows drag and drop techniques. Before starting a drag or drop operation, select the desired drop method using the option buttons in the Drop/Insert Deleted Options box. Notice the Instructions/Information box changes as you click on an item. Let's assume you do a lot of searching and you want everything in alphabetic order, with the exception of the Search Engines menu

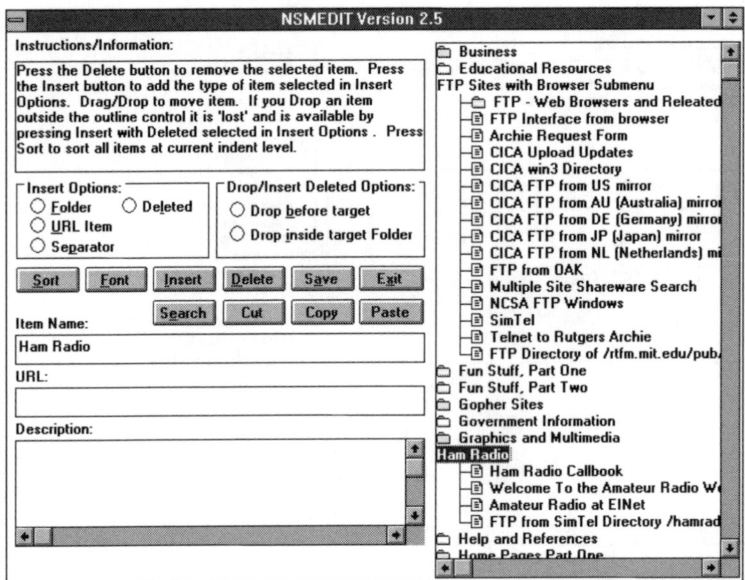

Figure 4.20 *Display expanded menus using NSMEDIT.*

item, which should appear first on the list. First, click on the Drop Before (Ctrl+B) option button, indicating the new place for a drop should be just before the item we drop on. Next, point to the Search Engines menu item with your mouse and, while holding down the left button, drag the menu to Business Resources and release the left button.

Do you remember how tough this would have been using Netscape? Remember our Fun Stuff workout? The top-level menu shows two Fun Stuff menu entries. Let's make Fun Stuff, Part Two a submenu of Fun Stuff, Part One. This time click on the Drop as Child option button since we want to make Part Two a submenu of Part One. Drag the Fun Stuff, Part Two menu item and drop it on Fun Stuff, Part One. Figure 4.21 shows both menus expanded. If the dropped item seems to have disappeared, don't panic—you probably just dropped it on the wrong item. To reverse the process, simply click on Drop Before, then drag Fun Stuff, Part Two onto the menu on the same level and just below Fun Stuff, Part One.

Individual bookmark items are movable within the same menu and between menus using the same drag and drop techniques. Use Drop Before to move an item within the same menu (drop the item on top of the item that will follow it). Use Drop as Child to make an individual entry subordinate to another (drop the item on top of the menu item where it will be placed at the end of the list).

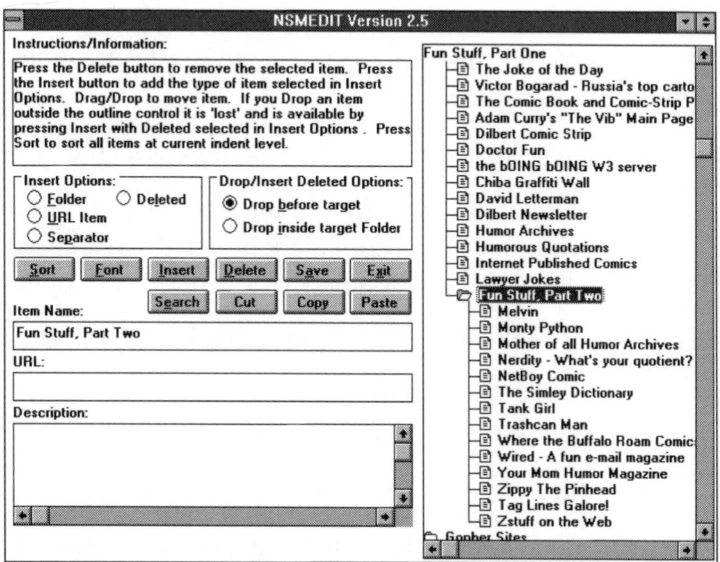

***Figure 4.21** The bookmark structure after making Fun Stuff, Part Two a submenu.*

Delete individual items by highlighting the item followed by clicking on the Delete button. Deleted items are copied to a backup buffer, not the Windows clipboard, and only one level of deletion is maintained—any recovery must be done before another delete or sort procedure. To recover a deleted item, first check the Deleted option in the Insert Options box. To place the deleted link in a specific location click on Drop Before. Highlight the item to follow the recov ered item and click on Insert to restore the item to the desired place. Restoring a deleted menu item follows the same logic. First click on the Delete option, then click on Drop Before, highlight the menu to follow the recovered menu, and finally, click on Insert.

NSMEDIT makes provisions for copying an item one field at a time using the Windows clipboard. To copy something, first highlight the item in the Item Name, URL, or Description field, then click on Copy (or Cut). If you are copying to a new item, select the radio button (or click in the Insert Options frame) corresponding to the new entry, then click on Insert. Place the cursor in the field in which you want to place the clipboard contents and click on Paste. Repeat this process if there is more than one field.

LET'S REVIEW

A Netscape bookmark list is a menu containing links to Web sites or submenus. A bookmark link provides mouse-clickable selections of important documents.

Netscape menu organization is hierarchically based. To see the set of menus available, click on the Bookmarks item on the menu bar. Each top-level menu may have any number of submenus.

Netscape lets you modify menus by using three different techniques:

- The easiest way is to press Ctrl+A to add the bookmark of the currently viewed document to the selected Bookmark group. This same action may be initiated by clicking on the Bookmarks | Add Bookmark option.
- Use Netscape's bookmark editor by clicking on the Bookmarks | View Bookmarks option.
- Modify the bookmark file using a text editor.

Adding the current URL as a bookmark is a two-step process:

1. Make the target menu group the default. If no menu group has been selected, the item will be added as a top-level entry.
2. Press Ctrl+A or click on the Bookmarks | Add Bookmark option.

To move a URL between menu groups, first highlight the item to be moved and repeatedly click on the Up or Down button to place it in the correct position.

bookmark.htm is the default bookmark file that Netscape uses unless you specify another file by using the Preferences dialog box. If a new bookmark file is specified, it doesn't become effective until the next Netscape session.

Use the following steps to add a submenu:

1. Click on the Bookmarks | Edit Bookmarks option.
2. Select the item to serve as the top level for the submenu.
3. Click on New Header.
4. Enter the menu's title.

You can delete a highlighted menu by clicking on Remove Item in the Bookmark List dialog box.

The shareware program NSMEDIT supplied on the companion CD-ROM as nsmed22.zip overcomes many of the deficiencies inherent in using Netscape to edit a bookmark file.

Inside URLs

Do you still feel in the dark when it comes to URLs? Read on and you'll find out how quickly they'll become as familiar as an old friend.

Did you learn to drive a car with a stick shift? Remember what it was like in the beginning? If you were at all like me, the car jerked a lot and it seemed to be stalling constantly. Recall the horror of stopping on a hill for a red light? I used to wait until another car would come up behind me and ever so gently, I'd let my rear bumper come to rest on its front bumper. As the light was about to turn green, I would slowly take my foot off my brake pedal until the car behind me was taking the full weight of my car. I only had to worry about my clutch and gas pedal; the other driver had to worry about braking for both of us. Great stuff!

URLs are like stick shift cars. Not only are they scary in the beginning, but to make matters worse, the whole URL process doesn't seem to make any sense. However, there is good news; if you make an effort to understand URLs—as opposed to simply using them—not only will they make sense, they'll actually start becoming second nature. This chapter will try to bridge the gap between confusion and understanding when it comes to URLs.

THE UBIQUITOUS URL

URLs (Uniform or Universal Resource Locator) are central to understanding, and formulating, pointers to Internet resources. The entire purpose of Netscape's bookmarks is to save URLs along with their plain-text descriptions. These saved pointers to interesting places we've visited, or pointers to practical things we've done, allow us to go back and visit a Web site or perform a previous task, without the labor of retyping a cryptic string of characters.

Think of a URL as a standardized pointer to an Internet resource. The resource might be a graphic, sound, or just a plain text file. URLs are also used to initiate Gopher, Telnet, and FTP (File Transfer Protocol) sessions. A URL may fetch the latest postings from one of our favorite newsgroups. URLs can also point to queries, which are documents stored deep within a database.

In many cases, it's convenient to conceptualize a URL as the network equivalent of the standard DOS pathname and filename. In fact, a URL can point to a file on our PC. A URL can also point to a specific file in a specific directory on a remote network machine. A target file may reside on a Web server located anywhere in the world. The general concept underlying a URL is, "If it's somewhere out there on the Internet, we can point to it." In this chapter we'll explore some of the more common URLs.

THE COMPONENTS OF A URL

First, let's start with the component parts of a URL. One of the most famous of all URLs is the one for Netscape's home page, as we've seen before:

```
http://home.netscape.com/home/welcome.html
```

A URL has several components. The first part, the "http" in this example, determines the protocol used by both the Web server and client. (Recall that Netscape is a Web client.) A protocol is a standardized method of communication that we humans call a language. If you speak French and don't understand English and I speak English and don't understand French, we can't communicate very well. Turning up the volume or trying very hard doesn't help. (I always love it when I hear one person address a question to another person in a language the second person can't understand. The person asking the question will typically ask the question a number of times, each time speaking louder and louder. It's as if speaking louder will suddenly make the listener understand a language he or she doesn't know!)

The idea behind a protocol is to have one language that is common to all parties. Some of the common Web protocols, in addition to http, are gopher, telnet, ftp, news, and file. A colon separates the protocol from the remainder of the URL.

URLs typically have a common syntax for the part of the object following the ":". The next section begins with the double forward slashes "//" and includes everything until the next slash. The second part of the URL, "//home.netscape.com/", is the Internet address that contains the server software. The general form of this part of the URL is:

```
//host[:port]/
```

In general, the syntax convention used in computer manuals is that anything enclosed between the "[" and "]" pair is optional. The bracketed text need not be entered, but if it is entered, it must conform to the stated syntax. Each protocol has a designated *port* (more on ports in a minute). Based upon the above syntax, the use of the designated port negates the necessity for explicitly designating the standard port.

The last portion of the URL in the example

```
/home/welcome.html
```

is the path designator. The interpretation of a URL's path component is dependent upon the protocol used. For the most part, the path represents a directory structure on which the target file resides. The starting "/" indicates the root directory of the remote network, while the directory home, in Netscape's home page example, is a subdirectory of the root and so on. If the specific URL type allows a file name as a component of the URL, it will appear after the rightmost slash; "welcome.html" in this example. The html extension is the convention designating the file as a Web standard HTML (Hyper Text Markup Language) document.

EXPLORER TIP

Using the "/" in a URL

Some Web servers strictly enforce the URL standard that states that a URL should be terminated with a "/" slash. If your browser chokes when given a URL as shown above, append a "/" at the end. As an example:

```
http://home.netscape.com/home/welcome.html/
```

You will frequently see an http:// type of URL without a file name at the end. Most Web servers (the software on the sending end that interfaces with your browser) are configured to look for a file named "index.html" (or "index.htm" on a PC server) if no file name is specified. Keep this in mind when you create your own home page.

The protocol designation, http is this case, is case-independent as is the URL's domain name. However, the path and file names are case-sensitive if the target resides on a Unix-based machine. When copying a URL, be safe by entering the URL using exactly the same case as used in the original.

Certain characters may not appear in a URL; the most notable prohibited character is a blank. To overcome this problem, there is a special encoding scheme used to represent prohibited characters. The scheme begins with a percent sign "%" followed by two hexadecimal digits (0..9, A..F). As an example, the code for a blank is "%20". (You technical types will recognize that hex 20 is ASCII 32, both of which indicate a blank.)

UNDERSTANDING NETWORK PORTS

All networks connected to the Internet have a series of ports. Conceptually, network ports are very much like the serial communication ports on your PC. You may have a mouse connected to COM1 and a modem connected to COM2. Your serial controller card expects rodent-type things on COM1 and telephone-type things on COM2. The default port for the http protocol is 80. It is not necessary to explicitly declare port 80. If the desired http port is something other than 80, it must specified. Each protocol has a different default port. Let's assume that the HTML document jems.html resides on port 1213 of network www.state.pen.edu in the directory /you-call/we-haul. Its URL would be:

```
http://www.state.pen.edu:1213/you-call/we-haul/gems.html
```

HTTP URLS

The most common of all URLs is http, which stands for Hyper Text Transport Protocol. HTTP servers are common because they deliver hyper text documents using a low-overhead protocol that takes advantage of the fact that a link pointer may be embedded directly in HTTP documents. The embedded pointers are efficient since HTTP doesn't have to support full features, such as those employed by FTP and Gopher.

The general form of an http URL is:

```
http://host[:port][/path-name][/file-name]
```

Remember that the port is explicitly specified only if it is something other than 80—its default. Many times the pathname and filename are omitted, such as:

```
http://www.charm.net
```

If no path is specified, the server looks in the defaulted path. As stated above, if a file is not specified, the server initially looks for a file named "index.html" in the specified, or default, path. The advantage of unspecified path and file names is that the location of the start-up file, and subsequently read files, may be moved to another location without the necessity of changing the URL sent by the client.

OTHER TYPES OF URLS

We just learned about http URLs, which are the most common. The Internet provides many other types of URLs including gopher URLs, ftp URLs, telnet URLs, Usenet newsgroup URLs, file URLs, and partial URLs. Each of these URLs has its own port and unique features. Let's take a closer look at each one.

gopher URLs

Gopher is a text search and retrieval system named after the mascot of the University of Minnesota, where Gopher was created. (Aren't you glad you didn't go to this school and have to wear their t-shirts?) A Gopher server treats the hierarchy of Internet databases, directories, and files as a series of menus, which you can browse through to find specific information. Of course, the easiest way to access Gopher sites is by using a gopher URL.

The general form of a gopher URL is:

```
gopher://host[:port]/document-type[/path-name][/file-name]
```

Gopher's default port is 70 and it does not have to be explicitly specified, unless it is something other than 70. The document type tells the Gopher server what file type is expected by the client. As an example, a document type of "1" represents a top-level menu. (More on this subject when we deal with Gopher in depth during a future exploration.) Once you get below a top-level menu, the gopher URL will have a file name and most likely a path name. The URL for the top-level menu at the University of Minnesota—where Gopher was invented—is:

```
gopher://gopher.micro.umn.edu/1
```

The URL to get to the New Jersey menu on the University of Illinois at Urbana-Champaign weather Gopher is:

```
gopher://wx.atmos.uiuc.edu/11/States/New%20Jersey
```

Note the "%20" encoding method to overcome the blank prohibition in a URL.

ftp URLs

FTP stands for File Transfer Protocol. Cooperating networks have dedicated portions of their disk storage system for anonymous public access. Anonymous access simply means that you can download a file from an FTP server even though you do not have an account on the host network system. A Web browser, such as Netscape or Mosaic, makes what is otherwise a fairly arduous process a snap. We'll also have a future exploration dedicated to FTPing. The general form of an ftp URL is:

```
ftp://[userid[:password]@]host[:port]/path-name][/file-name]
```

The default port for FTPing is 21, which does not have to be explicitly specified unless it is something other than 21.

Entering an ftp URL without a trailing file name causes the display of the path's directory contents. This may be a big help if you know the directory but you are not sure of the name of the latest version of the desired file.

While in the process of preparing this book, my editor and technical wizard Jeff Duntemann, frequently FTPed material that I had left for him on my network disk drive. I always named the file to be FTPed jeff.zip. The network hosting the file is acy.digex.net and the path name is /pub/lejeune. Jeff had to enter the following URL one time:

```
ftp://acy.digex.net/pub/lejeune/jeff.zip
```

He then saved the URL as a Netscape bookmark using the title, "The latest grammatical nightmare from Urb." From that point, downloading the latest version of jeff.zip during a Netscape session was as simple as clicking on the LGM (latest grammatical nightmare) item in the bookmark menu. How easy can it get?

The prevalent FTP mode is anonymous. An anonymous session is initiated by entering "anonymous" (must be lowercase; however, "ftp" usually works) as the user name followed by entering the user's full Internet e-mail address as the password. (Usually "userid@" is enough since the FTP server knows the domain name of the connected network.) If the [userid[:password]@] portion of the FTP's URL is omitted, anonymous mode is assumed. There are FTP servers that require something other than "anonymous" as a userid. Additionally, if you actually have an account on a remote network, you may perform an FTP login using your real login name and password. Let's assume that Jane Doe has an account on network "big.deal.com"; let's additionally assume that Jane's userid is janedoe, her password is 123abc, and that her home pathname is /home/janedoe. Jane's ftp URL would be:

```
ftp://janedoe:123abc@big.deal.com/home/janedoe
```

While running Netscape, the above entry would produce a listing of her home directory. Since she would have read and write privileges in her home directory, she could send and receive files. If either the userid or password is specified, the "@" character must be included.

telnet URLs

Telnet is a remote logon protocol. In its simplest form Telnet allows "live" connections to another network. An account on the remote system is typically required. Your initial login sequence looks exactly as it would if you were logging into the system from a local terminal. More advanced uses of Telnet, such as logging into a remote library, may not require an account or password. Telnet is more powerful than FTP because it lets you do more than just access files from a remote computer. With Telnet, you can actually log into a network and run programs and other services available on the network. Unfortunately, Telnet is text-based so it might seem a little in need of a graphical facelift—especially after you've used Netscape.

The general form of a telnet URL is:

```
telnet://[userid:[password]@]host[:port]
```

Telnet's default port is 23 and need not be explicitly specified. A very common use of Telnet is to do an Archie search for a file name that exists somewhere out there in cyberspace. (You guessed it; there will be more information on Archie in a later exploration.) The URL for the Rutgers University Archie server is:

```
telnet://archie.rutgers.edu
```

You would log in as archie (no caps) when prompted for a login name. Technically, you should be able to enter

```
telnet://archie@archie.rutgers.edu
```

avoiding the entry of a login name. Unfortunately, most Telnet clients do not support this form of the telnet URL. Try it and see if your client supports login names and passwords. Some Telnet clients tell you to enter "archie" as a login name, others just ignore the "archie@" prefix.

Another great Telnet server, at least for ham radio operators, is the Amateur Radio Callbook at the University of Buffalo. The URL for this service is:

```
telnet://callsign.cs.buffalo.edu:2000
```

Notice that port 2000 is explicitly stated.

A practical note: When you Telnet from a Web client such as Netscape, the browser passes the information concerning the host and port information to a "helper" program called a Telnet client. The Telnet client supplied with the Netmanage Internet Chameleon package supplied on the enclosed CD-ROM works fine with the port as shown above. However, the Telnet client supplied with the Chameleon sampler, which is also supplied on the enclosed CD-ROM, expects a space between the host name and the port number. The Chameleon sampler's Telnet client does not resolve the host domain name lookup when entering the URL as shown above. The workaround, if your Telnet client behaves in this fashion, is to enter the URL with a space in place of the ":", such as:

```
telnet://callsign.cs.buffalo.edu 2000
```

It's not a legal URL (no spaces allowed) but it fakes out Chameleon.

Usenet Newsgroup URLs

If you've spent any time at all on the Internet, you've probably heard about Usenet newsgroups. Usenet is a really massive networked collection of newsgroups, which in turn refers to special-interest forums where Internet users get together to share common interests. Newsgroups have sprung up for just about any topic you can think of from archery to Zen and the art of computer programming. Once you start using newsgroups, you'll be hooked for life.

The URL format used to retrieve a Usenet newsgroup is different from those we have previously seen. To "point" to a newsgroup, use the following format:

```
news:group-name
```

As an example, the URL to retrieve the newsgroup comp.internet.net-happenings would be:

```
news:comp.internet.net-happenings
```

Netscape, and other browsers that I have tested, will not let you specify a news server as you might expect, such as:

```
news://[news-server]/news-group
```

The Netscape configuration file netscape.ini does not initially specify a news reader so you may not be able to activate a newsgroup at this point. There will be a large section on using Netscape as a newsreader in a later chapter.

File URLs

First, let's assume we have copied the Netscape home page to a disk on our local computer. (We'll do exactly that in the Chapter 8 exploration.) Let's additionally assume that the name of our local hard disk file is "netscape.htm" and that it resides on drive "D:" in directory "WWWfiles". To have Netscape load the local file, the entered URL would be:

```
file:///D:/WWWfiles/netscape.htm
```

There are several points worth noting in this example. There are truly three consecutive slash characters "/" following "file:"; it's not a misprint. Remember from our URL introduction that protocols are delineated by a colon followed by a double slash, then the network host information, followed by a single slash. Three consecutive slashes indicate that the network host information is absent (or null as computer tekkies like to say); therefore, the remainder of the path name is on the local computer, not on a remote host. Technically the designation for a file read from a local disk is:

```
file://localhost/
```

Most browsers are forgiving when using the "///" in place of the "//localhost/" designation. However, when breaking apart URLs, as with many other factors, browser mileage requirements may vary. As we go to press, the Netcom NetCruiser requires local file URLs in the //localhost/ form. Hopefully, they will see the light before you read this.

The DOS path and file names' URL separators are also "/" not "\". Information component separators contained within a URL are delimited by a forward slash; the backward slash (used as a delimiter in DOS) is a reserved character in URL-speak because of its Unix heritage.

DOS path and file names are case-independent. I like to intermix upper- and lowercase for clarity and readability.

Partial URLs

Once you have successfully retrieved a document located somewhere on the Web, you can use a partial, or relative, URL to point to another file in the same directory, on the same network. To illustrate, assume we have read the Netscape home page, having entered the URL:

```
http://home.netscape.com/home/welcome.html/
```

The file home_igloo.gif contains the large graphic image at the top of the Netscape home page. Assume it's located in the same directory as welcome.html. (It's actually not.) Therefore

```
ihome_iglo.gif
```

would be a valid partial URL following the initial retrieval of welcome.html. It is a shorthand notation for:

```
http://www.ncsa.uiuc.edu/SDG/Sofware/Mosaic/mosaic.gif
http://home.netscape.com/home/home_iglo.gif
```

Partial URLs are an important consideration when creating, or modifying hyper text documents. A group of hyper text documents, residing in a common directory, may reference one another using only file names. These documents are said to be hyperlinked. The normal information, such as access method, hostname, port number, and directory name, are assumable based on the URL used to reach the first document.

LET'S REVIEW

This treatment of URLs is by no means complete. There are enough variations on gopher URLs to fill an entire chapter. There are also several URL types that are not used often enough to justify inclusion in this overview.

In the most unlikely event that this overview has piqued your interest, here are several URL references in URL format:

A Beginner's Guide to URLs
`http://www.ncsa.uiuc.edu/demoweb/url-primer.html`

Uniform Resource Locators
`http://info.cern.ch/hypertext/WWW/Addressing/URL/Overview.html`

For a more advanced treatment of URLs try:

Universal Resource Identifiers in WWW
`http://info.cern.ch/hypertext/WWW/Addressing/URL/uri-spec.html`

So there you have it—probably more than you really wanted to know about URLs. Try constructing some of your own URLs from scratch to build your skill and confidence. If you frequently FTP to the same site and download files from the same directory, build a URL and save it in a bookmark.

Enough for URLs—let's set sail and explore some alternative Web browsers.

CHAPTER 6

Lynx and Character-Based Browsers

Graphical-based browsers aren't the only game in town for surfing the Web. Here's a useful guide to working with character-based browsers.

The World Wide Web is a system for organizing, transmitting, and retrieving all types of information. Netscape, Mosaic, and their clones are graphical Web browsers. Graphical browsers represent the glamorous window into the Internet. It seems hard to believe, but Mosaic—the first user-friendly graphical Web browser—appeared on the scene in the spring of 1993. The introduction of Mosaic ushered in a new era in information communications. Prior to Mosaic, simple character-based Web browsers and hierarchical-based menu systems were the order of the day. Despite the obvious advantages of graphical Web browsers, there are still times when a character-based browser may be all that is available. Indeed, character-based browsers are substantially faster than Netscape or Mosaic. In this chapter we'll look at the original Web browser developed by those wonderful people who made yodeling a national pastime, and we'll also look at Lynx, arguably the best of the character-based breed.

Surfing the Web takes some practice since you follow a trail of links rather than searching for a key word or phrase. Your experience cruising the Web and the enjoyment you receive from the activity is strongly influenced by finding client software that adjusts to your style and liking. The ease of use and features of a Web client are much more important than those of any other Internet related application. This chapter will explore and summarize Web browsers to give you information about a few powerful Web surfing tools.

PLAIN VANILLA OR GRAPHICS

Web browsers come in two varieties, character based and graphically interfaced. Character-based browsers, such as WWW and Lynx, were the first widely used browsers. Since character-based browsers are universally adaptable, they worked on an endless variety of plain computer terminals. Additionally, character-based browsers are easy to learn and use. Early character-based browsers established the viability of the Web. These browsers also demonstrated the underlying genius that conceptualized the organization and easy retrieval of data. This information was previously hidden in an information wasteland. However, the 1993 introduction of Mosaic, with its graphical interface, took the Web from a "conceptual proving ground" to a household term. Despite the obvious advantages of graphical browsers, there are still times when character browsing is more efficient and faster.

WHERE IT ALL BEGAN

The initial conceptualization of the Web took place at the European Particle Physics Laboratory (CERN) in Switzerland. A project headed by Tim Berners-Lee and staffed by a dedicated group of scientists, produced the working model of what was to become the World Wide Web (WWW). It is easy to take the underlying organizations of the Web for granted since it has become so pervasive; however, doing so ignores the information and data chaos that existed out there in Internetland prior to the work at CERN. There was a vast reservoir of information "on" the Internet but it was almost impossible to find. Tim and his band of digital musketeers brought order to the information wasteland. Not only did they conceptualize, standardize, and subsequently implement their intellectual offspring, they freely shared the source code so that others building upon the early model had a convenient starting point. There has not been a major Web browser creation that hasn't been influenced by the original source code conceived and developed in Geneva. It is only fitting that we begin our Web exploration with a visit to the Web's birth site.

The WWW Client

If you have an account on an Internet-connected system, you probably have a WWW client. To check, simply enter WWW at your system's prompt. If your network doesn't have a resident WWW client, you may Telnet to telnet.w3.org to sample the original Web browser at the newly formed W3 Organization. (The client is no longer available at info.cern.ch.) The initial screen will look something like this:

```
Welcome to the World-Wide Web

                              THE WORLD-WIDE WEB

  This is just one of many access points to the web, the universe of
  information available over networks. To follow references, just type the
  number then hit the return (enter) key.

  The features you have by connecting to this telnet server are very primitive
  compared to the features you have when you run a W3 "client" program on your
  own computer.  If you possibly can, please pick up a client for your
  platform to reduce the load on this service and experience the web in its
  full splendor.

  For more information, select by number:

     A list of available W3 client programs[1]

     Everything about the W3 project[2]

     Places to start exploring[3]

  Have fun!

1-3, Up, <RETURN> for more, Quit, or Help:
```

The WWW character-based browser has much in common with Netscape, but typing a number as opposed to mouse clicking is one major difference. Additionally, there are no graphical capabilities with any character-based browser. Each reference has a bracketed number next to the anchor. You can obtain a listing of all link URLs by entering "list" at the command-line prompt. You can access the same document using Netscape, or any other Web browser, by entering its URL. The CERN home page URL is:

```
http://info.cern.ch/default.html
```

The command line is simplicity personified and starts with the range of available numeric links, 1 through 4 in this case. You may also enter q or Q to exit the browser and return you to the operating system prompt. You can enter h or H for help.

Evoking help produces the following information and list of commands:

```
WWW LineMode Browser version 2.12 (WWWLib 2.15)   COMMANDS AVAILABLE

You are reading
  "Welcome to the World-Wide Web"
  whose address is
  http://info.cern.ch/remote.html

  <RETURN>        Move down one page within the document.
  Bottom          Go to the last page of the document.
  Top             Return to the first page of the document.
  Up              Move up one page within the document
  List            List the references from this document.
  <number>        Select a referenced document by number (from 1 to 3).
  Go address      Go to document of given [relative] address.
  Verbose         Switch to verbose mode.
  Help            Display this page.
  Manual          Jump to the online manual for this program.
  Quit            Leave the www program.

1-3, Up, <RETURN> for more, Quit, or Help:
```

Some descriptions may end with an asterisk. The output of the asterisk-suffixed commands normally produces the "displayed" version of HTML documents. If you prefix the designated command with "source," the output will be the original HTML source documents. As an example, if you would like to save the HTML source of the displayed document as a disk file named "www.html" on your local system, enter the following at the WWW command-line prompt:

```
source > www.html
```

Selecting option 3 from the start-up screen, "Places to start exploring," produces the following selection:

```
GENERAL OVERVIEW OF THE WEB

   There is no "top" to the World-Wide Web. You can look at it from many points
   of view. Here are some places to start.
```

```
by Subject[2]          The Virtual Library organises information by subject
                       matter.

List of servers[3]     All registered HTTP servers by country.

by Service Type[4]     The Web includes data accessible by many other
                       protocols. The lists by access protocol may help if
                       you know what kind of service you are looking for.

  If you find a useful starting point for you personally, you can configure
  your WWW browser to start there by default.

_________________________________

1-5, Back, Up, <RETURN> for more, Quit, or Help:
```

The command-line options now include an expanded link list with a range encompassing 1 and 5. The first entry on the last line is 1-5, meaning that there are five selectable links in this document. Since the last displayed link is number 4 (of 5), there are additional pages to be displayed. Entering [b]ack ("b" must be entered, "ack" is optional) will return the display to the previous document. Pressing the return key will move to the next page, and entering u[p] will scroll back one display screen.

CERN type browsers are freely distributed with no strings attached. There are browsers available for most operating systems via anonymous FTP. For more information ftp to info.cern.ch and go to the directory /pub/www and get the file readme.txt.

Technically, the WWW browser is a line mode browser with all displayable lines inserted at the bottom of the screen. Insertion of additional lines forces the original lines up on the page, much like a typewriter. The big advantage of a line mode browser is that it doesn't care what type of terminal you are using. The disadvantage is that all of the "action" takes place on the last line. In summary, line mode browsers are easy to use, they are universally adaptable, but they are not much fun to use. Before moving on to screen mode browsers, I would personally like to thank Tim Berners-Lee and the dedicated staff at the European Particle Physics Laboratory for making the Web a reality. Without their pioneering work, we would probably be reading *Vogue* or *Sports Illustrated* instead of the *Netscape & HTML EXplorer*.

THERE'S A LYNX IN YOUR FUTURE

Lynx is a screen mode Web browser developed and maintained at the University of Kansas. A screen mode browser can write to any spot on the screen. Like their line mode counterparts, they only display characters, not graphics. They do, however, display enhanced characters such as highlighted and terminal characters that are provided with the enhanced character set.

A University of Kansas group headed by Lou Montulli took the original concept and implementation of the CERN staff and expanded it to become Lynx. The U of K group added features and increased user-friendliness. Lynx has been an evolving project ever since. Many people have contributed to the project either directly through bug reports or suggestion, or indirectly, through the development of parallel clients.

There are other screen mode Web browsers. Telnet to www.njit.edu or vms.huji.ac.il if you would like to see examples. (Log in as www.) Lynx is by far the most popular non-graphical interface to the Web; it is also the most feature rich and the best maintained. Much of what follows applies to the other browsers as well, but we'll stick to Lynx as the main model.

You should have a Lynx client on your Internet connected system; try it out by typing "lynx" at the command-line prompt. (If your system is Unix based, you must enter "lynx" in all lowercase letters.) If you don't have Lynx on your system, you should ask your system administrator to obtain the client. You'll probably not get much objection since Lynx is free for the asking. You may obtain Lynx using anonymous FTP from ftp2.cc.ukans.edu in the /pub/lynx directory.

Let's Tame Lynx

Start Lynx by entering "lynx" at your operation system command-line prompt. If your system does not have a lynx client, you can access lynx by Telneting to ukanaix.cc.ukans.edu, and enter www when prompted for a userid. If you have Lynx on your local system, it may not start with the University of Kansas home page. If not and you want to follow this exploration, enter the following at your command-line prompt:

```
unix% lynx http://www.cc.ukans.edu
```

In short order you are connected to the University of Kansas with its home page displayed. If you are using Netscape, Mosaic, or another graphical viewer connected to the Internet using a 14.4 Kbps—or slower—modem, you will be impressed with the document transfer speed. As with any communications link, the speed is a function of the slowest component. The transfer of data between connected networks is substantially faster than the transfer of information across a modem-connected telephone line. Your service provider only has to send terminal information one screen at a time. In addition, there is substantial time required to transmit graphic images over the modem line and to decode and display the transmitted images and display them on your local terminal. Progress does have a cost!

The University of Kansas home page will look something like the following:

```
About Lynx (p1 of 3)

                                ABOUT LYNX

   Lynx is a fully featured World-Wide Web browser for users on both UNIX
   and VMS platforms who are connected to those systems via
   cursor-addressable, character-cell terminals or emulators. That
   includes VT100 terminals, and desktop-based software packages
   emulating VT100 terminals (e.g., Kermit, Procomm, etc.).

   For information on how to use Lynx see the Lynx User's Guide, or the
   Lynx help files.

   Tell us how you use Lynx.

Credits and Copyright

   Lynx is a product of the Distributed Computing Group within Academic
   Computing Services of The University of Kansas. Lynx was originally
   developed by Lou Montulli, Michael Grobe, and Charles Rezac. Garrett
   Blythe created DosLynx and later joined the Lynx effort as well.
— press space for next page —
  Arrow keys: Up and Down to move. Right to follow a link; Left to go back.
 H)elp O)ptions P)rint G)o M)ain screen Q)uit /=search [delete]=history list
```

One of the anchors will appear in reverse video to indicate that it is the current default. You can make another link the default anchor by pressing the down arrow key to move down in the list, or by pressing the up arrow key to move up in the list. Press the right arrow key to activate a link and press the left arrow key to go back to the previous document. Entering "?" or "H" (must be capital H) will activate the following help screen:

```
Help! - Press the Left arrow key to exit help

                              LYNX HELP FILES
```

```
Choose a subject

     * Key-stroke commands
     * About Lynx
     * Lynx users guide version 2.3.7
     * New, improved Key-stroke commands for version 2.3.7
     * Lynx users guide version 2.3
     * Help on version 2.3
     * Help on HTML
     * HTML Quick Reference Guide
     * Help on URL's


Commands: Use arrow keys to move, '?' for help, 'q' to quit, '<-' to go back
  Arrow keys: Up and Down to move. Right to follow a link; Left to go back.
 H)elp O)ptions P)rint G)o M)ain screen Q)uit /=search [delete]=history list
```

At some point in your Lynx exploration, you will want to view the last three selections on the help menu. Since this is a browser chapter, not an HTML chapter, we'll stick to Lynx selections. Selecting the first option produces the listing of all the Lynx keystroke commands:

```
          MOVEMENT:

               Down arrow         - Highlight next topic
               Up arrow           - Highlight previous topic
               Right arrow,
               Return, Enter      - Jump to highlighted topic
               Left arrow         - Return to previous topic

        SCROLLING:
               + (or space)       - Scroll down to next page
               - (or b)           - Scroll up to previous page

        OTHER:
               ? (or H)     - Help (this screen)
               a            - Add the current link to your bookmark file
               c            - Send a comment to the document owner
               d            - Download the current link
               e            - Edit the current file
               g            - Go to a user specified URL or file
               i            - Show an index of documents
               m            - Return to main screen
               o            - Set your options
               p            - Print to a file, mail, printers, or other
               q            - Quit (Capital 'Q' for quick quit)
               /            - Search for a string within the current document
               s            - Enter a search string for an external search
               n            - Go to the next search string
               v            - View your bookmark file
```

```
z          - Cancel transfer in progress
[backspace]    - Go to the history page
=              - Show file and link info
\              - Toggle document source/rendered view
!              - Spawn your default shell
CTRL-R         - Reload current file and refresh the screen
CTRL-W         - Refresh the screen
CTRL-U         - Erase input line
CTRL-G         - Cancel input or transfer

H)elp O)ptions P)rint G)o M)ain screen Q)uit /=search [delete]=history list
```

Lynx has a bookmark function that is very similar to Netscape's bookmark. You save a pointer to your personal bookmark file by entering "a" at the command-line prompt. The next prompt is:

```
Save D)ocument or L)ink to bookmark file or C)ancel? (d,l,c):
```

If you want to save the pointer to the currently displayed document, press "d"; to save the pointer to the highlighted document, press "l". Be careful of this subtle distinction. Assume you are viewing document A and the default anchor is a hyperlink pointing to document B on another site. If you press "a" followed by pressing "d", you copied the link to document A to your bookmark file. If you press "a" followed by pressing "l", you've saved the link to document B.

The bookmarks are saved in a file named lynx_bookmarks.html in your home directory. As the extension implies, the file is an HTML document and is therefore a plain text file. You may edit any HTML file with any editor on your system that is capable of saving files in plain text format. You may view your bookmarks by entering "v" at any command-line prompt. A small sample of a bookmark file might appear as follows:

```
Bookmark file

   You can delete links using the new remove bookmark command. It is
   usually the 'R' key but may have been remapped by you or your system
   administrator.
   This file may also be edited with a standard text editor. Outdated or
   invalid links may be removed by simply deleting the line the link
   appears on in this file. Please refer to the Lynx documentation or
   help files for the HTML link syntax.

     1. Internet Course
     2. Help
     3. IST World Wide Web Menu
```

```
Commands: Use arrow keys to move, '?' for help, 'q' to quit, '<-' to go back
  Arrow keys: Up and Down to move. Right to follow a link; Left to go back.
 H)elp O)ptions P)rint G)o M)ain screen Q)uit /=search [delete]=history list
```

You cannot use the bookmark feature if you are accessing Lynx through a Telnet client. By definition, you have no local directory when you Telnet to a remote system. You also have no write privileges, so you cannot save a Web file to disk.

EXPLORER TIP

Kickstarting Lynx

A script is a Unix executable file much like a DOS batch file. Scripts are handy for a variety of purposes, especially when you would otherwise have to enter a series of commands.

I use a script called "links" when starting Lynx to accomplish the following:

1. Change directories to directory Lynx so that any files downloaded during the current Lynx session are saved in the same place.
2. Automatically start at the University of Kansas home page unless another URL is entered.
3 Eliminate the need to enter the "http://" portions of the URL when starting Lynx. Change back to my home directory when exiting Lynx.

The following is a listing of the script file links. You will find it on the enclosed CD-ROM in directory "scripts." Copy the file to your Unix home directory. At the command-line prompt (assuming that "unix%" is your prompt), enter:

```
unix% chmod 700 links
```

The change mode (chmod) command, using the parameter 700, makes the script file executable. To start Lynx at the University of Kansas, simply enter:

```
unix% links
```

To start at any other location, enter:

```
unix% links url
```

where url is the URL of the desired location, without the leading "http://". As an example, start Lynx at:

```
http://www.charm.net/~lejeune
```

which is my home page. Following is the listing of the script links. The "#" indicate a Unix comment.

```
unix% links www.charm.net/~lejeune

 # Script "links" to start a lynx session
 #
 # The syntax is:
 #             links [domain-name]
 # If a domain name is specified the lynx session will start at that site,
 # otherwise, the lynx session will start at the University of Kansas,
 # the home of lynx.  Do not enter the "http://" portion of the URL.
 #
 # The first thing this script does is change your directory path to
 # directory "lynx" which must be a subdirectory of your home directory.
 # To create the directory use the syntax unix% mkdir lynx
 # This directory will hold any material you download during a lynx session.
 # After quitting lynx this script will change back to your home directory.
 #
cd /$HOME/lynx # change to subdirectory lynx
if test -z "$1"
  then # There is no passed parameter
    lynx http://ukanaix.cc.ukans.edu
  else  # There is a passed parameter
    lynx http://$1
fi       # end if
cd $HOME # change back to home directory
```

LET'S REVIEW

If you are looking for an alternative to one of the graphical browsers such as Netscape or Mosaic for surfing the Web, Lynx is probably your best bet. You can try out Lynx by logging in your Internet connection and typing "lynx." If your Internet provider does not have Lynx available, you can get it by anonymous FTP from ftp2.cc.ukans.edu in the /pub/lynx directory. Its URL is:

```
ftp://ftp2.cc.ukans.edu/pub/lynx/
```

I suspect that few people will use the WWW browser since Lynx has so much more to offer. Lynx offers most of the functionality of Netscape or Mosaic, without the graphics. URLs can be loaded, bookmarks can be saved, and the same HTML document serves both masters. If speed, as opposed to glitz, is your prime surfing criterion, Lynx is hard to beat. To paraphrase the old commercial, "Try it, you'll like it."

Netscape: The Great Presentation Machine

Speeding up Netscape is simply a matter of learning how to download time-intensive Web pages. In the process, you'll discover that Netscape makes a great stand-alone presentation program.

I'll bet this scenario sounds familiar: You call up a friend or family member and the line is busy. After trying over and over you decide that something has "gone wrong." You then call the phone company or, if you're really paranoid, the police. Almost always the problem isn't an equipment glitch; it's the fault of the person you're trying to reach who has caught a bad case of wind-bag-itis.

The Internet equivalent of this telephone scenario typically occurs when you try to connect to a very busy computer such as Netscape's or the NCSA computer that Mosaic calls home. These computers are probably the two busiest computers on the Internet. Many monthly surveys show Netscape's home page is the most frequently accessed Web document, closely followed by the NCSA home page. Typically, the NCSA What's New page is in fourth or fifth place on the Web hit parade. (I'm not sure what the third most popular site is but it was probably Brandy's Cyberbrothel until it was taken off the air!)

Equipment and practical considerations limit access to these popular sites to a finite number of users. Forget trying to FTP from Netscape during prime time. After a major new version release it may be difficult making an FTP connecting to Netscape Central for several weeks. Many other Web sites have also imposed access restrictions. Don't forget that most of these computers have "real jobs" and their primary purpose in life isn't just to serve you information and entertainment on the Web.

The Web equivalent of a busy signal is usually a cryptic non-descriptive message. (Cryptic error messages are a carryover from the old days when systems programmers tried to fake out less sophisticated users.) If you have received an "Unable to connect to HTTP Server!" or "SOCKET: Connection has been refused" message, you've received a busy signal and most likely nothing is wrong with your Netscape installation or Internet access. Unfortunately, the connectivity problem is going to get worse because Web users are increasing faster than the facilities available to service their needs. NCSA specifically requests that Web users specify a startup site other than the NCSA home page to help reduce the strain on its network.

In this chapter I'll give you some alternatives to initially connecting to the home page of one of these busy sites. One of the techniques, loading copies of Web documents to your local hard drive, uses the fact that Netscape, in addition to being a great Web browser, is also an outstanding stand-alone presentation program.

TAKING THE STRAIN OFF THE WEB

You can easily reduce the strain on the prime Web machines when you start Netscape, or any other Web browser, by using one of these three methods:

- Start Netscape without displaying any document.
- Load a home page document from somewhere other than Netscape.
- Load the Netscape home page or any other document from your hard drive.

Let's examine these options one at a time. The last technique, loading from your hard disk, presents other interesting possibilities.

NO DOCUMENT ON STARTUP

Netscape, as orginally configured, loads its home page document from this URL:

```
http://home.mcom.com/home/welcome.html
```

The fastest way to speed up the loading of Netscape, and save valuable Internet resources, is by starting the program without displaying a home page. You can do this by executing the following sequence, Options | Preferences. Then, open the Set Preferences On menu and select Styles if it's not already selected. Figure 7.1 shows the radio buttons used to start Netscape with a blank page or a unique home page location. A startup URL can be entered even if the Blank Page radio button is selected.

If you select the Blank Page radio button and you have Netscape's home page URL (or any other URL) in the text box, you can bring up the home page at any time in the session by clicking on the toolbar's home page icon.

Turning off the display of inline images is another method to speed up the process of loading Web pages. The graphics associated with a Web document are typically much larger than the text portion of the file. As an example, the Netscape welcome page document is 3.4K in size while the GIF at the top of the page weighs in at 19.6K and the one at the bottom of the page is 5K. Text represents only 3.4K of the 37.9K total required to display the entire document. In addition, a graphic must be uncompressed and displayed, which takes addi-

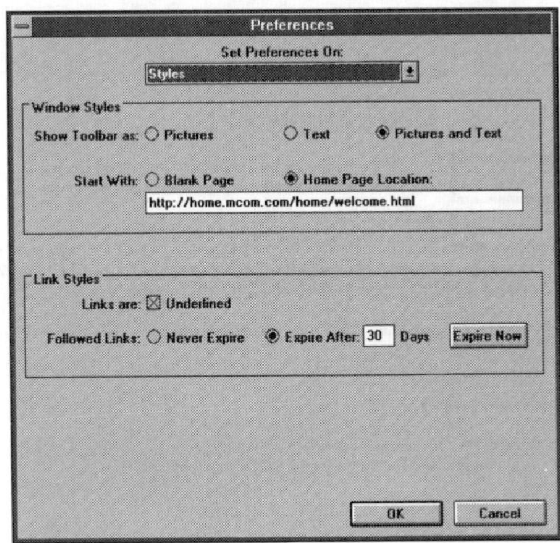

Figure 7.1 *Netscape's home page options from the Preferences' Styles menu.*

tional processing time at the browser end. All other things being equal, it takes ten times as long to load the graphic as it takes to fetch the home page document. To get Netscape to turn off automatic graphics display, open the Options menu and uncheck Auto Load Images. Thereafter, a locally supplied little graphic will appear wherever transferred graphics would normally appear. Figure 7.2 shows my home page without my smiling face staring out at you.

You can display the full graphic of an individual iconized image by clicking on it using the right mouse button, which brings up a menu of options. Click on Load this Image to display the individual image. You can also click on the Images icon on the toolbar to display all the document's images. After unchecking Auto Load Images, you can then turn image display back on by reversing the process.

SHIFTING THE LOAD TO SOMEONE ELSE

The second alternative for saving wear and tear on busy computer sites is to shift the burden to someone else. This does not save network bandwidth since you are still going to fetch a document, and maybe a graphic or two, but it will make the people at NCSA happy. (If no one called NCSA for a full day, do you think they would start checking their equipment?) I get the feeling that the Netscape people, unlike the folks at NCSA, enjoy a captive audience. They may not be happy if you don't call on a regular basis.

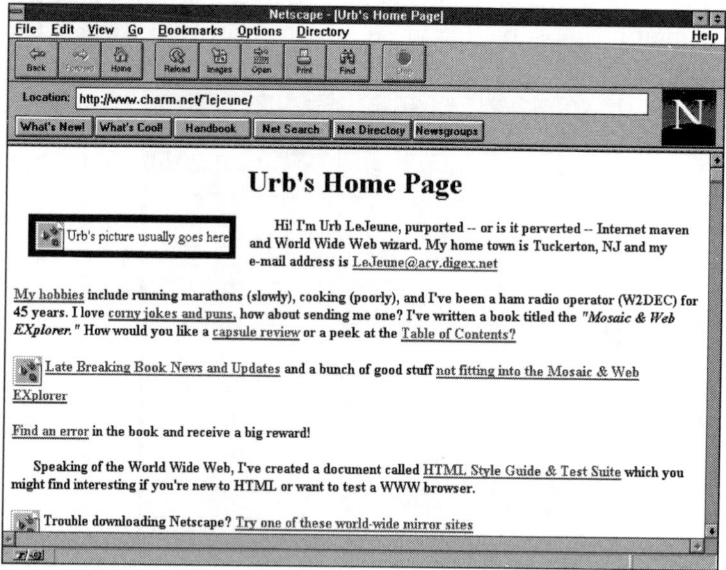

Figure 7.2 *Urb's home page without graphics.*

If you've discovered a nifty starting point for Netscape, by all means use it. I start my Netscape sessions with a large menu loaded directly from my local hard disk. More on this technique in a minute. To load a different starting home page, copy the URL for your favorite site and insert it in the text box in the Options|Preferences|Styles page. (If you're clever, copy it to the Windows clipboard and paste it into the text box.) A site with many well-maintained pointers to interesting places is a great Netscape starting point. An outstanding example of such a document is "Subject Based Information" on the University of Maryland, Baltimore Campus, machine. It contains pointers to over 200 web sites. Categories are alphabetically arranged. The URL for this wonderful document is:

```
http://umbc7.umbc.edu/~jack/subject-list.html
```

If you are going to change the Home Page document, it's a good idea to save the Netscape home page URL as a bookmark before making the change. There may still be times when you want to call up Netscape.

To configure Netscape to display the "Subject Based Information" document at startup, follow these steps:

1. Load the document.
2. Select the document's URL in the Location: text box using the mouse.
3. Copy the highlighted URL to the Windows clipboard by pressing Ctrl+C.
4. Execute the sequence Options|Preferences.
5. Select Styles from the Set Preferences On menu.
6. Highlight the Home Page URL.
7. Press Ctrl+V to paste in the new URL from the clipboard.

Loading Netscape from Local Files

If you want to become a good net citizen but you also like the look and convenience of the Netscape home page when Netscape starts, all is not lost. You can still reduce both your use of net bandwidth and the strain on the Netscape machine by first storing a document you normally retrieve from the Net on your hard disk. After you have brought all its associated files, if any, to roost on your computer, you can start Netscape and display the page by loading any files from your locally stored copies. Is this the best of all worlds or what?

Netscape, in addition to being a great Web browser, is also a great presentation program. You can use the techniques I'll present next to create your own presentations with the same look and feel that Netscape provides when you connect to the Web. The only difference in the operation of Netscape is that URL links point to your hard drive instead of somewhere out in Webspace. I frequently give Netscape presentations, using the Netscape home page, without using a modem or a phone line. All the required components, including graphics, are loaded from my laptop's hard disk. Extending the no-Internet-connection concept, I have developed Netscape presentations that have nothing to do with the Internet or the Web. Netscape's ability to present documents in a non-linear fashion is a major presentational advantage.

Having Netscape load hypermedia documents from your hard drive, instead of fetching them from Webland, is a two-part process:

1. Transfer the desired document from its host site.

2. Make any necessary changes to the links.

Let's look at each of these processes.

Downloading to Your Hard Disk

Ideally, you could load the Netscape welcome page directly from a hard disk. However, the page uses special bit-mapped graphics called *imaps*. The concept underlying imaps is that graphics images are treated as partitioned maps. You can activate a link in an imap by clicking someplace within the graphic image. We'll be exploring imaps a little later in this book, but for now let's use a simpler home page so that we won't have to deal with the complexities of imaps. For our example, we'll download the University of Maryland's Subject Based Information (UMD) page to disk for easy retrieval. Having the ability to load the UMD page from your hard disk requires transferring the UMD's main HTML document to your hard disk. Fortunately, you can easily download files from a Web site to your local disk using Netscape.

Start the process by creating a directory on your hard disk to hold Web documents. I keep all my Web documents in a directory called d:\WWWfiles. You may, of course, keep the file anywhere you choose.

Getting the University of Maryland's Subject Based Information Page

Let's go out and get the file for the University of Maryland's Subject Based Information page. Once you have this file, you can view it from your own PC.

Start by connecting to the UMD URL at:

```
http://umbc7.umbc.edu/~jack/subject-list.html
```

Save the Web page you are currently viewing by executing the sequence File | Save As. (The shortcut key for this process is Ctrl+S.) This action brings up the Save As dialog box as shown in Figure 7.3. The actual name of the file is subject-list.html. Let's save this document as subject.htm in the directory d:\WWWfiles.

Since the file name has more than eight characters, the default transfer file name will truncate to eight characters. The file extension will also default to the first three characters of the original extension. It truncates because DOS file names can only contain eight characters, and DOS extensions only three. Unix file names can be substantially longer and may also have multiple periods. Although DOS limits you to using eight characters, use a meaningful file name. After you enter the path and file name for your download in the Save As dialog box, click on the OK button or press Enter to start the transfer.

EXPLORER TIP

Getting Organized

If you plan on building a library of hard disk hypermedia documents, you may want a separate directory for each site from which you download files. As an example, you could create a subdirectory called Netscape immediately under d:\WWWfiles to store the files for various Netscape pages and graphics. Without such organization, you'll find it difficult to associate files with Web sites.

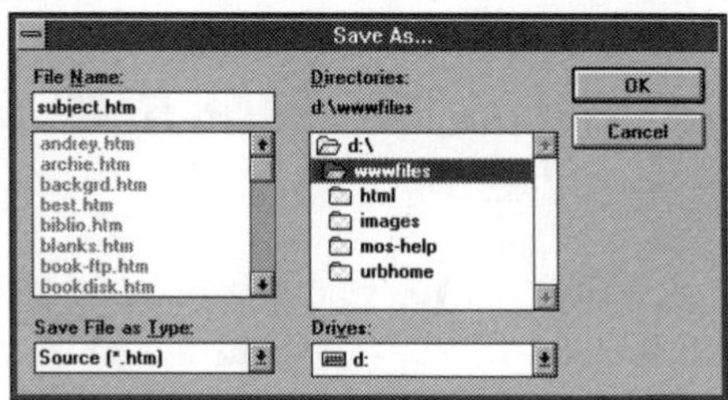

Figure 7.3 The Save As dialog box used to save the UMD HTML document.

In most cases, you'll need to download GIF graphical files that are associated with the Web pages you download. You'll also need to modify internal links that the documents use so that they can be loaded from your local hard drive. We'll get to these more exotic examples in a few minutes, but for now let's take our newly loaded document for a spin. Assuming the file was saved to your PC as d:\wwwfiles\subject.htm, enter the following URL:

```
file:///d:/wwwfiles/subject.htm
```

Note several things in this URL. First, there are three backward slashes ("/"), not two. If you recall our earlier URL exploration in Chapter 5, we usually place a domain name between the "file://" and the "/". Since we are reading the file from a local hard disk, we don't need to include a domain name. Some browsers may require the URL to be entered as:

```
file://local-host/d:/wwwfiles/subject.htm
```

But you don't need to do this with Netscape.

The second formatting issue to take note of is that the forward slash "/" (not the standard DOS backward slash "\") is used to specify the directory path for the file. Browsers are designed to speak Unix—not DOS—and Unix uses "/" instead of "\". Netscape will actually accept "\" slashes in the DOS portion, but most browsers are not as accommodating.

Figure 7.4 shows the document displayed after being loaded from my hard disk. When you load from your own hard disk, notice the relative speed between loading a document from disk as opposed to loading it from the net. The difference is especially pronounced when loading graphics.

Congratulations, you have just completed a major step. You might be surprised how often the question of how to load documents from disk comes up on the various discussion lists.

EXPLORER TIP

Getting Your Local HTML Documents to Load

Now that you've discovered one of Netscape's best kept secrets—it can load and interpret HTML documents stored on your hard drive—you might be tempted to use this feature often. Because you may be loading files without

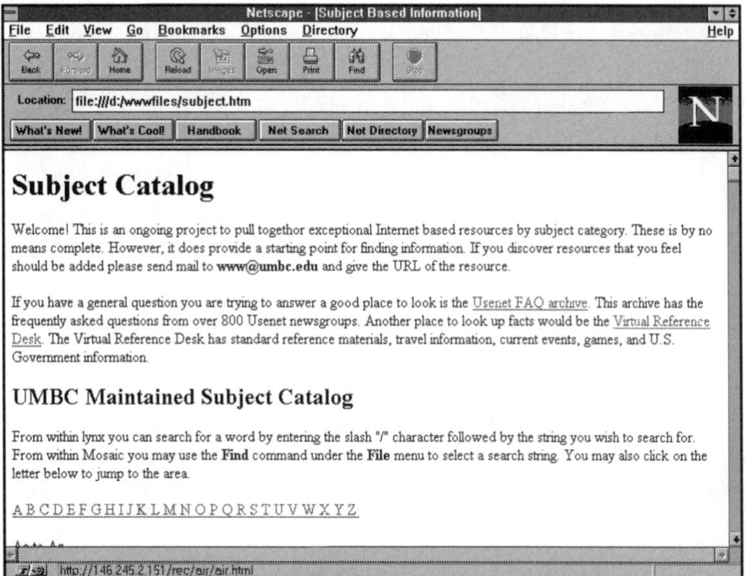

Figure 7.4 *Displaying the UMD home page after being loaded from a hard disk.*

being connected to the Internet, you might encounter occasional problems. The first, and easiest problem to fix, is when your local HTML documents might try to access other documents that aren't available on your hard disk. In this case you'll need to either download the files to your computer or make sure that you are connected to the Internet.

The other trick in loading local files is that you should make sure that your TCP/IP stack software is loaded in memory so Netscape will operate properly. This software performs the work of connecting your computer to the Internet. You don't actually need to dial to your provider and connect to the Internet; you just need to load the TCP/IP software so that Netscape will not give you any error messages.

Essentially, here's how Netscape operates. As it performs certain operations, it calls special functions that are stored in a file named winsock.dll in some directory accessible in your Path variable. These functions are known as the *WinSock API*. If the TCP/IP software is not loaded, some versions of Netscape and other browsers such as Mosaic may not be able to locate the WinSock API functions. If this happens, you'll receive an error message indicating that your browser could not find winsock.dll. To fix the problem, run the TCP/IP software you use to connect to the Internet and minimize it—the stack doesn't have to be logged into anything. You don't have to actually connect to your provider, only load the software. I'll cover TCP/IP software in much more detail in Part 4 of this book.

Another alternative, especially attractive if you are using Netscape on a laptop and never connecting to the Net via a modem, is something called a *NULLSOCK*. It's essentially a "fakeout" piece of software. Netscape, and many Netscape mirror sites, provide a program file named mozock.dll. This file is included on the companion CD-ROM for you to use. You can also get the latest version of this file by FTPing to the same site you would normally use to obtain Netscape. It may be in the same directory as the Netscape browser or it may be in another directory. The URL for FTPing mozock.dll directly from Netscape is:

```
ftp://ftp.netscape.com/unsupported/windows/mozock.dll
```

Copy mozock.dll to the same directory containing Netscape. Rename mozock.dll to winsock.dll and you won't need TCP/IP software to use Netscape to view Web pages stored on your hard drive. When you want to use Netscape to go back online to the Web, you'll need to change the name of winsock.dll back to mozock.dll.

Loading the Charm Net Home Page to Disk

Let's practice what we've learned and pick up a few new techniques by downloading the Charm Net home page. This is the Web site we first explored in Chapter 3.

Previously, we saved Charm Net's home page URL as a bookmark. If you still have it in your bookmark list, activate it now. If not, type http://www.charm.net/ in Netscape's Location: text box. The Charm Net home page appears as shown in Figure 7.5. The border around the top image indicates that the image itself is an anchor pointer. If you don't have a Charm Net entry in a bookmark list, save it now.

The actual HTML document used to produce the Charm Net home page is displayable using the View | Source sequence. You must click on the option, Source in this example, or make it the highlighted item using the down arrow key, then press Enter. Figure 7.6 shows how the charmnet.html source document is displayed when you select View | Source. Let's dissect the following portion of the second line:

```
<a href="charminfo.html"><IMG ALT="" SRC="logo.gif">
```

The first part, '<a href="charminfo.html">,' is called an *anchor reference*. If you click on the logo for Charm Net, a document named charminfo.html will be loaded. The second part, '<IMG ALT="" SRC="logo.gif">' is a pointer to an

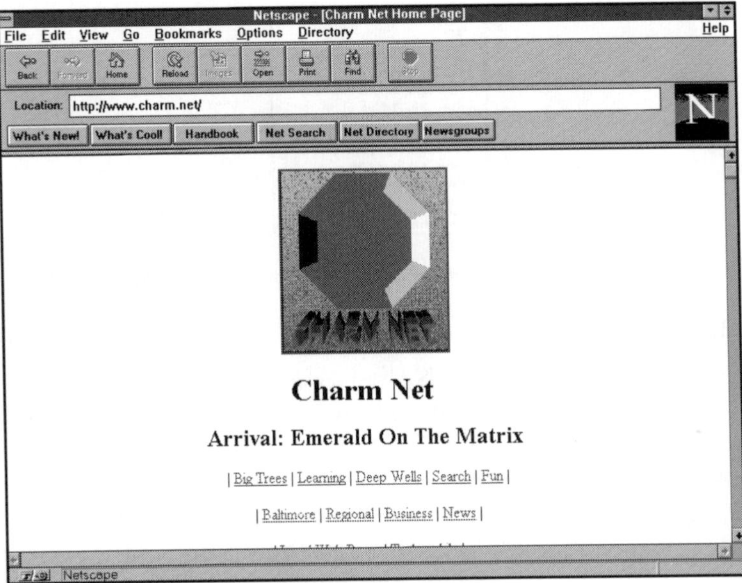

Figure 7.5 Viewing the Charm Net home page.

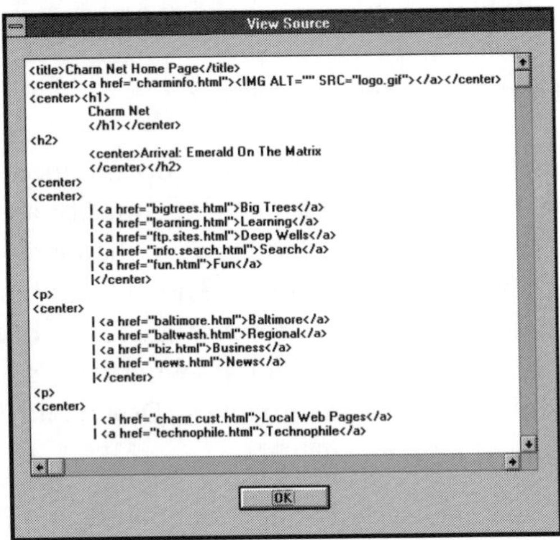

```
<title>Charm Net Home Page</title>
<center><a href="charminfo.html"><IMG ALT="" SRC="logo.gif"></a></center>
<center><h1>
        Charm Net
        </h1></center>
<h2>
        <center>Arrival: Emerald On The Matrix
        </center></h2>
<center>
<center>
        | <a href="bigtrees.html">Big Trees</a>
        | <a href="learning.html">Learning</a>
        | <a href="ftp.sites.html">Deep Wells</a>
        | <a href="info.search.html">Search</a>
        | <a href="fun.html">Fun</a>
        |</center>
<p>
<center>
        | <a href="baltimore.html">Baltimore</a>
        | <a href="baltwash.html">Regional</a>
        | <a href="biz.html">Business</a>
        | <a href="news.html">News</a>
        |</center>
<p>
<center>
        | <a href="charm.cust.html">Local Web Pages</a>
        | <a href="technophile.html">Technophile</a>
```

Figure 7.6 The HTML source document for the Charm Net home page.

image (.GIF file) having the same name, logo.gif in this case. Let's download the GIF and then we'll return to this anchor.

Close the HTML source document by clicking on the OK button. When the Charm Net home page is again displayed in the document area, click on the large logo graphic with the right mouse button. This will bring up a

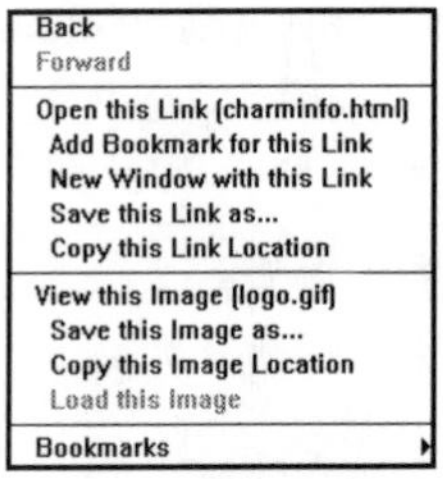

Back
Forward
Open this Link (charminfo.html)
Add Bookmark for this Link
New Window with this Link
Save this Link as...
Copy this Link Location
View this Image (logo.gif)
Save this Image as...
Copy this Image Location
Load this Image
Bookmarks

Figure 7.7 *The dialog displayed when you click on an image with the right mouse button.*

menu with a few options as shown in Figure 7.7. Just below the bottom third divider is an entry, View this Image (logo.gif). Viewing the image will simply display it all by itself on a page. This option would be handy if we had the Auto Load Images unchecked. However, we already know what the image looks like so let's download it. Click on the option, Save this Image as, and the familiar Save As dialog box will appear. Save the image as logo.gif in the same directory you used to download the Charm Net home page document.

Changing Pointers

Let's return to the HTML statement we were looking at earlier:

```
<a href="charminfo.html"><IMG ALT="" SRC="logo.gif">
```

The link reference in this address and the GIF document are in a form called a *relative reference.* Because the link does not specify a particular path for either of these files, charminfo.html and logo.gif, the browser expects to find both of them in the same directory where the home path is stored. The Charm Net home page and the logo.gif files are now stored on our hard disk, so no problem. However, charminfo.html is not anywhere to be found on our hard disk. We have the following two alternatives: Download the document, or point to the document at Charm Net.

charminfo.html is dynamic—it's modified frequently, reflecting the rapidly changing nature of Webspace. It is not normally good practice to download all of these documents to a local computer, unless you are going to use them strictly for demonstration purposes. Bringing the Charm Net home page to a computer near you is therefore a matter of copying the home page document and the associated GIF. After the two files are resting comfortably on your hard drive, you'll need to change the dynamic link pointers in the home page file so that they still fetch the documents from their original location on the Charm Net server.

Since the URL for the original Charm Net home page document was

```
http://www.charm.net/
```

we simply need to prefix our charminfo.html reference with this URL. It therefore becomes:

```
<a href="http://www.charm.net/charminfo.html">
```

Taking a close look at the charmnet.htm document shows many references having the appearance of the following:

```
<a href="bigtrees.html">Big Trees</a>
<a href="learning.html">Learning</a>
<a href="ftp.sites.html">Deep Wells</a>
<a href="info.search.html">Search</a>
<a href="fun.html">Fun</a>
```

Each of these documents must also be downloaded or the reference must be changed. Unless you're doing an entire presentation using local documents, you will most likely change pointers. If your favorite text or HTML editor has a global find and replace function, the task is easy. If your editor doesn't have a global find and replace, you may want to try the Windows Write editor. If you use Write, it will ask if you want to convert to Write format (.WRI extension) when you load the file charmnet.htm; reply, "No Way." When saving the edited file, make sure that it's saved as a text file. If you use a word processor to perform the search-and-replace task, make sure you save the file as a plain-text ASCII file.

After loading charmnet.htm in your seek-and-destroy editor, search for

```
href="
```

and replace that string with

```
href="http://www.charm.net/
```

My favorite HTML editor is Web Spinner. (It's included on the companion CD-ROM.) This editor has a search and replace option, making it easy to perform the above task. Highlight the text to be used for the search. Then, execute the sequence Search | Replace to display the Replace dialog box shown in Figure 7.8. The Find What text box is filled in with the highlighted text. Fill in the Replace With text box with the replacement text. Next, continuously click on Find Next and Replace to modify the links as necessary.

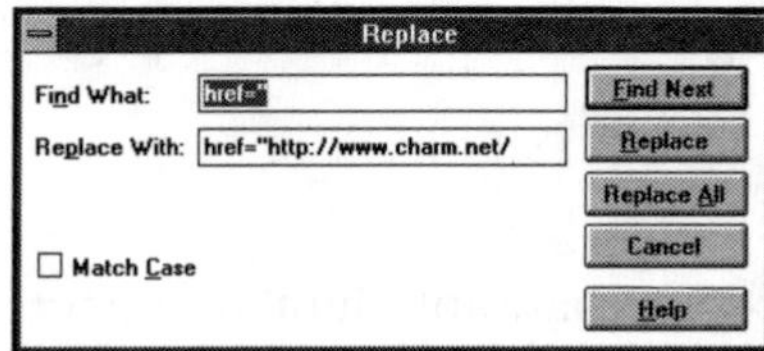

Figure 7.8 Using the Web Spinner Replace dialog box.

The modified charmnet.htm file should now look like the following listing:

```
<HTML>
<HEAD>
<title>Charm Net Home Page</title>
</HEAD>
<BODY>
<center><a href="http://www.charm.net/charminfo.html">
<IMG ALT="" SRC="logo.gif"></a></center>
<center><h1>
   Charm Net
   </h1></center>
<h2>
   <center>Arrival: Emerald On The Matrix
   </center></h2>
<center>
<center>
      | <a href="http://www.charm.net/bigtrees.html">Big Trees</a>
      | <a href="http://www.charm.net/learning.html">Learning</a>
      | <a href="http://www.charm.net/ftp.sites.html">Deep Wells</a>
      | <a href="http://www.charm.net/info.search.html">Search</a>
      | <a href="http://www.charm.net/fun.html">Fun</a>
   |</center>
<p>
<center>
   | <a href="http://www.charm.net/baltimore.html">Baltimore</a>
   | <a href="http://www.charm.net/baltwash.html">Regional</a>
   | <a href="http://www.charm.net/biz.html">Business</a>
   | <a href="http://www.charm.net/news.html">News</a>
   |</center>
<p>
<center>
   | <a href="http://www.charm.net/charm.cust.html">Local Web Pages</a>
   | <a href="http://www.charm.net/technophile.html">Technophile</a>
   |</center>
<p>
<center>
   | <a href="http://www.charm.net/pip.html">Connect</a>
   | <a href="http://www.charm.net/charm.pip.html">Connect To Charm Net</a>
   | <a href="http://www.charm.net/charminfo.html">About Charm Net</a>
   |</center>
</BODY>
</HTML>
```

I've added a few tags to this listing for consistency with other HTML listings in this book.

Great job! You're now ready to create your own hyper text slide shows. How does it feel to be a creative artist?

LET'S REVIEW

You can reduce the strain on the Web computers and be a good net citizen using one of three different methods:

- Have Netscape start without displaying any document.
- Load a home page document from somewhere other than Netscape.
- Load a document, complete with graphics, from your local hard drive.

The method you choose is a matter of personal preference.

Building a local copy of a starting home page, or any other HTML page, typically downloaded from a remote host, is a five-step process:

1. Capture the HTML text of the desired page to a local file with an .HTM extension.
2. Change the appropriate pointer using Netscape's Options | Preferences | Styles dialog box. Point to the entry of your choice, either a site on the Web or the location of the local file.
3. If the local file contains references to a non-text file, such as a graphic image, download the referenced file.
4. Change any links referencing downloaded non-text files so they point to the location of the local files.
5. If links to frequently changing sources do not contain external pointers, they must be added.

Save the displayed HTML document to disk by executing the sequence File | Save As. (You can also use the hotkey Ctrl+S.) This will bring up the Save As dialog box. Enter your desired file and path names.

To save an image file, click on the image with the right mouse button, which brings up a a few options. Click on the Save this Image as option.

This will bring up the Save As dialog box where you should enter your file name and path preferences.

After loading a home page or any document from your hard disk, check your links very carefully. Drag across all anchors in the displayed document to insure that they will not try to fetch a hard disk file that isn't there.

Well, there you have it, Netscape fans. What could be better than speeding up your Web surfing while simultaneously reducing net traffic? If you come up with interesting ways to use Netscape as a presentation tool, I would sure like to hear about them.

Publishing on the Web

Exploring the Power of Web Publishing

Get ready—the fascinating world of Web publishing is just around the corner. All you need is a little patience and some good ideas!

Now that we've mastered the art of exploring the Web with Netscape and using features like URLs and bookmarks, it's time to turn the corner and start our Web publishing explorations.

In the previous chapter, we learned how to prune and tune Netscape's home page so that Netscape could read it—including its embedded links—from your local hard disk. We've also pulled apart URLs in a recent chapter. This experience should give you the background you need so that you can jump in and learn how to create your own Web publishing documents and eventually publish on the Web.

In many ways, you'll be surprised at how easy it is to create your own Web pages, including a home page, and become a cyberspace publisher. If you have a talent for graphics and design, you'll really feel at home. But you don't need to be an artist, designer, or professional author to publish on the Web; you just need something interesting to tell the world.

I'll start Part 2 of this book by discussing what Web publishing is all about. You'll learn how to take advantage of this exciting medium by looking at the kinds of documents you can and cannot publish. After this introductory chapter, we'll start by creating a home page and then we'll learn how to use most of the key HTML features—including formatting codes, hyperlinks, and tables—to create exciting and useful Web pages. The more you learn about HTML, the more you'll appreciate the flexibility of this publishing tool.

Here are some of the questions that I'll answer in this chapter:

- What is Web publishing and what can be published on the Web?
- Why is Web publishing becoming so popular?
- What is the difference between a home page and a Web page?
- What exactly is a Web server?
- What is an HTML document?
- How are Web pages created?
- What is needed to publish on the Web?
- What does it cost to set up a publishing operation on the Web?
- What is involved in setting up a Web server?

THE WORLD OF WEB PUBLISHING

From using Netscape and surfing the Web, you already know that the Web is an interwoven network of computers and documents. With the powerful technique of hyperlinking, many different kinds of documents—from online newspapers to catalogs to complete electronic books—can be linked in interesting ways. New content and links can be added at any time and adding features like "point and click" navigational maps and interactive forms to Web publications makes them more interactive and useful.

The best part about Web publishing is that you don't have the kinds of limitations that you face with traditional publishing. Some of these limitations include:

- The high costs of paper and printing
- The cost and challenge of wide distribution (especially if you are a small publisher)

- The logistics problem of receiving feedback from people who read or view your publications
- The significant amount of time required for publishing and distributing material

Web publishing removes these obstacles because it is an electronic medium—a medium supported by the dynamic, global nature of the Internet. You don't need to be in any specific place in order to publish on the Internet. Also, the people who read or view what you've published don't have to go to central distribution centers, such as bookstores or newsstands, to get your latest publication. All they need is an Internet connection and access to the Web.

As the Web is becoming more widely used, more and more companies and individuals are setting up publishing operations. In some cases, material published on the Web can't be found in any other medium, including newspapers, magazines, or TV. Some companies are even using the Web to showcase new publications and get feedback from their audience before they publish their products in a printed or recorded format. For example, The Coriolis Group—the publisher of this book—often puts early chapters of some of their books on the Web before the book is printed and distributed. This allows readers to get information quickly and check out a book in advance.

A NEW KIND OF PUBLISHING

If anyone tells you that publishing on the Web is just a new form of desktop publishing or that it's just like creating online documentation, tell them you have ocean-front property in Arizona to sell them. Web publishing requires a completely different approach to designing and creating publications. Whether you want to publish an electronic newsletter or a catalog, your audience will have a completely different set of expectations. The information or *content* that you publish should be interactive, contain links that access other content, be up-to-date and as dynamic as possible, and should use different media—text, sound, images, video, and so on—whenever it makes sense to do so. Let's take a closer look at these different aspects of Web publishing.

Interactive Publishing

Many users look for an interesting home page with links to click on in order to access more information, or fill out a form. Often, users will be able to navigate by clicking on a visual map or icons. This gives the users the feeling that they can easily interact with the content they are exploring.

In traditional publishing, the audience is passive. They can't send a message to the author, ask a question, or click on a "link" to get more information. If you haven't worked with the interactive element before, this takes some getting used to. You need to learn how to design your publications so that your audience won't get easily bored or distracted and wander off to check out another site. Whether you are creating newsletters, books, magazines, newspapers, or personal content, the goal is to attract the reader's attention and keep it focused on your publication by offering the reader things to do. Some of the more useful techniques for accomplishing this include:

- Provide a set of links to other sites of interest so that your users can easily explore other places.
- Include features that users can click on to see more of a subject. For example, let users click on an image that will display a complete photo gallery.
- Add forms that users can fill out to send you comments or ask questions. (If you include features like this, make sure you set aside some time to respond to your users.)
- Provide searching features so that users can easily look up information.

Some of these interactive features require special skills to incorporate. However, as the Web is becoming more interactive, more and more tools are being developed to help publishers create interactive Web pages. And the best part is that many of the tools are free or very inexpensive. One useful system now available for setting up a "chat mode" feature is called WebChat. As shown in Figure 8.1, you can create a set of Web pages where users can come and leave messages for each other.

To learn more about WebChat or try out a live demo, use this URL:

```
http://www.irsociety.com/webchat/webchat.html
```

Publishing on Demand

People who are in traditional publishing businesses (books, magazines, newsletters, and so on) often talk about the ability to publish information "on demand." The underlying issue here is that most people don't need an entire book or magazine when they are interested in learning something new. Usually, they are looking for specific information and they end up having to

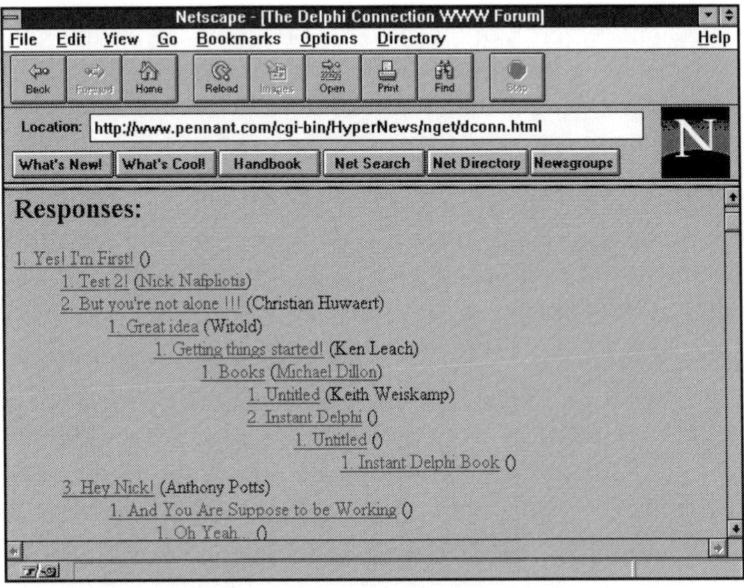

Figure 8.1 *Setting up an interactive chat mode with WebChat.*

purchase an entire book just to get access to one chapter they need. For example, let's say you are creating Web documents with HTML and you are interested in learning more about the newer features that have been added to HTML. Instead of buying a complete book on HTML that covers most of what you already know, what you really need is a straightforward guide with examples of the new features.

The Web easily makes this kind of publishing possible because of the "on demand" nature of Web pages. As you gain more experience publishing on the Web, you can even set up features such as a database of articles that your users can query to access important information.

ME MAGAZINE

The following article about the future of publishing appeared in the Oct/Nov 1994 issue of *PC TECHNIQUES* Magazine. In it, the author, Jeff Duntemann, discusses a new approach to publishing designed for the future. If you think about it, some of these ideas are starting to appear now.

> The Internet is a lot like NASA in some ways. It's a gigantic testbed for technologies we're going to need someday to serve the general

public. Client/server is one of these, and the more I play with the Internet, the more possibilities I see in really *really* sophisticated client/server publishing systems—systems good enough to put me out of a job.

In 2005 I see a new model for periodical publishing. The press syndicates have gone electronic and absorbed the editorial function. Writers sell *them* articles now, and the syndicates do the copy editing and proofing. Finished pieces are indexed and categorized and stored on a server on our information superhighway.

Publishers have mutated away from content generation toward a niche once filled somewhat gamely by clipping services. Subscribers subscribe to a *publisher*, not to any specific magazine. Each publisher has a very clever client application that maintains a subscriber interest profile and uses it to search the syndicates for articles, columns, and cartoons that seem to fit the subscriber profile.

Each month, or two months, or every 33 or 41 days (or whatever), the client goes out and finds as much stuff that fits the profile as the reader has requested and paid for. If, for example, I can only read 40 pages every month, I get 40 pages. If I know I'm going on vacation, I can request that the July issue be 70 pages long instead.

The profile is detailed indeed. I can request articles on any topic I'm interested in. I can ask for *Dilbert* and *Outland*; trends in copper prices; photos of classic Chevelles; and new recordings of music by Percy Grainger, Ralph Vaughan Williams, and Leslie Gore. The client digs up what it can, and then arranges it in a tidy if plain page layout and sends me the file. I can read it on the screen or print it to paper to take to the beach.

The free market works well here. If the publisher I subscribe to delivers stuff that I think misses the profile, I take my profile to a different publisher. The publisher prospers on the strength of its client application. The price I pay for my subscription depends on what percentage of ads I allow the publisher to sprinkle into my periodical, and how expensive the stuff I request happens to be. The publisher charges the advertisers to advertise in my periodical by how "valuable" my demographics are to them. Authors are paid by the request, and the more people who request their material, the more they get paid.

It's an *extremely* efficient system, especially with regard to wasted paper. About 50 percent of all magazines are never sold and go right from stores to landfills. (Sooner or later, the environmentalists are going to find out about that.)

Multimedia Publishing

If you think multimedia is one of those publishing buzzwords coined by computer people years ago to sell more computers, you're probably half right. Many brilliant people in the computer and publishing industries have made all kinds of predictions and promises over the past five years about multimedia; unfortunately, this technology hasn't quite taken over. One of the biggest problems with multimedia is that multimedia applications are difficult to develop and test. In addition, many users easily get bored with multimedia because it often offers nothing more than boring "point and click" slide shows.

Multimedia publishing on the Web offers something very important that can't be done with other publishing vehicles such as CD-ROMs—new content can easily be added. You can design Web pages that offer multimedia features such as sound, video, images, and so on, and then you can continually update your links so that your users don't get bored by seeing (or hearing) the same thing over and over.

The other major benefit of multimedia publishing on the Web—and one that is making it grow rapidly—is that it's easy to do. You don't need any special multimedia languages or engines to add multimedia links to your Web pages. In addition, you can easily create multimedia pages that can be "viewed" by users of a wide variety of computer platforms—from PCs to Macs to Unix machines.

Resource Publishing

When was the last time you bought a computer book or magazine, only to be disappointed that the publication didn't come with a disk or CD-ROM loaded with goodies for you to play with or try out? Although the costs of duplicating disks and CD-ROMs are decreasing, it's still an expensive proposition to produce them and get them in the hands of your users. Web publishing attacks this problem head on by offering users the ability to automatically download software, multimedia files, text, and other resources by simply clicking on a link.

This "dynamic download" feature opens up all kinds of new possibilities for publishing. Instead of displaying everything in your publications, you can easily provide links that will send material to the user's computer when selected. This approach can save you time and resources. The challenge is to determine what to display and what to include as a resource link.

New Technology—Virtual Reality on the Web

Just as I was in the final month of finishing the writing for this book, a new technology was introduced on the Web that introduces the fascinating world of virtual reality (VR) and 3-D like walkthroughs. Instead of clicking on two-dimensional maps to navigate, you can move around in a 3-D like environment and explore information. The driving force behind this new publishing technology is a language for creating Web pages called *Virtual Reality Modeling Language* (VRML).

Figure 8.2 shows a Web page created with this VR technology. Currently, popular browsers such as Netscape can't view VRML documents; however, the next generation of browsers should be able to. And in the Web browser business, a new generation appears every few months. To find out more about VRML, check out this site:

```
http://vrml.wired.com/
```

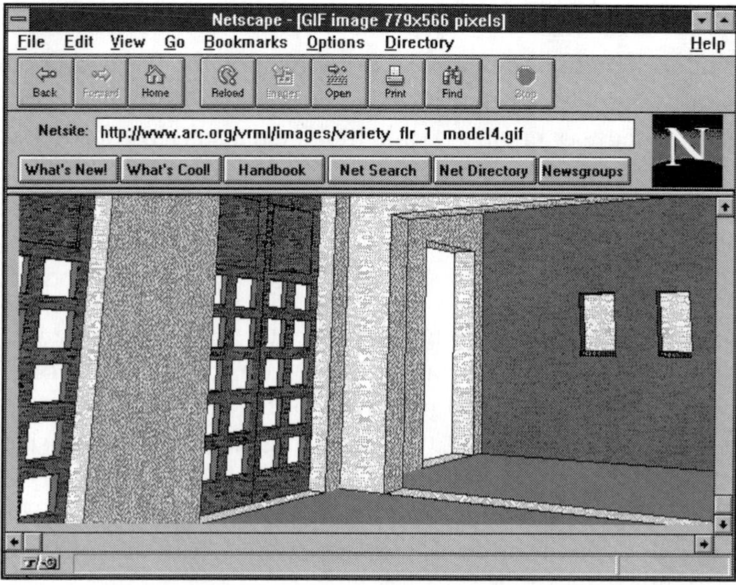

Figure 8.2 *Creating 3-D navigational systems for Web publishing.*

Growth of Web Publishing

Here's one of the most commonly asked questions on the Internet and in computer magazines these days: How fast is the Web growing? Nobody knows for sure but new Web sites are emerging daily. And the main reason most of these sites get set up in the first place is to publish material for others to explore.

Although Web traffic still accounts for only a small percentage of Internet activity, the Web is growing faster than any other Internet service. Popular Web sites that feature newly published home pages have become so popular that your chances are better at getting a parking place at the beach on the fourth of July than being able to connect to one of these sites.

This means the competition is heating up for people who want to publish on the Web and get others to view their publications.

What Can You Publish on the Web?

Since you've been surfing the Web with Netscape, you probably are already familiar with a few of the types of publications that can be successfully distributed. Here are a few additional suggestions, some of which you might not have encountered yet:

- **Specialty Newsletters.** The Internet is a great place for people with similar interests to get together. In fact, many people who have unique hobbies or professions join newsgroups so that they can share information—new ideas, gossip, horror stories, and so on. Newsgroups are one of the most widely used features of the Internet. As the Web is becoming more popular, specialty newsletters are being published that provide a useful supplement to newsgroups. These newsletters feature in-depth articles, interviews, tips and advice, and graphics and illustrations. To create your own specialty newsletter, all you need is a topic that you know something about and the ability to write, edit, or talk other people into writing and editing for you. Whether you are into hang gliding, stamp collecting, or traveling in foreign countries, you can turn your interests and knowledge into a publishing venture without spending a lot of money and resources on printing, paper, and postage.
- **Personal Profiles.** You might not have much to say about a particular topic, such as rock climbing, mountain biking, or gourmet cooking, but you should have a lot to say about yourself. Because of the high cost of traditional publishing, most people don't feel that they have the opportunity to share personal things with the world. Once you are on the Web,

you can publish any type of personal information, including your resume or a collection of poetry or short stories. Who knows? Maybe someone will read your stuff and offer you a job or a book contract.

- **Electronic Books and Magazines.** Many commercial publishers who are looking for new and innovative ways to distribute their publications are turning to the Web. In fact, some of today's publications exist only in an electronic format. Some readers who get both a printed and electronic version of a publication prefer the electronic version because they can search for information and get up-to-the-minute corrections and updates. Many tools and converters are being developed to help traditional desktop publishers transfer their publications created with programs like PageMaker to a Web page format. As the tools improve, more and more books and magazines are likely to appear on the Web.

- **Shopping Catalogs and Guides.** One concept with a very promising future in the Internet and the Web is the world of online shopping. Every day someone I know asks me, "Can you really buy things on the Internet?" Of course you can, In fact, you can buy anything from a luxury car to a wedding gift for a friend. If your company has products for sale, you can create electronic catalogs and brochures that feature pictures and descriptions of your products. You can even offer free samples by including links that your customers can click on. The best part about featuring products on the Web is that you can include ordering information so that customers can buy your products directly from you.

- **Directories.** The world is full of directories: white pages, yellow pages, *TV Guide*, *Literary Marketplace*, guides to U.S. colleges, lists of books in print, concert tours for rock bands, sports schedules.... The list goes on and on. The biggest problem with most of these printed directories is that they are quickly out of date. On the Web, you can publish electronic directories that can be updated weekly, or even hourly if you have a lot of free time on your hands. A good Web-based directory can easily link to other Web sites and resources to help the user better access referenced information.

- **Research Rep¡orts and Studies.** So many interesting studies and reports have been written about the world; unfortunately, many of these reports are hidden away in library basements. You can easily turn hard-to-find information into interesting reports, complete with illustrations and photography. You can also include information about yourself or the author of the reports so that readers can send in comments and critiques. The Web could even be a good place for you to test out your college term papers.

- **Annual Reports or Company Profiles.** Companies trying to get the word out about how well they've done throughout the year or who plan to introduce new products or services are turning to the Web in record numbers.

- **Literature, Fiction, and Poetry.** Surprisingly, this is still a relatively untapped corner of the Web. There are some good, interesting sites devoted to literature, but many of these are just lists of links for books or poems you can download. There are relatively few Web sites that offer truly interactive and visually oriented online books and magazines (sometimes called "ezines"). One of the best of the ezines is a Canadian online publication called *Teletimes.* You can view some of their back issues at:

  ```
  http://www.wimsey.com/teletimes/teletimes_home_page.html
  ```

  If you've got a literary bent and have always wanted to start a "small press" literary magazine, now's a good time to get your publishing operation going online. To exploit the full capabilities of the Web, be sure to include photos of authors, artwork, and links to other interesting literary Web pages.

- **Online Documentation.** The Internet is jam-packed with authors of shareware and freeware programs, and one of the main reasons these authors love the Internet is that they can publish their documentation online. Instead of having to run to the printer every time they add a new feature to a program, they can simply update their online manuals. This is a great way to introduce a product to the world and keep your manufacturing and support costs down.

- **Unique Projects.** Your Web publishing venture doesn't necessarily have to be oriented toward a traditional publication venue. Because the Web provides multimedia capabilities, you can provide anything from an online science experiment to an interactive game. The Web is rife with unique sites, from the outlandish (Talk to My Cat) to the fun (the URoLouette) to the educational (Dissect a Virtual Frog). Just let your imagination guide you.

If you are still not sure what you want to publish on the Web, you should spend a little more time exploring what others have done. The best part is that you can easily check out the work of others to see the mistakes they've made and "steal" some of their better ideas.

WHAT EXACTLY ARE WEB PAGES?

Before I can answer this question, there are few concepts and terms we need to discuss so that you can keep all of this new publishing technology in perspective. Here are the four important buzzwords of Web publishing:

- Web site
- Web server
- Web page
- Home page

Anything published on the Web must physically be located on a computer somewhere. This location is called the *Web site.* It could be anywhere in the world, from Hawaii to Australia. Three pieces of hardware are needed in order for the Web site to operate: a computer, a physical connection to the Internet, and a big hard disk. In order for users to be able to access the Web site at will, it must be connected to the Internet 24 hours a day.

Many Web sites that operate as major electronic publishing centers perform other operations as well. For example, you could connect up a computer to be your Web site and then use the same computer to run reports for your company at night. However, if your Web site gets really popular, your computer might be tied up all the time.

The Web site's mission in life is to broadcast (transmit) information and this is where a *Web server* comes in. Essentially, a *Web server* is specialized software that transmits information from a Web site to a user's computer. When you access a location on the Web such as Netscape's home page, you are sending a message to Netscape's Web server telling it that you want some information. The server responds by sending you back files that your Web browser can read and display.

What are the primary files that Web servers transmit? Web pages of course. All documents that are published on the Web are called *Web pages.* This term is a little misleading because a Web page is really not a page per se; it is simply a document—a text file with special formatting and linking instructions. The technical term for a Web document is the infamous *HTML document.* As you'll see shortly, HTML is the heart and soul of all Web documents, including home pages.

A *home page* is simply a Web page (or HTML document) that has a special function. It is the first document that is transmitted by a Web server when you access a Web site. Let's look at an example. If you give Netscape a URL such as

```
http://www.coriolis.com/coriolis
```

the Coriolis Group's home page will be transmitted by a Web server to your computer. When the server determines you are asking for something, it says "I guess they want the home page because they didn't ask for anything specific." Now, let's assume you use a slightly different URL:

```
http://ww.coriolis.com/coriolis/xyz.html
```

This time around, you'll get a different Web page—the file xyz.html, because that's the file you asked for.

People who publish on the Web use home pages as their front door. A good home page invites the user to come inside, look around, and spend some time.

What's a Markup Language?

We've been talking about HTML, but we haven't properly introduced it yet. HTML stands for *Hyper Text Markup Language*. Let me start by stating that a detailed reference guide on HTML appears in Appendix A. This appendix even covers the more widely-used features that have been introduced by HTML 3.0—the new emerging standard. (More on this in a moment.) In this chapter, we'll explore just the basics of HTML so that you can start constructing a cool home page using a minimum number of HTML features. In later chapters, we'll go a little deeper into HTML and you'll learn how to create more powerful Web pages. After you've finished reading all of the HTML chapters, you'll have the knowledge to create many types of Web pages and publish many different types of documents on the Web, including documents that incorporate multimedia features.

HTML is based on a language called *SGML* (Standard Generalized Markup Language), which has been around for years. Many people in the typesetting industry use it in one form or another to prepare documents for publication. HTML is actually a subset of SGML. It contains the more useful commands, which are called *tags*, for specifying how documents should be displayed and processed in Web browsers like Netscape.

If you have ever looked at what's stored in a word processor file, you've probably noticed that the file's data looks much different from what you see when viewing the file with the word processor. Within the file, you'll find special encoding data to indicate that certain text should be displayed in bold, italic, large type, double space paragraphs, and so on. This type of file stores data that is tagged with a special markup language so that a particular program will know how to interpret the data. Netscape and other Web browsers are similar to your word processor; they read a markup file and display the results on the screen in WYSIWYG (What You See Is What You Get) format. But one major difference between Web browsers, such as Netscape, and your word processor is that browsers do not write to a file; they only read from plain ASCII text files and reformat the input to produce those dramatic display effects, including both text and graphics. The other difference is that the information displayed in Web browsers is "interactive;" users can click on things that in turn cause other actions to occur.

One common misconception about HTML is the belief that it is a page layout or page description language like PostScript. HTML is actually a much simpler language and is designed to describe how documents are organized and not just how they should be displayed. For example, HTML doesn't allow you to specify the fonts you want to use in a document. It also doesn't allow you to indicate the leading (spacing) for how lines of text should be displayed. You might at first think that this is a big limitation, but it's actually a benefit in disguise. The actual formatting of HTML documents is left up to the browser program that views the document. This allows HTML documents to be interpreted and formatted in a number of different ways. The main benefit with this approach is that HTML documents can be read by a wide variety of browsers (HTML readers) running on literally every type of computer in the world. For example, if a user has a text-based browser such as Lynx running under Unix, they would be able to view the same document that a Power Mac Netscape user could view. In this respect, you can think of HTML as the universal publishing language.

GETTING STARTED

Before you start writing HTML documents and setting up a publishing center, you need to carefully plan what you want to accomplish. Otherwise, you'll end up with an assortment of documents that aren't as effective as you'd like. Publishing on the Web is a "trial and error," time-consuming activity, so you want to plan as much as you can in advance.

What Do You Want to Publish on the Web?

Okay, so you know you want to create your own Web pages. And maybe you have a general idea about what you want to include at your Web site. But unless you're only planning to create a simple "one-page" home page with maybe a graphic or two and a few links to other people's sites, you still have a lot of planning ahead of you.

The best way to begin planning is probably among the most obvious: Take a close look at what's already on the Web. But don't approach this by simply touring five or six or even a dozen Web sites at random. Purchase copies of *Wired, Internet World*, and other magazines and books that review Web sites and publish URLs. Then go visit Web sites that sound interesting .

Again, don't check out just a few sites. If you haven't yet spent a lot of time on the Web, you might not realize how easy and fast it can be to visit several sites in a relatively brief period. In two to three hours, you can easily tour 50 or more Web sites. If you haven't visited *at least* this many Web sites, you haven't even begun your homework.

When you find a Web page that is especially well designed or that has unique design concepts, print or download the page for future reference. All the elements of your pages don't have to be 100 percent original. If you borrow design concepts from other Web pages and then incorporate the best ones into your own Web pages, your published work will almost certainly look unique. In fact, your pages will look derived only if you model them based solely on one or two other Web pages, so "borrow" from as many sources as you can find.

Designing for the Web

In print media—regardless of whether we're speaking of books, magazines, newspapers, or newsletters—designing a publication is a critical, essential step. This is also true for broadcasting, although the design approach used in print and in broadcasting are a bit different.

Book, magazine, and newspaper designers and layout artists typically begin with a "dummy," which is simply a rough layout of the different components of the publication. A dummy shows where headings, body text, artwork, and other components will be placed and in what size and appearance. Often designers will come up with several dummies, or design versions, and then either select the one that seems to work best or select different elements from each dummy and then "mix and match" to incorporate the best concepts from each dummy into a single design.

In broadcasting, especially in TV advertising, designers use an approach called "storyboarding." A storyboard is much like a dummy, except that a collection of storyboards is created to show the sequence of events or scenes that will make up the complete broadcast. So storyboarding just takes the dummy approach a step forward to show sequential events. In other words, storyboards show how different events relate to one another and help designers and producers determine how the events will be arranged.

In designing effective Web pages, storyboarding is practically a necessity because the interactive nature of links will have your visitors jumping from one location to another in rapid-fire succession. You need to make sure you provide plenty of clear direction in how to navigate your Web pages so that your visitors don't become lost or frustrated between one link or page to another.

Remember, storyboards don't have to be fancy; they're just rough sketches that convey design and organization concepts. You can build your storyboards by using one sheet of paper for each Web page you want to create. For each page, a storyboard page should show what graphics are displayed on that page, what kinds of text are presented, any buttons or icons and what the buttons do, what kinds of links are on the page, and any check boxes or interactive forms that your visitors can fill in.

Then, you can shuffle your paper pages around to determine how you want to sequence your Web pages. You may find that you come up with new ways to combine pages. And, of course, your Web pages can have multiple links with each other. When you have an idea of what you want, create a smaller-sized, single-page version that shows all the pages with arrows indicating the links between pages and the direction of travel, as shown in Figure 8.3.

Time-Based Publishing

In broadcasting, each storyboard often includes a notation indicating how long the event or scene will last. (For instance, in broadcast advertising, commercials are typically 30 seconds or 60 seconds in length. Each event has to be timed carefully and compactly.) In Web publishing, time is also an important consideration, but for a different reason: When you design Web pages, you need to consider how long it will take for each page to *load.*

This is critical! If you load up your pages with graphics, your site may become too time-intensive for most visitors to tolerate. And while it's true that Netscape and most other Web browsers give users the option to turn off graphics view-

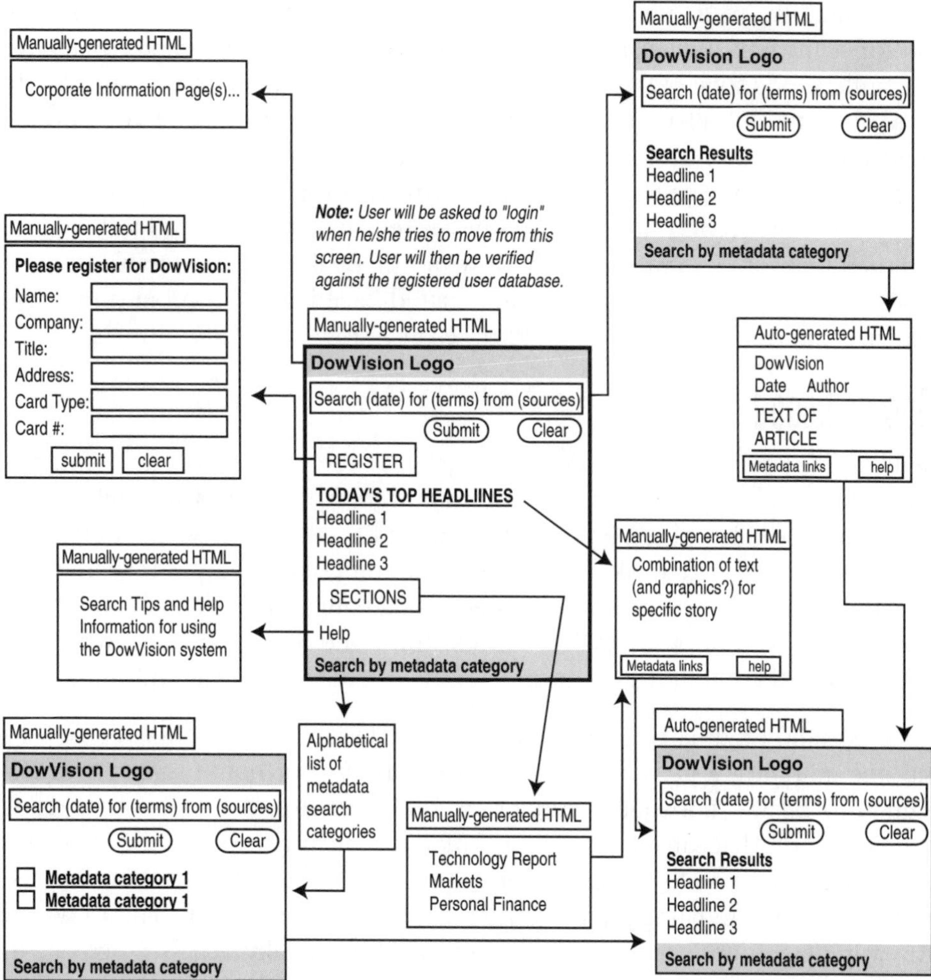

Figure 8.3 ***Several storyboards combined into a single chart to show the links and relationships among different Web pages.***

ing, a graphics-intensive site typically looks flat, boring, and empty when its most important elements (all those darned graphics) are eliminated.

A better approach is to mix graphics and text carefully for an attractive balance. And keep your graphics small (in bytes, not necessarily in physical size) wherever possible, although an abundance of small graphics is just as bad as having a few large graphics.

For instance, suppose you use an attractive spherical button with a drop shadow as a link to a different page. The button is only 16 K in size, so you figure that you're doing a good job in conserving space. Now suppose that button is the first "bullet" in a bulleted list of six items. That means you'll have six bullets for a total of 96 K. At 14.4 Kbps, it will take about 6 to 7 seconds to load all of these bullets. That's not too terribly long a wait. But if you add the text and any other icons and graphics that you're planning to put on that page, the time begins to add up, visitor frustration mounts, and guess what? People visit your Web site once and never return. You also need to take into account that some servers are very slow during peak periods of traffic. So that maximum 10-second wait you've anticipated based strictly on baud rate and file size can double, triple, or quadruple on a slow server.

Space-Based Publishing

With print media, designers define the size of the publication up-front. Because this size remains fixed, it's easy to design the layout of the publication within the specified height and width boundaries. Designing on the Web is not that simple. You need to take into account different screen sizes, because HTML tags do not include any provisions for adjusting your graphics content based on screen size. Web browsers will wrap text from one line to the next when the text reaches the right edge of the screen. But there's no way to wrap graphics.

So, logos and other large graphics need to be designed for small screens. Let's say the graphical logo that appears at the top of your home screen was designed to fill the horizontal margins of a 17" monitor, and your logo reads "Great Ideas." That same logo on a 14" monitor might read "Great Id," because the right end of your logo won't fit on the screen. True, visitors can scroll to the right to read the remaining part of the logo, but they might not think to do so. Anyway, it's an annoyance to have to scroll horizontally across a screen. In general, you're safe if you design your Web pages to fit within a 14" screen.

It's also a good idea to make sure that large graphics will entirely fit vertically on a single screen. If viewers have to scroll up and down to see different parts of a graphic, they lose the overall effect that you intended to create. It still amazes me to see so many otherwise well-designed Web pages that don't follow these simple guidelines.

Publishing with Levels

Depending on how you organize your Web pages, the links you create will either delight or confuse visitors. Because HTML makes it so easy to create links, it's just as easy for Web page designers to go a little bit overboard in the way links are placed. Sure, *you* know where each link takes you, but that's because you designed the links and the Web pages. For your visitors, the links will probably not be that intuitive. I can't tell you how many times I've visited a site and found myself linking to places I didn't want to go and being forced to use Netscape Forward and Back buttons to return to where I began and then try to find the link I *really* wanted.

This problem tends to be the most serious in Web pages that go overboard with links—where every graphic and every third word is a link to something. When you provide so many options, how can you expect your visitors to decide how to navigate effectively? They can't.

The key to effective organization of Web pages is to view the entire content of your Web site as representing a hierarchy, or series of levels. It's a lot like newspaper publishing. The first element in a newspaper article is the headline, which is designed to give readers a "feel" for what the article contains, using only a few carefully selected words to do so. After the headline comes the lead sentence, which includes general information that describes the who, what, where, why, and how of the article's content. Following the lead sentence, the most pertinent facts are presented, and the successive paragraphs contain less important and typically more specific information.

When you design the links for your Web pages, think in terms of these kinds of interest levels—moving from the general to the specific, from the most important information to the least important information. Your home page should provide general information about your Web site and briefly explain what's provided in lower-level pages. You'll then want to include links to the next two or three more specific pages at your Web site. Within these pages, you can include still more links to even more specific information or to other Web sites that provide related information.

The bottom line: Don't go crazy with links. There's an art to organizing links and Web pages, and most Web sites, unfortunately, demonstrate how few home page authors really understand this art. The key is to think like a visitor. Assume the role of a first-time visitor who knows nothing about the contents of your Web site. Then determine the easiest way to get this visitor to point A, point B, to point C, and back to any previous page they've visited. Make sure your links and buttons are very descriptive so that your visitors know precisely where they're headed or where they're heading back to. Don't send them off to Japan when they really wanted to go to Australia.

Evaluating Your Costs

Creating a simple home page typically costs you nothing but the time it takes to design and test your work. Because most, if not all, of the software you can use to design and edit your Web pages is freeware or shareware, all you'll end up paying is the registration fee for any shareware that you decide to use on a regular basis.

However, after you've created your home page and its associated Web pages, you'll still need to store the files on a server. So the big consideration at this point is whether you want your own computer to be the server or whether to locate your Web page on somebody else's server.

Setting up a Web server on your own computer is hardly a no-brainer; in fact, entire books have been written on this topic alone. If you're just getting started in Web publishing, you probably won't feel ready to tackle the additional effort of setting up a server. Fortunately, other low-cost and free alternatives are available.

Many Web publishing entrepreneurs turn to their Internet access provider for help in establishing their Web pages. Increasingly, Internet access providers offer their customers space on their server for storing their Web page files. Although many providers will give you server space for free as an incentive to sign up or to remain with that service, this offer is typically limited to the space required to set up maybe a single home page or a few simple Web pages. If your Web publishing plans are more elaborate than that, your provider will probably charge you a monthly fee to lease space on their server.

Unfortunately, most people who are new to Web publishing don't realize that there are a number of Web service bureaus in the U.S. and around the world whose main business is to provide server space for Web publishers. Often, these service bureaus can offer Web space at a lower cost than your own Internet access provider, and with more reliable results. Remember that you're publishing on the *World Wide* Web, so it doesn't matter where the physical server is located. It can be down the street or in Taipei, literally. Prices for server space on a service bureau's system typically begin at about $30 per month. That cost guarantees that your Web site will provide uninterrupted, 24-hour access, and usually service bureaus can support many more incoming lines than a local access provider. (There's nothing more frustrating than dialing into *your own* home page stored on your local provider's server and receiving a "connection refused by host" message.)

Other costs can be incurred if you want to create elaborate Web pages that have a truly professional appearance. For this level of sophistication, you might want to enlist help from others. For instance, you might want to pay a graphic artist to help design your Web pages or to create your home page logo. The Web service bureaus mentioned above often also offer the services of professional artists and other designers to help you create your Web pages, but fees for this kind of assistance typically *start* at $30 per hour, totaling hundreds or even thousands of dollars. The question you'll want to ask is: "How much of this can I do myself and how much will require assistance?" However, with all the Web publishing tools now available, you'll find that you can create some fairly elaborate designs on your own.

Tools of the Trade

There are several tools available on the Web to help you create and edit Web pages, along with several tutorials and other resources designed to help new Web publishers. Most of the best Web publishing tools available are on the companion CD-ROM. For descriptions of these tools, see Appendix E. To find out about additional resources to create Web pages, take a look at Appendix D.

LET'S REVIEW

There are several benefits of Web publishing over more traditional print publishing media. When you publish on the Web, you provide a way for your audience to interact with your Web pages through links, buttons, forms, and multimedia effects. Also, you can publish on the Web with little or no assistance from others. And the cost to publish on the Web is often free or as little as the leasing fee that you pay to a company that provides you with server space. Another benefit of Web publishing lies in timeliness. You can update your Web pages at any time to ensure that they also contain the most timely and accurate information.

One great feature of the Web is that "anything goes." In deciding what to publish, remember that the Web doesn't limit you to simple text and graphics. With links, you can create a truly interactive page, and with sound and video capabilities, you can extend your publishing effort into the multimedia arena.

Designing effective Web pages takes careful planning and requires that you give some thought to the needs and expectations of your audience. Using storyboards to create rough designs for all your Web pages can be a tremendous aid in visualizing how your Web pages will be linked and how your pages can interact with your audience. And make sure you consider your visitors' hardware—especially limitations that stem from slower modems or smaller screens.

Even if you create some of the most artistic and professionally designed Web pages this side of cyberspace, they'll do you no good until you get your files up on a server system. The easiest approach is to talk to your Internet access provider about acquiring free or inexpensive space on their Web server. Also look into the possibility of leasing server space from a national or international service bureau. The costs for these services have been decreasing in recent months as competition heats up.

Chapter 9

The Easy Way to Create Your Own Home Page

Now that you've explored the publishing potential of the Web, it's time to learn how to grab a few moments of publishing fame by creating your own home page.

After you surf the Web for about five minutes, the next thing you'll want to do is put up your home page. This urge seems to happen to everyone I know. I call it the *home page publishing obsession.* As soon as it happens to you, you'll start to frantically look around for information and tools to help you get your home page together.

First, you'll want to determine what you want to publish in the universe of Webspace. Perhaps you have an interesting story to tell or a great picture of yourself that you're dying to share with others. Or, you might want to put up a cool home page for your business. (In addition to acquiring fame, most Web users are frantically trying to figure out how they can make money or expand their business on the Web.) Once you gather the information for your home page, you'll need to figure out how to compose a home page document. This usually involves creating an HTML document with a text editor, but there is also a very quick way you can compose a basic home page.

Using the easy, step-by-step techniques presented in this chapter, you'll be able to create a home page in no time. Your home page can include text, images, your e-mail address, and even links to other Web pages. The best part is that you'll be able to do all this without writing any HTML! (The program I'll present creates the HTML file for you.) You'll then be able to take your home page creations and view them with Netscape or put them on a Web server.

I'll begin this chapter by showing you a few different ways to design your home page. Of course, the techniques I'll present also apply to creating other Web pages. Then, we'll use our secret weapon—a custom program named HomePage Creator that will automatically create a home page for you. This program queries you for information and then automatically creates an HTML document. In the last part of the chapter, I'll give you a few tips to help you get your home page published on a Web server.

IS THERE A HOME PAGE IN YOUR FUTURE?

The challenging part of creating a home page is coming up with something interesting to publish on the Web. So, how do you get started? First, you'll need to get organized. Then, you'll want to create a storyboard as I suggested in the previous chapter. If you plan to eventually publish more than just a home page, you'll want to think through a rough design for all the other pages.

To get started with a simple, standalone home page, create an outline for your text and sketch out a page design for your layout. In this respect, creating a home page is no different from creating another type of document, such as a report or newsletter. The big difference with Web pages is that you have so much more to work with because of the interactive nature of the Web.

But don't get carried away. The best home pages are those that are simple and clean. I always like to get the basic structure of my Web pages up and running first, and then go back and refine them. As you are typing the text, links, and references for images into an HTML document, it's hard to visualize exactly how the finished product will look when viewed with a browser.

Of all the Web pages you create and publish, your home page is the most important. It is the front door to your Web publishing enterprise, and needs to get across a number of ideas at once, including:

- Who you are
- What you have to offer

- What you have to offer that's new (this is important in getting users to return to your home page)
- The links that you have to other Web pages
- How users can navigate with your home page and explore further
- The type of service or product you have to sell (this is required if you are a business)
- An e-mail address for a contact person

Of course, you won't have much space to communicate all this information. If you're running tight on space, perhaps the most important information to emphasize is what's available from your home page, and an e-mail address for a contact at your Web site.

One way to determine how you should set up your home page is to surf the Web for a while looking at examples. In fact, let's do that right now. We'll start with the most simple type of home pages and work our way up to more complex (and unusual) ones. I'll present different types of Web sites to give you some idea of the variety of Web pages that can be created. As you explore them, you might want to keep in mind how they address the six points I just explained about effective home page (and Web page) design.

Text-Based Pages (Resources)

These are the simplest kinds of pages to create. All you need is text. The benefit is that they are fast. Unfortunately, text-based pages are going the way of the dinosaur, especially now that Web publishing is becoming more commercialized.

Text-based Web pages are often used for academic sites or research groups. You can use a text-based page to publish papers, provide listings of available research grants, or even include online documentation for a product or service you provide. You could even publish your resume as a text-based home page in hopes that someone might read it and e-mail you a job offer.

Figure 9.1 shows a good example of a text-based Web page. (This page actually provides one little image, so it's not entirely composed of text.) This page features useful links to all sorts of state agencies and departments across the U.S. This is not the kind of information you need to have at your fingertips on a daily basis, but when you need it, it's nice that one place has it all.

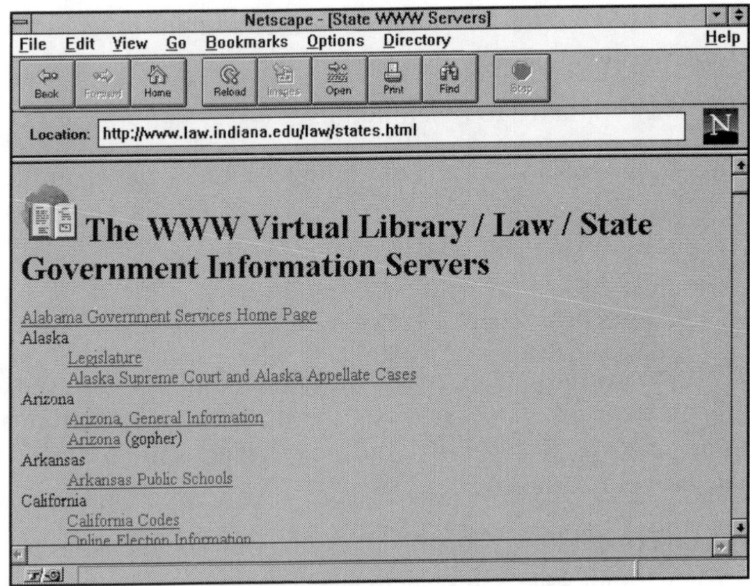

Figure 9.1 An effective text-based home page.

To explore this page, use the following URL:

```
http://www.law.indiana.edu/law/states.html
```

If you use a text-based approach like this, you must make sure that the information you present is high quality and that there is a good demand for it. Text-based pages typically serve as resource centers that are composed of links to other useful Web pages.

Typically, pages like the one shown in Figure 9.1 are organized as a hierarchical list. Publishing a document like this involves creating a simple but useful outline and then assigning links to some of the topics. If you take this approach, you'll need to make sure that you keep all of your links up to date. The main reason that users come to a Web page like this is that they believe they can quickly access reliable, up-to-date information.

Of course, the information you provide doesn't need to be boring. Here's a list of some text-based (or content-based) Web pages that provide great information with a twist.

- The TV home page with links to more TV-related sites than you could possibly surf in an evening:

  ```
  http://www.cs.cmu.edu:8001/afs/cs.cmu.edu/user/clamen/misc/tv/
  ```

- Zarf's list of Interactive Games on the Web (the name says it all) at:

  `http://www.cs.cmu.edu:8001/afs/cs.cmu.edu/user/zarf/www/games.html`

- Interesting Places for Kids home page, which features the best resources for young Web surfers:

  `http://www.crc.ricoh.com/people/steve/kids.html`

Personal Home Pages

Some Web publishers like to get personal. In fact, this was my approach in creating my home page, shown in Figure 9.2. Since this type of home page should make a personal statement, you can include whatever you like—photos of you, your bio, a picture of your house, the movies you've starred in, and so on.

One of the nice features about the Web is its informal and personal nature. I always enjoy surfing the Web and coming across pages by authors who have written other books or articles about the Web. Recently, I was looking into a new virtual reality language developed for the Web called VRML (http://www.eit.com/vrml/) and came across the home page of one of the develop-

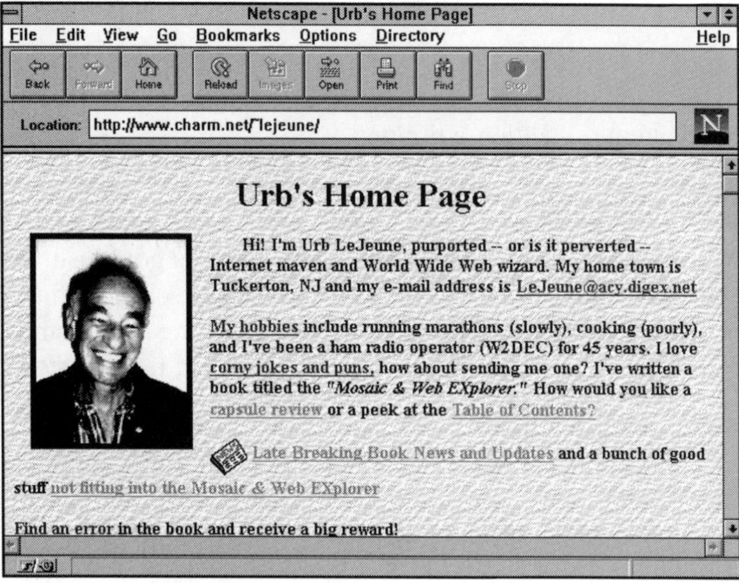

Figure 9.2 *Publishing a personal home page.*

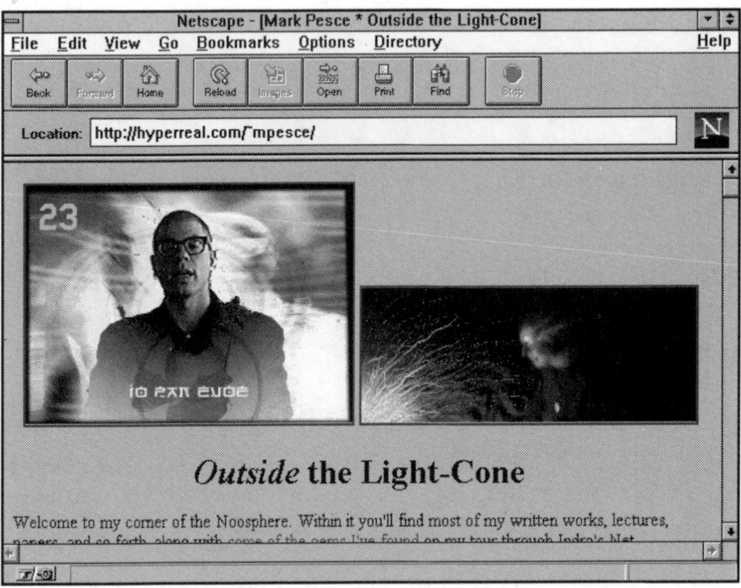

Figure 9.3 *Mark Pesce's personal home page.*

ers and visionaries behind this technology. Figure 9.3 shows this home page, which you can explore by using the following URL:

```
http://hyperreal.com/~mpesce/
```

This home page works well and probably gets good traffic. Personal home pages like this typically provide links to other interesting Web pages, unusual pictures, and attention-getting writing.

Commercial Home Pages

Someone recently said that the Web is like the California gold rush. Everyone's trying to get his or her business on the Web to stake a claim and start raking in those fortunes. Commercial home pages are popping up like mushrooms. Some of them are really interesting, and others are big time-wasters.

If you want to publish a home page to promote your business or to serve as a vehicle to sell products, check out the competition. In creating this type of home page, it's important to make it clear what your business does (unless you're IBM or Microsoft). In many commercial home pages I've seen, I can't figure out for the life of me what the business does or what products or services they're trying to sell.

A commercial home page is essentially the sign in front of your business. If your business is tucked away down a side alley or the sign is not visible or attention-getting, not many people are going to walk through your door. If you're trying to get a lot of attention, you'll need good graphics and something interesting to give away or offer.

Figure 9.4 shows one commercial spot on the Web that's a big success—the Sega home page. Notice how this home page is designed to invite both new and repeat customers. The interface is very simple and friendly, the graphics are eye-catching, and the "What's New" link is placed right at the top of the page to encourage customers to come back again and again. What more could you want?

To check out the Sega home page, use this URL:

```
http://www.segaoa.com/sega1.html
```

Most commercial home pages provide a banner to display their company name and logo. Make this image as small as possible without losing your message. You should also consider including a short description about what your company does—but keep it as brief as possible. Some key points to broadcast include special offers you are giving (especially if you have free samples to give away), products or services that are new, and unique information about your products or services.

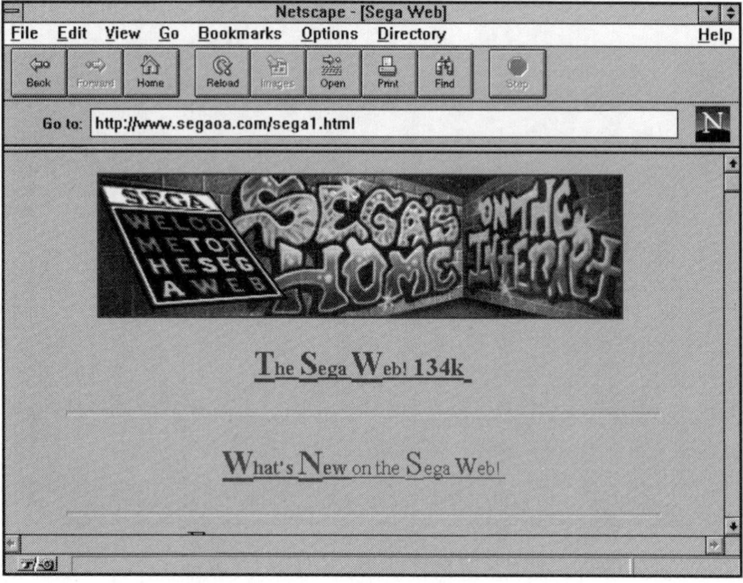

***Figure 9.4** The Sega home page—a very popular commercial hangout.*

Service-Oriented Pages

You sent a package yesterday to an important client in New York. Unfortunately, the package didn't arrive in time. Where is it? Who signed for it? What do you do? If you sent the package by FedEx, you're in luck because you can go to their home page and put a trace on your package. I've used this feature many times and it really works!

Figure 9.5 shows the FedEx home page, accessible with the following URL:

```
http://www.fedex.com/
```

Typically home pages that are designed for a service-oriented purpose are linked, in one fashion or another, to a database. They are relatively easy to design—however, they require some special CGI scripting (and possibly programming) features. For example, when you use the FedEx Web page to locate a package, a special script sends the airbill number of your package to the FedEx Web server. Then, the FedEx database is searched and a message is sent back to you.

Writing scripts for Web pages is a more advanced feature that we'll explore later in this book.

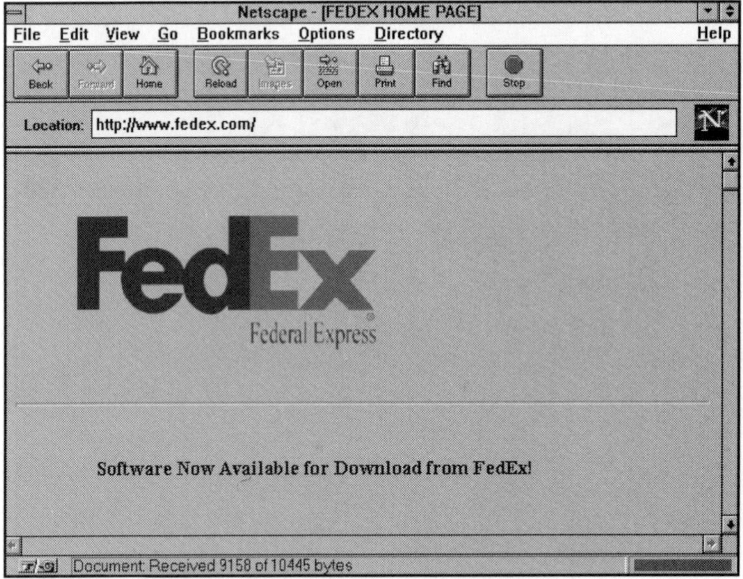

***Figure 9.5** The FedEx home page—your package is just a click away.*

Resource-Oriented Pages

Although the Web is getting very popular with commercial enterprises, historically it was used by academic organizations. This means there are a lot of home pages that serve only one purpose—to provide free resource information for other Web users around the world. Although this category overlaps with the text-based home page category we just discussed, good resource-oriented home pages often feature navigational graphics.

One of the more helpful resource-oriented home pages is the AskERIC Virtual Library, shown in Figure 9.6. To get there, use this URL:

```
http://eryx.syr.edu/COWSHome.html
```

Here you'll find easy access to electronic books through Project Gutenberg. Although this page uses just a few modest-sized icons, they are handy navigation tools. Just click on one of the icons as you scroll through the page, and you'll be taken to a corresponding Web page to get more information.

Resource-intensive Web sites often incorporate visual maps, called *image maps*. In an image map, different parts of an image can link to different Web pages

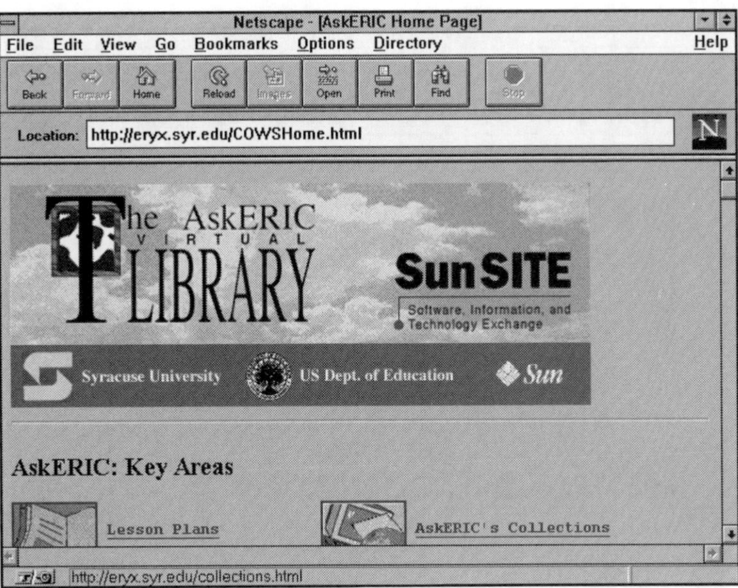

Figure 9.6 *AskERIC: A well-designed resource center.*

or sections within a Web page. This is a great technique for creating maps or visual clickable access guides to information on the Web.

Let's look at an example. The Coriolis Group, the publisher of this book, uses an attractive and very functional image map on their home page, as shown in Figure 9.7. You can get to this home page by using the following URL:

```
http://www.coriolis.com/coriolis
```

The displayed image is a single GIF file. However, it is divided into clickable regions. For example, if you want to tour their *Explore the Grand Canyon* multimedia CD-ROM/Web product, click in the upper-left area of the image. If you want to see "What's New" on their Web site, click in the bottom-left square of the image.

Image maps provide two benefits: They help make your home page more attractive and they help the user navigate. But don't fall into the trap that many Web page designers do—get caught up in the neat effects produced by image maps and make them way too large. I've also encountered countless image maps on home pages that are impossible to use because it isn't easily discernible what the different sections of the image link to. This defeats the whole purpose of using image maps.

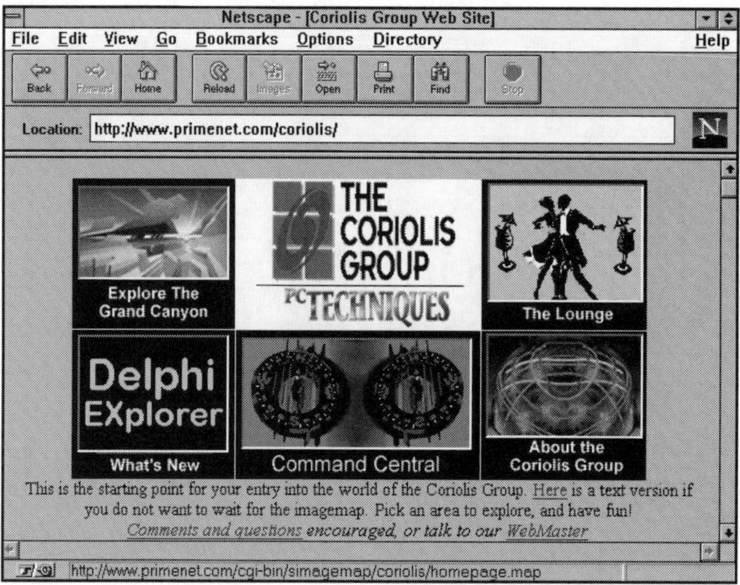

Figure 9.7 The Coriolis Group home page with its clickable image map.

Billboard Pages

In one sense, thinking of a home page as simply an electronic billboard is dumb. After all, the best feature of the Web is interactivity. On the other hand, if you have some incredible art and you want to show it off, go for it. Just keep in mind that many users won't wait for your very large images to download, especially if they've got a slow connection.

If you have the talent (and the time), you can go all out and create art that will knock people dead. Or, as one enterprising publisher thought of, you can exploit a certain celebrity and attract people to your Web site. Figure 9.8 shows a product concept featured on a billboard-style Web page that could actually be a big hit if it were ever released. (I won't give the URL for this home page because the jury is still out.)

Entertainment and Multimedia Pages

This category is growing rapidly. The twist here is that entertainment and multimedia home pages contain multimedia goodies or run on computers that are connected to multimedia devices such as video cameras.

To create effective multimedia home pages, you need to make them as interactive as possible. You can have buttons (links) to play sounds, video, or even

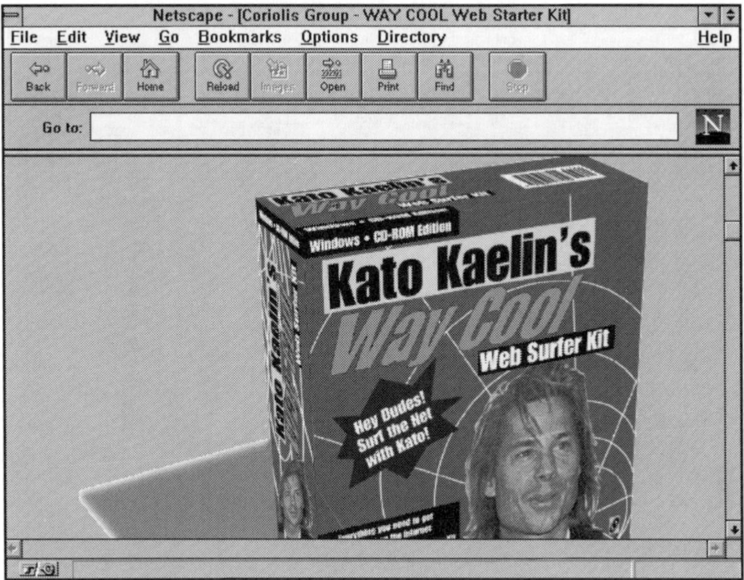

Figure 9.8 *Go for the billboard approach and really attract attention.*

animation. The technology is in place for all of this now, and there are a number of home pages on the Web that provide multimedia features. The big problem is bandwidth. Many Web users are too impatient to even wait for a simple graphics image to download, let alone a video clip that could take over ten minutes to download and play.

One commercial home page that uses multimedia effectively is Windham Hill Records' home page. Its URL is:

```
http://www.windham.com/
```

Windham Hill puts out popular CDs by talented recording artists. They are noted for having a unique "sound" in a business that doesn't always encourage creativity. Figure 9.9 shows the home page. Actually, this page doesn't directly include multimedia, but you can click on a link to select a particular recording artist. You can then listen to a sample from an artist's latest CD, or see a video clip of the artist in concert. This is the next best thing to having the artist come to your living room to put on a concert for you (if you don't mind waiting while large files are downloaded).

Another unique, emerging multimedia publishing approach combines interactive CD-ROMs with information published on the Web. The idea here is to link the relative static world of multimedia CD-ROMs that run on PCs with the

Figure 9.9 *The Windham Hill home page—an effective multimedia presentation.*

dynamic universe of the Web. With this approach, you can run multimedia software on a CD-ROM and then have it access the Web to get additional content or to view dynamic Web pages.

The pioneer behind this technology is The Coriolis Group. They've created a CD-ROM-based multimedia product called *Explore the Grand Canyon*. As you run the CD-ROM and visit the Grand Canyon, a special Web searching/publishing agent called NetSeeker accesses their Web site and links to additional multimedia content including sound, video, photographs, and text about the Grand Canyon. One of their Web pages, shown in Figure 9.10, features this technology. You can access the Grand Canyon Web page using this URL:

```
www.coriolis.com/coriolis/gc/gc_tips.htm
```

This approach to multimedia publishing opens up all kinds of design possibilities.

Humor-Oriented Home Pages

Everyone loves to have a good laugh, so why not use humor as the main theme of your home page? Here are some ideas that come to mind:

- Jokes page
- Cartoon-based page

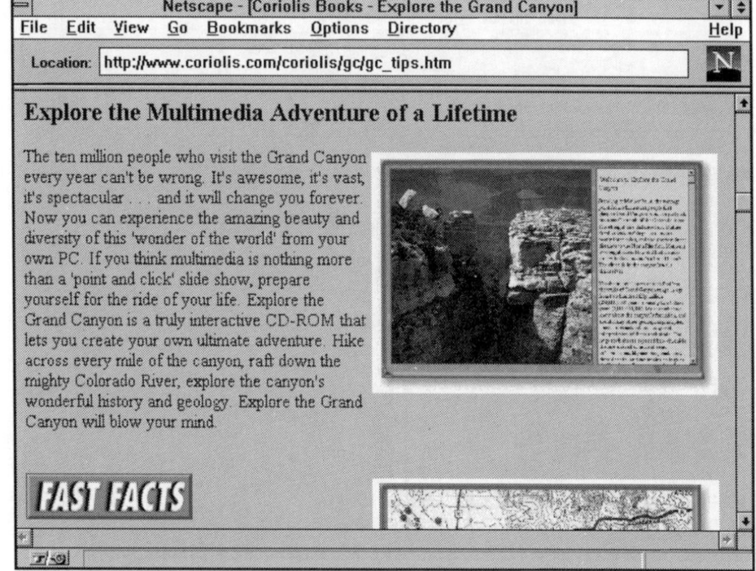

Figure 9.10 *The Coriolis Group's Explore the Grand Canyon CD-ROM/Web publishing project.*

- Humorous quotations page
- What's wrong with this picture page
- Outrageous headlines in the media page
- Political spoofs page
- Wacky (or really stupid) FAQs page

If you have a talent for drawing cartoons, funny pictures, or writing snappy copy, your home page could be a big hit. Figure 9.11 shows a very successful cartoon home page I came across recently. It's called *Where the Buffalo Roam* and features weekly cartoons created by Hans Bjordahl for the *Colorado Daily*. Here is the URL:

```
http://plaza.xor.com/wtbr/
```

Weird Home Pages

If you're looking to shock people, you'll need to come up with something *really* weird—the competition is stiff in this category. One popular, unusual home page is "Chat with a Cat." As the name suggests, this home page lets you talk to some guy's cat. Figure 9.12 shows the page created by Michael

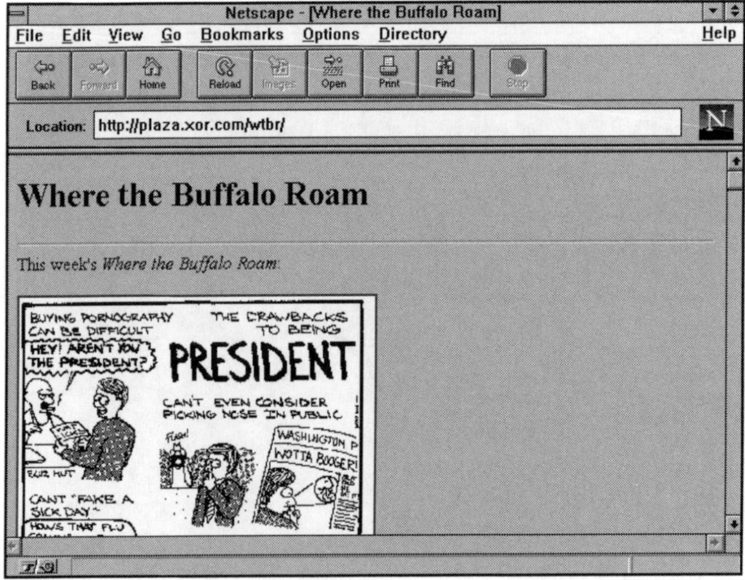

Figure 9.11 The Where the Buffalo Roam home page.

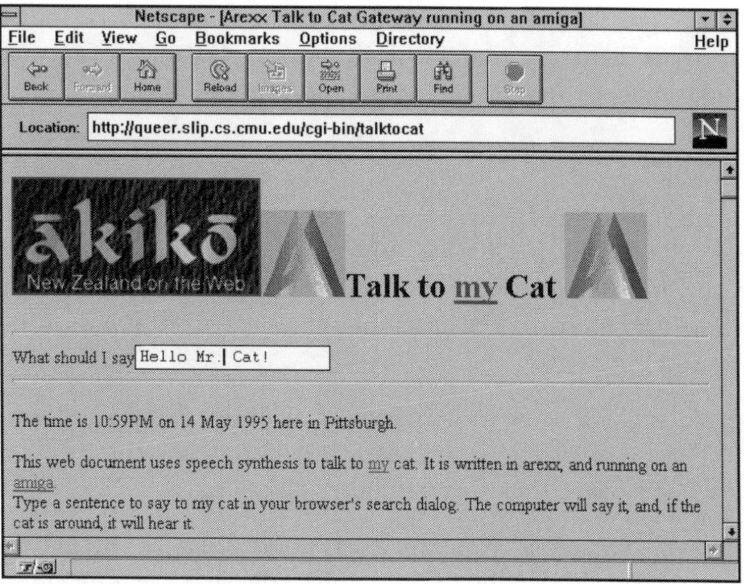

***Figure 9.12** Getting weird with "Chat with a Cat."*

Witbrok. This home page allows you to type messages that are then spoken to Michael's cat. Evidently, the computer running this home page is hooked up to a speech synthesizer, which "speaks" the messages that users type. You can also read the messages that other users have posted.

To check out this home page, point your browser to:

```
http://queer.slip.cs.cmu.edu/cgi-bin/talktocat
```

What are the guidelines for creating a weird home page? The sky's the limit.

HOME PAGE DESIGN 101

A wise saying coined years ago by a great architect sums up what we've been discussing about creating effective home pages: "Form follows function." Because of the highly interactive nature of home pages in particular and Web pages in general, a good design must do double duty. It must interest the user *and* allow the user to do something. If people land on your home page and the information presented doesn't get their attention or they don't know what to do next, your home page has failed.

I don't pretend to be an expert home page or graphics designer. The one thing I know is that there are about as many different home page design styles as there are actual home pages, but if you surf the Web long enough, you'll start to notice some general design principles that really work. (And you'll notice some techniques that really turn people off!)

Simple Is Good

Your first attempt might be to include everything you can think of in your home page. Stop right there, especially if you want other people to spend time at your home page and come back. Experienced designers are fond of repeating this word to designer newbies: KISS. It stands for Keep It Simple, Stupid.

A home page is like a New York apartment. You need to make the most out of the small space you have. Don't clutter it with information or pictures you don't really need—save them for another Web page.

If you start with very little, you can always add more. If you start with too much, you'll get attached to the information or the *way the information looks,* and you won't want to take things out.

Focus Is Better

Don't try to cover too much ground with your home page or any of your Web pages. If you have a lot of information to present, use one Web page as an entry point to link to other Web pages you provide.

Try to come up with one strong theme or message and stick with it. If you're not careful, your home page might end up looking like the *Time Online* page (http://www.timeinc.com/time/universe.html) shown in Figure 9.13. I realize that the *Time* folks have a lot of information to dish out, but give me a break! When I look at this Web page, I'm not sure what to do or where to go. There are so many pieces of information displayed here that it distracts the user. The graphics are great, but they are better suited for the company's annual report than their Web page.

Fast Is Best

I can't think of anything that annoys Web surfers more than Web pages that are really slow to load. The more stuff you put on your home page, the longer it will take to download, the longer the user will have to wait, and the less often the user will come back to see your page.

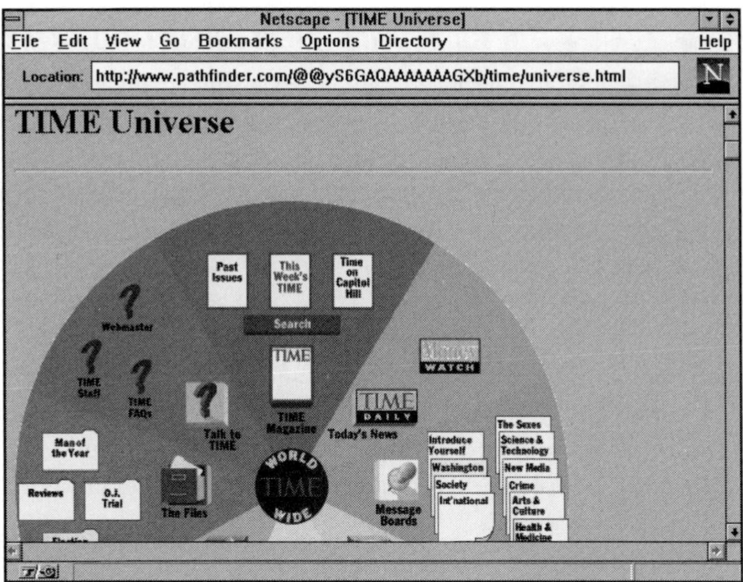

***Figure 9.13** Who has the time to decipher this confusing home page?*

When designing your home page, try to imagine your typical user surfing the Web at home on a 9600 baud modem (and during the commercial breaks of *Seinfeld* or at work when nobody's looking). If your home page needs to download ten minutes of data (text files, graphics files, and so on) when it first comes up, you're dead.

Many Web page publishers use fast connections, such as ISDN or T1, and they forget what it's like to access the Web with a slow modem. If you fall in this category, buy a 9600 baud modem and use it to test your home page. If it is too slow, simplify it.

If you can't simplify your Web page, offer a fast text-based version. Include a short message and link right at the top of your home page so that users can click on it and get the text version. But make sure you put the message and link before any graphics appear. Many home pages display a big, time-intensive image at the top of their home page and then they include a message at the bottom that says:

```
Click here for a text-only version.
```

Is this stupid, or what?

If You Provide a Text Version, Go All the Way

This tip comes from Vince Emery, author of *How to Grow Your Business on the Internet.* If your home page links to other Web pages at your site, don't just provide a text-only version of the home page. Otherwise, a user will access the text-only home page and click on a link to another Web page that contains a lot of graphics. The way to avoid this is to provide text-only versions of all your Web pages. This is more work, but your users will thank you by coming back.

Take a cue from magazine publishers. Years ago, magazine articles were long and very narrative. Today, most magazines provide much shorter articles with sidebars. Is it because people don't read any more? I don't think so. Publishers do this because people are overloaded with information, and prefer their information in bits and pieces.

Alternate Images and Text

If you use a lot of images, try my alternating method of first displaying a page with images, then a page that is text-based. For example, your home page could be displayed with a useful navigation image. When users click on a link, take them to a page that is more text-oriented. This way, users will see a much faster response time when they access the second page. Of course, to do this you'll need to first plan the organization of your links.

Truly inconsiderate designers create Web pages that display one time-intensive image after another. I hate clicking on a link after accessing a slow home page only to discover that I have to wait another five minutes to get to the actual information. Perhaps when *all* users are connected to the Web at high speeds, these issues will fade. But for now, do everything you can to get your user moving through your Web pages as quickly as possible.

Make Your Pages Readable

Netscape recently added support for an HTML extension called *backgrounds.* With it, you can add a neat background pattern to your home page. (I'll show you how to do this later in the book.) Unfortunately, Web publishers immediately went crazy and put backgrounds on everything. Overnight, already hard-to-read Web pages became *impossible* to read.

The moral of this story is *do everything you can to make your pages more readable.* Forget all of the neat visual effects, if they get in the way of your message. For many people, text is difficult to read on a computer screen, especially when they have to scroll through pages and pages of small type.

Come Up with an Angle

If you want other people to visit your home page (outside of your immediate family), you'll need an angle. This means you need to think like a marketing person. The Web is becoming crowded with new home pages, and it's getting harder to attract people to a new site. And this electronic publishing traffic jam is bound to get much worse before it gets better.

Try to think of a strategy that no one else has considered. This is your chance to unleash your creativity. If you are really stuck and can't come up with a good angle, try my favorite standby of the three best attention-getting words in the English language: "Win Free Sex". Seriously, think marketing. If you're not good at this, befriend people who are; take them out to dinner (marketing people love to spend time in restaurants) and make them give you an angle.

Use the Newspaper Approach

Reporters and designers at newspapers understand the main principle of presenting lots of information without losing their readers' interest. Here's the principle: Information is hierarchical in nature. When you scan a newspaper, the first thing that gets your attention is a headline:

"Giant Toads To Inherit the Earth"

Then, you start to read on:

"Scientists today announced recent findings: the population of giant toads is increasing 400 percent per year—a growth rate that will allow them to take over the earth by 1997. Top scientists from around the world attended the Chicago meeting, which made public the finding of a recent two-year survey..."

The goal is to present information in descending levels of detail. The general attention-getting stuff comes first. Then, the story starts and some of the details emerge. As you continue reading the story, you'll learn about a bunch of other facts. Often, you don't really care about all of the details, so you stop after the first few paragraphs. When was the last time you read a newspaper article from beginning to end?

The hierarchical approach is a good way to set up your home page and other pages on your Web site that you link to. Most users who read your pages will read the highlights. A much smaller percentage will click on links and examine the details. But that's okay—you've designed your pages with that in mind. Right?

Don't Ignore Your Links

As we learned in the previous chapter, users who come to your home page may often be more interested in where your page can take them than what you have to say. Here are some tips to help give your users *more* of what they want:

Add new links as often as you can. To keep users coming back, you'll want to offer new links at least once a week. (Some sites that are really popular provide new links daily!) If you're not convinced, just think of the reason you drive across town to your favorite store at the mall—you want to see what new goodies they have to offer. If the store stopped adding new products, you'd probably find a better place to spend your money.

Don't provide links to the same Web pages everyone else links to. Try to come up with the best links you can. Sure, you might want to provide a few of the links to popular pages like What's Cool on the Web or Yahoo, but don't neglect newer, out of the way places that are useful or interesting. Every time you surf the Web and find something that really grabs your attention, link your home page to it for a while.

Keep your links up to date. Things move around on the Web about as often as political leaders change their position on an issue. Don't let your links get rusty. Test them regularly. Think of this as a "must-do" activity, like backing up your hard disk. If you don't come up with a system and follow it religiously, you're asking for trouble.

Provide a good description for each link. Every link should have a description—and the description should be accurate. Recently I came across a home page that provided a link labeled "Cool places to explore in Hawaii." I clicked on the link and up came some boring Web page about government offices located in the Hawaiian Islands. Did I feel ripped off or what? I thought I was going to get pictures of secluded beaches or tips on locating secret waterfalls. Instead I got a listing of the hours for the Department of Motor Vehicles in Maui—what's so cool about that?

List file sizes for links that download files. Many Web pages provide links that will automatically download a file when the link is selected. The only problem is that the user's time might be limited and he or she won't know how long the download will take before the link is selected. You can really make your users happy by using labels like this for your downloadable file links:

Transcripts from the O.J Simpson trial (200 Mb)

THREE WAYS TO CREATE A HOME PAGE

There are three techniques you can use to create your own home page:

- Use HomePage Creator. (This requires no knowledge of HTML on your part.)
- Find a Web page that's similar to the one you want to create, obtain the HTML document, and then change it to meet your needs.
- Start from scratch using a text editor or special-purpose HTML editor that automatically creates a shell document for you.

The method you use depends on your personal preference and, of course, the amount of free time you have. But I think it's a good idea to look at all three of these approaches to gain a better understanding of HTML and the techniques involved in creating Web pages.

In this chapter I'll show you how to use the first method. Although somewhat limited, it will get you started in a flash. After we create a home page in this manner, we'll dig in and start writing our own HTML instructions in the next chapter.

Creating Your First Home Page with HomePage Creator

When my good friend Demetris Kafas, kafas@mars.superlink.net, was starting to get interested in the Web, I told him about Web publishing with HTML. Coming from a programming background, he was soon fascinated with HTML. "Isn't there a program that creates a basic home page?" he asked innocently one evening. To my knowledge there wasn't a tool available. I really set the hook when I told him, "If you really want to learn HTML, write a program that creates an HTML document." Soon thereafter he created a program called HomePage Creator (HPC).

What does HPC do? It builds a simple home page without requiring you to write any HTML. The program queries you for information for your home page and then presto, it creates the HTML document for you. This is a good place to start, especially if you want to learn HTML. You can use HPC to create a basic home page (HTML document) and then modify the document to your liking.

HPC presents a series of text boxes for you to enter your name, e-mail address, and so on. It also allows you to enter a GIF file name for displaying a picture as well as a few paragraphs to tell the world all about yourself. You can even include some of your favorite URLs to link to other Web pages.

Let's put this easy-to-use tool to work. First, you'll need to install it on your hard disk. To do this, run the SETUP.EXE program in the directory \tools\hpc on the companion CD-ROM. The setup program will ask you to provide the drive name where you want to install HomePage Creator. The setup program will then copy all of the files you need to your hard drive.

Start HPC by clicking on the program icon provided in the Windows Program Manager. Figure 9.14 shows the first screen that HPC displays. With this screen you can enter the following elements in your home page:

- A main heading
- A picture
- Your name

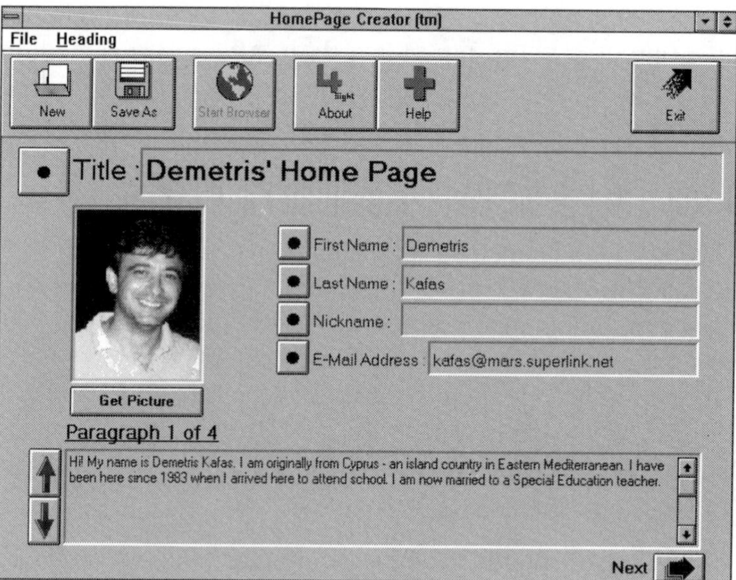

Figure 9.14 *The first screen of HomePage Creator with default entries.*

- Your e-mail address
- Up to four paragraphs of plain text

If you make a mistake while entering information, don't worry—you can delete it and enter the text correctly.

To get to the second page in HomePage Creator, click on the right arrow (Next) button displayed at the bottom of the window. Figure 9.15 shows the standard "favorite spots" default listing, which is displayed for the second screen. This is where you can add your own links to other Web pages. To change or insert a link, click on one of the buttons to the left of the site names that are displayed. HomePage Creator will then display the Site Editor dialog box that you use to enter both a site name and its URL. That's all there is to it.

Let's go to the first screen and fill in enough information for a basic home page. First, click on the New icon button to clear all the existing fields. Next, you can add a picture by clicking on the Get Picture button. This action displays the standard Windows Open File dialog box. This is where you select the name of the GIF file you want to display.

Figure 9.16 shows all the data that I entered to create my basic home page, including some personal information, my GIF file name, my address, and an introductory paragraph. After you enter your information, click on the Save As button to bring up the standard Windows Save As dialog box. Make sure

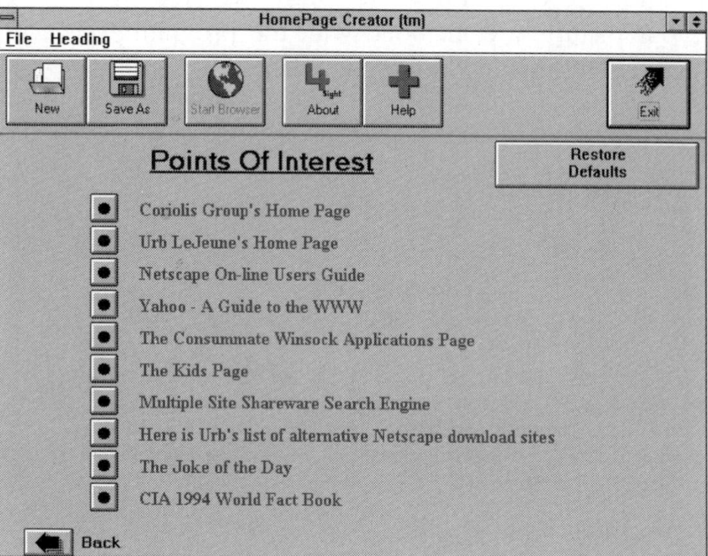

Figure 9.15 *The second screen of HPC.*

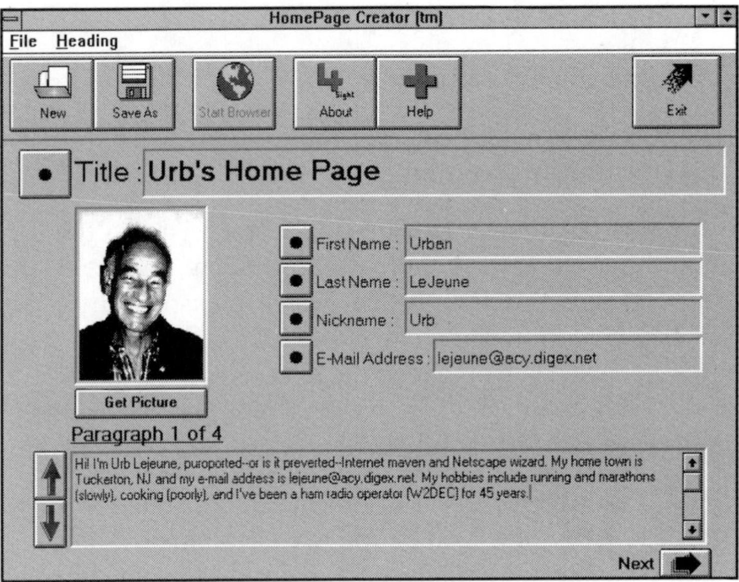

Figure 9.16 *The first page of HPC ready to go.*

you specify a file name for your HTML document and save it by clicking the OK button. If you want to insert some of your own Web pages as links, make sure that you click on the Next button and use the Site Editor to put in the names and URLs for your links.

Figures 9.17 and 9.18 demonstrate the output created by HPC. The GIFs, other than your picture, are included with the program. The actual HTML output created by HPC for my home page data is:

```
<HTML>
  <HEAD>
    <TITLE>Urb's Home Page</TITLE>
  </HEAD>

  <BODY>
    <CENTER><H1>Urb's Home Page</H1></CENTER>
    <IMG ALT="Urb's picture usually goes here" SRC="URB.GIF">

    Hi! I'm Urb LeJeune, purported - or is it perverted - Internet
    maven and Netscape wizard. My home town is Tuckerton, NJ and my
    e-mail address is lejeune@acy.digex.net. My hobbies include running
    and marathons (slowly), cooking (poorly), and I've been a ham radio
    operator (W2DEC) for 45 years.
    <P>

    <CENTER><IMG SRC="poi.gif"></CENTER><P>
    <UL>
```

```
    <LI><A HREF="http://www.yahoo.com">
        Yahoo - A Guide to the WWW</A><BR>
    <LI><A HREF="http://www.charm.net">
      Urb LeJeune's Home Page</A>
    <LI><A HREF="http://home.netscape.com/home/online-manual.html">
        Netscape On-line Users Guide</A>
    <LI><A HREF=""http://chef.sped.ukans.edu/cgi-bin/random"">
        URouLette - A different site every time</A>
    <LI><A HREF="http://www.infi.net/cool.html">
        The COOL site of the day</A>
    <LI><A HREF="http://www.pd.astro.it/kids.html">
        The Kids Page</A>
    <LI><A HREF="http://www.fagg.uni-lj.si/cgi-bin/shase">
        Multiple Site Shareware Search Engine</A>
    <LI><A HREF="http://www.charm.net/~lejeune/get-net.html">
        Here is Urb's list of alternative Netscape download sites</A>
    <LI><A HREF="http://bazaar.com/Jokes/jokeoftheday.htm">
        The Joke of the Day</A>
    <LI><A HREF="http://www.ic.gov/94fact/fb94toc/fb94toc.html">
        CIA 1994 World Fact Book</A>
  </UL>

  <A HREF="mailto:lejeune@acy.digex.net">
  <IMG ALIGN=CENTER SRC=mailbutt.gif>
  <B>Please mail me a comment about this home page.
  lejeune@acy.digex.net</B>
  <IMG SRC=line.gif>
  </A>
 </BODY>
</HTML>
```

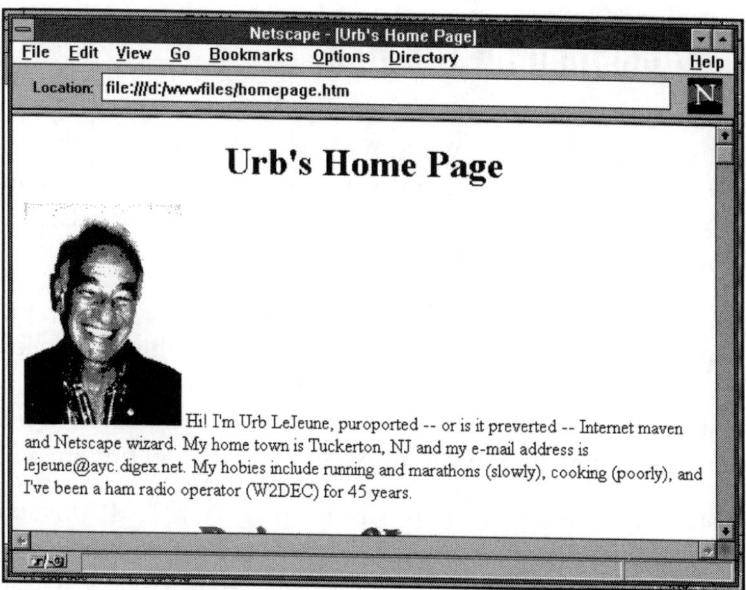

Figure 9.17 *The first part of HPC's finished product.*

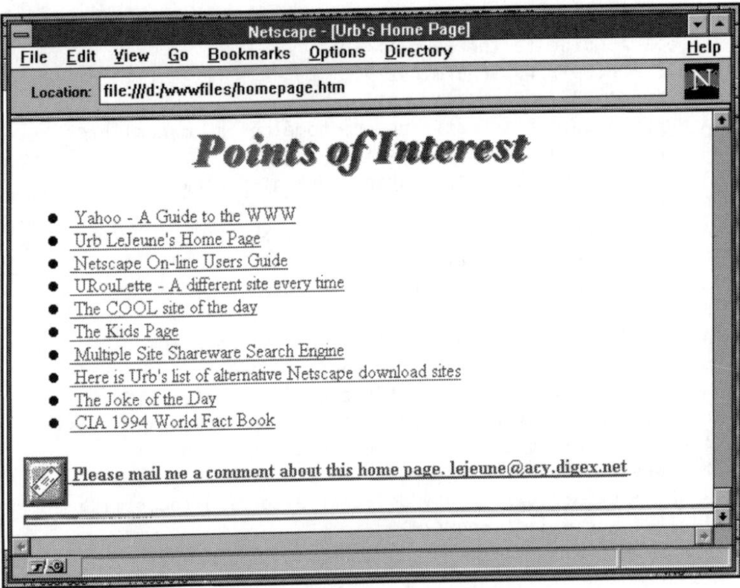

Figure 9.18 *The "Points of Interest" portion of HPC's output.*

Is this a piece of cake, or what? We've just created our very own home page without needing to know any HTML. This is the way Web publishing should be. Unfortunately, HomePage Creator can't do everything for us. You can, of course, take the HTML file created by HomePage Creator and add more to it.

GETTING PUBLISHED ON THE WEB

Now that you know how to create your own basic home page, you're probably anxious to publish on the World Wide Web so that the rest of the world can view your information. For many Netscape users, this is a frustrating task. The Web is like the "wild west"—there are very few standards for Internet service providers who provide Web access.

When I got into Web surfing, I lucked out. I was fortunate enough to have an account on Baltimore's Charm Net, where the forward-thinking folks managing this Internet provider allow all account holders access to a Web server so that they can show their home page to the world. The temptation to publish on the Internet was too much for me to resist, so I was up and running in no time.

To be "published" on the Web simply means that your HTML documents are available for other Web surfers to view. If you create a cool home page and just store it on your computer, no one will be able to view it unless you physically travel around the world and show it on your laptop computer.

Obviously, you won't get very far with this approach. You'd be better off trying to find an Internet service provider to help you go public with your Web creations.

If your company has its own direct connection on the Internet, you'll need to talk to the person in charge of your system's administration. He or she should be able to tell you everything you need to do to get set up. If you ask nicely (sometimes a gift of chips and salsa does the trick), the administrator will probably set up everything for you. Usually, this is simply a matter of creating a directory on a Unix machine or Windows NT and uploading a few files.

If you are considering using a service provider, the first thing you should do is ask if they can supply you with a Web server. If they can't, you'll need to look elsewhere. If they provide server capabilities but want to charge you an arm and a leg to get your home page on their server, tell them you'll trade them server space for the Brooklyn Bridge. Putting up a home page on someone else's server shouldn't be expensive—all that's required is a little storage space and a few setup instructions. Don't let anybody tell you otherwise.

If your service provider allows you to put up your own home page, you shouldn't have too much trouble getting set up. Let me walk you through a typical setup so that you can see what is involved. Of course, the actual details will vary a little, depending on which service provider you are using.

Setting Up Your Home Page with a Service Provider

Most service providers (if they are at all organized) will supply you with a set of instructions for getting your home page up on their system. In fact, you might find a reference to such a document by viewing the service provider's home page. If you can't find the information you need, call them. (That's why they are there—to provide you with service!)

Your provider will likely charge you for the space that your HTML and other documents take up on their computer. So, if you are just doing this for fun, don't go wild with your GIF files—you might get a big bill at the end of the month.

Once you have your home page HTML file and other necessary files, you'll need to get them on your provider's computer. This usually involves three steps:

1. Create a directory under your home directory (on their computer) to store your Web documents. This directory might have a name like *public_html*. This is the place that the Web server goes to locate your files. The directory must be named properly and set up with the appropriate permissions. (Your service provider will fill you in on the details.)

2. You must name your home page using a predetermined name. Many servers use the file name index.html. (Remember your files will probably be stored on a Unix computer and Unix uses different file name conventions than DOS.)

3. Upload your home page and other required Web documents to your newly created directory.

Keep in mind that these steps are typically completed by using Unix commands. The process involves logging on to your service provider's computer using your shell account and then executing some commands at a text prompt. Some service providers are even smart enough to give you a script to help you automate the process of setting up your Web documents storage area. For example, they might provide you with a script like

```
makehtml
```

which creates a directory for you and sets up the necessary server configuration so that you can be up and running in no time.

LET'S REVIEW

How's that for a crash course on creating a home page and getting it published on the Web? Of course, this is just a start—there are many other issues involved in creating HTML documents and Web publishing. Hopefully this is enough to whet your appetite so you'll continue to explore the other important HTML and Web publishing chapters in this book.

At its most basic level, Web publishing involves creating home pages, which in turn are written as HTML documents. HTML documents are text files that you can create with a text editor or a program like HomePage Creator.

Before you create your own home page, you'll want to create an outline for the content of your home page. A simple home page can include text, graphics, and links to other Web pages. With HomePage Creator, you can easily create your own home page (HTML document) by entering information into the program. The best part is that *you don't need to know any HTML to create a working home page.* HomePage Creator produces an HTML document, which you can use as is, or modify with a text editor or a special-purpose HTML editor.

To publish your home page on the Web, you'll need access to a Web server. Many Internet providers allow you to put up your own Web pages. To learn how to do this, you should ask your service provider for instructions.

Chapter 10

Creating Web Pages with HTML

It's time to learn how to create documents using HTML—the universal publishing language of the Web.

If you're like most budding Web publishers, you'll want to learn as much about HTML as possible so that you can publish better pages on the Web. Once you master the basics of HTML, you'll be amazed at how quickly you can create nice looking Web pages with hyperlinked text, graphics, and even multimedia features like sound, video, and animation. The best thing about working with HTML is that you can look at thousands of Web pages and easily examine the HTML used to create them. All you need is your Netscape browser and a little free time.

In this chapter we'll take a close look at HTML from the perspective of creating Web pages. Actually, we'll return to the topic of creating the types of home pages introduced in the previous chapter. We'll explore how home pages can be created by either modifying other HTML documents or writing HTML documents from scratch. To start, we'll borrow an HTML document from another Web site.

As we build a new version of our home page, you'll learn about the structure of HTML documents and some of the basic HTML features, including character and paragraph formatting, headings, images, and hotlinks. You'll be surprised at how little HTML you need to know to get up and running. If you make a mistake during the process of creating your home page using HTML, no problem. You can easily fix it using your favorite word processor or special-purpose HTML editor and test your updated version with your Web browser. To make it easier for you to create and edit your HTML documents, I'll also show you how to use a visual HTML editor called Web Spinner. This editor is very useful because it provides special features for creating HTML tags.

HTML FOR WEB PUBLISHING

When you first look at an HTML document like the one we created in the previous chapter with HomePage Creator, it's hard to see the correlation between the HTML instructions and a visual Web page. This takes some getting used to. As I mentioned in Chapter 8, HTML is not a language designed to describe page design or layout. Its strength is in describing how documents are organized and how they should link to other documents.

If your background is in traditional desktop publishing using programs like PageMaker, you'll need to adopt a different mindset to succeed with HTML. Basically, you need to keep in mind that HTML authoring involves working at a more basic, command level. Many of the design and layout tasks that can be automated with programs like PageMaker require actual coding with HTML. For example, with PageMaker you can put a word in bold type by selecting the word and clicking on a bolding option. In HTML, you need to write a special instruction called a *tag* to put a word in bold type. In this respect, HTML is a step backwards in the evolution of electronic publishing.

Fortunately, due to the popularity of Web publishing, HTML is evolving very quickly. Many automated Web publishing tools are in development and new features are continually being added to the current HTML standard. Even if you eventually have an automated tool that creates all of the HTML documents you need to publish on the Web, you'll want to understand how HTML documents are structured and how to write your own HTML commands. After all, if you want to "borrow" ideas from other Web publishers, you'll need to be able to read and understand their HTML documents.

What Is HTML+ or HTML 3.0?

If you've done much surfing on the Web or spent any time hanging out with people who publish on the Web, you've probably heard the term *HTML+* or *HTML 3.0*. (Have you ever noticed how programmers love to add plus signs to the end of their latest programming language creations? This is their way of saying "this latest version is new and improved.") HTML+ is essentially HTML with added features. If this isn't confusing enough, many people refer to this newer version of HTML as *HTML 3.0*.

Whenever new computer languages are unleashed on the world, those who use them come up with a million ideas for new features. Of course, HTML is no exception. HTML+ (or HTML 3.0) is not actually a standard yet—it's a specification for the extensions that are in development for HTML and Web publishing. Some of the new features in the works include:

- Tables
- Mathematical equations
- Text that can flow around images
- Figures with captions
- More sophisticated links so that you can create "guided tours"

You might not realize it, but some of the features in the HTML 3.0 specification are already supported by leading-edge browsers like Netscape. What this means is that you can get a jump on everyone else and start using some of these features right away. But if you use some of the HTML 3.0 features, such as tables and "flowable" text, remember not all Web browsers will support these features. If you want to learn more about HTML 3.0, point your Web browser to:

```
http://info.cern.ch/hypertext/WWW/MarkUp/HTMLPlus/htmlplus_1.html
```

Many of the HTML 3.0 features are so useful that I can't live without them. When I introduce them, I'll take special care to identify and point them out.

Learning HTML

The best way to learn how to create HTML documents (outside of using the HomePage Creator program introduced in the previous chapter) is to compose an HTML document that will become your home page. Even if you don't have access to a Web server yet, you can still view your home page with Netscape or another browser such as Mosaic, and show it off to your friends. If you later get access to a Web server, all you'll need to do is upload your HTML files. (See the previous chapter for suggestions on how to do this.)

I'm a big believer in learning new things by looking at what others have done. After all, why reinvent the wheel? Fortunately, the Web is full of many great (and some not so great) examples of home pages and HTML documents. And the best part is that you can easily check out the HTML documents used for any Web pages you locate. When an interesting display technique catches your eye, you can view or save its HTML document by using Netscape. Before we create any of our own HTML documents, let's go out and get the HTML document for the Charm Net home page.

EXPLORER PROJECT

Charm Net HTML Here We Come

In this project, we'll travel to Charm Net's home page and save the HTML for this page as charmnet.htm. We'll also get the GIF file this home page uses and save it as charmnet.gif This way, you can later view and modify the home page without having to go online to the Web. If you have already grabbed these files by following the projects in the previous chapter, you're all set.

The Charm Net home page uses a variety of interesting HTML styles and effects. To get this home page's HTML document, use the following URL:

```
http://www.charm.net/
```

Fire up Netscape and enter this URL in the Location: text box. When the document has loaded, execute the sequence File|Save As. Save the file as charmnet.htm. (Make sure you select the *.HTM option in the Save File as Type selection box. If you save the file as a *.TXT file, the HTML tags will be removed and you won't be able to use them.) To work with the Charm Net home page, you'll also need to get its logo. The URL for this image is:

```
http://www.charm.net/logo.gif
```

Go to this location and click on the logo that is displayed. Netscape will then display a list of choices. Click on the Save This Image As option, which will bring up the Save As dialog box. Accept the name logo.gif and save it in the same directory where you saved the HTML document for Charm Net's home page, charmnet.htm.

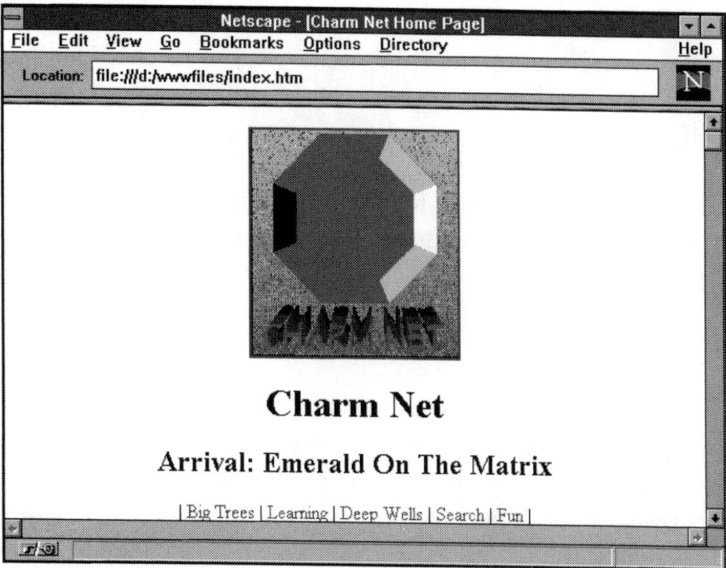

***Figure 10.1** The local disk copy of Charm Net's home page.*

Make a working copy of the HTML document by copying charmnet.htm to a file named index.htm. Figure 10.1 shows the Charm Net home page using our local disk document and GIF. You'll want to refer back to this figure as you are making changes.

Before we do anything with Charm Net's HTML file, let's take a little side trip, a sort of HTML crash course. We'll explore some basics and then return to our newly downloaded Charm Net home page and turn it into your home page.

> *Note: You can use any name you want to create an HTML file, as long as it has an extension of htm (for DOS) or an extension of html for other systems such as Unix. As a reference point for the remainder of this chapter, we'll call our evolving home page "index.htm". Let's assume that the Charm Net saved files and the files that we'll create will be stored on the "D:" drive in directory "WWWfiles".*

HTML 101

You've captured your first HTML document. So, now what? Since HTML documents are readable text files, you can view them using your favorite word processor, text editor, or HTML editor. In the examples I present, I'll be using an HTML editor called Web Spinner. Web Spinner is a custom HTML editor that I like to use to create and edit HTML documents. I've included a version of this program on the companion CD-ROM for you to use. I'll explain more about Web Spinner and other HTML editors later in the chapter when we create HTML documents from scratch.

Figure 10.2 shows the HTML tags for the index.htm file (the Charm Net home page). If you take a peek at the third line in this document, here's what you'll see:

```
<title>Charm Net Home Page</title>
```

This line actually reveals the essence of HTML. Look closely, and you'll see text inside angle brackets <>. These are called *tags*. Tags are what make this a "marked up" document. Text that has a special meaning is, for the most part, bracketed between a set of tags that have the same name. The trailing tag also has a slash between the "<" and the text inside the brackets. The text in this example is "Charm Net Home Page." The tag pair **<TITLE>** ... **</TITLE>** tells the browser how to treat the text between the tags. In this case, the text will be displayed as a title in the title bar for the Web page. Do you see how easy this HTML stuff is? Let's explore more.

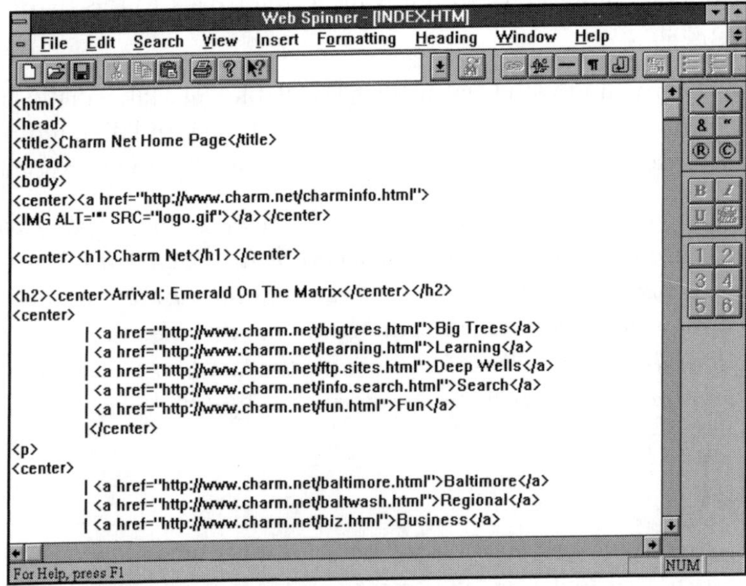


```
<html>
<head>
<title>Charm Net Home Page</title>
</head>
<body>
<center><a href="http://www.charm.net/charminfo.html">
<IMG ALT="" SRC="logo.gif"></a></center>

<center><h1>Charm Net</h1></center>

<h2><center>Arrival: Emerald On The Matrix</center></h2>
<center>
	| <a href="http://www.charm.net/bigtrees.html">Big Trees</a>
	| <a href="http://www.charm.net/learning.html">Learning</a>
	| <a href="http://www.charm.net/ftp.sites.html">Deep Wells</a>
	| <a href="http://www.charm.net/info.search.html">Search</a>
	| <a href="http://www.charm.net/fun.html">Fun</a>
	|</center>
<p>
<center>
	| <a href="http://www.charm.net/baltimore.html">Baltimore</a>
	| <a href="http://www.charm.net/baltwash.html">Regional</a>
	| <a href="http://www.charm.net/biz.html">Business</a>
```

Figure 10.2 Viewing the HTML document for Charm Net's home page.

Note: If you have any experience in graphic arts or typesetting, you can think of HTML tags as you would typesetting codes. In traditional typesetting systems, special codes are placed in front of words, sentences, and paragraphs to indicate how they should be printed. For example, a code such as <B> or <I> could indicate that text should be displayed in bold or italic, respectively. And this is exactly how HTML works!

A little further down in the index.htm file is this line of HTML:

```
<h1>Charm Net</h1>
```

This is the text for a heading. There are six tag pairs for headings; **<H1>** ... **</H1>** through **<H6>** ... **</H6>**. **H1** style headings are the largest and **H6** style are the smallest, providing nothing has been done to alter their size using Netscape's preference settings. Headings need not appear in any special order. Headings also generate a paragraph break; that is, the text that follows a heading will be displayed on its own line.

EXPLORER TIP

Centering Text with a Netscape HTML Enhancement

Netscape supports a useful HTML enhancement called centering. This feature is not part of the current HTML standard and is not supported by other browsers. In the Charm Net HTML example, you'll see that the main heading is enclosed within the **<CENTER> ... </CENTER>** tag pair. This tag tells the browser to center everything that appears between the two tags. Be aware that the center tags will be ignored by browsers other than Netscape. Part of the HTML standard states that unrecognized tags should be ignored—so there is no harm in using tags, even if the user's browser doesn't support them.

The text that is not a tag, or a component of a tag, is always considered plain text. A Web browser treats plain text as a continuous stream, which means that it continues to display the text using the currently selected format until a new format code is encountered. Embedded returns and multiple blanks are ignored. White space is also ignored. (White space can be a tab, return, and the like.) You cannot split a line by simply pressing the Enter key. Line breaks and paragraphs must be explicitly specified. I'll show you how to do some neat formatting a little later.

The important thing to keep in mind about tags is that they usually come in pairs. The first tag tells your browser how to handle the text that is about to follow and the second tag in the pair tells the browser that no more text is coming and that it should stop formatting and look for another command. As an example, one widely used command pair is **<B>** ... **</B>**, which is used to display text in bold. In a sentence like this:

```
HTML is really <B>easy</B> to learn
```

only the word "easy" would be displayed in bold. If the second tag, **</B>**, were missing, your browser would continue to format all of the text that it found in the HTML document using bold type.

HTML has two components, plain text and formatting controls. The formatting tags control the way plain text displays although the tags themselves are not displayed by the browser.

HTML Consistency Check

When creating HTML documents, you cannot assume that everyone else will see your text exactly as you see it on your screen. The display window size may differ. Additionally, there are differences in the various Netscape versions. Mosaic users may also change the font and point size for any display type in their mosaic.ini configuration file. Or, if someone is viewing your files within another browser such as Mosaic, your HTML documents could look a little different.

What you see on the screen is a function of three things:

- The specific browser being used. (A browser such as Mosaic will have different display features than Netscape.)
- The size of the window in which the browser output is displayed.
- Netscape's configuration parameters, which are set using the Preferences menu.

The HTML Shell Game

Now that we've explored tags, the basic building blocks of HTML documents, what else is there to an HTML file? Fortunately, the actual structure of an HTML document is quite simple; we can reduce the universe of standard HTML files to a working template or shell. If you were writing an article, you could think of this shell as your outline. Here's the shell that I recommend:

```
<HTML>
   <HEAD>
       <TITLE>document-title-here</TITLE>
    </HEAD>

    <BODY>
        <H1>major-document-heading-here</H1>
             text and markup
         < A  HREF="ur"l> anchor-title</A>

        <ADDRESS>
              author and version information
        </ADDRESS>
    </BODY>
</HTML>
```

Since HTML is case insensitive, tags can be in either uppercase or lowercase letters. For example, **<title>**, **<Title>**, and **<TITLE>** all are treated the same. I use uppercase letters for things that do not change and lowercase letters for things that could be deleted or modified.

At the top of our template, we have the pair **<HTML>** and **</HTML>**. Everything inside this part of the file is the information that a Web browser will interpret when it reads the file. These tags tell the browser that the file is an HTML document. If you place text before the first tag or after the second tag, the text will be ignored. This area is a great place to put notes to yourself to document what your HTML files do. You could also include the dates when you created and modified the file.

If you look closely, you'll see that only two main sections are within the **<HTML>** tags: a header indicated by **<HEAD>** and **</HEAD>** and a body indicated by **<BODY>** and **</BODY>**. The header section tells the browser what title to display at the top of the browser's window. The body, on the other hand, is where all the action occurs. Anything placed within the body will be displayed by the browser. Mostly that means text, but it can also include images and even sound files, which are "displayed" by the browser by playing them on the system speaker. As we create our own home page, you'll learn how to put all kinds of different things in the body of an HTML document—including hotlinks.

Inside the body I've placed some of the more widely used HTML tags, including a heading, **<H1>**, anchor, **<A>**, and a documentation section, **<ADDRESS>**. As we work our way through this chapter, you'll learn how these important tags are used.

The advantage of using a template like this to create your own HTML documents is that you won't have to look up the basic HTML tags. (You could also include some of the other formatting tags that we'll be exploring in this chapter and the next.) The template will also help you remember the order of the main sections. You might save this template to a file, and each time you want to start a new document simply make a copy of the template. I use the name SHELL.HTM for my template file.

> *Note: Take advantage of the fact that browsers ignore white spaces and adopt a style and adhere to it in all of your documents. I like to have my starting and ending tags line up and everything in between indented two positions from the tag margin. It sure makes it easier to find things that have gone wrong.*

Formatting Fun

You just saw how HTML is structured and how simple text is processed and displayed with HTML codes—in particular, titles for Web pages and headings. Of course, you can do much more with HTML, such as creating hyper text links, displaying images, formatting lists, setting up forms, and so on. We'll get into some of these techniques a little later. But for now, we need to take a closer look at some of the basics of formatting text.

In the document world, we can break things down into two levels: character formatting and paragraph formatting. At the character formatting level, you can format text like you would in a word processor. That is, you can put words or phrases in bold, italic, underline, and so on. Table 10.1 shows some of the more common HTML character formatting tags.

Let's look at a few examples:

```
<B>This is bold text.</B>
<I> This is italic.</I>
<B><U>This is bold and underlined.</U></B>
```

Here's how this text might look when it is displayed by a browser:

This is bold text.
This is italic.
This is bold and underlined.

Underlining is not currently supported by most browsers because underlined text looks too much like a link.

Table 10.1 *Basic Character Formatting Tags*

Tag	Description
<B> ... </B>	Bold
<I> ... </I>	Italics
<TT> ... </TT>	Typewriter style
<U> ... </U>	Underline

Notice that you can combine formatting tags for a single string of text. For example, the text in the third example is bold and underlined. When you combine tags, the order of them is not important. Just remember to include a closing tag for each starting tag you use. (The character formatting tags always come in pairs.)

You can also use character formatting tags with headings. But I recommend that you get in the habit of placing the character formatting tags inside the heading tags as shown here:

```
<H1><I>Welcome to the World of HTML!</I></H1>
```

In this case, the text would be displayed as a first level head in italic. I recommend putting the character formatting tags inside the heading tags because some older browsers may get confused if you do it the other way around.

Character formatting is the easiest HTML feature to master, although it limits you to simple display effects. Paragraph formatting is much more interesting and useful. Table 10.2 shows some of the basic formatting tags available for everything from inserting new paragraphs to creating lists to breaking a line of text within a paragraph.

We won't explore all of these now, but let's look at a few of them to get you started. As you work with paragraph formatting tags, the most important point to keep in mind is that browsers don't display text the way you format it within your HTML files. Text in an HTML file is treated as one big stream. The length of a line that a user sees when viewing a document in a browser is determined by the width of the screen or window. That means that the browser reformats the text to make it fit.

If you want to have your text displayed as different sections, such as headings, paragraphs, or lists, you'll need to put in some of the formatting tags. The most widely used tag, **<P>**, is not typically used as a tag pair. (There is a

Table 10.2 Basic Paragraph Formatting Tags

Tag	Description
  ... </BR>	Breaks a line
<DL> ... </DL>	Creates a directory list (a list that's indented)
<H1> ... </H1>	Creates a level 1 heading *
<HR> ... </HR>	Adds a horizontal rule in the displayed text
<LI> ... </LI>	Creates a list item
<OL> ... </OL>	Creates an ordered list
<P>	Starts a new paragraph
<PRE> ... </PRE>	Forces text to be displayed exactly as it is in the HTML document (this stands for "preformatted")
<UL> ... </UL>	Creates an unnumbered list

* Remember that HTML defines six different head levels, **<H1>** through **<H6>**.

</P> tag but it really doesn't do much.) This tag displays text as a new paragraph. For example, if you want to display two lines of text in a browser formatted as

```
HTML is easy to learn and use.

Let's start our HTML tour now.
```

the HTML version would look like:

```
<U>HTML is easy to learn and use.</U>
<P>
Let's start our HTML tour now.
```

If you omitted the **<P>** tag, both of these sentences would be run together.

EXPLORER TIP

How to Keep Your Lines from Wrapping

Because browsers ignore the format of text as it appears in an HTML document, text will wrap according to the width of the screen the user sees. In many cases, this is exactly what you want; however, there are times when you want to have more control over how text lines wrap.

The easiest way to get your text not to wrap is to use the **<ADDRESS>** ... **</ADDRESS>** tag pair. These tags are actually provided for documentation information, such as the author and revision dates, for an HTML document. But because they force text to appear exactly as it's written in the HTML document, with line breaks and line feeds as you've typed them, they are useful for controlling word wrap. The only limitation is that these tags force the text inside them to be displayed in italics.

Another tag pair you may want to try out is **<PRE>** ... **</PRE>**. Text placed between these tags will also keep its formatting as you entered it into the HTML file. But this time, it will force the text to a monospace font. This is useful for displaying computer source code or ASCII text, which is difficult to line up. The tag **
** causes a hard line break (carriage return). There is only a single **
** tag. The difference between the **
** and **<P>** tags is that the **<P>** tag causes a blank line while **
** simply advances to the beginning of the next line.

Displaying Images

One of the best things about Web pages is that they can display both text and graphics. Just think how boring the Web would be if you couldn't view pictures of things—it would be like reading a magazine without full color pictures.

As you learn more about HTML in this book, you'll discover a number of options for images in your Web pages including displaying:

- Full size images as standalone pictures
- Images as small thumbnails—a useful feature for minimizing the time it takes to display images
- Images as hyperlinks—when a user clicks on a hyperlinked image, he or she can be taken to another location in an HTML document or even to another Web site
- Images so that they can be used as navigational maps

Web browsers can easily display pictures if they are in a GIF format. If you have bitmap images in other file formats, such as PCX or BMP, you can easily convert them to GIF using a graphics imaging program. (In fact, I've included a program named Paint Shop Pro to help you convert your graphics files. We'll be using it in the next chapter.) The GIF file format is becoming so popular because it has been adopted as the standard by users of information services such as CompuServe, America Online, and of course, the Internet.

When browsers like Netscape and Mosaic first appeared on the scene, they didn't provide any special support to allow you to combine text with images.

If you wanted to display a small picture to the left of a paragraph of text, you were out of luck. Fortunately, HTML 3.0 provides new features so that you can easily wrap text around images. Using HTML 3.0, you can also display captions with your images.

The easy way to display a bitmap image on a Web page is to use the **<IMG>** tag. Here's the actual format for this tag:

```
<IMG SRC="filename">
```

When a browser encounters an **<IMG>** tag, it will load the file that is specified by the "*filename*" part. The filename is specified as a parameter assigned to the "**SRC**" subtag, which effectively tells the browser the name of the bitmap graphics source file.

> *Note: When a browser reads in a bitmap image and displays it, the image will be displayed using its original size. When you create your bitmap image files, you should make sure that you size them properly so that they will look good when they appear on a Web page. Most new Web page designers tend to make their images too big, and the user has to scroll quite a bit to completely see them. Small images also require less disk space and therefore load faster.*

The Magic of Hotlinks

Web pages really start to come alive when you add hotlinks. Hotlinks are essentially the text or pictures that you click on to take you to new Web-accessible locations or resources. For example, if you were creating a Web page that contained a list of your company's products, you could list each product with a small picture on one Web page. Each picture and product name could be set up as a hotlink. If a reader clicked on one of the product names or pictures, a new HTML document could be loaded to provide more detailed information.

Fortunately, hotlinks are very easy to create with HTML. Each hotlink you use on a Web page has two parts: an anchor and a hotlink location or resource. The anchor is the colored and underlined text or image that the users sees. The hotlink location is the place where your browser goes to fetch the next resource to display; typically, this hotlink location is a URL that references another HTML document. Since hotlinks can also be used to take a user to another location within the same HTML document, the hotlink location could be a tag that is placed somewhere else within the same document.

The more you know about anchors, the better you'll be at creating your own hotlinks. Let's explore the art of creating anchors with HTML. First I'll show you how to set up a link to a location within the same document, and then we'll create a link to reference a different HTML document.

Working with Anchor References

Anchor references are another pervasive HTML feature. Anchors are created by using the **<A>** ... **</A>** tag pair. This tag is easy to use; however, it will look a little awkward to you the first time you see it. Here is the general format for creating an anchor that allows you to set up a link to another location within the same HTML document:

```
<A HREF="#link-target"> anchor-text </A>
```

Notice that the formatting for an anchor tag is slightly different from the conventional <tag> ... </tag> pair. The first **A** tells the browser that it has encountered an anchor. The subtag, **HREF**, indicates that the anchor is linked to another location specified by the *link-target*. This is the location where the user will be taken when he or she clicks on the hotlink. Notice that you must place the character "#" at the beginning of the *link-target*, which can be any combination of letters. That's all there is to the first part of the **<A>** tag. In the middle goes the anchor—the text you want to highlight or define as the hotlink. The final **</A>** terminates the anchor.

In order for this type of anchor to work properly, you must also place the link-target used in the anchor definition at a another location in the HTML document. This is done by using another <A> anchor tag. This time the format is as follows:

```
<A NAME="link-tag"> target-text </A>
```

The **NAME** subtag tells the browser that this anchor is the location where the user should be taken when he or she clicks on its associated hotlink. Let's see an example:

```
This is our first Web page. It was a snap to create because
we had a great <A HREF="#htmllink">HTML guide</A> at our fingertips.
<P>
<P>
<P>
<HR>
<A NAME="htmllink">
<H2>The Easy HTML Guide</H2></A>
```

This is more actual HTML than we've written so far, but don't panic. It's actually very easy to follow. The first part is a paragraph of text that contains the hotlink or anchor "HTML guide." Then we have a few blank lines followed by a rule line. The last line is a level two head that is linked to the "HTML guide" hotlink. When the user clicks on the hotlink, he or she will be taken right to the level two head within the Web page. The target that ties both locations together is "htmllink." Wasn't that easy!

Linking to Another HTML Document

Setting up an anchor to link to another HTML document is similar to the technique we just explored; the only difference is that you must assign the path name of the target document to the **HREF** subtag. Here's the basic format:

```
<A HREF="file-pathname">anchor-text</A>
```

The *file-pathname* component can be a location on your hard drive or it can be a complete URL to another Web site.

To illustrate the use of an anchor tag that references another HTML document, let's use the URL for my actual home page, which is:

```
http://www.charm.net/~lejeune/
```

Now let's assume that you are creating an HTML document and want to say, "An interesting home page, demonstrating that one can be created by someone with marginal mental capability, is Urb LeJeune's. Another victory of perseverance over intelligence." Let's additionally assume that you want the text "Urb LeJeune's Home Page" to be the anchor. The body of your document might be:

```
<H2>The Original Big Dummy Creates Home Page</H2>
```

An interesting home page, demonstrating that one can be created by someone with marginal mental capability, is

```
<A HREF="http://www.charm.net/~lejeune/">
   Urb LeJeune's Home Page</A>

Yet another victory of perseverance over intelligence.
```

What might show up on the screen is:

```
The Original Big Dummy Creates Home Page

An interesting home page, demonstrating that one can be created by someone with
marginal mental capability, is Urb LeJeune's Home Page. Yet another victory of
perseverance over intelligence.
```

Pointing to the anchor Urb LeJeune's Home Page will result in "http://www.charm.net/~lejeune/" being displayed on the status line in Netscape, and when you click on this anchor, up comes my home page to a display near you.

CREATING A HOME PAGE USING CHARM NET'S PAGE

As promised, we'll return to the Charm Net home page, which now resides on our hard disk as index.htm. (We named the file index.htm—you'll see why in a moment.) I'll now show you a simple step-by-step procedure for turning this home page into your own home page. As you'll see, this is a good starting point for learning how to use some of the basic HTML tags. After we finish this project, we'll move down a level and create a home page from scratch using an HTML editor.

> EXPLORER TIP
>
> ***Using INDEX.HTM to Name Your Home Page***
>
> When you connect to a Web server using a URL that doesn't include a file name, the server will load a file named index.htm or index.html from the lowest order directory in the path name. Let's look at an example.
>
> My main URL on the Web server I use is
>
> ```
> http://ww.charm.net/~lejeune/
> ```
>
> If you point Netscape to this location, my home page document, index.html, will be loaded. Essentially, I placed this HTML file in my main directory /lejeune on the Unix system I share with other users. The nice feature here is that Web surfers who come to my home URL don't need to specify a filename. The Web server automatically knows what to do, which is to load in the file index.html stored in the current directory.

Step 1: View the File in an Editor

To start, load index.htm into your favorite editor. The first section of the file looks like this:

```
<html>
<head>
<title>Charm Net Home Page</title>
</head>
<body>
<center><a href="http://www.charm.net/charminfo.html">
<IMG ALT="" SRC="logo.gif"></a></center>

<center><h1>Charm Net</h1></center>
```

You might want to spend a few minutes looking over the file to get familiar with the different sections it contains. Since we are going to be changing the file, you might want to print the original to refer to if needed.

Step 2: Put in Your Own Title and Heading

Change the title and text between the **<HEAD>** tags to reflect the page's new mission in life—your home page. For my version, I use **<TITLE>**Urb's Home Page**</TITLE>**. You'll also need to change the main heading in the home page to make it your own. To do this, look for the **<h1>** tags and change the heading. I like to use the same text I use for the title. Thus, my change looks like **<H1>**Urb's Home Page**</H1>**. Here's the new version of the HTML with these changes made. Notice that I've changed the formatting slightly:

```
<HTML>
   <HEAD>
    <TITLE>Urb's Home Page</TITLE>
   </HEAD>

   <BODY>
   <CENTER>
      <A HREF="http://www.charm.net/charminfo.html">
      <IMG ALT="" SRC="logo.gif"></A>
   </CENTER>
   <CENTER>
      <H1>Urb's Home Page</H1>
   </CENTER>
```

Remember again, the text between the **<TITLE>** tags appears in the title area and the text between the heading tags appears in the document window area.

EXPLORER TIP

Better HTML Document Formatting

I like my HTML tags to be in uppercase to distinguish them from body text. I also like to use indenting to help keep track of how the HTML tags are being used. Although you can use whatever formatting techniques you like, this technique can help you better structure your HTML documents.

Step 3: Put in Your Own Image

The Charm Net home page displays a big green emerald. (This was the file logo.gif that we retrieved and saved earlier.) Let's replace this file with one of our own.

In the first section of the HTML document, you'll find the following line of text:

```
<A HREF="http://www.charm.net/charminfo.html">
<IMG ALT="" SRC="logo.gif"></A>
```

This is a hotlink instruction. It might look a little confusing to you at this point because it contains three components: a URL, an alternate name for the image, and the file name for the image. A hotlink is built using the form:

```
<A HREF="url"> anchor-text</A>
```

In this case, the "anchor-text" is actually the graphical image logo.gif. This indicates that it is a pointer to something. As you drag your mouse across the image, the URL "http://www.charm.net/charminfo.html" appears in the status bar. To put in our own image, just substitute your own GIF image file name for logo.gif, strip out the anchor, and include an alternate label for the image. Here's the change I made to put in my image file urb.gif:

```
<IMG ALT="Urb's picture goes here" SRC="urb.gif">
```

You might also want to change the placement of the picture on the home page. I like to have my heading above the image. Here's how I rearranged the HTML tags to accomplish this:

```
<BODY>
    <CENTER>
      <H1>Urb's Home Page</H1>
      <IMG ALT="Urb's picture goes here" SRC="urb.gif">
    </CENTER>
```

Again, this change is just a matter of personal preference.

Step 4: Add Your Story!

It's now time to tell the world all about yourself. Everyone has a unique story, and this is the place to tell it. Following the picture, insert a paragraph or two. Here's my version:

```
Hi! I'm Urb LeJeune, purported - or is it perverted - Internet
maven and Netscape wizard. My home town is Tuckerton, NJ and my
e-mail address is <B><I>LeJeune@acy.digex.net</I></B>.
My hobbies include running marathons (slowly), cooking (poorly),
and I've been a ham radio operator (W2DEC) for 45 years. I also love
corny jokes and puns, how about sending me one. I've written two books
titled the <B>Mosaic &amp; Web EXplorer</B> and the <B>Netscape &amp;
HTML EXplorer<B>.
<P>
```

Notice that I've used a few of the character formatting tags presented earlier. I also included a blank line after my paragraph of text.

Step 5: Change Some of the Hotlinks

The Charm Net home page provides links to other Web sites. It is always a good idea to add links to your home page. You can leave the links as they are, change them, or add new ones.

For my version, I changed a few links in the second section of links in the original Charm Net HTML document. This section starts with the HTML instructions:

```
<a href="http://www.charm.net/baltimore.html">Baltimore</a>
<a href="http://www.charm.net/baltwash.html">Regional</a>
```

Let's change them to point to the Yahoo database and the Cool Site of the Day home pages:

```
<A HREF="http://www.yahoo.com">Yahoo</A>
<A HREF="http://www.infi.net/cool.html">Cool Site</A>
```

Step 6: Save the HTML Document

Before you can test the changes you've made to the HTML document with a Web browser, you'll need to save the document. If you are using your favorite word processor, make sure that you save the document as a text file. If you use another format, such as Word for Windows, your browser will not be able to read the file.

Step 7: Test Your Creation

We've made enough changes for now. Fire up Netscape and load in the file using the instructions presented in the following section. Figure 10.3 shows

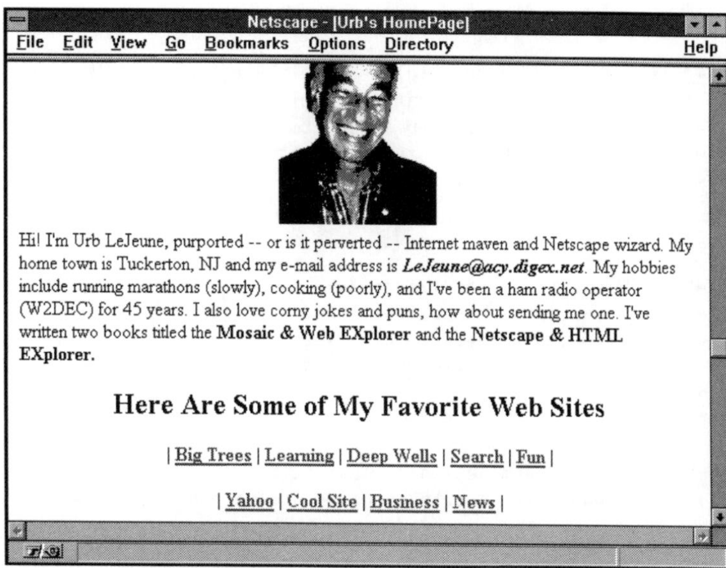

***Figure 10.3** The evolving home page.*

how Netscape displays our altered version of Charm Net's home page. The actual contents of the index.htm document are shown here:

```
<HTML>
  <HEAD>
    <TITLE>Urb's HomePage</TITLE>
  </HEAD>

  <BODY>
    <CENTER>
      <H1>Urb's Home Page</H1>
      <IMG ALT="Urb's picture goes here" SRC="urb.gif">
    </CENTER>

    Hi! I'm Urb LeJeune, purported — or is it perverted — Internet
    maven and Netscape wizard. My home town is Tuckerton, NJ and my
    e-mail address is <B><I>LeJeune@acy.digex.net</I></B>.
    My hobbies include running marathons (slowly), cooking (poorly),
    and I've been a ham radio operator (W2DEC) for 45 years. I also love
    corny jokes and puns, how about sending me one. I've written two books
    titled the <B>Mosaic &amp; Web EXplorer</B> and the <B>Netscape &amp;
    HTML EXplorer<B>.
    <P>

    <CENTER>
      <H2>Here Are Some of My Favorite Web Sites</H2>
```

```
     </CENTER>
     <CENTER>
    | <A HREF="http://www.charm.net/bigtrees.html">Big Trees</A>
    | <A HREF="http://www.charm.net/learning.html">Learning</A>
    | <A HREF="http://www.charm.net/ftp.sites.html">Deep Wells</A>
    | <A HREF="http://www.charm.net/info.search.html">Search</A>
    | <A HREF="http://www.charm.net/fun.html">Fun</A>
    |</CENTER>
<P>
<CENTER>
    | <A HREF="http://www.yahoo.com">Yahoo</A>
    | <A HREF="http://www.infi.net/cool.html">Cool Site</A>
    | <A HREF="http://www.charm.net/biz.html">Business</A>
    | <A HREF="http://www.charm.net/news.html">News</A>
    |</CENTER>
<P>
<CENTER>
    | <A HREF="http://www.charm.net/charm.cust.html">Local Web Pages</A>
    | <A HREF="http://www.charm.net/technophile.html">Technophile</A>
    |</CENTER>
<P>
<CENTER>
    | <A HREF="http://www.charm.net/pip.html">Connect</A>
    | <A HREF="http://www.charm.net/charm.pip.html">Connect To Charm Net</A>
    | <A HREF="http://www.charm.net/charminfo.html">About Charm Net</A>
    |</CENTER>
  </BODY>
</HTML>
```

Testing a Home Page

We're now ready to view the home page we've created. As you learned in the previous chapter, you can load an HTML file from your hard disk into Netscape by entering the URL in the Location: text box. You can also open an HTML file stored on your hard disk using File | Open File. When the standard File Open dialog appears, locate and select the index.htm file we've been creating. Netscape will take over and process the HTML file for viewing.

Wait a second, we're getting ahead of ourselves. Recall that to load a local HTML file, your TCP/IP stack must be active in memory so that WinSock API calls can be made by Netscape. You can easily set this up by first running your TCP/IP stack application and then minimizing it. If your stack isn't anywhere in memory, Netscape may refuse to run. It'll give you an error message stating that it can't find winsock.dll.

You can view your local handiwork using Netscape even if you aren't connected to the Internet. Refer back to Chapter 7 for instructions on how to do this.

CREATING A HOME PAGE FROM SCRATCH

We now know enough to be dangerous with HTML and put a home page together without having to steal someone else's. Although there are a lot of HTML examples on the Web, you'll eventually get to the point where you'll be creating your Web page documents from scratch. You can do this using a Word processor like Word for Windows, or you can use a custom HTML editor that will help you insert and modify HTML tags.

Whether you are just learning HTML or you have written hundreds of HTML documents, HTML editors can be a big help. Their advantage over conventional editors is that they make it easy to insert syntactically correct HTML tags in a document, which means that you won't have to memorize all of the HTML tags available. Most will allow you to view a document by launching a browser such as Netscape with the target document opened.

Some of the more popular editors that are available for Windows include:

- Hot Metal
- HTML Assistant
- HTML Write
- Web Edit
- Web Spinner
- Web Weave

I've included versions of some of these editors on the companion CD-ROM for you to try out and use. To locate them, look in the directory \tools. Some of them are shareware, so if you start to use them, please register them to support the developers of these great tools. I've also included another useful editor called Edit Master, which is a great Windows Notepad editor.

For the remainder of this chapter, I'll show you how to use one of these editors, Web Spinner, to create a new HTML document and include features like formatted text, images, and links. Once you learn the basic techniques of writing HTML with Web Spinner, you'll be able to easily use any of the other available HTML editors.

Creating a Home Page with Web Spinner

For our final home page adventure, we'll create an HTML document with Web spinner that you can use as the foundation for your own home page. The home page won't look too much different from the page we created earlier; however, this example will show you the steps involved in creating a new HTML document using a special purpose editor.

Let's use the Web Spinner editor provided on the companion CD-ROM. To use this editor, you must be running Windows 95 or Windows NT, or you must make sure Win32s is installed on you computer. Detailed instructions for installing Win32s are provided in Part Four of this book. To get you up to speed quickly, here are the steps you need to follow:

1. Run the program setup.exe located in the tools\winn32s\disk1 directory on the companion CD-ROM.

2. The setup program will take over and you'll see a window named "Microsoft Win32s Setup." Click on the Continue button. The installation program will copy the required files to your hard disk.

3. Restart Windows.

To start the editor, run the program webspin.exe located in the \tools\webspin directory on the CD-ROM. To create a new document, click on the File | New option or click on the New icon (the leftmost icon on the toolbar). The editor will create a skeletal document for you, as shown in Figure 10.4. Change the title text "Your title goes here" to your title choice. Add a new line just under the **<BODY>** tag, and enter the document heading and highlight the text by dragging the mouse across it. Figure 10.5 shows the highlighted text "Urb's Home Page."

Notice that many of Web Spinner's icons become active after text has been highlighted. (When they are grayed, they cannot be used.) The group of numbered icons on the right side of the screen represents the six heading tag pairs. Click on "1" and the tags **<H1>** and **</H1>** will surround your heading text. The entire text, including the heading tags, will also be highlighted. Open the Insert menu, select Netscape Symbol, and then select the Center option. The line you've previously selected becomes:

```
<CENTER><H1>Urb's Home Page</H1></CENTER>
```

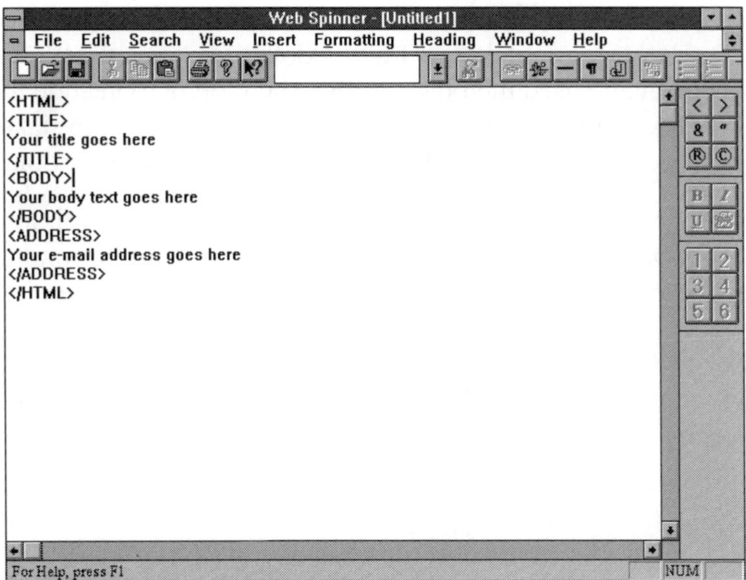

Figure 10.4 *Creating a skeletal document with Web Spinner.*

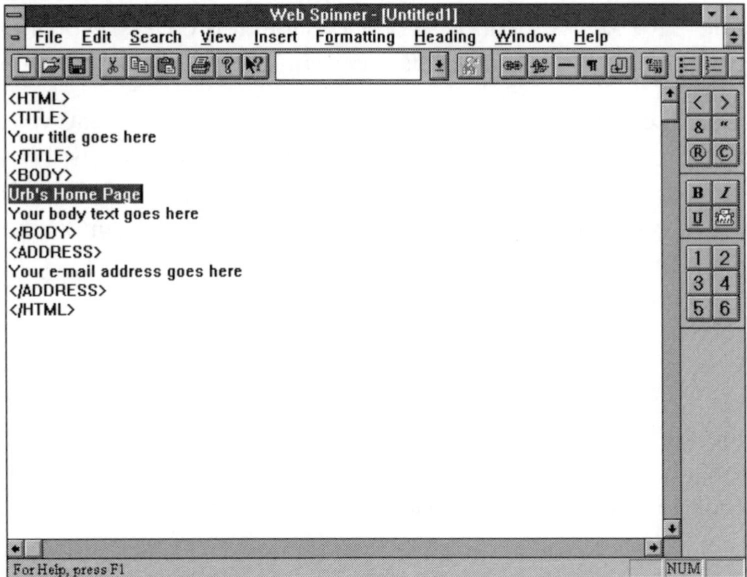

Figure 10.5 *Setting up a heading with Web Spinner.*

This technique for creating HTML documents is great because it can save you from making annoying mistakes. If I had a dollar for every time I created an HTML document and used the bold tag **<B>**, then forgot to include the terminating tag **</B>**, I'd be rich. (By the way, when you make this mistake, everything in your document from the first **<B>** tag gets displayed in bold type!)

Once you've centered the main heading, insert a short paragraph in the area defined "Your body text goes here." This is your second time around, so make up a good story. I like to use a segment of text that contains my e-mail address, and then I highlight the address. For example, to make "LeJeune@acy.digex.net" both bold and italicized, first highlight the address. Next, click on the "I" icon on the right side of the screen. Next, highlight the address again and click on the "B" icon. The sequence of imbedded tags is of no importance. Web Spinner creates the following line:

```
<I><B> LeJeune@acy.digex.net</B></I>
```

Repeat this process for any other special formatting effects you want to include.

Once you are finished creating your home page, save it as an HTML document by selecting File|Save As. As mentioned previously in this chapter, you'll probably want to name the file index.htm so that later you can put it up on a Web site.

Now we can take this home page for a spin. The best part is that we can do it right from Web Spinner! Click on the View|Options option to display the Options dialog box. One of the items provided is Web Viewer for Testing. Enter the path name and program name of your favorite browser. For example, here's the path and file name I use to have Web Spinner load Netscape:

```
J:\NETSCAPE\NETSCAPE.EXE
```

If Netscape (or some other browser) is not running, click on the View|Test HTML option If Netscape is already running, enter the URL of the document. If you are already viewing this document and you want to check out any modifications, just click on the Reload button on the toolbar.

Adding a Picture

After viewing the home page, let's return to Web Spinner to add a picture. If you have a GIF of yourself, use it—if not, practice with the logo.gif file we downloaded from Charm Net.

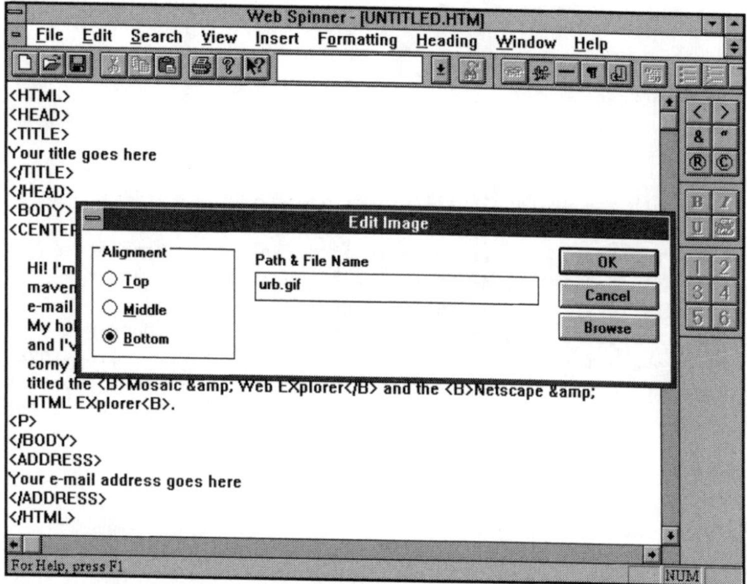

***Figure 10.6** Using Web Spinner's Edit Image dialog box to add a picture.*

Recall that the **<IMG>** tag is used to display a picture—in this case the GIF file yourname.gif or logo.gif. (Make sure that you have this file available on your hard disk; otherwise Netscape won't be able to display it when you view your home page.)

From the Web Spinner editor, create a blank line where you want the graphic to appear. Next, execute the sequence Insert | Graphic or click on the Graphic icon, which is just under the Windows menu item. An Edit Image dialog box will open, as shown in Figure 10.6. The radio buttons for Alignment will be explained in the next chapter. For now let's use the default setting Bottom. Enter the name of your GIF in the Path & File Name text box. Click on OK and an instruction like this

```
<IMG ALLIGN=BOTTOM SRC="urb.gif" >
```

will be added to the document.

That's all you need to do. Of course, save your file and take it for a trial run.

My completed version, with all HTML tags, looks like this:

```
<HTML>
  <HEAD>
    <TITLE>
      Urb's Home Page
    </TITLE>
  </HEAD>
  <BODY>
    <CENTER><H1>Urb's Home Page</H1></CENTER>
    <IMG ALLIGN=BOTTOM SRC="urb.gif" >
    Hi! I'm Urb LeJeune, purported - or is it perverted - Internet
    maven and Netscape wizard. My home town is Tuckerton, NJ and my
    e-mail address is <I><B> LeJeune@acy.digex.net</B></I>.
    My hobbies include running marathons (slowly), cooking (poorly),
    and I've been a ham radio operator (W2DEC) for 45 years. I also love
    corny jokes and puns, how about sending me one. I've written two books
    titled the <B>Mosaic &amp; Web EXplorer</B> and the <B>Netscape &amp;
    HTML EXplorer<B>.
   <P>

    <ADDRESS>
    lejeune@acy.digex.net
    </ADDRESS>
  </BODY>
</HTML>
```

We'll add some more features as we expand this page in the next chapter. Congratulations—you're well on your way to becoming a HTML expert.

Figure 10.7 shows the results of our initial handiwork. Our home page doesn't do much yet, but it's a start. Save the URL to a Netscape bookmark link, since we'll be displaying the home page quite a bit as we change it.

Notice that the text between the **<TITLE> </TITLE>** tags appears in the title bar following "Netscape -". The heading displayed within the document display window requires a pair of heading tags. As you can see, mine is:

```
<H1>Urb's Home Page</H1><P>
```

The text line in INDEX.htm following the heading is:

```
<IMG ALLIGN=BOTTOM SRC="urb.gif" >
```

Notice that it contains three parameters. The "IMG" parameter indicates an inline image, with the "SRC" parameter indicating the URL of the image file. The ALIGN parameter indicates where text is to be placed. Again, we'll go into the fancy details in the next chapter. Inline image files must be in either

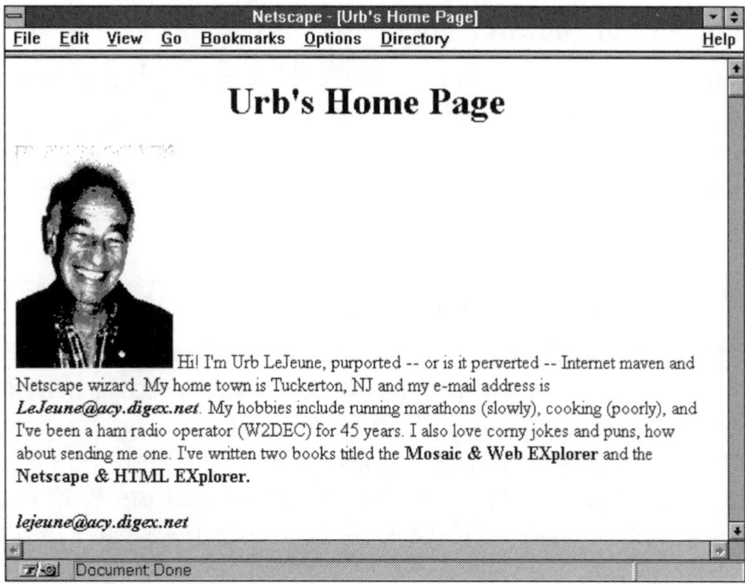

***Figure 10.7** Using Web Spinner's Edit Image dialog box to add a picture.*

a GIF or X Bitmap format and have either a .GIF or .XBM extension. Remember the partial URL concept from our URL explorations? If an explicit path is not specified, the browser assumes the target file has the same domain and path name as used for the parent document. As an example, if urb.gif is not in D:/WWWfiles, the URL must follow the **SRC=** parameter.

The **<P>** tag following the plain text is a "hard coded" paragraph. Recall that there is a corresponding **</P>** tag, but its use is optional since there is an implied **</P>** whenever encountering another **<P>** tag or a tag producing a formatting paragraph break such as a heading. Without a paragraph tag following the image designation, the bottom of the first line of display text would line up with the bottom of the image. We'll remove the **<P>** tag in the next version of our home page so that you can see what happens. We'll also add a few hotlinks to our document.

Now that the HTML document is displayed in the browser, you can see firsthand the difference between how paragraph text is placed in the HTML document and how it is displayed in the browser. The word wrapping is taken care of automatically. If you resize your Netscape window, your text will be adjusted so that it fits in the window. Try this out.

Adding Anchors to Your Web Pages

What good is a Web page without a few anchors? A Web page that doesn't allow you to link to another Web document isn't a whole lot of fun, or very useful, for that matter. In my home page, I wanted four anchors that would link to additional documents in the same directory. (External Web document links will be covered in a moment.)

> eXplorer TIP
>
> **Naming Your Files**
>
> If your documents are eventually going to reside on a Unix server, your HTM documents will become html. Remember, Unix cares about case. Most Unix file names are lowercase, so it's a good idea to use lowercase when entering your DOS file names since DOS doesn't care. If your file extension is longer than three characters, DOS truncates. We can use DOS truncation to our advantage and specify all text file names as html. DOS will fetch the HTM version.

I want my first anchor, "My hobbies," to point to an HTML document named urbhobie.htm; the second anchor, "corny jokes and puns," should point to urbjoke.htm; the third anchor, "Mosaic & Web Explorer," should point to mosbook.htm; and finally the last anchor, "Netscape & HTML Explorer," should point to net-book.htm.

The Web Spinner editor can easily help us add these new links. To do this, highlight the text to be used as the anchor. Then, execute the sequence Insert|Link (Ctrl+L) or click on the chain link icon. Then open the Server Type menu and select the local reference option. In the name field, enter the filename urbhobie.htm or whatever document you want to link to. Click on OK and an HTML instruction like the following will be added to your document:

```
<A HREF="urbhobie.html">My hobbies</A>
```

In this case, "My hobbies" is the anchor or hotlink. When the user clicks on it, guess what happens? Up comes the HTML document urbhobie.htm. When you start entering the actual text for tags like anchors within a document, use some conventions to help you remember the document's "innards" when you return at a later time. I like having the individual components of an instruction on separate lines and I also indent the information two spaces to the right of the tag margin.

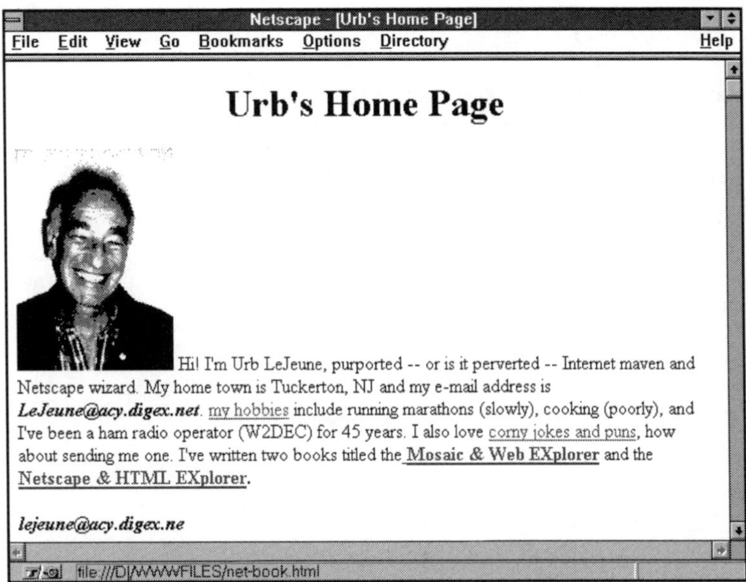

***Figure 10.8** Our home page with the latest links.*

To add a little pizzazz to the page, let's make my e-mail address both bold and italicized. Let's take a stab at simply editing the file, not using the Web Spinner editor's automatic tag insertion feature. Recall that enclosing text between the **<B>** ... **</B>** tag pair produces bolding, while italicizing occurs between the **<I>** ... **</I>** pair. Nested tags first require enclosing text between a starting and ending pair, next, enclosing the original with the second level tags. In this example the text, complete with tags, would be:

```
<B><I>LeJeune@acy.digex.net</I></B>
```

<B><I>text**</B></I>** will not work.

In this modified home page, I used urb.gif in place of logo.gif. A friend, with one of those new digital cameras, took a picture of me. I converted the camera's TIF file to a GIF format to shrink it; otherwise it's untouched.

Figure 10.8 shows how Netscape displays these new changes with all the bells and whistles index.htm has evolved to:

```
<HTML>
  <HEAD>
    <TITLE>
      Urb's Home Page
```

```
    </TITLE>
  </HEAD>
  <BODY>
    <CENTER><H1>Urb's Home Page</H1></CENTER>
    <IMG ALIGN=BOTTOM ALT="Urb's picture normally goes here" SRC="urb.gif" >
    Hi! I'm Urb LeJeune, purported - or is it perverted - Internet
    maven and Netscape wizard. My home town is Tuckerton, NJ and my
    e-mail address is <I><B> LeJeune@acy.digex.net</B></I>.
    <A HREF="urbhobie.html">my hobbies</A>
    include running marathons (slowly), cooking (poorly),
    and I've been a ham radio operator (W2DEC) for 45 years. I also love
    <A HREF="urbjoke.html">corny jokes and puns</A>,
    how about sending me one. I've written two books
    titled the<A HREF="mos-book.html">
    <B>Mosaic &amp; Web EXplorer</B></A> and the
    <A HREF="net-book.html"> <B>Netscape &amp; HTML EXplorer<B></A>.
    <P>

    <ADDRESS>
    <I><B> lejeune@acy.digex.ne</B></I>
    </ADDRESS>
  </BODY>
</HTML>
```

There are a few items in the revised document worthy of note. First, I included the structural tags, such as **<HTML>**, **<HEAD>**, and **<BODY>** in this second version of the home page. Although they are optional, it's a good idea to get in the habit of using them because they can help you better structure your HTML documents and they will keep you out of trouble if someone is trying to view your document with a browser that requires them.

Notice that the IMG declaration has an added parameter **ALT**. This parameter is used to display a plain text alternative to the image for those people viewing the document with a character browser such as Lynx. The new line is:

```
<IMG ALIGN=BOTTOM ALT="Urb's picture usually goes here." SRC="urb.gif">
```

Also note that parameters don't require enclosing quotation marks unless they contain embedded spaces. We'll explore this feature more in the next chapter.

Finally, notice the **<A>** anchor tags for each of four hotlinks. At this point, I suggest that you copy each of the four HTM files that this home page references from the companion CD-ROM to your hard disk, so that you can take this home page for a test drive. Make sure you also have the GIF file URB.GIF. (You don't want to miss the chance to have my picture on your Web page!) In the next chapter, we'll take a closer look at these other HTML documents.

HTML STANDARDS

Before we leave our exploration of creating Web pages in this chapter, there are a few standards issues for HTML documents that we should discuss. (See the URLs at the end of this exploration chapter for further reference.) Unfortunately, not everyone builds documents adhering to the standards. Netscape, and most other Web browsers, *currently* let you get away with some sloppy construction techniques. For example, the HTML standard specifies that the portions of the document to be interpreted by a browser must be enclosed between the **<HTML>** ... **</HTML>** pair. However, all browsers that I have tested, including the popular Netscape, correctly display documents that do not have the **<HTML>** tag pair. I don't think non-standard documents are a good idea if you are going to be serious about your HTML toils. There is no assurance that future version of Web browsers will ignore sloppiness and nonconformity. Let's produce standard documents while making life easy for ourselves.

LET'S REVIEW

So far, we've barely scratched the surface of available HTML mark-ups. Hopefully, you have seen that HTML documents are relatively easy to create and that you only need a handful of tags to produce nice-looking Web pages. Indeed, there is nothing stopping you from creating an HTML document without using HTML tags, but it wouldn't be much of a Web document if it didn't have hotlinks or special effects, such as graphics.

A simplistic group of HTML documents, such as the ones we've created here, can serve as your home page under construction, if you're lucky enough to have access to a Web server. If you don't have a server at your disposal, you can still create a home page, test it out, and refine it using Netscape. You just need to set up your HTML documents so that they can be loaded from your hard disk instead of an actual Web site. When I do a Netscape presentation, I find that interest always peaks when I demonstrate my own home page and tell people that they can easily do the same thing and publish on the Web.

To help you brush up on the HTML concepts we've explored so far, here's a quick summary.

The HyperText Markup Language (HTML) consists of three functional components:

- Plain text
- Tags that control the display and functionality of the plain text between the tags
- Hotlinks and the associated prompt enclosed by tag sets

HTML browsers do not recognize white space (multiple blanks, carriage returns, or tabs) embedded within plain text. Line breaks and paragraph breaks must be explicitly specified.

The basic form of an HTML tag is:

```
<tag>plain-text</tag>
```

where the tag determines the display characteristics of the plain text. The terminating tag is usually the same as the originating tag with the inclusion of the "/" between the "<" and the tag description. An example of a tag pair enclosing descriptive text would be:

```
<H1>This is Heading One</H1>
```

HTML tags are case independent; that is **<TITLE>**, **<title>**, and **<TiTLe>** are all acceptable.

An HTML document is enclosed between the tag pair

```
<HTML> . . . </HTML>
```

which is in turn constructed by these head and a body components:

```
<HEAD> . . . </HEAD>
<BODY> . . . </BODY>
```

The simple structure of a HTML document is therefore:

```
<HTML>
  <HEAD>
  </HEAD>
  <BODY>
  </BODY>
</HTML>
```

All of these tags are *currently* optional, allowing upward compatibility with older versions of HTML documents. However, you should get in the habit of using these structural tags so that your HTML documents will work correctly with all Web browsers.

The **<HEAD>** section of an HTML document typically contains the definition **<TITLE>** title-text **</TITLE>**. The title text appears in the Web page's Windows title bar.

There are two formatting tags that are not paired, the line break and paragraph break; **
** specifies a line break and **<P>** designates a paragraph break.

A hyperlink in an HTML document has two components, a reference address (URL) and an anchor. The general form of a hyperlink is

```
<A HREF=url>anchor-title</A>
```

where url specifies the complete location of the desired link and the *anchor-title* is the component that appears, usually underlined and colored, on the screen. Clicking on the anchor activates the URL. An example is the pointer to my home page:

```
<A HREF=www.charm.net/~lejeune/><Urb's home page</A>
```

A good way to learn about HTML concepts and expand your Web-publishing prowess is to be on the lookout for interesting effects as you surf the Web. When you find something that might prompt you to ask, "I wonder how they did that," take a minute to execute Netscape's View|Source or Mosaic's File|Document Source... sequence to look at the coding behind the display and find out how they did it.

Good luck with your home page publishing. Let me know when you get one up and going, I'd like to check it out.

Here are some places you can go on the Web to get additional information on creating Web documents with HTML:

A Beginner's Guide to HTML
`http://www.ncsa.uiuc.edu/General/Internet/WWW/HTMLPrimer.html`

The HTML Quick Reference Guide
`http://kuhttp.cc.ukans.edu/lynx_help/HTML_quick.html`

Information on the Different Versions of HTML
http://www.w3.org/hypertext/WWW/MarkUp/MarkUp.html

Composing Good HTML
http://www.willamette.edu/html-composition/strict-html.html

HTML+ Specifications
http://info.cern.ch/hypertext/WWW/MarkUp/HTMLPlus/htmlplus_1.html

HTML Specification Version 3.0
http://www.hpl.hp.co.uk/people/dsr/html3/CoverPage.html

HTML Editors
http://akebono.stanford.edu/yahoo/Computers/World_Wide_Web/HTML_Editors/

Resources for Converting Documents to HTML
http://info.cern.ch/hypertext/WWW/Tools/Filters.html

An Archive of Useful HTML Translators
ftp://src.doc.ic.ac.uk/computing/information-systems/www/tools/translators/

HTML in Style

We've only scratched the surface of exploring the power of HTML to create Web pages. In this chapter you'll learn how to use a number of HTML features to create effective documents.

While trying to conceptualize this chapter, I experienced a conflict of sorts. On one hand, an extensive overview of the Hyper Text Markup Language (HTML) at this stage might confuse you and it would be an overkill because Appendix A provides a detailed reference guide to the inner workings of HTML. On the other hand, presenting less than a major treatment of HTML would oversimplify and break the pattern of technical completeness from our previous explorations. Besides, you probably want to know as much as you can absorb about HTML so that you can add some of those neat effects to your Web pages that you see others doing.

To me, the learning process is about 50 percent luck, 49 percent serendipity, and 1 percent skill. I taught computer programming at the four-year college level and a former student recently reminded me of my opening monologue. "There's good news and bad news," I had started somewhat apprehensively. "The good news is that I'm an easy grader; the bad news is that you will be using Pascal to program your assignments and I don't know Pascal."

Serendipity helped me solve that educational dilemma. I learned Pascal that semester by helping students write and debug their programs. It was a great learning model—so why don't we use it here? Let's create more HTML instead of just describing more of its unique features. I'll cover as much as I can in the space available.

We'll begin where we left off in the previous chapter. We'll add more features, such as formatted text lists, to the home page we created. I'll also show you the contents of some of the other HTML files that my home page references. In the second part of this chapter, I'll introduce you to a useful HTML guide that I created as a Web page, which is called "HTML Style Guide & Test Suite." The guide is fairly complete, except that it doesn't cover HTML tables and forms. The guide is essentially one big HTML example that I've also included on the companion CD-ROM as the file style.htm. I plan to keep this guide up to date and post it on my Web server for you to view.

CREATING LISTS WITH HTML

When the designers of HTML decided to support lists, they went all out. The end result is that HTML now supports five different types of lists: bulleted, numbered, menu, directory, and description. There are enough list options to let you get very creative with your Web pages, although not all browsers support all of these list types. You can count on most browsers to support unordered, ordered, and description lists.

Bulleted lists are actually called *unordered lists* in HTML. They are probably the most widely used list type since they are great for creating everything from simple lists to more complex menus. Each item in an unordered list is typically displayed on its own line with a bullet symbol. Numbered lists, on the other hand, are called *ordered lists*. They look just like unordered lists except that each item of an ordered list is displayed with a number, starting with 1. Here's an example of each of these list types:

```
This is an unordered list:
· This is item 1
· This is item 2

This is an example of an ordered list:
1. This is item 1
2. This is item 2
```

The best part about these two list types is that they can be nested. For example, a bulleted (unordered) list could be formatted as:

```
· This is the first element of level 1
   · This is the first element of level 2
   · This is the second element of level 2
· This is the second element of level 1
```

But if you use nested unordered or ordered lists in your HTML documents, keep in mind that not all browsers will indent the nested list items. In addition, some browsers use different bullet symbols to indicate the difference between inner and outer list members.

Menu lists and *directory lists* are special types of unordered lists. A menu list is actually a compact version of an unordered list. The idea behind it is that all items should fit on one line. If you are really into compactness, directory lists are the way to go. With these lists, all items should have no more than twenty characters. This restriction allows the items to be displayed in three or more columns.

The last menu type is the *description list*. This list is defined and formatted differently from any of the other lists. Instead of a bullet or number, each list item can be displayed with special text that you provide (like a glossary).

Just as you might guess, HTML provides tag pairs to define each of the five list types. Appendix A shows the tag pairs that are available. The techniques for using the first four of these list tag pairs are essentially the same. The **<DL>** ... **</DL>** pair works a little differently because description lists can have list items that consist of text for a description and text for the actual item itself.

Introducing the Basic List Structure

I'm not going to show you how to create every type of list format that HTML supports (Appendix A provides a complete reference for creating lists); however, here's a useful template you can use to create either unordered or ordered lists:

```
<list-type>

<LI> List item 1 goes here
<LI> List item 2 goes here
<LI> List item 3 goes here
...
</list-type>
```

The *<list-type> </list-type>* tags define the list type. This is where you use either the pair **<UL>** ... **</UL>** or **<OL>** ... **</OL>**. For example, a numbered or ordered list in HTML is enclosed between the **<OL>** ... **</OL>** pair. Within the *<list-type> </list-type>* tags, start the individual list items with the tag **<LI>**. There is no terminating **</LI>** since the end of a list item is implied by the next **<LI>** that starts a new list item, or by the terminating *</list-type>* tag that terminates the list. List items do not have to fit on a single line; individual items may contain **<P>** paragraph tags and **
** line break tags. Now that we have a good template to work with, let's create some lists.

The Return of Urb's Home Page

Just when you thought you've seen enough of my home page, it's back again, sporting new features. A different second screen of the home page is shown in Figure 11.1. In addition to a few different heading styles, the page uses an HTML unordered list. The list format I'm using here is exactly as it appears in the NCSA home page where there are four groups of identically constructed lists starting immediately under the heading "NCSA Mosaic Flavors."

Adding a Second Page

For our next HTML project, we'll add a second page to the home page we created in the previous chapter. To view this Web page yourself, all you need to do is add the HTML instructions shown next to the end of the body section of the HTML file index.htm.

The HTML text in index.htm producing the new page is:

```
<P>
My beautiful wife Pat thinks all of us computer types belong in an
institution, and not the academic type. What can you expect from a
person whose first question, when shown a new application, is,
"How do I get out of this thing?"
<P>
<H3>These are some of my favorite things</H3>
  Living close by, I usually start Netscape sessions checking on the
  <A HREF=
      gopher://wx.atmos.uiuc.edu:70/00/States/New%20Jersey/Metro%20Area
        %20Zone%20Fcst%20%28Atlantic%20Cty%29">
     Atlantic City Weather Forecast
  </A>

<H5>What's New Pussycat</H5>
  To keep abreast of current net developments I frequently read posting
  the newsgroup
  <A
     HREF=news:comp.internet.net-happenings>
     comp.internet.net-happenings
  </A>
 Another great source of new Gopher and WWW servers and all around
 resource information is the
  <A
     HREF=http://netlink.wlu.edu:920/>
     Netlink Server at Washington & Lee University
  </A>
```

```
And certainly let's not forget the
 <A
   HREF="http://www.ncsa.uiuc.edu/SDG/Docs/whats-new.html">
   NCSA What's New
 </A>
document.

<H2>Interesting Starting Points for Explorations</H2>
  <UL>
    <LI>
    <LI> The University of Maryland's (Baltimore County) great list of
       <A
          HREF="http://umbc7.umbc.edu/~jack/subject-list.html">
          Subject based information
       </A>
    <LI> The
       <A
          HREF="http://www.charm.net/">
          Charm Net Home Page
      </A>
    <LI> Scott
       <A
         HREF="http://www.uwm.edu/Mirror/inet.services.html">
         Yanoff's List
       </A>
of dynamite Internet sites.
</UL>
```

This HTML example is worth a close look because it uses many of the features that we covered in the previous chapter, such as anchors, multiple levels of

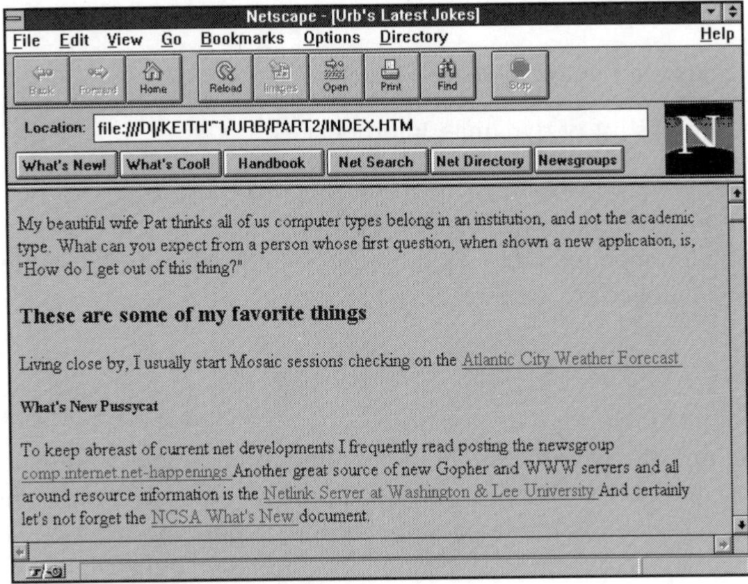

Figure 11.1 *The second page of Urb LeJeune's home page.*

heads, paragraph formatting tags, and character formatting tags. In a sense, you could say that it puts everything that we've learned into practice.

The first part of this section of HTML is simple enough: a new paragraph about my wife, a few headings, a few anchors to link you to some hot places on the Web, and so on. One part to note is the Atlantic City Weather Forecast anchor. Netscape does not ignore white space within a tag's parameters. The **HREF** parameter for the Gopher address connecting to this weather forecast appears on two lines in the listing only to show the URL without having to truncate it.

The section where things get interesting starts right after the heading "Interesting Starting Points for Explorations." Here you'll find a bulleted list structure, which HTML calls an unnumbered list. Notice that it's enclosed within the **<UL>** ... **</UL>** pair. For your reference, here's what the start of the list looks like:

```
<UL>
    <LI>
    <LI> The University of Maryland's (Baltimore County) great list of
       <A
          HREF="http://umbc7.umbc.edu/~jack/subject-list.html">
          Subject based information
       </A>
```

In the actual list on the Web page, I provide three options from which the user can select:

- The University of Maryland's list of subject-based information.
- The Charm Net home page.
- Scott Yanoff's list of dynamite Internet sites.

In each list item, which is set up using the **<L1>** tag, I've also defined an anchor to serve as a hotlink. This is a great way to set up a text-style menu. (I didn't use a terminating **</LI>** tag to define each list item because the end of a list item is implied by another **<LI>**.)

Land Ho!

The end of my home page exploration is in sight. Figure 11.2 shows Netscape displaying my joke page. There are a few interesting things to pursue in this document and then we'll call it quits. (You might want to look at the other two HTML files used in my home page, urbhobie.htm and urb-book.htm, on your own.) Here's the complete listing of the urbjoke.htm document:

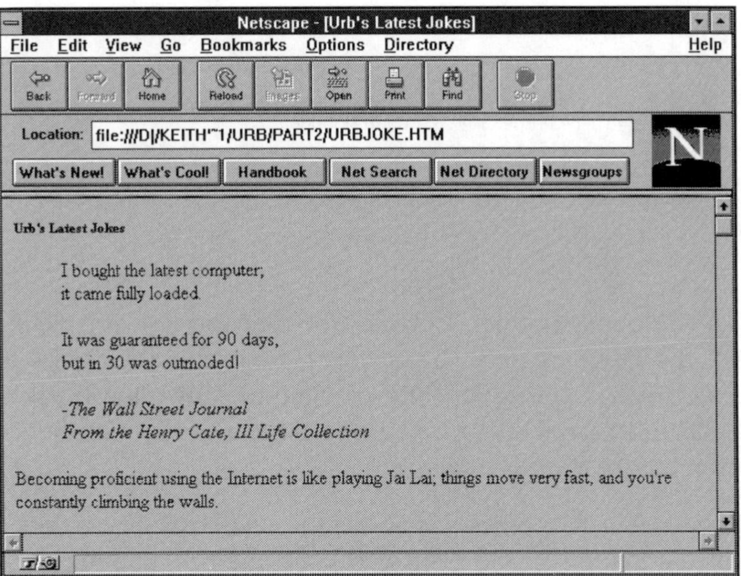

Figure 11.2 Displaying the joke page with Netscape.

```
<HTML>
   <HEAD>
      <Title>Urb's Latest Jokes</Title>
   </HEAD>
   <BODY>
      <H6><B>Urb's Latest Jokes</B></H6>
      <P>
      <DIR>
          I bought the latest computer;<br>
          it came fully loaded.
         <P>
          It was guaranteed for 90 days,<br>
          but in 30 was outmoded!
         <P>
         <I>
           -The Wall Street Journal<br>
           From the Henry Cate, III Life Collection
         </I>
      </DIR>
       <P>
        Becoming proficient using the Internet is like playing Jai Lai;
        things move very fast, and you're constantly climbing the walls.
       <P>
        Why do cook books outsell sex books? You eat three meals a day!
        <P>
        <B>How about sending a joke to Urb at LeJeune@acy.digex.net?</B>
        <P>
        <A
          HREF=urbhome.htm>
```

```
          Back to Urb's home page
        </A>
      <HR>
      <ADDRESS>
         Urb LeJeune  LeJeune@acy.digex.net<BR>
         43 Willis Drive<BR>
          Tuckerton, NJ 08087
        </ADDRESS>
    </BODY>
</HTML>
```

Notice that I've put in another list type—the directory list. It is defined using the **<DIR>** ... **</DIR>** tag pair. This is a neat compact list that's also indented. This specific list has embedded **<P>** paragraph, **
** line break, and **<I>** italic tags. In this case, I'm just using this list style to format the initial text quoted from the *Wall Street Journal*.

The **<HR>** tag, which appears just above the **<ADDRESS>** section, inserts a horizontal rule graphic in the displayed text. The rule graphic nicely delineates the logical parts of this document.

WORKING WITH SPECIAL CHARACTERS

All the text we've used in our HTML characters has consisted of standard alphanumeric characters. That is, all of the basic characters that you can type in from your keyboard. But what do you do if you want to include a special character such as a copyright symbol or a symbol that is used by HTML as a coding symbol such as "<" or ">"? Fortunately, there is an easy way to get symbols like these in your HTML documents. In fact, you can see these characters with their codes displayed in the "HTML Style Guide & Test Suite" presented later in this chapter.

You can use one of two methods to display a special character: Specify the numeric code of the character or use a pre-assigned symbolic name. Here's an example of how the numeric approach works:

```
&#169;
```

This would display a copyright symbol: ©. (The numeric code for this symbol is 169.) To specify a numeric code for a character, you must include "&#" in front of the number as shown. You can also specify multiple characters by separating each code with a semicolon. For example, this unusual looking line of HTML would display three spaces on a page (160 is the numeric code for a space):

```
     
```

If you don't like using hard-to-read numeric codes, you can use a symbolic name to represent a special character. Actually, this method only works for four characters: ", &, <, and >. The symbolic names for these characters are quot, amp, lt, and gt, respectively. Here's an example of how the pair of brackets, <>, can be displayed using their symbolic names:

```
&lt; &gt;
```

A LITTLE MORE ON IMAGES

In the previous chapter we only explored the basics of images. We experimented with the **<IMG>** tag to display bitmap images stored as GIF files. Recall that the format for this tag is

```
<IMG SRC = "gif-filename">
```

where *gif-filename* is the file name or the complete pathname and file name of the image to be displayed.

But there is much more to Web page images than this. You can also set up an image to be a hotlink just as you would set up a text hotlink. In addition, you can control the alignment of your images on a Web page by using special modifiers with the **<IMG>** tag. You can also include alternative text to be displayed if your image cannot be viewed.

The actual extended form of the **<IMG>** tag is:

```
<IMG [ALT = "alternative text"] [ALIGN=text-position] SRC = url-of-graphic>
```

Let's look at how these different features can be used to create more appealing Web pages.

Combining Images with Text

In most Web pages that you create, you'll want to combine images with text. With the first version of the HTML specification, you were not given a lot of options for displaying text with images. For example, you couldn't flow text around images like you would in a page layout program such as PageMaker. With HTML 3 features and a browser such as Netscape, you can now perform many types of text and image alignment features such as:

- Left, right, and center justify images and text
- Wrap text around left or right justified images using variable spacing
- Create variable-sized borders around images (or remove them altogether)

The important point to keep in mind when combining text with images is that an image does not force a paragraph break—all images are displayed inline with whatever text is displayed. Normally, any text in the same paragraph as an image will be lined up with the bottom of the image, and will wrap normally below the image. This works well if the text is essentially a caption for the image, or if the image is a decoration at the start of a paragraph. However, when the image is a part of a header, you may want the text to be centered vertically in the image, or to be lined up with the top of the image. In these cases, you can use the optional **ALIGN** parameter with the **<IMG>** tag to specify one of three settings: **TOP**, **MIDDLE**, or **BOTTOM**. As an example, the following HTML would display my picture with the bold text "This is me again" to the right of the picture, directly in the center of the picture:

```
<B>This is me again<B>
<IMG ALIGN=MIDDLE SRC = urb.gif>
```

If you wanted to display the text to the left of the picture and at the top, here's the HTML required:

```
<B>This is me again<B>
<IMG ALIGN=TOP SRC = urb.gif>
```

Later when I present the HTML for our style guide, I'll show you what the different alignment effects look like as they appear on a Web page. I'll also show you how to use some of the more advanced features provided with the HTML extensions.

Using Multiple Images per Line

Since an image is treated in some ways as a single (rather large) character, you can have more than one image on a single line. In fact, you can have as many images on a line as will fit in a browser window! Of course, if you put too many images on a single line, the browser will wrap the line, and your images will appear on two or more lines. Therefore, don't specify a series of images that must be displayed on one line. Conversely, if you don't want images to appear on the same line, be sure to place a **
** or **<P>** tag between them.

Displaying Text Instead of Images

You just created a fantastic HTML document with lots of images all designed to provide your user with important information. So what do you do if your user can only access your document with a text only browser such as Lynx? You could either ignore them (and really annoy them) or you could be considerate and add text descriptions to your images. The user would then see the text descriptions and they'd at least get an idea of what's included in your HTML document. (Maybe if your descriptions are good enough, they would be enticed to view your document with a visual browser such as Netscape or Mosaic.)

To define an alternate text description for an image, you use the **<IMG>** tag with the **ALT=** subtag. For example, this statement will either display my picture if the user has a visual browser or it will display the description "Urb LeJeune, author of Netscape and HTML Explorer" if the image cannot be displayed:

```
<IMG ALT="Urb LeJeune, author of Netscape and HTML Explorer" SRC="urb.gif">
```

You can use this feature with images you set up as hotlinks. (I'll show you how this is done shortly.) In fact, using the **ALT=** subtag is a good habit to get into for images that are either displayed as standalone pictures or as hotlinks. If an image is used as a hotlink, the text specified by the **ALT=** subtag will be the only thing a text-mode browser user will see. Without it, the user will miss out on the hotlink and they might get stuck somewhere in your document or not be able to access an important part of the document.

Using an Image as a Hotlink

Image hotlinks are set up just like hyper text links by using anchor tags **<A>** ... **</A>**. The only difference is that the image itself is used as the anchor text. Recall the format for defining an anchor:

```
<A HREF="file-pathname">anchor-text</A>
```

All we need to do is use the **<IMG>** tag to reference a picture in place of the anchor text. As an example, this anchor definition sets up the picture of you know who as a hotlink:

```
<A HREF = "UrbsBio.htm"><IMG SRC=urb.gif></A>
```

If you clicked on my picture, up would come the HTML document urbsbio.htm. (Just what you need, more information about me!) The user can tell that the picture is a hotlink because it will be outlined in a color. Netscape will outline images in blue that are set up as hotlinks.

In the previous section, I showed you how to include alternate text with an image. Let's combine what we learned with the anchor definition. The result is this line of HTML:

```
<A HREF = "UrbsBio.htm"><IMG ALT="Urb leJune, author of Netscape and HTML
   Explorer" SRC="urb.gif"></A>
```

If your user had a text-only browser, he or she would see the text assigned to the **ALT=** subtag as the hotlink. If this link were selected, the target document would still be displayed.

Linking a Picture to Itself

Here's a neat trick that many Web page designers incorporate into their Web pages. Define an anchor and link a picture to itself! I know this sounds weird, but follow along.

Here's how you can set up this type of anchor:

```
<A HREF=urb.gif><IMG SRC=urb.gif>
```

In this case, my picture is the hotlink. When the user clicks on the link, up I'll come. So why does it make sense to have an inline image point to itself? For one, many people turn off inline images to improve performance over a slow network link. If the inline image is an anchor for itself, they can then click on the placeholder graphic to see what they missed.

There is also an aesthetic issue at stake here. Some Web browsers do not "realize a palette" before displaying an image. Presumably this isn't a problem on a 24-bit display, but most of us have 256-color displays, and Windows maps the colors of inline images to the closest colors in the current palette. This can make for some funny looking images! If, however, the image is linked to itself, the readers can simply click on the image to load it into their favorite viewer, which will probably handle the colors much better.

Working with Thumbnails

A thumbnail is a small graphic image that points to a larger version of the same image. So why use them? They can greatly help you save transmission and loading time of Web pages. Let's say that you are creating a Web page that will serve as a catalog of jewelry that your company makes. You could create a Web page and put a sizable picture of each piece of jewelry with a one-sentence description. The problem with this approach is that when Web surfers (and potential customers) access your page, they might have to wait a very long time for all of the images to be downloaded and displayed on their computer. They might lose interest and go check out someone else's Web site.

The better approach would be to use thumbnails—little pictures of each item that link to the bigger and better looking images. The users could then click on one of the small images of their choice to view the image in full size. This approach would give you a "visual" table of contents.

If this description of thumbnails sounds like I'm describing anchors or hotlinks, you're right. In fact, you use the anchor tag to set them up, as shown here:

```
<A HREF=larger-graphic-file><IMG SRC=thumb-nail-graphic-file></A>
```

As an example

```
<A HREF=urb.gif><IMG SRC=urbsmall.gif></A>
```

would load the image urbsmall.gif as a thumbnail link. When the user clicked on this link, the image urb.gif would be loaded.

Processing and Sizing Your Images

We've explored many of the fine points for adding images to your Web pages using the **<IMG>** HTML tag, but what you also need to know is how to get your image files ready for displaying. There are many techniques and tricks for processing images for electronic documents that you'll discover over time. Right now let's discuss a few to get you started.

The first thing you'll need is a good image processing program to help you work with your images. There are many programs available, both shareware and retail products (and even a few freeware ones). I've included a powerful shareware program on the companion CD-ROM called Paint Shop Pro, as shown in Figure 11.3, to help you get started. I'll use it with a few of the image processing examples that I present here. If you have never used a program like this, I suggest you try it. You'll be amazed at many of the powerful image processing tasks you can perform, such as resizing and cropping images, editing your images, and saving them in different formats.

To display your images with Web pages, you'll need to make sure that they are converted to a GIF format. Most PC images are stored in a TIF, BMP, or PCX format. Converting your images is a snap if you have a program like Paint Shop Pro. You can either open one image at a time and save it as a GIF format or use a batch conversion process to convert all of your images at once. The batch conversion feature can be selected from Paint Shop Pro by selecting File|Batch Conversion. A dialog box will appear. You can then select the files you want to convert and the directory where you want to save the converted files. Also, make sure that you specify "GIF - CompuServe" as the Format option. (GIF files are widely used on CompuServe, also.) Click the OK button and Paint Shop Pro will convert the files.

Another technique you'll need to know is how to resize your images. Most images you get from different sources will probably be full screen images and they will be much too large for your Web pages. Fortunately, if you have a program like Paint Shop Pro, images are easy to resize. First, load in the image using the File|Open command. Then, select Image|Resize to display the dialog box shown in Figure 11.4. The standard size for a typical full screen image is 640x480. (Paint Shop Pro uses units of pixels to represent image dimensions.) To make your image smaller, you click on the Custom Size radio button and then enter your new sizes for the image's width and height in the two text boxes. The sizes shown in Figure 11.4 will make the image approximately 1" by 1". If you want to keep the width-to-height aspect ratio of your resized image the same as the original, you should select the Maintain Aspect Ratio check box.

Having a program like Paint Shop Pro can be a real asset, especially if you plan to include a number of thumbnails in your Web pages and you need a way to produce small versions of your larger GIF files.

Working with Multimedia

In addition to displaying images and setting up hotlinks to images, you can use multimedia files with your Web pages to really make things interesting. Basically, you can define a hotlink to a video file or a sound file by using the anchor tag pair **<A>** ... **</A>**. When the user clicks on the hotlink, the file will be sent to his or her computer, which in turn will "play" the file. This new area of the Web is just starting to explode.

As you work with multimedia files, keep in mind that most browsers can't actually play multimedia files. Browsers such as Netscape and Mosaic use what are called *helper programs* to load files that they can't internally read. For example, when you select a GIF file for viewing by clicking on a hotlink, Netscape calls a helper program to load and display the GIF image. These helper programs are set up by including special instructions in a browser's INI

Figure 11.3 *Using the Paint Shop Pro program to process your images.*

file. As an example, my netscape.ini file contains this instruction to tell Netscape to run the helper program lview31.exe whenever it encounters a file with the extension .GIF:

```
image/gif="C:\Internet\bib\lview31 %1s"
```

To set up a multimedia file as a hotlink, use the anchor tag pair **<A>** ... **</A>** as shown here:

```
<A HREF = "Gcanyon.wav">Sounds of the Grand Canyon</A>
```


Figure 11.4 *Using Paint Shop Pro's image Resize dialog box.*

When the users click on the text link, the WAV file gcanyon.wav will be sent to their computer so that they can play it. Of course, you are not limited to just sound files; you can create hotlinks for all types of files including video and animation.

Getting Smarter with Sound Files

One of the big problems with sound files is that they are typically very big and thus slow to download. If you include a sound file as part of a hotlink, the user must click on the link and then wait a long time for the file to be downloaded before it can be played. This is the kind of waiting that really turns off Web users—especially when the Internet has a lot of traffic.

One enterprising company, DSP Group, recently created a program called TsPlayer, which is billed as the first World Wide Web realtime sound player. TsPlayer lets you play any TrueSpeech sound file (.WAV) while you are downloading the file. The sound file is actually played by your favorite sound file player (Microsoft's Wave Mixer or Microsoft's built-in Windows 3.1 sound system), which is set up as the helper program. TsPlayer makes sure that the sound file starts to play as soon as you start the download. This means that your user can click on a hotlink that references a sound file, instantly start to hear the file, and then decide whether to continue downloading the file. What a dream!

I've provided the TsPlayer program on the companion CD-ROM. You can also download it using the following FTP site:

```
ftp://oak.oakland.edu/SimTel/win3/sound/tsplay100.zip
```

(If you need more help downloading files using FTP, you'll want to read Chapter 16.)

CREATING THE HTML STYLE GUIDE

You're now in for a real HTML treat. We're about to embark on an adventurous Web document project to surpass all other HTML documents we've created so far. What we'll do is create an interactive document that presents all the essentials of HTML. This is our first major Web publishing project. What's unique is that we'll use all the knowledge we've acquired to create a useful reference guide. We'll call the guide "HTML Style Guide & Test Suite." It is stored in the file style.htm on the companion CD-ROM. You can also access an "up-to-the-minute" version of the guide on the Web by pointing your browser to this location:

```
http://www.charm.net/~lejeune/styles.html
```

Of course, our HTML guide is not all-inclusive, nor will it provide detailed explanations of the HTML tags presented. The guide is mainly designed to be a quick reference. You'll find additional coverage of HTML topics, such as forms, in Chapter 15 and Appendix A. This appendix is an expanded guide to writing HTML. Our "HTML Style Guide & Test Suite" will be developed and discussed in 12 easy to follow sections; each section will represent roughly one page or screen of the guide. As we create the guide, I'll show you the section of the Web page in a Netscape screen along with the HTML that creates that particular page.

To get a real feel for HTML encoding, look at a listing of styles.htm while you are viewing Netscape's display of the file on your screen. Assuming that the file styles.htm is in the directory \WWWFiles on your D: drive, select the File | Open URL option from the menu line and enter

```
FILE:///D:/WWWFiles/STYLES.HTM
```

as the URL. (This is not a typo, there are actually three "/" following the ":".) If the file is stored on a different directory on your hard drive, make sure you specify the correct path name.

Without further fanfare, let's get started.

Screen 1—Creating the Table of Contents

Since our HTML guide provides a number of topics and scrollable pages, we'll need a table of contents for easy navigation. Figure 11.5 shows the first screen of the style guide as viewed in Netscape. Notice that the guide provides a range of topics from using special characters to working with graphics images to applying text formatting styles.

As you might guess, the table of contents is set up as an unordered list with anchors. In fact, the table of contents contains nested unordered lists. (This is our first chance to put some of our advanced list creation experience to work in a practical application.) When the user clicks on any of the highlighted hotlinks, he or she will be taken to a location (another page) in the document that corresponds with the topic selected. How's that for a truly interactive document!

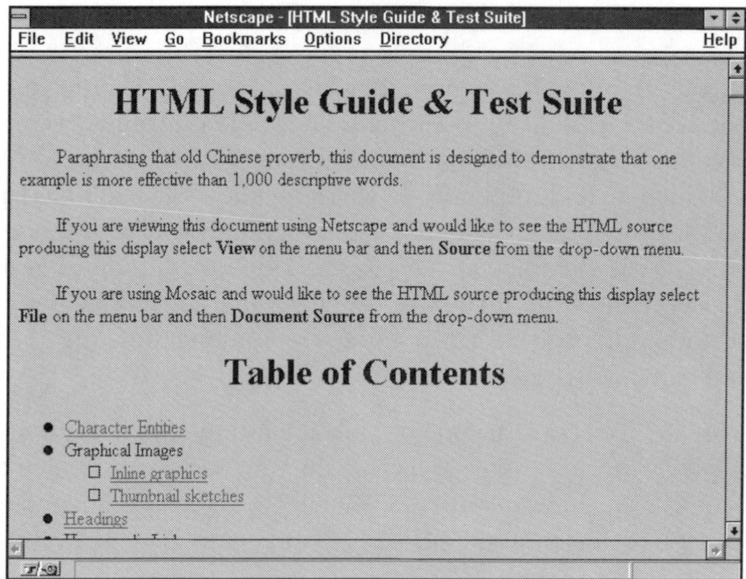

Figure 11.5 *The table of contents for the HTML style guide.*

Enough of the overview, let's create the HTML that sets up the first screen:

```
<HTML>
  <HEAD>
    <TITLE>HTML Style Guide & Test Suite</TITLE>
  </HEAD>

  <BODY>
    <CENTER><H1>HTML Style Guide &amp; Test Suite</H1></CENTER>

<! This is a comment and the pair of   below places two spaces
      at the start of the line. A comment ends with a greater than sign.>

           
    Paraphrasing that old Chinese proverb, this document is designed
    to demonstrate that one example is more effective than 1,000
    descriptive words.
    <P>
           
    If you are viewing this document using Netscape and would like to
    see the HTML source producing this display select <B>View</B>
    on the menu bar and then <B>Source</B> from the drop-down menu.
    <P>
           
    If you are using Mosaic and would like to see the HTML source
    producing this display select <B>File</B> on the menu bar and
    then <B>Document Source</B> from the drop-down menu.

    <A NAME="TOC"></A>
```

```
<CENTER><H1>Table of Contents</H1></CENTER>

<UL>
  <LI><A HREF=#SPECIAL_CHARACTERS>Character Entities</A>
  <LI>Graphical Images
  <UL>
    <LI><A HREF=#GRAPHICS>Inline graphics</A>
    <LI><A HREF=#THUMB>Thumbnail sketches</A>
  </UL>

 <LI><A HREF=#HEADINGS>Headings</A>
 <LI>Hypermedia Links
 <UL>
   <LI><A HREF=#GENERAL>General link information</A>
   <LI><A HREF=#SAME>To other places within the same document</A>
   <LI><A HREF=#OTHER>To other resources at the same Web site</A>
   <LI><A HREF=#OUTSIDE>Hypermedia links in Web Space</A>
 </UL>

 <LI><A HREF=#LISTS>Lists</A>
 <LI>Text Formatting Styles
 <UL>
   <LI><A HREF=#PLAIN>Plain text</A>
   <LI><A HREF=#LOGICAL>Logical text styles</A>
   <LI><A HREF=#PHYSICALL>Physical text styles</A>
 </UL>

 <LI><A HREF=#NETSCAPE>Netscape enhancements to HTML</A>
 <UL>
   <LI><A HREF=#CENTER>Centering Text and Graphics</A>
   <LI><A HREF=#BLINK>Blinking Text</A>
   <LI><A HREF=#FONTS>Font Sizing</A>
   <LI><A HREF=#BASE_FONT>Base Font Sizing</A>
 </UL>
 <P>
 <LI><A HREF=#AUTHOR>The author of this document</A>
</UL>
```

You shouldn't have much trouble understanding this section of HTML. The only new tag introduced is **<!>** which is used to create a comment section. The comment won't show up when the document is viewed by a Web browser.

The first part of the document takes care of all the required setup work. Here you'll find tags for the document's title, body, level one head, and so on. Notice that the special character code ** ** (space) is used to indent the introductory text over a few spaces. (Remember that Web browsers do not indent text so we have to do this manually.)

Next, we get to the menu or contents section. This anchor kicks things off:

```
<A NAME="TOC"></A>
```

It defines the anchor target named "TOC". We need this target so that we can link back to the menu from any of the other nine sections. (This is the location the user returns to whenever he or she clicks on an anchor that is assigned **HREF=#TOC**.)

The actual navigation menu is created by using nested **<UL>** pairs. There's nothing tricky here, but keep your eye out for the anchor link targets that are being defined here, such as **#SPECIAL_CHARACTERS**, **#GRAPHICS**, **#THUMB**, and so on. You'll see these in action when we create the next sections.

One nice feature of the HTML style guide that we are building is that it contains information about some of the enhanced HTML features that Netscape supports such as centering text and graphics, blinking text, and font sizing. These new features will be placed in the section of the document that is referenced by the **#NETSCAPE** anchor.

Screen 2—Here Come the Headings

As Figure 11.6 shows, screen 2 of the HTML guide is used to display samples of each of the six HTML headings, **<H1>** through **<H6>**. Even without seeing

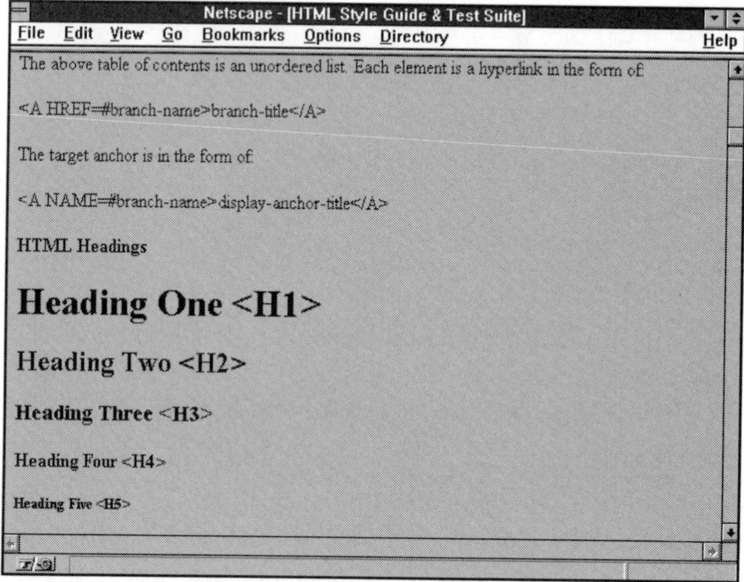

Figure 11.6 Screen 2 of the style guide—HTML headings.

the HTML for the main part of this screen, you can probably guess that it looks like:

```
<P>
The above table of contents is an unordered list. Each element
is a hyperlink in the form of:
<P>
&lt;A HREF=#branch-name&gt;branch-title&lt;/A&gt;
<P>
The target anchor is in the form of:
<P>
&lt;A NAME=#branch-name&gt;display-anchor-title&lt;/A&gt;

<H4><A NAME="HEADINGS">HTML Headings</A></H4>

<H1>Heading One &lt;H1&gt;</H1>
<H2>Heading Two &lt;H2&gt;</H2>
<H3>Heading Three &lt;H3&gt;</H3>
<H4>Heading Four &lt;H4&gt;</H4>
<H5>Heading Five &lt;H5&gt;</H5>
<H6>Heading Six &lt;H6&gt;</H6>
<P>
<A HREF=#TOC>Back to Table of Contents</A>
```

Actually the first part of this HTML belongs with the previous section. It didn't all fit in the previous browser screen, so I'm showing it here. Basically, the text explains how the menu system was set up. If you look closely, you'll see the rather strange-looking line of HTML

```
&lt;A HREF=#branch-name&gt;branch-title&lt;/A&gt;
```

which gets translated into:

```
<A HREF=#branch-name>branch-title</A&>
```

Some people say that HTML is hard to read. If you had to read HTML lines like this all day, you'd probably agree. The code **<** represents the less than symbol (<) and the code **>** represents >. Remember that all of the unique symbols that HTML supports are presented in the style guide. When using these codes, you must place a semicolon after the end of each code.

The remainder of the screen displays the six different heading formats. Note also that this HTML section contains an anchor with a reference to the **TOC** target that links the reader back to the table of contents.

Screens 3 and 4—Exploring the Basics of Links

We now come to our part of the guide that covers hypermedia links. There is more to say here so we'll easily fill up two pages. First, we start with screen 3. This screen features the text that describes general link information and techniques for defining links that reference other locations within the same HTML document. Figure 11.7 shows the actual browser window.

The HTML required to display this screen is:

```
<H4><A NAME="GENERAL">General Link Information</A></H4>

A hyper text link has two components, the visible and invisible
parts. The visible part, called the anchor, is the highlighted
portion that you see on your display. The invisible part is the
component instructing the browser where to find the desired resource.
The general format of a link is:
<P>
&lt;A HREF=[transfer-protocol][web-location]resource-name&gt;
anchor-prompt&lt;/A&gt;
<P>
<A HREF=#TOC>Back to Table of Contents</A>
<H4><A NAME="SAME">Links to Other Places Within the Same
  Document</A></H4>
<P>
The table of contents in this document uses internal links. There
are two components required, the pointer and the branch location
within the document. The pointer takes the form of:
<P>
&lt;A HREF=#branch-label&gt;title&lt;/A&gt;
<P>
The pointer to this section is:
<P>
&lt;A HREF=#SAME&gt;To other places within the Same Document&lt;/A&gt;
<P>
The desired location tag pair takes the form of:
<P>
&lt;A NAME=&quot;branch-location&quot;&gt;&lt;title&lt;/A&gt;
<P>
The target tag pair for this section is:
<P>
&lt;A NAME=&quot;SAME&quot;&gt;&lt;Links to other places within
the Same Document&lt;/A&gt;
<P>
<A HREF=#TOC>Back to Table of Contents</A>
```

Sorry, but the first heading disappeared from the browser window in Figure 11.7. (Space is getting tight.) The first paragraph of text, labeled with the anchor **NAME="GENERAL"**, describes the general information about defining hyper text links. The second paragraph, labeled with **NAME="SAME"**,

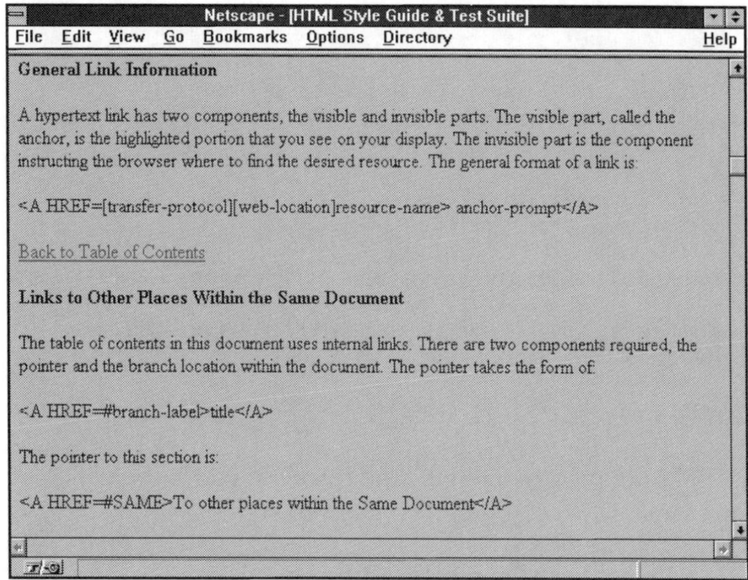

Figure 11.7 Screen 3 of the style guide—exploring links.

illustrates the process of pointing to links within the same document. Notice that at the end of both paragraphs a **TOC** return link is provided to take the user back to the table of contents. The text for this link, "Back to Table of Contents," is underlined in the screen shown in Figure 11.7. Providing the user with an easy way to always access the top level menu is good style; your users will thank you if you design your Web pages this way.

Okay, on to screen 4. Figure 11.8 shows the second part of the hyperlinks reference. This time, we need to cover two topics: linking two other resources at the same Web site and linking to files at other Web sites. Here's the required HTML:

```
<H4><A NAME="OTHER">Links to Other Resources at the Same Web Site</A>
</H4>

<P>
If the desired resource is located at the same Web site and uses
the same protocol, all that is needed is the name of the resource.
This pointer takes the form:
<P>
&lt;A HREF=resource-name&gt;anchor-prompt&lt;/A&gt;
<P>
To illustrate, a file named SECOND.HTM that is located at the
same site and in the same directory as the document currently
being viewed would be fetched using the link:
```

```
<P>
&lt;A HREF=SECOND.HTM&gt;Click here to activate SECOND.HTM&lt;/A&gt;
<P>
<A HREF=#TOC>Back to Table of Contents</A>
<H4><A NAME="OUTSIDE">Hypermedia Links in Web Space</A></H4>

<P>
An external link points to a resource at another Web site. As
an example, my home page link is:
<P>
&lt;A HREF=HTTP://www.charm.net/~lejeune&gt;Urb's Home Page&lt;/A&gt;
<P>
It would appear on your screen as: <A HREF=HTTP://www.charm.net/
~lejeune>Urb's home page</A>
<P>
<A HREF=#TOC>Back to Table of Contents</A>
```

Notice that links are provided to take the reader to either the table of contents or my home page.

Screen 5—Using Text Formatting Styles

As we work our way through the HTML document, we come to the part of the guide that covers text styles. As Figures 11.8 and 11.9 show, we cover both logical and physical text styles. If you look closely, you'll see that Netscape does not support all HTML text styles. The HTML for this section follows.

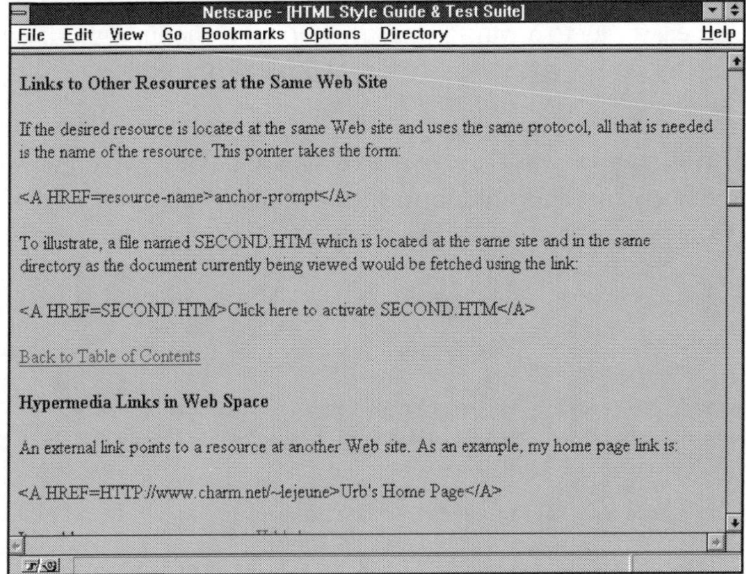

Figure 11.8 Screen 4 of the style guide.

```
<H4><A NAME="PLAIN">Plain Text</A></H4>

<P>
Most Web pages consist of plain text, which is any text appearing
outside of an attribute tag pair. Web viewers ignore multiple
spaces, tabs, and line breaks while &quot;word-wrapping&quot;
text. You have no control over the display of plain text. If you
desire a line break inserted in your text use the &lt;BR&gt; tag.
To force a paragraph use the &lt;P&gt; tag.
<P>
Line one. &lt;BR&gt; Line two. &lt;P&gt; appears as: <BR>
Line one.<BR>
Line two.
<P>
If text is to be displayed with formatting retained, as an example
a program listing, use the &lt;PRE&gt; &lt;/PRE&gt; tag pair.
<P>
    Paragraphs are not indented, however, multiple blanks are
inserted using a series of &quot;&amp;#160;&quot; groupings. This
paragraph starts with two such groupings.
<H4><A NAME="LOGICAL">Logical Text Styles</A></H4>

<P>
This sentence is normal text. Each of the following styles is
enclosed between the tags indicating the style. <EM>Emphasized
Text</EM>
<P>
<STRONG>Strong Text</STRONG>
<P>
<CITE>Cited Text</CITE> line break is next.<BR>
<A NAME="PHYSICALL"> </A>
<H4>Physical Text Styles</H4>

<P>
<B>Bold Text</B>
<P>
<I>Italics Text</I>
<P>
<U>Underlined Text</U>
<P>
<TT>Typewriter Font</TT>
<P>
Horizontal Rule &lt;HR&gt; is next<HR>
```

In Chapter 10 we presented all of the physical text style tags that HTML provides—**<B>**, **<I>**, and so on. In addition to these styles, HTML provides *logical* tags for character formatting. Logical styles are used to mark text according to its meaning. For example, if you were writing a sentence like this that referenced the name of a book

```
The Netscape and HTML Explorer is a great read.
```

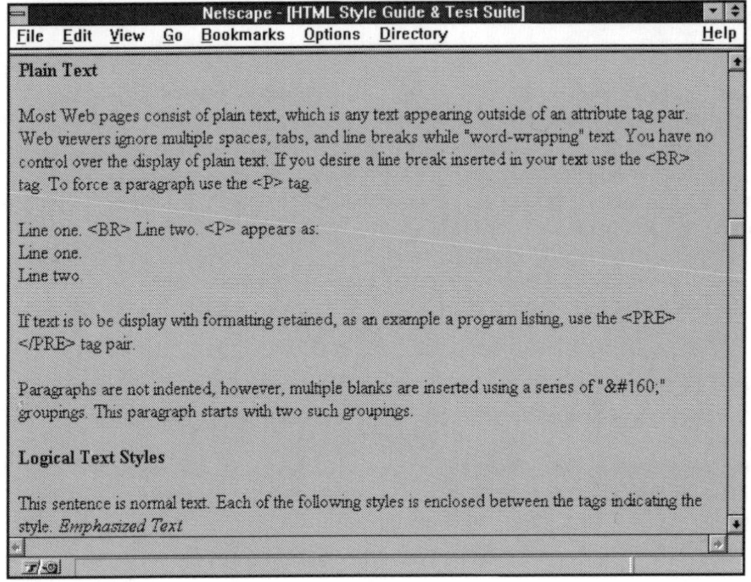

Figure 11.9 *Screen 5 of the style guide.*

the name of the book is considered a citation. In this case, you could use a special HTML logical tag named **<CITE>** to mark the citation.

It turns out that many of the logical tags cause text to be displayed in one of the three physical styles: bold, italic, or underlined. For example, text marked with **<CITE>** will appear as italic text; text marked as **<STRONG>** will appear as bold text. I've included some of the more widely used logical tags in the style guide so you can see how they are used and how they change the appearance of displayed text. The complete set of logical tags is presented in Appendix A.

Blinking Text for Netscape Users

If you are a Netscape user, there is a logical style you just have to check out. Its tag is **<BLINK>**, and as you might guess, it makes text blink on the screen. This is a good way to really get a user's attention. To use this feature, simply format the text like this:

```
<BLINK>This is blinking text!</BLINK>
```

Don't forget to include the terminating tag. If you forget, all of your text will blink and your Web page will look like it belongs in Las Vegas!

Screens 6 and 7—Displaying Inline Graphics and Thumbnails

This is your chance to check out many of the inline graphics features we've been exploring in the first part of the chapter. Screen 6, shown in Figure 11.10, presents some of the different image display options supported by the **<IMG>** tag. This is your chance to see the different effects produced by the **ALIGN** modifier. For example, the text displayed with the first picture is positioned by using the statement **ALIGN=TOP** within the **<IMG>** tag.

The HTML that produces this screen is:

```
<H4><A NAME="GRAPHICS">Inline Graphics</A></H4>

<P>
An inline graphic is treated like a character, albeit a very large
one, by graphical WWW browsers. The format for displaying an inline
image is
<P>
&lt;IMG [ALT=&quot;alternative-text&quot;] [ALIGN=text-position]
SRC=url-of-graphic&gt;
<P>
Where &quot;alternative-text&quot; is the text that will be displayed,
in lieu of the image on a non-graphic browser such as Lynx.
<P>
The parameter for ALIGN= may be TOP, CENTER, or BOTTOM. This determines
where one line of text will be displayed within the same paragraph.
<P>
Align Top <IMG ALT="Netscape Image Goes Here" ALIGN=TOP SRC=big-net.gif>
Align Top
<P>
Align Middle <IMG ALT="Netscape Image Goes Here" ALIGN=MIDDLE SRC=big-
net.gif>
Align Middle
<P>
Align Bottom <IMG ALT="Netscape Image Goes Here" ALIGN=BOTTOM SRC=big-
net.gif>
Align Bottom
<P>
<A HREF=#TOC>Back to Table of Contents</A>
```

First, we set an anchor target "Inline Graphics" to reference this section from the hotlink in the table of contents. We also need to use some of the HTML special characters to display the full form of the **<IMG>** tag. Next comes the HTML to display the Netscape image in three different ways. In each variation, different text alignment options are used to show you the HTML required to combine text with images. Notice that the paragraph tag **<P>** is placed after the HTML instructions used to display each group of images and text. If we omitted this tag, the browser would try to display all three images on the same line. Always keep in mind that a graphic image is treated like a

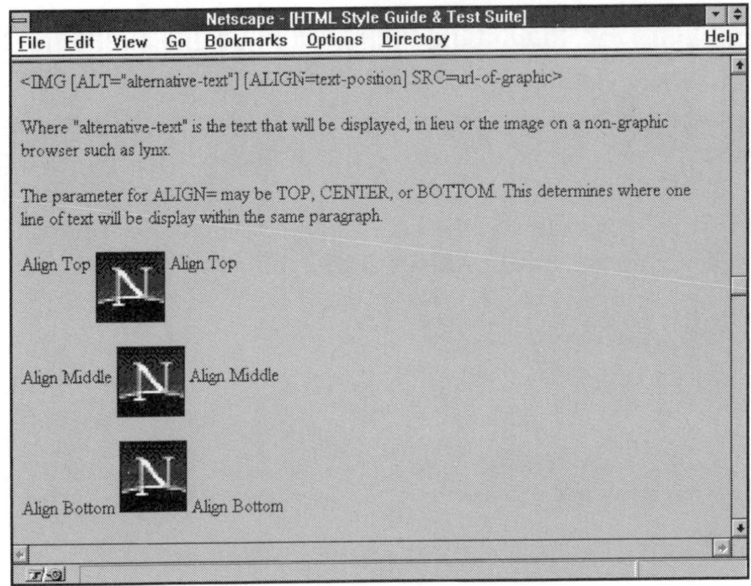

Figure 11.10 *Screen 6 of the style guide—inline images and text.*

single character, albeit a large one. Future versions of the HTML standard may contain multiple display column capabilities for displaying images.

Our next stop is thumbnails. Figure 11.11 shows the basics of how a thumbnail is defined using the anchor tag **<A>**. Notice that a heavy border is displayed around the image to indicate that it is a hotlink. When the users click on it, the file urb.gif will be transmitted to them for viewing. Here's the HTML for screen 7:

```
<H4><A NAME="THUMB">Thumbnail Sketches</A></H4>

<P>
A thumbnail sketch is small graphic display that points to a larger
version of the same graphic. It has the advantage of not requiring
the full graphic to be transmitted and displayed unless the user
specifically requests the larger display.
<P>
&lt;A HREF=large-graphic-file&gt;&lt;IMG SRC=thumb-nail-graphic-file&gt;
&lt;/A&gt;
<P>
<A href=urb.gif><IMG SRC=urbsmall.gif></A>
<P>
Click on the thumbnail graphic to activate a larger graphic.
<BR>
The heavy border around the graphic indicates that the image is
a pointer.
<P>
<A HREF=#TOC>Back to Table of Contents</A>
```

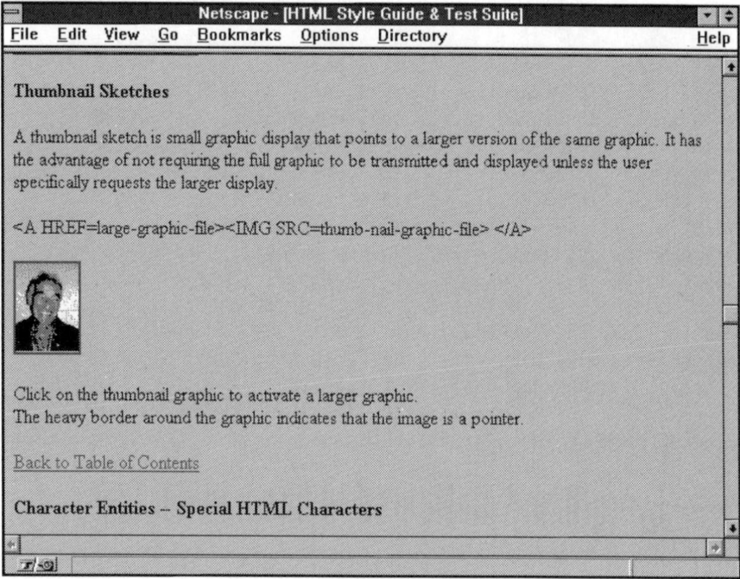

Figure 11.11 Screen 7 of the style guide—thumbnails.

Screen 8—Inserting Special Characters

Screen 8 gives our viewers a chance to see all of the special characters that HTML supports. I found this to be a very helpful reference as I was creating other HTML documents. After all, it's very easy to forget the actual code for a special character like the copyright sign. Figure 11.12 shows the browser window with some of the symbols and their codes displayed. The HTML to display this table of special characters is actually quite simple (although I did have to type a lot of code to create the table!):

```
<P>
These characters are formed using either the &quot;&amp;special-name;&quot;
or the &quot;&amp;#nnn;&quot; (where nnn is the numeric code)
format conventions. As an example the double quote is &amp;quot;
and the Yen symbol (&#165;) is &quot;&amp;#165 ;&quot;.
<P>
quot=&quot;, amp=&amp;, lt=&lt;, gt=&gt;, iexcl=&#161;, cent=&#162;,
pound=&#163;, curren=&#164;, yen=&#165;, brvbar=&#166;, sect=&#167;,
uml=&#168;, copy=&#169;, ordf=&#170;, laquo=&#171;, not=&#172;,
shy=&#173;, reg=&#174;, hibar=&#175;, deg=&#176;, plusmn=&#177;,
sup2=&#178;, sup3=&#179;, acute=&#180;, micro=&#181;, para=&#182;,
middot=&#183;, cedil=&#184;, sup1=&#185;, ordm=&#186;, raquo=&#187;,
frac14=&#188;, frac12=&#189;, frac34=&#190;, iquest=&#191;, Agrave=&Agrave;,
```

```
Aacute=&Aacute;, Acirc=&Acirc;, Atilde=&Atilde;, Aumi=&Auml;,
Aring=&Aring;, AElig=&AElig;, Ccedil=&Ccedil;, Egrave=&Egrave;,
Eacute=&Eacute;, Ecirc=&Ecirc;, Euml=&Euml;, Igrave=&Igrave;,
Iacute=&Iacute;, Icirc=&Icirc;, Iumi=&Iuml;, ETH=&ETH;, Dstrok=&ETH;,
Ntilde=&Ntilde;, Ograve=&Ograve;, Oacute=&Oacute;, Ocirc=&Ocirc;,
Otilde=&Otilde;, Oumi=&Ouml;, Oslash=&Oslash;, Ugrave=&Ugrave;,
Uacute=&Uacute;, Ucirc=&Ucirc;, Uuml=&Uuml;, Yacute=&Yacute;,
THORN=&THORN;, szlig=&szlig;, agrave=&agrave;, aacute=&aacute;,
acirc=&acirc;, atilde=&atilde;, aumi=&auml;, aring=&aring;, aelig=&aelig;,
ccedil=&ccedil;, egrave=&egrave;, eacute=&eacute;, ecirc=&ecirc;,
euml=&euml;, igrave=&igrave;, iacute=&iacute;, icirc=&icirc;,
iuml=&iuml;, eth=&eth;, ntilde=&ntilde;, ograve=&ograve;, oacute=&oacute;,
ocirc=&ocirc;, otilde=&otilde;, ouml=&ouml;, oslash=&oslash;,
ugrave=&ugrave;, uacute=&uacute;, ucirc=&ucirc;, uuml=&uuml;,
yacute=&yacute;, thorn=&thorn;, yuml=&yuml;
<P>
<A HREF=#TOC>Back to Table of Contents</A>
```

Screen 9—Everything You Wanted to Know About Lists

By now you probably know that lists are one of the most useful HTML constructs. And what could be better than a Web page that shows you the syntax for creating each of the list types supported by HTML? The complete HTML that creates the screen shown in Figure 11.13 follows

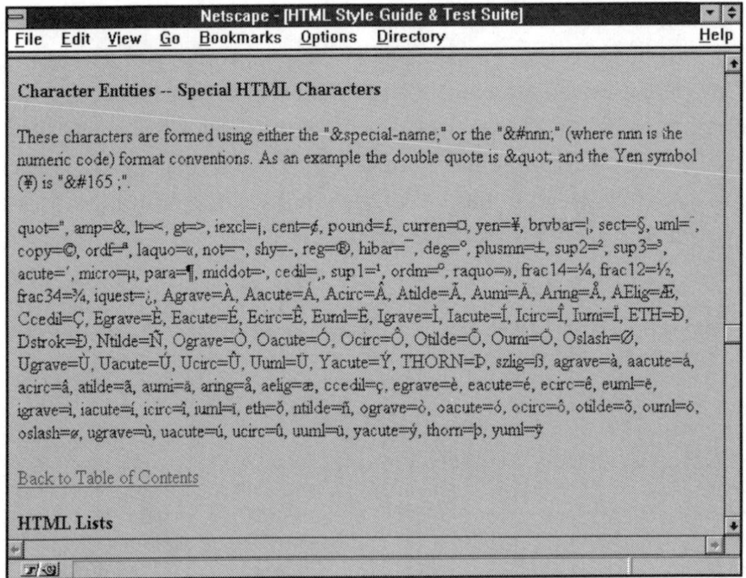

Figure 11.12 *Screen 8 of the style guide.*

```
<H4><A NAME="LISTS">HTML Lists</A></H4>

<H6>Ordered List &lt;OL&gt; </H6>

<OL>
<LI>&lt;LI&gt; Ordered List Item One
<LI>&lt;LI&gt; This is Item Two
</OL>

<H6>Unordered List &lt;UL&gt;</H6>

<UL>
<LI>&lt;LI&gt; Unordered List Item One
<LI>&lt;LI&gt; This is Item Two
</UL>

<H6>Directory List &lt;DIR&gt;</H6>

<DIR>
<LI>&lt;LI&gt; Directory List Item One
<LI>&lt;LI&gt; This is Item Two
</DIR>

<H6>Definition List &lt;DL&gt;</H6>

<DL>
<DT>&lt;DT&gt; Definition List first entry to be defined
<DD>&lt;DD&gt; Definition of first entry
<DT>&lt;DT&gt; Second entry to be defined
<DD>&lt;DD&gt; Definition of second entry
</DL>

<H6>Two Unordered Lists &lt;UL&gt; Nested within an Ordered List
&lt;OL&gt;</H6>

<OL>
<LI>&lt;LI&gt; Major List Item One
<UL>
<LI>&lt;LI&gt; First Nested List Item One
<LI>&lt;LI&gt; First Nested List Item Two
</UL>

<LI>&lt;LI&gt; Major List Item Two
<UL>
<LI>Second Nested List Item One
<LI>&lt;LI&gt; Second Nested List Item Two
</UL>

</OL>

<H6>Menu List &lt;MENU&gt;</H6>

<MENU>
```

```
    <LI>&lt;LI&gt; First Menu List Item
    <LI>&lt;LI&gt; Second Menu List Item
    </MENU>

    <P>
    <A HREF=#TOC>Back to Table of Contents</A>
```

Every type of list is coded here: ordered, unordered, directory, definition, and menu.

One feature we didn't explore in our HTML guide is the use of images with lists. You can easily combine inline graphics, especially if they are small images like thumbnails, with list items. As an example, let's recode one of the menus shown in Figure 11.13. This time around, I'll add a thumbnail to the first unordered list item:

```
<H6>Unordered List &lt;UL&gt;</H6>
    <UL>
      <LI>&lt;LI&gt;  Unordered List Item One <A href=urb.gif><IMG
      SRC=urbsmall.gif></A><P>
      <LI>&lt;LI&gt;  This is Item Two
    </UL>
```

This is the same anchor definition used before to define a thumbnail. You might want to experiment with this feature on your own to see how useful it is.

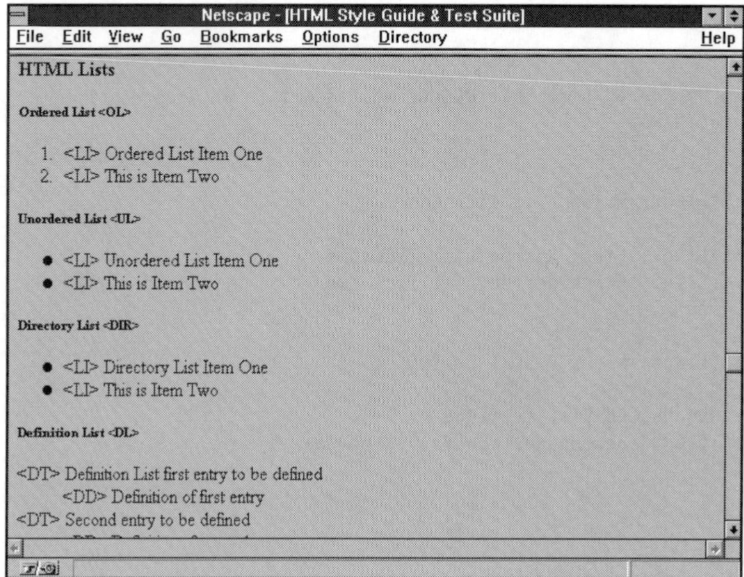

***Figure 11.13** Screen 9 of the style guide.*

Screens 10 and 11—Applying Netscape's Enhancements to HTML

If you are tired of standard font sizes and stationary text, you'll enjoy playing around with some of the newer Netscape HTML enhancements. Figure 11.14 shows the first screen of some of the text-related enhancements that I've added to our style guide. The HTML to create this first screen of enhancements is:

```
<H2><A NAME="NETSCAPE">Netscape's enhancements to HTML</A></H2>

<P>
Netscape has added a series of enhancements to the existing HTML
standard. Be aware, the use of these additional constructs are
NOT supported by other browsers. Check the effect of these tags
when viewing documents using other popular browsers before adopting.
<H2><A NAME="CENTER">Centering Text and Images</A></H2>

<P>
The most popular of Netscape's enhancements is the text centering.
<P>
<CENTER><IMG SRC=home.gif> <B>Centering Example</B> </CENTER>
<P>
The above example is produced by
<P>
&lt;CENTER&gt;&lt;IMG SRC=home.gif&gt; &lt;B&gt;Centering Example&lt;/
B&gt;&lt;/CENTER&amp;GT;
<H2><A NAME="BLINK">Blinking Text</A></H2>

<P>
Blink is the most derided Netscape's enhancement. People either
love it or hate it, with the later predominating. Use it sparingly.
<P>
<BLINK><B>Cool</B></BLINK> Dude
<P>
The above example is produced by
<P>
&lt;BLINK&gt;&lt;B&gt;Cool&lt;/B&gt;&lt;/BLINK&gt; Dude
<P>
Both Center and Blink can be used with relative impunity. If a
browser doesn't support the enhancement it is ignored. The text
will still be produced, without the centering or blinking.
<H2><A NAME="FONTS">Font Sizing</A></H2>
```

In addition to formatting your Web pages by centering text and graphics or displaying blinking text, you can change the size of your text on a Web page using another useful HTML extension. Figure 11.15 shows the next screen of our style guide that shows off this new feature. Here's the HTML for specifying font sizes:

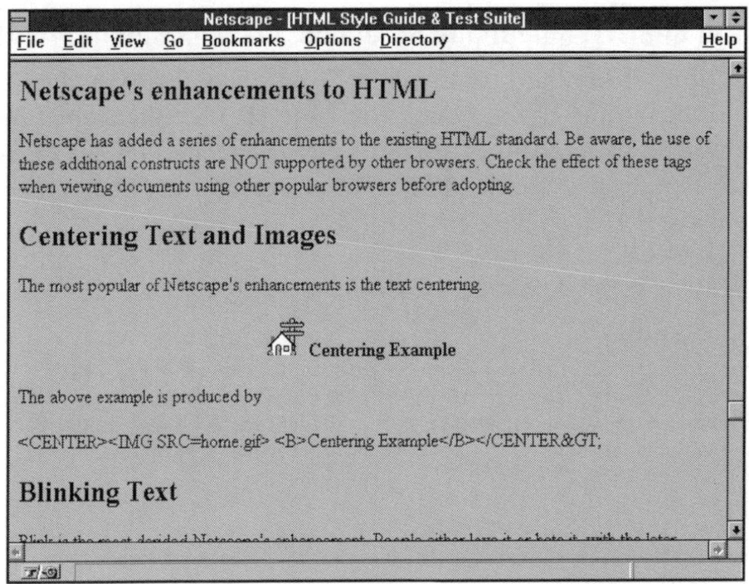

Figure 11.14 *Screen 10 of the style guide—Netscape's centering and blinking feature.*

```
<P>
Font size can be changed on the fly using the FONT tags in the
form:
<P>
&amp;ltFONT SIZE=N&gt;text&lt;/FONT&gt;
<P>
Where N is an integer between 1 and 7 with 3 being the default.
<P>
The following examples were started with:
<P>
&lt;FONT SIZE=1&gt;One&lt;/FONT&gt;&lt;BR&gt;
<P>
Through
<P>
&lt;FONT SIZE=7&gt;Seven&lt;/FONT&gt;&lt;BR&gt;
<P>
<FONT SIZE=1>One</FONT><BR>
<FONT SIZE=2>Two</FONT><BR>
<FONT SIZE=3>Three</FONT><BR>
<FONT SIZE=4>Four</FONT><BR>
<FONT SIZE=5>Five</FONT><BR>
<FONT SIZE=6>Six</FONT><BR>
<FONT SIZE=7>Seven</FONT><BR>
An interesting (?) effect is produced when placing varying font
sizes on the same line, as in the following example. The first
letter is FONT SIZE=1 and each letter increases by one through
7 and then decreases by 1.
```

```
<P>
<FONT SIZE=1>A</FONT><FONT SIZE=2>B</FONT><FONT SIZE=3>C</FONT>
<FONT SIZE=4>D</FONT><FONT SIZE=5>E</FONT><FONT SIZE=6>F</FONT>
<FONT SIZE=7>G</FONT> <FONT SIZE=6>H</FONT><FONT SIZE=5>I</FONT><FONT
SIZE=4>J</FONT>
<FONT SIZE=3>K</FONT><FONT SIZE=2>L</FONT><FONT SIZE=1>M</FONT>
<H2><A NAME="BASE_FONT">Base Font Sizing</A></H2>

<P>
Font size may also be changed using the BASEFONT tag &lt;BASEFONT
SIZE=N&gt;, where N in an integer in the range of 1 to 7 which
represent the range of font sizes. The sizing integers are identical
to the font sizes produced by the FONT SIZE pair. A major difference
is the absence of a closing tag. Once the font size is changed
it remains in effect until a new BASEFONT tag appears. If there
is an embedded FONT SIZE pair, the font size returns to the stated
BASEFONT size following the closing &lt;/FONT&gt; tag.
I would strongly suggest that you either don't use this enhancement
- since it tends to be at odds with conventional HTML matching
tag pair wisdom - or that you immediately enter a &lt;BASEFONT
SIZE=3&gt; as a pseudo closing tag which will set the font
size back to normal.
<P>
<BASEFONT SIZE=1> This line produced a &lt;BASEFONT
SIZE=1&gt; tag<BR>

&lt;FONT SIZE=4&gt;
<FONT SIZE=5>Embedded FONT SIZE=4 pair</FONT>&lt;/FONT&gt;<BR>
This line follows the embedded tag pair and is back to the BASEFONT
size of 1
<P>
<BASEFONT SIZE=3> <!- set font size back to normal ->The previous
line is: &lt;BASEFONT SIZE=3&gt; &lt;!- Set font
size back to normal -&gt;
<P>
<B>Stayed tuned. More Netscape HTML enhancements are on the way.</B>
<P>

<A HREF=#TOC>Back to Table of Contents</A>
```

As Figure 11.15 shows, seven font sizes are supported. The new HTML tag for specifying a font size is:

```
<FONT SIZE=N>Text goes here</FONT>
```

where *N* must be a number from 1 to 7. The default font size setting is 3.

In addition to setting the font size, a new tag is provided so that you can set the size used for all of your text in a document. This tag, formatted as **<BASEFONT SIZE=*N*>** serves as a global setting. Again, *N* must be a value

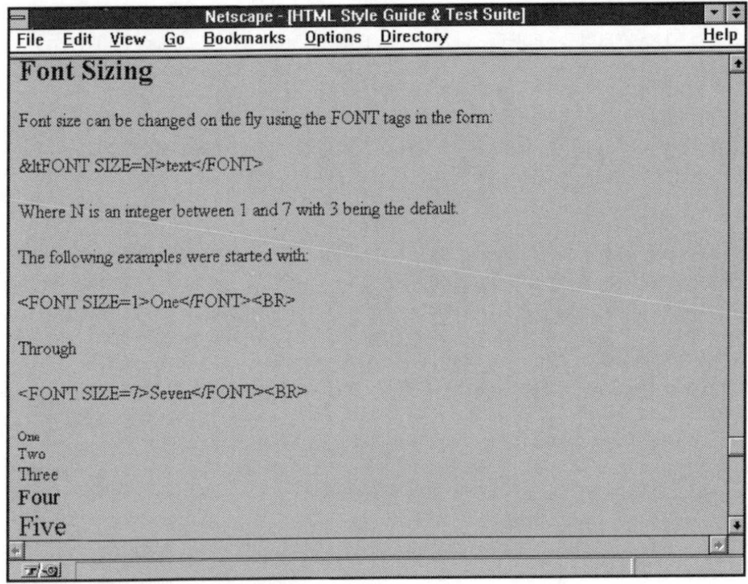

Figure 11.15 *Screen 11 of the style guide.*

from 1 to 7. Once this tag is encountered in a document, all of the text will be displayed using the specified setting. Of course, you can override the base font setting at any time by using the **<FONT> ... </FONT>** sizing tag pair.

Screen 12—Is There an Author in the House?

We've finally arrived at the end of our style guide. The reward is that I get to tell the world who created this document (see Figure 11.16). Here is the final section of HTML:

```
<P>
<A NAME="AUTHOR"> </A>

<A HREF=HTTP://www.charm.net/~lejeune/><IMG ALIGN=CENTER SRC=home.gif>
 Check out my home page. </A><P>

Document Last Updated May 11, 1995

<P>
&copy; 1995 by:<BR>
Urban A. LeJeune<BR>
43 Willis Drive<BR>
Tuckerton, NJ 08087<P>

<B>Please mail any comments or suggestions about this document to:
</B><BR>
```

```
    <A HREF="mailto:lejeune@acy.digex.net">
    <IMG ALIGN=CENTER SRC=mailbutt.gif>
    lejeune@acy.digex.net

    <IMG SRC=line.gif></A>
  </BODY>
</HTML>
```

The anchor target name that takes the reader to this section is AUTHOR. The <BR> tags at the end of each address line caused a "hard" line break at that point, allowing you to format short text lines precisely as given. (The <PRE> tag pair is another way to do this.) Be careful not to put <BR> at the end of too long a line; if the browser tries to wrap a line ending in <BR>, what the user sees will be unpredictable at best. See Figure 11.16 for the on-screen results.

The last section of the style.htm file demonstrates a feature I haven't introduced yet—a "mailto" URL. The mailto protocol allows you to e-mail a message while viewing a document. The last block of HTML contains the following instructions:

```
<B>Please mail any comments or suggestions about this document to:
</B><BR>

<A HREF="mailto:lejeune@acy.digex.net">
<IMG ALIGN=CENTER SRC=mailbutt.gif>
lejeune@acy.digex.net
```

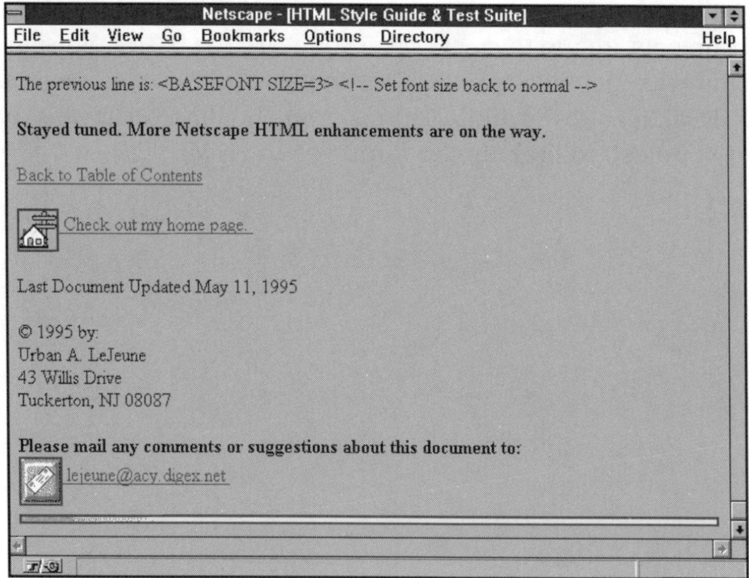

Figure 11.16 *Screen 12 of the style guide.*

If you would click on the "lejeune@acy.digex.net" anchor, you would be taken through a series of prompts that would conclude with e-mail being sent to me. Unfortunately, older versions of Mosaic and several other Web browsers do not support the "mailto" URL. Netscape, on the other hand, will pop up a window so that a user can easily type the e-mail message and then send it.

Finally, note that I've created an interesting effect by including an inline image as part of the **<ADDRESS>** section, as this is the last bit of HTML. The graphic is enclosed in a blue border indicating that it is part of the mailto anchor. The original graphic is a yellow line, which blends nicely with the blue border. This isn't exactly what you'd call very functional, but what the heck—we at least get to finish our project with style!

LET'S REVIEW

HTML provides support for five types of lists: ordered, unordered, menu, directory, and description. Each of these list types can be defined using special tags. For example, the tag pair **<UL>** ... **</UL>** defines an unordered list. Some of the list types can also be nested to create more functional lists.

A number of options are available for displaying images with the **<IMG>** tag, including displaying images with optional text descriptions and aligning images.

HTML documents are fun to create once you learn the basics of using the key HTML features. Appendix A provides a complete reference guide to all of the standard HTML features including forms. You should refer to this appendix whenever you need to look up the format of an HTML tag.

Web Publishing Tips and Techniques

Are you wondering how to add special features to your Web pages such as colored or textured backgrounds or text that can flow around images? This collection of FAQs and tips will show you how.

We've covered a lot of HTML ground in the previous three chapters; however, you still probably have a number of questions, especially if you've surfed the Web and seen some of the neat features you can add to your Web pages, such as custom rules, shaded backgrounds and colors, and text that flows around images.

Many features like these are possible because several extensions have been added to HTML. Some extensions are part of the HTML 3.0 specification and others have been introduced by Netscape. In this chapter, I'll show you how to do much more with HTML so that you can liven up your documents. I'll start with a set of useful HTML FAQs (frequently asked questions) and then we'll look at some clever Web publishing tips.

In the final part of the chapter, I've put a tips and techniques guide of what's available on the Web to help you create HTML documents and publish, and also to show you how to design and create better Web pages. I'll present a few projects to show you how to apply some of the more useful tools.

HTML FAQS

Whenever I'm trying to master something new, I love to read useful FAQs and tips to jump-start the learning process. FAQs are great because they often cut right to the chase. And HTML and Web publishing are two important subjects that could really use a good set of FAQs and tips.

In this section I'll give you some answers that will help you write better HTML documents and add features to your Web pages—such as custom horizontal lines, resizable images, images without borders, and so on.

What happens if I use an HTML+ (HTML 3.0) extension that is not supported by a browser?
The HTML standards police will take your Web publishing license away. (You do have a license, don't you?)

Actually, nothing will happen. If you use a feature that isn't supported by a browser, the browser will just ignore it. For example, let's say you use the **<CENTER> ... </CENTER>** tag pair to center text in an HTML document. If someone is using an older version of Mosaic, the text will be displayed as left-justified.

If you are really concerned about including a feature that can't be viewed by all browsers, my advice is to avoid all of the HTML extensions. If you feel that Netscape is the best thing since the invention of hot showers and that everyone should be using it (or will be in the near future), go ahead and use the extensions.

Do I need to always use HTML tags such as <HTML>, <HEAD>, and <BODY> to create my HTML documents?
No. I've been using them in this book to help standardize the format for our HTML documents. These tags are provided to help you keep your HTML documents structured.

Should I be concerned that my HTML documents will become obsolete and won't work with newer Web browsers?
At the rate the Internet and World Wide Web are changing, I would be concerned. Is there anything you can do about this? Try not to worry too much. So far, every new browser or new version of an existing browser has been backward compatible. But to be safe, try to use HTML features that you know work with most browsers. Once a feature is in wide use, it's unlikely that it will go away.

Will desktop publishing programs like PageMaker or QuarkXpress output files in an HTML format?

Yes and no. Currently, these popular page-design programs don't create HTML documents. However, independent developers are adding extensions so that PageMaker or Quark files can be converted to HTML. For instance, a program (available now) called *Dave* will convert Mac PageMaker files to HTML. To find out why this program is named Dave or to retrieve it, here's where you should go:

```
http://www.bucknell.edu:80/bucknellian/dave/
```

How can I incorporate Acrobat PDF files into my Web pages?

Acrobat PDF files are Postscript files (which are generated by desktop publishing programs) that have been converted to a special format so that they can be read by the Acrobat electronic viewer. Web browsers don't currently read PDF files; however, you can easily set up the Acrobat Reader as a player or helper program with Netscape. Then, when you select a PDF file from a Web page, the file will automatically be displayed.

The Acrobat Reader can be freely distributed. You'll find a copy of this program on the companion CD-ROM in the directory \helpers\acrobat. For more information on how to set up player programs, see Chapter 23, *Netscape's Helpers*.

Can I include a comment in an HTML document?

You're in luck. HTML provides a special tag that allows comments to be inserted in your documents. When HTML documents are read by a browser like Netscape, the comments will *not* be displayed. To include a comment, here's the tag you use:

```
<!-- Your comment text goes here -->
```

Don't forget to include the closing "-->". If you leave this out, everything else in your document will be ignored. If this happens to you, don't call me at midnight to ask me where your document went.

How can I add a horizontal line to a Web page?

You're in luck again because HTML provides a standalone tag that performs this task. To display a horizontal line across a page, you use **<HR>**. For example,

```
This text is above the line<BR>
<HR>
This text is below the line
```

would display a horizontal line between the two lines of text.

How do I change the size and look of horizontal lines?
By default, a horizontal line is displayed as a thin shaded line across a page when you use the **<HR>** tag. The width of the displayed line is two pixels. If you are using a browser like Netscape that supports extended HTML features, you can change a line's thickness, width, and alignment, and turn off the shading.

So, how do I use this extended tag?
The **<HR>** tag provides special modifiers or settings that you can include. The actual format for this tag with all its bells and whistles is:

```
<HR SIZE=pixel-setting-for-thickness
    WIDTH=pixels-or-percent
    ALIGN=Left|Right|Center
    NOSHADE>
```

Let's look at some examples. To change the thickness of a line, you would use a tag like this:

```
<HR SIZE=5>
```

This displays a line that is five pixels thick. To change the width, you could use

```
<HR WIDTH=100>
```

or you could use this format:

```
<HR WIDTH=30%>
```

The first version displays the line as 100 pixels in width. The second version says "display the line by taking up 30 percent of the document window width." In either case, the line will be centered across the screen.

So, how can I change the alignment of the horizontal line?
Use one of these options:

```
<HR ALIGN=Left|Right|Center>
```

For example, this tag would display a horizontal line that is right-justified and 200 pixels in width:

```
<HR ALIGN=Right WIDTH=200>
```

How can I turn off the shading from a displayed horizontal line?
Another easy answer. Try this:

```
<HR NOSHADE>
```

Should I care whether users with slow Internet connections have to wait a long time to view my Web pages because they have a lot of graphics?
Imagine you are taking your family on vacation to Colorado and you get stuck behind a big fat motorhome. If you had to travel like this for a few hours on those famous steep and winding Colorado roads, you'd be mad as hell. It would probably ruin your vacation.

Thousands of people are still surfing the Web at very slow speeds. In fact, many people are starting to use relatively slow electronic services like CompuServe or America Online to access the Web. If you don't care about these users, go ahead and be a road hog. But if you do, think about streamlining your Web pages.

Ok, but I'm too attached to my great images; is there anything I can do?
First, make sure that you save your GIF files using the lowest resolution possible. Instead of creating images with 2 million colors, try to use some images that will still look nice with only eight colors. You can use programs like Paint Shop Pro, included on the companion CD-ROM, to convert the resolution of your images and the number of colors used. Remember that an image can only be displayed at 72 dpi on the screen. Therefore, if you use an image that has a higher resolution than this, no one will be able to enjoy the higher resolution while viewing it on the screen.

If you are willing to make two versions of your bigger images, there is an extended HTML feature you can use to speed up the process of displaying images. See the next question.

I've seen Web pages with images that seem to display very quickly from low resolution to high resolution. How can I set up my images to be displayed like this?
Here's a neat trick that you can add to your Web pages if you're using Netscape. It's a great way to make readers of your Web pages feel they're getting a very quick response even when you are displaying large images.

This sample HTML tag shows how the feature works:

```
<IMG SRC="HIGHRES slow.gif" LOWSRC="fast.gif">
```

As shown, the **<IMG>** tag supports two modifiers: **HIGHRES** and **LOWSRC**. The high resolution file is specified first and then the low resolution file is listed. When this command is processed, Netscape will first display the low resolution file.

This tag speeds up the display process because Netscape can quickly determine how much room to leave for the image and then it can go about its business filling in the details. To see how this feature works, try out the Coriolis Group home page at http://www.coriolis.com/coriolis.

Should I create Web pages that both Netscape users and text-based browser users can access and read?
Sure. Why leave anybody out? The best way to achieve this goal is to create both text- and graphics-based versions of your Web pages. Include an option on your home page that users can click on as soon as the page starts to appear so that they can access the text-based version.

Can I use an image that's not saved as a GIF file?
Many browsers only support GIF files, although some browsers do provide built-in support for JPEG images. If your image files are in another format such as TIF or PCX, you'll need to convert them to GIF so that all users can view them with their Web browsers. I like to use the Paint Shop Pro program to convert my images because it provides a "batch conversion" feature to automate the process of converting multiple files.

How do I remove a border from a linked image?
Suppose you have an image that you want to display without a border to appear like a clickable button or icon. (Those big blue borders that Netscape displays can overpower a small icon.) To do so, use this version of the **<IMG>** tag:

```
<IMG BORDER=0 SRC="mybutton.gif">
```

The **BORDER** parameter specifies the line width of the border in pixels.

How do I place left-justified and right-justified images on the same line?
Suppose you're creating a catalog or brochure and you want to position pictures at the margins, with text in the middle. Fortunately, the **<IMG>** tag provides a parameter called **ALIGN** for controlling the alignment of an image. Here's how you can use this feature to sandwich text between two images:

```
<IMG ALIGN=LEFT SRC="leftp.gif"> <IMG ALIGN=RIGHT SRC="rightp.gif">
Text goes here!
<BR CLEAR=LEFT>
More Text here!
<BR CLEAR=ALL>
```

How can I display two images side by side, with about 4 to 5 spaces between them?

There are three ways that I know of. The first is easy: Use the special code for a space—** **. This example puts three spaces between two images:

```
<IMG SRC="image1.gif">     <IMG SRC="image2.gif">
```

The second method for doing this is to create a "spacing" image and display it between the two images.

The third is to put the images in a table without borders. But keep in mind that only the latest versions of Netscape and Mosaic support tables. I'll show you how to create and use tables in Chapter 13, *Mastering Tables.*

How can I resize an image?

Again, the **<IMG>** tag comes to the rescue. Here's the format for this tag when using it to resize an image:

```
<IMG HEIGHT=pixels WIDTH=pixels SRC="filename">
```

As an example, this tag would display the image stored in pict.gif as 32x40 pixels:

```
<IMG HEIGHT=32 WIDTH=40 SRC="pict.gif">
```

You can specify a height and width that is either larger or smaller than the original image. When the image is displayed, it will be scaled to fit the dimensions you specify. The image will not be cropped. So, no matter what size you provide, you'll still see the entire image.

This tag provides a hidden advantage even if you don't need to resize an image. If you know the size of an image, you can specify its dimensions using the **HEIGHT** and **WIDTH** parameters and Netscape will be able to display your HTML document much faster. Let's look at an example. Assume that Netscape is reading the following HTML:

```
<IMG HEIGHT=100 WIDTH=100 SRC="pict1.gif">
<IMG HEIGHT=100 WIDTH=100 SRC="pict2.gif">
<BR>
Welcome to my home page.
<P>
<IMG HEIGHT=100 WIDTH=100 SRC="pict3.gif">
...
```

Each time Netscape encounters the **HEIGHT** and **WIDTH** parameters, it knows exactly how much space to leave for an image. This allows it to quickly put up a border (bounding box) for the image and then move on to create the remainder of the page. The details are then filled in later.

If you have a little extra time on your hands, you can determine the width and height of all your images, and then update your **<IMG>** tags so that your pages will display quicker. Your fellow Web surfers will thank you.

When I use the ALIGN=Middle with the <IMG> tag, my text isn't truly centered. How do I fix it?
Write to the people who invented HTML and complain. Actually, I think enough people have complained about this because they've added a new alignment feature called **Absmiddle**. Here's how it works:

```
<IMG ALIGN=Absmiddle SRC="pict.jif">
```

How do I change the size of my text (font size)?
A new tag has been added to HTML to allow you to change the size of your text at any time. Here's the basic format:

```
<FONT SIZE=size> text </FONT>
```

The *size* parameter can be a number from 1 to 7. The default font size is 3. Once the size has been changed with this tag, all of the text within the tag will be displayed using the specified size.

How can I include my Internet address on a Web page so that users can click on it and send me e-mail?
This is easily accomplished using the *mailto* protocol. When you define a link using the **<A HRREF>** tag, you include the mailto protocol instead of the typical http protocol that you'd use to link to a Web page. As an example, let's assume that your e-mail address is johnsmith@surfstuff.com. Here's how you would define an anchor:

```
<A HREF="mailto:johnsmith@surfstuff.com" Send me mail, please!></A>
```

When a user clicks on the link, "Send me mail, please," a message box will pop up so that a mail message can be entered.

How can I set up a link on a Web page so that a user can access an FTP area on a Web site?

This is another protocol variation. This time, instead of using http or mailto, you use FTP as the link protocol. Here's an example:

```
<A HREF=FTP://coriolis.com Click here to download something special!></A>
```

How do I display a background image on a Web page?

This question is a good one, but it deserves a special section just to answer it. So, let's roll up our sleeves and explore backgrounds....

ADDING BACKGROUNDS AND COLORS

The recently proposed HTML 3.0 specification provides a feature for adding backgrounds to Web pages. The background attribute, as implemented by Netscape, allows your documents to override the background specified by a local browser. The attribute specifies a URL that, in turn, points to an image used as the document's background. Netscape supports additional enhancements so that you are even able to control the color of your backgrounds.

If you've never seen a Web page containing a background, check out:

```
http://home.netscape.com/assist/net_sites/bg/index.html
```

Figure 12.1 shows how Netscape will display this document. Netscape calls this background "Brushed Aluminum." It's difficult to identify in black and white, but the GIF image, brushed_aluminum.gif, is tiled to fill the entire screen.

A simplified outline of the **<BODY>** portion of the Netscape page that displays this background is:

```
<BODY BACKGROUND="metal/brushed_aluminum.gif">
     Remainder of Document
</BODY>
```

Netscape maintains an interesting *Background Sampler* that you can access by pointing your browser to:

```
http://home.netscape.com/assist/net_sites/bg/backgrounds.html
```

This collection includes more than 50 background GIFs. Figure 12.2 shows some available images, of which Netscape allows free use. There are two ways to use them:

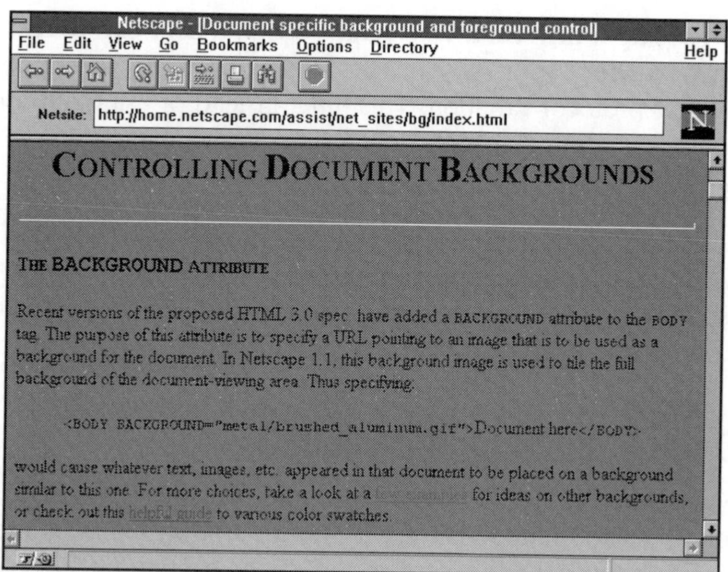

Figure 12.1 *Displaying the "Brushed Aluminum" background with Netscape.*

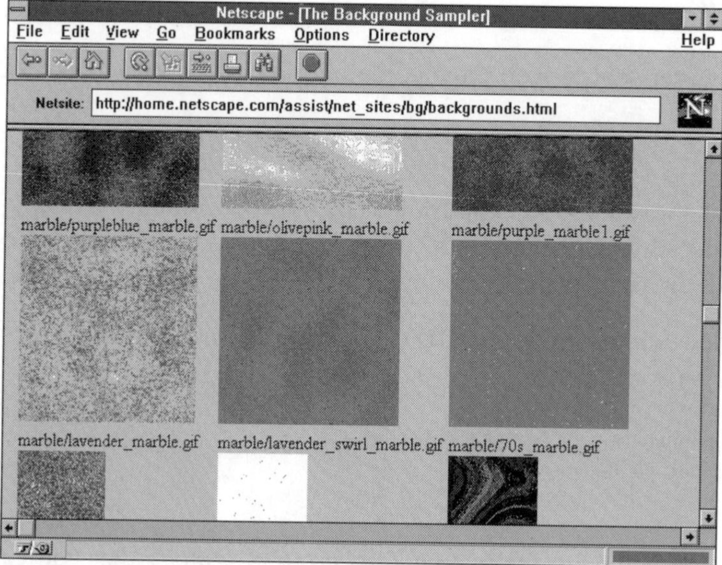

Figure 12.2 *A portion of Netscape's collection of background images.*

- Download an image to your HTML server and reference it in your document.
- Leave the image at Netscape; reference the Netscape URL in your document.

Building a Document with a Background

In this project we'll actually build a document using a Netscape-provided GIF. We'll first download the image to our PC and reference the local copy. Then, we'll modify the document to fetch the image from Netscape.

First, connect to Netscape's Background Sampler at:

```
http://home.netscape.com/assist/net_sites/bg/backgrounds.html
```

Find a background you like. This could take a while (because the Web page loads slowly). The image I've selected is Netscape's 70s_marble.gif. I saved it as marble.gif in my Netscape directory. Next, I created a new file using Web Spinner. In the document's **<BODY>** tag I put:

```
<BODY BACKGROUND="marble.gif">
```

That's all there is to it. Figure 12.3 shows Netscape displaying the document. Unfortunately, the document's title and other text are barely visible. I'll show you how to fix this in a minute.

Let's modify marble.htm so the background image is fetched directly from Netscape. The sampler document uses this URL:

```
http://home.netscape.com/home/bg/fabric/gray_fabric.gif
```

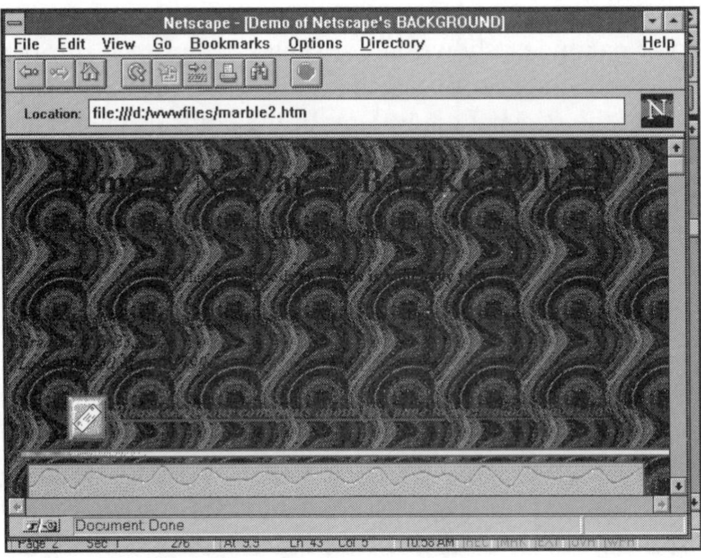

***Figure 12.3** A document displayed using a marble background.*

The last part of the URL, /fabric/gray_fabric.gif, is the directory and file name for the image. So, the URL to use when fetching your choice is

```
http://home.netscape.com/home/bg/
```

plus the directory and file name shown on the swatch background image collection. My choice was in the directory /marble and the file name was 70s_marble.gif. So, the new **<BODY>** tag in the modified marble.htm is:

```
<BODY BACKGROUND="http://home.netscape.com/home/bg/marble/70s_marble.gif">
```

If you use a background image that does not contrast with the black text normally displayed when viewing Web documents, you'll want to specify different text colors. Netscape to the rescue.

Changing Various Document Colors

The proposed HTML 3.0 specification contains the **BACKGROUND** attribute, which is placed in the **<BODY>** tag. Several newly introduced attributes from Netscape can be used in the **<BODY>** tag. They all take the same general form, namely:

```
<BODY attribute="RGB-color">
```

One of the available attributes is **TEXT**. Could this be the answer to our contrast dilemma? You bet!

The RGB-color parameter shown in the syntax template is a triplet of color numbers. The numbers must be specified in hexadecimal. Don't panic—yet! Let's first look at the decimal equivalent. In the color palette, 0 is the lowest intensity and 255 is the highest intensity. The first number in the triplet series is the red specification, the second is green, and the third is blue. If we want to specify bright red, the specification would be 255, 0, 0. That is, give red the maximum intensity and don't muck it up with any green or blue. Conversely, all green would be 0, 255, 0 and drop-dead blue would be 0, 0, 255. The RGB triplet tells Netscape how to combine the three basic colors.

Netscape's Built-in Color Sampler

Colors and colorization are tough for me conceptualize. Fortunately, the Netscape folks have provided a great tool, only they apparently don't know about it. Here's what to do:

1. Execute the sequence Option|Preferences|Fonts and Colors.
2. Click on one of the Choose Colors buttons in the Colors frame. This brings up the Color dialog box.
3. Click on the Define Custom Colors button to expand the dialog box and expose the color palette.
4. In the lower-right corner you'll find three fields showing the Red, Green, and Blue decimal representation of the selected color. Click on the white square in the Basic Color selection and the RGB numbers become 255, 255, and 255. Click on the black square and the numbers become 0, 0, 0. Click anywhere in the color palette and the RGBs are mixed right before our eyes.

You can also manually enter the appropriate decimal number in each of the three boxes to view the represented color in the box marked Color|Solid. Use the palette to pick colors for your various **BACKGROUND** attributes.

I suggested to Netscape that another column of numbers be added to the right of the decimal numbers to display the hex number equivalents. That sure would save a lot of conversion consternation, as I'll explain in a moment.

Modifying the Color of Textual Information

In this project we'll take the HTML document created in the previous project and modify it. We'll change the displayed color of a document's normal text and also the color of the various links.

Selecting Text Color

As I mentioned earlier, the color parameter for the **TEXT** attribute must be specified in hexadecimal. Programmers sometimes use hex when it's more convenient to do so for computer representations. Hex is a base 16 numbering system. Each placeholder can have 16 different characters, as opposed to the decimal system's 10 (0 through 9). Hex character representation uses 0 through 9 in addition to A through F. Decimal 9 is hex 9, decimal 10 is hex A, 11 is hex B and so on. Decimal 15 is hex F, the last available character.

So, then what would decimal 16 be in hex? You use the same placeholder principle that you would use with decimal numbering. In decimal, if we count to 9 (the largest character) and want to add 1, we put 0 in the current placeholder and add 1 to the next-higher order place holder, giving us 10. Decimal 15 is hex F, so decimal 16 would be hex 10. In hex-speak, decimal 0 is 0 and decimal 255 is hex FF.

As Artie Johnson used to say on *Laugh In*, "Very Interesting, but stupid." Requiring a non-programmer to enter hex numbers is another example of programmers forgetting about those of us in the real world. Having said that, we still need to use hex numbers.

Let's skip the hex conversion problem for just a minute. As we've seen, a totally white display is decimal 255, 255, 255. We've also seen that decimal 255 is hex FF. To have Netscape display normal text (non-link text) in white, we would use the following:

```
<BODY TEXT="FFFFFF">
```

As is true with the **<BODY>** tag, **TEXT** allows multiple attributes. Let's modify marble.htm to include the following **<BODY>** tag.

```
<BODY BACKGROUND="marble.gif" TEXT="FFFFFF">
```

Figure 12.4 shows the effect this tag produces. The text went from non-readable to something my granddaughter Lauren describes as "cool." If for some reason the specified background image is not loaded, the other color attributes are ignored. This is really a good idea. If I had specified my background color preference as white (which I have) and displayed marble.htm,

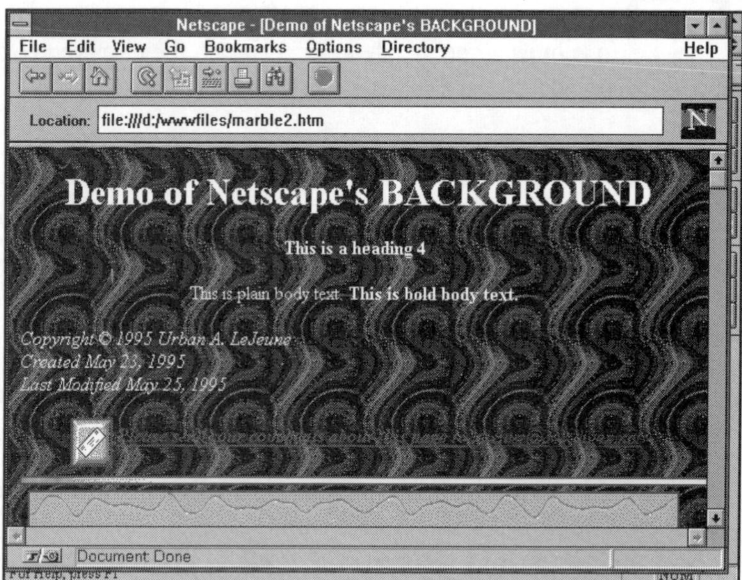

***Figure 12.4** The modified document now displays white text on the marble background.*

sans marble.gif, I would be looking at white text displayed on a white background—just a wee bit tough to read.

We still have a little problem with the display. The link text is blue (or whatever color the user specifies from within the Font and Colors preferences dialog box), which makes for difficult reading. There are three other optional link attributes—**LINK**, **VLINK**, and **ALINK**. **LINK** is used when displaying an unfollowed link, while **VLINK** is used when displaying an anchor that has previously been followed. I don't have a clue what an active link (**ALINK**) represents.

To make the link display in white, add the following attribute:

```
LINK="FFFFFF"
```

But now we have yet another problem with the display. White is fine for unvisited links, but after the link is made, the anchor displays in the user-specified color, which may represent a poor contrast. Red contrasts well with the marble display. So, add the following attribute to our growing list:

```
VLINK="FF0000"
```

Figure 12.5 demonstrates the results of our handiwork, showing the mailto anchor displayed in red. Take a closer look at the bottom of the screen in

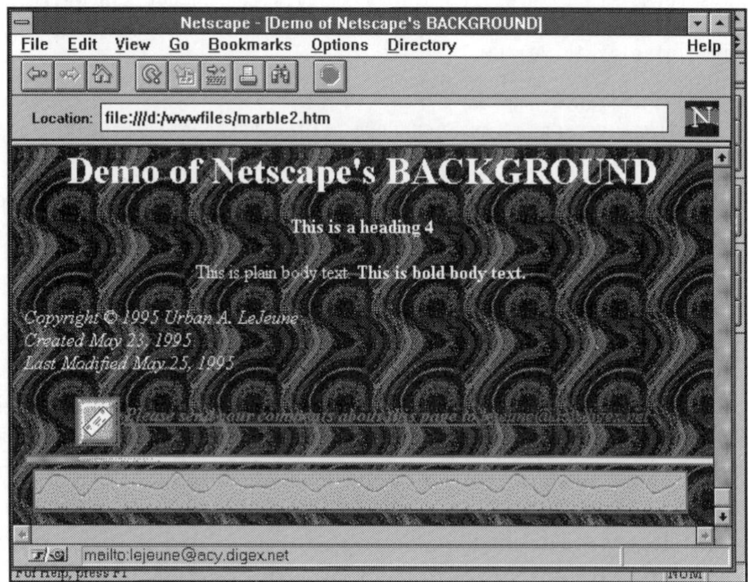

Figure 12.5 The modified document with a red followed link on the marble background.

Figure 12.5. The mail button and everything displayed below the button has a border that's the same color as the mail link. I once forgot to include a closing **</A>** at the end of my mail link. Everything below that point was treated as part of the anchor. I really like the effect and now do it on purpose. Here's the code:

```
<CENTER>
    <A HREF="mailto:lejeune@acy.digex.net">
    <IMG ALIGN=CENTER SRC=mailbutt.gif>
    <B>Please send your comments about this page to</B>
     lejeune@acy.digex.net</ADDRESS>
    <IMG SRC=line.gif>
    <IMG SRC=sine.gif></A>
</CENTER>
```

For consistency, let's add colorization for an active link. Yellow also contrasts well with the marble background. By using yellow, we can see if and when an active link ever shows up. If you find one, let me know. Yellow is 255, 255, 0 or FFFF00. So, the active link attribute is:

```
ALINK="FFFF00"
```

Here's what we end up with:

```
<!--
     The following BACKGROUND attributes use a marble background-
     displays normal text in white, displays unvisited anchors in white.
     Visited anchors are displayed in red  and  active links, whatever
     they are, display in yellow.
 -->
  <BODY BACKGROUND="marble.gif"
               TEXT="FFFFFF"  LINK="FFFFFF"  VLINK="FF0000"  ALINK="FFFF00">
```

Notice that HTML has a provision for comments. They are enclosed between the <!-- remarks --> pair. I like to add a comment before any lines that might lead me to ask myself at a later date, "Why the heck did I do that?"

Solid Background Colors without Images

Netscape has made an addition to the proposed HTML 3.0 specification: There are times when you simply want a plain, patternless background. This next attribute will override the user's background specification (made in the Font and Color preferences dialog box). For instance, if you think your document would look better with a black background, you could use the new background color (**BGCOLOR)** attribute to change the background color.

Let's once again modify marble.htm to make a negative display—white text displayed on a black background. The background color attribute is **BGCOLOR**. The modified **BODY** tag for our reverse image display would look like this:

```
<BODY BGCOLOR="000000" TEXT="FFFFFF" LINK="FFFFFF" VLINK="FFFFFF">
```

Figure 12.6 shows the result. It's interesting, but a little spooky. Try a blue background with white text, something I find soothing. The value for a simple blue background would be 0000FF.

Aesthetics aside, there's also a pragmatic reason to use **BGCOLOR**. Establishing a background image requires the fetching of an image from a second server connection. The second connection will slow down the loading of a document. In other words, none of your document will display until the image is loaded and decoded. When you use a background color, as opposed to a background image, everything is accomplished in one fetch. This speed issue is also a good reason to keep your background images small.

Biting the Hex Bullet

Now that you've see the great effects you can produce by using the various color attributes, it's time to deal with hex. Once you decide which decimal color numbers to use to produce the desired color, you can convert them to

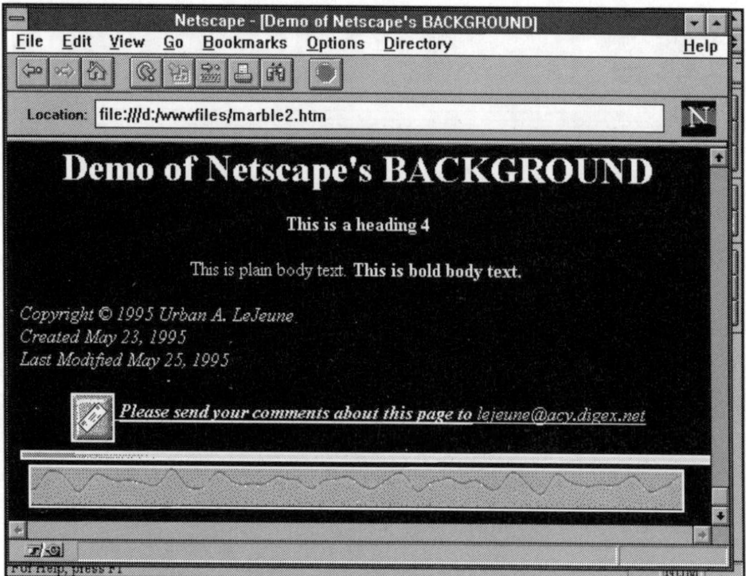

***Figure 12.6** The modified document with white text displayed on a black background.*

hex by using a scientific calculator. The easiest approach is to open the Accessories group window, start the Calculator, and change the View to Scientific (from the main Calculator menu, click on View | Scientific). Enter the decimal number you want to convert, say, 255, and click on the Hex button, which in this case displays FF, the corresponding hex value.

If you don't have the Windows Calculator, you can use Laura Lemay's online script. Point your browser at:

```
http://www.lne.com/lemay/rgb.html
```

Figure 12.7 shows this little gem. You just enter the red, green, and blue decimal values and then click on the Submit values. For instance, if you submit RGB 55, 119, and 222, the script will return 3777DE.

Also, a listing of colors is available at:

```
http://www.infi.net/wwwimages/colorindex.html
```

Another nice resource is "Colors and Their Hex Equivalents," by Rich Barrette, a graduate student at Ohio University. This document is part of the Webaholic home page. Check it out at:

```
http://www.ohiou.edu/~rbarrett/webaholics/ver2/colors.html
```

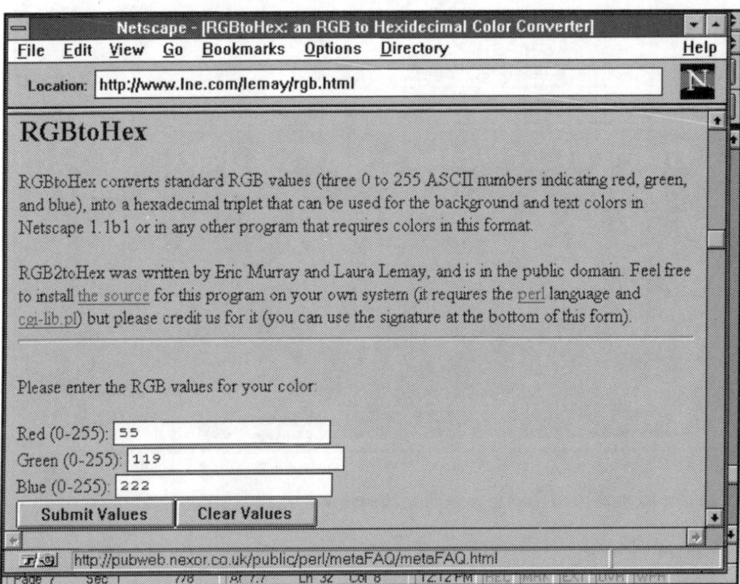

Figure 12.7 Laura Lemay's Decimal to Hex converter.

I would also appreciate it if you would send me any examples of interesting backgrounds you create or find. E-mail me at:

```
lejeune@acy.digex.net
```

GREAT WEB PUBLISHING TIPS

Since you've probably been surfing the Web for a while, you must realize that it is bursting at the seams with great publishing resources and tips and techniques to help you create HTML documents and publish on the Web. If you know where to look, you can find useful information and tools to help you design pages, add great icons and images, design your own graphics, check your HTML documents for errors, convert documents created by other desktop publishing applications such as PageMaker to HTML, and much more.

In this section, I'll show you some of the better places to go to help you create better Web pages. But we won't just explore lists of resources. I'll also show you how to use resources and tools on the Web to perform a number of useful tasks, including:

- Creating custom graphics for your Web pages
- Spell checking your Web pages
- Checking your HTML documents for proper formatting

Creating Your Own Graphics

Wouldn't it be nice if you could design your own graphics as you were surfing the Web? Sure, you can find graphics you like and download them as GIF files, but a much more useful technique would be to build them on the fly while you're surfing the Web.

Patrick Hennessey, spectre@ksu.ksu.edu, has created what I think is one of the most innovative publishing/design tools I've seen on the Web. His creation, called the Interactive Graphics Renderer page, is located at:

```
http://www.eece.ksu.edu/IGR/
```

When you get to his home page, click on the button that takes you to the Interactive Graphics Renderer tool. Figure 12.8 shows the form that you'll get.

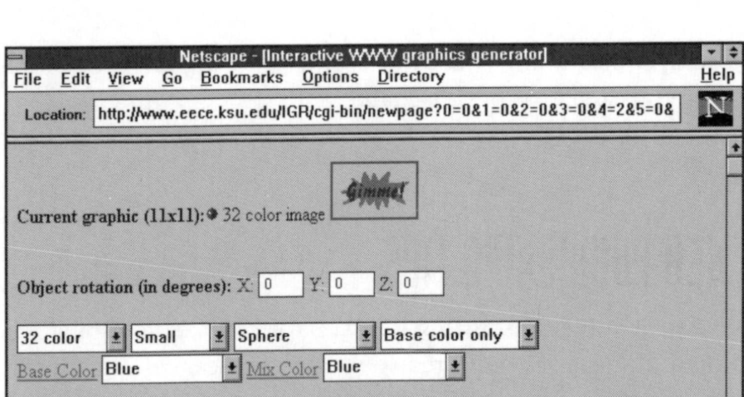

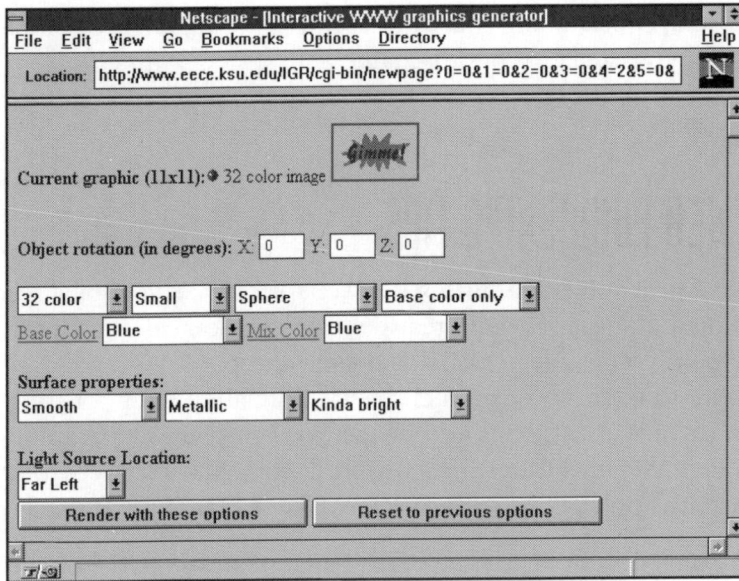

Figure 12.8 The Interactive Graphics Renderer tool for creating your own graphics.

To use this tool to build your own images, here are the steps to follow:

1. Select the settings for the image using the text boxes and option boxes. You can rotate your object, select a size and object type, change its colors and surface properties, and so on.
2. Click the "Render with these options" button to create the image. If it doesn't come out the way you want, just change some of the settings and create it again.
3. When you finish, click on the Gimme button and the GIF image you've created will be downloaded. I don't know anyone else on the Web who offers service like this!

Creating a Home Page

In Chapter 9, I presented our very own HomePage Creator that you can run from Windows to help you create your own home page. There is also another program you can download from the Web that offers this service. This program is called Web Wizard and you can locate it at:

```
http://www.halcyonon.com/webwizard/webwiz16.htm
```

Web Wizard works a little differently than HomePage Creator; it interviews you for the information to put on your home page and then it generates an HTML document for you. Try it out. Everyone can always use an extra program to help generate a home page.

Checking a Web Page

If you are concerned about the accuracy of your HTML documents, there is a neat tool available on the Web you can use to check them. The tool is called Weblint; it reads an HTML document and checks for a number of possible errors in your documents, including:

- Incorrect structure
- Unsupported HTML tags
- Mismatched tags
- Obsolete tags

You can think of this tool as the HTML style enforcer. It will even complain if you use the word "here" as anchor text. I like to use Weblint to check whether an HTML document uses HTML tags that are not supported by most browsers.

Checking Coriolis Group's Home Page

Let's take Weblint for a test drive and have it check Coriolis Group's home page, which is at the following location:

```
http://www.coriolis.com/coriolis
```

But first, to use Weblint, point Netscape to this site:

```
http://www.unipress.com/weblint/index.html#form
```

Figure 12.9 shows the Web page that is displayed. You'll need to scroll down until you see the Weblint Form shown in Figure 12.10. Next, enter the URL for the Coriolis Group home page and click the Check it... button. Weblint will then go to work and analyze the HTML document specified by the URL we entered.

Did this Web page pass? Sure. In fact, I would give them a B. Figure 12.11 shows the results of the test. As you can see, Weblint is pretty picky. When it finishes checking an HTML document, it displays the errors or inconsistencies

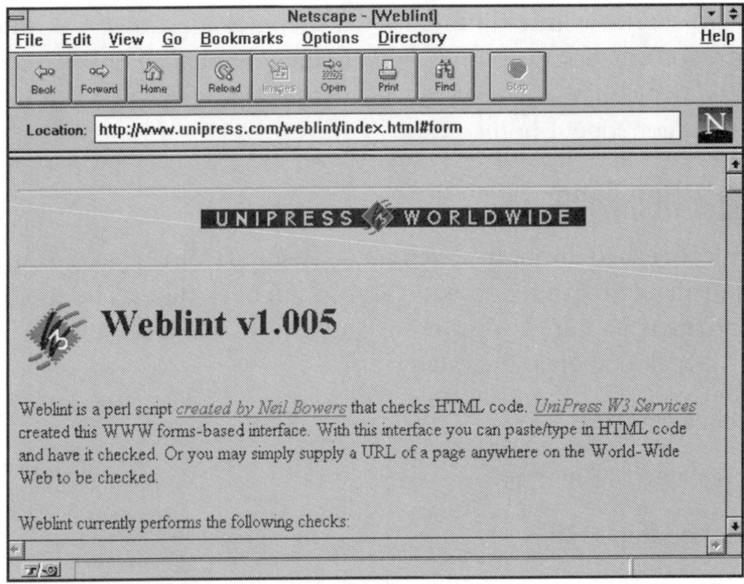

Figure 12.9 *The Weblint page for checking HTML documents.*

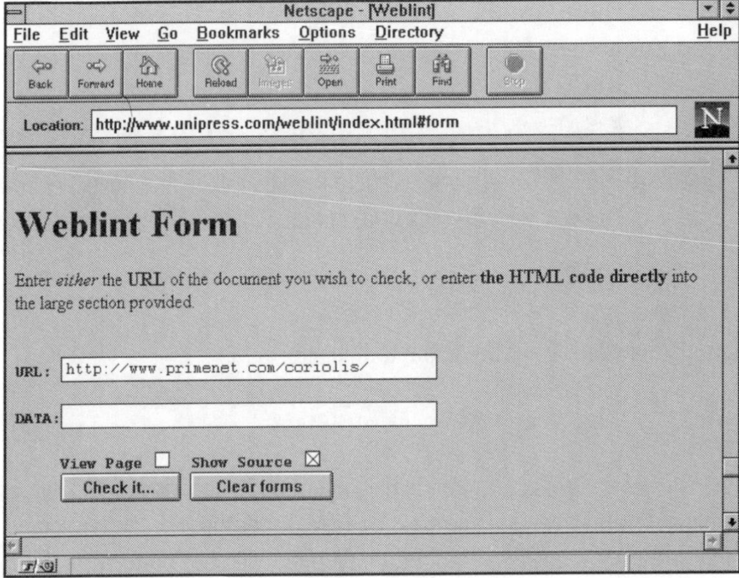

Figure 12.10 *The Weblint Form you fill out to check a document.*

it finds, along with the HTML tags for the document. This is a nice feature because you can see exactly where and why errors have occurred. Try Weblint on one of your HTML pages.

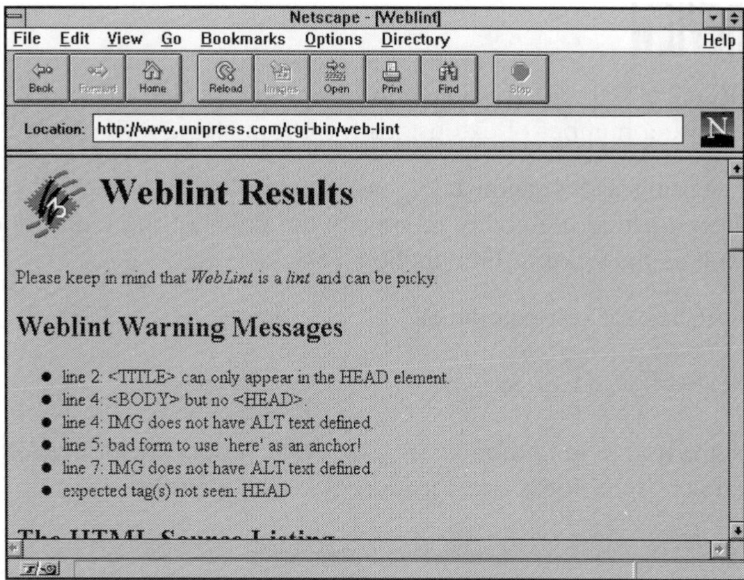

Figure 12.11 *The Weblint Results page, which shows the errors found in an HTML document.*

If you are interested in this type of Web page verification, you can find another tool at this location:

```
http://www.halsoft.com/html-val-svc/
```

Spelling Bee

If you're like me, you'll agree that one of the best inventions to come along in ages is the spelling checker. I couldn't live without mine. Unfortunately, most of the HTML editors available don't provide any spell checking features. So, you're likely to find a lot of Web pages out there in cyberspace that have a lot of typos. One solution to this problem is the automatic spell checker called WebSter's Dictionary that you can run right from the Web. To use this tool, go to:

```
http://www.eece.ksu.edu/~spectre/WebSter/spell.html
```

Once you are there, you can enter a URL for an HTML document and the program will produce a Web page showing all of the words that are misspelled. You might be wondering, how good is this tool? I haven't fully tested it but I did try testing it on itself. That is, I entered the URL for the WebSter's Dictionary HTML document and guess what happened? I got a list of misspelled words. Oh well, I guess the person who created this tool was so busy programming that he or she forgot to spell check the page!

LET'S REVIEW

The proposed HTML 3.0 specification, frequently called HTML+, makes it possible to use a number of extensions from font sizing to backgrounds.

Netscape, starting with version 1.1N, had also implemented several enhancements. These include the ability to specify the color of the entire document area, as well as the color of link anchors.

The basic format for colorization is:

```
<BODY attribute="RGB-colors-in-hex">
```

Attributes are usable in combination. The HTML code (including Netscape's enhancements) used in the specification of colors include:

Opening Tag	Closing Tag	Description
<BODY>	</BODY>	No special color effects
<BODY BACKGROUND="URL">	</BODY>	Use the image stored at URL to construct background
<BODY BGCOLOR="RGB-in-Hex">	</BODY>	Solid background color display specified in Hex
<BODY TEXT="RGB-in-Hex">	</BODY>	Normal, non-link, text color display specified in Hex
<BODY LINK=""RGB-in-Hex">	</BODY>	Link anchor display color specified in Hex
<BODY VLINK=""RGB-in-Hex">	</BODY>	Visited link anchor display color specified in Hex
<BODY ALINK=""RGB-in-Hex">	</BODY>	Active link anchor display color specified in Hex

Colors are specified in the range of 0 through 255 (hex 0 through hex FF) with 0 being the lowest intensity and 255 the highest. Colors are specified in red-green-blue order. Bright red would be 255,0,0 or FF0000 in hex.

The existing HTML+ specification is certain to undergo changes and additions. Do not use colorization unless you're prepared to perform fairly heavy maintenance on your documents.

Different color effects may look different, or may not display at all, on different browsers, or even when using the same browser with different user-specified values. Don't assume that a person viewing your document will see what's identical to your screen.

Mastering Tables

Are you looking for a better way to display lots of data on your Web pages. Look no further, because you're about to see how you can use tables to publish more information in less space.

"People," I was saying at a recent meeting of the South Jersey Internet User's Group, "can be divided into two groups—those who divide people into groups, and those who don't."

The dividers are those people—me for one—who prefer placing objects in neatly defined pigeon holes; we love spreadsheets and any extensively organized system. Conversely, the non-partitioners are those people who have been given the gift of creativity. These creative people, most of who prefer Macs, disdain anything with a straight line while the left side of their brain cranks out another work of art. Somehow it just doesn't seem fair—we denizens of the neatly structured world truly admire the creative output of our gifted counterparts, while they routinely relegate our predictable, organized output to the trashbasket.

In this chapter I'm going to take up my role as divider as I present HTML tables. Both Netscape and Mosaic have implemented HTML table tags in their latest beta versions. This chapter will show you how to use the basic HTML 3.0 table tags as implemented by Netscape. Keep in mind that HTML 3.0 is a proposal, not a standard. The HTML tags used for creating tables will probably change in the final HTML 3.0 standard when it is eventually adopted. You should also be aware that Netscape has added enhancements to the proposed standards, which we'll also explore in this chapter.

GETTING STARTED WITH TABLES

Tables are interesting critters. Many people prefer information presented in the two-dimensional linear format offered by tables. It's no accident that a spreadsheet program provided the catalyst for the desktop computer revolution—desktop revolting, some might say.

On the other hand, highly creative people aren't big fans of tabular displays of data. They prefer presentations with more pizzazz. Whatever your bag, the addition of tables to the proposed HTML 3.0 standard creates display options previously unavailable for your Web documents.

As you will see, very creative things can be done with tables. In essence, each cell in a table is its own miniature HTML document. You can even create tables without borders and produce neat effects in your Web documents like text flowing around images—something not very easily done without tables.

HTML tables are easier seen than talked about. For this reason I have built a tutorial HTML document called tables.htm. The file is in the \urbstuff\html directory on the companion CD-ROM. In the event you don't have a CD-ROM drive, I have also put the document "on the air" at:

```
http://www.charm.net/~lejeune/tables.html
```

I'll try to keep the "live" version up to date with any standards changes and added tutorial information. The online document will also have links to table information on the Web. In addition to tables.htm, the individual tutorial components are kept in a file of their own. This arrangement allows you to copy a specific table construction and use it as a starting point for your own table publishing projects.

All the tables presented in the tutorial, with the exception of the first one, will show the actual table, immediately followed by the HTML construction that produced the table.

Let the Tutorial Begin

First, we need to get a few simple conventions out of the way. Tag labels in the examples I present will be all uppercase. Anything within a table shown in either upper or mixed case is something you must construct.

Let's start our tutorial by looking at the results rather than the process. Figure 13.1 shows the first page of the table tutorial. Here we are looking at two tables. The upper table, which contains the three images, is a two row by three column table. The lower table is a one row by two column table. (The number list displayed is actually two lists that take advantage of Netscape's **START=** option.)

Another interesting use of a table is the BrowserWatch home page as shown in Figure 13.2. This page displays information about Netscape in a large table. The URL for this site is:

```
http://www.ski.mskcc.org/browserwatch
```

The basic HTML tags used to construct tables are shown in Figure 13.3. This example table is a whopping seven rows by three columns. The table also has a visible border. (The tables presented in Figure 13.1 did not use borders.) Netscape treats borders in tables a little differently depending upon the back-

***Figure 13.1** The opening page of the Table Tutorial showing two interesting tables.*

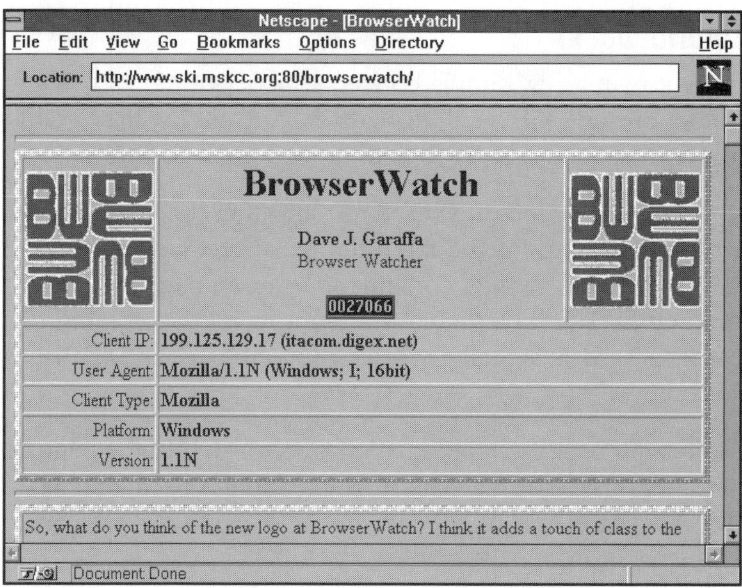

Figure 13.2 The BrowserWatch home page showing a large bordered table.

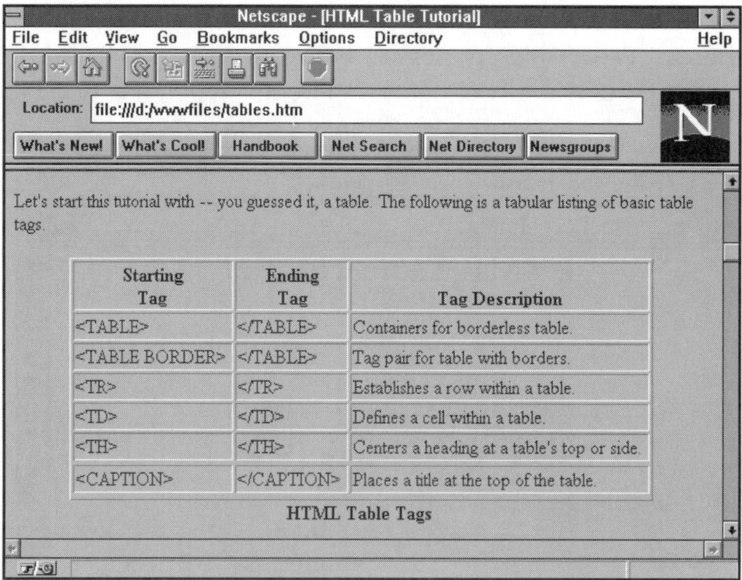

Figure 13.3 HTML table tags in a bordered table.

ground color that is selected. As with almost all Web publishing activities, don't assume what you see on the screen will be what someone else sees, even if they are also using Netscape.

Table 13.1 HTML Table Tags

Starting Tag	Ending Tag	Tag Description
<TABLE>	</TABLE>	Container for a borderless table.
<TABLE BORDER>	</TABLE>	Tag pair for a table with borders.
<TR>	</TR>	Establishes a row within a table.
<TD>	</TD>	Defines a cell within a table.
<TH>	</TH>	Centers a heading at a table's top or side.
<CAPTION>	</CAPTION>	Places a title at the top of the table.

Summary of HTML Table Tags

Table 13.1 lists all of the main HTML tags that are used to create tables. As you explore the examples presented in this chapter, you'll want to refer back to this table to look up the function of a particular tag.

The World's Simplest Table

Conceptually, an empty table is the simplest table. However, an empty table is not very useful—it doesn't even look good! The simplest practical table would be a one row by one column structure. Here's an example:

```
<TABLE>
    <TD>Row One - Column One</TD>
</TABLE>
```

Each table is enclosed between the **<TABLE> ... </TABLE>** tag pair. A *cell* (table data) is enclosed between the **<TD> ... </TD>** tag pair. A non-empty table is assumed to have one row; therefore, the **<TR> ... </TR>** tag pairs (which are used to define a new row) may be eliminated for a one row table. There is never a designation for a column. The position of cells within a row determine the column location.

A table, by default, has no border. Typically, a table with a border is cosmetically more appealing than a borderless table. All bets are off however, if we want to use the capabilities of a table without tipping our hand that it is a table. The table shown next is the same 1x1 table shown above with a border:

```
<TABLE BORDER>
     <TD>Row One - Column One</TD>
</TABLE>
```

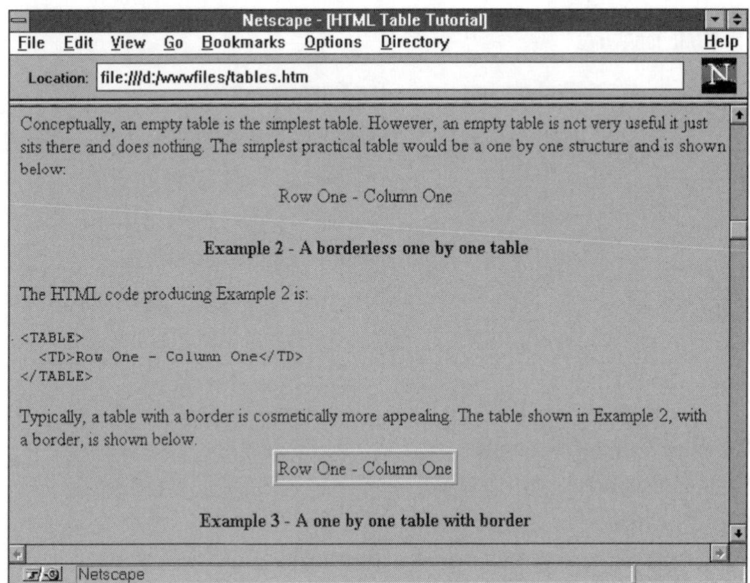

Figure 13.4 *Two 1x1 tables, the upper without a border and the lower with a border.*

The upper table in Figure 13.4 shows a borderless one row by one column table. The lower table demonstrates the effect of adding the **<TABLE BORDER>** tag.

Here's a basic shell for a one row by two column table:

```
<TABLE>
     <TD>Row One - Column One</TD><TD>Row One - Column Two</TD>
</TABLE>
```

Remember, your mileage with borders may vary. A table will have a different appearance if the background color changes, even if it is using the same document, browser, and computer.

Two-Dimensional Tables

A table row is defined using the **<TR> ... </TR>** tag pair. A two row by two column example would be:

```
<TABLE>
     <TR><TD>Row One - Column One</TD><TD>Row One - Column Two</TD></TR>
     <TR><TD>Row Two - Column One</TD><TD>Row Two - Column Two</TD></TR>
</TABLE>
```

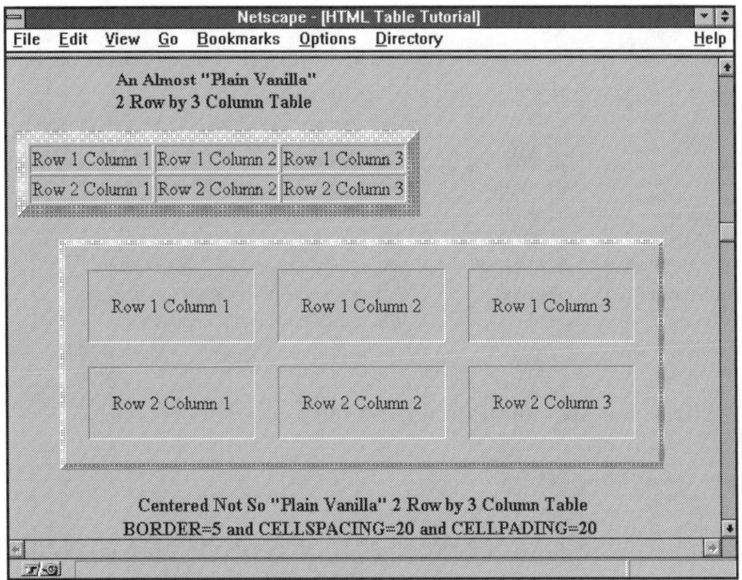

***Figure 13.5** Two identical tables showing the special effects created by sizing.*

Are you ready to get a little fancy? Let's again look at the actual table before we write the HTML. Figure 13.5 shows two *Not So "Plain Vanilla" Two by Three Column Tables.* Both tables have captions and sizing and effect attributes, but otherwise they are the same.

A table may have an optional caption enclosed between, you guessed it, the **<CAPTION> ... </CAPTION>** tag pair. As we have seen with other Netscape HTML enhancements, tags may frequently contain attributes. The opening **<CAPTION>** tag may have an optional alignment tag. The formats are:

```
Opening Tag                   Closing Tag
< CAPTION>                    </CAPTION>
<CAPTION ALIGN=TOP|BOTTOM>    </CAPTION>
```

If the **ALIGN=** option is used, it must immediately be followed by "**TOP**" or "**BOTTOM**". The default is **ALIGN=TOP**. I once wanted to move a caption from the top to the bottom of a table. I changed **TOP** to **BOTTOM** and the caption still showed up on the top of the table. About five microseconds before I was about to send a message to Netscape reporting a bug, I noticed that I had started the attribute with ALIGH. If a browser doesn't recognize an HTML tag or modifier, it ignores it. Since Netscape didn't recognize "ALIGH" it ignored the attribute; without the **ALIGN** attribute, **TOP** was meaningless.

The upper table in Figure 13.5 contains a **TOP** aligned caption while the lower caption is **BOTTOM** aligned. Both tables have enhanced **<TABLE>** tags. Table tags may take the following form:

Opening Tag	Closing Tag	Description
<TABLE>	</TABLE>	No border or special effects
<TABLE BORDER>	</TABLE>	Default border size of 1
<TABLE BORDER=n>	</TABLE>	Where n is border size in pixels
<TABLE CELLPADDING=n>	</TABLE>	Where n is cell padding size in pixels
<TABLE CELLSPACING=n>	</TABLE>	Where n is cell spacing size in pixels
<TABLE WIDTH=n>	</TABLE>	Where n is table width in pixels
<TABLE WIDTH=%>	</TABLE>	Where % is table width in % of page width

The table attributes are combinable. To illustrate, this HTML

```
<TABLE BORDER=5 WIDTH=50%>
```

would create a table with a border size of 5 pixels and it would take 50 percent of the page width. If the natural size of the table exceeds any of the attribute sizes, the attributes are ignored.

The HTML producing the upper table in Figure 13.5 is shown here:

```
<TABLE BORDER=10>
      <CAPTION ALIGN=TOP>
         <B>A Not So &quot;Plain Vanilla&quot;<BR> 2 Row by 3 Column Table</B>
      </CAPTION>
      <TR>
         <TD>Row 1 Column 1</TD> <TD>Row 1 Column 2</TD> <TD>Row 1 Column 3</TD>
      </TR>

      <TR>
        <TD>Row 2 Column 1</TD> <TD>Row 2 Column 2</TD> <TD>Row 2 Column 3</TD>
      </TR>
</TABLE>
```

Just as a refresher, unadorned double quotation marks are not useable in an HTML document since they have special meaning in HTML. The """ special character causes the display of the double quotation marks.

The table has a caption and a border size. The default border size is 1. The lower table in Figure 13.5 has a few bells and whistles. The HTML code is:

```
<CENTER>
 <TABLE BORDER=5 CELLSPACING=20 CELLPADDING=20>
      <CAPTION ALIGN=BOTTOM>
          <B>Centered Not So &quot;Plain Vanilla&quot; 2 Row by 3 Column
               Table<BR>
```

```
    BORDER=5 and CELLSPACING=20 and CELLPADDING=20</B>
  </CAPTION>
  <TR>
    <TD>Row 1 Column 1</TD> <TD>Row 1 Column 2</TD> <TD>Row 1 Column 3</TD>
  </TR>

  <TR>
    <TD>Row 2 Column 1</TD> <TD>Row 2 Column 2</TD> <TD>Row 2 Column 3</TD>
  </TR>
</TABLE>
</CENTER>
```

In addition to being centered, the table has **BORDER**, **CELLSPACING**, and **CELLPADDING** attributes. The **BORDER** attribute controls the size of the 3-D effect. The **CELLPADDING** controls the width of the cells while **CELLSPACING** controls the size between the cells both vertically and horizontally.

Text Formatting within Cells

Now we're getting to my favorite part of table construction: *cells*. Each cell within a table has a life of its own. A cell may contain anything you would normally find in the body section of an HTML document, including nothing or another table! Indeed, empty cells and nested tables produce interesting effects. A cell's content doesn't need to have any logical relationship with the contents of its neighboring cells.

Within a table, the widest cell in any column determines the width of the column. Likewise, the height of the highest cell determines the height of all the cells in the same row. The contents of a cell are left aligned and vertically centered. Netscape has added optional cell width and alignment attributes. More on these in a minute.

Let's take a look at our old reliable two by three table containing some HTML formatting. Figure 13.6 shows the table with all kinds of goodies. The text within the cells determines the size formatting. The center cell in the second row is empty, while the cell in the lower right corner contains an image. The code producing this gem is:

```
<TABLE BORDER>
  <TR>
    <TD><EM>This is Emphasis</EM></TD>
    <TD><H3>Heading 3</H3></TD>
    <TD>Unformatted text</TD>
  </TR>

  <TR>
    <TD><B>Bold<BR>with<BR>three lines</B></TD>
```

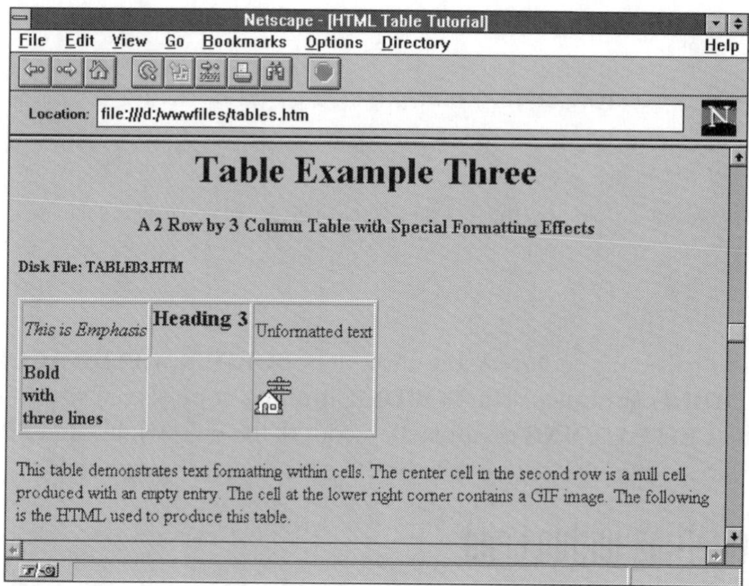

Figure 13.6 *A table containing special effects including an image and a blank cell.*

```
        <TD></TD> <!-- This is a null cell -->
        <TD><IMG SRC="home.gif"></TD>
    </TR>
</TABLE>
```

Surprisingly simple, isn't it? The content of a cell is alignable both vertically and horizontally. The following are more Netscape HTML table enhancements.

```
Opening Tag                    Closing Tag   Description
<TD>                           </TD>         No special effects
<TD ALIGN=LEFT|RIGHT|CENTER>   </TD>         Horizontal alignment within cell
<TD VALIGN=TOP|MIDDLE|BOTTOM>  </TD>         Vertical alignment within cell
<TD WIDTH=n>                   </TD>         Where n is cell width in pixels
<TD WIDTH=%>                   </TD>         Where % is percentage of table width
```

Both vertical and horizontal alignments, as well as width attributes are permitted within the same cell. Figure 13.7 shows the same table shown in Figure 13.6 with alignment and width attributes. The HTML for this table is:

```
<TABLE BORDER>
     <TR>
         <TD WIDTH=50%><EM>This is Emphasis</EM></TD>
         <TD><H3>Heading 3</H3></TD>
        <TD>Unformatted text</TD>
     </TR>
```

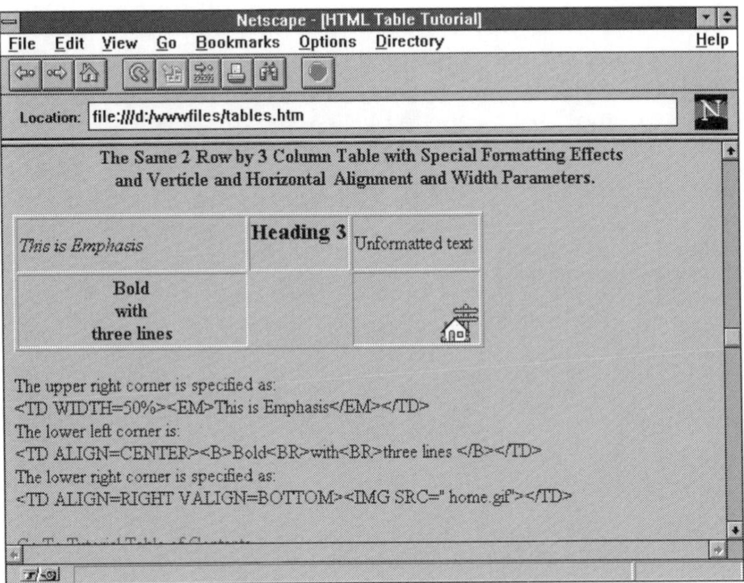

Figure 13.7 *Vertical and horizontal alignment applied to the table in Figure 13.6.*

```
    <TR>
        <TD ALIGN=CENTER><B>Bold<BR>with<BR>three lines</B></TD>
        <TD></TD> <!-- This is a null cell -->
        <TD ALIGN=RIGHT VALIGN=BOTTOM><IMG SRC=home.gif></TD>
     </TR>
</TABLE>
```

The cell in row one, column one has the **WIDTH** set to 50 percent of the total table size. The **WIDTH** attribute establishes the size of all cells in the same column. The text in the lower-left corner is centered because of the **ALIGN=CENTER** attribute. The GIF in the lower right corner is horizontally right aligned and vertically aligned at the bottom of the cell because of the **ALIGN=RIGHT** and **VALIGN=BOTTOM** attributes.

Cell Spanning

All the tables we have created and viewed so far have been symmetrical. All rows contained the same number of cells, and all columns contained the same number of cells. This is certainly not a requirement. Both rows and columns may be spanned by connecting two or more cells through the use of the **ROWSPAN** and **COLSPAN** attributes. The syntax of these attributes is:

```
<TD COLSPAN=n>  </TD>   Where n is the number of columns to span
<TD ROWSPAN=n>  </TD>   Where n is the number of rows to span
```

Let's first look at some rowspans. Figure 13.8 demonstrates the use of row spanning. The center column is just one big row because of the **ROWSPAN=3** specification. The right column has the lower two rows connected using the **ROWSPAN=2** attribute. The required HTML for these effects is:

```
<TABLE BORDER>
    <TR>
       <TD>Row 1 Col 1</TD>
       <TD ROWSPAN=3>ROWSPAN=3<BR>Element 1,2</TD>
       <TD>Row 1 Col 3</TD>
    </TR>

    <TR>
       <TD>Row 2 Col 1</TD><TD ROWSPAN=2>ROWSPAN=2<BR>Element 2,3</TD>
    </TR>

    <TR>
       <TD>Row 3 Col 1</TD>
    </TR>
</TABLE>
```

Since the center cell of the first row specifies **ROWSPAN=3** there are no **<TD> ... </TD>** tags for the center column in the second and third rows. The phantom cells tend to be confusing when you're constructing the table.

Hold on to your hat, we're now going to get really fancy with column spanning and special formatting. Figure 13.9 shows a table with column spanning

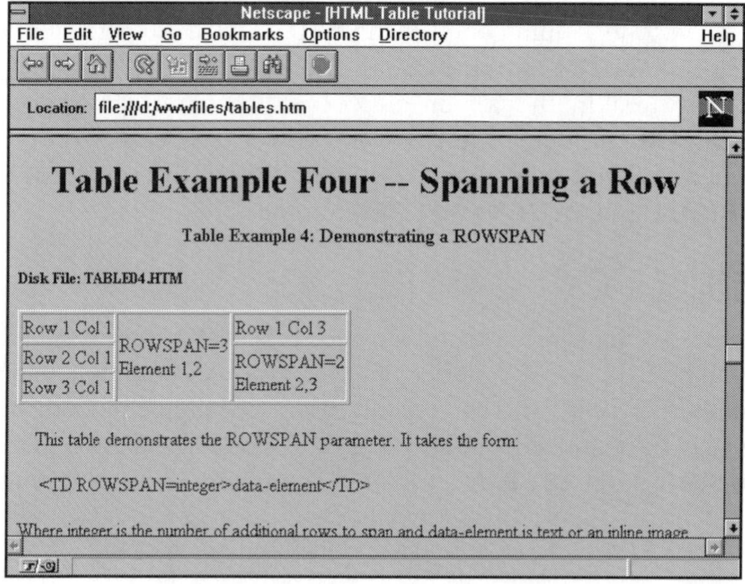

***Figure 13.8** The use of the ROWSPAN attribute to combine multiple rows.*

and some other formatting effects. Row two spans all three columns, while the upper-right corner spans two. The center row is interesting because it contains a link and GIF image which is part of the anchor. The anchor text is also center aligned. The HTML code is:

```
<TABLE BORDER>
    <TR>
        <TD>Row 1 Col 1</TD>
        <TD COLSPAN=2>COLSPAN=2<BR>Element 1,2</TD>
    </TR>

    <TR>
         <TD ALIGN=CENTER COLSPAN=3><A HREF=http://www.charm.net/~lejeune>
          <IMG ALIGN=CENTER SRC="home.gif">
           Urb's Home Page</A><BR> COLSPAN=3 - Element 2,1</TD>
    </TR>

    <TR>
      <TD>Row 3 Col 1</TD><TD>Row 3 Col 2</TD><TD>Row 3 Col 3</TD>
   </TR>
</TABLE>
```

The second row's starting table data tag has both a **COLSPAN=3** attribute and an **ALIGN=CENTER** attribute. The link reference

```
<A HREF=http://www.charm.net/~lejeune> <IMG ALIGN=CENTER SRC="home.gif">
```

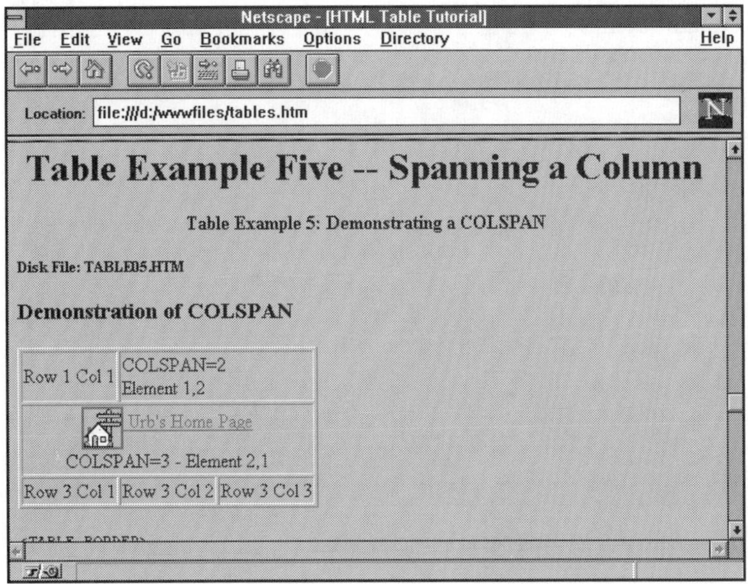

Figure 13.9 *The use of the COLSPAN attribute to connect multiple columns.*

contains both the address reference and an image. When an image is included in this fashion, it is bordered with the specified anchor color. Since the image is part of the anchor, clicking on it activates the link.

Top and Side Table Headings

A table heading is much like a cell element; the difference is that the content is centered and bolded. The table heading is enclosed between the **<TH> ... </TH>** tag pair. Table headings have much the same syntax as **<TD>** elements. Here they are:

<table>
<tr><th>Opening Tag</th><th>Closing Tag</th><th>Description</th></tr>
<tr><td><TH></td><td></TH></td><td>No special effects other than bold and centered</td></tr>
<tr><td><TH ALIGN=LEFT|RIGHT|CENTER></td><td></TH></td><td>Horizontal heading alignment within cell</td></tr>
<tr><td><TH VALIGN=TOP|MIDDLE|BOTTOM></td><td></TH></td><td>Vertical heading alignment within cell</td></tr>
<tr><td><TH WIDTH=n></td><td></TH></td><td>Where n is cell width in pixels</td></tr>
<tr><td><TH WIDTH=%></td><td></TH></td><td>Where % is percentage of table width</td></tr>
<tr><td><TH ROWSPAN=n></td><td></TH></td><td>Where n is heading span in number of rows</td></tr>
<tr><td><TH COLSPAN=n></td><td></TH></td><td>Where n is heading span in number of columns</td></tr>
</table>

Figure 13.10 demonstrates how the **<TH> ... </TH>** pair can be used to create column headings for our old reliable two by three table. The code is:

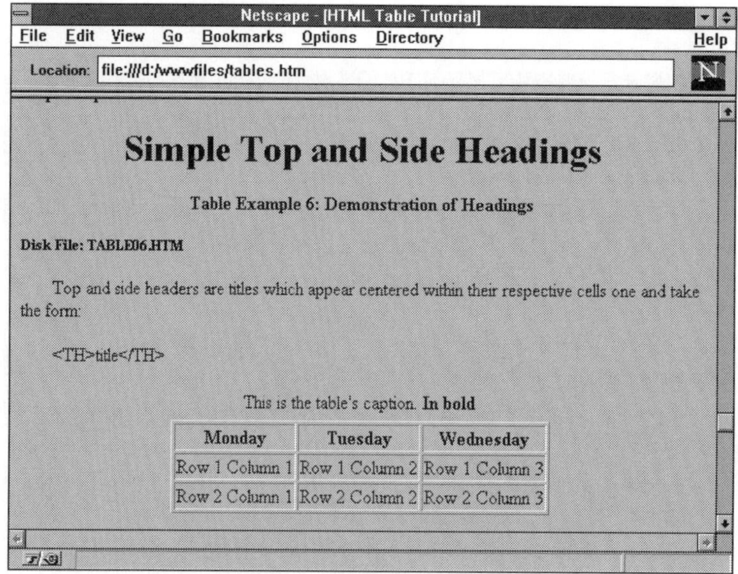

Figure 13.10 The use of top headings in a simple table.

```
<TABLE BORDER>
   <CAPTION>This is the table's caption. <B>In bold</B></CAPTION>
    <TR>
     <TH>Monday</TH><TH>Tuesday</TH><TH>Wednesday</TH>
   </TR>

      <TR>
           <TD>Row 1 Column 1</TD><TD>Row 1 Column 2</TD><TD>Row 1 Column 3</TD>
      </TR>

      <TR>
     <TD>Row 2 Column 1</TD><TD>Row 2 Column 2</TD><TD>Row 2 Column 3</TD>
     </TR>
 </TABLE>
```

Figure 13.11 again shows off a variety of effects. The purpose of the formatting is illustration, not cosmetic purity. The entire row with the "Week One" heading is left aligned with the **<TR ALIGN=LEFT>** starting tag. The row title "Week Two" is right aligned using the **<TR ALIGN=RIGHT>** starting tag. The caption demonstrates **BOTTOM** alignment and also the use of Netscape's **<FONT SIZE>** pair. The complete code is:

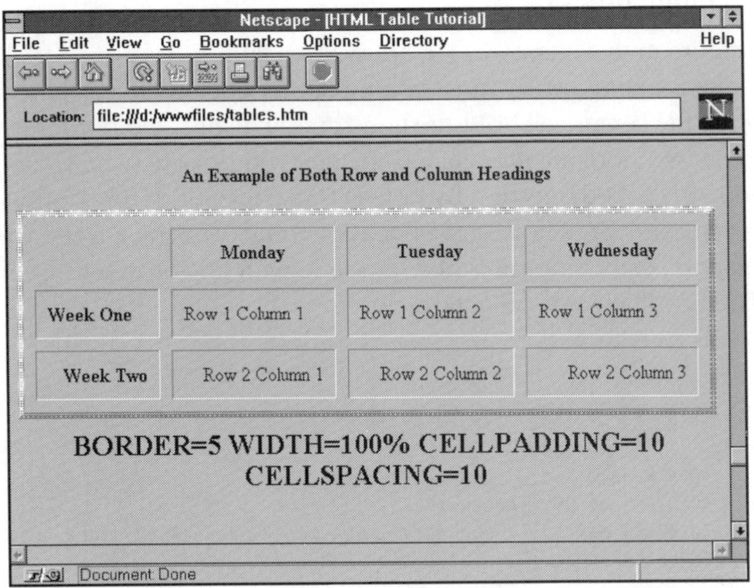

Figure 13.11 Multiple effects coupled with row and column headings.

```
<CENTER>
 <TABLE BORDER=5 WIDTH=100% CELLPADDING=10 CELLSPACING=10>
    <CAPTION ALIGN=BOTTOM>
           <FONT SIZE=5>
             <B>BORDER=5 WIDTH=100% CELLPADDING=10 CELLSPACING=10</B>
           </FONT>
     </CAPTION>
     <TR>
         <TD></TD> <!-- This is a null cell -->
         <TH>Monday</TH><TH>Tuesday</TH><TH>Wednesday</TH>
     </TR>
      <TR ALIGN=LEFT>
          <TH>Week One</TH>
           <TD>Row 1 Column 1</TD><TD>Row 1 Column 2</TD>
           <TD>Row 1 Column 3</TD>
      </TR>
      <TR ALIGN=RIGHT>
           <TH>Week Two</TH>
           <TD>Row 2 Column 1</TD><TD>Row 2 Column 2</TD>
           <TD>Row 2 Column 3</TD>
      </TR>
</TABLE>
</CENTER>
```

Practical Applications

The first figure in this chapter, 13.1, shows two tables that use special effects. The first one is a one row by three column table. The outer cells each hold an image while the center cell holds text and an e-mail link. No border is used so the effect is two horizontally aligned images with text between. One of the most frequently asked question by new HTML coders is, "How do I wrap text around an image?" Until now, it was possible only by using a Netscape HTML enhancement. Text wrapping is now possible with any browser that supports tables. The HTML code for this table is:

```
<TABLE>
     <TR>
         <TD><IMG SRC="table.gif"></A></TD>
        <TD>
            <B>HTML 3.0 Table Tutorial</B><BR>
            <CENTER> by Urb LeJeune<BR>
            <A HREF="mailto:lejeune@acy.digex.net">LeJeune@acy.digex.net</A>
            </CENTER>
        </TD>
        <TD> <IMG SRC="table2.gif"></TD>
    </TR>
</TABLE>
```

The lower table in Figure 13.1 demonstrates another interesting construct. HTML lists frequently have large amounts of blank space since they often take less than half a page. This representation is a one row by two column table. Each column holds an ordered **<OL>** list. What makes it work is Netscape's enhancement of **<OL START=n>** where n is the number starting the list. The right ordered list starts with 5. The code for this table is:

```
</CENTER>
 <TABLE>
     <TR>
        <TD>
          <OL>
            <LI><A HREF=#TABLE01>
                Tutorial and Conventions</A>
            <LI><A HREF=#TABLE02>
                A Simple 2 Row by 3 Column Table</A>
            <LI><A HREF=#TABLE03>
                A 2 Row by 3 Column Table With<BR>
                Special Effects</A>
            <LI><A HREF=#TABLE04>
                Spanning Rows</A>
          </OL>
        </TD>

        <TD>
          <OL START=5>
            <LI><A HREF=#TABLE05>
              Spanning Columns</A>
            <LI><A HREF=#TABLE06>
              Simple Top and Side Headers</A>
            <LI><A HREF=#AUTHOR>
              Urb LeJeune, your friendly<BR>
              Table Tutorial tour guide</A>
             <BR><BR><BR>
          </OL>
        </TD>
    </TR>
 </TABLE>
 </CENTER>
```

Interesting Online Uses of Table

Here are some Web pages you can check out:

Browser Watch by Dave J. Garaffa, d-garaffa@ski.mskcc.org
http://www.ski.mskcc.org/browserwatch

Browser Watch What's New Table
http://www.ski.mskcc.org/browserwatch/whatsnew-table.html

Business trips to Canada. Multiple examples.
http://www.bizserve.com/canadian-detroit/busntrav.html

Colors and their HEX equivalents. An interesting use of a table.
http://www.ohiou.edu/~rbarrett/webaholics/ver2/colors.html

David Rosborough Resume. A large table and background example.
http://trinculo.educ.sfu.ca/David/persinfo/resume.html

Premier League Table
http://www.ccnet.com/people/jmcgough/table-1.1.htm

'Resources' Interesting use of borderless tables and black background.
http://www.ot.com/~stefeb/restab.html

Welcome to CyberCat Technology</A> GIFs and Anchors in table.
http://www.eskimo.com/~scrufcat/cyber.htm

Online References

An HTML 3.0 page to cut your browser's teeth on.
http://gummo.stanford.edu/html/hypermail/www-html-1995q1/0266.html

Homepage construction kit
http://www.digital.com/gnn/netizens/construction.html

HyperText Markup Language Specification Version 3.0 Cover Page
http://www.hpl.hp.co.uk/people/dsr/html/CoverPage.html

NCSA Mosaic Tables Tutorial
http://www.ncsa.uiuc.edu/SDG/Software/Mosaic/Tables/tutorial.html

NCSA Tables on the Web!
http://www.ncsa.uiuc.edu/SDG/Software/Mosaic/Tables/Overview.html

Netscape Extensions
http://home.mcom.com/home/services_docs/html-extensions.html

Netscape Table Sampler
http://home.netscape.com/home/demo/1.1b1/tableSample.html

Netscape's Background and Foreground Control Tutorial
http://home.netscape.com/home/bg/how.html

Online HTML Training Course
http://www.usask.ca/dcs/courses/cai/html/

Yahoo HTML Listings
http://www.yahoo.com/Computers/World_Wide_Web/HTML/

Yale WWW style manual
http://info.med.yale.edu/caim/StyleManual_Top.HTML

LET'S REVIEW

Tables have traditionally been used to display tabular data. The ability to display a table without borders and the fact the each cell is essentially a miniature HTML document presents the opportunity to create interesting and useful effects.

The HTML code, including Netscape's enhancements, used in the construction of table include:

Opening Tag	Closing Tag	Description
Table Definition		
<TABLE>	</TABLE>	No border or special effects
<TABLE BORDER>	</TABLE>	Default border size of 1
<TABLE BORDER=n>	</TABLE>	Where n is border size in pixels
<TABLE CELLPADDING=n>	</TABLE>	Where n is cell padding size in pixels
<TABLE CELLSPACING=n>	</TABLE>	Where n is cell spacing size in pixels
<TABLE WIDTH=n>	</TABLE>	Where n is table width in pixels
<TABLE WIDTH=%>	</TABLE>	Where % is table width in % of page width
Table Data		
<TD>	</TD>	No special effects
<TD ALIGN=LEFT|RIGHT|CENTER>	</TD>	Horizontal alignment within cell
<TD VALIGN=TOP|MIDDLE|BOTTOM>	</TD>	Vertical alignment within cell
<TD WIDTH=n>	</TD>	Where n is cell width in pixels
<TD WIDTH=%>	</TD>	Where % is percentage of table
<TD COLSPAN=n>	</TD>	Where n is the number of columns to span
<TD ROWSPAN=n>	</TD>	Where n is the number of rows to span
Table Heading		
<TH>	</TH>	No special effects other than bold and centered
<TH ALIGN=LEFT|RIGHT|CENTER>	</TH>	Horizontal heading alignment within cell
<TH VALIGN=TOP|MIDDLE|BOTTOM>	</TH>	Vertical heading alignment within cell
<TH WIDTH=n>	</TH>	Where n is cell width in pixels
<TH WIDTH=%>	</TH>	Where % is percentage of table
<TH ROWSPAN=n>	</TH>	Where n is heading span in number of rows
<TH COLSPAN=n>	</TH>	Where n is heading tspan in number of columns
Caption		
<CAPTION>	</CAPTION>	Caption with no special effects
<CAPTION ALIGN=TOP|BOTTOM>	</CAPTION>	Caption above or below the table

Tables are part of the proposed HTML 3.0 standard, sometimes called the HTML+ standard. Some things are almost certain to change and additional constructs may be added. Do not use tables unless you're prepared to perform fairly heavy maintenance on your documents.

Different table effects may not look the same, or may not display at all, on a different browser, or even using the same browser with a different user-specified background color. Don't assume that the viewer of your document will see the same screen that you see.

Chapter 14

Unlocking the Mysteries of CGI

The world of truly interactive Web pages is waiting for you. All you need to know is a little about Common Gateway Interface (CGI) scripting.

My editor, Jeff Duntemann, jokingly calls us Webheads. My wife lovingly calls us Webaholics. I prefer something less pejorative, like slightly dysfunctional Web reclusives. Whatever the title, we've arrived at this lofty station in life by passing through three highly distinguishable phases on our way toward becoming a certified Web maniac: surfer, author/publisher, and programmer.

After operating as a Web surfer for a while, you'll know you're ready to move on when you have voluntarily visited ten different governmental home pages looking for design ideas. Another obvious sign is when you visit URoLette and the same site comes up for the third time. URoLette is a page at the University of Kansas that brings up a random site from a massive database each time you visit. The URL is:

```
http://www.cc.ukans.edu/cwis/organizations/kucia/
   uroulette/uroulette.html
```

The second phase (Web authoring) begins innocently enough when you decide that you want to publish your own home page. Of course, before you know it, you'll become a web publishing mogul and your home page directory will contain hundreds of html or htm documents. But the real fun (and obsession) begins when you start becoming interested in the *Common Gateway Interface* (CGI) and start writing your own scripts.

In this chapter I'll show you the basics of how to write CGI scripts. These scripts are very useful because they allow you to make your Web pages much more dynamic. With them, your users will be able to search for information, fill out forms, and send you feedback, and you can send custom messages back to your users. We'll start by discussing what CGI scripts are and how they work. Then, we'll create a few of our own. If you get the scripting bug, you can take the sample scripts presented and modify them to create your own custom scripts. In the next chapter we'll go one step further and look at how scripts work with HTML forms.

MEET JON, THIS CHAPTER'S CO-AUTHOR

One of my favorite discussion lists is html-list@netcentral.net. (The subscription details for this list are presented at the end of this chapter.) As the name implies, this group discusses HTML issues such as standards, problems, and tools. Jon Lewis, jlewis@inorganic5.chem.ufl.edu, is a major contributor to the list. He also runs a Web server at the University of Florida, http://inorganic5.chem.ufl.edu. Jon is a walking depository of information about HTML, servers, and—you guessed it—CGI. After several e-mail discussions with Jon, I convinced him that if he helped with this chapter, he would become instantly famous. After a little arm-twisting, he agreed. Am I a smooth-talking Yankee, or are graduate students just gullible? We ultimately decided to co-author this chapter and the next one by splitting the work equally. I did all the easy parts and Jon did all the difficult parts—as I said, 50/50.

WHAT IS A SCRIPT?

Your first question might be, what are Common Gateway Interface scripts? The vast majority of documents you have retrieved on the Web are purely passive. You retrieve them and they arrive just as their authors wrote them, weeks or even months before. Your home page is one example. You create a document with an .html extension (.htm if you're on a DOS server) and everyone in the world visiting your home page sees pretty much the same thing. Web browsers read in the HTML codes stored in the document and display appropriate text and graphics. When you are accessing an HTML document, all you can do is view what is displayed and select links to view additional information. HTML by itself provides no direct way for you to receive customized information or to send information back to a Web server.

A script, on the other hand, is an executable file of some type. It serves as the dynamic communication link between a Web server computer and a computer that is running a Web browser like Netscape. The purpose of a script is illustrated in Figure 14.1. As you can see, a script gathers information from a user, sends the information to a host computer and performs specialized commands, and then sends the results back to the user. In a nutshell, these are the general operations that a basic computer program performs. When a script needs to communicate with a user, it generates custom HTML documents "on the fly" and sends them down to the user's Web browser.

Now that you know that CGI scripts are your two-way link to the outside world, your next question might be, what are scripts used for? Let's look at an example. Assume you have a database on your computer of the best bird watching sites in your part of the country. You could create a script so that Web surfers who come to your Web site could access your database using a simple fill-in-the-blanks form. They could query for information, such as where is the best place to look for cardinals or brown towhees, and the results could be displayed—complete with nice pictures of the requested bird species. Of course, gathering and processing information is just one type of operation that can be programmed with CGI scripts. You can also use them to process forms, display information like the date and time, or keep track of the number of people who come to visit your home page.

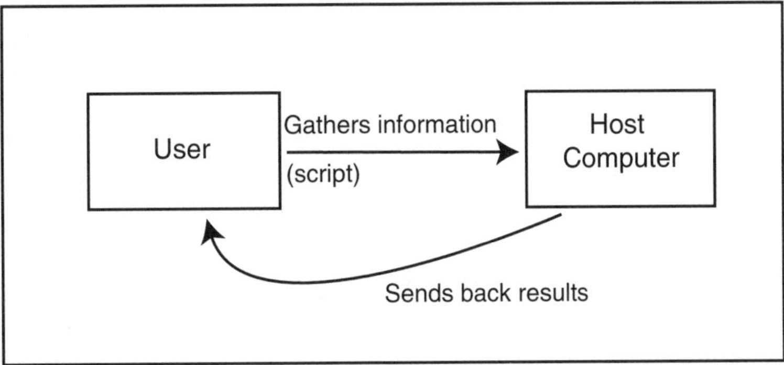

Figure 14.1 *How CGI scripts work.*

How Can You Tell when Scripts Are Used?

When you are accessing a Web site that uses CGI scripts, you can sometimes tell that a script is being executed when you see the words "cgi-bin" in a URL as you are accessing a specific "document." This isn't always the case—but it's an important hint. A better clue is the presence of any "control" on an HTML form—a push button, an edit box, a group of check boxes or radio buttons—anything by which the user can enter data into the HTML document and thus "talk back" to the Web server. Other clues are the presence of customized information in an HTML document—the current time or date, or some other data that seems specific to the time you fetched the document or to your location.

How Are Scripts Executed?

When the URL of an HTML document with an associated CGI script is selected by clicking on a link in a Web page, the script (which is named in the HTML file) is located on the server computer and then launched for execution. The script will take input from the browser (if it needs any) and perform a specific action, such as searching a database or performing some calculation. It may then respond to the user by issuing customized, script-generated HTML to the user's Web browser.

Do You Need to Use a Programming Language to Create Scripts?

Yes and no. The real answer to this question depends on what you consider a programming language. If you have never written a computer program before, or used or written batch files such as DOS .bat files, you might be feeling a little put off by all of this talk about scripting, programming, and writing batch commands. But don't panic yet. The basics of script writing are easy to master. In fact, you're halfway there if you already know HTML, because you know how to compose commands to display output in a Web browser.

The best part about CGI scripts is that they can be written using a number of different languages and techniques. The actual executable script on a Web site may be a Unix script file, which functions much like a DOS batch file. It contains relatively simple Unix commands. This type of CGI script may also be an executable program produced by a programming language. One widely used language for doing this is called *Perl*. Fairly complicated scripts are frequently written in the C programming language. (Don't worry—we won't be programming in C in this book!)

Don't make the mistake of assuming that CGI itself is a programming language. It's actually just a set of conventions or protocol for setting up two-way communication between a computer running a Web browser and a computer running a server. The script itself may be written in a traditional programming language like C, C++, or Pascal, or the script may be written in a higher-level "shell" language. In this book, I'll be using the Unix bourne shell called *sh* to write scripts. This is a good place to start because most Web servers run on Unix machines and this Unix shell language is easy to learn. If you are writing scripts for a server that runs on another type of computer such as a PC, you should easily be able to convert the scripts presented.

What Do You Need to Run Scripts?

The only thing you'll need to run the scripts you write is access to a Web server. You can write your scripts on your own PC and download them to your server, or you can log onto your server and create your scripts there. If you are running your own server, you're all set.

When you copy a script file to the server you are using, you must make sure that you put it in a directory where it can be located. You'll need to make sure that your server is configured to accept script requests from Web browsers. If you are not sure how to do this, you'll need to talk to the person in charge of running your Web server. Most servers set aside a subdirectory named /cgi-bin for storing script files. When a user performs an action with a Web browser, such as clicking on a hyperlink or selecting a form button, the corresponding script is located and executed.

What's the Best Way to Learn How to Create Scripts?

The first phase of scripting involves creating a simple but customized HTML document, such as one to display the current date to the user. The script's simple job is to merge "boilerplate" HTML lines with customized text and send the generated HTML document to the user.

The second phase gets a little more mystical. It involves setting up the interaction between the script and the user. The script initially prompts the user for some information and does something with the information. Then, it sends the results back to the user. As an example, I could ask you for an e-mail address and subsequently display the resulting "finger" information. We might also ask a user for a file name, then perform an Archie search and subsequently display the results. The trick here is to have the same script do both parts of the transaction. It must first ask for information and then the same script must respond to the information in some fashion.

These more sophisticated scripts set up and process HTML forms, which can be used to process more than one piece of information at a time. Handy features such as radio buttons and check boxes may be included on forms, increasing the user-friendliness. We'll take a closer look at forms in the next chapter.

Unlike HTML files, which you can view with Netscape, scripts are usually tucked away in special directories on Web servers, and they typically can't be accessed from outside the server system. If you're friendly with the person who runs your Web server, you might ask him or her to show you some scripts that others have written.

As you are surfing the Web, you might want to keep a close eye out for Web sites that use CGI scripts. Although you won't be able to look at the actual scripts, it will give you more insight into the type of operations that can be performed with scripts. As an example, if you are using a Web page such as the WebCrawler and you click on the Search button, a script named WebQuery will execute. This process is illustrated in Figure 14.2. Notice that the Location: text box contains a URL that references the script:

```
http://webcrawler.cs.washington.edu/cgi-bin/WebQuery
```

The giveaway is the part of the URL that contains /cgi-bin/WebQuery.

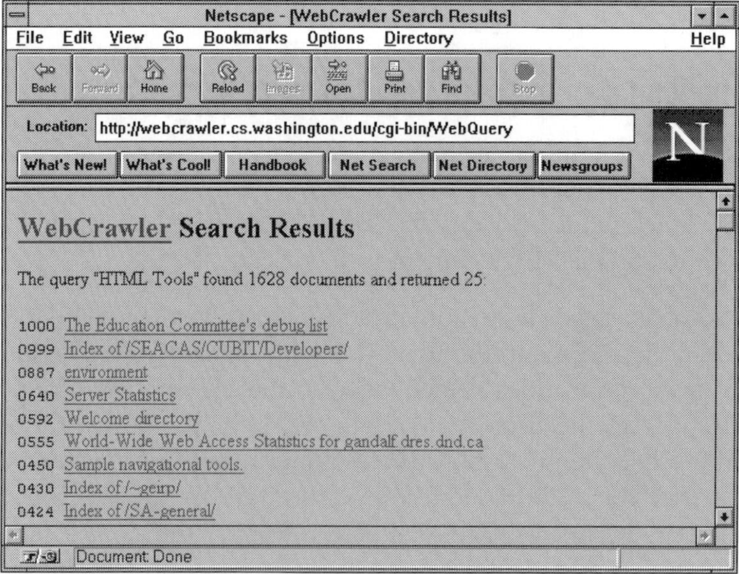

Figure 14.2 How the WebCrawler uses a script to search a database.

The first script we'll build in this chapter will display the current date and time on the user's screen. Whenever the user immediately reloads our URL, a new time will be delivered. (Maybe even a new date will be displayed if they are literally burning the midnight oil.) This script will get you started. If you are feeling really brave, you'll want to modify it to add other features.

Do You Need to Become a Unix Expert?

I've tried to shield you from dreaded Unix commands up until now. Unfortunately, we can't put it off any longer. Since some readers may already know Unix, I'll skip the basic Unix introductions in this chapter. But don't despair if you are not one of the chosen few, because Appendix B provides a Unix survivor's guide. As the name implies, it's a gentle introduction to Unix and it covers much of what you need to know so you can get started down the path of CGI scripting. Appendix C is a guide to Unix macros and scripts. The general concept of performing quasi-programming is explained in this appendix. Unless you're a Unix whiz, you might want to at least skim those two appendixes.

What Time Is It in Tuckerton?

In this project we'll develop a CGI script that will return your Web server's local time and date when queried by a remote browser. Once you know how to create a functional script, you'll be surprised how easy it is to expand.

To create our first script, we'll work backwards starting with something we already know how to do—HTML coding. We'll set up a simple HTML document and then convert it into a CGI script using Unix shell commands. Once the script is finished and loaded on your Web server, you can link one of your Web pages to it by setting up a simple link.

Figure 14.3 shows how Netscape displays a Web page that uses our script. What distinguishes this document from many other Web documents is that the time and date will be different each time the URL is accessed.

The first step for creating our script is to build a file representing a minimal HTML document structure. Although most Web browsers will recognize a document without **<HTML>**, **<HEAD>**, and **<BODY>** tag pairs, let's conform to the standard and get into the habit of producing *good* HTML—as opposed to HTML that simply works. Open your favorite editor and enter:

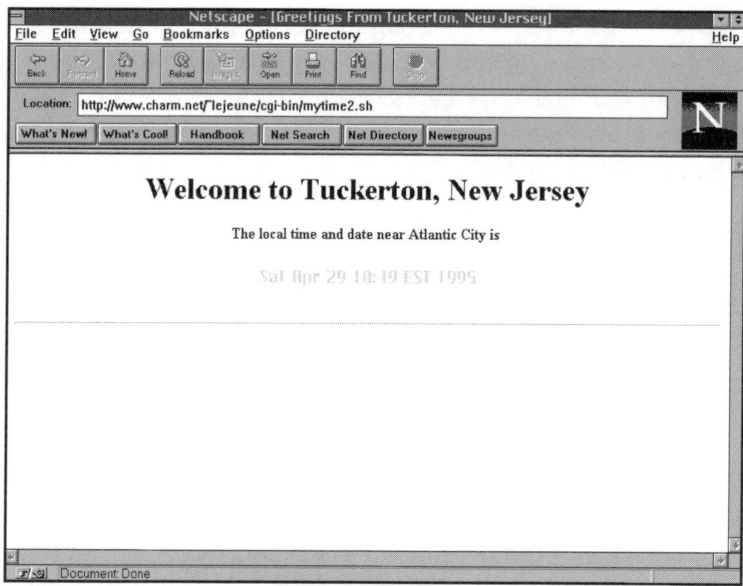

Figure 14.3 *Netscape's display of our first CGI script.*

```
<HTML>
   <HEAD>
   </HEAD>

   <BODY>
   </BODY>
</HTML>
```

You might even want to use the *Web Spinner* or the *HTML Assistant* editor provided on the companion CD-ROM, which will help you automate the work of entering the HTML tags. Remember that everything in the document is between the **<HTML>** pair; therefore, the **<HEAD>** pair is indented as is the **<BODY>** pair. Let's now add a few components to make this HTML document more specific for our local date and time example:

```
<HTML>
   <HEAD>
     <TITLE>Greetings From Tuckerton, New Jersey</TITLE>
   </HEAD>

   <BODY>
      <H1>Welcome to Tuckerton, New Jersey</H1>
      <H4>The local time and date near Atlantic City is</H4>
      The local date and time will go here.
   </BODY>
</HTML>
```

To get a little more creative, we could also add a little Netscape centering. The new centering feature is one of the few Netscape HTML enhancements we can use with impunity. If a visitor's browser doesn't support centering, the output is left justified as if the center tags weren't even there. Here's the final (for a while, at least) version of the body section:

```
<BODY>
   <CENTER>
     <H1>Welcome to Tuckerton, New Jersey</H1>
     <H4>The local time and date near Atlantic City is</H4>
     The local date and time will go here
  </CENTER>
</BODY>
```

In a Unix environment, you'll want to save this file as mytime.html. (If you're working on a PC, give the file an .htm extension for now. If you later need to copy the file to a Unix server, you may need to change the extension to .html when you copy the file.)

Next, let's test the file. Fire up your Web browser, and open the HTML file. When you're satisfied the file works as planned, you'll be ready for step two—turning the file into a real script.

I like to use the extension .sh to name my script files. If you are working on a PC, copy mytime.htm to mytime.sh. If you are working on a host Unix server, copy mytime.html to mytime.sh so you can transform it into a Unix executable script. The copy command for Unix is:

```
unix% cp mytime.html mytime.sh
```

By storing all of my Unix script files with the "sh" extension, I can perform directory listings like:

```
unix% ls -la *.sh
```

and easily view all of my script files.

Creating the Script

What we must do now is modify the newly created mytime.sh file to become an executable script. This involves creating an executable program of some sort that issues the text that makes up your HTML file, line by line. When executed, the script will produce an HTML document on the fly and send it down to the user's browser. The HTML output will be the same as the output from the original file. We can test the script by capturing its output to a file so that it can be checked before putting the script on a Web server.

A script is a series of lines, each of which is an executable statement. Technically, more than one statement can appear on a line, but let's keep life simple. A Unix script, as with a DOS batch file, executes when its name is entered as a command.

The file we've created so far simply contains HTML tags, which unfortunately are not executable statements. There are two different ways we can covert the HTML so that it can be executed as a script which produces output. The first method involves using the DOS-like **echo** command. Here's an example:

```
echo "<HTML>"
```

This statement is now a valid Unix command, which will output **<HTML>** as text. To preserve indentation in the output, you can use leading spaces, such as:

```
echo "  <HEAD>"
```

I'll show you the second method (which Jon prefers) for building scripts from HTML files shortly.

Using the **echo** statement, we can easily convert our complete HTML file into an executable script:

```
echo "<HTML>"
echo "   <HEAD>"
echo "     <TITLE>Greetings From Tuckerton, New Jersey</TITLE>"
echo "   </HEAD>"
echo "   <BODY>"
echo "     <CENTER>"
echo "        <H1>Greetings From Tuckerton, New Jersey</H1>"
echo "        <H4>Tuckerton in near Atlantic City, New Jersey</H4>"
echo "        The local date and time will go here."
echo "      <CENTER>"
echo "   </BODY>"
echo "</HTML>"
```

Notice how the double quotation marks are used to preserve formatting.

Now that we have a file in script form, the next step is to make it executable. We'll use the Unix change mode command, **chmod**, to make the transition.

Here's the command that should be executed to convert mytime.sh to an executable script:

```
unix% chmod 700 mytime.sh
```

Here I'm using the prompt "unix%" to indicate a Unix command line. This prompt will certainly be different on your system. The **chmod** command simply converts the file attributes of the mytime.sh file so that Unix will treat it as an executable file. Without doing that, it's simply text.

Now we're ready to take our script for a spin. Enter this command at the Unix command line:

```
unix% mytime.sh
```

You'll the see this output:

```
unix% mytime.sh
<HTML>
  <HEAD>
    <CENTER>
    <TITLE>Greetings from Tuckerton, New Jersey</TITLE>
    </CENTER>
  </HEAD>
  <BODY>
    <CENTER>
    <H1>Welcome to Tuckerton, New Jersey</H1>
    <H4>The local time and date near Atlantic City is</H4>
     local time and date will go here.
    </CENTER>
    <HR>
  </BODY>
</HTML>
unix%
```

We now have a program that emits HTML. We're looking good! Let's now make this script display the current time and date. We can use the Unix **date** command to do exactly that. (Remember, the purpose of a script is to execute Unix commands.) Change the line containing:

```
echo "      local time and date will go here."
```

to:

```
/bin/date
```

Notice that we are also specifying the path (/bin/) where the **date** program is located. It's a good idea in Unix (or DOS for that matter) to include a path to the desired executable file. (More on this shortly.)

Since the **echo** command directs its output to the terminal, let's redirect the output from our script to a file using the ">" redirection command. And now, here's the acid test:

```
unix% mytime.sh > temp.html
```

This command looks a little strange but it's actually easy to understand. It simply executes the script mytime.sh and redirects its output to a file named temp.html. But here's a general word of caution about using the Unix ">" redirection symbol. If the file on the right side of the ">" already exists, it's history when you execute the command. If the file doesn't exist, it's created.

If you are using a Unix system that has the Lynx program available, you can test your script in text-mode by entering this command at the Unix command line:

```
unix% lynx temp.html
```

This command passes the newly created output of our script to Lynx. The result, which will appear on the screen, should be:

```
Greetings from Tuckerton, New Jersey

                      WELCOME TO TUCKERTON, NEW JERSEY

    The local time and date near Atlantic City is

   Fri Apr 21 09:27:29 GMT 1995
__________________________________________________
```

We made it! You might want to take a look at the contents of temp.html. The Unix **more** command displays on the screen, one screenful at a time. Enter:

```
unix% more temp.html
```

To finish, you'll want to add the following five lines at the top of your script:

```
#!/bin/sh
# Script mytime.sh - displaying local time and  date - was written by Urb
   LeJeune, lejeune@acy.digex.net
echo Content-type: text/html
echo
```

The first line is an incantation telling Unix which script to run rather than any script just hanging around doing nothing. The script "sh" is conceptually somewhat like the DOS program command.com, in that both are command interpreters. The Unix script interpreter is usually called a *shell*, hence the term "shell account." Unix installations typically support a variety of shell scripts so the first line

```
#!/bin/sh
```

explicitly states *which* shell should be executed. The default shell on systems may vary, and explicit statements like this guarantee uniformity of command response when your script runs. This is very important because there are many syntactical differences in scripting languages.

The second line is a comment attesting to your authorship and script purpose. In Unix the "#" symbol starts a comment. Everything between a "#" and the end of the line is considered a comment and is not executable. The "#" tells Unix to ignore anything following the symbol. It's a good idea to use comments so others can understand your logic.

The fourth line, starting with **echo** is a message the server sends to the browser, stating the sort of creature to expect—in this case an HTML document. A browser typically knows what to expect based upon the file extension specified in the URL. For example, index.html tells the server the name of the document to return, and it also tells the browser to expect an HTML formatted document.

There is a snag with scripts, however. When a script creates a dynamic HTML document on the fly, there is no file extension to guide the browser. The first thing our dynamic HTML document must send to the browser is "Content-type: text/html" (followed by a mandatory blank line) indicating that an HTML or text document will be arriving shortly. The fourth line in the script, which contains only the command **echo**, is necessary to produce the mandatory blank line following the "Content-type: text/html" statement. Simply leaving a blank line in the script file won't do it!

Here is the script mytime.sh in its final form:

```
#!/bin/sh
# Script mytime.sh - displaying local time and  date - was written by Urb
   LeJeune, lejeune@acy.digex.net
echo "Content-type: text/html"
```

```
echo
echo "<HTML>"
echo "  <HEAD>"
echo "    <CENTER>"
echo "    <TITLE>Greetings from Tuckerton, New Jersey</TITLE>"
echo "    </CENTER>"
echo "  </HEAD>"
echo "  <BODY>"
echo "    <CENTER>"
echo "    <H1>Welcome to Tuckerton, New Jersey</H1>"
echo "    <H4>The local time and date near Atlantic City is</H4>"
  TZ=EST5EST /bin/date
echo "    </CENTER>"
echo "    <HR>"
echo "  </BODY>"
echo "</HTML>"
```

There's still one line in this file that needs a little explanation:

```
TZ=EST5EST /bin/date
```

When executed, our previous script produced output in Greenwich Mean Time (GMT). The prefix "TZ=EST5EST" is required to produce an output in Eastern Standard Time (EST). You may or may not need it. Try /bin/date, without the prefix first. If you're not in the EST zone, check with your system administrator for the correct syntax.

Using the Script

Where you put the script, if indeed you can use scripts at all, depends upon your Internet provider. Check with them for details. As I mentioned before, the script will almost always go in a subdirectory called /cgi-bin.

To use the script with a Web page, I include an anchor, such as the following:

```
<A HREF="http://charm.net/~lejeune/cgi-bin/mytime.sh">Show me the date and
time</A>
```

When a user clicks on the hyperlink, "Show me the date and time," the script that is stored on my server executes. Typically, when you click on a link, an HTML file is loaded. But in this case, the link accesses the /cgi-bin subdirectory where my scripts are stored and it runs mytime.sh. The script itself returns a set of HTML commands that are displayed in Netscape.

Now you see how easy it is to use CGI scripts to communicate with a Web server. We've already seen the Web page created by this script in Figure 14.3.

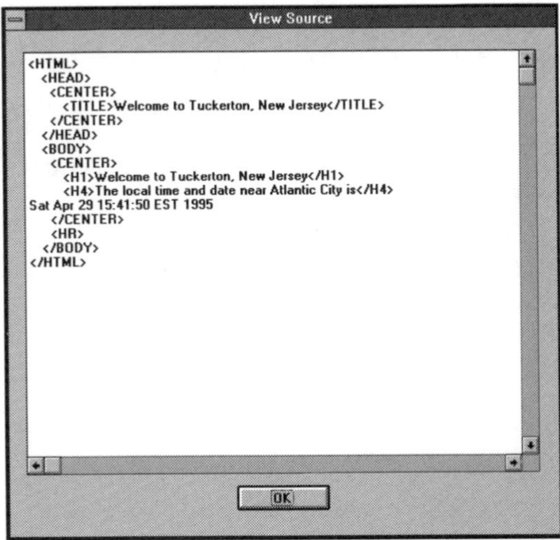
View Source
<HTML>
<HEAD>
<CENTER>
<TITLE>Welcome to Tuckerton, New Jersey</TITLE>
</CENTER>
</HEAD>
<BODY>
<CENTER>
<H1>Welcome to Tuckerton, New Jersey</H1>
<H4>The local time and date near Atlantic City is</H4>
Sat Apr 29 15:41:50 EST 1995
</CENTER>
<HR>
</BODY>
</HTML>
OK

***Figure 14.4** The "document" that was sent by executing script mytime.sh.*

If you execute Netscape's sequence View | Source, the HTML that is received by Netscape is displayed as shown in Figure 14.4.

EXPLORER
PROJECT

What Time Is It in Tuckerton? Part 2

In this project we'll develop a CGI script that improves upon the script created in the first project. We'll use a different method of building the script and we'll also get fancier with some time and date formatting.

We'll name the new script that we create mytime2.sh. We'll actually be building this script in a few parts. The first part will contain the main text for the Web page that is produced by the script. Then, we'll use a special form of the Unix **date** command to display the date and time in a unique format. Finally, the last part of the script will contain the closing HTML tags for the script.

If you recall from the previous script project, we needed to use a number of **echo** commands to transmit HTML lines from a Web server (where the script is running) to a Web browser. Fortunately, Unix provides a command we can use to get rid of all of those **echo** commands. This command **cat**, for concatenate, allows us to join multiple text lines into one long string. Here's how this command is used:

```
cat<<user-supplied-label

user-supplied-label
```

Essentially, **cat** tells Unix to treat everything between the two statements as multi-line input. The labels may be anything you choose, but they must both be the same. Remember once again, Unix is case sensitive.

In the first part of the mytime2.sh script, here's how the **cat** command is set up:

```
# Script mytime2.sh by Urb LeJeune lejeune@acy.digex.net and
# Jon Lewis, jlewis@inorganic5.chem.ufl.edu. Demonstrates formatted date
cat << Part1
Content-type: text/html

<HTML>
   <HEAD>
      <CENTER>
         <TITLE>Welcome to Tuckerton, New Jersey</TITLE>
      </CENTER>
   </HEAD>
   <BODY>
       <CENTER>
         <H1>Welcome to Tuckerton, New Jersey</H1>
         <H4>The local time and date near Atlantic City is</H4>
Part1
```

Here we start out with two comment lines. Next, comes the **cat** command. Notice that the label used to group the text is "Part1". Note also the blank line following the "Content-type: text/html" line. A Web browser will not handle the document properly unless there is a blank line following the "Content-type" line. (The blank line indicates to the browser that the "Content-type" header ends and that the content itself follows.) That's all there is to the first part of this script. Let's now add the **date** command.

The Unix **date** command has a variety of formatting switches. Formatted date output is indicated by an argument enclosed within double quotes. Date formatting begins with a "+", followed by the information telling the command what information to display and how to display it. The format specifications use the percent sign "%". A few of the more common ones are seen in Table 14.1.

Let's use a few of these formatting codes to display the date and time. Here are the commands needed to do this work:

```
TZ=EST5EST /bin/date "+The time in Tuckerton is %I:%M %p %Z or %H:%M if \
you like 24 hour time."
echo "<BR><BR>"
TZ=EST5EST /bin/date "+Today is %A: %B %d, which is day %j of %Y"
```

Table 14.1 Formatting Switches for the Unix date Command

Description	Switch	Parameter
Year	y	95
	Y	1995
Month	m	12
	b	Dec
	b	December
Day	a	Mon
	A	Monday
Day of Month	d	18
Hour	I	00 to 12
	H	00 to 23
Minute	M	23
Second	S	58
AM/PM	P	pm
Time	t	12:45:58
Day of Year	j	145

Produce Your Own Manual

You can get documentation for all the Unix commands available on your server computer by entering this command:

```
unix% man <command-name>
```

This command produces a manual for the specified parameter. Here's an example of how you can view the manual for the **date** command:

```
unix% man date
```

To create your own copy of the manual, use the Unix redirection symbol ">", as shown:

```
unix% man date > date.man
```

This produces a file named date.man to store the output of the **man date** command.

We're now ready to finish the last part of our script. Here's all we need:

```
cat << Part2
   </CENTER>
    <HR>
</BODY>
</HTML>
Part2
```

The output from this script is shown in Figure 14.5.

Let's Get Fancy

To update our script we'll want to add a little pizzazz. Let's display a few GIFs and add some gingerbread to the bottom of the "document." As mentioned earlier, most CGI scripts are placed in a Unix subdirectory called /cgi-bin. The majority of time this directory is directly subordinate to the directory holding the conventional HTML documents. Let's assume this is the case.

When referencing URLs within a document, it is highly desirable to preserve relative addressing. On my provider's machine, HTML documents for use by a Web server are placed in a directory called public_html. The use of a directory named public_html is rapidly becoming a standard. The URL

```
http://www.charm.net/~lejeune/cgi-bin/mytime2.sh
```

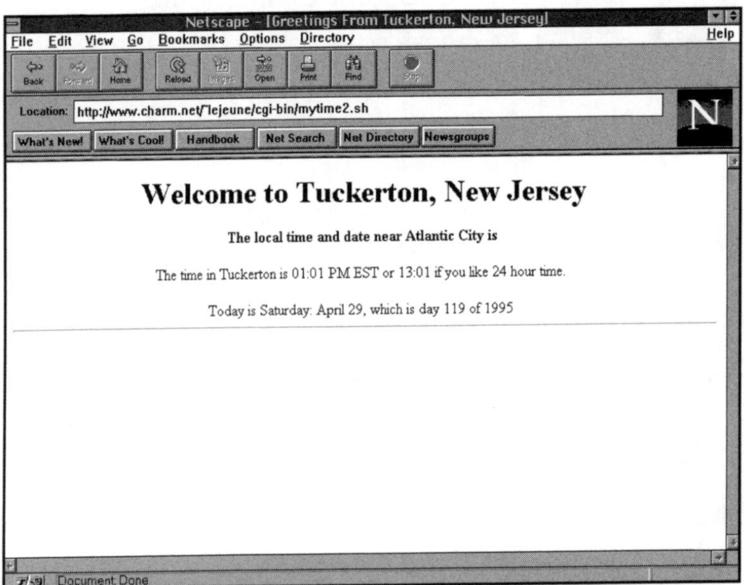

Figure 14.5 The output from the CGI script mytime2.sh.

indicates several things. First, "~lejeune" is a *symbolic link.* This link is shorthand for a much longer path name. In addition to brevity, symbolic links permit changing paths, or even servers, without the outside world being aware that a change has been made. Again in my specific—although common—case, the symbolic path terminates in a directory named public_html. The subdirectory /cgi-bin is therefore a child of directory public_html. Most administrators managing Web servers only allow executable files in the directory /cgi-bin. If we want our script to include a reference to a graphics file such as a GIF, we must "point" to another directory. To illustrate, assume directory public_html holds a graphic called home.gif. In Unixspeak (as well as DOS) a parent directory may symbolically be referenced by "..". Our pseudo document may therefore include a graphics link to home.gif in the following form:

```
<IMG SRC="../home.gif">
```

This is functionally the same thing as saying:

```
<IMG SRC="/public_html/home.gif""
```

The advantage of this notation is portability. If I were to move to another provider having a directory structure of

```
/html/cgi-bin
```

the first notation would still work, but the second would not.

Here's the complete listing of our new fancy-smantzy Tuckerton time script:

```
#!/bin/sh
# Script mytime2.sh by Urb LeJeune lejeune@acy.digex.net
# Jon Lewis, jlewis@inorganic5.chem.ufl.edu. Demonstrating
# Date formatting and relative graphics referencing

cat << Partl
Content-type: text/html

<HTML>
  <HEAD>
     <CENTER>
        <TITLE>Greetings from Tuckerton, New Jersey</TITLE>
     </CENTER>
  </HEAD>
  <BODY>
```

```
      <CENTER>
      <H1>Welcome to Tuckerton, New Jersey</H1>
      <H4>The local time and date near Atlantic City is</H4>
Part1

      TZ=EST5EST /bin/date "+The time in Tuckerton is %I:%M %p %Z or %H:%M if \
      you like 24 hour time."
      echo "     <BR><BR>"
TZ=EST5EST /bin/date "+Today is %A: %B %d, which is day %j of %Y"

cat << Part2

     <P>
       <A HREF="../index.html"l>
         <IMG ALIGN=CENTER SRC="../home.gif">
           Visit my home page</A>

       <A HREF="../urb-book.html">
         <IMG ALIGN=CENTER SRC="../up-arrow.gif">
         The Netscape EXplorer Main Page</A><BR>

       Created by Urb LeJeune
       <A HREF="mailto:lejeune@acy.digex.net">
         <IMG ALIGN=CENTER SRC="../mailbutt.gif"> lejeune@acy.digex.net<P>

       <IMG SRC="../line.gif">
         </A>
     </CENTER>
   </BODY>
</HTML>
Part2
```

The URL that executes this script is:

```
http://www.charm.net/~lejeune/cgi-bin/mytime3.sh
```

The output of this script is shown in Figure 14.6.

A PEEK AT OTHER LANGUAGES

As scripts get more complicated they frequently are written in a scripting language called Perl or in the C programming language. Perl is somewhat like a hybrid between a Unix shell language and the C language. When learning any programming language, a student's first program is usually an ultra-simple one producing as output "Hello World." To give just a little taste of programming, here is a Perl "Hello World" script:

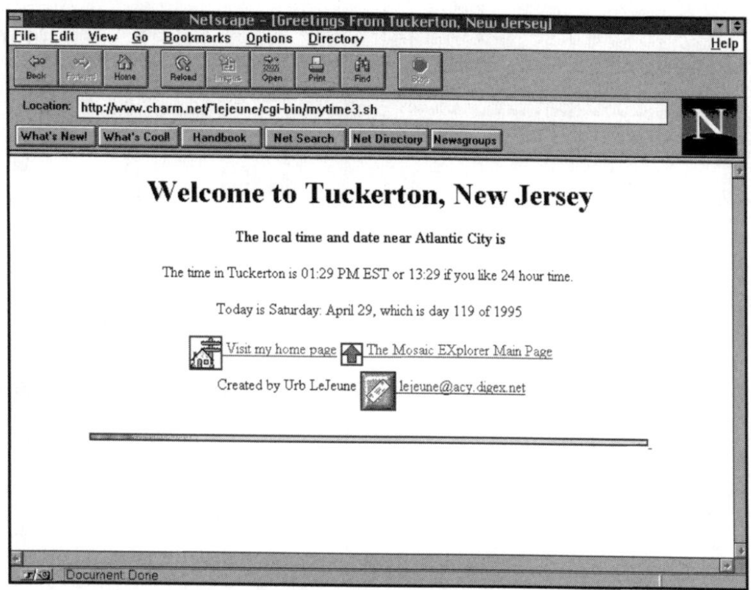

Figure 14.6 *The output produced when executing script mytime3.sh.*

```
#!/usr/bin/perl
# Script hello.pl is a demonstration "hello world" program by
# Urb LeJeune, lejeune@acy.digex.net.
print "Content-type: text/plain\n\n";
print
print "Hello, world!\n";
print "My name is Urb LeJeune\n";
print "My e-mail address is lejeuen@acy.digex.net\n";
```

Again note the empty print statement to produce the requisite blank line after the "Content-type" header.

Figure 14.7 demonstrates the output from one of the world's most useless programs. We'll look at some meaningful Perl in a future chapter. If you're desperate for things to do, check the output of this Perl script by pointing your browser to:

```
http://www.charm.net/~lejeune/cgi-bin/hello.pl
```

LET'S REVIEW

The Common Gateway Interface (CGI) is a standard that allows executable files to run as "custom extensions" of a Web server. These executable files are

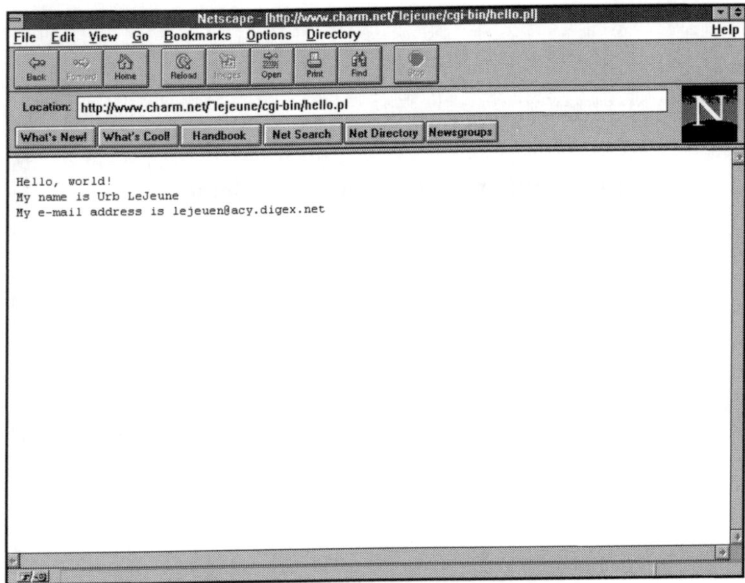

***Figure 14.7** The output produced by the world's most useless program.*

called *CGI scripts*. They can (as demonstrated in this chapter) create customized HTML content and (to be demonstrated in the next chapter) allow information to be sent to a Web server via HTML forms.

The simplest kind of CGI script is an executable program of some sort that creates lines of text formatted as HTML. This output is sent by the server to the Web browser as a dynamic HTML "document" created "on the fly." Ordinary, static HTML documents, by contrast, are created once and never change, and are always the same when downloaded.

A CGI script is an executable program written in any language capable of reading from standard input, writing to standard output, and accessing environment variables. Under Unix, most scripts are written in a scripting language such as Perl, although some more advanced scripts are written in C.

More advanced CGI scripts allow two-way communication between the browser and server. The output of a script may vary depending upon the input supplied by the user. This topic will be covered in the next chapter.

If you're starting to get into more exotic HTML, you might want to give the discussion list html-list a try. To subscribe, send a message to

```
listserv@netcentral.net
```

and in the body of the message put:

```
sub html-list <your-first-name> <your-last-name>
```

Well, there you have it. You're on your way to becoming a CGI junkie. Be forewarned, if you proceed into the next chapter and look at interactive scripting, there is no turning back.

Publishing with Forms

In the next leg of our Web publishing exploration, we'll look at techniques for using HTML forms and document queries to make our Web pages more interactive.

In the previous chapter we explored the CGI (Common Gateway Interface). We learned that CGI is used to communicate between a client and a server to perform all kinds of tasks, such as searching databases, performing calculations, and displaying such information as the current date and time. Although gateway scripts are extremely useful, they can't do everything by themselves. To really extend the power of scripts, we need a better way to get information from a Web page to a Web server and back again. That's where HTML document queries and forms come in.

In this chapter we'll explore the basics of using HTML to create document queries and forms. We'll also look at how we can write some basic scripts to process HTML forms. If you've never used forms in your Web pages, you'll be surprised at how flexible and powerful the key HTML tags are, such as **<FORM>** and **<INPUT>**.

Instead of jumping in and showing you how to compose forms using HTML tags, I'll first present the basics of document query techniques so that you can see the process involved in having interactive Web pages communicate with Web servers. Then, we'll start to build an HTML document that uses different form components—including text boxes, radio buttons, checkboxes, and menus. If you want to continue further by using other powerful form features, be sure to read Appendix A.

GETTING INPUT

To make the Web pages you publish more interactive, you'll need a way to get information from your users. For example, let's assume you want to publish a catalog featuring the products your company sells. To make this catalog a true sales-getter, you'll want to have an online order form that users can fill out. You can even provide a questionnaire to obtain important information about your customers. With HTML forms, gathering this kind of information is possible with only a little effort.

Without the ability to get input from users, your Web pages would be very limited. Sure, you could display information and provide links to hot Web sites, but you wouldn't be able to engage in two-way communication with your users. Fortunately, techniques for getting input from a user on the Web have been around for a while, even before features like graphical forms and buttons were implemented in HTML. Some of the earliest browsers were designed to be interactive. A user could enter a keyword; the keyword would then be sent to a Web server, and the server would search a database and return the result, nicely formatted. The original HTML specification provided a feature that sent a single piece of user-supplied information to a server. After this, the demand for more interactive communication grew so quickly that the HTML 2.0 specification provided the basis for reasonably complex interactive forms.

So, how does the communication system between a Web browser and a Web server operate? In a nutshell, this interactivity involves a five-step process:

1. The Web server script requests information from the user.
2. The user's Web browser supplies the requested information (input).
3. The server script processes the user-supplied information.
4. The server script returns the information (output) as a (hopefully) nicely formatted document.
5. The user tells everyone about the script writer's cleverness.

Okay, so it's really a four-step process. Of course, the CGI script is the glue that makes the communication process possible. As we learned in the previous chapter, a script is an executable set of computer instructions that can be written in many different languages, including Perl or the workhorse of all languages, C. But our mission in this chapter isn't to cover everything there is to know about scripting with CGI. (That would take a rather large book.) Instead, we'll focus on the interactive portion of the information exchange concept, with enough scripting thrown in to give you some examples that will get you started publishing more interactive Web pages.

DOCUMENT- AND FORM-BASED QUERIES

I'll be using the word query a lot in this chapter, so let's come up with a good definition: A *query* is essentially a request for information. When you run your favorite database program and it displays a field asking you to enter a specific piece of information, such as a customer's phone number or social security number, you are being queried by the program.

The interactive Web pages that you create can communicate information to Web servers in one of two ways: by *document-based queries* or *form-based queries*. The query used is actually performed by a CGI script; however, HTML does the work of setting up the query. Document-based queries have been around since the first version of HTML was unleashed. Form-based queries arrived with HTML 2.0 and continue to move into center stage with the evolution of the HTML 3.0 specification. The best way to understand the differences between these two types of queries is to look at an example.

A document-based query uses a special tag named **<ISINDEX>**. This tag is placed in the **<HEAD>** section of an HTML document. When the **<ISINDEX>** tag is encountered by a Web browser, some type of input prompt would be displayed so that the user could enter information. A script for a document-based query would generate HTML that would look something like this:

```
<HTML>
  <HEAD>
    <TITLE>Document Based Forms Demo</TITLE>
    <ISINDEX>
  </HEAD>

  <BODY>
    <H1>Document Based Forms Demo</H1>
        Your Body Text Goes Here
  </BODY>
</HTML>
```

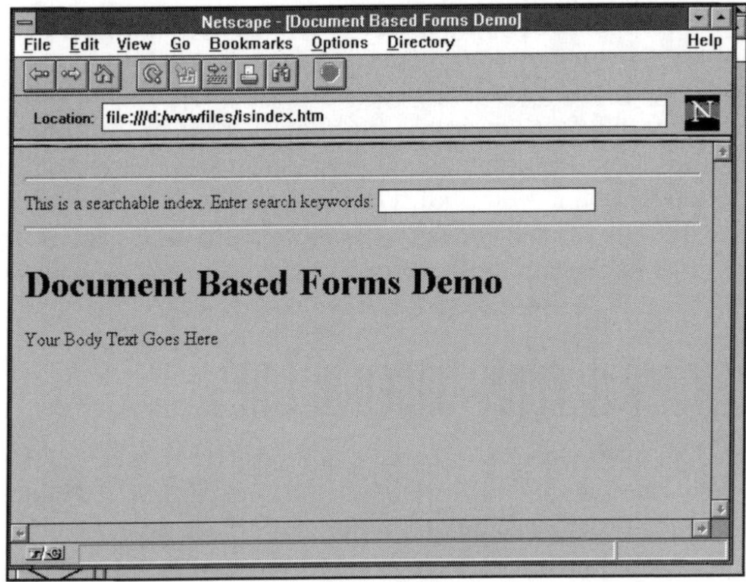

***Figure 15.1** The world's simplest document-based query.*

Figure 15.1 shows what this document looks like when it is displayed by Netscape. As you can see, it is a really simple query. When Netscape reads the **<ISINDEX>** tag, it displays a text box. The big drawback with a query like this: You can't select your own prompt. Another disadvantage is that you can't ask for more than one piece of information from the user. And there's yet another limitation: You can't place the text box that queries for information in a specific location relative to the remainder of the document. What you see in Figure 15.1 is all you get.

Anything this simple turns out to be rather inflexible. Form-based queries, on the other hand, allow you to support a substantial amount of interactive features. If you've seen any of the forms that have been included on Web pages during your surfing explorations, you know that form-based queries look much more interesting than the simple document-based query we just looked at. With forms, you can include text boxes, pop-up selection boxes, buttons, scrolling text windows, radio buttons, and a few other elements. And the best part is that you can place these objects wherever you want on your Web pages. This type of flexibility opens up a lot of publishing possibilities. Forms capabilities have even led to businesspeople staying up nights contemplating the kinds of businesses they can set up and the money that will pour in from their interactive, online ordering systems.

Until recently, lack of security has been a real deal breaker, putting a damper on the commercialization of the Internet. In theory, almost anyone can publish a set of Web pages that provides interactive forms to capture sensitive information, such as credit card or bank account numbers. Unfortunately, it's easy for unauthorized "information scoopers" to get at this data as it is being sent, especially if they are dedicated hackers. Secure Web servers, such as those supplied by Netscape, should make commercial use of the Web a reality. Experienced forms designers and CGI script writers may soon be in be high demand and short supply. So, read this chapter closely, do your homework, and get your resume out.

USING DOCUMENT-BASED QUERIES

Before we roll up our sleeves and start creating powerful forms, let's take a closer look at document-based queries. This will give you some techniques to help you better understand how communication links are established between Web pages and Web servers. Since the HTML part of document-based queries is really simple, we'll spend our time in this section discussing the role that CGI scripts play in processing simple queries. Here are the questions we'll answer:

- How does one script perform two jobs?
- How does a script receive its parameters?
- How are parameters used to perform different tasks?
- How are HTML documents sent?

Once you know how to set up communication links between a Web browser and a server, all you'll need to learn to create forms for Web pages are the basic HTML tags required for displaying and processing forms.

Performing Two Jobs with a CGI Script

A little sleight of hand occurs when a document-based query is processed. First, your browser sends a request and back comes a simple page with a single field that needs data. You enter the data and click on Submit, or in some cases you press Enter. Then, the information gets sent to the server and the same script executes, but this time the response is a formatted reply. What's going on here? How can the script know what to do each time it is called?

The script performs double duty by sensing the nature of the request. (Actually, the script only knows if the first request it receives is in fact the first one.) The difference between the requests is the presence (or absence) of the user-supplied data. In the world of computer programming, the supplied information is called a *parameter* or an *argument.* I prefer the term parameter; however, you will see both terms used in the scripting literature.

You've actually used parameters many times without realizing it. When you enter DIR (or dir) at the DOS command-line prompt, DOS supplies you with a directory listing of all file names and all file types in the current directory path. You receive a display of all files because the default parameter is *.*. (A default is what happens if you don't specify something else.) When you enter the command

```
C:\> DIRr *.BAT/P
```

DOS gives you a listing of all file names with a BAT extension (*.BAT) and it stops when the screen fills up waiting for you to press any key because you included the /P (for page) switch parameter. The output of the DIR command changes depending on the parameters you provide. Several different DIR commands each would produce different results; the same is true for CGI scripts that use parameters. Now you know the secret.

Creating a Document-Based Script

For this project we'll create a simple script to process a document-based query. The query will ask the user to input a string. The script then echoes the user's response. The trip we need to make goes like this:

1. From browser to server: request the URL
2. From server to browser: supply the simple form (document query)
3. From browser back to server: return the completed form
4. From server back to browser: process the supplied information and send a response

A script's ability to recognize whether a request is a "first request" requires a little programming logic. So, put your programming hat on. The logic that makes this black magic work looks something like this:

```
if this is the first time
  then
     send the user a simple fill-out form (document-based query)
```

```
  else
     process the passed parameter(s)
     create and send a report
end if
```

Let's write at an actual Unix script to perform the if-then-else logic, complete with feedback results.

```
#!/bin/sh

if [  $#  =  0  ]
  then # There is no passed parameter
    echo "There are no passed parameters."
  else  # There is a passed parameter
    echo "Whoopie! There is at least one passed parameter."
fi # end if
```

(If Unix scripts still make you feel nervous, spend a few minutes reading Appendix A and Appendix B.) The first line in our script is an incantation that tells Unix to execute the script using the sh shell. The syntax for the Unix **if** construct requires that we start with the keyword **if** and end with the keyword **fi** (which is "**if**" spelled backwards, of course). These Unix people are just too cute for words.

The **[$# = 0]** test looks scary. Actually, though, it simply asks if the number of passed parameters (**$#**) is equal to zero. Any number of statements may follow the required **then** keyword. The statements to be executed if our test is true must be enclosed between the **then** keyword and either the **else** or **fi**. The keyword **else** is optional, but if used, any number of statements may be embedded between the **else** and the **fi**. Anything between a **#** character and the end of the line is treated as a comment for humans and ignored by Unix. Try the above script to get the hang of it.

Parameter Magic

Let's now create a real script to see how a parameter can be passed. The script we'll use is named isindex.sh. (The complete script is shown at the end of this section.) What does the script do? When it starts, it displays an HTML document like the one shown in Figure 15.2. At first glance, you'll notice that the script looks like one we created in the previous chapter. The Web page displays a greeting, along with the current date and time. But the difference with this script is that a text box is displayed so that you can enter some information. If you look at the script, you'll see that the **<ISINDEX>** tag is included in the **<HEAD>** section of the HTML document generated by the script:

***Figure 15.2** The document returned when "isindex.sh" was executed for the first time.*

```
<HTML><HEAD>
    <CENTER>
        <TITLE>Welcome to Tuckerton, New Jersey</TITLE>
    </CENTER>
    <ISINDEX>
</HEAD>
```

The second part of the script performs some parameter magic. When the script is called with a parameter, a different HTML document will be displayed. We'll see what the second page looks like in a moment, but first let's see how the script is used.

As we learned in the previous chapter, executable scripts are almost always placed in a directory called /cgi-bin. The URL I use to activate the script on my Charm Net account would therefore be:

```
http://www.charm.net/~lejeune/cgi-bin/isindex.sh
```

When this URL is entered, the browser tells the Web server at www.charm.net to execute the script isindex.sh without any parameters. The script in turn generates an HTML document and sends it back to the browser. (This is the page shown in Figure 15.2.) The document displayed requests the user to enter a string in the text box at the top. If I enter "Search_Forms" the browser takes this string and appends it to the URL following a "?". The browser then sends the newly formulated URL back to the server. This time the URL will look like:

```
http://www.charm.net/~lejeune/cgi-bin/isindex.sh?Search_Forms
```

As you might have guessed, "Search_Forms" is the parameter for the isindex.sh script. The server then removes the URL component following the "?" and passes it to the script. The script can access the first parameter as **$1**, the second as **$2**, and so on. The script, using the if-then-else logic we explored in the previous section, gets the parameter to produce a second document.

Figure 15.3 displays the returned document. Notice the URL in the Location: box. The complete script for this act of magic is shown next. I've included the complete script file on the companion CD-ROM as isindex.sh. To use it, just copy it to your Web server and place it in a directory that you can access. Then, run Netscape and enter the URL and name of the script, just as I did earlier.

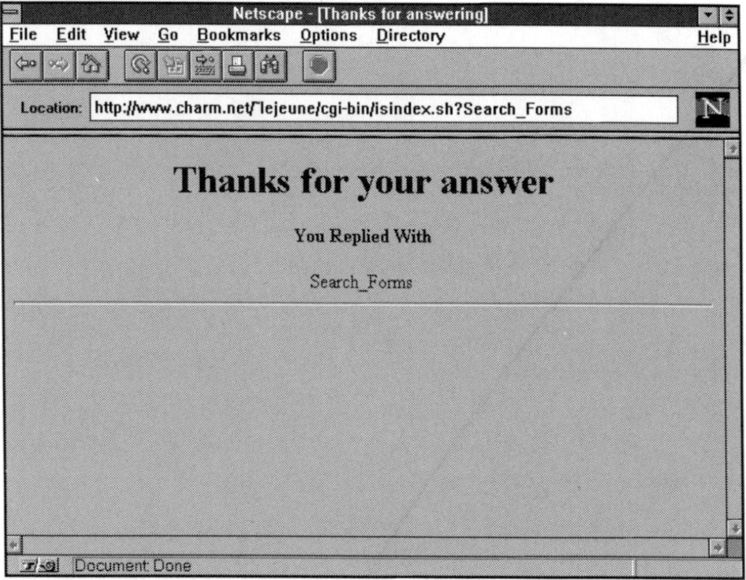

Figure 15.3 *The document returned when isindex.sh was executed with a parameter.*

```
#!/bin/sh
# Script isindex.sh by Urb LeJeune lejeune@acy.digex.net

if [ $# = 0 ]
  then # There is no passed parameter

cat << Part1
Content-type: text/html

<HTML><HEAD>
    <CENTER>
        <TITLE>Welcome to Tuckerton, New Jersey</TITLE>
    </CENTER>
    <ISINDEX>
</HEAD>
<BODY>
    <CENTER>
        <H1>Please enter a test string above</H1>
        <H2>Welcome to Tuckerton, New Jersey</H2>
        <H4>The local time and date near Atlantic City is</H4>
Part1

TZ=EST5EST /bin/date "+The time in Tuckerton is %I:%M %p %Z or %H:%M if \
   you like 24 hour time."
echo "<BR><BR>"
TZ=EST5EST /bin/date "+Today is %A: %B %d, which is day %j of %Y"

cat << Part2
   </CENTER>
    <HR>
</BODY>
</HTML>
Part2

else # There is a passed parameter
    # Create a document
cat << Part3
Content-type: text/html

<HTML><HEAD>
    <CENTER>
        <TITLE>Thanks for answering</TITLE>
    </CENTER>
</HEAD>
<BODY>
    <CENTER>
        <H1>Thanks for your answer</H1>
        <H4>You Replied With</H4>
$1

   </CENTER>
    <HR>
</BODY>
</HTML>
Part3
fi # end if
```

The **$1** about three-quarters of the way down in the listing references the first passed parameter. When the executing script encounters the **$1**, it expands the parameter and displays the value it contains. If any part of the isindex.sh script doesn't make sense, you may want to review the CGI chapter.

Supporting Multiple Options

A script may first request information. Next, it may do different things depending upon the parameters that are sent. Let's assume your first form requests the user to enter "m" for male or "f" for female. Different HTML documents could be returned by the script, based upon the user's gender answer. Here's an example of how this type of system could be set up:

```
#!/bin/sh
if [  $#  =  0  ]
  then # There is no passed parameter
     send form requesting information
  else  # There is a passed parameter
     if [  $1 = "m" ]
         then #  It's a male reply
           send male-related document
    else # There is a passed parameter but not "m"
      if [ $1 = "f" ]
        then # It's a female reply
          send female related document
    else # Invalid reply
        send error message and request "m" or "f" again
fi # end if
```

First, the script checks to see if a parameter has been sent. If one hasn't, the basic document-based query is sent to ask the user to enter a gender. The first **else** statement checks to see if an "m" response has been entered. In this case, the male-specific document would be sent to the user's browser. The second **else** statement looks for an "f" response and sends the female-specific document. Finally, notice that a third **else** statement handles an error condition. This is good practice, especially if you think your users might enter an incorrect response and you want to tell them what they've done wrong.

Sending Actual HTML Documents

In the above example, I showed how an actual prewritten HTML document could be sent by a script instead of having the script create the document on the fly. The syntax for doing this is:

```
Location: URL
required blank line
```

The **Location** line replaces the normal script output. When you use **Location**, you don't need to use Content-type (nor *can* you use it). The URL may be actual or relative. Let's assume we have two documents named male.html and female.html. They reside in the directory just above the /cgi-bin directory. The script shown above could then be written as:

```
#!/bin/sh
if [  $#  =  0  ]
  then # There is no passed parameter
     send form requesting information
  else  # There is a passed parameter
     if [  $1 = "m" ]
         then #  It's a male reply
           echo Location: ../male.html    # return male.html
           echo                                    #  required blank line
   else # There is a passed parameter but not "m"
      if [ $1 = "f" ]
        then # It's a female reply
           echo Location: ../female.html    # return female.html
           echo                                    #  required blank line
   else # Invalid reply
        send error message and request "m" or "f" again
fi # end if
```

The ".." instructs Unix (and DOS) to look one directory above the current directory. I've left the error processing for you to complete, as an exercise. (This is frequently a textbook author's euphemism for "I don't feel like doing it.")

FORM-BASED QUERIES

Now we're ready to move ahead to the good stuff. The document-based queries we've been exploring are not only limited but are also cumbersome to develop and write. Form-based queries, on the other hand, use prewritten HTML documents to request information from the user. CGI scripts only come into play when the server receives the user-supplied information.

Keep in mind that forms are a recent innovation and not all browsers support them. If you want to create interactive documents that will work with all browsers, you'll need to use the document-based query technique we introduced earlier.

Getting More Information About Forms

The National Center for Supercomputer Applications (NCSA) has an incredibly good forms tutorial set up as a set of Web pages you can explore. It's called *Supporting FORMS with CGI.* The tutorial contains an assortment of sample forms that illustrate many techniques for creating and processing forms. The URL for the tutorial is:

```
http://hoohoo.ncsa.uiuc.edu/cgi/forms.html
```

The NCSA folks have also provided two test servers to help you develop and test your forms. The server for testing forms using the POST method is:

```
http://hoohoo.ncsa.uiuc.edu/htbin-post/post-query
```

The server for testing forms using the GET method is:

```
http://hoohoo.ncsa.uiuc.edu/htbin/query
```

Creating Form-Based Queries

In this project we'll take the HTML document created in the previous project and modify it so that it uses HTML-generated forms. For a little fun, we'll change the displayed color of the document's normal text and also the color of the various links.

There is a lot to learn, and many obstacles to overcome before you can truly master forms. But creating forms is fun and rewarding once you get the hang of it. To get good at creating your own forms, you'll need to master these three different skills:

- Creating form components using HTML tags.
- Decoding the input the user replies to your forms.
- Creating scripts that process the user input.

In this section we'll concentrate only on the first skill, building HTML query forms. NCSA has provided test servers that will take the output from a completed form and echo the results. Even if you do not have access to a server, you can create interactive forms using a NCSA test server. Once you have fully tested your Web documents that use forms, you can write the scripts you need to perform the needed tasks at the server side.

Creating Forms with HTML

The general format of an HTML document that uses forms is:

```
<HTML>
    <HEAD>
        Normal heading stuff
    </HEAD>
    <BODY>
        Normal body stuff
        <FORM  form-specifications, normal text, and regular HTML formatting
           tags  </FORM>
        More normal body stuff
    </BODY>
</HTML>
```

The tag pair **<FORM> ... </FORM>** does the work of setting up a form. Within these tags, other form-related tags are placed—as you'll see shortly—to define the components of the form. A form-based query must have at least one input field. The input field can be a text box, radio buttons, drop-down menus, or check boxes. The components used in a form (text, input boxes, selection buttons, and so on) can be arranged in any combination. You can also use as many of these components as you like. Of course, if you clutter up your forms with too many options, they might become hard to use. As you gain more experience creating forms, you'll want to use such features as large text boxes with scroll bars, password fields, and even image maps.

Let's construct a simple form that uses a text box as the input field. We'll look at the important sections, then we'll build the whole enchilada. Here's the first part of our HTML document:

```
<HTML>
  <HEAD>
    <TITLE>Form Example One</TITLE>
  </HEAD>

  <BODY>
     <H1>One Text Box Form</H1>

     <H2>An example of a simple fill-out form using a text box</H2>
     <H4>The forms portion is enclosed between the two &lt;HR&gt;.
     <HR>
```

Everything in this listing should be familiar HTML stuff at this stage. Next, we need to set up the form:

```
<FORM METHOD="POST"
      ACTION="http://hoohoo.ncsa.uiuc.edu/htbin-post/post-query">
```

This is the start of the **<FORM>** section. Each form *must* have a **METHOD** attribute and an **ACTION** attribute. The **METHOD**, which can be either **POST** or **GET**, tells the script that processes the form how to handle the information the user provides when filling out the form. The **POST** setting tells the script that information is being sent to the server. The **GET** setting tells the script that information is being requested. The parameter for the **ACTION** attribute is a URL. It points to a program that decodes and processes the information. In this case, I'm using a script at NCSA called post-query to process the form.

Are you ready for the next step? To make the form useful, we need to have a way to get some input:

```
Input your name here: <INPUT TYPE ="text" NAME="USER-NAME">
Note that it has no default value. <P>
```

The **<INPUT>** tag is the component used to indicate that some type of input object should be displayed. In our case, we'll be displaying a text box. Two things are at work here. First, the **<INPUT>** includes the **TYPE** parameter to indicate the type of input item that is being created—a text box. Second, the **NAME** parameter assigns a name to the input field. You can supply any name that you like.

Next, we need a way to send form data to the server:

```
To submit the query, click on this button
<INPUT TYPE="submit"
       VALUE="Submit Query"> and you're done.<P>
```

We use another **<INPUT>** tag to define an additional **<FORM>** component. But this time, we are creating a submit button. The **VALUE** parameter is used to specify an initial value for the input item—in this case, the submit button. The following closing tags, and the second **<HR>** finish our document.

```
         Since there is only one field you can press Enter to submit.
     </FORM>
     <HR>
  </BODY>
</HTML>
```

One underlying concept in creating forms is something called *name/value* pairs. Each form component (text box, radio button, and so on) has a name assigned by the document's author. The name part is assigned a value when the user enters data. You can think of the *name* part as a placeholder (the slot) and the *value* part as the piece of information stored in the slot. If you have any programming experience, you can think of the *name* as the variable and the *value* as the variable's content. If you worked for the post office, you could think of the *name* as a mailbox and the *value* as the letter you need to stuff in the mailbox.

Figure 15.4 shows how Netscape displays our HTML document with our first form. If you enter "Urb LeJeune" in the requested field and click the Submit Query button, you'll get the NCSA server's reply, shown in Figure 15.5 The complete listing for forms1.htm is displayed next. Look at the output in Figure 15.4 and try to figure out what's happening. The file forms1.htm is also on the companion CD-ROM for you to experiment with.

```
<HTML>
  <HEAD>
    <TITLE>Form Example One</TITLE>
  </HEAD>

  <BODY>
     <H1>One Text Box Form</H1>

     <H2>An example of a simple fill-out form using a text box</H2>
     <H4>The forms portion is enclosed between the two &lt;HR&gt;.
     <HR>
     <FORM METHOD="POST"
                ACTION="http://hoohoo.ncsa.uiuc.edu/htbin-post/post-query">

          Input your name here: <INPUT TYPE="text" NAME="USER-NAME">
         Note that it has no default value. <P>

        To submit the query, click on this button
        <INPUT TYPE="submit"
                   VALUE="Submit Query"> and you're done.<P>
         Since there is only one field you can press Enter to submit.

     </FORM>
     <HR>
  </BODY>
</HTML>
```

How Do Forms Work?

In true explorer fashion, we've built a form without understanding how it actually works. So let's now review what we've done. **<FORM>** tags are paired, so there is always a closing **</FORM>** tag. All of the other form-related tags must be placed within this pair. Any HTML document syntax may come before or after the **<FORM> ... </FORM>** pair. A form's opening tag, **<FORM>** requires at least two components, the **METHOD** and **ACTION** attributes. The

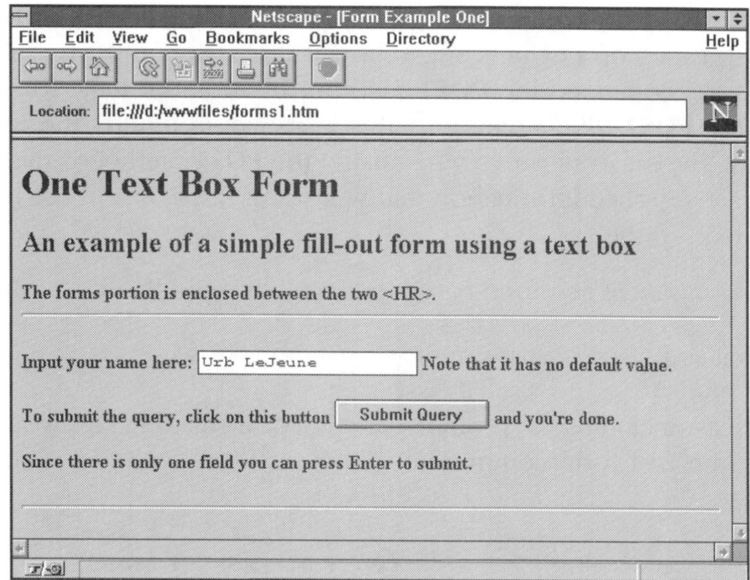

Figure 15.4 *An example of a one text box form- based query.*

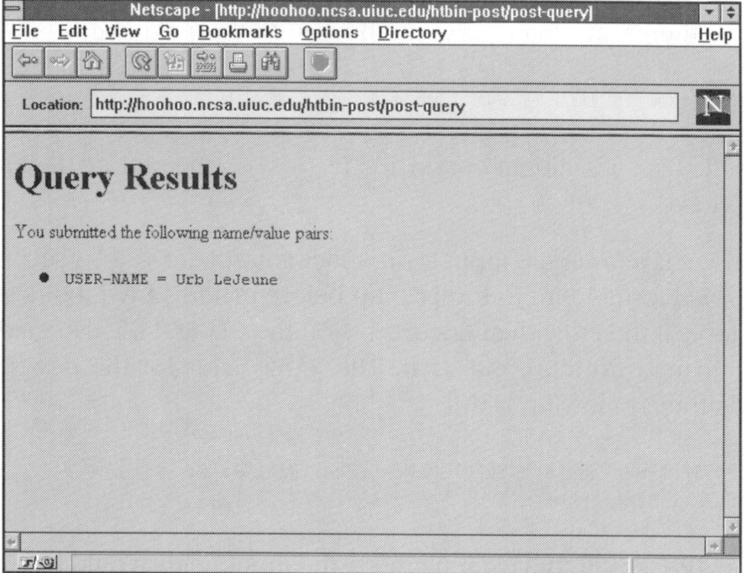

Figure 15.5 *The NCSA server's response to the submission of the form shown in Figure 15.4.*

ACTION attribute, which is a URL, points to the script that is called when the user submits the form. In our previous example (and the other examples in this chapter), we use the script available at the NCSA server.

The **METHOD** attribute has one of two possible parameters—namely, **POST** or **GET**. Let me cop out of a big technical discussion and say NCSA and CERN both recommend the **POST** method. In addition, most form-based queries use **POST**. Explaining why this is so would muddy the waters at this point. The major negative when using the **POST** method is the truncation of user-supplied information that will occur if the size of the information passed is large.

The first component in a form-based document is typically:

```
<FORM METHOD="POST|GET" ACTION="URL">
```

Normal text—including the prompt—and HTML formatting tags would most likely be the first form component. The next form construct would normally be:

```
<INPUT NAME="assigned-name" TYPE="TEXT|RADIO|CHECK|SUBMIT|PASSWORD|RESET">
```

If the **TYPE** attribute is omitted, **TEXT** is assumed. The **INPUT** attribute may also have a **VALUE** parameter. The value parameter is the starting value in a text box or the prompt on the submit button. In this example,

```
<INPUT TYPE="submit" VALUE="Submit Query">
```

indicates the type is a submit button and the text on the button, the **VALUE**, is Submit Query.

Now that we have a simple input form under control, let's add a second input field. I copied forms1.htm to forms2.htm before making any modifications so you can look at the individual documents on the CD-ROM. I also made a few cosmetic changes to titles and such. The input fields for the new form are created with the following HTML:

```
Input your first name here: <INPUT NAME="FIRST-NAME"><P>
Input your last name here: <INPUT NAME="LAST-NAME"><P>
```

Notice the **<P>** tags. If they weren't there, the input fields would be displayed on one line. Figure 15.6 shows the form with the two new input fields, while Figure 15.7 displays the results of submitting Urb as a first name and LeJeune as a last name. We could expand this form by adding as many additional input fields as needed.

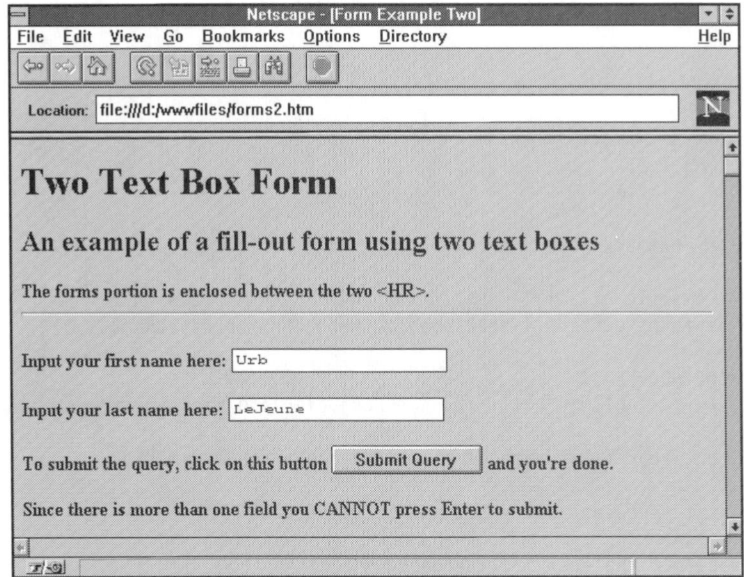

Figure 15.6 An example of a two text box form-based query.

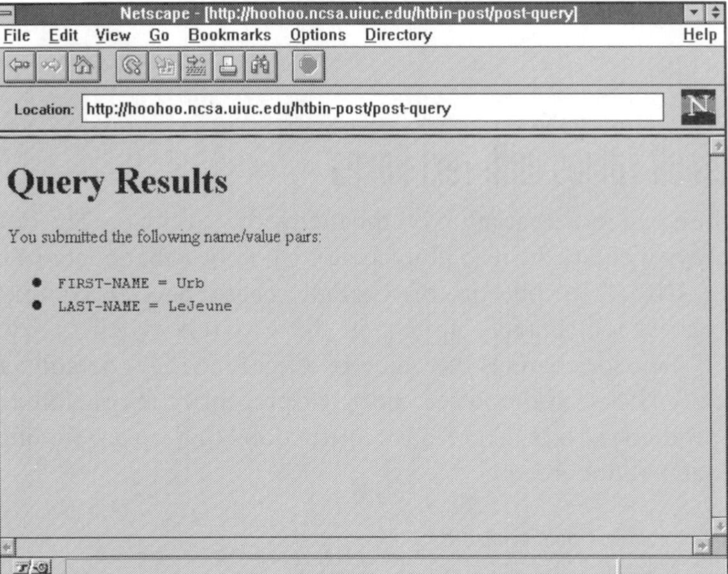

Figure 15.7 The NCSA server's response to the submission of the form shown in Figure 15.6.

The complete listing of forms2.htm is shown here:

```
<HTML>
  <HEAD>
    <TITLE>Form Example Two</TITLE>
  </HEAD>

  <BODY>
     <H1>Two Text Box Form</H1>

     <H2>An example of a fill-out form using two text boxes</H2>
     <H4>The forms portion is enclosed between the two &lt;HR&gt;.
     <HR>
     <FORM METHOD="POST"
                 ACTION="http://hoohoo.ncsa.uiuc.edu/htbin-post/post-query">

         Input your first name here: <INPUT NAME="FIRST-NAME"><P>

         Input your last name here: <INPUT NAME="LAST-NAME"><P>

        To submit the query, click on this button
        <INPUT TYPE="submit"
                    VALUE="Submit Query"> and you're done.<P>
         Since there is more than one field you CANNOT press Enter to submit.

     </FORM>
     <HR>
  </BODY>
</HTML>
```

Using Default Values with Text Boxes

Let's explore one more variation on the theme of text boxes. The next HTML document we'll create, forms3.htm, creates a text box that contains a default value. The **INPUT** attribute in this example uses a **VALUE** parameter. The text "Netscape" will initially appear in the text box when the document displays. If the user changes the value of a field having a default value and subsequently clicks on the Reset button (if present), the original value will reappear in the text box. The HTML instructions that set up the input field with a default value are:

```
What is your favorite Web Browser?
<INPUT NAME="Browser-Preference" VALUE="Netscape">
Notice default value<P>
```

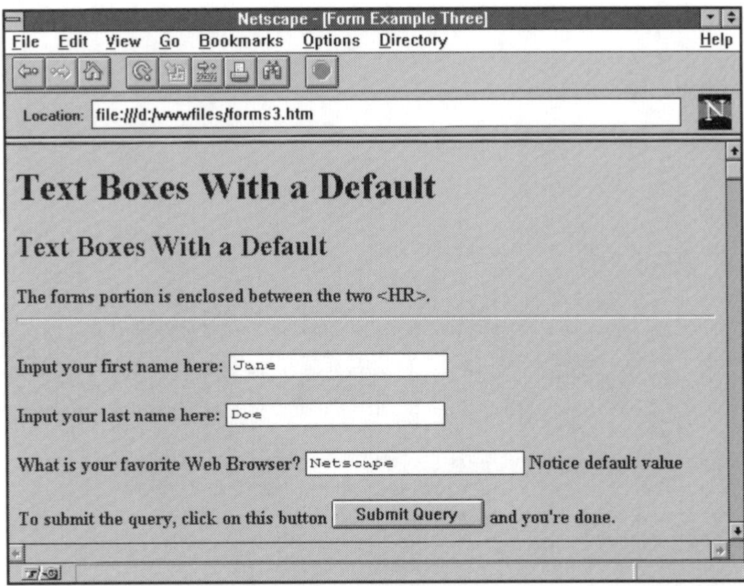

Figure 15.8 *An example of a three text box form-based query with "Netscape" being a default value.*

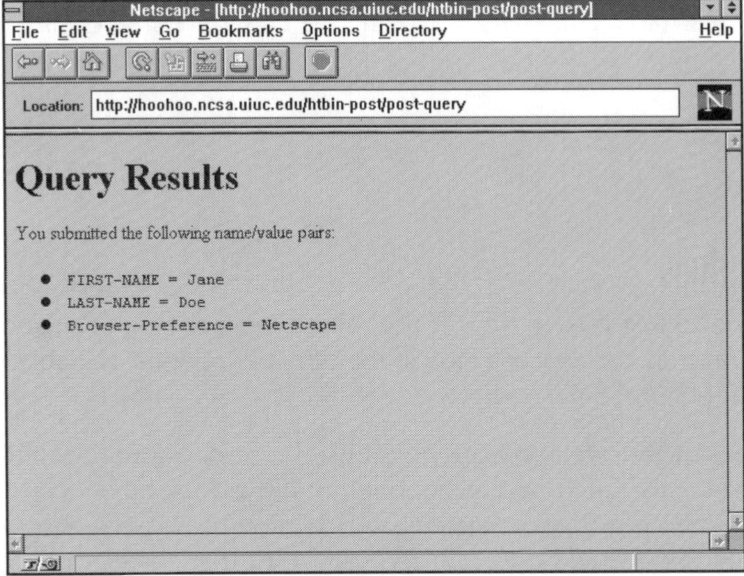

Figure 15.9 *The NCSA server's response to the submission of the form shown in Figure 15.8.*

Figure 15.8 and Figure 15.9 again show the form submission and server response pair. In this case "Netscape" was not typed into the browser question shown in Figure 15.8.

Here's the complete listing for forms3.htm:

```
<HTML>
  <HEAD>
    <TITLE>Form Example Three</TITLE>
  </HEAD>

  <BODY>
     <H1>Text Boxes With a Default</H1>

     <H2>Text Boxes With a Default</H2>
     <H4>The forms portion is enclosed between the two &lt;HR&gt;.
     <HR>
     <FORM METHOD="POST"
                  ACTION="http://hoohoo.ncsa.uiuc.edu/htbin-post/post-query">

         Input your first name here: <INPUT NAME="FIRST-NAME"><P>
         Input your last name here: <INPUT NAME="LAST-NAME"><P>
         What is your favorite Web Browser?
         <INPUT NAME="Browser-Preference" VALUE="Netscape">
         Notice default value<P>

        To submit the query, click on this button
        <INPUT TYPE="submit"
                    VALUE="Submit Query"> and you're done.<P>
         Since there is more than one field you CANNOT press Enter to submit.

     </FORM>
     <HR>

  </BODY>
</HTML>
```

Radio Buttons

In addition to text boxes, we can use other types of components to obtain information from a user. Let's look at the different options available, starting with radio buttons.

Any type of Windows application you use these days provides radio buttons (sometimes called option buttons) to allow a user to select different options. When a group of related radio buttons is displayed, a user can select only one of the buttons in the group. In this respect, radio button choices are mutually exclusive. To see how radio buttons are defined, let's change the form we created in the previous section and add a group of radio buttons that query the user about sex. Often, a list construct is used to set up radio button choices. Here's the HTML we need to compose our set of radio buttons:

```
What is your sex?<BR>
<DL>
      <DD><INPUT TYPE="radio" NAME="SEX" VALUE="Female" CHECKED> Female
      <DD><INPUT TYPE="radio" NAME="SEX" VALUE="Male"> Male
      <DD><INPUT TYPE="radio" NAME="SEX" VALUE="Not-Sure"> Unknown
</DL>
```

The **TYPE** parameter is set to **radio**. All of the associated choices must have the same name (**SEX** in this example). The browser sends the **VALUE** parameter to the server if the user checked the corresponding selection. The item listed with the **CHECKED** option indicates the radio button that will be selected by default when the document is displayed. One, and only one, item in the list of choices can be **CHECKED** and one *must* be **CHECKED**. The last item, outside the closing > specifies the text that is displayed with the radio button. Using a list to display radio buttons is certainly not mandatory, but is very convenient. Figure 15.10 and Figure 15.11 once more show the execution of the document and NCSA's reply.

The complete HTML document that uses the radio buttons is named forms4.htm.

```
<HTML>
<HEAD>
  <TITLE>Form Example Four</TITLE>
</HEAD>
<BODY>
   <H1>Text Boxes With Radio Buttons</H1>
   <HR>
   <FORM METHOD="POST"
              ACTION="http://hoohoo.ncsa.uiuc.edu/htbin-post/post-query">
       Input your first name here: <INPUT NAME="FIRST-NAME"><P>
       Input your last name here: <INPUT NAME="LAST-NAME"><P>
       What is your sex?<BR>
    <DL>
       <DD><INPUT TYPE="radio" NAME="SEX" VALUE="Female" CHECKED> Female
       <DD><INPUT TYPE="radio" NAME="SEX" VALUE="Male"> Male
       <DD><INPUT TYPE="radio" NAME="SEX" VALUE="Not-Sure"> Unknown
     </DL>
      To submit the query, click on this button
      <INPUT TYPE="submit"
                 VALUE="Submit Query"> and you're done.<P>
   </FORM>
   <HR>
 </BODY>
</HTML>
```

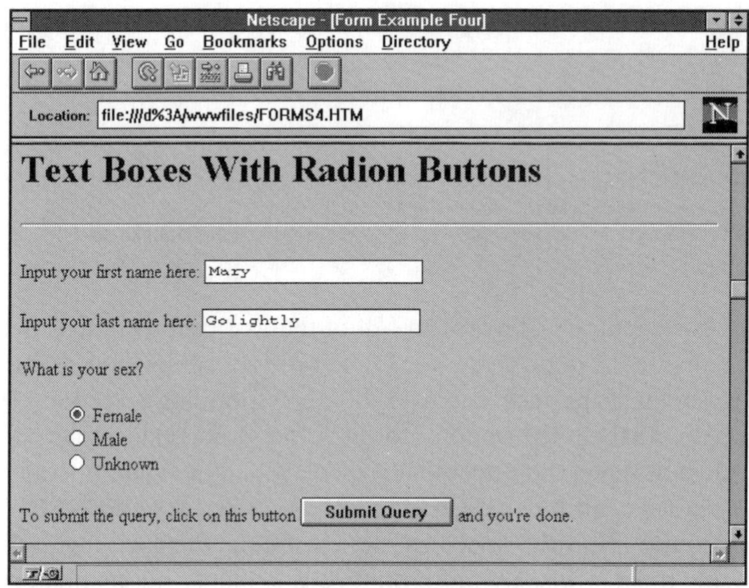

Figure 15.10 A two text box form-based query, also using radio buttons.

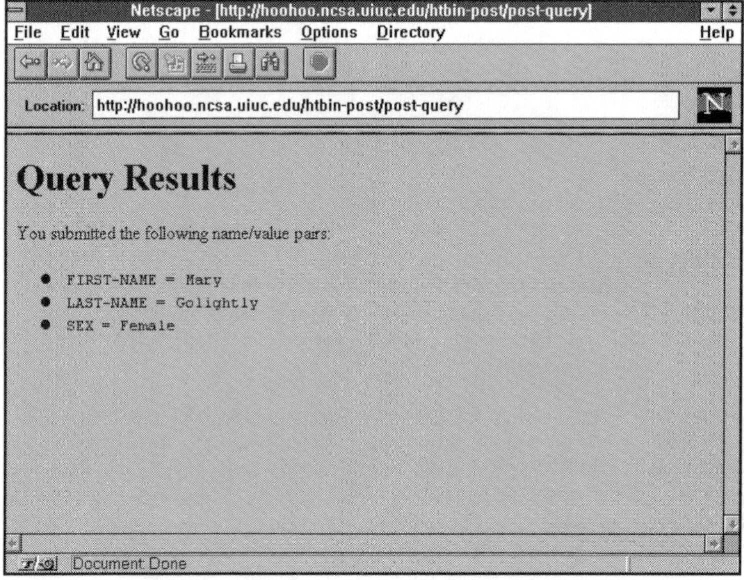

Figure 15.11 The NCSA server's response to the submission of the form shown in Figure 15.10.

Checkboxes

Checkboxes are similar to radio buttons except they are not mutually exclusive. No checkboxes need be selected and any number may be selected. Let's add a few checkboxes to our existing form to see how easy they are to create:

```
<INPUT TYPE="checkbox" NAME="Browser1"
       VALUE="Netscape" CHECKED> Netscape
<INPUT TYPE="checkbox" NAME="Browser2"
       VALUE="Mosaic"> Mosaic
<INPUT TYPE="checkbox" NAME="Browser3"
        VALUE="Cello"> Cello
...

<INPUT TYPE="checkbox" NAME="Browser8"
         VALUE="CompuServ"> CompuServe
<INPUT TYPE="checkbox" NAME="Browser9"
         VALUE="NetCom"> NetCom
<INPUT TYPE="checkbox" NAME="Browser10"
         VALUE="Others"> Others
```

The **TYPE** parameter in this case is set to **checkbox**. Each input item defined (checkbox) must have a different name. Notice that the prompt or label for the checkbox appears outside the closing tag. When a group of checkboxes is defined, you don't need to specify a default item, but I did in this example. The **CHECKED** parameter is included with the first **<INPUT>** tag so that this checkbox will automatically be selected (checked) when the form is first displayed. Because multiple checkboxes in a group can be selected, we could use the **CHECKED** parameter with any of the other **<INPUT>** tags defined here as well.

Adding Formatting Features

Now that we have a handle on text boxes, radio buttons, and checkboxes, let's add some more interesting formatting features to the document that uses the form we've been constructing. The file name for the new version will be forms5.htm.

To get a better idea of where we are headed, take a peek at Figure 15.12. Unfortunately, what doesn't show up in the black and white screen shot is the nice light blue background. The HTML instruction used to produce this effect is:

```
<BODY BGCOLOR="7FFFFF">
```

I'll also use text formatting—the **<B> ... </B>** tag pair—to highlight our checkboxes. In addition, I've increased the font size of the checkboxes by using the **SIZE=+1** parameter. I've also placed the checkboxes in a table containing one row and two columns. The first column contains an ordered list **<OL>** while the second column also contains an ordered list, starting with 6. This is probably not a good idea since only Netscape supports the **START=** attribute for an ordered list. However, let's have some fun while we try out some of the more interesting Netscape enhancements. The skeletal syntax for all this gingerbread is:

```
<TABLE>
       <TR>
          <B>
          <TD>
              <OL>
                  <FONT SIZE=+1><B>
                   <LI><INPUT TYPE="checkbox" NAME="Browser1"
                        VALUE="Netscape" CHECKED>
...
                 </FONT></B>
              </OL>
           </TD>
           <TD>
              <OL START=6>
                  <FONT SIZE=+1><B>
                  <LI><INPUT TYPE="checkbox" NAME="Browser6"
...
                  </FONT></B>
              </OL>
          </TD>
        </TR>
</TABLE>
```

Notice that the Netscape item is **CHECKED**, meaning it is preselected. The default size for a text box is 20 characters. More text may be entered, but only 20 characters will be listed. You can change the size by using the **SIZE** parameter. Here's how we've used this feature in our new form:

```
<INPUT NAME="E-MAIL" SIZE=40><P>
```

Our form also has a reset button created by this tag:

```
Click on this button to clear:
<INPUT TYPE="reset" Value="Reset Form">
```

Figure 15.12 displays the form in all its glory. The NCSA response in shown in Figure 15.13.

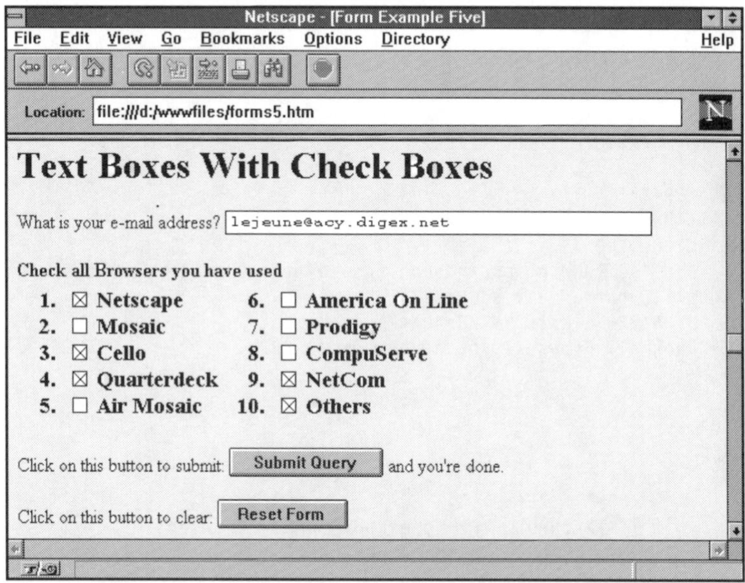

Figure 15.12 *A query form demonstrating checkboxes replete with special effects.*

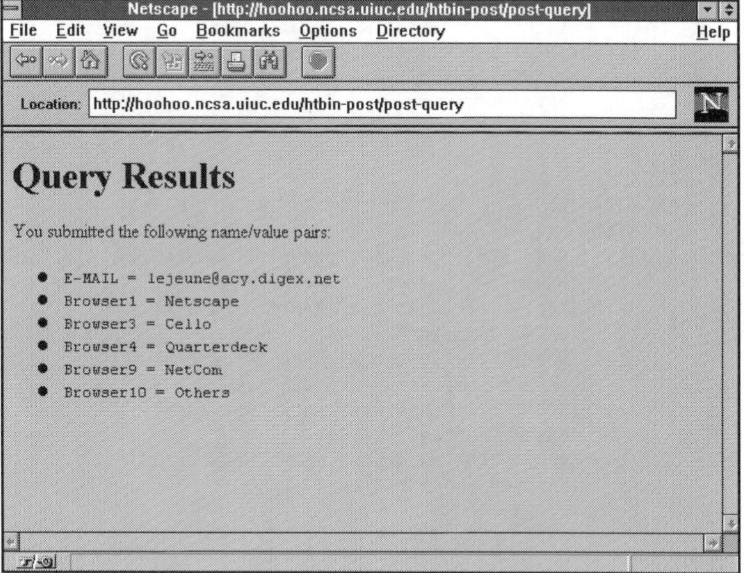

Figure 15.13 *The NCSA server's response to the submission of the form shown in Figure 15.12.*

The complete listing for forms5.htm follows.

```
<HTML>
   <HEAD>
     <TITLE>Form Example Five</TITLE>
   </HEAD>
   <BODY BGCOLOR="7FFFFF">
      <H1>Text Boxes With Check Boxes</H1>
      <FORM METHOD="POST"
                  ACTION="http://hoohoo.ncsa.uiuc.edu/htbin-post/post-query">
          What is your e-mail address?
         <INPUT NAME="E-MAIL" SIZE=40><P>
         <B>Check all Browsers you have used</B><BR>
    <TABLE>
       <TR>
          <B>
          <TD>
              <OL>
                  <FONT SIZE=+1><B>
                   <LI><INPUT TYPE="checkbox" NAME="Browser1"
                        VALUE="Netscape" CHECKED>
                        Netscape
                   <LI><INPUT TYPE="checkbox" NAME="Browser2"
                        VALUE="Mosaic"> Mosaic
                   <LI><INPUT TYPE="checkbox" NAME="Browser3"
                         VALUE="Cello"> Cello
                   <LI><INPUT TYPE="checkbox" NAME="Browser4"
                        VALUE="Quarterdeck"> Quarterdeck
                   <LI><INPUT TYPE="checkbox" NAME="Browser5"
                        VALUE="Air Mosaic"> Air Mosaic
                   </FONT></B>
              </OL>
           </TD>
           <TD>
              <OL START=6>
                  <FONT SIZE=+1><B>
                  <LI><INPUT TYPE="checkbox" NAME="Browser6"
                       VALUE="AOL"> America Online
                  <LI><INPUT TYPE="checkbox" NAME="Browser7"
                       VALUE="Prodigy"> Prodigy
                  <LI><INPUT TYPE="checkbox" NAME="Browser8"
                       VALUE="CompuServ"> CompuServe
                  <LI><INPUT TYPE="checkbox" NAME="Browser9"
                       VALUE="NetCom"> NetCom
                  <LI><INPUT TYPE="checkbox" NAME="Browser10"
                       VALUE="Others"> Others
                  </FONT></B>
              </OL>
          </TD>
       </TR>
     </TABLE>
       Click on this button to submit:
       <INPUT TYPE="submit"
                    VALUE="Submit Query"> and you're done.<P>
       Click on this button to clear:
          <INPUT TYPE="reset" Value="Reset Form">
```

```
      </FORM>
      <HR>
   </BODY>
</HTML>
```

Drop-Down Menus

Last on our forms hit parade is drop-down menus. A drop-down menu, created using the **<SELECT>** tag, is conceptually much like a radio button. Only one choice can be made from a list of displayed items. The basic format for this tag is:

```
<SELECT> NAME="name"
         SIZE=number
         MULTIPLE> text or option list </SELECT>
```

The **SIZE** and **MULTIPLE** parameters are optional. If **MULTIPLE** is provided, the menu will allow the user to select more than one option. The individual items in a menu are defined using the **<OPTION>** tag. To see how this is done, let's look at the HTML required to define the actual menu used in the previous version of the HTML form presented in this chapter:

```
<B>Select your highest level of education:</B>
<SELECT NAME="Education">
       <OPTION>Less than 8 years
       <OPTION>Grammar School
       <OPTION>High School
       <OPTION>Some College
       <OPTION>College Graduate
       <OPTION>Master Degree
       <OPTION>Earned Doctorate
</SELECT><P>
```

The first option item is the default. The prompt will appear in the box when the form is first displayed. If there is an **<OPTION>** tag with no prompt, the starting value would be null and the selection box would be empty. The **<OPTION>** tag may also contain a **VALUE** attribute, in the form:

```
<OPTION VALUE="My Choice">
```

If used, the **VALUE** parameter is sent to the server when the item is selected. If **VALUE** isn't used, the prompt becomes the value and is sent to the server. Use caution on the placement of the drop menus. Make sure the menu, when dropped, doesn't exceed the screen size for a variety of different browsers and terminals.

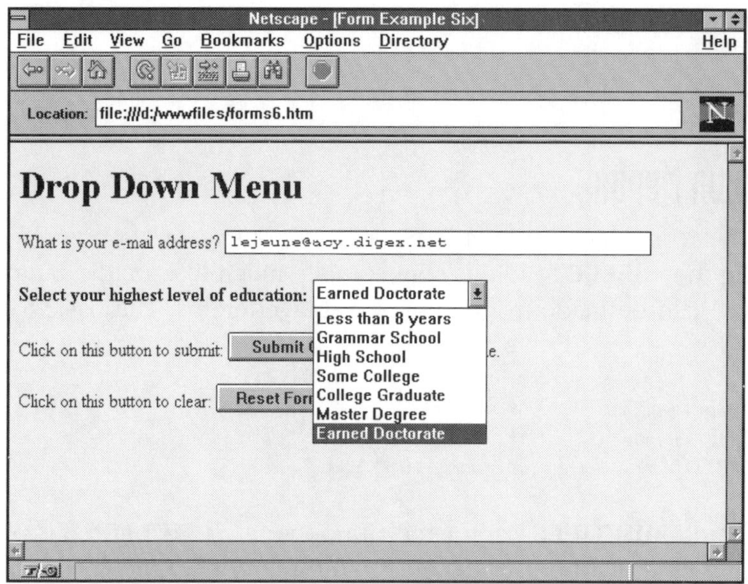

Figure 15.14 An example of a drop-down menu used in a form.

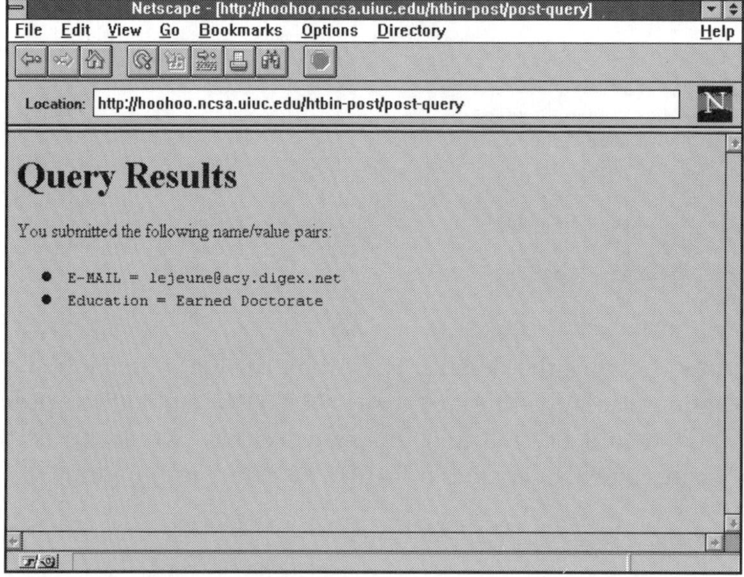

Figure 15.15 NCSA's Query Results display.

Figure 15.14 displays a form employing the drop menu, while Figure 15.15 shows NCSA's reply to the entries shown in Figure 15.14.

The complete HTML file for the final version of our example document is forms6.htm. Here it is:

```
<HTML>
   <HEAD>
     <TITLE>Form Example Six</TITLE>
   </HEAD>
   <BODY BGCOLOR="FFFF00">
      <H1>Drop Down Menu</H1>
      <FORM METHOD="POST"
                  ACTION="http://hoohoo.ncsa.uiuc.edu/htbin-post/post-query">
          What is your e-mail address?
         <INPUT NAME="E-MAIL" SIZE=40><P>
         <B>Select your highest level of education:</B>
         <SELECT NAME="Education">
                <OPTION>Less than 8 years
                <OPTION>Grammar School
                 <OPTION>High School
                 <OPTION>Some College
                 <OPTION>College Graduate
                 <OPTION>Master Degree
                 <OPTION>Earned Doctorate
         </SELECT><P>
        Click on this button to submit:
        <INPUT TYPE="submit"
                     VALUE="Submit Query"> and you're done.<P>
        Click on this button to clear:
           <INPUT TYPE="reset" Value="Reset Form"
         </FORM>
      <HR>
   </BODY>
</HTML>
```

Decoding Name/Value Pairs

If you plan to get serious about forms, you'll need to decode the name/value pairs supplied by the browser. Thankfully, robust scripts to accomplish this task are available. A commonly used parser is the one supplied with the CERN HTTPD server. It's called cgipars and may be available on your system in the /usr/local/bin/cgiparse directory. NCSA also makes C source code available to parse the name/value pairs. Their FTP URL is:

```
ftp://ftp.ncsa.uiuc.edu/Web/httpd/Unix/ncsa_httpd/cgi/cgi-src/
```

There are many CGI scripts available on the Web simply for the asking, or downloading. Visit some of the sites listed in the resource guide that follows. Existing scripts serve two purposes—they prevent you from reinventing the wheel if you can find a script that come close to doing what you want it to do, and they are great learning vehicles.

It is always a good idea to check on script availability with your Internet service provider or system administrator. You may have to look no further.

Resources

The following may be helpful when exploring the construction of forms.

Ask Dr. Web
`http://WWW.Stars.com/Email.html`

CGI (Common Gateway Interface) Reference material
`http://WWW.Stars.com/Vlib/Providers/CGI.html`

CyberWeb's Virtual Library
`http://WWW.Stars.com/Vlib/Search.html`

W3 Browse at NASA - Super Examples
`http://guinan.gsfc.nasa.gov/cgi-bin/StarTrax/w3browse.pl`

The following is especially useful. It is a good example of a complex form; it also will validate an HTML document from a provided URL.

HTML Validation Service by HaL Computer Systems
`http://www.hal.com/users/connolly/html-test/service/validation-form.html`

Super NCSA Forms Tutorial
`http://hoohoo.ncsa.uiuc.edu/cgi/forms.html`

Web Developer's Virtual Library</A> This is a gold mine!
`http://WWW.Stars.com/`

Production version of StarTrax
`http://heasarc.gsfc.nasa.gov/StarTrax/Browse.html`

Supporting forms with CGI
`http://hoohoo.ncsa.uiuc.edu/cgi/forms.html`

WebCommunications forms information
`http://www.webcom.com/~jbd/rtc/rtc.html`

An FTPable public-domain Perl forms script
`ftp://ftp.cc.utexas.edu/pub/output/www/form-mail/form-mail-1.3/form-mail.pl`

WWW FAQ in HTML
`http://sunsite.unc.edu/boutell/faq/www_faq.html`

Yahoo CGI list
http://www.yahoo.com/Computers/World_Wide_Web/CGI_Common_Gateway_Interface

LET'S REVIEW

Form-based queries became a reality with HTML 2.0. However, care must be taken when using forms since some browsers may not support forms and some support forms poorly.

Document-based queries have been with us since the beginning of HTML. Only one input field is supplied with a document-based query. The tag **<ISINDEX>** must appear in the **<HEAD>** section of a document-based query. A script must be used to generate the input form and to format a report based upon the user's input.

Forms-based queries are much more flexible and much easier to write and test. The document supplied to the user is actually a conventional HTML document with a **<FORM>** section.

The basic format for creating a form is:

```
<FORM METHOD="POST|GET" ACTION="URL">
</FORM>
```

A form-based query must have at least one input field. The input fields can be text entry boxes, radio buttons, drop-down menus, or checkboxes. These components can be arranged in any combination and you can use any number of them. You can also use more advanced features, such as large text boxes with scroll bars, password fields, and image maps. The general format of a forms-related document is:

```
<HTML>
    <HEAD>
        Normal heading stuff
    </HEAD>
    <BODY>
        Normal body stuff
        <FORM  form-specifications, normal text, and regular HTML formatting
           tags  </FORM>
        More normal body stuff
    </BODY>
```

Once a user completes a form—by clicking on the submit button—name/value pairs are sent to a server. Public domain scripts are available to decode these pairs.

Doing More on the Web

CHAPTER 16

Finding and Retrieving Files

There are gigabytes of free files out there on the Net, ready for you to download. The trick is finding them...but with a little help from some searching tools, you'll be able to find what you want in no time at all.

One of the joys of being connected to the Internet is the ability to download the latest programs and other goodies from a seemingly inexhaustible supply. Indeed, new files and programs are being placed "out there" faster than anyone could possibly hope to download and evaluate them.

Many of these downloadable programs are absolutely free and others are low cost "shareware" that may be tested before you buy. (More on the notion of shareware shortly.) The process of first finding and then downloading files can be frustrating unless someone has told you the precise location of a particular program and its exact file name. This chapter will do just that.

In this chapter I'll take you out into these uncharted waters and direct you through the process of finding and downloading files from remote sites in cyberspace. Don't despair! The process seems complicated at first, but it becomes second nature by the time you have filled your hard disk—at least twice.

FILE COMPRESSION PROGRAMS

Programs that compress and uncompress files have gone from an exotic luxury to an absolute necessity in recent years. Stac's patent infringement suit against Microsoft, over a compression utility, was page one news in the mainstream press, and the battle was frequently mentioned on national TV during the 11 o'clock news. Until a few years ago, only aficionados of online services even knew about file compression. Then, along came Windows and its voracious memory appetite—and a market was born.

Why File Compression?

My first word processor was WordStar. I think it was version 3.0, if my rapidly failing memory serves me correctly. WordStar ran very nicely on a two diskette XT machine; 360Kb diskettes at that. Disk swapping was required only when I wanted to spell check or do something else really out of the ordinary. Not being content to swap diskettes simply because I wanted to run a different program, I installed a hard disk.

My first hard disk was a Seagate ST232, a 32MB workhorse that changed consumer attitudes about hard disks. After installing this behemoth drive, I was king of the hill, since all my friends only had 10 or 20 MB hard drives. To put 32MB of hard disk space into perspective, a few years earlier I was providing mini-computers with 12MB of disk space to businesses with 50 or so employees. We did everything on those machines, including payroll and many thousands of inventory items.

I think I paid about $500 for my 32MB drive plus another $50 for a controller. I remember thinking, "I'll have enough disk space to last for years." Now, neither WordPerfect for Windows nor Microsoft's Word for Windows would fit on that ST232 hard disk, if they were installed with all the accompanying bells and whistles. Worse yet, a quick look through *Computer Shopper* shows dozens of listings for gigabyte (that is, *billion*-byte) drives that can be purchased for far less than I paid for my beloved "232" and its controller.

The arrival of Windows, coupled with the desire to have lots of software and especially graphics on one's disk, accelerated both the need and development of compression techniques. As a consequence, almost all files stored on BBSs or at FTP sites store files in compressed form. The only exceptions are typically very small text files. Without going into the gory details, compression reduces a file's storage requirements, often by as much as half, and sometimes by up to 80 or 90 percent. That's the good news...the bad news is that a compressed file is absolutely useless unless you can uncompress it. Another piece of bad news is that there often seems to be an infinite number of compression techniques—and at least ten more at any given time than you know how to handle. As many of my online friends would say, :-(

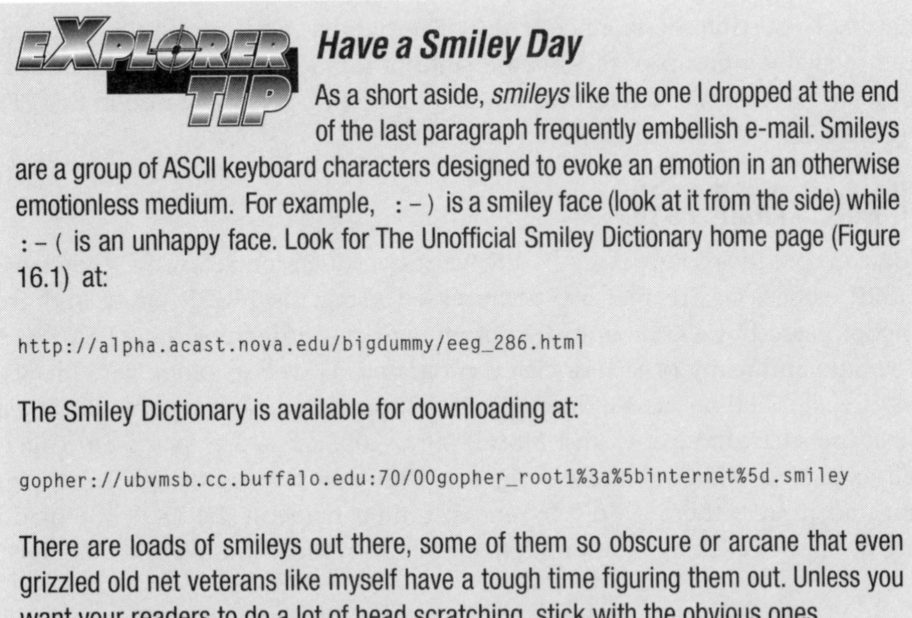

Have a Smiley Day

As a short aside, *smileys* like the one I dropped at the end of the last paragraph frequently embellish e-mail. Smileys are a group of ASCII keyboard characters designed to evoke an emotion in an otherwise emotionless medium. For example, :-) is a smiley face (look at it from the side) while :-(is an unhappy face. Look for The Unofficial Smiley Dictionary home page (Figure 16.1) at:

```
http://alpha.acast.nova.edu/bigdummy/eeg_286.html
```

The Smiley Dictionary is available for downloading at:

```
gopher://ubvmsb.cc.buffalo.edu:70/00gopher_root1%3a%5binternet%5d.smiley
```

There are loads of smileys out there, some of them so obscure or arcane that even grizzled old net veterans like myself have a tough time figuring them out. Unless you want your readers to do a lot of head scratching, stick with the obvious ones.

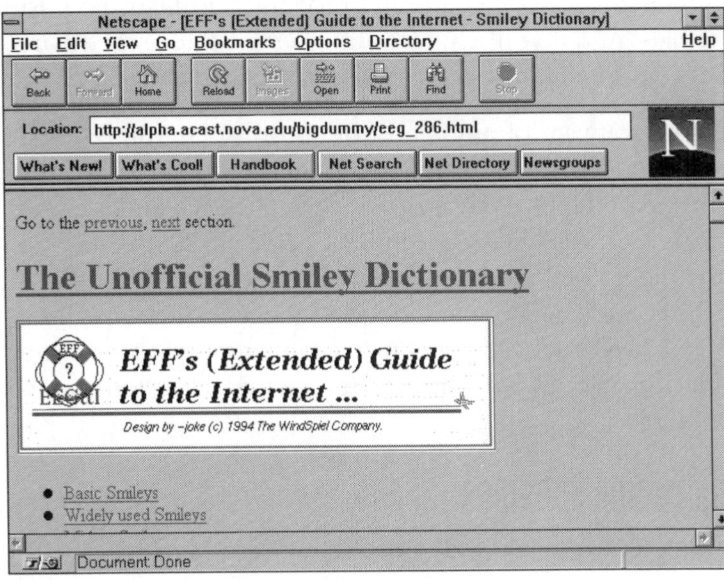

Figure 16.1 *The Unofficial Smiley Dictionary home page.*

The most commonly used compression scheme is one developed by a company named PK Ware ("PK" for Phil Katz, the company founder). Files compressed using their technique have a file name with a .ZIP extension, and are typically called "ZIP files" or simply "ZIPs." Let's start our FTPing career by finding a specific file located somewhere "out there," and then we'll transfer that file to our Internet-connected PC. The file that we'll use in this exploration (actually a group of files) is the suite of utilities used to create and manipulate ZIP files. We'll return to other compression schemes used in the FTP business after this initial exploration.

PK Ware's PKZIP 2.04G

You can spot files compressed by PK Ware's products a mile away—they have a .ZIP extension. ZIP files are compressed using the PKZIP utility and are uncompressed by a companion program named—you guessed it—PKUNZIP. Netscape and many of its associated programs, as well as other Web browsers, are supplied on the Net in compressed form. The more recent version of Netscape—n1re1b3.exe— and Mosaic—mos20b$.exe—are in a form called self-extracting. Although these programs were compressed using PKZIP, you can uncompress them simply by entering their name at the DOS command line prompt or clicking on their filename while in the Windows' File Manager.

If a program or application has a ZIP extension, PKUNZIP Version 2.04G (or a later version) is required to uncompress these programs. If you do not have PKUNZIP, you will need to acquire the program and learn how to use it to uncompress files. And if you're new to transferring files over the net, obtaining PK Ware's compression suite is a great place to start.

When acquiring software of any kind from a BBS or the Internet, it's important to make certain you are downloading the latest version. At this writing, the latest version of the PK Ware's zipper suite is 2.04G, and it comes in a file named pkz204g.exe. The utilities are indeed inside pkz204g.exe in compressed form, but the file is combined with a simple uncompression utility that rides along with the compressed files and obviates the need for a separate unzipper utility. The PKZ204G package contains the program—zip2exe—used to perform the "black magic" of converting a file with a ZIP extension into a self-extracting EXE file.

Other Compression Schemes

If life were simple, we would only need to concern ourselves with the ubiquitous ZIP-compressed files. As you might suspect, life is not that simple.

Before you can uncompress a file, you must know the compression technique used to compress the file in the first place. Although ZIP compression predominates, there are hundreds of different file compression methods in use on the Internet, and you'll encounter most of them if you cruise the world's FTP sites regularly.

This implies a problem: How are you ever going to navigate the "compression seas" and figure out the compression method employed by a given file, where it isn't obvious from the file extension? Most FTP directories have a read.me or index file (or something similar) listing all the files that are in that directory. Some considerate FTP site administrators have created expanded read.me files that include information about the compression method utilized. Some *exceptionally* considerate administrators even tell you where to obtain the software needed to uncompress the files.

Failing specific uncompression instructions, look at the file extension of a stored archive file. Table 16.1 shows some of the most popular extensions that you may find during your visits to FTP sites worldwide. The list also shows the transfer modes needed to retrieve files with these extensions and which uncompression software package you will need to uncompress the retrieved files. The list, derived from "The EFF's Guide to the Internet," is by no means all-inclusive, but it should cover about 98 percent of the FTPable files you will find.

Fortunately, most uncompression software is either public domain or shareware. Public domain is free but shareware authors expect you to send some money for the program (typically less than the commercial counterpart) if you decide to keep and use the program on a regular basis. Thankfully, most uncompression software is available for FTPing.

FILE TRANSFER PROTOCOL (FTP)

There are currently over 1,200 Internet sites making files available for downloading by people who do not have accounts on these remote systems. The downloading (and uploading, if you have write privilege on the remote site) is accomplished by a protocol named FTP, for File Transfer Protocol. This transfer process by system "outsiders" is called *anonymous FTP* because you don't need an account on the host system to avail yourself of their largess. You simply log in as user "anonymous" and enter your e-mail address as your password.

Just so you don't get the idea that FTPing is a minor undertaking, there are over 2.5 million unique filenames out there in cyberspace, consuming over

200 gigabytes of storage space. (That's 200,000,000,000 bytes.) CICA, one of the major software depositories, adds about 20 new programs a day! The database holding information on all available FTPable files, complete with file and path names, requires about 400MB of storage space for the reference material. Managing all the data in this massive database is a serious challenge, one handled fairly well by a client/server system called Archie. The database is stored on an Archie server and it is accessed by an Archie client. We'll take a closer look at Archie a little later in this chapter. If we can drag him away from Veronica (more on Veronica later), maybe he'll perform a file search for us.

EXPLORER TIP

What Time Is It in Tokyo?

Consider the following information before connecting to an external Internet computer. Most Internet resources (like FTPable files) reside on computers primarily engaged in other activities. Most employees would be annoyed to discover their paychecks are late because their employer's computer was busy servicing FTP requests from people on the other side of the world. Internet services on these machines have a very low priority. Many sites that normally allow anonymous FTP will not permit, or severely limit, outside access of their systems during normal local business hours. Even those permitting the service may be very sluggish during periods of high "local" activity.

Much of the traffic on the Internet moves at close to the speed of light. Limitation in traffic flow is usually the result of low priority rather than low transmission speeds. Resource-intensive tasks frequently complete more quickly when connected to a system on the other side of the earth, when the local inhabitants are fast asleep at what they see as 3:00 AM—even if it's 3:00 in the afternoon where you live.

The sun rises in the East, so remote time—that is, the time as perceived by the other person—gets progressively farther ahead of local time as we go east. The rate is approximately 45 minutes for every 1,000 miles. London is five hours ahead of New York and eight hours ahead of San Francisco. The time on the opposite side of the earth is 12 hours different from local time. Keep that in mind the next time you want to transfer a large file from an FTP site.

It's a Shareware World. Although there are only 90,000 different programs available at these depositories, compared to over 2.5 million files of all sorts available for FTPing, depository programs represent about 99 percent of all FTP downloads. Major software depositories have four distinguishing characteristics:

- They're designed to hold large numbers of programs and files.
- They have user-friendly directory structures.

Table 16.1 Commonly Used File Extensions on the Internet

Extension	Mode	Transfer Comments and Uncompression Program, if Needed
.arc or .ARC	Binary	An early compression scheme rarely found anymore. Requires the use of ARC or ARCE to uncompress.
.doc or .DOC	ASCII	Usually another common extension for text documents. However, .doc and .DOC extensions are also used for Microsoft Word documents, which must be transferred as binary files. Try previewing the file with a plain ASCII editor, such as DOS's EDIT. If you see strange graphic-like characters, it's a binary file.
.gz	Binary	This is a Unix version of a ZIP file and is uncompressed with a program named gunzip. At the Unix command line enter: `unix% gunzip filename.gz`
.hqx or .Hqx	Binary	Macintosh compression format requiring the BinHex program to uncompress.
.LZH	Binary	A DOS format in widespread use.
.ps or .PSASCII		A PostScript document that does not need uncompressing. You may print this file on any PostScript capable printer or use a special program called GhostScript. PostScript is Adobe's page description language.
.shar or .Shar	Binary	Another Unix compression scheme. Use unshar to uncompress.
.sit or .SitBinary		A Macintosh format requiring StuffIt to uncompress.
.tar	Binary	Yet one more Unix compression scheme that is frequently used to compress many related files into one large file. Unix systems typically have a program called tar to uncompress or, as the Unix types say, "un-tar," these files. The "tarred" file could be compressed with the .gz compression method. You first have to use uncompress and then tar.
.txt or .TXT	ASCII	A file with a .TXT extension indicates that the file is a document rather than a program. It does not need uncompression.
.Z	Binary	A Unix compression method. To uncompress a file with a .Z extension, enter the following from within a Unix shell account: `unix% uncompress filename.Z` u16.zip is a DOS program that uncompreses downloaded .Z files on your PC. A Mac-equivalent program is called MacCompress.
.zip or .ZIP	Binary	Uncompress using PKUNZIP or WinZip. You may uncompress a ZIP from within a Unix shell using a program called unzip.
.zoo or .ZOO	Binary	These extensions may be either a Unix or a DOS compression scheme. To uncompress use a program called zoo.

- They have an index file in each directory containing a one-line plain text description of each program in addition to the file's name and size.
- They have *mirror sites* (ideally at wildly different geographical locations) to minimize the distance files have to travel to any given requester.

A mirror site has the same files as the parent site and a similar (and often identical) directory structure.

The Virtual Shareware Library, located at the University of Ljudljana in Slovenia, has a wonderful service that permits querying a database of software depository file names and their descriptions. The breakthrough in the "Shareware archives search engines" (SHASE) database lies in its ability to search by program description or program file name, and not simply by file name as required by Archie. We'll devote an entire section to this service shortly.

Public Domain, Shareware, and Freeware

There is much confusion on the Internet, and elsewhere, concerning the differences among public domain, freeware, and shareware. There are no restrictions on the use or distribution of software placed in the public domain. You may do anything you choose with it, and may copy, sell, or modify the software as you like. Public domain software is frequently, but certainly not always, developed with government funding.

Freeware is software that is distributed without charge, but is nonetheless protected by the author's copyright. The owner of the copyright may state conditions for no-charge usage of the software, as in non-commercial applications, and may require some sort of license and fee for commercial use. Several Web browsers, including Netscape and Mosaic, fall into this category. Netscape may be used without charge by people affiliated with academic institutions or non-profit organizations, or by people evaluating the browser. There is currently a $39.00 charge for people not falling into one the above catagories. I'm not aware of a time limit imposed upon the evaluation period :-) Mosaic has a little less restrictive policy; individuals may use the software without charge. With most freeware, there is no charge for individual users but commercial users must often pay for the use of the software. As with most software, you may not sell or modify the programs without the written permission of the copyright owner.

Shareware is very much like regular commercial software, with a few twists. It is essentially commercial software that you pay for on the honor system. The full, non-crippled copy of the software is distributed widely, and you are encouraged to pass it along to as many people as you like. You may try shareware before you purchase it—but you are morally and legally bound to pay for the software if you retain it and use it regularly. The quality of shareware runs the gamut from poor to superior. (Why should the quality of shareware be different from the quality of commercial software?) But you're at least allowed to see how good it is (and decide whether you want to keep it) before you're actually out any money.

Shareware is different from "demo software." A demo copy is frequently limited or disabled in some way, and after you've played with the demo a while, you have the opportunity to upgrade to the full commercial product. Some features may not work, or the product may only work for a short period of time or access a limited amount of data. For example, the Air Mosaic demo limits a Web surfing session to six external links. Other demo software may not be able to print, save data to a file, or save more than a small amount of data to a file. The idea is to let you see clearly how the software works and what it can do, but not give you enough functionality to allow you to use the demo copy as though it were the product itself.

SEARCHING TECHNIQUES

There are two different techniques for finding FTPable files: word of mouth and database search. The word-of-mouth method is certainly the oldest and may also be the most reliable. Plug into a newsgroup dealing with your favorite subject to get the latest on program uploads. Database searches may use Archie or search the Virtual Shareware Library using the SHASE engine.

Let's take a look at Archie first. The Archie database is searchable using five different techniques; they are:

- Use an Archie gateway from within a forms-capable Web browser.
- Telnet directly to an Archie server using a Telnet client.
- Use an Archie Client, such as the one provided with the Internet Chameleon.
- Send an e-mail request to Archie.
- Telnet to an Archie server from within a Telnet-capable Web browser.

Let's look at these options one at a time.

Querying Archie Using a Web Form

The simplest of the five techniques, especially for new Archie users, requires filling out a form from a Web browser, such as Netscape or Mosaic, and sending it to an Archie gateway. A fill-in-the-blanks Archie request form may be completed from within a Web browser. Be aware, not all Web browsers support forms. Earlier versions of Mosaic and the current version of Cello do not support forms; most others browsers do support forms.

Trying Out a WWW Archie Server

For this project we'll use a WWW Archie server to locate a copy of PKZIP—the file pkz204g.exe. We'll initiate the search by filling out an easy-to-use Archie Request Form on the Web.

To initiate an Archie request, start your favorite Web browser and bring up the dialog that allows you to manually enter a URL. This happens in slightly different ways for different browsers. Enter the following URL:

```
http://http2.sils.umich.edu/utility/archie.html
```

Next, press enter to activate the URL. The server at the University of Michigan is frequently busy. For a list of alternative sites point your browser to:

```
http://pubweb.nexor.co.uk/public/archie/servers.html
```

Figure 16.2 shows part of an Archie Request Form about to be sent to the University of Michigan Archie server. Figure 16.3 shows the second half of the Archie Request Form. The only entry that I've made on the form is the target search string of "pkz204g." The target search string may be a substring (as it is in this example) of the full string "pkz204g.exe". We could have entered the entire file name of pkz204g.exe, but let's assume (as may often happen) that we don't know the file's extension.

There are several search methods available, but notice we're about to use the "Case Insensitive Substring Match" technique. When you're ready to initiate the search, click on the Submit button at the bottom of the form as shown in Figure 16.3. As the heading in the display window states, "Archie searches can take a long time," so be patient.

As you might expect with a file having the popularity of pkz204g, there are literally hundreds of locations on the Internet containing the file. In fact, it's a

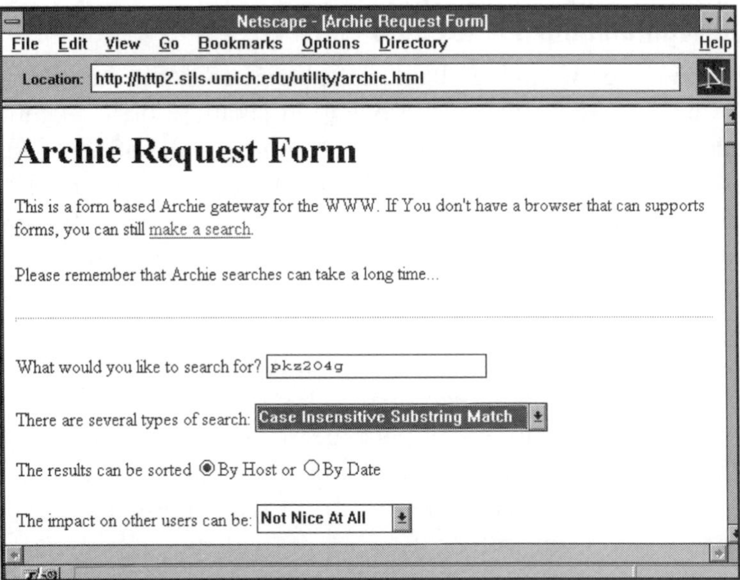

***Figure 16.2** Filling in the first half of an Archie Request Form.*

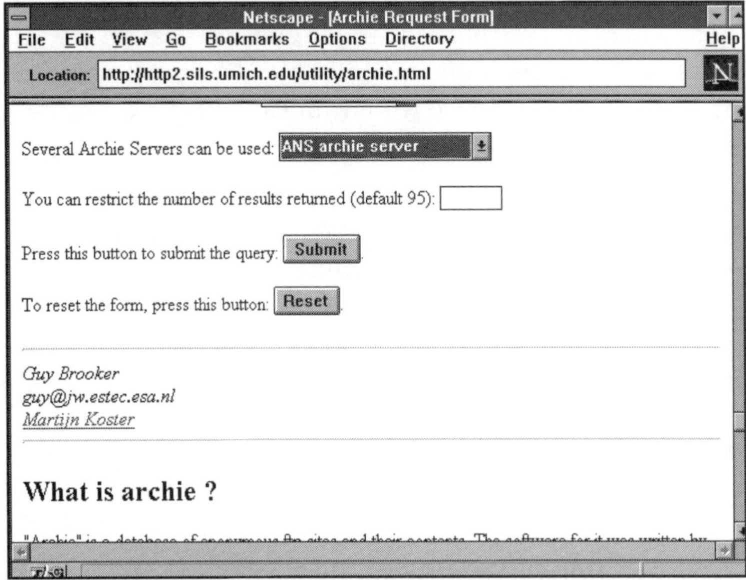

***Figure 16.3** The second half of an Archie Request Form.*

rare site that doesn't have a copy of pkz204g lurking in one of its directories. So how do we know that pkz204g.exe is the latest version? Good question! Partial string searches to the rescue.

Partial Strings and Sorting by Date

The version number of much FTPable software is embedded in the file name, so if you develop some naming convention smarts, you'll be much more successful in searching for software. The naming convention of PK Ware's compression archive uses the template pkz*mnna*.exe where "m" is the major version of the release, "nn" is the minor version, and "a" is the alphabetic maintenance update of the release. Following the PKZ prefix, the next most important character is the "m" or major version, followed by the "nn" or minor version update, and finally the maintenance release letter. What all this means is that pkz300a.exe would be a later version than pkz299z.exe. pkz205a.exe would be a later release than pkz204g.exe. If you want to search for the latest version of PK Ware's compression package, look for the highest three numbers following the "pkz" and, in case of a tie, the highest letter preceding the EXE extension. When you start the search, all you'll know for certain is that the file's name will begin with "pkz."

Look at Figure 16.2 again and notice the radio buttons on the form. (Windows radio buttons allow exactly one selection from several options. If you click on an unchecked button, it becomes the checked button and the previously checked button becomes unchecked.) The results of a search are sortable By Date or By Host. A descending name sort would be preferable in this case since the newest version of the file would appear first in the results. (More on name sorting when we speak of Telnetting to Archie.)

The date sort is actually a descending sort with the most recent file creation dates appearing first on the list, for files matching our search key. There is nothing to prevent someone from uploading an outdated pkz204a.exe after uploading many copies of pkz204g.exe. In this case, the outdated file has a later *creation* date than current versions of the file. Since the most recently dated matching file appears first on the returned list, an outdated file would be on the top of the list sorted by date. However, if you closely review the returned list and look past the first few entries, you'll almost certainly spot any such date anomalies.

Downloading pkz204g.exe

Since all we know for sure about our target file is that it will begin with the string "pkz", we'll perform another Archie search using "pkz" as the target string. This time we'll also check the By Date field to select sorting by date.

When I tried to submit the Archie search request, the default server was busy. Taking my own advice, I opened the Archie Server menu and selected an Archie Server in Japan. (At the time of my search it was early afternoon on the East Coast.)

Figure 16.4 shows the results of the search in this project. The first entry lists files contained on the host ftp.ipc.chiba-u.ac.jp, which is in Japan. pkz204g.exe is in directory /.1/pub/kosahara/msdos/Archive-tool/pkzip. It is not unusual for a popular file to appear in more than one directory on the same server. If we move down through the listing, we would see that pkz204g.exe is indeed the most recent version of the program.

At this point, you'll probably want to transfer the file to your PC. The returned query, as shown in Figure 16.4, is actually an HTML document complete with active links. As you drag the mouse pointer across the underlined anchor associated with the file pkz204g.exe, notice the URL that appears on the status line:

```
file://ftp.ipc.chiba-u.ac.jp/.1/pub.kosahara/msdos/Archive-tool/pkzip/pkz204g.exe
```

This indicates that the file is a few clicks away from residing on your PC. The URL protocols (the first part of the URL) file: and ftp: are used interchangeably under most simple circumstances.

Figure 16.4 The results of an Archie search.

Before downloading an archive containing a number of files, I always like to create a temporary directory, download the archive into that directory, and unzip the archive so that its component files remain in that directory. If I later decide to trash the entire file and all its component pieces, it's simply a matter of deleting the directory. In this case, let's assume the creation of a directory named D:\PKZIP. This directory will receive the downloaded file.

To download the file, prepare your browser to receive a file to disk rather than simply displaying it. Click on the pkz204g.exe anchor to activate the transfer. In short order the Save As dialog box appears, as shown in Figure 16.5. This is a standard Windows dialog box much like the familiar Windows Open File dialog. The default file name is the name of the file you're requesting, as it is stored on the remote site, provided it's a legal DOS file name. Change the file name if you prefer a different name for the file as it will exist on your disk, and click on the Drives drop-down menu to change the drive designation, if necessary. When the desired file name appears in the File Name edit box and the desired path name appears under the Directory title, you're ready to download. Click on OK and the download will begin.

The browser absolves you from all login details, which is a major difference compared to performing FTP from an Internet shell account. You do not have to enter "anonymous" at the login prompt, and you do not have to enter your e-mail address at the password prompt. The HTTP FTP protocol (with the

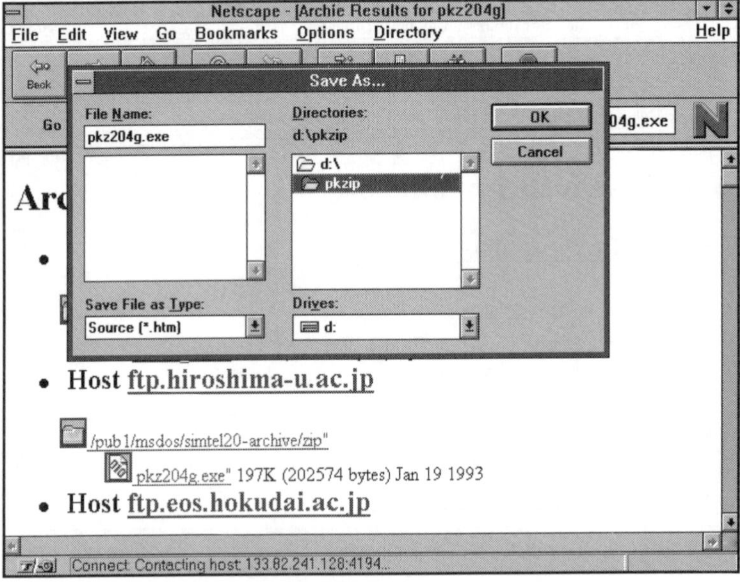

Figure 16.5 Selecting a name and location for a saved file.

browser in command) takes care of these details automatically. The browser furthermore decides to employ either binary or ASCII mode for the transfer based upon the target file's extension.

Now we have to uncompress the package. You could switch to Windows Program Manager and select the menu option File | Run, then enter

```
D:\PKZIP\PKZ204G
```

in the Command Line edit field. Alternatively, you could shell to DOS by clicking on the MS-DOS Prompt icon. When at the DOS prompt, make d:\pkzip the default directory. Then, enter

```
PKZ204G
```

at the command-line prompt. The self-extracting archive will kick into high gear and extract all of its component files into the current directory.

After expanding pkz204g.exe, do a directory listing (DIR). You should see something similar to the following:

```
 Volume in drive D has no label
 Volume Serial Number is 13D2-044A
 Directory of D:\PKZIP

.           <DIR>       12-12-94  11:32a
..          <DIR>       12-12-94  11:32a
PKZ204G     EXE         202,574 10-28-94      4:10p
README      DOC         741 02-01-93          2:04a
SHAREWAR    DOC         573 02-01-93          2:04a
WHATSNEW    204         2,430 02-01-93        2:04a
V204G       NEW         0,704 02-01-93        2:04a
HINTS       TXT         4,109 02-01-93        2:04a
LICENSE     DOC         3,707 02-01-93        2:04a
ORDER       OC          3,304 02-01-93        2:04a
ADDENDUM    DOC         19,361 02-01-93       2:04a
MANUAL      DOC         202,252 02-01-93      2:04a
AUTHVERI    FRM         2,330 02-01-93        2:04a
PKZIP       EXE         2,166 02-01-93        2:04a
PKUNZIP     EXE         29,378 02-01-93       2:04a
PKZIPFIX    EXE          7,687 02-01-93       2:04a
ZIP2EXE     EXE         27,319 02-01-93       2:04a
PKUNZJR     COM         2,750 02-01-93        2:04a
OMBUDSMN    ASP         591 02-01-93          2:04a
          19 file(s)    571,976 bytes
```

After you have expanded the files, you may delete pkx204g.exe—or perhaps, to be safe, archive it to tape or diskette. If you are new to ZIPing, take the time to read the files readme.doc, hints.doc, and at least skim through manual.doc. You may want to print manual.doc for future reference. Since we will be using pkzip.exe, pkunzip.exe, and zip2exe.exe on a regular basis, and pkzipfix.exe on a (with some luck) infrequent basis, copy these files to some directory that is on your path, perhaps DOS or a UTILS directory.

If you're like me, you will use PKUNZIP more that any other DOS utility program. Then again, maybe you're not as compulsive about trying new things as I am.

Creating a Self-Extracting Compressed File

Let's assume you have a group of files you have FTPed in your DOS directory c:\big-deal that you want to send to several friends. Your friends have yet to read this book so they may not know about PKUNZIP.

First, compress and include all files in a single file named goodies.zip. At the command line enter

```
C:\BIG-DEAL> pkzip  goodies  *.*
```

This creates goodies.zip. If you don't enter an extension, pkzip assumes you want a .ZIP extension. Next enter this command:

```
C:\BIG-DEAL> zip2exe goodies
```

You now have a file goodies.exe that your friends may extract simply by entering its name at the command line prompt.

Using Archie from a Unix Shell

Using Telnet to directly access an Archie server is number two on our searching technique hit parade. Telnetting from within a Web browser is essentially the same as using its Unix shell account counterpart, so let's go with good old Unix first. I'm going to make the heroic assumption that you understand and know how to use Telnet. If you don't, you are missing out on a very valuable tool—but, alas, I don't have the space to provide a detailed tutorial on its use. I would strongly suggest that you find out more about Telnet by reading one of the reference books available. It may be a bit of a handful, but it is definitely worth learning.

Locations of Archie Servers

There are currently 25 Archie servers worldwide. Despite the number of servers, establishing a Telnet connection to Archie can frequently be difficult due to congestion on the servers and the low priority of Internet traffic at most sites. Using the guidelines from the first tip presented in this chapter, select an Archie server located somewhere in the world where it is *not* local business hours. Figure 16.6 shows the Archie Server's drop-down menu on an Archie Request Form.

A representative geographic sample of Archie servers follows:

```
Australia     archie.au
Canada        archie.uqam.ca
Finland       archie.funet.fi
Israel        archie.cs.huji.ac.il
Ireland       archie.doc.ic.ac.uk
Japan         archie.wide.ad.jp
USA-NJ        archie.rutgers.edu
```

If you are building your own bookmarks, or if you just want a listing of all active Archie servers, send an e-mail message to archie@archie.rutgers.edu (or any other Archie, for that matter). In the subject area or in the body of the message, put the one word *servers*. (That's all!)

When Telnetting to Archie from within a Unix shell account, enter the following at the Unix command line prompt

```
unix% telnet archie-domain-name
```

where "unix%" represents the prompt on your system. (Don't type the prompt!) An Archie domain name might be archie.rutgers.edu. When presented with the "login:" prompt, enter "archie" without the quotations. (Don't forget: This is Unix and *case counts*. Make sure you enter "archie" using *only* lowercase

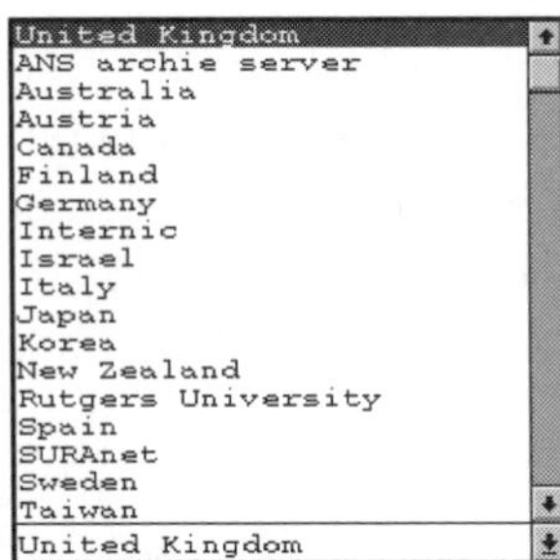

Figure 16.6 *The available servers on an Archie Request form.*

letters.) Requests for Archie services represent one of the Internet's most popular activities; don't be surprised if your connection request is refused. Most Archie hosts limit the number of simultaneous connections. If you do connect successfully, you'll be greeted with the prompt "archie>".

Archie commands take the following form

```
archie> command
```

where "archie>" is the prompt and "command" represents your chosen command. The basic command to query the Archie database is "find". There are many variations on the Archie search theme; see the EXplorer TIP near the end of this chapter for information on obtaining your very own Archie manual at no charge. The manual describes a great many options and additional features that we don't have the space to cover here. The "sortby" command is especially useful. There are many sort variations; the one that helps us identify the most current version of a software package is the command "sortby rfilename", which instructs Archie to sort the results of the search and list the output by file name, in descending order.

If you would like the search results mailed to you, use the command:

```
mailto your-e-mail-address
```

The default number of search matches is 100. If you think you need more or fewer, use the command

```
set maxhits nnn
```

where *nnn* is the number of matches you desire. (Use as few as you think you need to save time and resources.) The listing can be generated in compact form with one line per entry if you issue the command:

```
set output_format terse
```

Return for a moment to the pkz204g.exe download. If we search for "pkz" and set the sortby parameter to return the search in descending order, the most recent version would be on top of the list. All files starting with "pkz" (or "PKZ") would produce a sort tie. The next character would be the tie breaker. Since we elected to sort in reverse order "2" would appear before "1". If all returned file names tied with "pkz2", the fourth character would be the tie breaker, and so on.

Using Archie to Find the Latest Versions of Mosaic

To illustrate the power of searching with Archie, let's look for the latest version of NCSA Mosaic. In actuality, there are two current version of Mosaic and Netscape. There is an "alpha" version and a "beta" version. The alpha version, which is frequently called the production version, has been well tested while the beta version is newer and has more features. The decision to use the alpha or beta version is usually the choice between relative bug-free stability and buggy features. (I keep both available.)

For the sake of simplicity and to keep the size of the search under control, I'll assume we know the current version of NCSA Windows Mosaic is 2.x and we therefore know that the file name will begin with "mos2". (In most real-life searches you'll have heard at least some clues as to the current major release of a piece of software.)

The following is the listing of an actual Telnet session to an Archie server in Taiwan. Do we have a global information superhighway or what?

```
unix% telnet archie.ncu.edu.tw
Trying 192.83.166.12...
Connected to spc11.ncu.edu.tw.
Escape character is '^]'.

SunOS UNIX (spc11)

login: archie
Last login: Wed Dec 14 00:07:20 from acy1.digex.net
SunOS Release 4.1.3 (BAU) #1: Tue Jan 11 09:29:51 CST 1994
# Bunyip Information Systems, 1993, 1994

# Terminal type set to 'vt100 24 80'.
# 'erase' character is '^?'.
# 'search' (type string) has the value 'sub'.

archie> set sortby rfilename
archie> set maxhits 200
archie> find wmos2
# Search type: sub.
# Your queue position: 1
# Estimated time for completion: 12 seconds.
working...
```

After the search's output was displayed, I entered

```
archie> mail lejeune@acy.digex.net
archie> quit
```

so that the output would be mailed to me. The following is a portion of the search results Archie mailed to me:

```
Host ftp.rrzn.uni-hannover.de    (130.75.2.2)
Last updated 23:24 23 Mar 1995

    Location: /pub/systems/msdos-local/tcpip/Mosaic
      FILE    -rw-rw-r—  947877 bytes  22:52 30 Jan 1995  mos20a9.exe

(LOTS OF STUFF DELETED TO SAVE SPACE)

Host ftp.sunet.se    (130.238.127.3)
Last updated 18:10  1 Apr 1995

    Location: /pub/pc/windows/winsock-indstate/WWW-Browsers/Mosaic
      FILE    -r—r—r—  947877 bytes  08:24 28 Jan 1995  wmos20a9.exe
      FILE    -r—r—r—  955546 bytes  07:45 22 Dec 1994  wmos20a8.exe
      FILE    -r—r—r—  288404 bytes  03:55 22 Oct 1994  wmos20a7.zip
      FILE    -r—r—r—  292878 bytes  03:55 22 Oct 1994  wmos20a6.zip
      FILE    -r—r—r—  272435 bytes  03:55 22 Oct 1994  wmos20a5.zip
      FILE    -r—r—r—  263431 bytes  03:55 22 Oct 1994  wmos20a4.zip
      FILE    -r—r—r—  263306 bytes  03:55 22 Oct 1994  wmos20a3.zip
      FILE    -r—r—r—  243749 bytes  03:55 22 Oct 1994  wmos20a2.zip

    Location: /pub/pc/windows/mirror-cica/winsock
      FILE    -r—r—r—  288404 bytes  16:07 26 Sep 1994  wmos20a7.zip
```

The first portion of the listing shows a site archiving only the latest version of Mosaic. The second host has Mosaic packages in two different directories, /pub/pc/windows/winsock/-indstate/WWW-Browsers/Mosaic and /pub/pc/windows/mirror-cica/winsock. The first directory has seven older versions but illustrates the effect of the Archie command "sortby rfilename."

The Host name in these listings is the site to which you would FTP. The Location portion of the listing is the path name containing the directory, and the last item in the FILE line is the actual name of the file. The FTP URL to transfer mos20a9.exe from the first site shown above would be:

```
ftp://ftp.sunet.se//pub/pc/windows/winsock-indstate/WWW-Browsers/Mosaic/wmos20a9.exe
```

Again, remember that most FTP host machines are Unix-based and as such, case is significant. The "WWW" substring in the above path name would not be recognized if you entered "www", nor would "Mosaic" be recognized if you entered "mosaic".

Using an Archie Client

The Internet Chameleon, which is included on this book's CD-ROM, contains a suite of Internet client packages. The Internet Chameleon will be discussed, in detail, later in the book. As a functional preview of a dedicated client, let's take a look at the Chameleon Archie. Figure 16.7 shows the results of an Archie search on the string "mos20." As you can see, the files mos20aN.exe and mos20bN.exe are available, where "N" represents the version number. The "a" or "b" coming before the version number represents the release level of the software: "a" indicates the software is an alpha version and "b" indicates the software is beta software. The listing in Figure 16.7 shows the availability of alpha versions a8 and a9 and beta versions b1, b3, and b4. As an example, the file mos20a9.exe indicates the program is Mosaic 2.0, alpha 9.

One of the nice features of the Chameleon Archie client is a seamless transition to FTPing a display file. Highlighting a file and clicking on the Retrieve button, or simply double clicking on the file name will bring up the FTP dialog box as shown in Figure 16.8. If the default directory or file name is not what you would prefer, click on the file folder icon, which will bring up the Select target file dialog box as shown in Figure 16.9. Clicking on the OK button in the FTP dialog will start the FTP download.

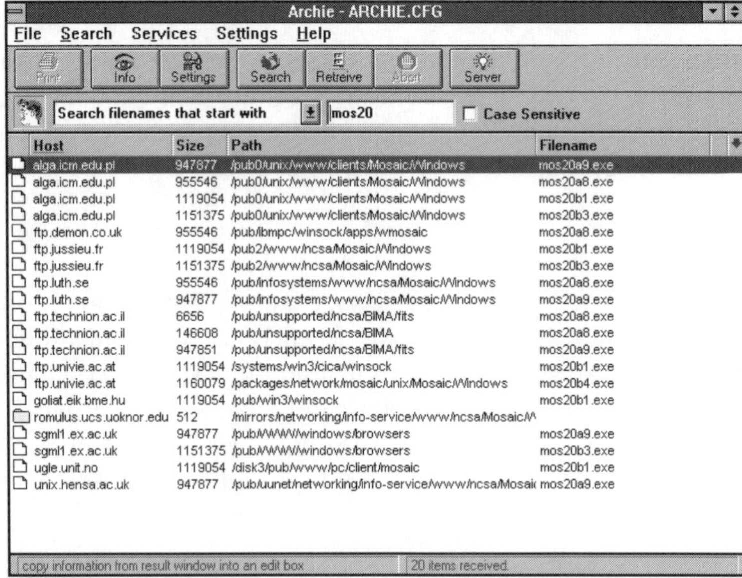

***Figure 16.7** The results of an Archie search using the Chameleon Archie client.*

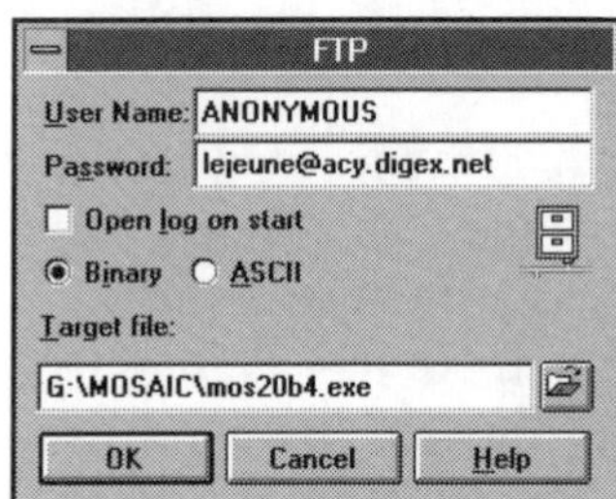

Figure 16.8 Going from an Archie search to an FTP download in one easy step.

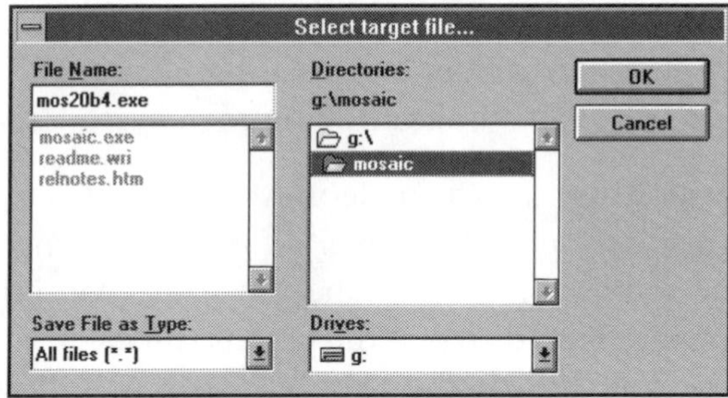

Figure 16.9 Selecting a path and file name for the FTPed file.

Advanced Archie: Send Him Some Fan Mail

Archie is frequently inaccessible; I hear it has something to do with Veronica. E-mailing Archie can be a big-time frustration saver if you are not in a major rush for the results of your search. You can send mail to any Archie server requesting a search or any other available information. The address is in the form:

```
archie@archie-domain-name
```

The address archie@archie.rutgers.edu is an example. Put the same commands in the body of the message that you would enter at the command line. Send it off and in due course your mail box will hold the results. If you have access to a Unix shell account, you may want to use the script file that I present below. (It's on the supplied CD-ROM as "findfile" in the \urbstuff\unix directory.) If you transfer the file to your Unix host and make it executable, you need only enter:

```
unix% findfile search-target
```

To conduct the same search as listed in the above example, with terse output formatting thrown in for good measure, enter:

```
unix% findfile wmos2
```

The listing of the script file follows.

```
 # Script "findfile" used to send an e-mail search request to an archie server #
 #
 # The syntax is:
 #             findfile string
 # replace string with the file name (or substring) to find.
 #
 # Test to see if there is a passed parameter
 #
if test -z "$1"
  then # There is no passed parameter
    echo
    echo "The syntax for this script is:"
    echo "     find <search-string>"
    echo "replacing <search-string> (without the <>) with"
    echo "a string, or substring, that is the name of the"
    echo "file you are trying to locate"
    echo
  else  # There is a passed parameter
    # Create a file archie.tmp and write the following six string
    echo "set search sub" > archie.tmp    # Perform a substring search
    echo "set output_format terse" >> archie.tmp # Produce one line listings
    echo "set sortby rfilename" >> archie.tmp # Sort in descending order
    echo "set maxhits 200" >> archie.tmp # Allow 200 matches
    echo 'find' $1 >> archie.tmp         # Write string with passed parameter
    echo "quit" >> archie.tmp            # End of request
    # Mail file archie.tmp to archie server
    # Substitute your favorite archie server below
    #
    mail archie@archie.rutgers.edu < archie.tmp
    rm archie.tmp  # Delete file archie.tmp
fi # end if
```

Telnetting to Archie from within Netscape

Telnetting to an Archie server from within a Web browser is the last technique we'll cover here. If your Web browser supports Telnetting and you have a Telnet client, you can connect directly to an Archie server. Your provider may have given you a Telnet client program on that install diskette you were handed when you signed on. The Chameleon Sampler product supplied on the companion CD-ROM contains a nice Telnet client. See Chapter 26, *SLIP/ PPP and the Chameleon Sampler*, for instructions on using the Chameleon

Telnet client. See Chapter 22, *Setting Your Netscape Preferences*, to configure Netscape to look for an external Telnet client.

The URL format for Telnet is:

```
telnet://domain-name
```

To initiate a Telnet session from within Netscape, insert the following URL in the Location: field

```
telnet://archie.ncu.edu.tw
```

(or any other Archie site) and click OK. If you have successfully configured a Telnet client program as the Telnet helper utility and you get connected to the Archie server, you'll be presented with a "login:" prompt. This prompt is exactly the same as the one discussed in the Unix shell example earlier. Figure 16.10 shows a portion of a Telnet session to archie.ncu.edu.tw using the Chameleon Sampler Telnet client. The search was initiated using the command:

```
archie> find winweb
```

WinWeb is a Web browser. The listings are in the same format as those in the Unix Telnet session.

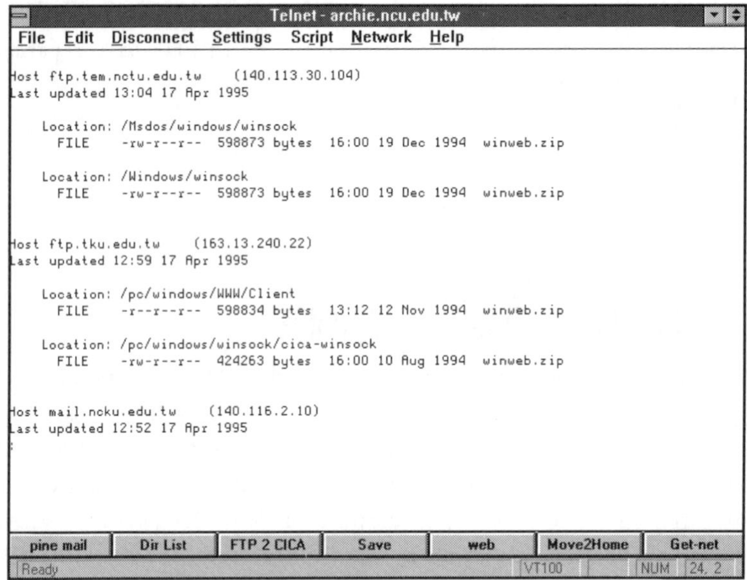

Figure 16.10 A Telnet session to Taiwan's ARCHIE>NCU.EDU.TW.

Downloading Using FTP

After having found the file of your choice, the next step is to download it to your PC. We discussed using Netscape to download a file a little earlier in this chapter by clicking on the hotlink returned as part of the Archie search results. You may also FTP a file from Netscape by manually entering its URL. Let's return to the Windows Mosaic 2 example begun earlier and download the file mos20a9.exe.

The host name contained in an Archie search listing is the site to which you would FTP. The location portion of the listing is the path name containing the directory, and the last item in the FILE line is the name of the file. The FTP URL to transfer mos20a9.exe from the first listing in the above example would be:

```
ftp://cc04.ccit.edu.tw/pub2/WWW/ncsaMosaic/Windows/wmos20a7.zip
ftp://ftp.sunet.se//pub/pc/windows/winsock-indstate/WWW-Browsers/Mosaic
  wmos20a9.exe
```

Again, remember that most FTP host machines are Unix based and, as such, case matters. Enter the above URL in Netscape's Location box and click on OK. When Netscape encounters a file with an extension it doesn't know how to process, such as .EXE in this case, it brings up the Unknown File Type dialog box as shown in Figure 16.11. In this case, click on the Save to Disk button.

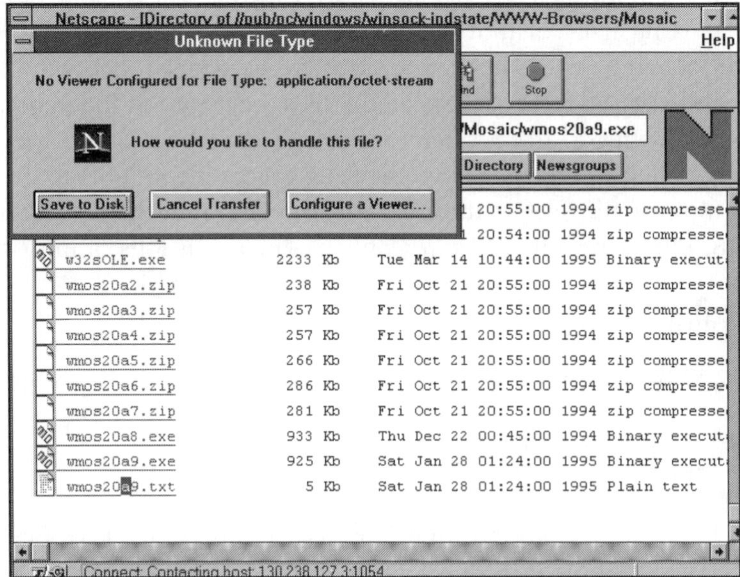

Figure 16.11 Using the Unknown File Type dialog box.

This will bring up the Save As dialog box with the name of the file as you want it stored on your disk. Make any necessary adjustments in name or path and click on OK, and—here it comes!

THE VIRTUAL SHAREWARE LIBRARY

As mentioned earlier in this chapter, the Virtual Shareware Library, located at the University of Ljudljana in Slovenia, has a service called SHASE (SHareware Archives Search Engine) that permits querying a database of software depository file names and descriptions. The breakthrough in the database lies in the ability to search by program description or file name, not only by file name as required by Archie.

These major software depositories all have a file named "index" (or something very similar) in every directory. File names on Unix systems are usually composed of lowercase letters. Directory contents are listed in ascending order. Since uppercase comes before lowercase, INDEX will usually come first in a directory listing.

Each entry in the index file has a short (about 40 characters) plain text description of the program's function. A search of the SHASE database attempts to match the search key to the file's description as well as its name. Among the software sites SHASE scans on a nightly basis are the massive software goldmines called CICA (University of Indiana's *Center for Innovative Computer Applications)*, Garbo, and SimTel. These major sites are so popular that many "mirror" sites of each exist. A mirror site has all the files contained in the parent site. If you want to download from a mirror site, you must be a little careful since there can be a delay of a day or two between uploading of a file to the parent and spawning of the file to the mirror sites. The Yanoff list, described in Chapter 18, *Comparing WWW and Gopher*, contains listings of mirror sites.

SHASEing Around

Access the Virtual Shareware Library's home page by pointing Mosaic to:

```
http://www.fagg.uni-lj.si/cgi-bin/shase
```

http://www.fagg.uni-lj.si/cgi-bin/shase

Figure 16.12 shows a portion of the Library's "Front Desk." Let's find a program called Paint Shop Pro—it's a great image processing application you might want to use to create graphics for your Web pages. A major problem

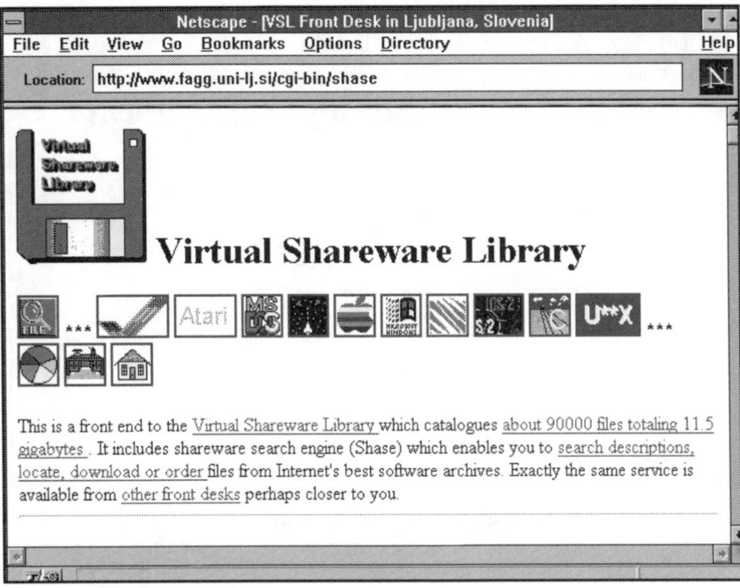

***Figure 16.12** The Virtual Shareware Library's home page.*

when using Archie to find a file is the fact that only file names and directories are searched in the FTPable database. Since most program packages have a version number imbedded in the name, it is very difficult (read impossible) to predict what file name will be given to the name of the program. SHASE comes to our assistance when navigating FTP sites.

Getting Some Great Windows Software

CICA, at the University of Indiana, is a massive depository of Windows software. Sim-Tel is another outstanding depositor,y as is the Microsoft FTP machine. Let's use a combination of all three as an exploration to find some useful Windows software.

Since we know Paint Shop Pro is a Windows program, click on the Windows icon. There are 14 searchable shareware depositories available with SHASE. Clicking on the Windows icon will result in searching the CICA, Sim-Tel Windows directories, and the Microsoft database. This will in turn bring up the form shown in Figure 16.13. If we only wanted to search the CICA depository, we could uncheck the other two archives.

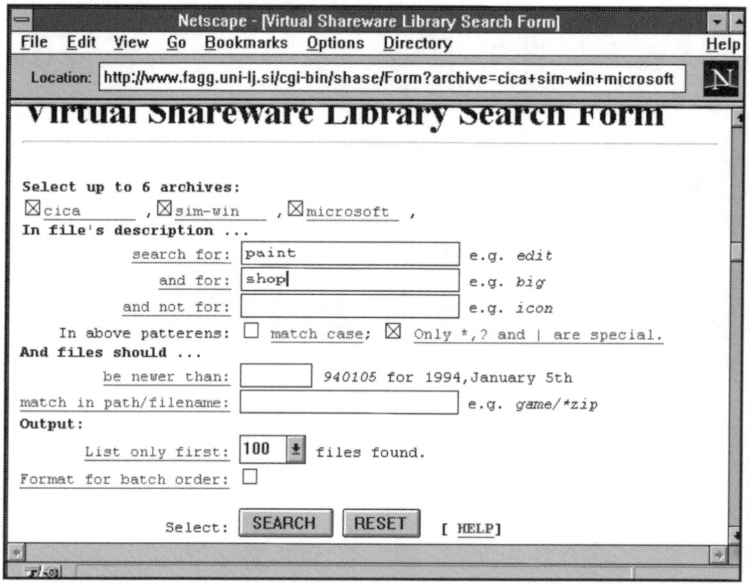

Figure 16.13 Using the SHASE search form.

Enter "paint" in the form's first "search for" field. Next enter "shop" in the "and for" field. A Boolean "and" requires that both string must be present to establish a hit.file description field. Click on Submit at the bottom of the form to initiate the search. Figure 16.14 shows the search results.

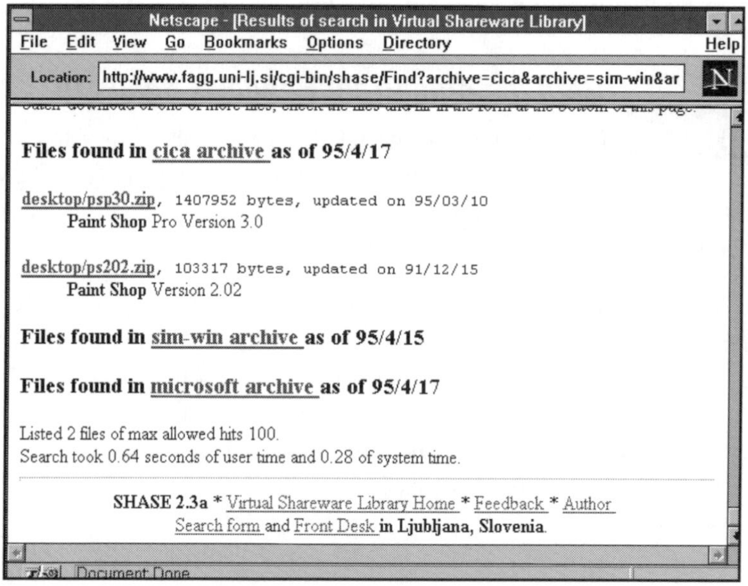

Figure 16.14 The results of a SHASE search.

As a final step, you may download a displayed file. As shown in Figure 11.14, there are two different versions of Paint Shop Pro found in the CICA depository. Clicking on

```
desktop/psp30.zip
```

will bring up the list of CICA, and CICA mirror, sites hold psp30.zip. Clicking on a site will start the FTP process as described in the earlier section, *Downloading Using FTP*.

The incredible Virtual Shareware Library was conceived and implemented by Ziga Turk, an Assistant Professor of Computer Science at Slovenia's University of Ljubljana. His e-mail address is ziga.turk@fagg.uni-lj.si. I'm sure he would enjoy hearing your comments about his brainchild.

Getting the Archie Manual

Archie is an extremely versatile system with a host of options and features that we cannot begin to cover in this book (which, after all, is a book about the World Wide Web). There is a detailed manual that you can receive at no charge that covers the rest of its very rich feature set. To get the official Archie manual, send an e-mail message to archie@archie.rutgers.edu (or any other Archie server). In the body of the message put the one word *manpage*. That's all you need to do. The manual document will be sent to you via e-mail.

EXPLORER TIP

Using WinZip

If you're a confirmed Windowholic, you will love the shareware package WinZip. As the name implies, it's a Windows front end for combining all the PK Ware zip functions as well as the ability to configure many other compression utilities. A Virus scanner may also be configured. Figure 16.15 shows WinZip after having opened easyicon.zip. It not only displays the components of the ZIP file, you may also read the TXT files without uncompressing them. Check it out.

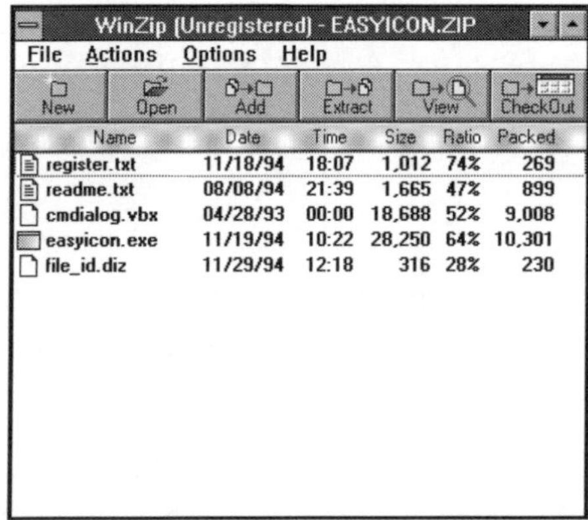

Figure 16.15 *The WinZip Open Window.*

LET'S REVIEW

Locating programs and other useful documents and downloading these files to your PC makes the Internet both fun and rewarding. With a little practice you'll become an old hand at these complementary skills. The HTML document master.htm, which is included on the supplied CD-ROM, contains links for all of the URLs contained in this book. In addition, the HTML document urb-menu.htm is a menu that I have built for my frequently visited sites. The menu contains over 300 sites listed by category. I use the menu as my Netscape starting document. Many FTP sites and utilities are included in the menu.

Let's get some rest before starting our next exploration; this has been a big one.

Gopher, Gopherspace, and the Web

The easy-to-use hierarchical menu structure imposed on the Internet by Gopher may be used seamlessly and efficiently from inside Netscape.

The Internet tools we encountered in our earlier explorations each accomplishes a dedicated task. Archie helps find the location of a file, provided we know the file's name, or at least a portion of its name. FTP allows fetching a file from a distant location, if we know the location of the file, including the site and its directory tree structure. Telnet enables logging onto remote networks in faraway places. The more advanced Web browsers like Netscape and Mosaic provide windows into these services without the need to use the dreaded Unix command line interface. Gopher continues the process of building our ever-expanding Internet toolbox.

The World Wide Web is the primary thrust of this book, but Netscape and its friends provide a window into the separate world of interlinked Gopher directories that aficionados call *Gopherspace*. Gopher is also interesting because it is accessible by anyone connected to the Internet, as opposed to Netscape's requirement that the user's computer be "on" the Internet via a SLIP or PPP account.

Even users having only e-mail access to the Internet can use the full facilities of Gopher, albeit slowly. Information search and retrieval using Gopher tends to mimic most people's experiential background, so it's easy to catch on once Gopher is in front of you.

As with Netscape, Gopher knows the proper tools to use when helping us to move around and retrieve what we want. The best part of Gopher, from our perspective as Internet explorers, is that the entire process is effortless and transparent.

GOPHER AND MY FRIEND VIN

Many years ago a ham radio friend of mine (Vin Hoyes, VP5BL, later 9Y5BL) encouraged me to come to Jamaica for a visit. At the time I had never been further south of New Jersey than the state of Virginia, and northern Virginia at that. Finally, I packed my new bride and myself into my old car, drove to Florida, and flew to Jamaica. We were late in arriving and we didn't want to disturb our friend Vin at work, so we just rode into town and checked into the best known hotel in Kingston. After dinner I called Vin. After I explained why we were at the hotel, Vin simply said, "Check out, I'll be at the main entrance in 15 minutes!" I tried to protest, saying that we had already paid for a day and eaten dinner, to which he again admonished, "Check out!" After an enjoyable visit with Vin and his family, he drove us to the top of the highest hill on his end of the island. He had us check into a beautiful hotel having a glorious view of the entire Kingston area. The rooms were twice as large, the food was substantially better, and the price was exactly half the rate being charged by the downtown tourist hotel. Later, Vin performed the same magic when we spent a few days on the hilly north shore of Jamaica. Gopher is much like my friend Vin.

Why Did Gopher Come into Being?

Prior to the introduction of Gopher in 1991, the Internet was a vast depository of information that no one knew how to access effectively. Gopher was the right software at the right time. The original development of Gopher took place at the University of Minnesota. The university's sports teams are the "golden gophers." The software is designed to "go fer" information—and with that in mind, the origin of the name should be obvious.

The design concept underlying Gopher was brilliant: To organize available Internet resources and make them easy to access. From that rather humble beginning, Gopherspace—the domain of all Gopher servers—has expanded far beyond anyone's original expectations. As we go to press, approximately 2,300 organizations and institutions host a Gopher server, and new ones are being added at the rate of about 35 per week. If we count each Internet-accessible Gopher site, including those at the department level, there are over 5,000 publicly accessible Gopher networks. These sites contain more than 150,000 menus and 10 million individual resources, such as text and graphic files. The spectacular growth in the number of Gopher sites, although impressive, is not the total story. The addition of new sites presents only one aspect of information expansion, since existing sites continue to expand their offered information.

If Netscape could not access Gopherspace and I could choose only one Internet utility, I would be hard pressed to choose between Netscape and Gopher. With Gopher I can do almost everything I normally do using other software, with the exception of sending and receiving mail and viewing (as opposed to fetching, which it can do) graphics. Gopher is the next logical stop on our exploration of major organized informational resources.

What Is a Gopher?

Technically, the Internet Gopher is a hierarchical, menu-driven software system that searches for and retrieves resources from participating networks on the Internet. Resources may be menus, text files, graphic images, sound files, video clips, and other types of non-textual information. Gopherspace sounds a lot like the World Wide Web because it is. All the methods used to access Internet information have liberally borrowed from one another. For a few minutes, let's look at Gopher as a stand-alone system, and then we'll return to using Netscape to access Gopher sites.

The power of Gopher stems from its two types of functions: First, it is a protocol that sends and retrieves information over the Internet. Second, it is a methodology used to organize information. Gopher permits "burrowing" through the vast informational structure of the Internet by using a network of related menus.

Gopher is a superb browsing tool. When using Gopher, you don't concern yourself with details like the location of information or how to transfer the information to your local computer. Gopher manages all details of an online session, including the selection of the appropriate tools. Indeed, some of my favorite Internet resources have been serendipitous "finds" while on a Gopher "surfing the net" exploration.

Before the advent of Gopher, the organization of information stashed away on the Internet could be charitably described as abysmal. Knowing about

Internet information was similar to knowing a great big-mouthed bass lake existed somewhere in the Midwest; however, Lake Big Bass didn't appear on any map. To further compound the problem, few people knew the location of Lake Big Bass. To be sure, Archie helps locate a file available for downloading, provided we know the file's name. Much like folk tales, pointers to Internet resources were largely transmitted by word of mouth. When Internet contained only a few dozen sites, and everyone knew everyone else, there was little need for organization. The "tela-buddy" form of communications, however, became obsolete when the number of Internet nodes exceeded the average IQ of its users. When the nodes crossed into the 100,000 range, the existing data organization scheme—or lack thereof—bordered on the comical.

Gopher First Organized the Internet

Gopher servers were the first structured attempt to create a user friendly interface on the Internet. In addition to providing ease of use, Gopher added the means for information organization. Gopher technology was originally designed to serve the needs of a multi-network university, not the voracious information appetite of the Internet.

It is fortunate for all of us latter-day Gopher users, and indeed Web surfers, that the software was conceived, went through a short gestation period, and spent its early childhood in academia. Academic institutions, by their very nature, are bureaucratic organizations. As such, these institutional guardians husband their resources and authority with religious fervor. In its early incarnations Gopher was conceptualized as a central information server. Students, faculty, and staff would connect to a common computer to retrieve a broad range of university information. Alas, it was not to be. Each department envisioned itself as an independent entity, creating and maintaining its own rules and its own information.

Then, as now, individual departments in large universities tend to control all of their own resources, including individual computer networks. The implementation of a university-wide data pool had two requirements: The first was a central network that would receive all requests for information. The second was the central network's ability to direct any department-specific requests to the appropriate subordinate network. For reasons that will shortly become clear, imbuing an information system with the ability to connect to another network also gave it the ability to communicate with a cooperating computer anywhere on the Internet. From a technical standpoint it doesn't make an iota of difference whether another network is on the next floor or halfway around the world. A URL by any other name is still a pointer to an Internet resource.

Had Gopher been developed in a highly efficient profit-making enterprise, it would have emerged in a different form. Had the form been different, it would in all likelihood now be extinct, or at least endangered. The bureaucratic nature of a university environment forced the necessity of dealing with distributed information upon the original software developers of the Gopher system. These external forces positively influenced the development of Gopher, just as external forces have frequently influenced many other great inventions.

GOPHER AS A CONCEPT

Gopher shares a characteristic common to all well-functioning systems, namely, the underlying technology is transparent to the user. When you pick up a phone, all you want to hear is the dial tone. When you dial a long distance number, you have absolutely no interest in the fact that your connection may indeed be traveling through the facilities of many different service providers. Gopher is like that. To help us understand these concepts, let's first take a look at a Gopher-like application with no technical bells or whistles.

Imagine we are taking a vacation to historic cities on the east coast. While in Philadelphia we walk into the lobby of Liberty Bell One, a large modern office building. As we enter the concourse, we notice one wall lined with a row of brightly colored computer terminals. We walk up to one and on the screen is:

```
                Welcome to Liberty Bell One

—>1. Liberty Bell One - Introductory Video <Video>
   2. Liberty Bell One - Facilities/
   3. Liberty Bell One - Frequently Asked Questions (FAQ).
   4. Accounting Firms/
   5. Philadelphia Lawyers/
   6. Local Points of Interest/

Enter the number of your choice, or q to quit   Enter ? for help
```

The Liberty Bell One menu is much like the top-level menu at any Gopher site. When you start a search of Gopherspace, you initially see the main menu for the site that you select as a starting point. In this example, notice that some lines end with either a slash character "/" or a period. If this were a fancy Windows-like interface, graphic icons would start each line. Each item on the menu represents a pointer of sorts to another object. The object may be a directory (another menu, in other words) or an actual resource like a file. The "/" indicates a more detailed menu "under" the selection. In this example, and those to follow in this chapter, an entry ending with a period indicates a pointer to a plain text file. (Not all Gopher menus use the period convention; some indicate a text file simply by the omitting any other notation.) A menu selection may point to many different types of resources. In this example items 2, 4, 5, and 6 point to submenus. Item 1 points to a video and item 3 points to a text file. Later on we'll discuss other possible terminators.

At this point you can select one of the six numeric choices by entering the appropriate number. Alternatively, you may move the arrow to your choice by pressing the keyboard's up and down arrow keys. Finally, select your choice by pressing Enter. You may also enter "?" for more information about the menu and its commands. If you enter "q" you will quit and disconnect. If you select "1" on this menu, you will see a video describing the beauty of Liberty Bell One. Selecting "3" will produce a plain text listing of frequently asked questions about Liberty Bell One. Although both of these resources will appear on the terminal being operated, the actual resources may reside anywhere in Gopherspace. This illustrates one of the major benefits of both Gopher and the Web: You don't need to know the actual location of a resource, and you don't need to know the transportation details required getting from "over there" to your computer. However, if you do care about the location of resources, Gopher provides a way to find out.

Starting Down a Gopher Hole

Continuing our quest, we select option "5", expecting a more detailed submenu because the selection ends with a "/". The screen next displays:

```
           Philadelphia Lawyers

—>    1. Philadelphia Legal Aid Society.
      2. Ethical Conduct of Philadelphia Lawyers (Short Document).
      3. Stickem & Upham/
      4. Suet, Brewitt & Clewless/
      5. Philadelphia Area Law Schools/
      6. Philadelphia Bar Association/

Enter the number of your choice, q to quit, u to go up a level or ? for help
```

The title of the main menu's item 5 is "Philadelphia Lawyers." An item's description (Philadelphia Lawyers in this case) becomes the title of the next menu upon its selection. As we descend the menu structure, this pattern will prevail at all levels. At each level of the descent the selected menu will become progressively more detailed. Notice the "u to go up a level" addition to the status line when we arrive at this level. Once you go below the main menu, you may work your way back up one level at a time by pressing "u", or you may skip the intermediate menus and press "m" and return to the main menu. An example of a comment—generally enclosed within parentheses—is item 2's "Short Document."

Although we are on vacation, it is hard to pass up looking at the information provided by that internationally famous firm of Philadelphia barristers Stickem & Upham. Not only is Stick Up (as the firm Stickem & Upham is lovingly known to many of their clients) located in a building other than Liberty Bell One, it is on a totally different network. However, both the Stick Up network and the Liberty Bell One network are connected to the Internet. The fact that we are now going to another network is of no concern in our world of transparent functionality.

If we choose menu selection "3" the next screen might look like this:

```
                Stickem & Upham
                 Attorneys at Law

            "You Call, We Haul, That's All, You All"

—>     1. Ethics of the firm  (Not currently functional).
       2. List of Satisfied Clients (Short list).
       3. Partners/
       4. Wannabe Partners/
       5. Client Services/

Enter the number of your choice, q to quit, u to go up a level, or ? for help
```

And so it goes. As we descend into the Gopher hole, the selections get progressively more detailed. Can you take a guess as to what the level below this menu will look like? If we select item 3, we expect another menu since the line ends with a "/". What would that menu contain? Most likely a listing of partner names, each of which would lead to a text file with information about that specific lawyer. A search culminates when we find the search object, or we reach the bottom of the shaft and come up empty handed. Once you reach a document that looks interesting, you may transfer it to your own computer for later reference. You may also fetch graphic files and all kinds of other goodies.

Gopher's underlying tree structure is much like an organization chart. To take a little peek ahead at one of Gopher's outstanding features, you may instruct your client to remember where you were by placing a "bookmark" at the current location. A few keystrokes at any time will return you to the site of your bookmark. You can actually start your Gopher journey with your bookmarks, which will be displayed just like any other Gopher menu.

A Little Background

Before starting our first Gopher exploration, it will be helpful to define a few terms. Gopherspace comprises the totality of all Gopher installations and the information contained within them. When we begin our quest for information stored within Gopherspace, it makes little difference where we start. As you become more proficient gophers, you may want to begin all your Gopher sessions at a site with an abundance of the type of information for which you typically look.

Gopher is a client/server system. Clients and servers are two terms that you'll see frequently in today's technology press. A *server* is a computer program having access to a database of information, typically (but not always) on a "big" system like a mainframe. A *client* is a computer program specifically designed to retrieve information from a server. Clients usually (but not always) run on desktop systems. The Gopher program you'll use will normally be a Gopher client.

ACCESSING A GOPHER SERVER

Four methods may be used to explore gopherspace:

- Use a Gopher or Web client residing on your PC.
- Use a Gopher or Lynx client residing in your local host's system.
- Telnet to a public access Gopher or Lynx client.
- Use GopherMail.

If your individual computer connects directly to the Internet through SLIP or PPP (as opposed to a connection via an intermediate host, which is in turn directly connected to the Internet), you'll ideally have a Gopher client on your PC. Many Internet providers will hand you a freeware Gopher client when you sign up. A local Gopher client is a program that runs on your host machine; in most cases, that means your provider's minicomputer or mainframe. If your Internet access is via a dial-up shell account, you'll ideally use a Gopher client on that host computer.

You can Telnet to a public Gopher site that allows remote access to its Gopher client program. Utilizing a local Gopher client is preferable to using a public access Gopher. A local Gopher client is almost always more feature-rich than a public access Gopher. If you are not sure if your local host machine has a Gopher client, enter "gopher" at your shell command line prompt. In short order you see either a main Gopher menu at some particular installation, or else an error message indicating that the furball just isn't there. A Gopher main menu indicates that you have a local client; otherwise you don't have a local client.

You can perform some useful Gopher explorations using a public access Gopher, but be aware that Telnetting to a remote host to do something normally done on your local host is not the best use of Internet bandwidth. However, if you decide that you like Gopher and intend to use it on a regular basis, you should contact your service provider's system administrator and request they obtain a Gopher client. Clients are now available for almost all hardware and operating system configurations. Since Gopher clients are available free of charge, a request to install a client is not likely to run into serious opposition from your local system administrator.

GopherMail literally entails e-mailing a Gopher search request to a Gopher server, and having the Gopher server mail you the results. It's slow, but it was very useful in the days when getting e-mail access to the Internet was a lot easier than getting full access. We won't discuss GopherMail in detail in this chapter.

Now that we have nailed down the background and fundamentals, let's start some Gopher explorations.

Gopher for the Computerphobic

I met my wife during a weekend seminar course. We were both doctoral students at Temple University, two divorced grandparents in a sea of super-bright and highly aggressive twenty-year-old students. Pat was tough to miss in a crowd; her eyes twinkled and her smile was captivating. Her voice was clearer and slightly stronger than all the other women in the crowd. If you missed these characteristics, her sentences usually began with, "What do you mean I can't do...," as the educational system tried to place yet another obstacle in her path.

On the way home from that eventful seminar I startled my car-pool partner by announcing, "I'm going to marry that woman." It took about seven and a half years of persuading before Pat would take the big step, but we are now a "Paradox," as it were.

Pat's involvement with computers is best summarized by her frequent observation that, "Anyone who voluntarily spends more than fifteen minutes staring at a blinking cursor has taken leave of their senses." (I must in fairness tell you that she word processed her own dissertation.) Early one morning, while mentally preparing this chapter, I casually mentioned to Pat that I could teach a computer illiterate the basics of Gopher in about two minutes. My first mistake was bringing up anything about computers before noontime. When she expressed skepticism that I could teach her something meaningful about a computer in anything under an hour, I invited her to sit at the terminal. Second mistake!

I had her type "gopher" from the "unix%" prompt. Presto! Up pops the main menu at the University of Minnesota, the mother of all gopher sites. So far so good. I patiently explained that the characters at the end of each menu entry had special meaning. Those with a slash at the end would produce a submenu. Bravely continuing, I pointed out the bottom line. Enter the number corresponding to your desired menu choice. Should there be any confusion with the visible menu instructions, press the question mark and help will be forthcoming. (Notice how I tactfully avoided saying, "If you get confused.") Press lowercase "u" to go up one menu level, and when you are all finished, press either upper- or lowercase "q" to quit.

I pointed out proudly, while glancing at my watch, that the Gopher Instructional session had taken exactly one minute and forty-five seconds. "Now do something," I enthused. Without hesitation, Pat pushed the "q" key and headed for the garden.

ACCESSING GOPHER VIA SLIP/PPP OR WITH A LOCAL CLIENT

If you access the Internet through a SLIP or PPP account, you may have a Gopher client that came as part of the access software included when you signed up and got your account. Look for a Gopher icon in your Internet program group. If you have one, connect to the Net and double-click on Gopher. Most Gopher clients you receive from a provider will connect directly to the provider's Gopher server and present you with their default menu. You will have to "repoint" Gopher (see below) for the purposes of this exploration.

If you access the Internet through a shell account and your provider has a local client, enter "gopher" at your command line prompt. If you don't have a local Gopher client, skip to the next section titled *Using A Public Gopher Client.* The configuration of a local Gopher always "points" to a particular Gopher site. If you are starting Gopher from a site having its own Gopher server, you are first connected to the main Gopher server at your location. The default Gopher site is the one established by your system administrator during the initial installation, and is not under your control. Our initial explorations are going to illustrate connecting to the "mother Gopher" at the University of Minnesota.

Regardless of how you access Gopher, you may start at the University of Minnesota even if your default site is somewhere else. "Pointing" a Gopher client is the process of entering a specific Gopher address when starting a session. You can do this from your host's Unix prompt by entering the following:

```
unix% gopher gopher.micro.umn.edu
```

This is the functional equivalent of entering a Netscape URL.

There's no standard way to repoint a Windows-based Gopher client, but you should be able to dope out the method used by your particular client by following the menus and (if all else fails!) reading the online help. Use the same address shown above.

Using a Public Gopher Client

Failing the options I just described, you may be able to Telnet to a public access Gopher server. Once connected, it will function much like a local client except for a few, but important, functions. Two of the most important public access Gopher shortcomings are the inability to use individualized bookmarks and the inability to download resources. When you are accessing a Gopher server using a public client, you do not have disk space at the location of the public server so you cannot transfer a file, or other resources, from some remote location.

The list of Gopher public access servers, like all resources on the Internet, is subject to change. At press time the list includes:

I would highly recommend that you run local client software instead of logging into public Gopher sites through Telnet. A client can use the custom features of the local machine (mouse, scroll bars, and so on), which gives faster response. A client also allows the use of bookmarks and the transfer of information from remote sites—which is probably what you're doing this for, after all.

Host Name	IP#	Login	Area
consultant.micro.umn.edu	134.84.132.4	gopher	North America
gopher.uiuc.edu	128.174.33.160	gopher	North America
panda.uiowa.edu	128.255.40.201	panda	North America
gopher.msu.edu	35.8.2.61	gopher	North America
gopher.ebone.net	192.36.125.2	gopher	Europe
info.anu.edu.au	150.203.84.20	info	Australia
gopher.chalmers.se	129.16.221.40	gopher	Sweden
tolten.puc.cl	146.155.1.16	gopher	South America
ecnet.ec	157.100.45.2	gopher	Ecuador
gan.ncc.go.jp	160.190.10.1	gopher	Japan

The public gopher concept is worth knowing, however, just in case. Assuming that you are starting your session from a host using Unix, you would enter:

```
unix% telnet consultant.micro.umn.edu
```

Once successfully connected, the "login" prompt appears. At that point enter "gopher" in lowercase letters:

```
login: gopher
```

In short order the prompt "Term = (VT100)" appears. If you are running VT100 emulation (a good bet) simply press "Enter" without typing anything else. Then the main menu will appear.

EXPLORER TIP

Up-to-the-Minute Public Gopher Sites

The Yanoff list, described in the next chapter, contains a multitude of Internet resources gathered by master Internet surfer Scott Yanoff. Included in the list, which is available via Gopher or Netscape, is the current listing of all public access Gopher sites. If you are going to access Gopher by Telnetting to a public Gopher, you might want to glance ahead to acquire Scott's latest list, which by its very nature will usually be more up-to-date than a book printed on paper. The HTML version is at:

```
http://www.uwm.edu/Mirror/inet.services.html
```

The Gopher version of the Yanoff list is at:

```
gopher://alphal.csd.uwm.edu:70/00/UWM%20Information/
Information%20Technology/Misc%20Documentation/inet-services
```

THE MAIN MENU

Most Gopher clients have some way of telling you that something is happening. Unix shell clients display the following on the bottom line whenever it's bringing data home:

```
Retrieving Directory..
```

To the right of this message you'll see something that looks like a spinning rotor that is actually several characters in rapid alternation. If the rotor stops, something may be wrong with your connection. If your connection is successful, the main menu at the University of Minnesota will display:

```
                Internet Gopher Information Client 2.1.0

                 Root gopher server: consultant.micro.umn.edu

--> 1.  Information About Gopher/
    2.  Computer Information/
    3.  Discussion Groups/
    4.  Fun & Games/
    5.  Internet file server (ftp) sites/
    5.  Libraries/
    6.  Mailing Lists/
    7.  News/
    8.  Other Gopher and Information Servers/
    9.  Phone Books/
    10. Search Gopher Titles at the University of Minnesota <?>
    11. Search lots of places at the University of Minnesota <?>
    12. University of Minnesota/

Press ? for Help, q to Quit
Page: 1/1
```

Items 1 through 9 and 12 are pointers to submenus. The "<?>" at the end of items 10 and 11 indicate those menu choices will lead to a search entry prompt. The item "Page: 1/1" shows that this is menu page one of one; in other words, the entirety of the menu is visible at once, and no further selections remain to be displayed. Entering "?" at any menu will bring up a detailed help screen.

Traversing a Gopher Menu Structure

A Gopher menu always will have one default item. An arrow to the left of an item indicates the default. Pressing the Enter key will select the default item. You can change the default menu item by moving the arrow with the up and down arrow keys. Entering the number corresponding to the desired menu item will select and activate that menu item.

The main menu at virtually all sites has an entry that is essentially a selection to produce additional information on other Gopher sites. On the University of Minnesota main menu the entry is:

```
8.  Other Gopher and Information Servers/
```

Selecting this item makes the following screen appear. (Please note that the actual screen changes from time to time and may have changed between the time I wrote this chapter and the time you read it.)

```
                    Internet Gopher Information Client 2.0 pl11

                       Other Gopher and Information Servers

  -->1.  All the Gopher Servers in the World/
     2.  Search titles in Gopherspace using Veronica/
     3.  Africa/
     4.  Asia/
     5.  Europe/
     6.  International Organizations/
     7.  Middle East/
     8.  North America/
     9.  Pacific/
     10. Russia/
     11. South America/
     12. Terminal Based Information/
     13. WAIS Based Information/
     14. Gopher Server Registration <??>

Press ? for Help, q to Quit, u to go up a menu                  Page: 1/1
```

All menu items in this submenu point to additional submenus, with one exception. Item 14 points to a registration form that is used to put a new Gopher server into the University of Minnesota database.

Since you know that I received a degree from Temple University, you might propose that we continue our exploration by seeing if Temple has a public Gopher. When searching for something, we would typically try to narrow down our search by big incremental amounts. In this case we would select item 8 corresponding to the North America selection. (One would think that there would be a separate menu listing for the United States.) However, I want to give you some idea of the magnitude of Gopherspace so let's go with the first selection and request All the Gopher Servers in the World.

After much wheel spinning the following menu appears:

```
                Internet Gopher Information Client v2.1.0

                   All the Gopher Servers in the World

    --> 1.  Search Gopherspace using Veronica/
     2.  AARNET/
     3.  ACADEME THIS WEEK (Chronicle of Higher Education)/
     4.  ACES - Educational Service Agency Gopher/
     5.  ACLU Free Reading Room/
     6.  ACM SIGDA/
     7.  ACM SIGGRAPH/
     8.  ACTLab (UT Austin, RTF Dept)/
     9.  AMI -- A Friendly Public Interface/
     10. ANS (Advanced Network Services)/
     11. ANS gopher/
     12. APS-Academic Physician and Scientist/
     13. AREA Science Park, Trieste, (IT)/
     14. ARPA Computing Systems Technology Office (CSTO)/
     15. AT&T Global Information Solutions (formerly NCR) Info Server/
     16. Academia Sinica, Taiwan, ROC./
     17. Academic Physician and Scientist/
     18. Academic Position Network/

Press ? for Help, q to Quit, u to go up a menu                  Page: 1/126
```

This menu begins to show something of the international presence of Gopher. AARNET is located in Australia, AREA Science Park is in Trieste, Italy, while Academia Sinica is coming to us from Taiwan. The very first item

```
  --> 1.  Search Gopherspace using Veronica/
```

points to a fabulous searching tool. Veronica searching will be discussed in Chapter 19, *Searching for the Holy Grail.*

When asking for information, such as this listing or the output of a Veronica search, Gopher presents the details in the familiar form of a Gopher menu. In this specific case, Gopher has presented an ascending alphabetically sorted listing containing all the registered top-level Gophers in the entire world. There is only one top-level Gopher per site. The top-level may and usually does access subordinate public access Gophers. An example would be a university such as the "mother Gopher" at the University of Minnesota. The main menu is a product of the top-level Gopher. Working our way down this particular Gopher shaft will, at some point, connect us to a subordinate Gopher. It might be a Gopher managed by the computer science department or the admissions office. The nifty part is that the transition is transparent to us as users.

The "biggie" on the above menu is the last line. If all the requested information does not fit on the first menu page, the remainder becomes the second page...or as pages many as it takes. You can press the space bar to move to the next page, or the "b" key to move to the previous page ("Back"). The last line item reading "Page: 1/126" indicates that this is the first page of 126 pages! The maximum number of items per page is 18. Does this mean that there are about 2,268 Gophers listed for our perusing pleasure? That's *exactly* what it means. Numbered menu items are a circular list. If item 1 is the current default and you press the Up-Arrow key one time, you are then viewing menu 126/126, or page 126 out of a total of 126 pages. If you are at the last menu item and you press the Down-Arrow key, you will be placed in the first menu.

The last few items in the menu seems to be out of alphabetical order. That's something you'll often see when server names mix upper and lowercase characters heavily rather than all names simply having an initial capital. Case on the names is significant, and the sorting order places uppercase characters before lowercase letters. If you want to create a Gopher site that will appear dead last on the list, call it "zzzzzzz."

Pressing "?" will bring up the "Page Help" menu, which summarizes the options you can press at that point. If you ever get confused, just punch "?" and you will be enlightened.

EFFICIENT PROBLEM SOLVING

How do we navigate to the Temple University Gopher in the shortest period of time? Search strategy becomes a progressively more important consideration as the sheer quantity of available information increases. Search strategies fall into three general categories:

- Brute force
- Moderately effective
- Elegant

Brute force searching would require continually pressing the Down-Arrow key until arriving at Temple, or a menu entry higher in the collating sequence indicating that there is no Temple Gopher. This would exercise your fingers until they could crush rocks. What most people do is moderately more effective: They scan a full page at a time by eye, and move a page at a time by using the space bar and "b" key rather than the arrow keys. Keep in mind that a numbered menu item is selectable even if it's not currently displayed. If we knew the menu number corresponding to the Temple entry, we could simply enter it at any menu in the series. Either of the above methods will work...but there should be—and are—better ways.

Elegant Solutions to Common Problems

What would be an elegant approach to this problem? Think for a moment about what would constitute the ideal solution: Find Temple in one shot. To accomplish this lofty goal, we must have Gopher itself perform the search. Hey, that's what computers are supposed to be good at, right?

If you press "?" and bring up the "Page Help" screen, you'll see (among many other things) the following line:

```
  /                          : Search for text
```

Pressing the "/" key brings up the text search dialog box, which will look something like this:

```
+-----------All the Gopher Servers in the World-----------+
|                                                         |
| Search directory titles for:                            |
|                                                         |
|    _                                                    |
|                                                         |
|         [Cancel: ^G] [Erase: ^U] [Accept: Enter]        |
+---------------------------------------------------------+
```

Enter "temple" without the quotation marks. Gopher searches are case insensitive, so upper- or lowercase data will yield the same results. This menu appears:

```
              All the Gopher Servers in the World

     1243. Technical University of Hamburg-Harburg, (DE)/
     1244. Technical University of Nova Scotia (Canada)/
     1245. Technion - Israel Institute of Technology/
     1246. Technion Building Technologies Gopher/
     1247. Technische Universitaet Berlin, Informatik, (DE)/
```

```
    1248. Technische Universitaet Cottbus, (DE)/
    1249. Technische Universitaet Muenchen, (DE)/
    1250. Techno/Rave gopher/
    1251. Tecnopolis CSATA Novus Ortus (Master Gopher)/
    1252. Tel Aviv University Information Server/
    1253. TeleEducation New Brunswick/
    1254. Telerama Public Access Internet - Pittsburgh, PA/
    1255. Telerama Public Access Internet - Pittsburgh, PA/
 -> 1256. Temple University/
    1257. Temple University SYNERGY project/
    1258. Tennessee Technological University/
    1259. Tex-Share Gopher/
    1260. Texas A&M University/

Press ? for Help, q to Quit, u to go up a menu              Page: 80/126
```

Not only have we found the pointer to the Temple Gopher, we have traversed 80 menus in the process and didn't even see them go by. In addition, Temple is now the default selection, so we only need press Enter to begin a Temple University Gopher exploration.

Accessing Gopher Using Netscape

Graphical Web browsers, such as Netscape, may also be used to access Gopher menus and documents. Figure 17.1 shows Netscape's display of the University of Minnesota's main Gopher menu. It is the same menu as shown above. To access the site we would point Netscape at the University of Minnesota's main menu by entering the following URL:

```
gopher://gopher.micro.umn.edu
```

Compare the graphical icons preceding each item with the information contained in the character-based version. The same pointing technique can access any Gopher site for which you have the address.

Before concluding this chapter, let's do a Gopher exploration using Netscape as our Gopher client.

What's the Weather Forecast?

I start most of my online sessions by checking the local weather forecast. One mouse click later and I'm reading the National Weather Service's latest forecast. You might also want your local area weather forecast available as a bookmark; let's create one.

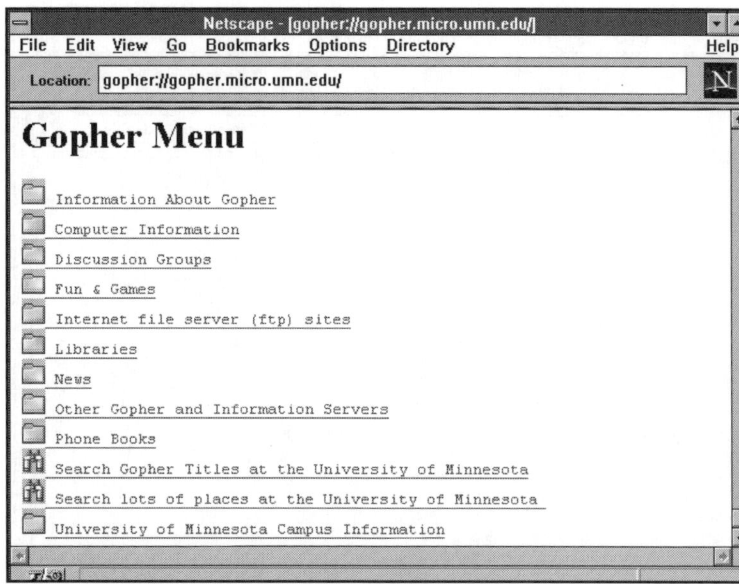

Figure 17.1 *Netscape's display of the University of Minnesota's main Gopher menu.*

The University of Illinois has a Gopher-based "Weather Machine." (You can get the innermost details online if you're interested.) To start the exploration, enter the Weather Machine's URL:

```
gopher://wx.atmos.uiuc.edu
```

You can take a shortcut. Start by placing the cursor in the left side of the Netscape edit box normally containing the URL of the displayed document. Press Ctrl+Delete to remove the existing URL. Enter the new URL and press Enter to activate.

Figure 17.2 is the opening menu of the University of Illinois Weather Machine. Much additional information appears below the portion shown on the screen. Scroll down until you see an entry "States." Notice that the icon associated with the "States" entry is an open file folder. This icon indicates that this link will take us to another menu.

Click on "States" and a menu of states will appear, as shown in Figure 17.3. Click on your home state.

I clicked on New Jersey and yet another menu, as shown in Figure 17.4, appeared. The U.S. Weather Service metropolitan forecasts are available for

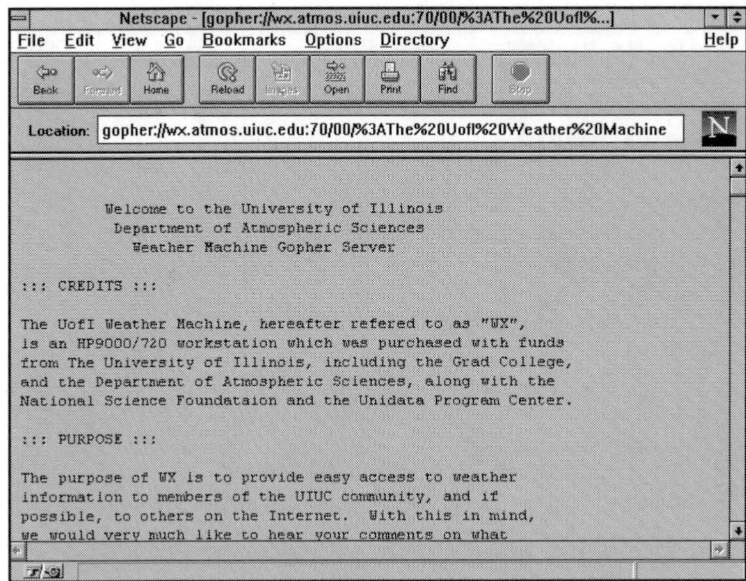

Figure 17.2 The main Gopher menu at the University of Illinois Weather Machine.

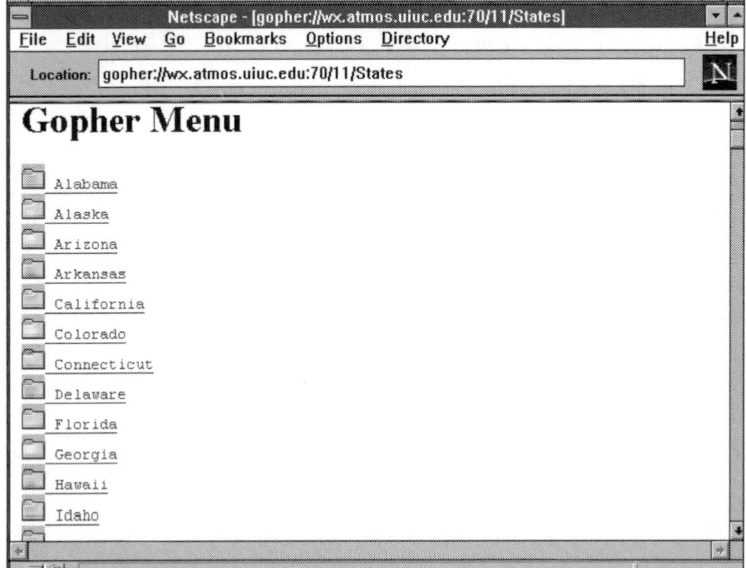

Figure 17.3 UI Weather Machine state selection menu.

most cities with major airports. Notice that on the Figure 17.4 menu display there are icons depicting a piece of paper with the corner folded over. This

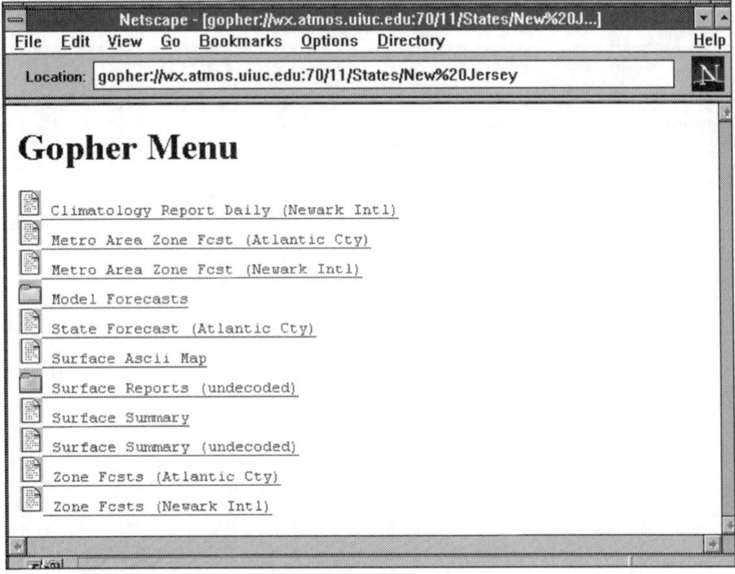

Figure 17.4 *State options available on the UI Weather Machine.*

indicates that the end is near and we've reached the bottom of the Gopher shaft. The next entry, represented by the familiar page icon, is a document rather than another menu.

Clicking on "Metro Area Zone Fcst (Atlantic Cty)" produced the display in Figure 17.5. I frequently find that this weather information is more current than information broadcast on local radio stations. But then again, this is Atlantic City, which is not known as the broadcast news capital of the world.

When you've located the weather forecast for your local area, save its pointer as a bookmark, thereby creating a "two click return path." Make sure your current bookmark file is the one you want to hold the weather forecast pointer and click on the sequence Bookmark | Add Bookmark, or simply press Ctrl+A. If you need a review on these procedures, go back to Chapter 4. Netscape makes bookmark additions very easy.

In the next chapter we'll look at one of Scott Yanoff's famous lists of Internet resources. Scott has posted resources on a Gopher server for a long time. He now ports the list to HTML. This creates the opportunity to objectively look at the same set of information as accessed by both Gopher and Netscape.

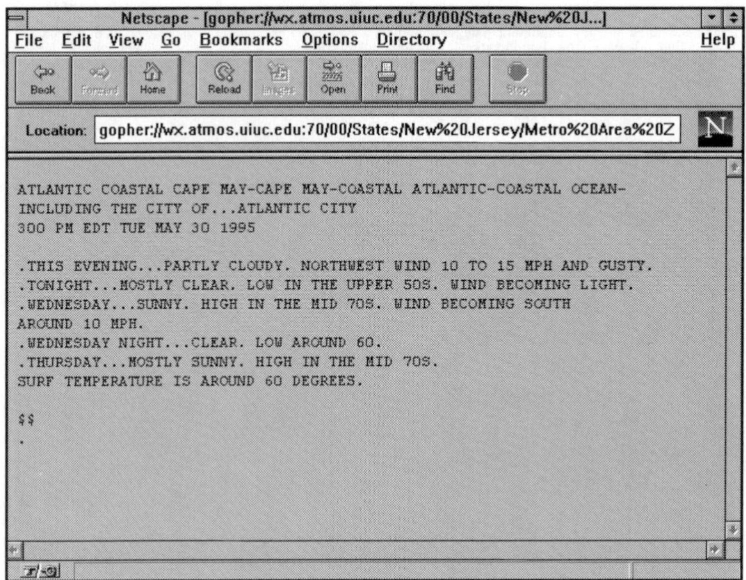

Figure 17.5 *Weather forecast for Atlantic City.*

LET'S REVIEW

Gopherspace is hierarchical in nature. A Gopher menu item leads either to another menu or to a file. You keep searching menus until you find the file you need. Menus may be searched visually, or through a built-in string search feature.

To perform a text-string search from any menu, enter the "/" character at the menu prompt. When a dialog box appears, enter your search string. A string may be any group of characters, not necessarily a complete word. String searches are case insensitive. Searching Gopherspace using Veronica will be covered later.

When dealing with this vast amount of information, an efficient search strategy is critical. Thinking about how you will efficiently find something, as opposed to doing the same simplistic things over and over again, will pay off tremendously in saved time. Don't use brute force techniques when you can be clever. Also, let the machine do the tough and boring stuff!

We can explore the entirety of Gopherspace, once we understand its overall design, from within the friendly confines of our favorite Web browser. Any Gopher address can be expressed as a URL (beginning with "gopher://") and the Gopher menu structure displays beautifully. In Netscape, pressing Ctrl+A will add the URL for the currently displayed page in the bookmark list. This provides "a two click return" to any point in Gopherspace.

Comparing WWW and Gopher

The two leading schemes for organizing Internet information are by no means mutually exclusive, and if you know the strengths and weaknesses of each, you'll be much better off.

You may find this difficult to believe, but I haven't always been an Internet maven. If the truth be known, I haven't been in any specific profession for very long. I tend to change careers more often than most people change phone numbers. My career path started with driving a truck and has included portfolio management and teaching computer science. I think the willingness to change careers demonstrates versatility; although others have argued that it also shows lack of focus.

My computer career started quite innocuously. I was introduced to amateur radio at the age of 13. In 1949, when I was 16, I was licensed as W2DEC, which I still hold. In the mid 1970s I observed that the price of computers was dropping and they were becoming available to hobbyists.

Way back in 1976 I said to myself "One of these days you're going to be able to afford one of these things—then what?" So at age 44, I trotted off to my local community college to take a course in computer programming. The first night was a harrowing experience. In a cold sweat, I drove in and out of the parking lot twice. I was afraid I'd make a fool of myself in front of a bunch of barely post-pubescent teenagers. Finally I walked past the classroom and saw a person in the back of the room who actually looked to be a few years my senior, so I went in.

When we went to the lab and keyed in our first Basic program, I thought I had died and gone to Heaven. When I decided to take a second programming course (remember COBOL?), a dedicated counselor lead me to Thomas Edison State College (TESC).

Now, Edison is not your traditional college, but is in fact the first fully accredited non-traditional college in the country. There are no classrooms or dorms—and, horrors—no Thursday-night beer bashes. The school's namesake was not a college graduate, and good old Tom gave the school its major mission when he said, "The whole world is a classroom." You earn Edison credits by taking courses at other colleges, taking tests, and through the evaluation of your college-level life experience. Not only did I earn a degree at Edison, I went on to earn two masters and a doctorate at Temple University. As an interesting aside, I started my teaching career in the same classroom in which I took my first college course.

I would like to start this exploration visiting the Edison State College Gopher site as a token of appreciation to the school that helped change my life.

WHAT ARE GOPHERSPACE AND WEBSPACE?

The terms Gopherspace and Webspace are used rather loosely in this book, at least until now. Let's tighten up the definitions of these two terms so we can establish a framework for this chapter. First, let's review the concept of client/server software applications.

A *server* is a software program, usually running on a relatively powerful machine, whose purpose is to distribute information over a network of some kind. (To add some confusion to the stew, the computers that server software runs on are often called servers as well.) The receivers of this information are *client* programs. The client makes a request over the network to a server, and the server satisfies the request (if it can) by sending down the requested information to the client, often after processing it in some way.

Most Internet informational systems are based upon the client/server relationship. Netscape is a client program and receives all those graphical goodies from a Web server. FTP servers have within their local jurisdiction a set of files that can be requested by any remote FTP client or a client, such as Netscape, supporting the FTP way of communicating. The heart of the client/server relationship is something called a *protocol.* A protocol is an agreed-upon group of commands and responses understood by both the server and client. It's kind of like a complex secret handshake that serves a particular purpose, and unless both sides know the handshake, nothing useful gets done.

Terms like Gopherspace or Webspace represent a number (perhaps a large number) of client/server programs accessing and distributing information stored and maintained at server locations, using an established protocol that everyone agrees upon. Loosely stated, Gopherspace is the worldwide body of information and software used to access and distribute this information using the Gopher protocol, and likewise for the Web within Webspace and FTP within FTPspace. Each has a protocol, and each has a body of information and software that supports and distributes it. Some of these "spaces" overlap; because you can access both Gopher and FTP sites while using a Web browser, Webspace, Gopherspace, and FTPspace cannot be considered isolated universes. Webspace, especially, has this way of absorbing everything else on the Internet—which is one reason I'm writing this book the way I am. Gopherspace, properly speaking, is part of Webspace, because you can access Gopher servers and obtain Gopher information from most Web browsers.

How does Webspace differ from Gopherspace? There are two very important differences:

- Webspace, as strongly influenced by the introduction of Mosaic, uses a set of resources specifically formatted to maximize the usefulness of graphical and multi-media presentation, and also to enable non-linear, hyperlink-style access. Gopherspace is linear and hierarchical, and while Gopher can deliver graphical and multimedia files to the user, it typically does not *present*—that is display or play—such files.
- The Web protocol is not exclusive. Web browsers like Netscape are "multilingual" and recognize many protocols, and will almost certainly absorb whatever new protocols happen in the future. Gopherspace, by contrast, does one thing and one thing well.

As we have previously observed, we can use our trusty Web browsers—if they support the functionality—to retrieve files (FTP) from participating sites, perform interactive connectivity (Telnet), and freely navigate Gopherspace. What we haven't seen in this book is the ability of some browsers, most notably Netscape and newer commercial browsers like Internetworks, to function as Usenet Newsreaders and electronic mail processors. We can therefore define Webspace as, "An integrated information system composed of tools to interactively locate and deliver the totality of Internet accessible resources, emphasizing multimedia presentation and nonlinear retrieval."

Comparing Gopherspace and Webspace

We'll use two techniques to compare and contrast Gopherspace and Webspace. First, let's look at different methods for exploring Gopherspace and Webspace, and then, at the differences in information presentation and retrieval.

This book is targeted to users of the World Wide Web and Web browsers. Our Gopher explorations, for the most part, have used Web browsers such as Netscape. However, Gopherspace may perhaps be best used from text mode and the Unix command line. Speed of data access is the compelling reason. Although it is certainly true that Windows implementations of Gopher are capable of supporting graphical wizardry to the same extent as Netscape, in reality, few Gopher sites include much in terms of images and sound effects. Gopher was originally designed as a plain text document processing system. Whatever eye, or ear, pleasing effects exist were plugged in as an afterthought. If we want plain text browsing, why use a system containing a weak link that can be "losslessly" excluded? The lethargic component is, of course, our modem.

It's this simple: Less data has to travel through your modem when using a Unix shell account than when using SLIP or PPP. Shell account transfers of Gopher menus and documents are performed at whatever speed your provider uses when connecting to the Internet backbone—typically T1 speeds. (T1 is a technical term cooking down to "very fast digital transmission"—use it at cocktail parties and people will be most impressed.) There is no comparison between the coaxial cable or fiber optic line connecting your provider to the Internet backbone and the twisted pair of copper wires connecting your modem to the phone line. "Well," you might ask, "doesn't the information still have to get to my computer via modem?" Sure, but the character-mode stuff your provider's computer sends to your computer (which is actually working as a dumb terminal during your Gopher shell account session) is much more easily processed by your desktop computer than the stream of addressed packets that runs in both directions over a SLIP or PPP connection. What you've done, in essence, is "offloaded" some of the computational burden of connecting to the Internet onto the shell account host. You pay in reduced richness of format—but that may be a tradeoff you're willing to make.

Surfing Gopherspace Using Different Client Programs

Let's compare Gopher's various presentation methods by fetching the Thomas Edison State College menu. Figure 18.1 shows the Edison menu as accessed from a Unix shell account. Figure 18.2 shows the same Edison menu as viewed using Netscape. The same information is contained in both displays. Icons appear in the Web browser, as shown in Figure 18.2, rather than simple item numbers in the character interface, as in Figure 18.1. The graphical interface uses point-and-click navigation rather than the typing required in the Unix command-line version.

```
                   Internet Gopher Information Client v2.1.0

                          Thomas Edison State College

-->  1.  ...... Introducing Thomas Edison State College (TESC)
     2.  ...... TESC gopher service
     3.  ...... TESC Computer Assisted LifeLong Learning (CALL) Network
     4.  ...... TESC On-line Computer Classroom                    /
     5.  ...... TESC CALL Network connection (Telnet to CALL.TESC.EDU).. <TEL>

                                 Other Services

     9.  ...... Libraries and References                                  /
     10. ...... News and Weather                                          /
     11. ...... Phone Books and E-mail Addresses                          /
     12. ...... Explore the Internet Services                             /



Press ? for Help, q to Quit, u to go up a menu                 Page: 1/1
```

***Figure 18.1** The Edison main Gopher menu viewed with a Unix command-line Gopher.*

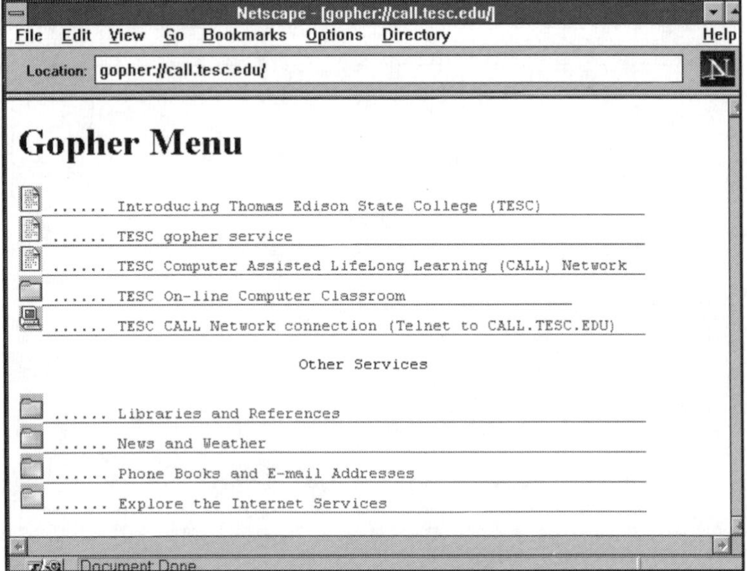

***Figure 18.2** The Edison main Gopher menu viewed with Netscape.*

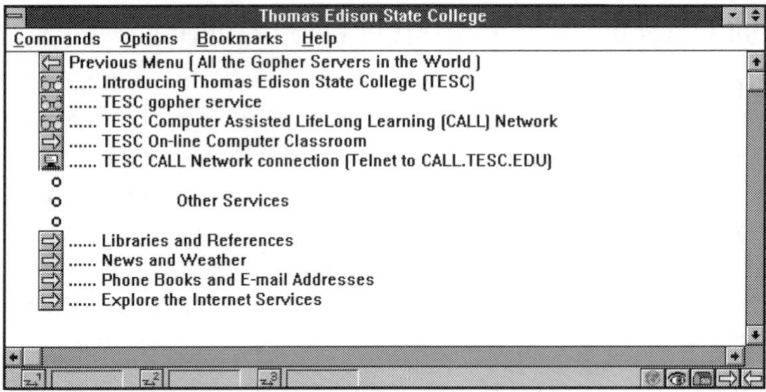

***Figure 18.3** The Edison menu viewed with HGopher.*

Next, take a look at the display of Edison's main menu using two different dedicated Windows Gopher clients: HGopher, shown in Figure 18.3, and Chameleon's Gopher, shown in Figure 18.4. There are no substantive differences between HGopher and Netscape—shown in Figure 18.2—when viewing Gopherspace, at least until we get down to subtle details. There are Gopher-specific features—such are the ability to open three different documents simultaneously—contained in HGopher, but I'll leave this discovery as an exercise. Essentially, you have little need for additional Gopher features, unless you're really into Gophering big time.

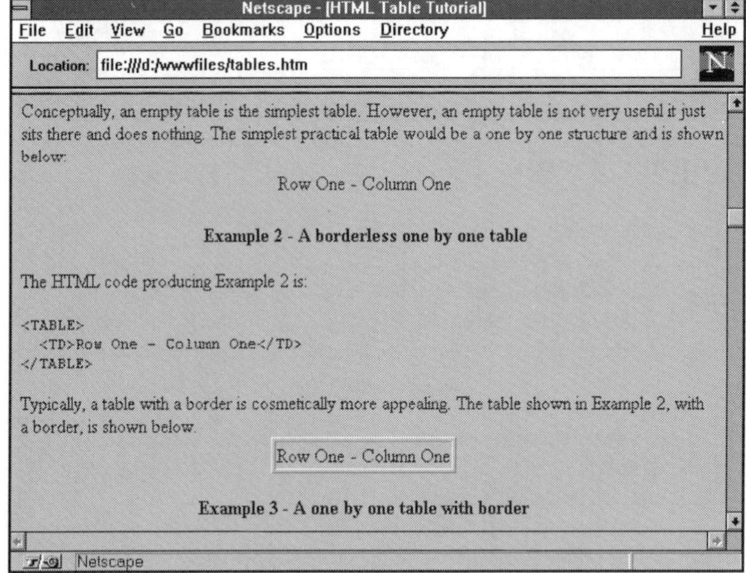

***Figure 18.4** The Edison menu as initially displayed by Chameleon Gopher.*

The Gopher bundled with Netmanage's Chameleon is a very well-trained rodent. As you descend the Gopher shaft, multiple levels of the menu hierarchy are displayed, as shown in Figure 18.4. A nice feature of this Gopher is the identification of icons. When the Figure 18.4 screen shot was snapped, the mouse was pointing to the icon in front of the line starting with "TESC CALL Network...." The type of icon the mouse is pointing to, Telnet in this case, is displayed on the status line.

The right pane of Chameleon's adjustable split screen contains the most recently accessed menu. The left pane contains the tree structure above the menu in the right pane. Figure 18.5 is the right pane of Figure 18.4, the currently accessed menu, expanded to fill the entire screen. Figure 18.6 shows the left pane of Figure 18.4 expanded to give some idea of the hierarchical tree structure. This innovative design permits "leapfrogging" over several menu levels. Smacks of the Web, doesn't it?

Another feature of Chameleon Gopher is the ability to click on the Properties button and bring up the Item Properties dialog box as shown in Figure 18.7. An extension to the standard Gopher protocol, called Gopher+, allows attachment of an administrator address and an abstract. The item shown in Figure 18.7 doesn't contain Gopher+ data (very few servers are using it) but Chameleon Gopher does support it on the client side.

One aspect of the Chameleon Gopher that appeals to me is the ability to display text files in the Windows Notepad editor, as shown in Figure 18.8. (You can change to another editor of your preference if you like.) Using Notepad as a viewer makes all Notepad features available for use with the

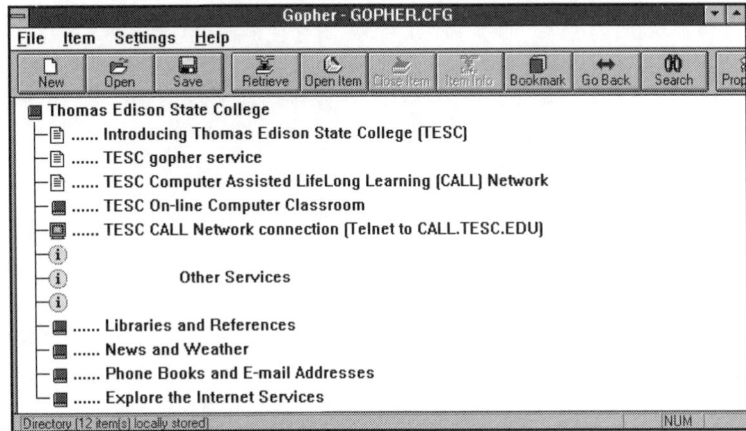

Figure 18.5 *The Edison menu expanded to fill the full screen.*

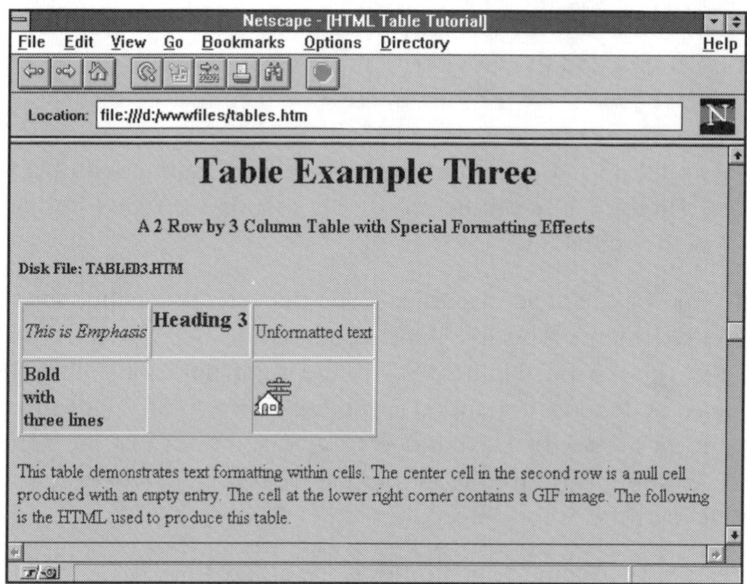

Figure 18.6 *The tree structure leading to the Edison menu.*

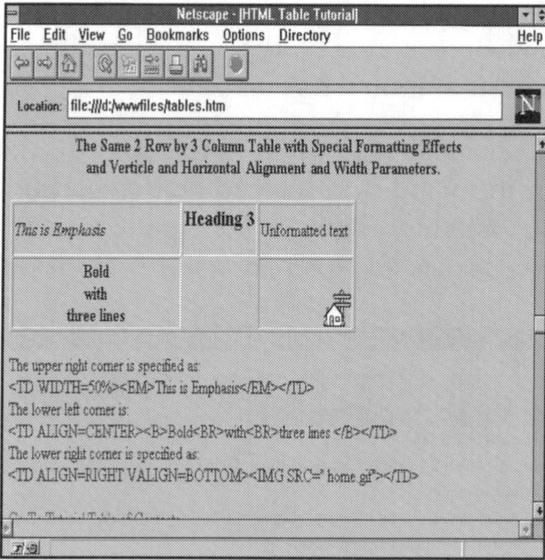

Figure 18.7 *Item Properties dialog box from Chameleon Gopher.*

document being accessed, including the ability to search the document and save it to local disk. As with HGopher, Chameleon Gopher has other nice features, which I encourage you to discover firsthand.

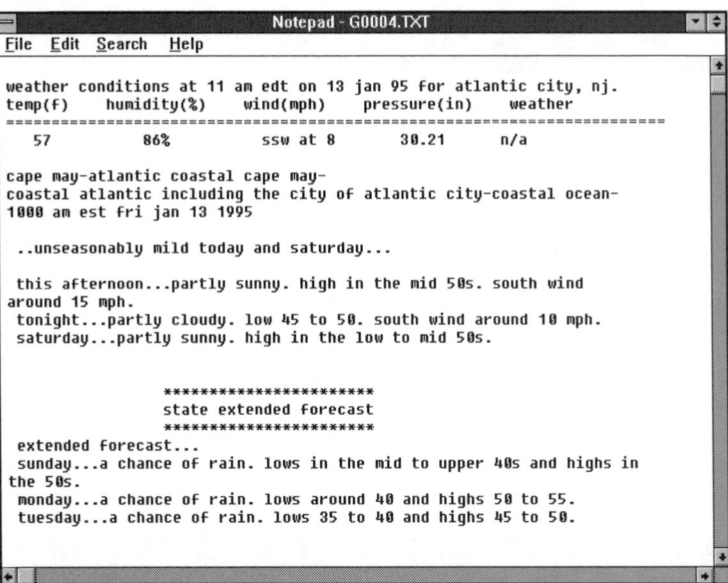

Figure 18.8 *Chameleon Gopher's use of Windows Notepad.*

Gopher Resources for Web Surfers

The Yanoff list (learn how to obtain the latest version in the tip given later) is an incredible resource, especially if you're relatively new to the Internet. This list, officially titled *Special Internet Connections*, was one of the first comprehensive compendiums of generally available Internet resources. The list's evolutionary composition parallels the evolution of the Internet. First available as a plain text file, the document was e-mailed to anyone asking for inclusion on Scott Yanoff's distribution list. Later, many people starting including the list on their Gopher servers.

Resources on the Internet tend to become dated very quickly. The timeliness of this list is highlighted by the fact that at any given point in time there are versions of the Yanoff list out there spanning a six month period. Scott distributes the list twice a month, which only underscores the timeliness problem. The e-mail distributed list is now sent as two separate mailings, since many mailers will not accept a document over 5 KB in size. More recently, the list is being constructed and distributed as an HTML document as well as an ASCII text file.

Figures 18.9 and 18.10 show the first two screens of the Gopher version of the Yanoff list. Figures 18.11 and 18.12 show the same information from this list in HTML format, with active anchor links. The difference in functionality is dramatic.

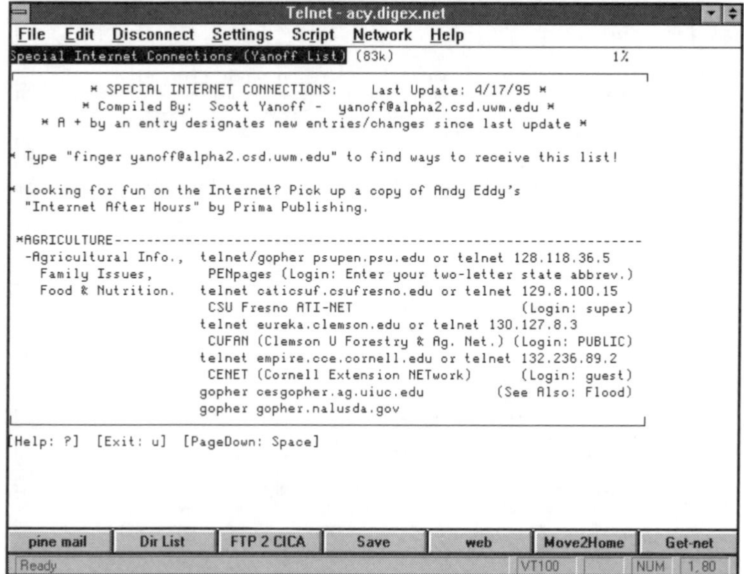

Figure 18.9 *The Yanoff list via Gopher, page 1.*

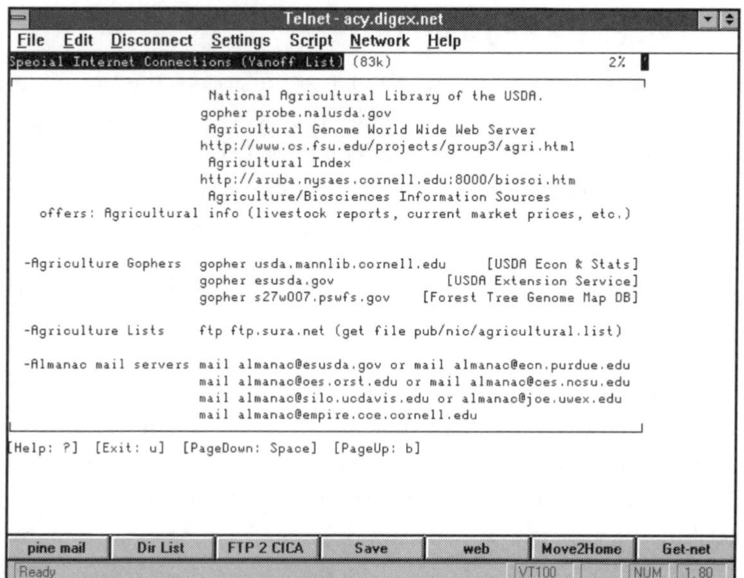

Figure 18.10 *The Yanoff list via Gopher, page 2.*

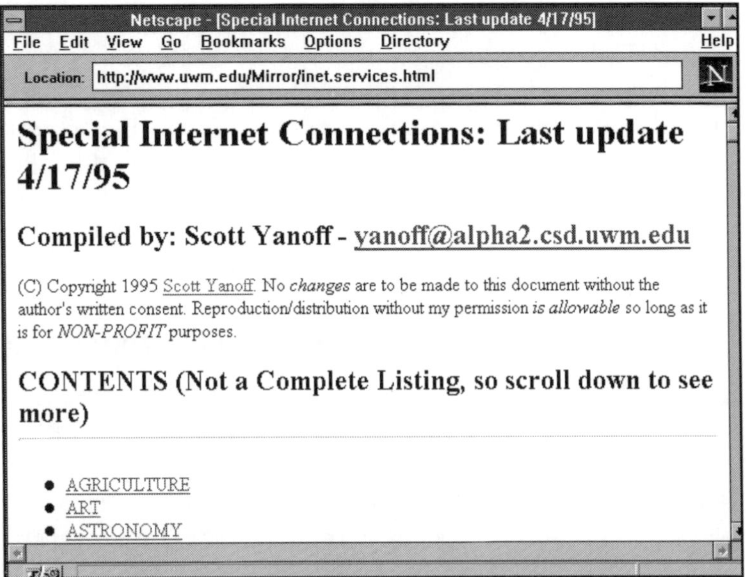

Figure 18.11 *The Yanoff list on the Web, page 1.*

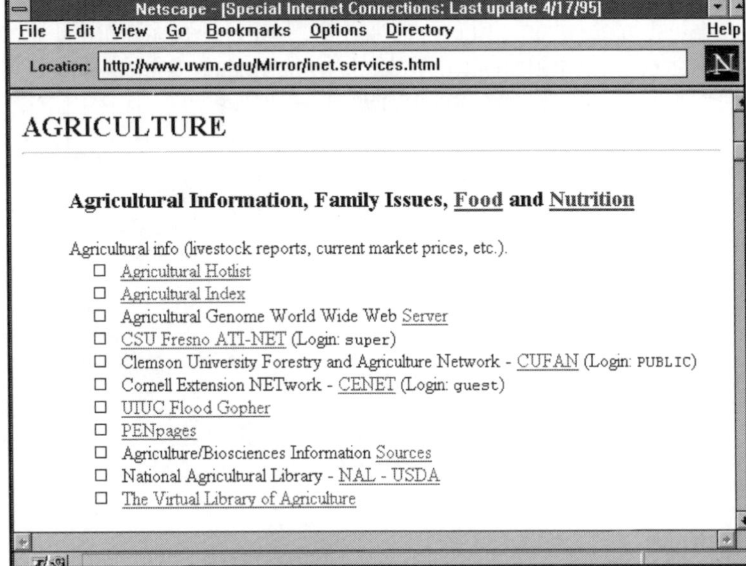

Figure 18.12 *The Yanoff list on the Web, page 2.*

If you're currently surfing the Web using a graphical browser, I would suggest you access the HTML version of the Yanoff list from Netscape or your favorite Web browser. If your Internet access is limited to shell account access, use the Unix command line browser Lynx to access the Yanoff list, as opposed to using a Gopher browser to access the Gopher version. Enter the following on the Unix command line:

```
unix% lynx http://www.uwm.edu/Mirror/inet.services.html
```

The Latest Version of the Yanoff List

To access the Yanoff list via Gopher, point your client to gopher.csd.uwm.edu. From the main menu, select "Remote Information Services." From the next menu select "Special Internet Connections (Yanoff List)" and you have it. The WWW version is even more comprehensive than the Gopher version and has links allowing actual connection to the various resources without leaving your browser.

To access the HTML version, point your Web browser to:

```
http://www.uwm.edu/Mirror/inet.services.html
```

To get the latest information on downloading the text file version of the Yanoff list, finger Scott's account. In addition to downloading information, Scott's "finger" file contains an interesting ASCII graphic of the Milwaukee skyline.

```
unix% finger yanoff@alpha2.csd.uwm.edu
```

The methods as we go to press are:

```
1) newsgroup alt.internet.services
2) ftp ftp.csd.uwm.edu  (get /pub/inet.services.txt) (Login: anonymous)
3) gopher gopher.csd.uwm.edu (select Remote Information Services...)
4) mail inetlist@aug3.augsburg.edu  (Auto-replies with lists)
5) URL: http://www.uwm.edu/Mirror/inet.services.html (for WWW, Mosaic)
6) mail listserv@csd.uwm.edu     and in the mail say:
    SUBSCRIBE INETLIST <your full name>
```

Gopher Jewels

One test that I use to determine the best of just about anything is to ask, "If you could only have one (fill in the blank), which one would it be?" Gopher Jewels is the Gopher bookmark that wins hands down. In addition to being a great resource, the Gopher Jewels Project exemplifies all that is good about the collaborative nature of the Internet. The extraordinary achievement that culminated in

Gopher Jewels demonstrates the contributions of a group of individuals, lead by Dave Riggins and his band of merry gopherites, who make substantial contributions of their own time so that we needn't waste so much of our own.

Gopher Jewels is a list of resources, but it's much more than that. Gopher Jewels offers a unique approach to Gopher subject tree design and content. It is an alternative to the more traditional subject tree design. The combined set represents the best Gopher sites from around the world. The "Jewels" have in fact become a part of the Internet culture. There's a Jewels discussion newsgroup, a Jewels FAQ document, and soon maybe even Gopher Jewels t-shirts.

Gopher Jewels offers the following:

- Over 2,000 pointers to information, organized by category
- Jughead (a recent development and relative of Archie and Veronica) search of all menus in Gopher Jewels
- The option to jump up one menu level from any directory
- The option to jump to the top menu from any directory
- Gopher Tips help documents
- Gopher Jewels list archives
- Gopher Jewels—Talk list archives
- Other Gopher related archives
- Help and WAIS-searchable archives

To access the Jewels, point your browser to:

```
gopher://cwis.usc.edu:70/11/Other_Gophers_and_Information_Resources/Gopher-Jewels
```

Alternatively, point to:

```
gopher://cwis.usc.edu
```

Then click on Other Gophers and Information Resources, and then click on Gopher Jewels. Figure 18.13 is the Gopher Jewel's opening menu. Search the entire Gopher Jewels structure by clicking on the Search Gopher Jewels Menus entry.

The basic Gopher Jewels structure was converted into a series of HTML documents by Bruce Speyer, speyer@einet.net. The Web version of Gopher Jewels, as shown in Figure 18.14, can be accessed on the EINET Webserver; the URL is:

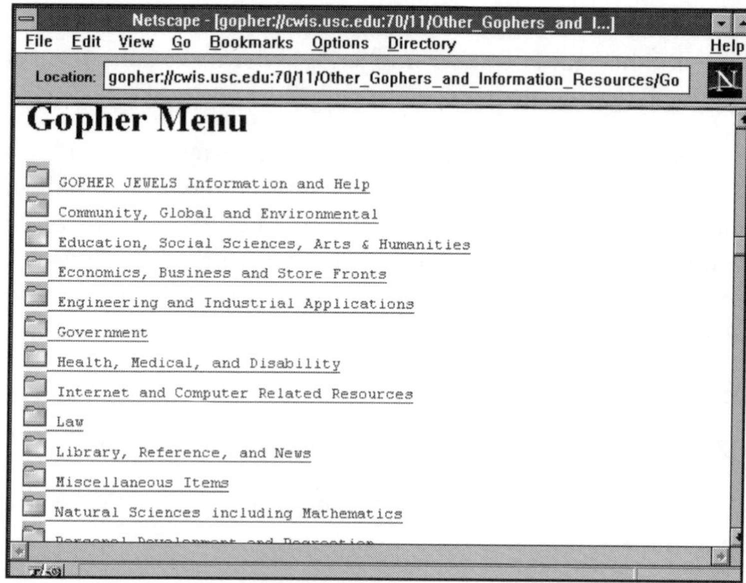

Figure 18.13 The Gopher Jewels main Gopher menu.

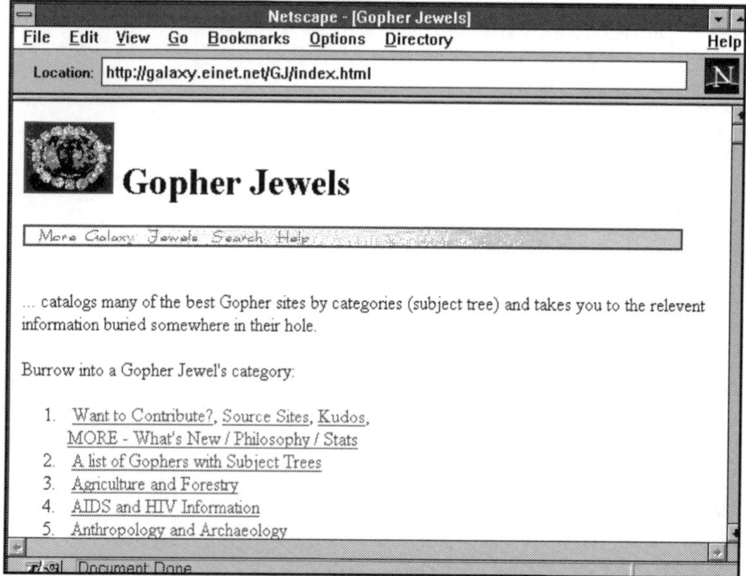

Figure 18.14 The first part of the HTML version of the Gopher Jewels.

```
http://galaxy.einet.net/GJ/index.html
```

David Riggins, david.riggins@tpoint.com, is the developer and maintainer of the Gopher Jewels list. Special thanks also go to Pete Siemsen, siemsen@usc.edu, and the University of Southern California for giving Gopher Jewels a home on the USC Gopher machine.

GOPHERJEWELS@EINET.NET is a list service with over 3,200 subscribers. The purpose of the list is to share interesting Gopher finds. To subscribe to the list, send a message to:

```
LISTPROC@EINET.NET
```

Leave the subject blank and in the body of the message enter the following:

```
subscribe gopherjewels your-first-name your-last-name
```

As an example:

```
subscribe gopherjewels Urb LeJeune
```

A Free Gopher Course

During the late part of 1993 there was an online course called "Navigating the Internet: Let's go Gopherin'." The e-mail course lasted three weeks. Its developers described it this way: "An electronic mail, distance-education course that introduces the new and intermediate user of the Internet to the popular navigating tool—Gopher." The organizers of the course were Jim Gerland, gerland@ubvm.cc.buffalo.edu, the Technology Manager of Network User Support Services at the State University of New York at Buffalo, and Richard J. Smith, smithr@clp2.clpgh.org, who was at The Carnegie Library of Pittsburgh while conducting the course.

The course consisted of e-mail instructions and illustrations. All the course messages are available online at the USC site shown above. There were over 17,000 participants! Point Netscape at:

```
gopher://cwis.usc.edu:70/11/Other_Gophers_and_Information_Resources/Gopherin
```

Alternatively, point your Gopher client at the USC Gopher:

```
cwis.usc.edu
```

From the main Gopher menu, enter and select Other Gophers and Information Resources, and then select How to use Gopher (free course). The course contains a very good section on finding resources.

LET'S REVIEW

Web browsers frequently support the display and traversal of Gopher menu trees, and the intensively competitive browser market will certainly force more Gopher functionality in new Web browsers coming down the pike. However, currently available Web browsers are a compromise when viewing Gopherspace, compared to the more feature-laden dedicated Gopher clients. Chameleon Gopher, for example, is far better for viewing Gopherspace than Netscape.

If response time is a serious consideration, you might strongly consider the use of a character-based Gopher browser that runs under the Unix shell. SLIP and PPP connections place a computational burden on the desktop machine that the host handles under the Unix shell. In other words, if I'm simply collecting reams of boring data from the last Federal census, I may not want to get bogged down waiting for the display of pretty pictures on my monitor.

On the other hand, there is no comparison when evaluating a Web browser as compared to a Gopher browser, if traversing the underlying data in a non-linear fashion is your goal. This point is dramatically driven home when the targeted information contains references to significant amounts of data stored off-site.

As with almost all questions asked of computer systems, the query, "Which is better: Gopher or the World Wide Web," is best answered with, "it depends on what you want and how you want it—and how you intend to search for it." Experience, as always, will teach you how to make this decision work in your favor every time.

Searching for the Holy Grail

Data doesn't become information until you know where to find it. Your Web browser is the ideal vehicle for data reconnaissance, regardless of the undiscovered countries where the objects of your desire may be hidden.

They say you can never step into the same river twice—the river flows by without pause, and the water you see today will be lapping at the shores of Arkansas tomorrow morning. The Internet is in some sense a river of data, updated continually and without notification. Items—nay—*whole sites* full of useful files come and go with regularity. Every time you fire up your Web browser and venture forth for a short trip, you will discover something of interest, and perhaps something that will (when brought home) become a permanent part of your information landscape.

Initially, entertainment rather than knowledge rules the day. However, there comes a time when serendipity (that is, just tripping upon things) will no longer get you everything you want or need. A friend may ask if you can find information on obtaining a National Science Foundation educational grant. Your quiz-kid progeny may want to find out the Catholic population of Spain for a school project. Your boss walks into your office and admonishes, "Either you have that census data for me by this afternoon or I'll find someone who can." Just how do we go about finding the answers to such highly specific, Internet resource related questions?

FINDING THINGS

Finding Internet information typically requires the use of a search engine to ferret out elusive data. Before jumping into the review of different search engines, let's first look at a few general concepts used when searching for information.

OK. How do queries work? In detail, this depends heavily on the individual search engine you use. Each engine does things in its own way, but the broad strokes follow the same general principles.

Before getting into the arcane details of database searching, let's look at a real example. The Yahoo database has come from relative obscurity to prominence within a year. This type of phenomenon is not unusual in an arena where a product's half-life is measured in months, not years. Dial the following Yahoo URL into your Netscape Location box:

```
http://www.yahoo.com
```

Figure 19.1 shows the home page at this extraordinary site. The second line has an anchor named "Search." Clicking on the search item brings up the

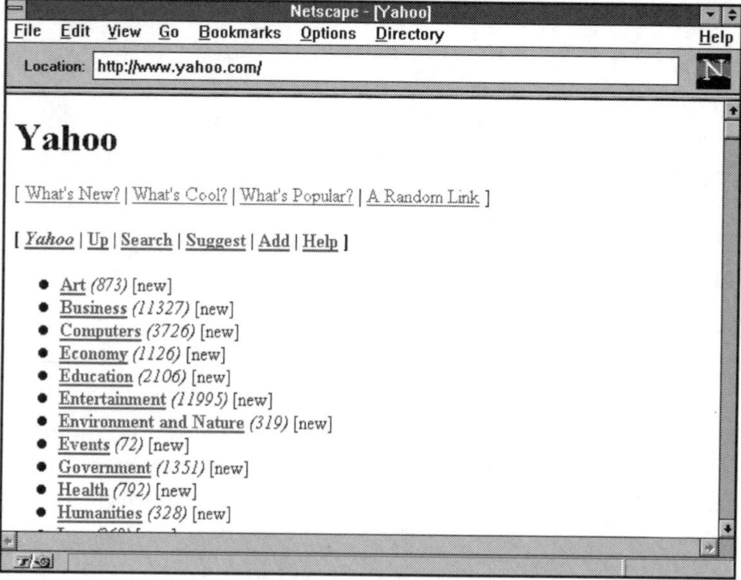

Figure 19.1 *The Yahoo home page.*

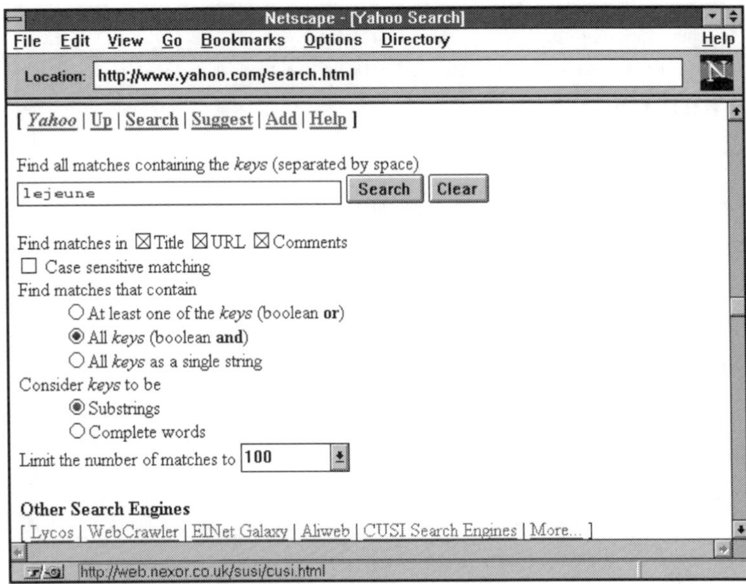

***Figure 19.2** The Yahoo search page.*

page shown in Figure 19.2. We could have taken a shortcut and entered the search URL directly. Here it is:

```
http://www.yahoo.com/search.html
```

I've entered "lejeune" as the search key in the Yahoo search text box. Let's keep life simple for a few minutes and leave the other fields with their default values. Figure 19.3 shows the partial results of Yahoo searching for entries with your trusty tour guide.

Searches can get a lot more complicated, but you get the general idea. Let's get back to some general concepts.

Finding Things, Continued

Most keyword queries search an established database. Databases are frequently constructed by parsing search strings into words based on space and punctuation boundaries. Each component word is frequently (but not always) converted to lowercase to facilitate searching—"Netscape" becomes "netscape." Checking parsed words against a "don't-include" list eliminates those that are trivial or in other ways meaningless in the search context.

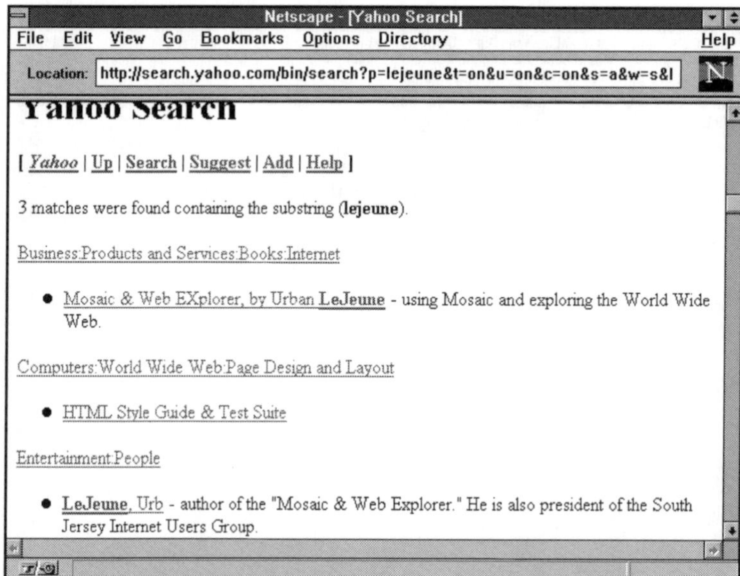

Figure 19.3 *The partial results of a Yahoo search.*

To help illustrate some of these concepts, let's take a look at a few examples. A database constructed by scanning all Web documents for URLs and breaking the URL's components into a record would take

```
http://zeus.oxford.edu.uk/Public/QUEEN.gif
```

and parse it into a case-insensitive record containing the words:

```
zeus oxford edu uk public queen gif
```

The "http" is ignored, since its inclusion in a search string would not help to narrow the range of the quest. "QUEEN" and "Public" become "queen" and "public." A database record, in this case, would have two components: the collection of individual pieces and the assembled object. In the above example, the record (with the two components separated by "^") would be:

```
zeus oxford edu uk public queen gif ^ http://zeus.oxford.edu.uk/Public/QUEEN.gif
```

If we wanted a list containing GIF files on Web servers in England, we would search the above database with the query:

```
uk and gif
```

One of the returned entries would be:

```
http://zeus.oxford.edu.uk/Public/QUEEN.gif
```

AND and OR

There are two possible ways of searching for multiple words. In a search with a two-word search key, you might want to find only those database entries containing *both* words, or you might be happy bringing home any entry containing either one word or the other. You generally have to tell the search engine what sort of search you want to do. This is an issue of Boolean logic in the query, and a matter of AND and OR. An AND search requires the presence of all stated keys; for example, to find entries on computer science you would search for "computer" AND "science" in the same entry. To search for items relating to DOS or Windows (which stand independently) you would want to do an OR search. AND is usually implied in the absence of an explicitly stated operator.

AND and OR operators can be present in a single query. Continuing the previous example, if we wanted a list of graphic files in the two major formats (GIF and JPEG) on Web servers in England, we would query using:

```
uk (gif or jpeg)
```

This query requires the satisfaction of two conditions: "uk" (the top level domain for England) along with either "gif" or "jpeg". Note that the AND operator is not explicitly stated. In this fairly common scheme,

```
http://zeus.oxford.edu.uk/Public/QUEEN.gif
```

would be a search "hit" as would:

```
http://scotland.yard.gov.uk/Private/bobby.jpeg
```

More detailed explanations of the key building process appear near the end of this chapter.

Gopherspace, as a universe of generalized information, has been with us longer than any other organized collection of data. "Generalized" is the operative word here. Archie was the first Internet search engine available for general use; however, Archie dealt with finding files and not topic-specific information. Since Gopher has a long history and plenty of "time-in-grade," it should not be surprising that Gopherspace has a versatile and mature search engine. The name of the Gopher searcher is Veronica, which stands for Very Easy Rodent-Oriented Net-wide Index of Computerized Archives. Do I sense an *a priori* acronym here? (Someone obviously didn't want Archie to get lonely.)

We'll have a tutorial explaining how to compose efficient Veronica queries near the end of this chapter. We'll also discuss the composition of the Unix-based search key used in most Web search engines. First, we'll have a little fun....

LET'S HAVE VERONICA FIND SOME HUMOR

Let's get down to business. I love lawyer jokes. You know the type: "How do you get a dead lawyer out of a tree?"—"Cut the rope." The nice thing about lawyer jokes is they lack protection under the Political and Environmentally Correct Anti Terrorist law, usually known as the POLECAT act. Lawyers don't appreciate these jokes, but then again, what can you expect from a group of professionals whose idea of fun is watching the blood drain from a client's face when presented with the bill? I've heard that a great list of lawyer jokes is stored at several different sites on the Internet. Veronica can help us find the lists.

Veronica searches the Gopherspace menu system for key words. It (or is it *she?*) does *not* search documents at the end of the Gopher shaft. You can start a Veronica search using either Gopher (client or server) or a Web browser. If you wish to start by using the Unix command line, point Gopher at

```
unix% Gopher Gopher.micro.umn.edu
```

or just about any Gopher site. From virtually any Gopher main menu, there is usually an entry called, "Other Gopher and Information Services." Selecting the "Other Gopher" entry will in turn produce a menu having an entry called something close to "Search titles in GopherSpace using Veronica." We'll pick up at this point using Netscape.

Figure 19.4 shows the Search Engine's submenu from my Netscape bookmark menu. (My complete Netscape menu system is on this book's CD-ROM as urb-menu.htm. It can be used as a Netscape bookmark.htm replacement.) Clicking on "Veronica Search" brings up the next menu. Figure 19.5 shows a portion of the menu. From this menu select a Veronica site, one that is not likely to be busy. A remote site at 3:00 AM would be ideal—people awake at that hour are unlikely to be composing Veronica searches. Since it's currently

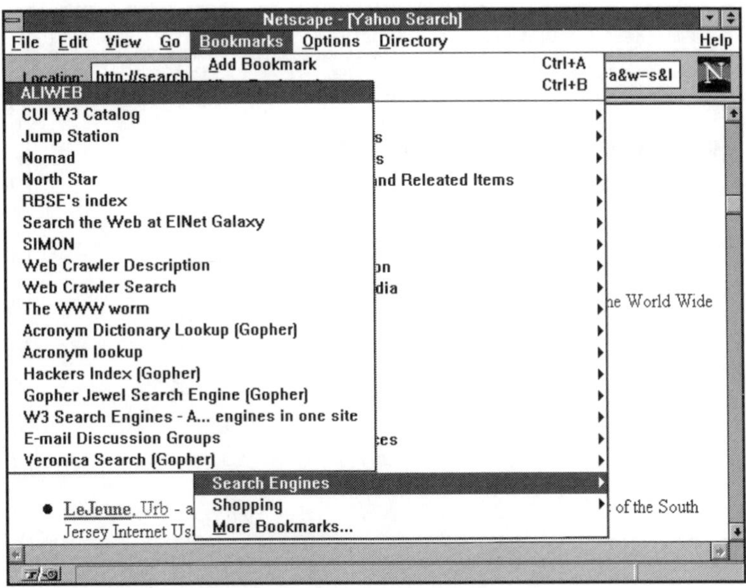

Figure 19.4 *The Search submenu from Urb's urb-menu.htm bookmark file.*

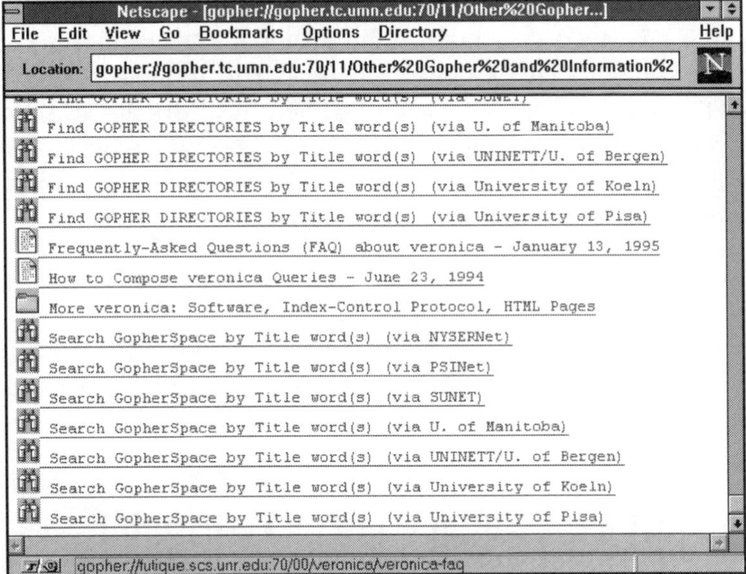

Figure 19.5 *The Gopher menu produced by clicking on "Veronica Search".*

9:00 PM on the East Coast, let's try Italy's University of Pisa. (It's the selection leaning to one side.) Click on the item, "Search Gopherspace by Title word(s) (via University of Pisa)" to display the query form shown in Figure 19.6.

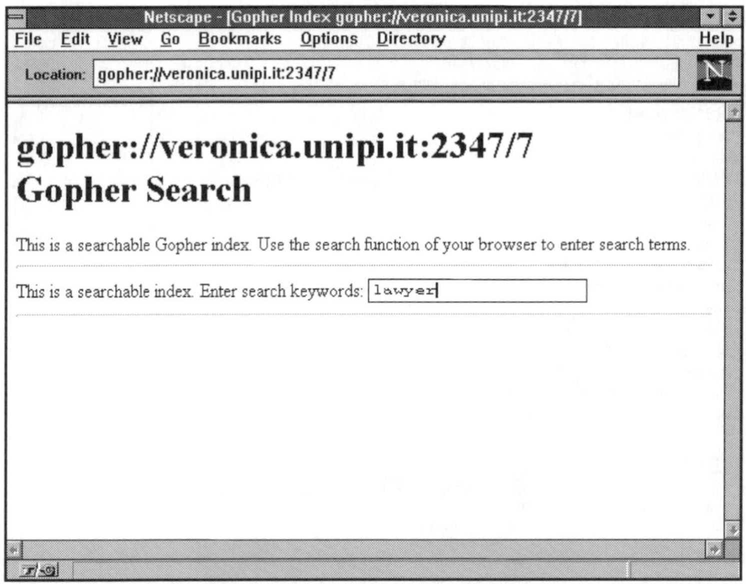

Figure 19.6 A Veronica search form.

Fill in the search index as shown in Figure 19.6 and submit the form by pressing Enter. We need a bit more sophistication in our search keys, but we'll narrow down search strategies shortly. After what frequently seems like an interminably long wait, back comes a list. Veronica formats a list of entries matching the search string so it appears just like any other Gopher menu, as shown in Figure 19.7. Somewhere in the middle of a rather long list is a likely looking candidate, "Canonical list of Lawyer jokes."

Paydirt! Clicking on the "Canonical list" yields the long list of jokes shown in Figure 19.8. At about 75 Kb of "yucks," this is not a trivial list. A fascinating aspect to this type of information retrieval is not knowing the source of these wonderful jokes, unless you're experienced enough to recognize an institution or business by its URL. If you access this list using a Gopher client, you won't even see the URL.

STEVEN FOSTER'S VERONICA QUERIES TUTORIAL

Steven Foster is one of the original members of the Gopher development team at the University of Minnesota. Steve is currently the Veronica Project Manager at the University of Minnesota and has written the terrific treatment of query techniques that we're reprinting here. Steve has graciously agreed to share his work with the readers of this book, for which I would like to express my deepest thanks.

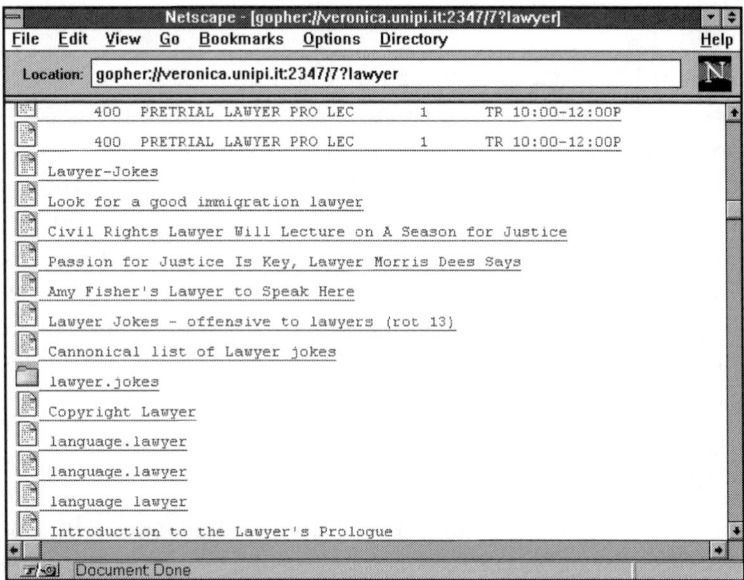

Figure 19.7 *A Gopher menu produced by a Veronica search.*

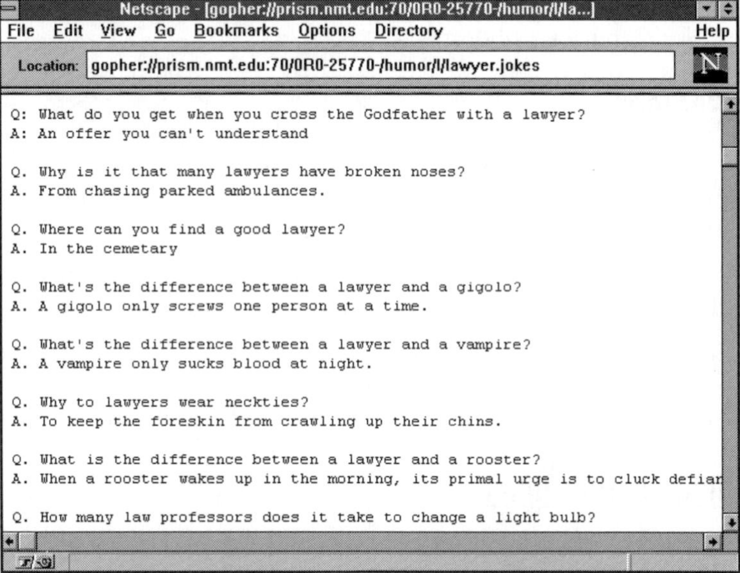

Figure 19.8 *The world's largest collection of lawyer jokes.*

The original (and possibly updated) versions of this document are obtainable by Gophering to:

```
Gopher://Veronica.scs.unr.edu:70/00/Veronica/how-to-query-Veronica
```

Introduction

The Veronica index contains about 10 million items from over 6,000 Gopher servers (as of this writing). Veronica finds resources by searching for words in titles. It does not do a full-text search of the contents of the resources; it finds resources whose titles contain your specified search word or words. The "title" is the title of the resource as it appears on the menu of its home Gopher server. Veronica is used with a Gopher client. You will choose "Veronica" from the menu of some Gopher server, and enter a set of query words or special directives. When the search is finished, the results will be presented as a normal Gopher menu. You may browse the discovered resources in this menu, as you would use any other Gopher menu.

Types of Searches

Most Veronica-access menus offer several types of searches. In addition to these pre-defined types, you can compose Veronica queries using a number of special options to focus your search more precisely. You should use these options when appropriate, as they will make it much easier to locate resources. (See sections below on "Pre-Defined Search Types" and "Finding Resources of a Certain Gopher Type.")

Multiple Servers

Many Veronica-access menus offer a list of various Veronica server sites; in this case, you will have to choose a server site to use. Ideally, it does not matter which server you use, as all servers will give the same answers. In practice, the servers do not all update the index at the same time, so there will be some difference in the results. Some servers will return an answer faster than others, depending on load and network traffic. Many other Veronica-access menus offer a single entry rather than a list of servers. In this case, simply click on the search type desired, and submit your query in the dialog box.

Pre-Defined Search Types

Most access menus offer two predefined search types. Here's one:

```
> Search GopherSpace by keywords in Titles.
```

This search will find *all* types of resources whose titles contain your specified search words. The resources may be of any Gopher data type; for example, ASCII documents, Gopher directories, image files, binary files, and so on.

And here's the other:

```
> Search Gopher DIRECTORIES ONLY for keywords in Titles.
```

This search will find only Gopher *directories* whose titles contain the specified words. This search can be very useful to find only major holdings of information that relate to your query. After Veronica finds the Gopher directories, you can open any of them to see the contents in more detail. This is especially useful to avoid being overwhelmed by too many results if you are searching with a common word such as "women" or "Internet"! You can define your own query, specifying only certain types of Gopher resources, by using the -t option. For instance, you could search for *only* image files by including the phrase "-tI" in your query. See below for more about the -t option.

Entering a Query

When you select a query type, your Gopher client will present a dialog box. Enter your query words. The search is *not* case-sensitive. You may get better results by entering a multi-word query rather than a single word. Multiple word queries will find only those items whose titles contain ALL of the specified words. For instance, "women" will find 5223 items; but "league women voters" will find 126 items. Be as specific as you can. It also helps to be imaginative. Think about how gophers are organized; the information you want may not be found under "league of women voters", but under the more general heading of "politics". A multiple word query does not require that the words be adjacent in the title, nor that they appear in any particular order. So, "marx brothers" will locate the same items as "brothers marx". There is more information on composing queries below.

Default Maximum Items and the "-m" Option

By default, most Veronica servers will deliver only the first 200 items that match your query. You can request any number of items by including the "-mX" command phrase in your query. X is the number of items you wish. If X is omitted ("-m"), there is no limit to the number of items delivered. For instance:

```
"women" will provide 200 items.
"women -m1000" will provide 1000 items.
"women -m" will provide all available matching items.
```

You may find a message at the end of your Veronica results menu, like "*** There are 576 more items matching your query." If you are not satisfied with the 200 items you got, you can resubmit the query, requesting more items with "-m".

Note that some Veronica servers will provide more than 200 items by default.

Query Logic, Boolean Searching, and Wildcards

The search understands the logical operators AND, NOT, OR, (, and). If you use a simple multiple word query, it is the same as using AND between the words. For instance "acid rain" is the same query as "acid and rain". "League women voters" is the same as "league and women and voters". As noted above, we recommend using AND to create a tightly focused query. We recommend that the word "OR" be used very rarely. Usually, OR will just produce thousands of hit-or-miss results. OR is best used in conjunction with other operators, as "rice and (fried or curr*)". An asterisk ("*") at the trailing end of a query word will match anything.

The asterisk character may be used *only* at the end of words; the search will fail if an "*" is placed within a word or at the beginning of a word. Search words must be at least two characters long. Shorter words are ignored. Interpretation of the query starts from the right-hand, interpreting operators as encountered. If in doubt about order of interpretation, *use parentheses!* The Veronica server at University of Koeln (as of June 94) interprets the query logic from left-to-right.

Finding Resources of a Certain Gopher "Type" using the "-t" Flag

You can use Veronica to find resources of a specified Gopher type and that type only. You specify the type or types of interest by adding the "-tX" option phrase to your query. The -t flag may appear anywhere in the search specification. For example:

```
"women-t1"
"-t1 women"
```

Either of these search phrases will find resources with the word "women" in the title. All the resources will be Gopher *directory* items (type 1). There must *not* be any spaces between the -t and the type specifier.

You may specify more than one type in the query. Do *not* use separate -t options to do this; simply put all the types together (with no spaces) after the

-t. For example: "-tgs mac" returns a menu of GIF images or sounds with the word "mac" in the title.

Official Gopher types, from the Gopher Protocol Document, are:

```
0 – Text File
1 – Directory
2 – CSO name server
4 – Mac HQX file
5 – PC binary
7 – Full Text Index (Gopher menu)
8 – Telnet Session
9 – Binary File
s – Sound
e – Event (not in 2.06)
I – Image (other than GIF)
M – MIME multipart/mixed message
T – TN3270 Session
c – Calendar (not in 2.06)
g – GIF image
h – HTML, HyperText Markup Language
```

Summary of the Options

Here's a summary of the key Veronica search options:

- -t Limits the search to items of specified data types.
- -m Specifies maximum number of items to find.
- -l Creates a file of links for the discovered resources. The file will be displayed as the first item on the Veronica results menu. You can then retrieve that file and include the links in menus that you may be building. Note well that not all Veronica servers support the "-l" option.

Just include the options in the search query. They will work with any Gopher client. You can put options before the query words, after the query words, or even between query words.

Do *not* cluster more than one option behind a single hyphen; instead, use a separate hyphen for each separate option. For example:

```
Gopher -t1s -m400
```

This example requests 400 items containing the word "Gopher" and specifies that we want only items whose type is "directory" or "sound".

Examples (from Fred Barrie)

Here are some simple examples:

- Search on the word "internet". This will return a menu list of (at most) 200 records that have the word "internet" in the title field. Just type:

  ```
  internet
  ```

- Search on the word "internet", but specify 1000 items instead of the default 200. Type:

  ```
  internet-m1000
  ```

  or

  ```
  -m1000 internet
  ```

- Search on the words "chicken" and "wine". This returns a menu list of (at most) 200 records that have *both* "chicken" and "wine". Type:

  ```
  chicken and wine
  ```

- Search for the keywords "chicken" or "wine", specifying directories only. This returns a menu list of resources that have *either* chicken or wine, and which are Gopher directory entries. Type:

  ```
  chicken or wine -t1
  ```

  or

  ```
  -t1 chicken or wine
  ```

- To use the operator NOT in a query, type:

  ```
  chicken not wine
  ```

  This will search for all titles with the word "chicken" but *not* the word "wine". Type

  ```
  chinese food not msg
  ```

  to search all the titles with the words "chinese" *and* "food" but *not* "msg". Remember there is an implied AND between two words.

- To use parentheses in queries, type

  ```
  chicken (wine or curry) -m
  ```

to list all titles with the words "chicken" and either "wine" or "curry". The -m asks for *all* records. Now type

```
(chicken or wine) not (msg or growing)
```

to search for titles with the words "chicken" or "wine" but not "msg" or "growing".

- The metacharacter "*" matches anything at the trailing end of a search word. Type

  ```
  chicken*
  ```

  to search for all titles with the word "chicken", "chickens", and so on. Type

  ```
  chicken* or wine*
  ```

  to search for all titles with the word "chicken", "chickens", ... or "wine", "wines", "wineries"....

WORLD WIDE WEB SEARCHING

Veronica is virtually the only search engine in common use for exploring Gopherspace. Another utility called Jughead performs a Veronica-type search on a Gopher database confined to a single institution. (What's next: Moose, for brute-force searches?)

Unfortunately, there is no clear front runner when it comes to WWW searching. From a user interface perspective, Web search utilities work in much the same way: You bring up an HTML search form (this requires any version of Netscape or Mosaic 2.x or one of the other, newer Web browsers) and enter some search criteria. At minimum this can be a word or multiple words; at best it can be a full Unix regular expression as used in the famous (or infamous) grep utility. Let's save the topic of Unix grep expressions for a tutorial at the end of this chapter. For now, let's plunge into the uncharted waters of Web searching.

THE WORLD WIDE WEB WORM

Let's begin the discussion of World Wide Web search engines with an award winner. Oliver McBryan, McBryan@cs.colorado.edu, developed the World Wide Web Worm (WWWW or simply the Worm). Oliver is a Professor of Computer Science at the University of Colorado at Boulder. The '94 Best of the Web contest awarded Oliver's WWWW first place in the Navigational Aid category. The Worm is one of the most popular (if not *the* most popular) search engine on the Web. Current Worm queries exceed 500,000 every month—which testifies to its quality, although such volume can cause problems, as I'll explain later. To converse with the Worm, tune in to this URL:

```
http://www.cs.colorado.edu/home/mcbryan/WWWW.html
```

The concept underlying the Worm's database is quite simple: A special program called a *Web robot* goes out onto the Web and gathers information by automatically loading and scanning Web pages, and the information is then compiled into a database. (There are other Web robot search systems out there. The WebCrawler is one, and we'll discuss it shortly.) A Web robot is much like an automated Netscape user, though one with considerably more patience than you or I. The World Wide Web Worm's robot goes out to a list of URLs, loads them, and grabs their titles and any hyper text links that those titles contain. It then traverses any hyper text links to linked documents, and looks for more hyper text links to more URLs, recording HTML page titles and hyper text citations as it goes. (Hyper text citations are the blue-colored text you see in HTML documents that lead to other places on the Web.) As you might imagine, given the connectedness of the Web, such a system can automatically generate a massive database of information if allowed to run long enough. (One hopes robots don't get as bored with Netscape's animated symbol as humans do.)

The Worm stores URLs, page titles, and hyper text citations found within the pages that its robot reads. It can search on substrings for any of those three categories of data, and provide a cross-reference of all citations of a given page, as well. (This could have some vanity value if you get a kick out of knowing how many other Web pages contain links to your own personal home page.)

The hyper text citations may contain useful information ("Click here to see pictures of Jupiter") or text that is pointless without context ("Click here to go back"). Because the pointless citation contains words unlikely to be used in any significant search ("here" or "click"), they factor out and don't get in the way.

One unavoidable shortcoming of the Worm is that it cannot know of a URL's existence unless either the URL exists in the initial list examined by the Web robot, or a URL is cited by a Web page that the robot visits. The list of URLs examined by the robot grows all the time as people submit newly created Web pages to the Worm's database. (This is necessary because newly-created pages are by definition not cited by existing Web pages.) Eventually there will be nowhere to hide from the Worm's tireless robot.

The Worm uses the Unix egrep utility to perform searches. We'll summarize the basics of grep-style string searches at the end of this chapter. It's a complicated subject, so if you really choose to become a crackshot Web searcher, crack a Unix text and bone up on grep, particularly on the building of regular expressions.

Figure 19.9 shows the Worm's home page. The first list box toward the bottom of the page contains a drop-down menu showing the four search types available through the Worm. To perform a Worm search, you can either go with the default of "Search all citations hyper text" or select a search type from the four listed. Next, enter the keywords into the edit field labeled "Keywords." Finally, click on the Start Search button. Figure 19.10 shows the results of a Worm search I performed for the string "census". There were more than the defaulted 50 matches, so only the first 50 are displayed. Looks to me like item 3, "All About The 1990 U.S. Census" should keep your boss happy for at least another day.

If the Worm is unusually busy when you try to access it, your search may fail even though there was nothing wrong with the regular expression you entered, and the information is in fact in the Worm's database. If you try to search for a common and obvious key word such as "Clinton" and the Worm comes back empty, try again, ideally when Boulder, Colorado (where the Worm lives) is relatively quiet.

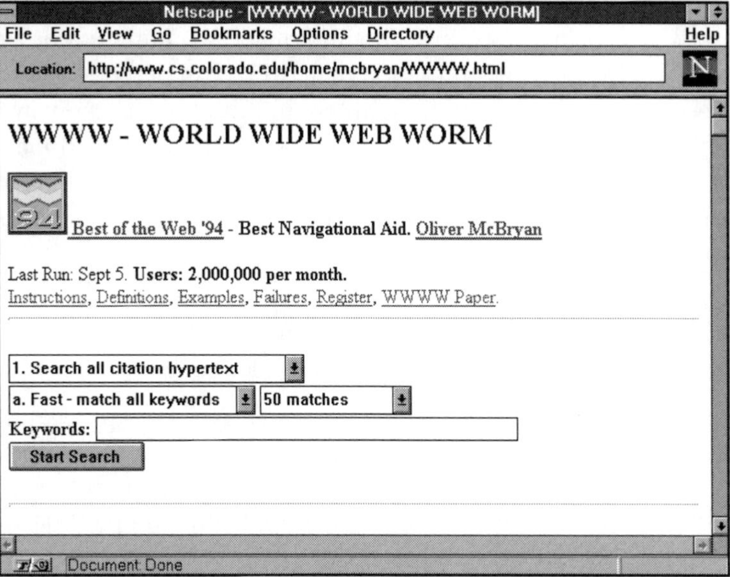

Figure 19.9 The World Wide Web Worm's home page.

Figure 19.10 *Worm search results for "census".*

HARVEST

Harvest is an ambitious, innovative entry into the field of Web search engines. Developed at the University of Colorado, Harvest is an information discovery and access system using a set of distributed utilities running under Unix. This system is definitely not your "run of the mill" Web searcher, but a next-generation architecture that promises to have an enormous effect on the way information will be handled over the Internet in years to come. It indexes *content* (that is, the material inside a Web page rather than just its URL, title, or hotlinks) and can handle more than Web-based material, such as Gopher and FTP data as well.

The Harvest architecture addresses three critical problems, namely:

- Providing the means for efficiently and flexibly indexing widely distributed information, thereby supporting knowledge discovery.
- Providing network-adaptive means of caching and replicating heavily accessed information, thus preventing processing bottlenecks.
- Providing support for accessing and manipulating complex data.

From your standpoint (that of a Web user working from a Web browser like Netscape), using Harvest is very similar to using the World Wide Web Worm or WebCrawler (which we'll discuss later). You bring up a Harvest query form and enter a query, which may be as simple as a single word or quoted phrase, or as complex as a roaring Unix regular expression. The Harvest server fielding the query returns an HTML page to you containing the results of the query.

Behind the scenes, however, is a *lot* of machinery. The Harvest people at the University of Colorado have given a lot of thought to both the requirements of an information index system and the peculiarities and limitations of the network (Internet) over which it operates. Harvest's design recognizes that the Internet is a huge and highly diverse collection of data. The tasks of gathering, indexing, and distributing the data are split into several nearly autonomous subsystems that can work in parallel, and consideration is given to the fact that some data is very popular and accessed many times by many people. One main goal of the Harvest system is to make the impact of information management on the Net itself as low as possible, by distributing the various jobs to make the best possible use of Net bandwidth.

Raw data is collected from where it resides (HTML pages, Gopher sites, FTP sites) by servers called *gatherers*. Rather than indiscriminately scouring the entire Internet (which is now arguably impossible) gatherers are given a focused task to gather a particular type of data (say, PC software or telephone numbers) from a limited number of places. Once data is gathered, it is managed and made available by servers called *brokers*. Brokers are the key to the Harvest system, and the only part of it generally encountered by end users like you and me. Brokers index the data and provide query interfaces to both end users and other brokers in the Harvest system. Brokers accept queries and run them, and package the discovered data for return to the end user, typically through a Web browser. (There is no Harvest-specific client software, as there is for the Web or Gopher.)

If a given broker is frequently parceling out certain data, the data is copied out to a sort of virtual broker (called a *cache)* by yet another type of server (called a *replicator)*. By automatically setting up frequently-accessed data in multiple caches, Net traffic is spread around and more efficient use is made of our increasingly precious bandwidth.

The design of the system minimizes the impact of information indexing on the Internet, making the best possible use of Internet processing and bandwidth. Harvest's developers claim that Harvest reduces server load by a factor of 6,600, network traffic by a factor of 59, and index space requirements by a factor of 43. Calculation of these numbers is obscure, but overall the idea makes an enormous amount of sense. You can get to the Harvest home page via the following URL:

```
http://rd.cs.colorado.edu/harvest/
```

Figure 19.11 shows the Harvest home page. Read as much of the documentation at the site as you can, but keep very plainly in mind that most of what you will read is for the benefit of people who want to set up their own Harvest servers on their Unix machines, not for ordinary Web users who simply want to present queries to Harvest brokers.

Harvest Brokers

Brokers are the "big guys" you will talk to when requesting Harvest data. Like Web servers and Gopher servers, they are Unix programs running on Unix systems connected to the Internet. When you access them from a Web server, they show you a form-based query entry page with an edit field and a "search" button.

Brokers are created to serve a certain type of information; you can't just search any broker blindly for anything. Harvest has created an index of servers, so you can first search for a server that handles the type of information

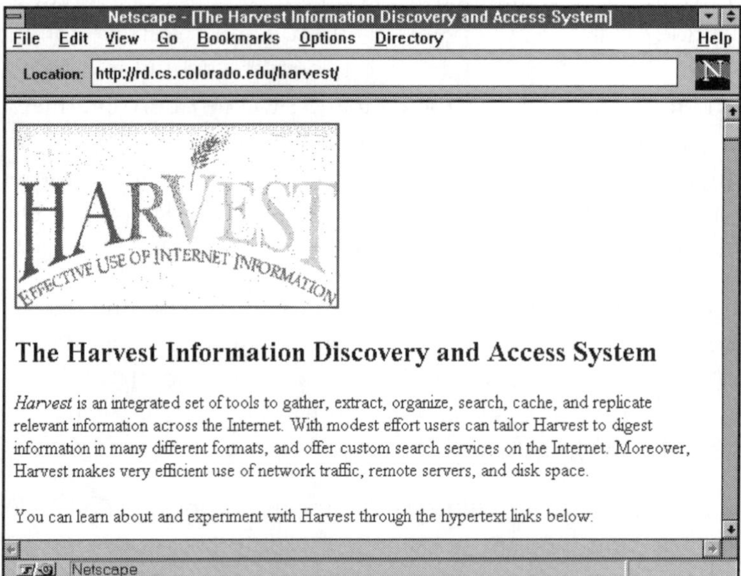

Figure 19.11 The Harvest home page.

you want to examine. There are several demonstration brokers currently reachable from the Harvest home page. Available demonstration brokers include:

- The University of Colorado CS Department index lets users search for documents in many different formats. This index is available through the department's WWW, FTP, and NetNews servers. It demonstrates how a Broker can be customized to support queries of interest to a user community, and how a Broker can be customized to use local site document naming and organization conventions to provide high-quality indexing terms for documents.

- The SEC EDGAR index lets users search forms that have been filed with the Securities and Exchange Commission in 1995. It demonstrates how a Broker can make use of SGML-tagged data to provide a powerful search service, with query fields based on the tagged data.

- Query Access to the AT&T 1-800 Telephone Directory. This Broker was gathered from AT&T's 800 Web pages, which currently only supports browsing by category or name. With a modest amount of effort we were able to build:

  - A customized Harvest Gatherer that collected the 4,000+ Web pages that hold these data and extracted categories according to the particular data formats being used.

  - A Broker that lets users browse by category, search by category, search by business name, and search by telephone number, including support for misspellings.

  In addition to using this Broker, users can retrieve the indexing data we gathered in a single compressed stream of object summaries, and construct their own indexes of the data without incurring the additional server and network load needed to gather the data themselves. For example, while it took about 10 hours to gather the data from across the Internet, it only takes a few minutes to retrieve the compressed summary stream for these data from across the Internet. To learn more about doing this, see the Harvest help screen about finding Harvest servers with the Harvest Server Registry (HSR), and search the HSR for GATHERER AND "telephone directory" (note that the quotation marks are significant).

- Web Home Pages. Here we used Harvest to create an index of 45,000 Web home pages. Because we index content summaries rather than just anchor and HTML strings, this index captures much of the content of Web sites without having to collect every last Web page—providing a useful index at lower cost and much less duplication of information than that found in the World Wide Web Worm or Lycos (TM).

- PC Software. This index demonstrates Harvest's ability to incorporate information in a variety of formats from other sources, including high quality, manually-generated information sources. Because each indexed site uses a somewhat different format, we used Harvest's customizable extraction features to collect indexing information in site-specific ways and place this information into a uniform format. As a result of this effort, we were quickly able to incorporate high quality indexing information about nearly 35,000 publicly available PC software distributions. This index provides better search support than more general-purpose software indexes (such as Archie), because it contains conceptual descriptions of a focused collection of information. For example, searching for "batch programming language" will locate the "RAP" package, while Archie could only locate this object if you searched for "RAP".
- There is also a Gatherer translation script for some other manually created indexing information formats, including the "Linux Software Map" (LSM) format and the Internet Anonymous FTP Archives IETF Working Group (IAFA) format. At present we have a Broker running for LSM data but none for IAFA data, because there are not yet enough sites using the IAFA format to warrant building a Broker.
- Computer Science technical reports. This index covers content summaries of over 32,000 reports from 280 sites, published in a variety of formats (such as ASCII, PostScript, DVI, and HTML). Content summaries support more powerful searches than the titles or abstracts covered by previously existing CS technical report indexes (such as those offered by Monash University, Indiana University, and the University of Karlsruhe). The current index is possible because Harvest provides a very space-efficient indexing architecture. This Broker also demonstrates Harvest's integration with a commercial search engine (from Verity Inc.).
- Networked Information Discovery and Retrieval (NIDR) software and documents, and a software index built by cascading the separate indexes into a combined index (at no additional network or server load). These indexes underscore the scaling advantages of topic-specific indexing. For example, the query "approximate" will locate a grep (an approximate

match tool embedded in Harvest's indexing system), while the same query at our more general Computer Science technical reports index locates many unrelated papers.

- Documents referencing the Santa Fe Institute time series competition data. This index demonstrates Harvest's structured indexing capability and its indexing customizability: In addition to supporting the usual content summary index, the SFI time series broker allows all users to search by time series reference. These references are generated by a specific script attached to the indexing process that matches each document content summary against approximately 70 regular expressions, to heuristically determine the referenced time series.
- The NetNews index demonstrates how Harvest can work with a rapidly changing database such as network news. Rather than indexing individual messages, here we only use the newsgroup "overviews." An overview is a list of the subject, sender, message-id, and other information for each message in a newsgroup. This allows us to create a good index of news articles without needing to retrieve each article individually. Unfortunately, an article's subject line often does not reflect its content. Currently this broker contains only newsgroups from the 'comp' hierarchy. Updating the database occurs every other day. Figure 19.12 shows the Demonstration Brokers page.

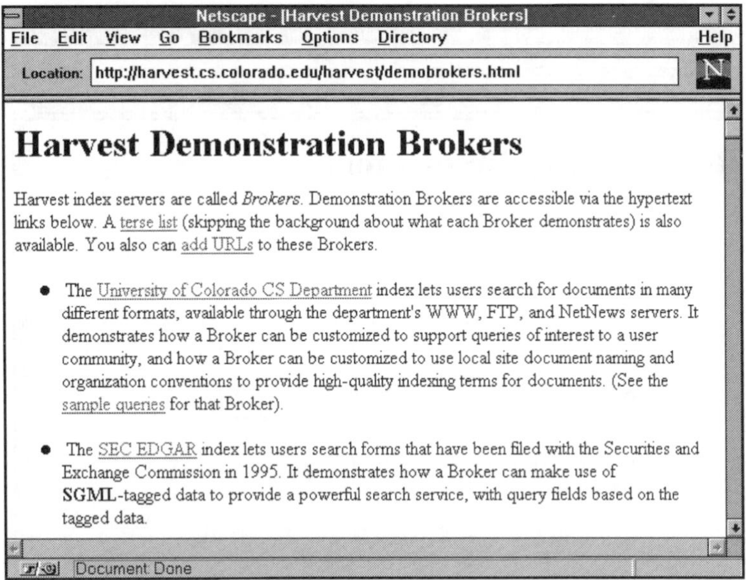

***Figure 19.12** The Harvest Demonstration Brokers.*

Harvest Queries

Let's use the 1-800 directory broker to demonstrate Harvest queries. All 1-800 numbers are not necessarily included, because the broker index was built using data from AT&T's 800 information service.

Enter a search keyword to match individual entries or categories. The 1-800 broker has a browse-by-category interface. A query has several selectable options, as listed below. You can set them all or simply use the defaults:

- Case insensitive—the default is the entire keyword must be matched
- Number of spelling errors allowed
- Maximum number of "hits" to be returned
- Broker Server Options
- Broker Host

Let's look for 800 numbers belonging to airlines. Your search key is the simple word "airline". Enter your search key, leave the other options alone, and click on Submit. The broker will perform the search and return an HTML document containing the results, if any. Figure 19.13 shows a portion of the results of the "airline" query. Harvest returned 32 phone number in 16 categories.

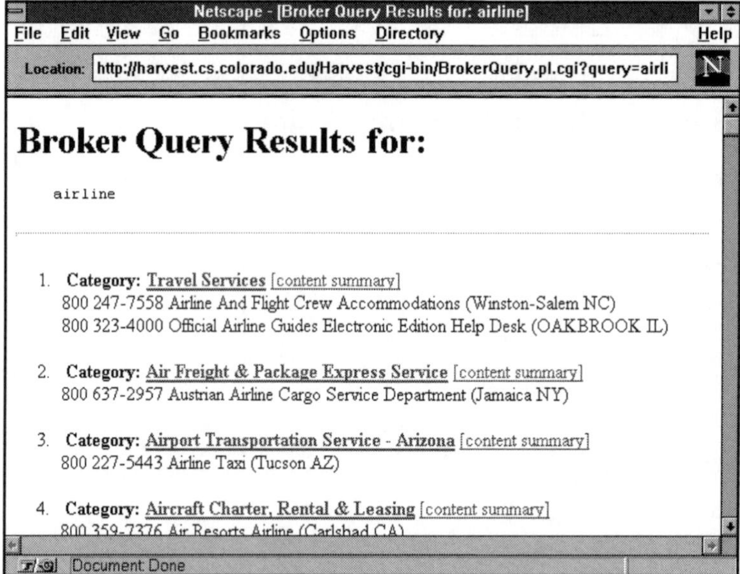

***Figure 19.13** Querying the 1-800 broker for "airline".*

Sometimes a response will come back indicating that your selected broker host isn't online. You are often given a choice of multiple hosts for a given broker, and if one isn't working, you can select another through the final option on the query form.

The Harvest people have set up an exceptionally useful help page on broker queries. Make sure you read it before attempting any but the simplest searches using a broker:

```
http://harvest.cs.colorado.edu/Harvest/brokers/queryhelp.html
```

The other demonstration brokers are well worth checking out. One of the demonstration brokers indexes several of the world's largest software repositories, including CICA, SimTel, Garbo, and Hobbes. If you're looking for a shareware or freeware package for your PC, boy, they don't come much better than this—and it's a superb demonstration of just what Harvest may grow to be in coming years, as it matures and people begin to use it in earnest. To get the PC software broker, go to:

```
http://harvest.cs.colorado.edu/brokers/pcindex/query.html
```

Hey, Linux fans: There is a Harvest broker that indexes over 1200 different software packages available for the freeware Linux operating system, which may well be the fastest-growing variant of Unix. This broker is unusually valuable because most Linux software is freeware and thus rarely advertised or promoted in any way. You often have to "ask around" to find anything, and even then you'll only hear about what your friends have discovered somehow. Using Harvest, you can "gather" as much information on available Linux software as anyone has available right now. To get to the Linux software broker, go to:

```
http://harvest.cs.colorado.edu/Harvest/brokers/lsm/query.html
```

Harvest is very new, and new Harvest brokers are being created all the time. Fortunately, the Harvest folks have created a Harvest broker called the Harvest Server Registry that indexes known Harvest servers of any type, including brokers, gatherers, and caches. Servers can't be listed, obviously, unless their creators inform Harvest that they exist. If you want to see the list of known Harvest servers, go to the following Harvest Query page and submit the query BROKER AND GATHERER AND CACHE, as explained in the query page's comments:

```
http://harvest.cs.colorado.edu/brokers/hsr/
```

There's a lot more to Harvest than we can even summarize in one portion of a chapter. Certainly this is the future of Internet information management. For the time being, check out the Harvest FAQ file, which is nicely done and will answer most of your unanswered questions:

```
http://harvest.cs.colorado.edu/harvest/FAQ.html
```

NIKOS—THE NEW INTERNET KNOWLEDGE SYSTEM

NIKOS is another recent and promising information discovery system. A joint project between California Polytechnic Institute and Rockwell Network Systems, NIKOS is a text-based search engine referencing over 100,000 documents. According to its creators, the number of documents in the NIKOS database is increasing at the rate of five per minute! A query summary lists documents in their likely relevance to the query, much as WebCrawler does. Figure 19.14 shows the NIKOS home page. The URL for NIKOS is:

```
http://www.rns.com/cgi-bin/nikos
```

I used the key "NSF" to query NIKOS, with the results shown in Figure 19.15. NIKOS returned 253 entries. Clicking on the "Global Schoolhouse - Thomas

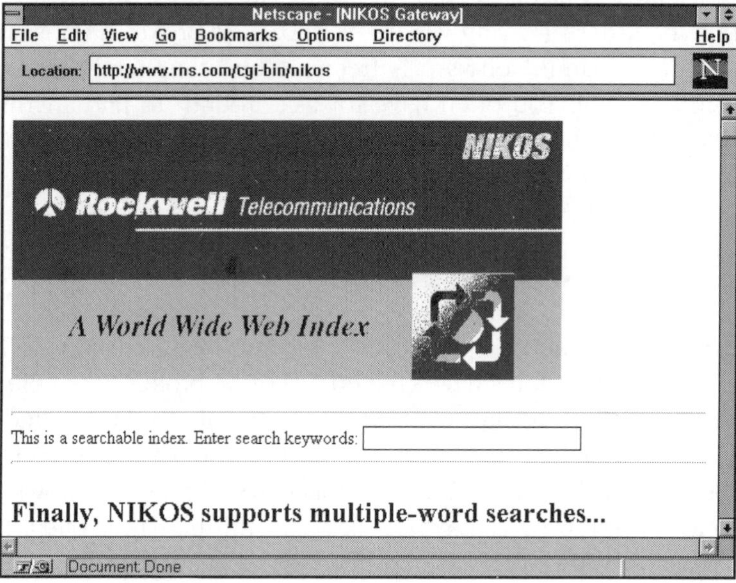

Figure 19.14 The NIKOS home page.

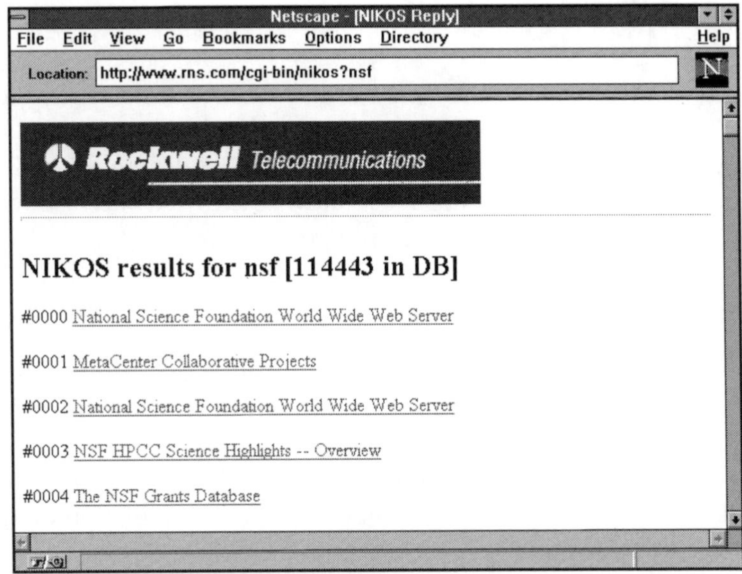

***Figure 19.15** NIKOS search results on "NSF".*

Jefferson Middle School" anchor loaded the page shown in Figure 19.16. Returning to the results of the "NSF" search and following the trail of funding guides there were several entries representing the grant solicitation information your hypothetical friend requested at the beginning of this chapter.

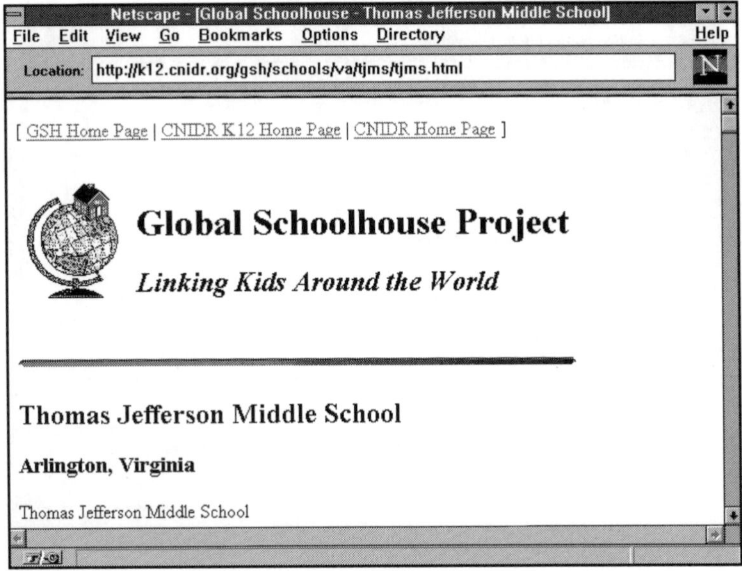

***Figure 19.16** Following the NIKOS search links to the NSF page.*

EINET GALAXY

EINet is the firm that created the WinWeb browser for RAM-challenged Windows machines. Their Galaxy page is a guide to worldwide Internet information and services. EINet Galaxy contains a searchable database in addition to a hierarchical subject index. Figure 19.17 shows the EINet Galaxy home page, which can bet reached by pointing Netscape to:

```
http://www.einet.net/galaxy.html
```

EINet Galaxy is a good jumping-off location for Internet searches. Searching from this starting point takes some adjustment, since there are different search modes present on the page. In addition to a form-based search option, there are topics categorized by content and subtopics within the broader topics. As an example, let's see if we can ferret out the Catholic population of Spain for our in-house honor student.

One of the most difficult aspects of searching is the development of a strategy. Understanding the nature of the database you want to search is key to the process. Some databases—Harvest and WebCrawler are good examples—index *content* as well as titles, URLs, and citations. Many other systems, like the World Wide Web Worm, index only the titles, URLs, and

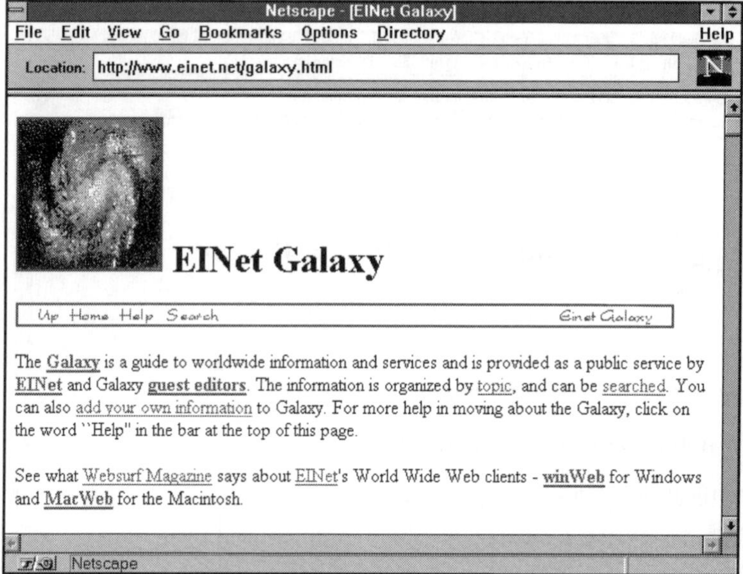

Figure 19.17 The EINET Galaxy home page.

citations. Galaxy is one of those that does not search on index content, so searching for "spain and catholic", as key words in the content, might not produce useful results. The successful approach would probably address the question, "What type of document would contain the information of my desires?"

The Galaxy home page (Figure 19.17) shows the first of many topics, Arts and Humanities. What broad or general topic would have the answer to our prime question—"What is the Catholic population of Spain?" Moving down the Galaxy page, we find the general topic Social Science. This topic has two promising subtopics, Geography and Sociology. Let's try Geography.

Figure 19.18 shows a portion of the Geography page. An entry that catches my attention is one with the word "searchable" in the title. Let's try the CIA World Factbook. This is a famous Internet resource maintained by America's superspy agency, and contains a multitude of useful facts about countries around the world. (You might get the impression, however, that they have kept the most interesting data themselves.) Following the trail, we next have a form for searching the CIA World Factbook. Entering "spain" brings up a Gopher menu, a portion of which is shown in Figure 19.19. Notice the seamless transition from the Web to Gopher. The entry "Spain, People" sounds pretty good to me. Following the Spanish People link brings up the fact sheet

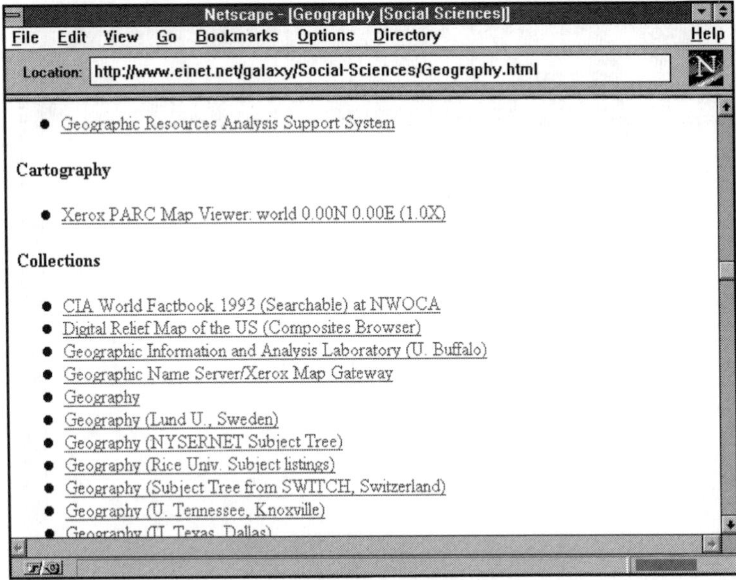

Figure 19.18 *A partial entry from the Galaxy Geography category.*

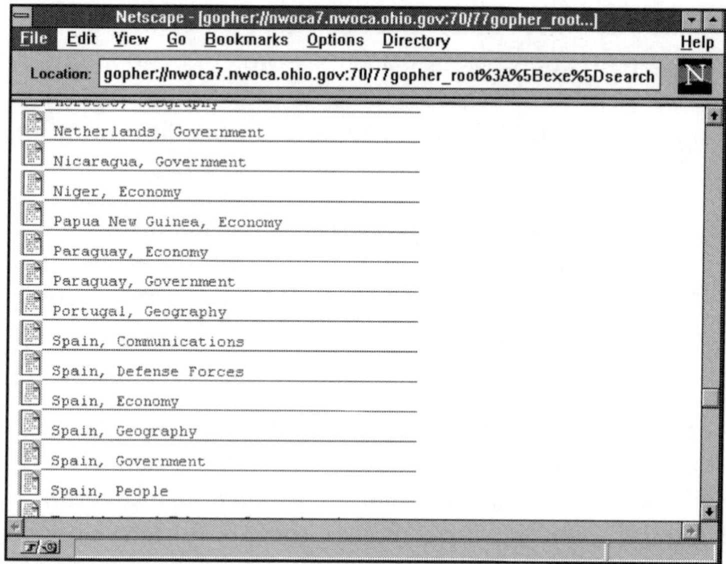

Figure 19.19 *A Gopher menu produced by searching the CIA World Factbook for "Spain".*

shown in Figure 19.20. There it is, right in the middle of the scrolled page. Spain has a Roman Catholic population of 99 percent. If your company makes elementary school uniforms, you may want to run out and get a Spanish export license.

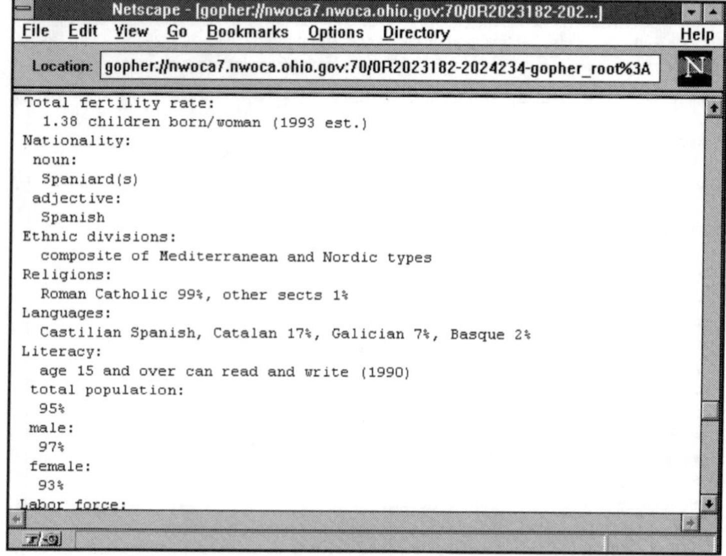

Figure 19.20 *The CIA Factbook document on Spain.*

THE WEBCRAWLER

Like the World Wide Web Worm, the WebCrawler is a Web-search system based on a Web robot that scours the contents of Web documents. The Crawler database is one of a small group of search systems that actually indexes the contents of Web pages in addition to their titles, URLs, and internal hyper text citations.

The WebCrawler has a very easy user interface, with the downside that it is not as powerful as some and does not allow the entry of grep-style regular expressions. You simply enter the key word or words and click on the Search button. If your key consists of multiple words, you have the option (through a Windows check box) of selecting the AND operator for the search, such that to be a hit, a document must contain all the specified key words and not simply one or two. The default operator is AND. Figure 19.21 shows the WebCrawler search form.

To get to the query page for the WebCrawler, journey to this URL:

```
http://webcrawler.cs.washington.edu/WebCrawler/WebQuery.html
```

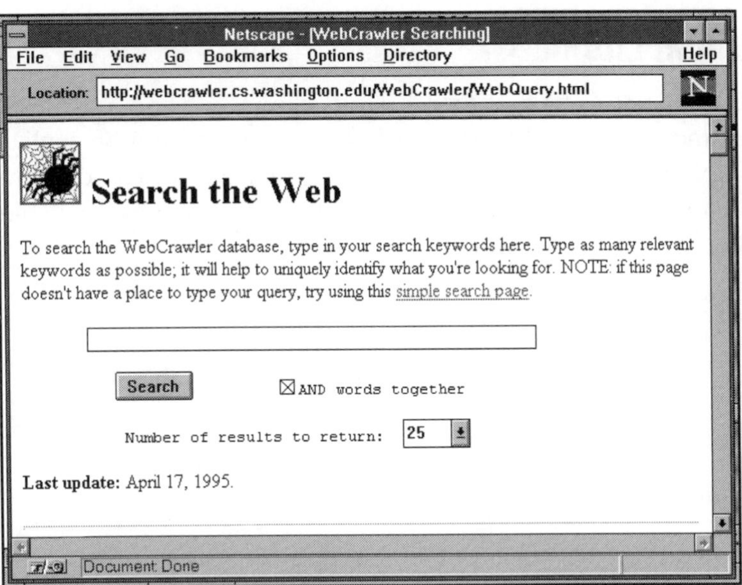

Figure 19.21 *The WebCrawler query form.*

The query responses sent back to you by WebCrawler contain a "pertinence index" on their left margin. This number indicates how likely it is (according to WebCrawler's logic) that the selected item will pertain to your query. "1000" is always the top number, and they scale down from there. You can set a maximum number of responses through an edit field on the query form; 35 is the default.

As with most such utilities, it pays to read whatever documentation the developer has provided. The WebCrawler query page has links to its documentation. In another slightly odd development, WebCrawler has "sponsoring" corporations who are obviously lending financial support to the project. A hotlink in the WebCrawler page invites you to check out the sponsors and their products. This is an interesting notion, and worth watching to see if similar projects obtain sponsors to help them foot the bills for providing free services like this.

As an aside, I've found that WebCrawler is one of the most reliably available Web search schemes. If the Web is really cooking and you get locked out of other search schemes, try the WebCrawler before you despair and throw something at the wall.

W3 SEARCH ENGINES

The URL pointing to a page in Switzerland called W3 Search Engines is, to me, the single most valuable link on the Internet. This page represents the "one stop shopping center" of Internet searching machinery. The document contains pointers to some of the most useful search engines available on the WWW. You can access it through this URL:

```
http://cuiwww.unige.ch/meta-index.html
```

The major search topics, as shown on its first-level menu, are:

- Information Servers
- Software
- People
- Publications

- News/FAQs
- Documentation
- Other Interesting Things (Jargon, Acronyms, WIRED...)

W3 Search Engines contain links to most of the search resources I've listed in this chapter, and to many more than I could possibly cover, even if I had an entire book at my disposal. You'll have to explore most of them on your own. Be aware that there is very little standardization in query formats; at best you'll be able to use Unix grep syntax, and at worst you'll have to learn the peccadilloes of a whole new system. Many of the resources you'll find through W3 Search Engines are special-purpose in nature, and some may be of no particular interest to you, but I recommend becoming familiar with the breadth of resources you'll find there—just in case you need to look for something tomorrow that you've never had to look for before.

The following section lists some of the search resources you can access by starting from this single page. To avoid blowing the size of this chapter out of the realm of reasonableness, about all I can do is list. But hey, by this time you're a seasoned explorer, right?

Information Servers

- Lycos WWW search engine at Carnegie Mellon University
- The Whole Internet Catalog
- Veronica (Gopher directory search)
- Search the Web at EINet Galaxy
- Veronica subset (Gopher directory search) at EINet Galaxy
- Jughead (Gopher directory search)
- WAIS directory-of-servers index (gateway access)
- WAIS directory-of-servers index (direct access)
- Thesaurus Search

Software

- Archieplex (Swiss server at SWITCH)
- The Language List
- The Free Compilers List
- The Free Database List
- keyword in SW archive using SHASE

People

- Netfind gateway (name key...)
- Finger gateway at mit.edu
- Finger gateway at Digital CRL
- Ph gateway at ms.uiuc.edu
- UFN Search (X.500 directory)
- FOUR11 Directory Services Back to Top

Publications

- Rik Harris' Abstracts Index
- The Unified CS TR Index
- Computer Science TR Archive Sites
- OO Bibliography (object-oriented and related papers)
- Gopher Catalog of Electronic Texts
- Cornell University's Technical Report Library

News/FAQs

- WAIS FAQ Search at Utrecht University
- HTTP FAQ Search

- Gopher FAQ Search
- Search news.announce.conferences
- Search today's Usenet news

Documentation

- Big Dummy Search
- NCSA Docfinder
- BSD/386 Hypertext Man Pages
- CUI Computer Science Library
- Nexor's Public Services
- RFC index at Nexor
- Internet Draft Index at Nexor

Other Interesting Things

- Hacker's Jargon
- Acronym Search
- Say (Text to Speech Translator)
- American recordings
- WIRED Archive

Miscellaneous

- CUI's collected search engines
- NCSA's Experimental Search Engine
- Meta-Index

Quite a collection, huh? Figure 19.22 shows the beginning of the meta search form derived from the W3 Search Engines master. See the tip, *Load W3 Search*

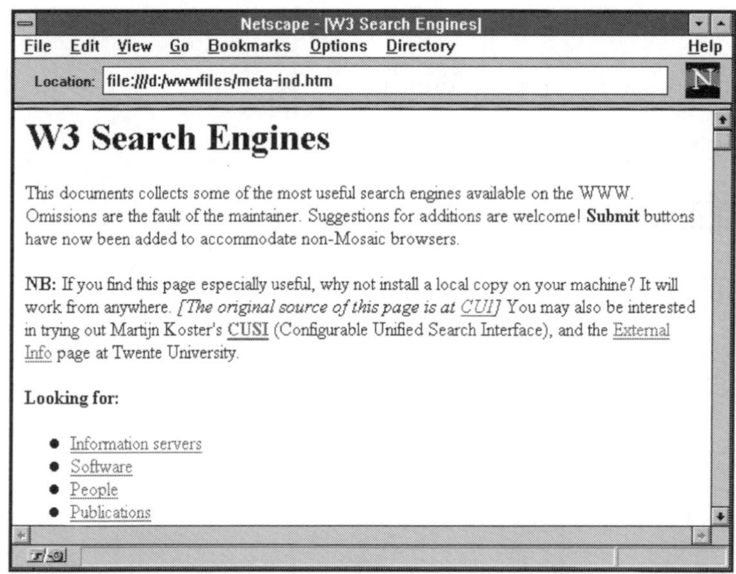

***Figure 19.22** W3 Search Engines loaded from local disk.*

Engines from Local Disk, for details on loading this form directly from your PC's disk rather than fetching it from the Net. Figure 19.23 shows one small portion of the available search forms.

Netscape - [W3 Search Engines]
File Edit View Go Bookmarks Options Directory Help
Location: file:///d:/wwwfiles/meta-ind.htm
List-based WWW Catalogs
submit CUI World Wide Web Catalog
submit Global Network Academy Meta-Library
submit Aliweb (Archie-like Indexing for the Web)
See also:
Aliweb at Nexor
Spider-based WWW Catalogs
Search WebCrawler (Search WWW document content)
☒ AND words together

***Figure 19.23** The W3 Search Engines search forms.*

Load W3 Search Engines from Local Disk

You can accelerate the loading of the W3 Search Engines HTML document by copying the form that originally resided in Switzerland to your PC's hard disk. Transatlantic loads can be time-consuming, and if you use a page a lot (as I use this one) there's no reason to haul it across the pond every time you want to use it. If loading speed concerns you more than cosmetics, edit out the document's anchors that specify graphic images. Locally loading the search form, without images, is lightning fast.

Start the process by first loading the W3 Search Engines' document by entering the URL:

```
http://cuiwww.unige.ch/meta-index.html
```

Next, select File|Save As. Note the filename has been truncated to meta-ind.htm. Select your desired stored path when the Save As dialog box appears. Accept the default file name of meta-ind.htm. Let's assume you have saved meta-ind.htm to d:\WWWfiles.

As I said earlier, edit out any references to GIF files, as there's not much point in saving the HTML file to disk and still going out on the Net to fetch images. If you're a purist, download the GIF files and change the addresses so they're also fetched from local disk—though even that takes some time while the files decode. Next, activate the URL by entering:

```
file:///d:/wwwfiles/meta-ind.htm
```

making any adjustments for your pathname.

(The D: could of course be some other drive specifier on your machine.) Last, enter the URL and title as a bookmark in an appropriate category. I also keep the original transatlantic cuiwww URL in my Search Engines menu (as I'll describe later in this chapter) so I can periodically check to see if any new search links have been added.

URB'S HOT SPOTS

I keep a Search Engines submenu as part of my Hot Spots bookmark list. The following is the applicable portion of my urb-menu.htm bookmark file. You'll find it on the companion CD-ROM as the file urb-menu.htm in the directory \urbstuff\netscape.

```
<H3 ADD_DATE="799098009">Search Engines</H3>

    <DL><p>

        <DT><A HREF="http://web.nexor.co.uk/aliweb/doc/aliweb.html"
             ADD_DATE="799093568" LAST_VISIT="0">ALIWEB</A>

        <DT><A HREF="http://cui_www.unige.ch/w3catalog" ADD_DATE="799093568"
             LAST_VISIT="0">CUI W3 Catalog</A>

        <DT><A HREF="http://www.stir.ac.uk/jsbin/js" ADD_DATE="799093568"
             LAST_VISIT="0">Jump Station</A>

        <DT><A HREF="http://www.rns.com/www_index/intro.html"
             ADD_DATE="799093568" LAST_VISIT="0">Nomad</A>

        <DT><A HREF="http://comics.scs.unr.edu:7000/top.html"
             ADD_DATE="799093568" LAST_VISIT="0">North Star</A>

        <DT><A HREF="http://rbse.jsc.nasa.gov/eichmann/urlsearch.html"
             ADD_DATE="799093568" LAST_VISIT="0">RBSE's index</A>

        <DT><A HREF="http://galaxy.einet.net/www/www.html" ADD_DATE="799093568"
             LAST_VISIT="0">Search the Web at EINet Galaxy</A>

        <DT><A HREF="http://web.elec.qmw.ac.uk/simon/welcome.html"
             ADD_DATE="799093568" LAST_VISIT="0">SIMON</A>

        <DT><A HREF="http://webcrawler.cs.washington.edu/WebCrawler/Home.html"
             ADD_DATE="799093568" LAST_VISIT="0">Web Crawler Description</A>

        <DT><A HREF="http://webcrawler.cs.washington.edu/WebCrawler/
             WebQuery.html" ADD_DATE="799093568" LAST_VISIT="0">Web Crawler
             Search</A>

        <DT><A HREF="http://www.cs.colorado.edu/home/mcbryan/WWWW.html"
             ADD_DATE="799093568" LAST_VISIT="0">The WWW Worm</A>

        <DT><A HREF="gopher://info.mcc.ac.uk:70/77/miscellany/acronyms/.index/
             index" ADD_DATE="799093568" LAST_VISIT="0">Acronym Dictionary
             Lookup (Gopher)</A>

        <DT><A HREF="http://curia.ucc.ie/htbin/acronym" ADD_DATE="799093568"
             LAST_VISIT="0">Acronym lookup</A>

        <DT><A HREF="gopher://gopher.mcs.kent.edu:4320/7hackindex"
             ADD_DATE="799093568" LAST_VISIT="0">Hackers Index (Gopher)</A>

        <DT><A HREF="gopher://cwis.usc.edu:3456/7" ADD_DATE="799093568"
             LAST_VISIT="0">Gopher Jewel Search Engine (Gopher)</A>

        <DT><A HREF="http://cuiwww.unige.ch/meta-index.html"
             ADD_DATE="799093568" LAST_VISIT="0">W3 Search Engines - All known
             search engines in one site</A>
```

```
<DT><A HREF="http://alpha.acast.nova.edu:80/listserv.html"
     ADD_DATE="799093568" LAST_VISIT="0">E-mail Discussion Groups</A>

<DT><A HREF="gopher://gopher.tc.umn.edu:70/11/
     Other%20Gopher%20and%20Information%20Servers/Veronica"
     ADD_DATE="800137768" LAST_VISIT="800137711">Veronica Search (Go-
     pher)</A>

</DL><p>
```

UNIX GREP STRING SEARCHES

As promised earlier, here is a mini-tutorial on the construction of Unix grep-style search keys. Many WWW search engines perform grep searches. Grep, like many other Unix command names, doesn't necessarily mean anything. (It helps to remember that Unix was designed to impress heavy-duty computer geeks and, secondarily, to scare others away from this most obtuse operating system—with the slow speed of ancient ASR33 teletypes contributing to its terseness.) This might be a good point to distinguish between a nerd and a geek. Nerds are people who don't realize that they are totally consumed by computers. Geeks, on the other hand, are people with an all-consuming addiction to technology who wear their affliction like a badge.

Done exhaustively, grep syntax and searching techniques would fill a volume at least as large as this book. Fgrep and egrep are variations on the basic grep theme. Fgrep allows searching for multiple targets. Egrep encompasses a richer set of searching expressions, in addition to allowing multiple targets.

Essentially, grep—and its cousins fgrep and egrep—locate lines in a file matching a target search pattern. The World Wide Web Worm conducts egrep searches using a database of URLs, titles, and citations (hotlinks.) Since the last component of a URL is typically a pointer to a stored hypermedia resource, an fgrep search will efficiently ferret out pointers to a specific type of resource such as mpeg movie files. Searches may use combined descriptors, so that a conceptual search for "uk" and "au" and "edu" would produce a listing of all audio files (au) on Web servers at educational institutions (edu) in the United Kingdom (uk). Because words typed separately with no other text between them implies the AND operator, a successful "hit" requires the simultaneous presence of all three substrings—uk, au, *and* edu—in a line for the line to qualify as a hit.

Regular Expressions

A *regular expression*, in grep parlance, is a standard syntax for symbolic expressions. Table 19.1 contains an abbreviated listing of elements of regular expressions.

***Table 19.1** Regular Expressions in grep and egrep*

Common grep Regular Expression Symbols

Symbol	**Meaning**	**Example**	**Matches**
.	Match a single character	urb	urban, suburban
*	Match zero or more repetitions of preceding character	sp*ort	sport, sort
[ ]	Match any character(s) enclosed in the brackets	[Uu]rb	Urb, urb
^	Match only if at beginning of a line	^Urb	Urb at start of line
$	Match only if at end of a line	rice$	I like fried rice
\<	Match the character only if at beginning of a word	\i	it - not split
\>	Match the character only if at end of a word	p\l	pl - not place

Additional egrep Regular Expression Symbols

<table>
<tr><th>Symbol</th><th>Meaning</th><th>Example</th><th>Matches</th></tr>
<tr><td>+</td><td>Match one or more occurrences of the preceding character</td><td>no+n</td><td>noon - not nn</td></tr>
<tr><td>?</td><td>Match zero or one repetition of the preceding character</td><td>lo*se</td><td>lose, lse - not loose</td></tr>
<tr><td>|</td><td>Match either x or y</td><td>x | y</td><td>x, y</td></tr>
<tr><td>( )</td><td>Use enclosed text as a group</td><td></td><td></td></tr>
</table>

Don't forget Rule #1: The grep family (as with most search engines) assumes a Boolean AND in the absence of an explicitly specified connecting symbol between subexpressions. The expressions (lawyer joke) or "lawyer joke" would successfully identify a line if it contained *both* "lawyer" and "joke". However, the expression (lawyer|joke) would successfully identify any line containing *either* "lawyer" or "joke".

The World Wide Web Worm's home page contains a group of example searches that adhere to the egrep syntax. Reading them is a good idea—and actually trying them out on the Worm to see them in action is very good practice. To access them, point your browser to:

```
http://www.cs.colorado.edu/home/mcbryan/WWWW.html
```

To display a short manual for the grep family, get into your shell account and enter the following command at the Unix command line prompt:

```
unix% man grep
```

If you would like a hard copy of any Unix manual (keeping in mind that Unix manuals were written for the enjoyment of Unix geeks), redirect the output of the "man" command to a file using the following command syntax:

```
unix% man grep > grep.man
```

The output of the command "man grep" appears in the file "grep.man." Transfer the file down to your PC and print a hard copy. That's all there is to it.

LET'S REVIEW

After the initial rush from surfing the Web, your enjoyment tends to be a function of your ability to find the things you want, rather than simply accepting what's there as you explore. Make it a habit to use searches early and often in your Web journeys. The Yahoo search engine is an especially good place to start.

Successful searching requires practice. The W3 Search Engines page contains links to about 45 different searching forms. So experiment and try things—remember, you're an explorer. However, recognize that knowing the *nature* of what you search for is far more important than its name or where you choose to search. The WebCrawler has a great page dedicated to searching hints. The WebCrawler searching guidelines formed the basis for the following query suggestions.

Most search engines know a lot about Web information and documents, so it pays to make precise queries—within limits. You can, however, be too precise. Finding what you want frequently requires multiple queries—multiple spellings, perhaps, and certainly multiple approaches. If you don't get the results you desire, use the following suggestions to recast your query.

Now, what to do when your search produces no results at all? First, check your spelling! If that looks okay, then try to be less specific in your query. For instance, the query "molecular biotechnology DNA sequencing genetics chromosome human genome project" is probably a touch too specific. Very likely no one document contains all, or even most, of those keywords—as valuable as such a hypothetical document might be to your current line of inquiry. Don't jump in with an indiscriminate Boolean OR hoping to find sources containing at least one of the descriptors. Think about the range of documents, or even titles, containing the common words "human" or "project" or "molecular" or ... I'm sure you get the point. Instead, try something like "molecular DNA sequencing."

Suppose your search produces too many results? Be more specific—but even before that, make sure that you have the AND button checked. Try to think of words that uniquely identify the object of your affection—without also identifying a lot of other things as well. Some words are of little value, because they will match many database indexes. The words "information" and "university" even when taken together identify a lot of the entries in almost any database, and as such, are of little value in trying to narrow down the search.

Search engine errors don't always mean that you made a mistake. Sometimes they can indicate that the engine is busy, or that the server in question is down for maintenance. Generally they don't indicate bugs in the software, so please be merciful about flaming the creators of a service—they're giving you an extraordinarily valuable service for free.

Be aware of characteristic terms or acronyms associated with your search goal. For instance, if you're looking for information on the band They Might Be Giants, you can search for "They Might Be Giants," or remember that insiders sometimes refer to the band as just "TMBG."

Some keywords pop up in many places. Ada is a programming language, but it's also an acronym for the Americans with Disabilities Act and probably many other things. (Many search engines cannot discriminate based on case.) For example, instead of searching for "ADA" use something more descriptive such as "ada programming" or "ada computer". (Make sure the AND button is checked, if there is an AND button.) If you want to find something instead of other things that talk about that something, add a qualifier to its name. In other words, to find pointers to the *New York Times* (and not a host of unrelated documents that cite the Times by name), try the query "New York Times online newspaper".

One final piece of pragmatic advice: As you become expert in the fine art of information procurement, don't tell anyone. This goes double if you're in earshot of a high school or college student. If you're foolish enough to boast about your wizard status as data snooper, be prepared to spend all your spare time doing other people's homework. It happened to me. It can happen to you.

Let Your "finger" Do the Walking

Here's a protocol that provides you with up-to-the-minute information from people to earthquakes to sports scores. It will also provide you with your own "home page," whether or not your provider has a Web server!

As I stated in the previous chapter, the focus of this book is the quest for information. Information acquisition includes the techniques for finding information and retrieving things of value. This chapter shifts gears a little, since it's a humanistic sort of exploration. We'll find people instead of "things" and retrieve information associated with people.

The finger program (which is actually a protocol; the finger programs themselves are nearly trivial) allows finding information about the users on your host network, in addition to finding information about users having accounts on cooperating networks. As we shall see, users are not always people. They may also be interesting (if inanimate) things like coke machines. Additionally, finger gives you a convenient method for posting information that may change frequently, in the fashion of an Internet billboard.

The operation of finger may vary from system to system. Some networks do not allow fingering at all, while others do not allow fingering from an external system. Don't be surprised if you receive a "Connection Refused" message in response to your finger request. Use the information in this chapter as a guide and explore. One thing the Internet *cannot* be accused of is gratuitous consistency.

RUNNING FINGER

When we get around to installing Netmanage's Internet Chameleon in Chapter 26, *The Fastest Road to the Web*, we'll have our own finger client installed on our Internet-connected PC. For the purpose of being complete in this chapter, we'll assume that a resident Windows finger is available for current use. In general, anything you do with the Unix command line finger utility you can do with a Windows finger client. However, keep in mind that your individual Internet-connected PC may represent a network unto itself. Fingering your "own" network will come up void unless you have also installed a finger server on your PC.

If you're using the Unix shell version of finger, you should enter the command in the following form:

```
unix% finger
```

Finger will then produce a listing of users currently logged onto your system. The output will look something like this:

```
Login        Name           TTY   Idle   When    Where
lejeune      Urb LeJeune    p0    Wed    00:04   pm1.acy.digex.ne
stuartm      STUART MASLOW  p1    Tue    20:55   pm1.acy.digex.ne
tconova      Tracy Conova   p2    Tue    22:35   pm1.acy.digex.ne
skylar       Skylar         p3    Wed    00:27   pm1.acy.digex.ne
zzazeron     Ken Matheson   p4    Tue    23:28   pm1.acy.digex.ne
```

A cooperating network may be fingered remotely using only the domain name of the network preceded by the "@" sign. I fingered San Diego State University for the following example

```
unix% finger @bestsd.sdsu.edu
```

and it produced the following listing:

```
 [bestsd.sdsu.edu]
Wednesday, December 22, 1994 12:18AM-PDT   Up 7 09:02:54
2+0 Jobs    Load ave  0.05 0.02 0.02
```

```
User       Personal Name    Job   Subsys  Idle   TTY    Console Location
REGAN1019  Susanne Regan    20E0  TELNET         .nty3  TCP: nunic.nu.edu
SYSTEM     System Manager   15E7  TELNET  1:34   .opa0  The VAX Console
```

Not much activity at San Diego State at 18 minutes after midnight, huh?

Finding the Hard to Find

Here's a sneaky tip: If you're trying to make contact with people at a specific company or institution but don't know their e-mail address, finger their network host system between midnight and 6 AM. Send an e-mail request for information to anyone you find logged on at that time. Any users who are active during those wee hours are likely to respond to an e-mail message. I've had great success with getting e-mail addresses this way. Late night people tend to be very cooperative once they get over the shock of learning how you found them. Maybe it's the lack of human contact at that hour in the morning. Maybe it's the shock of human contact of any kind, irrespective of the hour.

Many networks support finger servers that can perform a database search based upon first name, last name, or user-name (that is, login name). To find information about a specific user on your own network, whether logged on or not, use finger in the form:

```
unix% finger user
```

To illustrate the principle:

```
unix% finger urb
```

produced:

```
Login name: lejeune                     In real life: Urb LeJeune
Directory: /homeb/lejeune               Shell: /bin/csh
On since Apr 22 00:04:32 on ttyp0 from pm1.acy.digex.ne
Mail last read Sat AprJun 22 00:11:04 1994
No Plan.
```

My last name and my user identification are identical, so fingering lejeune@acy.digex.net would have produced the same result.

As you might suspect, there are rules for performing a finger search. A database "hit" requires an exact match and additionally requires satisfying one of the three following conditions:

- A case-sensitive match of the user's login name
- A case-insensitive match of the user's first name
- A case-insensitive match of the user's last name

Finding someone this way is not as difficult as it sounds. Most host systems are Unix based, therefore, login names are almost always in lowercase only. In addition, most Unix systems limit a user login name to a maximum of eight characters. If the last name of the person you're looking for has over eight characters, try the first eight. If the last name is less than eight characters long, try the first letter of the first name plus the last name, all as one word (no space separating the two). Since first and last name searches are case-insensitive, you can always use lowercase when trying names since you might get a hit on user login id. If you don't get a match of any kind, you will see something like the following:

```
Login name: xxx                          In real life: ???
```

Customizing Your "finger" Information

There are two ways to change the personal information displayed when someone "fingers" you. On a Unix system some, or all, of your basic display block information may be changed with the chfn command, although for security reasons that command may be disabled on your network. Entering

```
unix% chfn
```

will interactively take you through the process. The results are not always immediately updated. You may have to log off and then log back on again to see your changes take effect. Other information that may be displayed is contained in two files that are located in your home directory. These files are called ".project" and ".plan". (The names must be preceded by the period, which indicates a Unix system file.) The project file can be only one line, whereas your plan can be as long as you like. The personalized information can be anything you choose. Create either, or both, of these files using the least undesirable Unix text editor. (There is no such thing as a desirable Unix text editor.) If you really can't abide Unix, you could create the files on your PC and transfer them to your network host. Finger yourself to see if you like the effect. After adding .plan and .project files, my display had this look:

```
unix1% finger urb
Login name: lejeune     (messages off)  In real life: Urb LeJeune
Directory: /homeb/lejeune               Shell: /bin/csh
On since Apr 25 08:56:23 on ttyp5 from itacom.digex.net
Project:              The Netscape & HTML EXplorer
Plan:

     My plan is to work at least two hours a day on the
"Netscape & HTML EXplorer."

     Any suggetions or errors from the "Mosaic & Web EXplorer"
would be most appreciated.

     I aim to please, it's not my fault that I'm a poor shot.

Urb
lejeune@acy.digex.net or check my home page at:
http://www.charm.net/~lejeune
```

Once you're satisfied that your creative best is ready for the outside world, you must make both your home directory and these files visible to the universe. Of the two commands that follow, the first will open your directory, and the second will make these files readable by anyone.

```
unix% chmod a+x  ~
unix% chmod a+r  .plan  .project
```

In the first chmod command the "~" represents your home directory. The "a+x" part is saying, for all users (a) let them execute (x) things in my directory. The second states, for all users (a) let them read (r) files .plan and .project. The period before the plan and project file names are required.

There is a small disadvantage to opening your directory to outsiders. Other users on your network will be able to view the contents of your directory. They will not have the authorization to view the contents of files that have not been made readable as shown above. (Of course, if you have files lying around with names like GIRLS.GIF or PLAYMATE.JPG, they won't have to view the files to know what kind of guy you are...) So if you're a privacy buff, you may want to forego these finger enhancements.

Using Windows Finger

Let's assume a Windows finger client is already in place on your computer, and let's also repeat the last example using the Windows version of finger. Activate finger by double clicking on its icon. Using the Internet Chameleon's Finger client (which is supplied on the companion CD-ROM) I entered acy.digex.net in the Host: text box and lejeune in the User: text box. Click on

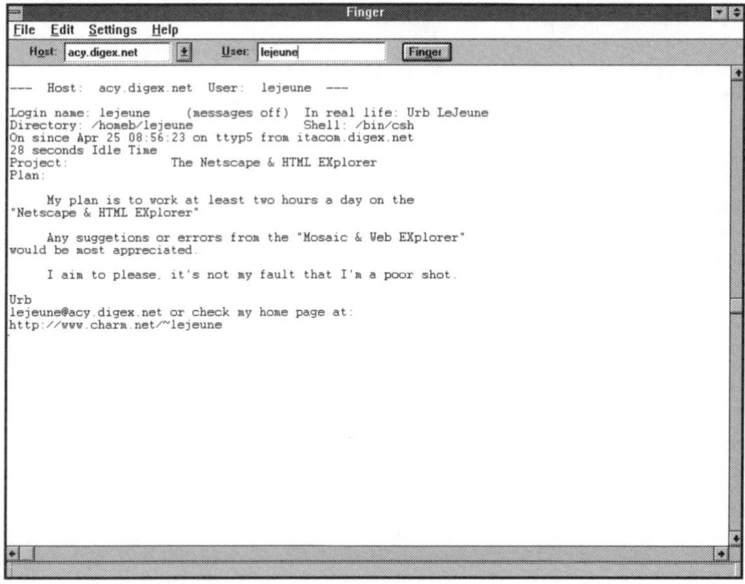

Figure 20.1 The results of the finger query.

the Finger button, or simply press Enter, to initiate the query. Figure 20.1 shows the results of the finger query for lejeune at acy.digex.net.

USING INTERNET BILLBOARDS

An interesting byproduct of a Unix .plan file is the ability to let other users conveniently receive information that may be subject to very frequent change—as often as several times a day. As we'll see in a minute, there are finger .plan files with daily sports scores and earthquake activity.

Scott Yanoff, a computer scientist at the University of Wisconsin, maintains an incredibly useful guide called the Internet Services List. Don't leave your home network without it! There are several methods that may be employed to obtain this list. To get the latest distribution details, finger Scott at yanoff@csd4.csd.uwm.edu. Figure 20.2 shows Scott's billboard-like "plan."

Let's Explore

Finger is an interesting and simple way of creating and distributing small amounts of information, especially information that changes on a regular basis. The ".plan" file may be easily changed using any Unix text editor. The plain text file then becomes instantly available to anyone fingering the creator's plan file. The finger functionality leads to many interesting uses of these Internet "billboards."

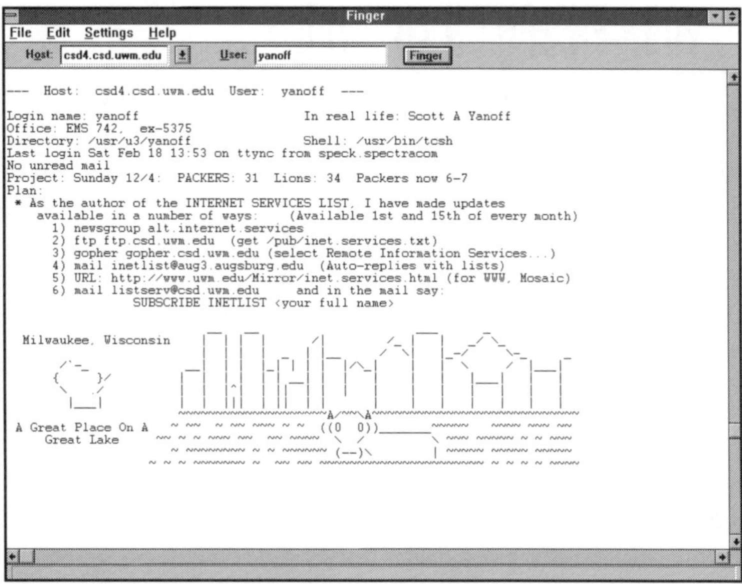

Figure 20.2 *Scott Yanoff's creative.plan file.*

An example of frequently changed information in a .plan file is the earthquake update at the University of Washington. I fingered quake@geophys.washington.edu to produce the output shown in Figure 20.3. Actually there is another half-screen of information to be perused beyond what can be shown on a single screen.

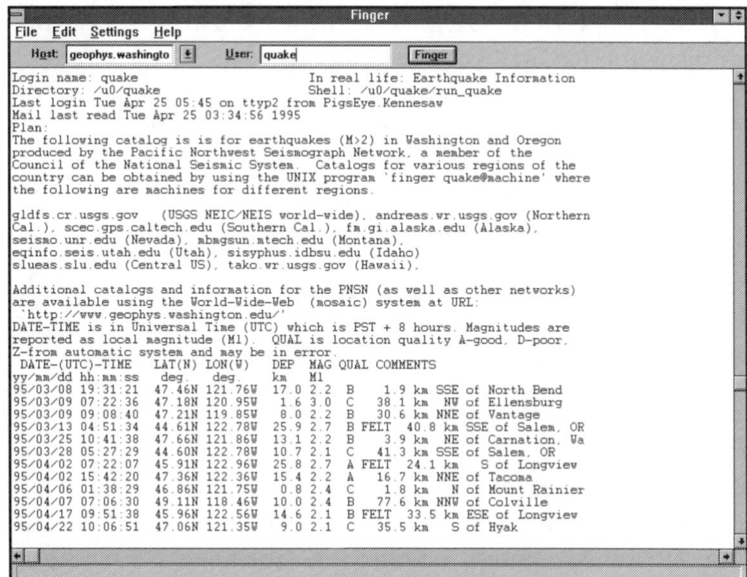

Figure 20.3 *The University of Washington's earthquake activity update.*

PUTTING YOUR FINGER ON THE WEB

It is also possible to use finger from within Netscape and other Web browsers. The University of Indiana has a finger gateway at the disposal of Web citizens. A *gateway* is essentially an interconnection between two otherwise unrelated networks or protocols. You send a finger request to the University of Indiana, and it gateways your request to the appropriate network site. When some response occurs, the gateway then passes the information back to you. To use the Indiana finger gateway, enter a URL in the form

```
http://www.cs.indiana.edu/finger/host-domain-name/user-id
```

where *host-domain-name* is the host name to be fingered and *user-id* is the login name of the user you wish to finger. For example, if you wanted to finger me from within Netscape, you would click in the Location text box (the one displaying the URL for the current document). Then, press the Home key to go to the left border of the text box, and press Ctrl+Del to clear out the field and enter the following URL

```
http://www.cs.indiana.edu/finger/acy.digex.net/lejeune
```

and as the last step, press Enter.

If you would like an update on baseball sports scores, they are available via finger thanks to Joseph Hernandex, jtchern@headcrash.berkeley.edu. To finger Joseph using the Indiana gateway, enter this URL:

```
http://www.cs.indiana.edu/finger/headcrash.berkeley.edu/jtchern
```

Figure 20.4 shows the results of fingering Joseph in last April 1995. As you can see, Joseph was not thrilled with the baseball strike.

A good example of the degree of diversity of applications that creative Internauts have discovered for finger is Cyndi Williams' Trivia Time. Finger Cyndi at cyndiw@magnus1.com using any of the techniques described in this chapter. Figure 20.5 is the display of the first page of Cyndi's Trivia Time.

The list goes on and on, and, yes indeed, there are fingerable Coke machines on the Internet. The first Coke machine came "online" in the mid-1970s. It served the Computer Science department at Carnegie-Mellon University. Everyone knows that programmers need periodic caffeine fixes to help sort out those ones and zeroes. The Coke machine in question was located quite a

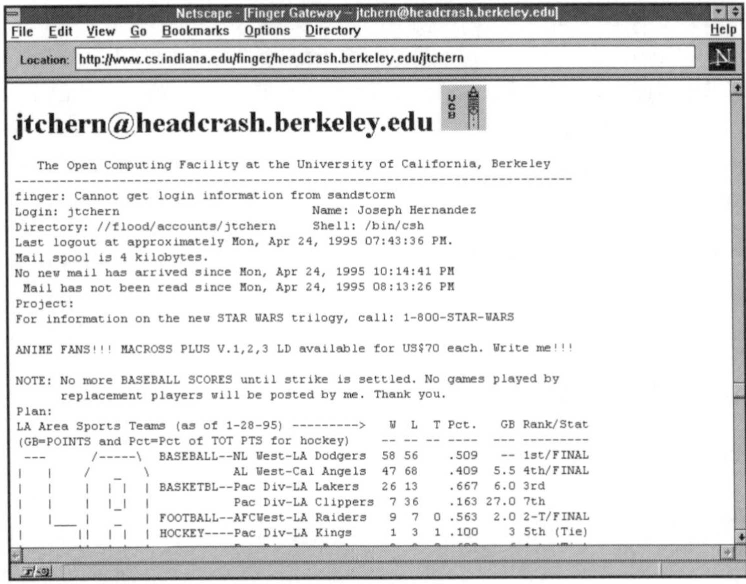

Figure 20.4 *Joseph Hernandez' baseball score finger file.*

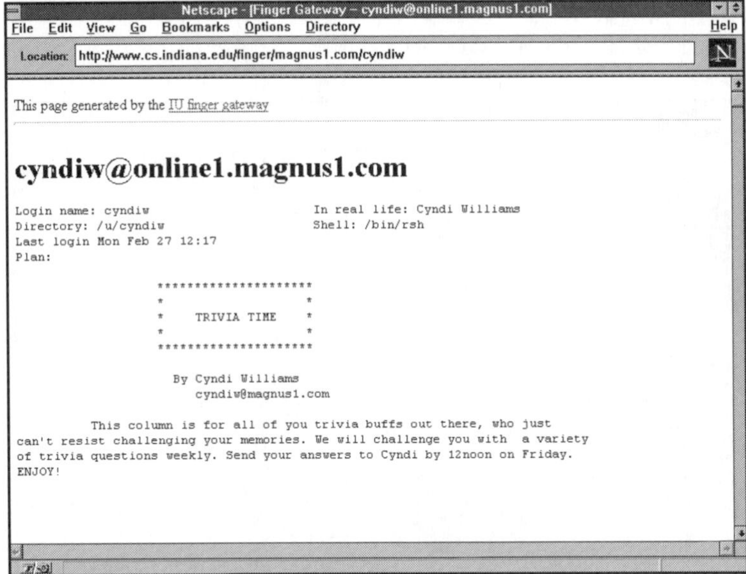

Figure 20.5 *Fingering Cyndi Williams' Trivia Time.*

distance from where many of the programmers were caged. Total frustration ensued when one of these guys, complete with pocket protector, trotted up a long flight of stairs, only to find that other caffeine-deprived programmers had already emptied the machine. Almost as bad, they might deposit their trusty quarter only to find that the forthcoming Coke was warm. Their solution was to make the machine a node on the Internet so that it could be interrogated remotely. Alas, the wonderful coke machine, coke@elab.cs.cmu.edu, at Carnegie-Mellon no longer seems to exist. CMU also had a special machine created for those needing a sugar fix as opposed to a caffeine fix, but mnm@elab.cs.cmu.edu also seems to be extinct.

Bennet Yee maintains a list of pointers to these sites around the world, as shown in Figure 20.6. You can access Yee's coke machine list at: http://www.cgi.cs.cmu.edu/afs/cs.cmu.edu/user/bsy/www/coke.html.

Other Interesting Sites

A few other interesting finger sites are:

```
Crossword Puzzle trinkets galore
   xword@acy.digex.net

Events on This Day in History
   copi@oddjob.uchicago.edu

Tropical Storm Forecast
   forecast@typhoon.atmos.colostate.edu
```

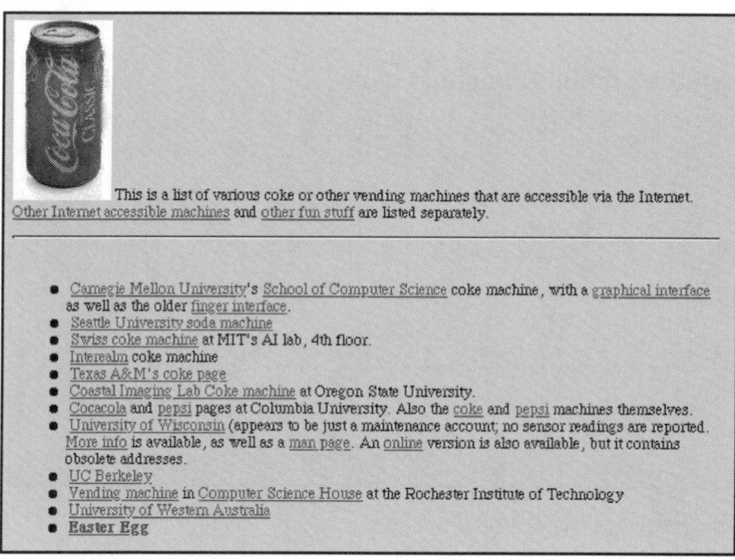

Figure 20.6 *Bennet Yee's list of worldwide coke machine servers.*

Scott Yanoff's Internet Services List, usually known as the Yanoff list, has lots of interesting places to finger. If you access the World Wide Web version of Scott's list, you can activate the finger command right from within the document. The HTML list is available for Netscape browsing at:

```
http://www.uwm.edu/Mirror/inet.services.html
```

The Gopher version of the list has more "finger" entries. To retrieve the Gopher version enter the following URL:

```
gopher://gopher.csd.uwm.edu
```

and then select Remote Information Services; next select Special Internet Connections (Yanoff List).

A Home Page for (Almost) Everyone

The Netscape Web browser introduced an interesting feature that may create a universal "home page" capability, even for people without access to a Web server. As explained in this chapter, a finger client, once it discovers the target of a finger request, looks for a file with the name ".plan". If the file is present and accessible, its contents are displayed by the finger client.

While browsing the Web using Netscape, try fingering someone via a finger gateway. If that person has created his or her .plan file as an HTML document, Netscape will display the document as it would any other HTML document, hotlinks and all. (Well not quite, formatting is somewhat different.)

Try it by entering this URL

```
http://www.mps.ohio-state.edu/cgi-bin/finger
```

and fill in the form with the e-mail address of the person (or Coke machine) that you want to finger. Figure 20.7 shows the results of fingering my account at Charm Net.

If your network system allows external fingers, you can now have a home page. Power to the people!

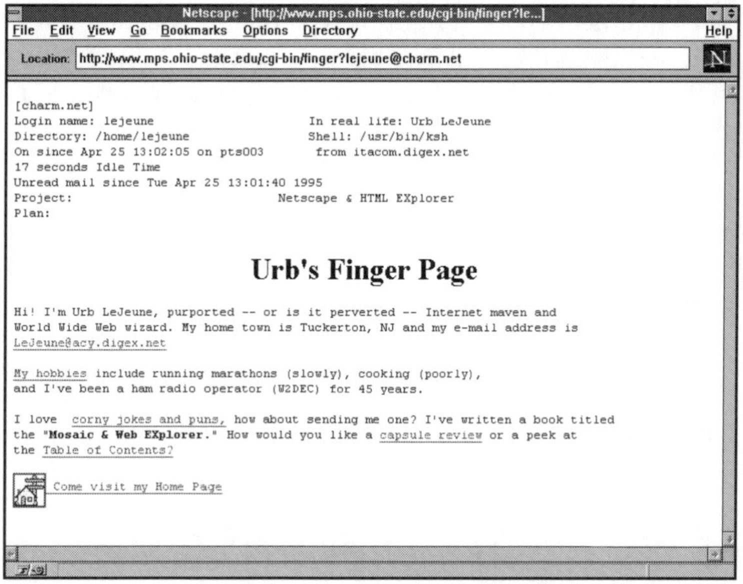

Figure 20.7 Urb's .plan file when viewed using Netscape via the Ohio State gateway.

LET'S REVIEW

Using finger to find the e-mail address of people on the Internet requires that you find the name of their host network, which is their domain name. Once you have found the domain name of a remote network, you may use the following Unix shell form of finger:

```
unix% finger name@host
```

where *name* conforms to the rules stated above and *host* is the domain name of the remote network.

Finger may also be invoked from Internet-connected PCs if you have a finger client installed. (I'll show you how to install a finger client, in addition to many other Windows clients, later in this book. The companion CD-ROM is full of 'em!)

You may also use finger from within a Web browser, taking advantage of the finger gateway at the University of Indiana. Enter a URL in the following form:

```
http://www.cs.indiana.edu/finger/host-domain-name/user-id
```

where *host-domain-name* is the host name to be fingered and *user-id* is the login name of the user you wish to finger.

If a user has created his or her .plan file as an HTML document and you are using Netscape, try the finger gateway at:

```
http://www.mps.ohio-state.edu/cgi-bin/finger
```

Since many administrators consider finger to be a security risk, they have disabled finger servers, or at least disabled them to outside users. Don't be surprised if you receive a message

```
Connection Refused
```

in response to a finger request. It's the price we pay when people abuse the system.

Even if you have to be clueless, don't be planless! If this chapter inspires you to take the plunge and set up a truly creative .plan file, please let me know. Do send a note to me at lejeune@acy.digex.net.

Just the FAQs, Ma'am

To avoid looking like a goof by re-asking questions that get asked almost daily, learn how to look for a FAQ, which contains the most frequently needed answers.

Pat, my beautiful wife, frequently states my life has become just one great big balancing act. Her observation usually occurs within a second or two following the sound of breaking china as yet another of my spinning plates comes crashing to the ground. Surfing the Net is a lot like keeping a whole group of plates spinning on sticks, all at once. New things are happening all the time, and there is just so much "out there" requiring attention.

In Chapter 19, we explored ways of finding information through the use of Internet-based search engines. We dealt with generalized searching and questions in the form of "what is or where is...?" In this chapter we'll look at another category of information, the type of questions frequently asked in the form of "how do I...?"

After the initial excitement of discovery begins to abate, it's fairly typical to sit back and reflect upon the gaps in one's knowledge base. How best to catch up? Can I go to a public forum and ask some questions without making a pain, or perhaps a fool, of myself?

FAQS TO THE RESCUE

In the parlance of the Internet, a FAQ is a list of Frequently Asked Questions. There are FAQs for an amazing number of topics. These are not trivial lists or casual lists put together on a whim. Most FAQ lists have evolved over a period of years. Each of these lists represents a substantial body of topical knowledge, and collectively has become a set of encyclopedias available for our use while surfing the Net.

At the end of this chapter, we'll take a look at the general concept of Usenet newsgroups and listserv discussion lists. For the moment, let's generalize and say newsgroups and discussion lists collectively represent over 10,000 different topics. I like to consider them "asynchronous cocktail parties," that is, groups of people sharing a common interest gathered to share information and one another's company. The topical content of these groups ranges from the esoteric to the bizarre. And when I say bizarre, I mean *bizarre!*

The two primary reasons for obtaining a FAQ for your specific area of interest are:

- being a good net citizen
- procuring the latest version of information that changes unpredictably

Most Usenet newsgroups and listserv discussion groups support and maintain FAQs pertaining to the specific interests of the group. There are several reasons for a group with common interests to support a FAQ. The first reason is somewhat obvious: People enter the Internet community at various points in time. If you're new to the Internet, any question that you might ask has probably been asked hundreds, if not thousands, of times. The quickest route to the answers for many of your questions lies in a FAQ. The Internet community is very collaborative; nevertheless, it does get somewhat trying when reading the same question several times a week or (as occasionally happens) several times in an afternoon. You don't want to be thought a pest or (gasp!) a perpetual newbie. Checking for FAQs first makes you a good netizen (net citizen) because you're not taking up a lot of Net bandwidth and other people's valuable time asking questions that have been already answered in detail.

FAQs are a great source of current information since updating takes place on a regular and ongoing basis. The currency of FAQs contrasts well with material contained in a book such as this. Any Internet resources listed in a book may well be out of date by the time you read the material. It's not always the case, obviously, but try as we might to pin it all down, the electronic universe changes all the time.

Many FAQs are available using the Web and Gopher, while others require FTP downloading. We'll start by looking at some online resources and then detail how to FTP interesting FAQ documents to your PC.

THE MIT FAQ DEPOSITORY

Many Usenet newsgroups have FAQs associated with their groups. There is a massive depository of these FAQs at the Massachusetts Institute of Technology (MIT). We'll come back to the MIT listings in a few minutes.

Thomas Fine, fine@cis.ohio-state.eud, a systems programmer at Ohio State University (OSU), has started taking the MIT depository and converting the FAQ documents to HTML. Hypertext FAQ documents ease the effort required when accessing a knowledge base as vast as the composite FAQ depository. The opening page of the Usenet FAQ processor is shown in Figure 21.1. The second part of the opening page is shown in Figure 21.2. The URL for the OSU FAQ list is:

```
http://www.cis.ohio-state.edu:80/hypertext/faq/usenet/FAQ-List.html
```

Figure 21.2 shows the alphabetized lookup listing. If your "how do I" question is fairly general and you don't know the name of an appropriate newsgroup, this home page also has a pointer to a key word search form.

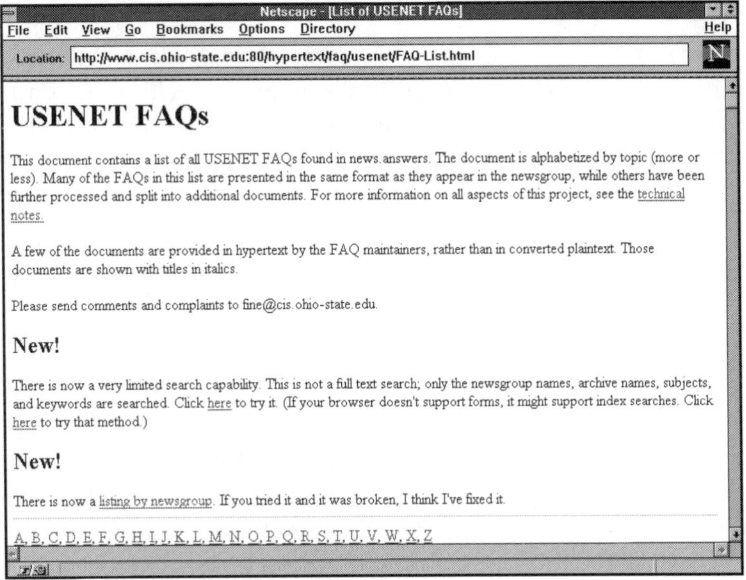

***Figure 21.1** The home page of the Ohio State FAQ list.*

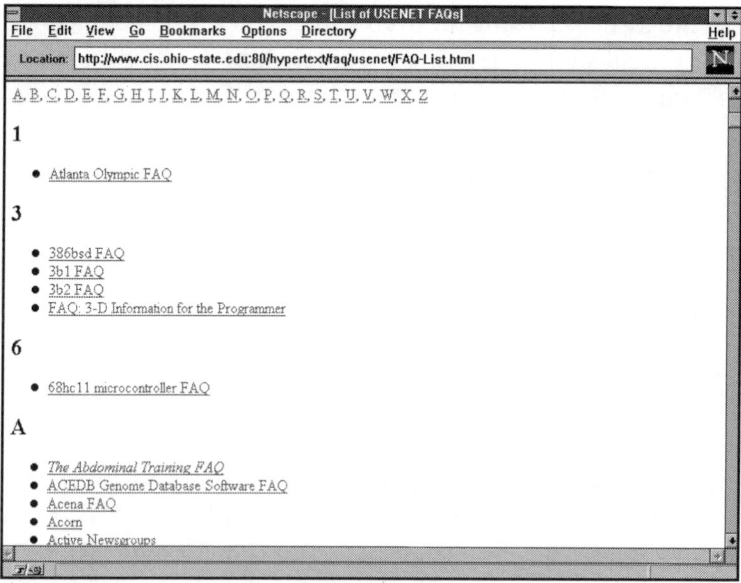

Figure 21.2 *The second part of the Ohio State FAQ home page.*

Creating a Signature for E-Mail

In this project we'll learn how to add a personal signature to an e-mail message. This will give you a chance to really add your personality to your messages.

I think every e-mail user since the beginning of time has asked the question, "How do I include one of those cute little signature blocks at the end of my e-mail messages? I know darn well nobody types them in every time!" You know the ones, they tend to be little commercials or funny sayings. Me, I like the one stating:

```
If you can remain calm and keep your head,
when all around you have panicked,
perhaps you just don't understand the situation.
```

Let's go to the search form and see what we can find. As with most searches, there are probably many paths to the same destination. Let's try a few. Pine is probably Internet's most popular Unix shell mail program. If you are using pine and a pine FAQ exists, there is an excellent chance that the signature block question and answer appears in the FAQ. Figure 21.3 is a copy of the OSU form used to search the FAQ database for "pine". The search returned two interesting FAQ hyperlinks, Signature and Finger and Filtering Mail. As

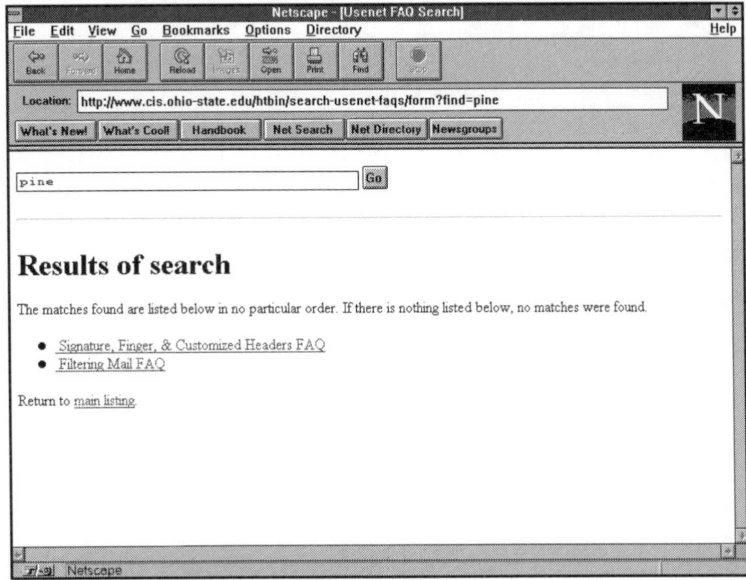

Figure 21.3 *The results of searching the FAQ database for "pine".*

you might suspect, the Signature portion of the first FAQ is more than we ever wanted to know about "sigs." Figure 21.4 shows a portion of the results from following the "Signature, Finger, and Customized Headers FAQ" link.

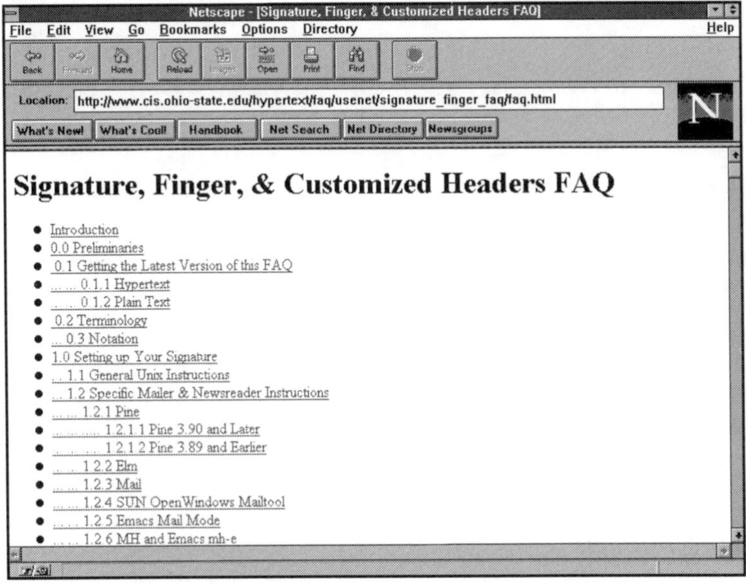

Figure 21.4 *Partial results of following the "Signature, Finger, and Customized Headers FAQ" link.*

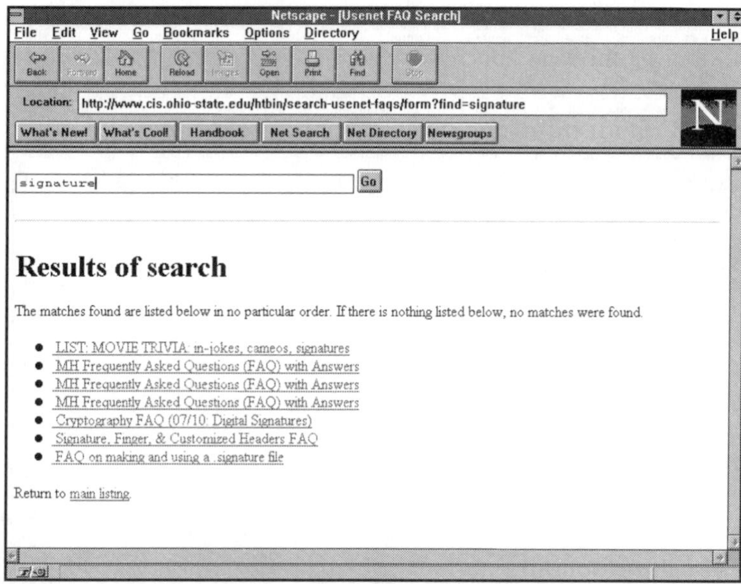

***Figure 21.5** The results of searching the FAQ database for "signature".*

You don't use pine, you say. OK, let's try a search simply on "signature" and see what mail wisdom we can discover. This search, as shown in Figure 21.5, turns up a few unrelated FAQs and the Signature and Finger FAQ from the last search as well as a new one on making and using a signature file.

What are the interests of Internet surfers? The FAQ list keeps running statistics on database accesses. To get the latest version of the statistics, point Netscape at:

```
http://www.cis.ohio-state.edu/hypertext/faq/usenet/technical-notes/faq-doc-7.html
```

Figure 21.6 shows the ranking by top level use groups categories. "alt-sex" was first with 3,031 accesses, followed by "nude-faq" at 2,005. The "TV" faq—entertainment of a different type—came in third place. "Investment-faq" was well down the list in fifth place. Figure 21.7 shows the popularity contest by document with "alt-sex" items in the first three places. Indeed, alt-sex and other forms of erotica occupied 11 of the 20 top spots! Investing was well down the list (16th place) with a few computer related FAQs in between the sex items. Just goes to show, Internet surfers prefer sex, computers, and money—in that order.

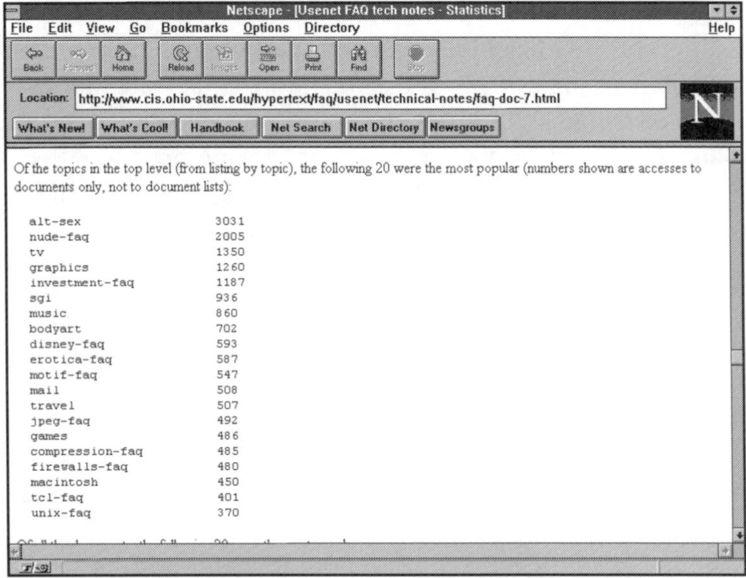

Figure 21.6 *The OSU FAQ access statistics by Usenet categories.*

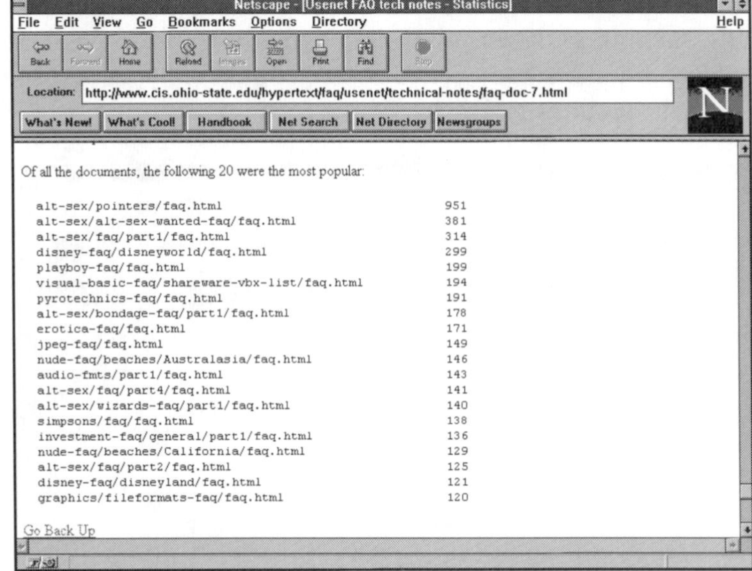

Figure 21.7 *The OSU FAQ access statistics by individual document.*

Finding FAQs about WAIS

WAIS is an acronym for Wide-Area Information Servers. WAIS, pronounced "wayz," is a powerful system for searching large amounts of information very quickly. WAIS resulted from a collaborative effort by Apple Computer, Dow Jones, and the Thinking Machine company. WAIS searching is rather difficult (much more difficult than it should be!) and space considerations preclude detailed WAIS coverage in this book. Let's take one last look at the Ohio State FAQ machine and its WAIS machinery before moving on. I would encourage you to spend a little time at the WAIS way-station. Maybe you'll bolster the intellectual portion of the OSU's Usenet FAQ tech notes statistics.

Point your Web browser toward

```
http://www.cis.ohio-state.edu:80/hypertext/faq/usenet/FAQ-List.html
```

to bring the OSU FAQ home page back to life. Select the "W" index listing, and the group shown in Figure 21.8 appears. (The comp.windows.misc FAQ entry is also a great list.) Follow the WAIS FAQ anchor, which brings up two pointers:

- freeWAIS-sf Frequently Asked Questions [FAQ] with answers
- comp.infosystems.wais Frequently asked Questions [FAQ] (with answers)

Selecting the first brings up the WAIS FAQ hyper text startup page. This FAQ is an excellent tutorial on WAIS, and a good example of hyper text spicing up dull plain-vanilla documents.

Figure 21.8 *The "W" portion of the OSU FAQ index.*

FAQs Via FTP

Not all of the available Usenet FAQ lists are on the OSU machine. If you want any excluded lists, or if you like your data in raw form, go directly to the source. Load the following URL into your favorite Web browser:

```
ftp://rtfm.mit.edu/pub/usenet/news.answers/
```

This is the FTP machine at MIT. The whole FAQ business, or so it's rumored, started when the early "flame wars" erupted on Usenet. The term flame is netspeak for an inflammatory remark. In the beginning, someone would ask a question that someone else considered stupid. The reader of the question would post a message to the effect of, "Read the fine manual;" that's not exactly what was said, but you get the idea. In time, all common usage phrases seem to get reduced to acronyms, and it happened that "read the - - - - ing manual" became RTFM. Note the machine name in MIT's URL above—and you thought engineers didn't have a sense of humor.

Figure 21.9 is the start of the "news.answers" directory at MIT. Download the individual document if you like your FAQs in hard copy. The listings of FTPable FAQs use the following format:

```
rtfm.mit.edu/pub/usenet/news.answers/gopher-faq
```

Netscape - [Directory of /pub/usenet/news.answers]

File Edit View Go Bookmarks Options Directory Help

Location: ftp://rtfm.mit.edu/pub/usenet/news.answers/

Current directory is /pub/usenet/news.answers

Up to higher level directory

Name	Size	Date	Type
.#index	312 Kb	Wed Apr 26 16:19:00 1995	
1996-olympics-faq	15 Kb	Mon Apr 24 07:34:00 1995	
386bsd-faq/		Thu Apr 20 12:57:00 1995	Directory
3b1-faq/		Sat Feb 11 01:55:00 1995	Directory
3b2-faq/		Mon Nov 21 01:25:00 1994	Directory
3d-programmer-info	35 Kb	Thu Apr 20 12:26:00 1995	
Arabic-software-map	40 Kb	Tue Apr 18 08:49:00 1995	
AudioFAQ/		Sun Apr 16 07:58:00 1995	Directory
Brazil-faq	87 Kb	Sat Feb 25 01:32:00 1995	
C++-faq/		Mon May 23 00:00:00 1994	Directory
C-faq/		Thu Apr 20 13:09:00 1995	Directory
CPM-faq	44 Kb	Tue Apr 25 12:32:00 1995	
ForthFaq/		Wed Dec 15 00:00:00 1993	Directory
GNU-Emacs-FAQ/		Sat Apr 22 11:48:00 1995	Directory
LANs/		Sat Apr 22 12:36:00 1995	Directory
LEGO-faq	39 Kb	Thu Mar 02 01:24:00 1995	
Modula-2-faq	20 Kb	Tue Feb 28 08:29:00 1995	
Modula-3-faq	66 Kb	Tue Feb 14 00:40:00 1995	
Oberon-FAQ/		Wed Dec 21 01:18:00 1994	Directory

Figure 21.9 *The news.answers FAQ directory at MIT.*

The part preceding the first "/" is the domain name of the network hosting the resource. In this illustration "rtfm.mit.edu" is the domain name of the remote server. You would FTP to this site. The item to the right of the last "/" is the actual name of the file, in this example, "gopher-faq". The part between these two items is the directory path containing the resource, in this example "/pub/usenet/news.answers".

The site

```
rtfm.mit.edu/pub/usenet/news.answers
```

is the primary site for the Usenet FAQs. There are many "mirror" locations. It may be difficult to log onto an anonymous FTP server during certain times of the day. Use an alternative site or try during non-peak hours. There is, however, always the possibility that a mirror site may not have the latest version of the FAQ. If you doubt that you've cornered the latest scoop in a particular FAQ, perform an Archie search and then compare file creation dates. This is always a good idea when downloading important files, especially when the download takes a significant amount of time.

A Sample FTP Session

The following is the transcript of the actual FTP session used to download the file "gopher-faq". Remember that Unix is case-sensitive.

```
unix%  ftp rtfm.mit.edu
Connected to BLOOM-PICAYUNE.MIT.EDU.
220 rtfm ftpd (wu-2.4(21) with built-in ls); bugs to ftp-bugs@rtfm.mit.edu
Name (rtfm.mit.edu:lejeune): anonymous
331 Guest login ok, send your complete e-mail address as password.
Password:  < Enter your full e-mail address here >
230 Guest login ok, access restrictions apply.
ftp> cd /pub/usenet/news.answers
250 CWD command successful.
ftp> get  gopher-faq
200 PORT command successful.
150 Opening ASCII mode data connection for gopher-faq (27603 bytes).
226 Transfer complete.
local: gopher-faq remote: gopher-faq
28270 bytes received in 1.9 seconds (14 Kbytes/s)
ftp> quit
221 Goodbye.
```

If you prefer that the remote file be transferred to your host system with a different name, use the following command format:

```
ftp> get gopher-faq gop-faq.txt
```

In this format, the first parameter is the name of the file on the remote site and the second parameter is the name that you desire on your local host.

USENET AND LISTSERV GROUPS

A short description of Usenet newsgroups and LISTSERV lists follows. These few paragraphs are brief introductions. I recommend checking a basic Internet book for a complete description of these groups.

Usenet Newsgroups

One of the earliest forms of "group electronic mail" were the Usenet newsgroups. (Most people today glue "news" and "group" together into "newsgroup" when speaking in the generic.) The early Bitnet and Internet culture was richer because of these groups, back when there was nothing like Gopher or the Web to feel good about. There are currently about 10,000 different newsgroups, with a new group being added almost daily. (Groups are also periodically retired, but overall the number is steadily growing.)

Getting started with newsgroups is a little trying. You must first subscribe to a group that seems to hold some promise for you. Selection is typically accomplished by eliminating groups from a list that includes all known newsgroups—which is not a lot of fun. Once subscribed to a newsgroup, you periodically go pick up the latest listings with a news reader, which is a utility that understands the newsgroup protocols. Netscape has a good news reader built into it, something Mosaic users as yet only dream about. You may post to any group to which you subscribe, and you may answer the postings of others. There are many powerful Winsock compliant news readers; several are included on the enclosed CD-ROM.

Newsgroups bear considerable resemblance to the public forums on CompuServe. People post messages to a newsgroup, and then anyone who subscribes to the newsgroup can read that message. If a particular message piques their interest, readers can post a reply or follow-up to a particular message. Follow-ups can have their own follow-ups, and so on, resulting in strings of messages on a given topic, the whole of which is called a thread. Most news readers know how to identify threads and display messages hierarchically, indicating dependence of one message on another by way of indenting.

Vast and complex arguments occur in newsgroups (some of them mostly hot air, which rapidly degenerates into pointless nastiness), but mostly people post messages or questions and two or three comments are posted as follow-ups. One can often question how useful the information exchanged in a newsgroup actually is, but one can take some comfort at least in knowing that people are getting some practice at writing.

Usenet newsgroups are the primary attraction to many Internet users. Be careful, they can be addictive. There are books exclusively devoted to newsgroups, so we will not devote any additional time to the topic in this chapter. We visit newsgroups again in Chapter 24, *Advanced Netscape Features*, when we take a look at the Netscape news reader.

LISTSERV Lists

Listserv lists are conceptually much like Usenet newsgroups, only they work by way of e-mail rather than a separate newsgroup protocol. When someone posts a message to a list, that message is distributed to all subscribers of the list as regular e-mail that you fetch with pine or Eudora or some other mail reader. Listserv is a Unix program used to manage a list on a server somewhere. When you want to communicate with the software, you send mail to listserv, and when you want to post something for human beings to read, you send it to the list. Let's look at a few examples.

The first task is finding a list that piques your fancy. Let's be somewhat generic and assume we're newcomers and want a list that gives us general "help." The address of the big listserv in the sky is listserv@listserv.net, so we send a message to:

```
listserv@listserv.net
```

and in the body of the message use the form:

```
list global <topic>
```

The first two words are required. "list" tells the software that we want a list of listserv lists. "global" instructs the software to search the big database of close to 10,000 lists. We substitute our topic of interest where <topic> appears. In this case the entire body of the message would be:

```
list global help
```

Don't place anything in a message to a listserv that is not a recognized command of some sort. (In other words, don't feel obliged to say "Hi!" or include your signature block. It's only software and courtesy to software is not yet required of us.) You may make several "list global" requests in the same e-mail message; simply begin each different request on a new line. In short order you will receive something resembling the following in your e-mail from the listserv:

```
******************************************************************************
* To subscribe, send mail to LISTSERV@LISTSERV.NET with the following
* command in the text (not the subject) of your message:
*
*                        SUBSCRIBE listname
*
* Replace 'listname' with the name in the first column of the table.
******************************************************************************

Network-wide ID  Full address and list description

HELP-NET         HELP-NET@VM.TEMPLE.EDU
                 Bitnet/Internet Help Resource

GNAHELPW         GNAHELPW@MITVMA.MIT.EDU
                 Globewide Network Academy Help Wanted Ads

HELPDESK         HELPDESK@IBACSATA.BITNET
                 Info DIR-ITA Heldesk
```

Help-net looks as if will fit the bill, so let's subscribe. Again, we want to communicate with the software managing the details of the list. Subscription directions are shown in the first part of the message. Send another message to:

```
listserv@listserv.net
```

In the body of the message include:

```
sub help-net <Your-first-name> <Your-last-name>
```

Be careful to add the "-" if you're subscribing to help-net. (There is another list called helpnet without the hyphen.)

Notice the list:

```
HELPDESK         HELPDESK@IBACSATA.BITNET
                 Info DIR-ITA Heldesk
```

The address is a BITNET address, as are many listserv hosts. Many mail programs will not accept an address in BITNET form. In these cases, the mail must be routed through something called a "gateway." A BITNET address in the form:

```
user@host.bitnet
```

would be converted to:

```
user%host@internet-gateway
```

An actual address, using the above list, would be:

```
helpdesk%ibacsata@cunyvm.cuny.edu
```

If you encounter this problem, check with your system administrator for your preferred Internet gateway address.

There may be times when the query results shows a list that is distributed from two different servers. As an example,

```
PASCAL-L         PASCAL-L@VM3090.EGE.EDU.TR
                 Pascal Language Discussion List
                 PASCAL-L@VMD.CSO.UIUC.EDU
                 Pascal Language Discussion List
```

In the case of duplicate locations the server must be explicitly stated when subscribing. You can also send your subscription request to the appropriate listserv when subscribing to the list. In this example PASCAL-L is distributed from two different machines. To subscribe to the UIUC list, send a message to:

```
listserv@listserv.net
```

In the body enter:

```
sub pascal-l@VMD.CSO.UIUC.EDU <Your-first-name> <Your-last-name>
```

help-net is an excellent list if you are new to the Internet. One nice thing about subscribing to a list like help-net is that you will receive mail almost every day.

In all subscription requests, you may optionally include your first and last names, but you don't have to include your name if it also appears in your mail message. Shortly you will receive a message announcing the acceptance of your subscription. This message contains much useful information, such as how to unsubscribe. (Some listserv lists—especially the ones of broader interest than to iguana fanciers—generate huge numbers of messages every day. You may want out after a day or two of e-mail deluge.) It's a good idea to keep the message saved on disk for future reference.

From this point on, you will receive a copy of all posted messages. If you want to send a message for other people to read, send it directly to the list. In this case, send a regular e-mail message to help-net@vm.temple.edu.

Another list you will probably find of interest is:

```
NETSCAPE          NETSCAPE@IRLEARN.UCD.IE
                  Discussion of Netscape
```

Send a message to listserv@irlearn.ucd.ie and in the body enter:

```
subscribe netscape   <Your-first-name> <Your-last-name>
```

LISTSERV FAQs

Many listserv lists also have their own FAQs. Send a message to the listserv hosting your favorite list; let's use help-net as an example. help-net is domiciled at Temple University so we would send a message to:

```
listserv@vm.temple.edu
```

In the body put:

```
index help-net
```

Back comes a list of archived documents, a portion of which would include:

```
FILE
Name        Type    Description
FAQ         FILE    Frequently asked questions
BABEL94C    TXT     Irving Kind's glossary of computer abbreviations and
                    acronyms
FINDING PEOPLE  How to find the E-mail address of a friend or colleague
```

To obtain one of these files, you must once again send a message to the listserv hosting the list in the form of:

```
get file-name file-type list-name
```

To get the help-net FAQ, send a message to:

```
listserv@vm.temple.edu
```

In the body enter:

```
get faq file help-net
```

Some of the questions answered in this document are:

```
1)   What is archie?
2)   What is telnet?
3)   What is ftp?
4)   What are USENET/BITNET/FREENET/FIDONET/UUNET?
5)   What are *.tar files and what can we do with them?
6)   How can we get to Compuserve, MCI, etc. mail from the Internet?
7)   What is the LISTSERV service?
8)   How can I find someone's e-mail address?
9)   What are the *.gif files and how can we view them?
10)  How can I add my "signature" to outgoing mail?
11)  Interactive commands to write and talk to other users.
12)  What is gopher & irc?
13)  Books and Periodicals that may be of use.
14)  VMS, BITFTP, and those pesky binary files
15)  Files files files, what do all those extensions mean?
16)  Job sources via The Internet
```

Almost all listserv lists archive the postings to this list. If you want to get the "feel" of a list, retrieve a few of the recent archive listings. When you issue the command:

```
index <list-name>
```

to the listserv hosting the list, the returned document contains the name of the files, and the dates of inclusion, of the archives.

LET'S REVIEW

Frequently Asked Questions (FAQs) represent the collective wisdom of the Internet, gathered into the well-known question-and-answer format. The topical broadness of the subject material practically guarantees that answers are waiting to virtually any question you might have about almost any topic held as interesting by more than three people in the Internet community. The instantaneous availability of the large database makes accessing this information easier now than in the past.

Most FAQs have come about through the efforts of people participating in Usenet newsgroups, which are "asynchronous cocktail parties" of people with common interests posting messages of interest to the group where subscribers to the group can read them. Many FAQs are distillations of the discussions of these groups gathered over a period of years.

There is a list of FAQs available in HTML format, for viewing with your favorite Web browser, at:

```
http://www.cis.ohio-state.edu:80/hypertext/faq/usenet/FAQ-List.html
```

The primary site for the MIT collection of FAQs is:

```
rtfm.mit.edu/pub/usenet/news.answers
```

The Usenet newsgroup and the LISTSERV discussion group descriptions in this chapter are intended only as a brief introduction. If you are not already using these resources, take the time to learn more about them by reading other books more focused on the subject.

III

Setting Your Netscape Preferences

Netscape is a highly configurable creature; alas, configuring it can be pretty involved. But with the right tips and techniques, you can make Netscape work the way you want.

In most cases, flexibility equals power. The more flexible a tool is, the more you can do with it—kind of like that all-purpose thingamajig that hammers nails, pulls nails, grabs wire, cuts wire, and clubs rattlesnakes—all depending on how you wave it. The snag, of course, is that flexibility can also equal difficulty, and, at worst, total obscurity. If a tool becomes so flexible that it grows obscure, it loses its utility for all but the initiated. (Unix is a lot like that. You can do almost anything with Unix except understand it.)

Netscape is a Web browser of extraordinary power, mainly because you can set it up in a number of different ways. Of course, you have to know how to set it up—or most of its flexibility becomes thoroughly obscure. That's what this chapter is about: configuring Netscape. Most of our discussions in this book have focused on the Web itself—what's out there and how you can publish on the Web. Now we're going to take a little detour. The greater part of Netscape's configurability does not require editing a very large, frighteningly obtuse INI file. (Earlier versions of most Web browsers required the scary process of editing a configuration file.)

However, you'll work (and sleep) easier if you take a few precautions while jiggering Netscape's configuration and the configuration file netscape.ini along the guidelines presented in this chapter:

- Always make a backup copy of netscape.ini before making major configuration changes or editing the file (if you discover you need to).
- If you change the INI file, comment out parameters; don't delete them.
- Make changes to the INI file one parameter at a time, and test the results of that one change before making any additional changes.

If you follow these three simple steps, there is nothing to fear, since you can always return to netscape.ini as it was when you began to fuss with it.

Netscape reads netscape.ini only when it starts up. To see the effects of some of the configuration changes that you make, you need to exit Netscape and restart the program.

USING THE OPTIONS MENU

Let's start at the top and explore the simplest configuration options first. A few common preferences may be easily changed by using Netscape's Options menu as shown in Figure 22.1. From this menu you can perform any of the following:

- Display or hide Netscape's toolbar
- Display or hide the URL (Location) text box
- Display or hide the directory buttons
- Tell Netscape to automatically load new images
- Display or hide FTP file information when links are selected

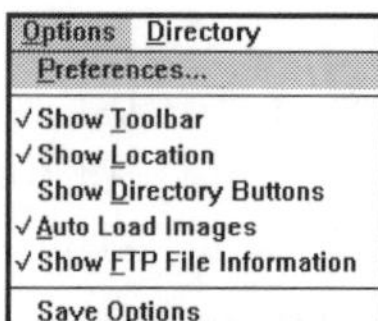

***Figure 22.1** Using Netscape's Options menu to select configuration options.*

If an item has a checkmark next to its name, you'll know that the option has been selected. To turn off an active option, simply select it and the checkmark will disappear. Keep in mind that any changes you make using the Options menu only affect the current session. To make a permanent change, you need to select the Options | Save Options item.

If the Auto Load Images option is selected, all images will be displayed when you download a Web page. If this option is turned off, images may not be displayed when you load in a new Web page. In place of an actual image you'll get a small built-in icon that will appear where the graphic is normally displayed. To fetch and display the image, click on the icon place holder with the right mouse button and then select the Load This Image option.

Making More Room for Netscape

One of the options you might want to turn off is Show Directory Buttons. The What's New and What's Cool buttons provided with the group of displayed buttons are interesting in the beginning but take up space that could otherwise be used for documents. Most of the URLs underlying the directory buttons are available by using the Directory menu.

USING THE WONDERFUL PREFERENCES MENUS

There was a time in the evolution of Netscape (a few versions ago) when all the useful Netscape configuration options needed to be set by changing the NETSCAPE.INI configuration file. Fortunately, the latest version of Netscape allows you to change settings directly from within Netscape. The best part is, you can do most of the configuration work by selecting options with the mouse.

To view or change preferences, select the Options | Preferences option. There are eight Preferences menus from which you can select:

- Styles
- Fonts and Colors
- Mail and News
- Cache and Networks
- Applications and Directories
- Images and Security

- Proxies
- Helper Applications

Let's look at these groups of preferences one at a time. To select a particular Preferences dialog box, click on the down arrow to the right of the Set Preferences On edit box. Then, click on the desired preference.

Styles

The Styles Preferences dialog box is shown in Figure 22.2. The upper frame of this dialog box is named Window Styles. The top set of radio buttons controls how the toolbar is displayed. The individual icons can be displayed as pictures, text only, or as a combination of the two—the default. The advantage of either of the first two options is that they allow more space for displaying your documents.

The lower portion of the upper frame specifies which starting document is displayed. The default, as configured by Netscape, is Netscape's Welcome Page. Here you can specify any page you want by entering its URL in the text box. I start my Netscape session by displaying my menu of over 300 frequently visited sites. (This file is provided on the companion CD-ROM as urb-menu.htm.) You can even load a starting page document from your hard disk

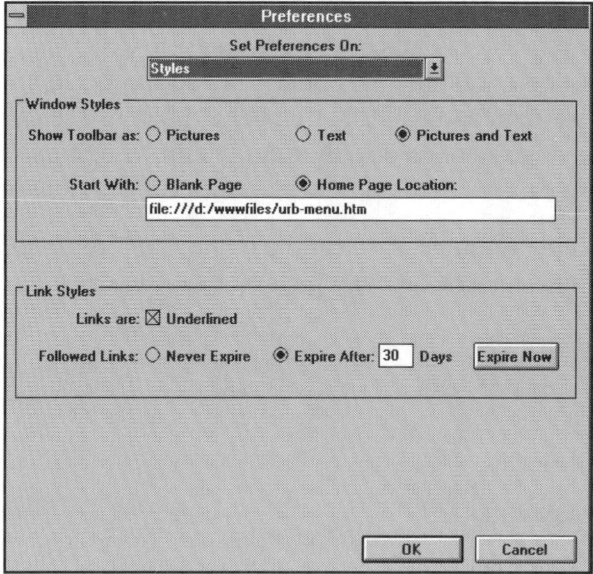

Figure 22.2 *Netscape's Styles Preferences dialog box.*

to speed up the startup process. If the Blank Page radio button is selected, the specified document may be retrieved at any time by clicking on the tool bar's Home icon.

The lower frame, titled Link Styles, configures links. If the option, Links are Underlined, is not selected, your documents will load a little faster. Why? Netscape won't need to display all of the links in your documents as underlined text.

Another useful option you can set in this section is the history file. Netscape keeps a history file of all the sites you visit. The default setting for the history file is a 30-day period. Links visited within the specified period appear in a different color in the document area. Clicking on Expire Now erases the history file without changing the retention parameters.

When you are finished with the Styles Preferences dialog, click OK to accept any changes or click on the Set Preferences On down arrow to select another preferences dialog. If you decide you don't like your changes, click Cancel to revert back to the original settings.

Fonts and Colors

The Fonts and Colors Preferences dialog box is shown in Figure 22.3. The upper frame of this dialog box is named Fonts/Encodings. The two drop-

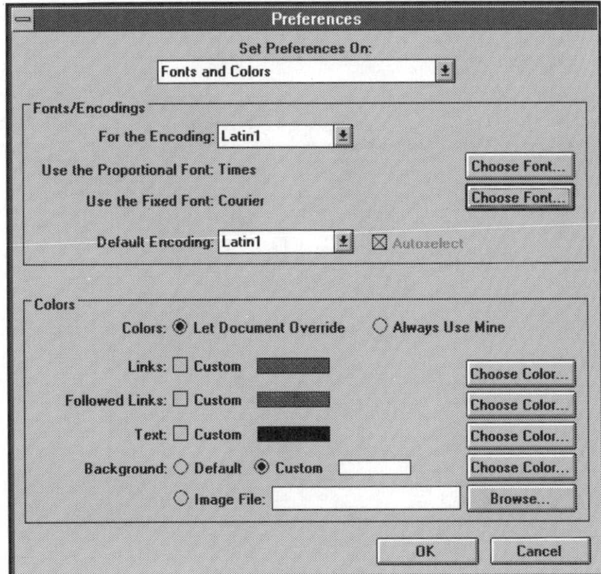

***Figure 22.3** Netscape's Fonts and Colors Preferences dialog box.*

down menus aren't useful unless you are viewing documents in Japanese. The two center options, Use the Proportional Font and Use the Fixed Font, are used for determining font style and size. The proportional font is used to display portions of documents, including scaled headings. The fixed font is used for special effects such as Gopher menus, FTP listings, and forms.

You can select a different font or font size by clicking on the desired Choose Font button. Figure 22.4 shows the Choose Base Font dialog box. Scroll through the Font selections or the Size options to adjust specifications. Changing fonts periodically tends to add a little spice to Web browsing. If you're spending too much time surfing the Web and your eyes no longer can see the small print, you may want to increase the font size. On the other hand, you may want to decrease the size to display more information on each Web page.

The lower frame, titled Colors, also changes how Netscape displays documents. The radio buttons at the top of the frame are used to indicate if your color preferences should override any colors specified in a document. I suggest you select the Let Document Override option. A Web author like yourself may spend hours getting a document just right, and you don't really want to miss out on all this hard work, do you?

The four selections to the left of the Choose Color buttons determine the color of links, followed links, text, and the background. An actual swatch of

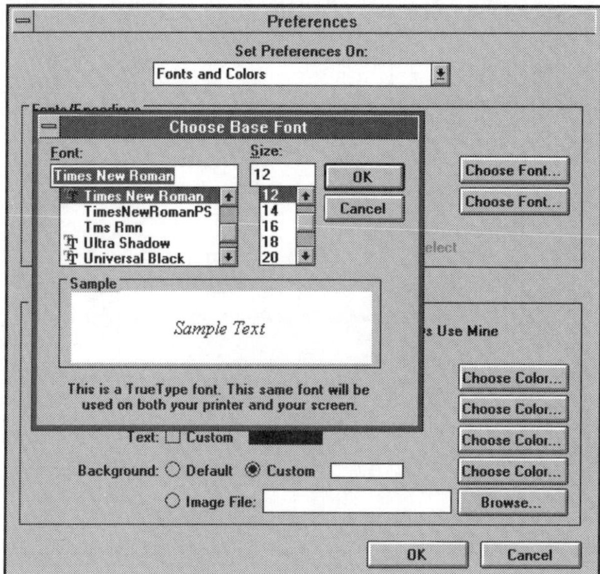

Figure 22.4 *Selecting a different base font and size.*

the specified color is displayed to the right of the word Custom. Clicking on a Choose Color button brings up the initial Color dialog box as shown in Figure 22.5. Clicking on the Define Custom Colors option expands the dialog box to include a color palette as shown in Figure 22.6. Select a Basic Color by clicking on your choice. Select a Custom Color by clicking somewhere in the palette or by editing the color numbers. If you select a custom color, add it to your color repertoire for future use by clicking on Add to Custom Colors. The custom color will then appear in one of the Custom Colors boxes.

EXPLORER TIP

Getting the Best Contrast

Most people prefer to display text using as much contrast as possible. If you've spent any amount of time surfing with Netscape, you've seen the result of ill-conceived background color schemes. To get the most contrast possible, use black text on a white background. Try changing the default gray background to white and see if it doesn't make viewing easier. If you decide you prefer the original gray color, just select the Background Default radio button.

When selecting background and text colors, don't choose closely related colors. Low color contrast can make long term viewing tedious. You can always choose black text on a black background when you get tired of viewing (grin).

The last item at the bottom of the Colors frame is Image File. If you have seen a background image you like (not a background color) you can use it for all your documents by downloading the image to your hard disk and specifying its name and location in the text box. Even though you select an image file, you must still select the radio button to the left of the Image File prompt for it to take effect.

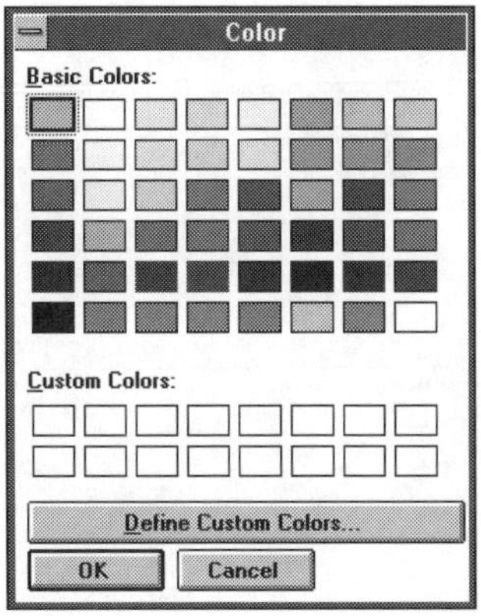

Figure 22.5 *The initial Color dialog box.*

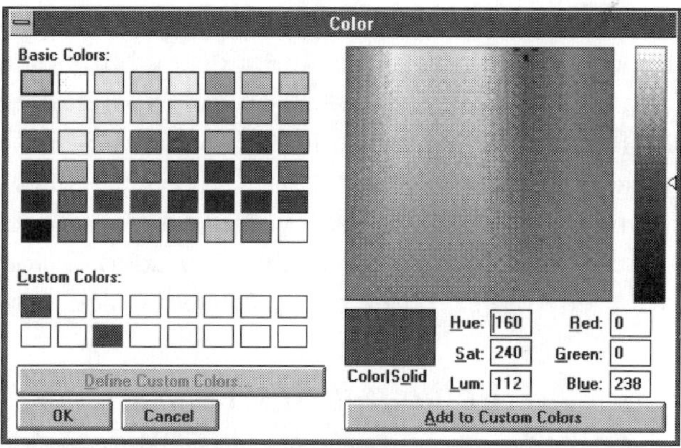

Figure 22.6 *The Color dialog box expanded to include custom colors.*

As usual, click on OK to accept any changes or click on the Set Preferences On down arrow to select another preferences dialog box.

Mail and News

The Mail and News Preferences dialog box is shown in Figure 22.7. The upper frame of this dialog box is named Mail while the lower frame is named News. The Mail Server entry is the domain name of your Simple Mail Trans-

Preferences
Set Preferences On:
Mail and News
Mail
Mail (SMTP) Server: acy1.digex.net
Your Name: Urb LeJeune
Your Email: lejeune@acy.digex.net
Your Organization:
Signature File: J:\NETSCAPE\SIG.TXT Browse...
Send and Post: Allow 8-bit Mime Compliant (Quoted Printable)
News
News (NNTP) Server: news1.acy.digex
News RC Directory: j:\netscape\news
Show: 100 Articles at a Time
OK Cancel

Figure 22.7 *Netscape's Mail and News Preferences dialog box.*

port Protocol (SMTP). Your Internet service provider or system administrator provides the mail server's domain name. Your name is what your parents hung on you or what you choose to call yourself. Netscape uses your name entry when constructing a bookmark file title and a mail heading. Your e-mail address is the user identification given to you, or selected by you, when you opened your account, followed by "@" then your provider's domain name. There are never any spaces in an e-mail address. Your Organization is typically your work affiliation if you choose to use one.

Many people like to have a small message appended to their mail messages. The message—called a sig block—may be a cute little saying or, heaven forbid, a quasi-commercial. You too can personalize Netscape mail by creating your own sig block. Create a file using a text editor and add the text you would like included in your signature. Save it and specify its name and path in the Signature File text box. Good taste dictates holding a signature block to five lines or less.

EXPLORER TIP

Using the Correct E-mail Address

Be very careful when entering your e-mail address in your Netscape Mail and News Preference. If you make a mistake when entering your address and someone subsequently replies, the returned message will not reach you. It's a good idea to send mail to yourself and then select "Reply" (if your mail reader supports the function) to ensure everything is OK.

The Send and Post radio buttons control how Netscape deals with sending mail attachments. Unless you are into MIME encoding, check the Allow 8-bit button.

The lower frame, titled News, has three entries dealing with News. If you don't read news using Netscape, you can skip this section. The name of your News Server, as with the Mail Server, is provided by your Internet provider or Network administrator. The News RC Directory is a directory path where Netscape keeps news related items. I like to keep life simple and keep all my Netscape related files in the same directory as the executable program and the directories immediately subordinate to the Netscape directory. (It does add a complication when configuring a second version of Netscape such as a beta release.)

The last entry, Show Articles at a Time, is the count of unread Newsgroup articles displayed at one time. Since the icons used to bounce around while processing news appear only at the start and finish, pick a number that you find agreeable. I'll cover more techniques on using Netscape's Newsreading feature in Chapter 24, *Advanced Netscape Features.*

Once again, click on OK to accept any changes or click on the Set Preferences On down arrow to select another preferences dialog box.

Cache and Networks

Figure 22.8 shows the Cache and Networks Preferences dialog box. The upper frame of this dialog box is named Cache while the lower frame is named Network Connections. Since this section is somewhat complicated, you might want to leave the options at their default setting.

The idea behind caching is to hold things in main or disk memory that might be used again in the future. If a required file is held in cache memory, Netscape does not need to fetch it from the Internet. That's the good news; the bad news is that caching takes both disk and main memory space. Memory Cache specifies how much memory will be set aside for caching. Unfortunately, memory dedicated to cache memory cannot be used for anything else during an active Netscape session. Disk Cache, on the other hand, is used to specify the size and location of space on your hard disk used to hold stored files between Netscape sessions.

If you look at the directory specified as the Disk Cache Directory, you will see many files with an .MOZ extension. Most of these files are actually the GIF files that were loaded when you visited various sites.

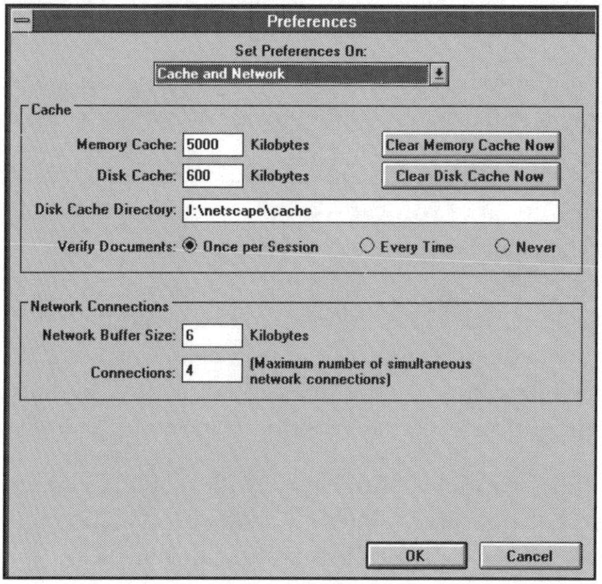

Figure 22.8 *The Cache and Network Preferences dialog box.*

Viewing Stored GIF (MOZ) Files

Paint Shop Pro, included on the companion CD-ROM, comes with a program called PSP Browser, which is a very clever and useful utility. If you run PSP Browser and point it to your Disk Cache Directory, it recognizes which files are GIF images despite the .MOZ extension. PSP Browser gives you thumbnail sketches of all your image files. Be careful of copyrights and ask for permission before using any GIF you find in your cache. I have never had anyone tell me no when I asked for permission to use an image—I've had people ignore my request, but then again, I don't always answer all of my mail.

The first time a page is requested, Netscape downloads the page from the Internet. Each page you retrieve is temporarily stored in a cache. If you subsequently request a page you have previously acquired, Netscape checks to see if the page is available in the cache. If you click on the Back button, you'll notice that cached documents are displayed much faster than when you first displayed the document.

There are times when you don't want to use cache retrieval. The page you fetched initially may have changed. If this happens, you typically want to see the updated page, not the original. This is especially noticeable when you perform multiple searches. When you click on a link, choose a bookmark, enter a URL, or press the Reload button, Netscape checks to see if an update has occurred before loading a page from cache. If a change has occurred, the new version is fetched. If no change has occurred, the faster loading cache version is retrieved.

Netscape does not check for different versions when you choose a history item or press the Back button. If you have reason to suspect a document has changed (you may have changed it yourself), click on the Reload button, which manually overrides the process.

Caching sizes are a tradeoff between processing speed and maximizing memory resources. Memory cache sizes between 200 and 400 Kilobytes are typically used with computers having 4 megs of main memory. 600 Kilobytes to the-sky-is-the-limit are used when you have more memory. I would recommend you select the Once per Session radio button in the Verify Documents section. Disk cache sizes are typically set to about 2,000 to 8,000 Kilobytes (2 to 8 megs).

There may be times when you suspect your cache is acting incorrectly, or maybe you just want to free up some memory space. The caches are clearable by pressing the Clear Memory Cache Now and Clear Disk Cache Now buttons.

The lower frame, Network Connections, contains a Network Buffer Size and a Connections limit. The defaults for these settings are 6 Kilobytes and 4 simultaneous network connections. These are fine for most uses. You don't really want to be using more than 4 simultaneous connections if you're using a 14.4 Kb modem.

EXPLORER TIP

Opening Multiple Netscape Windows

Netscape provides the ability to have multiple windows open simultaneously. This can be a major advantage when you are FTPing a large file or you want to rapidly switch between sites to make a comparison. To open another window press Ctrl+N or select the File|New Window option. A new window always starts by opening your designated home page. (A good reason to load it from local disk.) After your home page is displayed, you can select a different URL. To switch between windows, press Ctrl+Tab.

To close a window press Ctrl+W or select File|Close. Don't click on the button in the upper left corner; this will end your entire Netscape session.

Moving right along, click on OK to accept any changes or click on the Set Preferences On down arrow to select another preferences dialog box.

Applications and Directories

Figure 22.9 shows the Applications and Directories Preferences dialog box. The upper frame of this dialog box is named Supporting Applications and the lower frame is named Directories.

Netscape needs help with certain applications; Telnet is one example. Netscape does not handle a Telnet or TN3270 request directly. If you have a Telnet client, such as the one furnished with the Internet Chameleon, specify its location in the Telnet Application text box or use the Browse button to search for its program.

TN3270 sessions are much like Telnet sessions where you connect to an IBM mainframe. Although TN3270 clients are available, I have never found the need to have one.

The View Source application is the editor used by Netscape, if specified, to view the source of an HTML document by executing the sequence View | Source. If you specify an HTML editor, as opposed to letting Netscape display the document, you have the advantage of modifying and saving the document. The disadvantage is longer loading times.

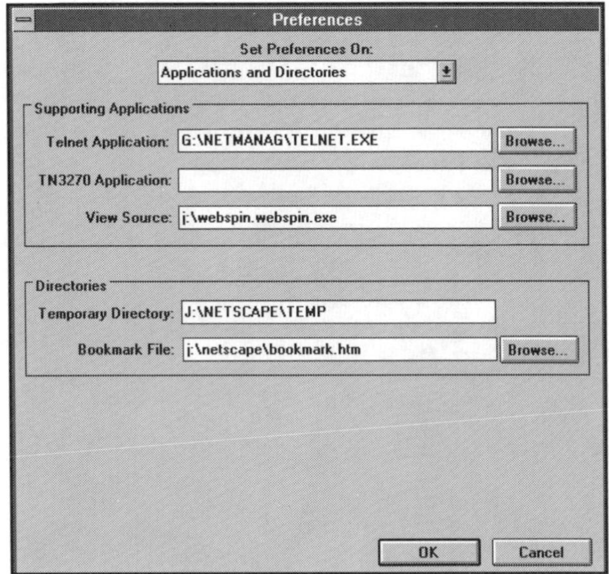

***Figure 22.9** Netscape's Applications and Directories Preferences dialog box.*

The lower frame, Directories, contains the specifications for a Temporary Directory and the location and name of your Bookmark File. The Windows' Temporary Directory is typically specified as the default setting. I prefer to use another directory. There is enough junk in the Windows \temp directory already. We discussed the Bookmark file back in Chapter 4. Remember, changes made to the bookmark file do not take effect until after terminating and restarting a Netscape session.

Yet again, click on OK to accept any changes or click on the Set Preferences On down arrow to select another preferences dialog box.

Images and Security

Figure 22.10 shows the Images and Security Preferences dialog box. The upper frame of this dialog box is named Images and the lower frame is named Security Alerts—what a shock!

Frankly, I don't see much difference when selecting either the Dither to Color Cube or Use Closest Color in Color Cube radio button when specifying the Colors option. You might want to experiment with the settings on your system.

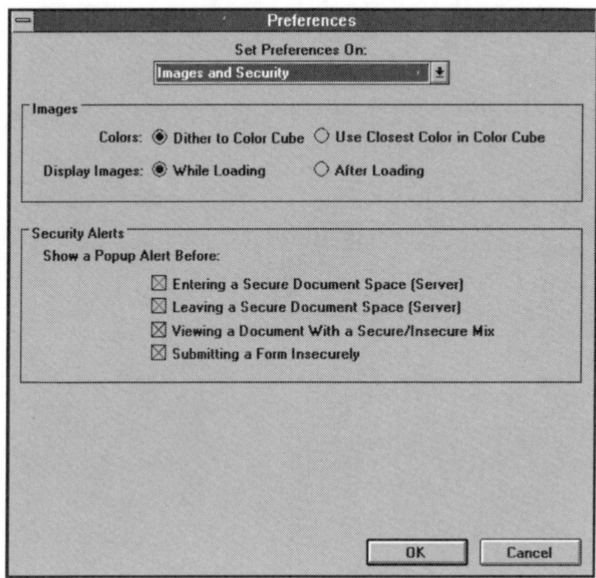

***Figure 22.10** Specifying Netscape's Images and Security preferences.*

Having images displayed While Loading or After Loading is again a matter of personal preference. I like to watch my images being displayed as they are loading. But then again, maybe I'm just weird.

The lower frame represents a not-so-subtle commercial reminding us that Netscape Communications supplies secure servers.

Proxies

The Proxies Preferences dialog box is shown in Figure 22.11. If you already know about proxies, you don't need me to tell you about them. If you are accessing the Internet using a standalone PC, you definitely don't need to use proxies.

If you are running Netscape through a security firewall, you will need to access one or more proxy servers. A *firewall* is a security protection device. The use of firewalls occurs when accessing the Internet through a network and security is a concern. If your system uses a firewall, I would suggest that you leave the configuration of this section to your system administrator.

Let's leave proxies well enough alone and move on to Helper Applications.

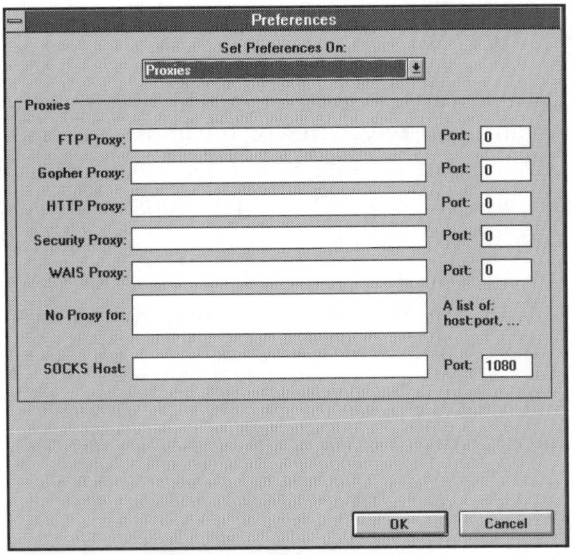

Figure 22.11 Netscape's Proxies Preferences dialog box.

Helper Applications

The Helper Applications Preferences dialog box is shown in Figure 22.12. Configuring Helper Applications requires a reasonable degree of support material. Since you're probably up to your eyeballs in preferences, let's hold off discussing Helper applications until the next chapter, *Netscape's Helpers.*

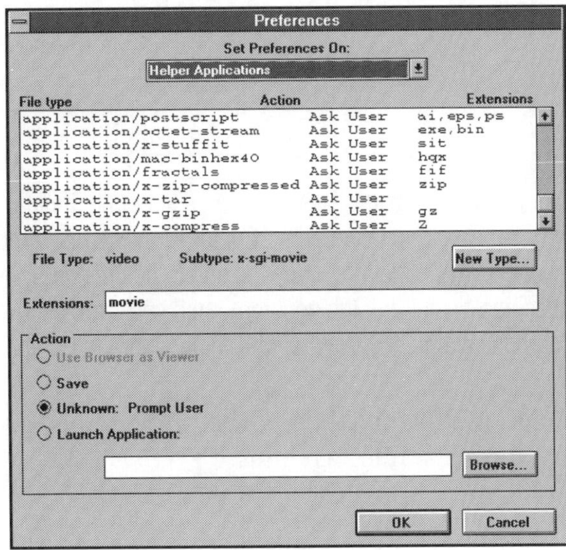

Figure 22.12 The last preferences dialog, Helper Applications.

EDITING NETSCAPE.INI

Windows configuration files, frequently called initialization files, are essentially lists of program directives. One of the most important files on your entire system is named win.ini—the Windows initialization file. This file resides in your main WINDOWS directory. The initialization file that Netscape uses is netscape.ini. It's a good idea to become as familiar as you can with both of these files so that you can better troubleshoot any problems that might occur with Netscape. My first rule of computer management is, "Don't try to understand how things should work after they don't."

> *Note: Never edit netscape.ini while Netscape is running. Netscape only reads netscape.ini when it starts, and overwrites the original version when it finishes. Any editing done in the interim is lost.*

Saving Backup Copies of netscape.ini

Before manually editing any configuration file, I suggest you make a copy of the INI file using its actual name and an extension of "ORG" (for original). Alternatively, you can do what I do and number your versions using the scheme, netscape.000, netscape.001, and so on. This technique allows you to return to older versions at any time.

I also include the following lines in my autoexec.bat file:

```
copy c:\autoexec.bat c:\*.org
copy c:\config.sys c:\*.org
copy c:\windows\win.ini c:\windows\win.org
copy j:\netscape\netscape.ini j:\netscape\*.org
```

You get the idea.

Here are a few other points to consider. Use comments to notate original lines and make changes one at time. Any line beginning with REM (or rem) is considered a comment. If you are going to change something, first copy the line to be changed. Next, put a "rem" in front of one of the lines. Lastly, edit the uncommented line. After each change, test the INI file. If something goes wrong, it's easy to determine where the problem occurred.

INI files have a common structural theme. They are grouped into sections. For example, the Netscape section in win.ini is:

```
[Netscape]
```

Each new section contains a label enclosed in square brackets.

INI files also contain what are called *embedded program directives*. These directives allow you to include parameters to define values. Here's the format:

```
keyword=replacement-value
```

Where Is netscape.ini?

If you search your hard disk for netscape.ini files, you may find several. Which is the one Netscape reads when it starts? The answer can be found by looking at the main Windows configuration file, win.ini. Within this file is a special Netscape section as shown here:

```
[Netscape]
ini=J:\NETSCAPE\NETSCAPE.INI
```

Essentially, this tells Windows where to look for the file—in the directory \netscape. I once spent three days working on a problem with a friend. He kept changing the netscape.ini file and restarting Netscape, but couldn't solve his problem. Finally, it dawned on me; he was editing the wrong file.

When you install a new version of Netscape, the installation program looks for an existing netscape.ini. If it finds one, it does not overwrite the original. Earlier versions of Netscape installed netscape.iniI in the c:\windows directory. Check win.ini to see which one you are using. It is also a good idea to check the netscape.ini that comes with a new release. As we'll see in a minute, the file frequently contains troubleshooting comments.

Let's look at a netscape.ini section.

```
[User]
User_Name=Urb LeJeune
User_Addr=lejeune@acy.digex.net
Sig_File=J:\NETSCAPE\SIG.TXT
User_Organization=
```

Recognize these settings from our Preferences editing? Sections may come in any order and frequently get rearranged when the program rewrites the file. However, all the components for a specific section must occur within that section.

NETSCAPE.INI File Comments

Recall that INI files use the keyword REM or rem to indicate a comment line. The netscape.ini file for version 1.1N, for example, starts with the following comment:

```
rem  This is the default initialization file for Netscape.  Netscape
rem  will look in win.ini in the [Netscape] section for the ini
rem  entry and expect this file to be there.  Failing that, Netscape
rem  will look in the directory where it was launched for this file.
rem
rem If you install NetScape in a directory other than c:\netscape
rem  you should make sure that you update the "History File"
rem  and "File Location" (under "Bookmarks") to be pointers to
rem  files in valid directories that NetScape can write to or
rem  else you won't get global history or bookmarks across
rem  sessions.  In addition, you should make sure the directory
rem  specified by "Cache Dir" exists and is writable.
rem
rem If you are having winsock problems you should try setting
rem
rem     [Network]
rem     Use Async DNS=no
rem
rem you might also need to set
rem
rem     [Network]
rem     Max Connections=1
rem
```

Had my friend read the first section, about where Netscape looks for netscape.ini, he would have saved both of us three days of aggravation.

There are a few settings that are not changeable from within a preferences dialog box. In the history section, the location of the history file, as shown next, cannot be modified from within a preferences dialog box. The Expiration setting, however, can be modified.

```
[History]
History File=j:\netscape\netscape.hst
Expiration=30
```

The Network section contains the Use Async DNS setting, which can cause the problem described in the remarks section above. If you are having DNS problems, try changing the Use Async DNS=yes and Max Connections=4 settings to:

```
[Network]
Use Async DNS=no
Max Connections=1
```

If the **<BLINK>** tags in Web pages drive you crazy, you can change the Blinking parameter in the Settings section from Blinking=yes to:

```
[Settings]
Blinking=no
```

Finally, there is the mysterious Cookies section and file. I don't have a clue what it does, nor can I find anyone who does. If you find out, please let me know.

```
[Cookies]
Cookie File=j:\netscape\cookies.txt
```

So there you have configuration in all its glory, or is it gory? It wasn't all that scary, was it?

Using Editors

You can edit netscape.ini using one of the following text editors: Windows Notepad, DOS EDIT, or any other ASCII editor such as an HTML editor. Notepad is probably the most convenient to use. You can also use a full-featured word processor like Word for Windows or WordPerfect, but you'll need to make sure that you save any files you change as text files. The native format for a word processor contains all sorts of binary information that will be appended or prefaced to netscape.ini, and this will prevent Netscape from reading and using the file.

LET'S REVIEW

Most Netscape user-modifiable parameters are modified using a series of Preferences dialog boxes. These parameters let Netscape adjust to your preferences rather than the other way around.

The notion of modifying Netscape's configuration file netscape.ini is unnerving to some people, but there is truly nothing to fear if you follow the golden rule, "Always make backups." Before editing any configuration file (and this could apply to any Windows INI file) follow these three simple rules:

- Make a backup of the file you are about to edit.
- Comment out parameters, don't delete them.
- Make changes one parameter at a time and test the result before making additional changes.

INI files typically have section names enclosed between square brackets. Here's an example:

```
[Main]
```

Sections may come in any order but individual items must be in the proper section. Within sections, there are parameters typically having the form:

```
Parameter=replacement-value
```

Replacement values may sometimes be a simple "yes" or "no". The replacement value may also be a file name or a server name. The URL used for the starting home page would be another example of a replacement value.

Netscape's Helpers

When you must "view" a file not anticipated by Netscape's designers, you can install helper programs that Netscape can launch to present the file, from a graphics image to a video clip.

Obsolescence is a serious matter in the computer field. Sometimes it seems like you can't even get a new machine home before someone down the street has a more powerful one. As with hardware, so it is with software—especially software within a field that is evolving as rapidly as the Internet. The recent brouhaha over who owns the GIF file format is a case in point. If GIF is indeed retired to its dog-in-the-manger owner Unisys (as many people say it should be), some other format will have to take its place, and indeed a new format is on the drawing board. But that makes all the existing Web browsers that display GIF files obsolete, no?

Not quite.

Netscape and other Web browsers have anticipated this problem, which is evident in the way they handle the display of multimedia data. The hyperlinks in HTML documents scattered across the Web point to text files, images, sound files, movies, and potentially, any kind of data you can store in digital form. When a link points to a resource Netscape cannot process internally, the file is "displayed" using an external viewer. The term "viewer" may be slightly confusing when used in a Web context. To Netscape, a viewer is a program that presents to the user (most people still say "views") an external file that Netscape cannot process internally. An example of this type of software is a graphical image viewer that displays a JPEG or Targa file. A different sort of "viewer" also "plays" a sound file—you can see why "viewer" isn't exactly the best word. More and more people are calling them *helper applications.*

When Netscape, or any other Web browser, receives a file from a Web server, the server identifies the file's MIME (Multipurpose Internet Mail Extensions) type. The server furnishes a MIME code, which is a standardized method for defining a group of different file types. When a browser receives a file of some sort from a server, the browser determines if the file can be processed by the software's built-in capabilities. If the browser cannot in fact handle the file format, a helper application (assuming one is available) is executed to "view" the file. The concept is the same for all browsers. (Keep in mind that browsers differ in their capabilities to process file types internally—that is, without having to resort to a viewer.)

Some earlier Web servers don't provide a MIME type code. In these cases (which are increasingly rare), the browser uses the file's extension to type the incoming file. For example, the .JPG (of JPEG) extension in the file name urb.jpg indicates a file in the JPEG graphic format.

INSTALLING HELPER APPLICATIONS

This chapter is about installing helpers and then instructing your browser about available helpers and the extensions associated with those helpers. Implementing a helper application is a four-part process:

1. Obtain the program from the companion CD-ROM (if it is available) or FTP it down to your PC.

2. Install the helper on your PC.

3. Tell your browser where the helper resides.

4. Tell your browser the extensions associated with each helper.

Steps 3 and 4 are performed using a Netscape Preferences dialog box. Earlier versions of both Netscape and Mosaic frequently required the tricky editing of the program's initialization file.

To illustrate the viewer concept, we might want to tell Netscape to send a file with a JPG extension to a helper program called lview.exe, which is a commonly used image viewer. Likewise, the program wham.exe can play audio files. Helper programs are not restricted to multimedia files; as you may remember, we configured the use of a Telnet helper client in the previous chapter.

Netscape's use of external programs for handling specific data types is configurable by entering the required information in a Preferences dialog box. If you obtained the Netscape Navigator by downloading the program from Netscape or a mirror FTP site, you must also obtain and install the external viewer programs. If you obtained your Web browser from your provider, you may also have been given a set of helpers for common data types.

All the programs mentioned in this chapter are contained on the companion CD-ROM. In the event you do not have a CD-ROM drive, FTP sites containing the helper files are listed in this chapter. Since the programs are periodically updated, it's also a good idea to check the listed FTP path from time to time to ensure that the program found on the CD-ROM is the latest version.

You do not necessarily have to use the specific viewers mentioned in this chapter. You can use any viewer capable of processing the desired file type—and new viewers appear all the time. The only requirement of a viewer, in addition to performing the decoding task, is the viewer's ability to accept the name of a data file to be presented as its first command line argument.

Netscape Viewers List and WinSock Client Listing

Netscape maintains a list of viewers tested and known to work with Netscape. The URL for Netscape's Release Notes, which contains the external viewer information, is:

```
http://home.netscape.com/eng/mozilla/1.1/relnotes/windows-1.1.html
```

The viewer information is listed under the heading "*Helper Applications.*" The URL shown above is specific for Netscape version 1.1. If you are using a different version of Netscape, use the URL shown under "*Release Notes*" when you open the Help menu. The pertinent information from the document is:

```
Helper Applications

For telnet, ftp, and for displaying audio and video, Netscape uses "Helper
Applications". These applications are configured in your Preferences window. For
help configuring this window, check out our documentation: Helper Applications
```

```
On Windows, LVIEW31.EXE (for JPEG images), MPEGPLAY.EXE (for MPEG movies), and
WHAM.EXE (for audio files) are all useful applications. One site where these can
be found is

ftp://ftp.cica.indiana.edu

but that site is often difficult to reach. You can also try the mirror site on

ftp://gatekeeper.dec.com/pub/micro/msdos/win3/

The files you want are:

Gif/Jpeg:

ftp://gatekeeper.dec.com/pub/micro/msdos/win3/desktop/lview31.zip

MPEG:

ftp://gatekeeper.dec.com/pub/micro/msdos/win3/desktop/mpegv11d.zip
ftp://gatekeeper.dec.com/pub/micro/msdos/win3/desktop/mpegw32g.zip

Video for Windows (AVI)

ftp://gatekeeper.dec.com/pub/micro/msdos/win3/desktop/avipro2.exe

Audio

ftp://gatekeeper.dec.com/pub/micro/msdos/win3/sounds/wham133.zip
```

The document also has anchors containing the full FTP URLs for the listed programs so you can easily click and download the ones you want.

Obtaining Current Helper and WinSock Information

Current and comprehensive information on helper applications and WinSock compliant programs is available from two different sources. Forrest H. Stroud, Neuroses@mail.utexas.edu, maintains a set of online documents called The Consummate WinSock Apps List. The home page URL is:

```
http://uts.cc.utexas.edu/~neuroses/cwsapps.html
```

Figure 23.1 shows a portion of The Consummate WinSock Apps List home page. These are invaluable documents in keeping current on Web browsers and support applications. Included on the home page are links to reviews of programs, complete listings, and—notice the last line—a pointer to the E-Z Net's WinSock Archive. E-Z Net, whose home page is shown in Figure 23.2, represents "one-stop" FTP shopping for WinSock and related applications. All

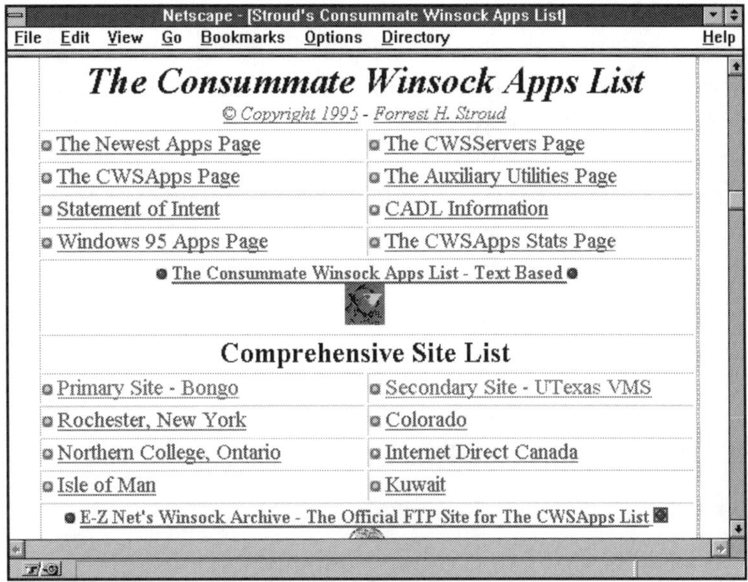

Figure 23.1 *The Consummate WinSock Apps List home page.*

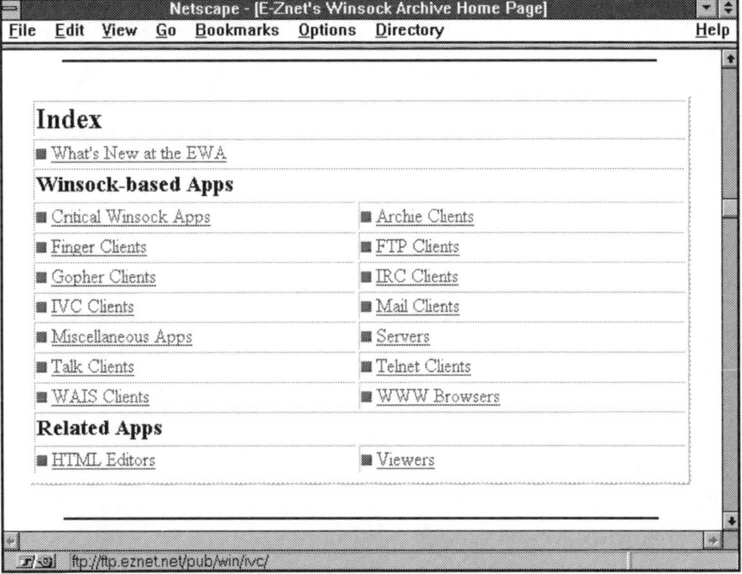

Figure 23.2 *E-Z Net's one-stop shopping for FTPable WinSock applications.*

the programs mentioned in The Consummate WinSock Apps List are available at the E-Z Net site. If you want to go directly to E-Z Net's home page, the URL is:

```
http://homepage.eznet.net/~rwilloug/ewa.html
```

The second source for WinSock and Web programs is *The WinSock Client Listing*, maintained by Ed Sinkovits, edsink@mail.mbnet.mb.ca. This 90-page document is a storehouse of information and could well be called, "Everything You Always Wanted to Know About the Care and Feeding of Netscape and Associated Programs—But Were Afraid to Ask." Ed publishes a new version on almost a monthly basis. The file name is winterxx.zip where xx is a version number. (The version at this writing is 13.) This file contains the document in both Windows' Write and Microsoft Word for Windows format. It is available for FTP download from:

```
ftp://ftp.cica.indiana.edu/pub/pc/win3/winsock
```

Installing Helper Applications

Here are the steps for installing a helper application:

1. Create a new directory to hold the program files.
2. Copy the file from the CD-ROM or FTP the file to your new directory.
3. Uncompress the file (which is typically inside a ZIP archive).
4. Create a Windows Program Manager icon for the program.
5. Enter the helper information in Netscape's Helper Applications Preferences dialog box.
6. Test the helper application.
7. Delete any unneeded files.

If you obtained a helper via FTP download, you might also archive the downloaded program onto diskette for safekeeping.

We'll perform a fairly detailed installation of Lview Pro shortly. (This is a must-have viewer and all-around image program!) The Lview installation process can then be used as a template for installing additional viewers. If you're inexperienced at the art of finding and downloading files, take a few minutes to review Chapter 16, *Finding and Retrieving Files.*

There are two possibilities for installing any program under Windows. Simple programs often require nothing more than a simple unzipping into their home directory and the creation of a Program Manager icon. More complex programs often have their own setup.exe or install.exe programs that handle the creation of directories and any possible install-time configuration. It isn't always possible to tell which sort of installation a program will need just by looking at its ZIP archive; very often you will have to unzip the archive into its directory and then double check the read.me file. The presence of a file named setup.exe or install.exe and most files existing in the form abc.ex_ (with the underscore as the last character) are good tipoffs that the program needs to be installed through an included installer utility.

For reference from this chapter's discussion, I've compiled information about helper applications into tables. Each table suggests a directory to hold the program, and recommends files to delete after the program is installed and tested. In some cases the ZIP file is deleted; in others, an entire temporary directory of files can be deleted. In the latter case, the use of a directory in the form of h:\temp (where "h" is just an arbitrary drive; use whatever drive your system uses) shows the purpose of the directory and also serves as a reminder that the directory, along with its contents, can be deleted after installation.

The tables use the following format:

Program Name:
Version:
Path on CD-ROM:
FTP URL:
Status:
Download To:
Installation Action:
Netscape Preferences **File Type:** **Extensions:**

Action After Installation:

The first four table entries are self-explanatory. The fifth, Status, will indicate whether a program is freeware, or if it's shareware, its cost. If the program uncompresses into files requiring additional uncompression and installation with a SETUP program, the suggested download directory is h:\temp. Call it what you like (and put it where you like), but I suggest that you use a directory named \temp. If no additional uncompression is required and there is no SETUP program, the download directory can be the program's final resting place.

The entries for Netscape Preferences represent the File type and Extensions that are selected from the Helper Applications Preferences dialog box. The majority of multimedia files you will encounter on the Web are preconfigured in the Helper Applications dialog box. The default actions for these file types are either Ask User or use Netscape, which is shown as Browser in the text box. The purpose of the preference configuration is to associate helper applications with MIME types and file extensions. The process will soon be clearer when we actually configure Lview Pro.

Configuring Viewers

After a viewer is installed, Netscape must be informed of its location and the types of files it views. Netscape looks to its configuration file, netscape.ini, for this information. Fortunately, all viewer configuration is accomplished directly from the Helper Application Preferences dialog box.

AN INSTALLATION TEMPLATE

The next section is a detailed set of instructions for installing Lview Pro. This Netscape image helper will serve as a model for other helper applications.

GIF and JPEG Viewer Lview Pro

Program: lviewp1b.zip
Version: Version 1.B
Path on CD-ROM: x:\\helpers\lview\lviewp16.exe
FTP URL:
`ftp://ftp.eznet.net/pub/win/viewers//lviewp1b.zip`
Status: Shareware, $30 plus shipping
Download To: h:\lviewpro
Installation Action: Uncompress, create new Program Manager item, select icon.
Netscape Preferences

File Type:	Extensions:
image/gif	gif
image/tiff	tiff, tif
image/jpeg	jpeg, jpg, jpe

Action After Installation: Delete h:\lviewpro\lviewp1a.zip

Lview and Lview Pro are two widely used GIF, JPEG, and Targa file viewers. Lview is a freeware program available for quite some time. Lview Pro is the professional version of Lview (with more features), and is shareware.

Now let's go through the process step by step. You'll perform very much the same steps for installing other simple helpers.

Step 1 Create a directory to hold the program. Create the directory shown in the table's entry "Download To."

Step 2 Copy or FTP the file into the directory. Simply copy the files in the \helpers\lview directory on the CD-ROM to the new directory if you want to use the version from this book's CD-ROM. If not, bring it down to your PC using FTP, which you can do in two ways. One is to start from the Netscape's Release Notes page and go to the Helper Applications section. The URL for this page is:

```
http://home.netscape.com/eng/mozilla/1.1/relnotes/windows-1.1.html
```

NCSA maintains a FTP directory for helper applications; its URL is:

```
ftp://ftp.ncsa.uiuc.edu/Web/Mosaic/Windows/viewers/
```

Once you get to the appropriate FTP directory, click on lviewp1b.zip and choose Save to Disk when Netscape prompts you for directions to process the file. This will bring up the Save As dialog box as shown in Figure 23.3. Select the target directory for the program.

Step 3 Uncompress the file. Unless you have a Windows-based uncompression utility (and Niko Mak's WinZip shareware product is excellent in this category), shell to DOS by clicking on the MS DOS icon in the Main group, and uncompress the file lviewp1b.zip from the command line. Make h:\lviewpro (or whatever directory you used) the default directory, and enter:

```
H:\LVIEWPRO>pkunzip lviewp1b
```

A directory listing of h:\lviewpro should look something like this:

```
 Volume in drive H has no label
 Volume Serial Number is 13DC-3628
 Directory of H:\LVIEWPRO

.            <DIR>          01-22-95   8:33a
..           <DIR>          01-22-95   8:33a
LVIEWP1B EXE       552,576 05-01-95   2:29a
LVIEWP1B ZIP       312,747 05-22-95   5:37p
LVIEWP   HLP       110,105 05-03-95   8:27p
README   TXT         3,055 04-25-95   5:44a
IREGISTR TXT         2,047 05-03-95   8:19p
SREGISTR TXT         2,542 04-26-95   4:32a
CHANGES  TXT         9,370 04-26-95   4:13a
CTL3DV2  DLL        21,648 08-17-93   8:22a

       10 file(s)      1,014,090 bytes
                       6,414,336 bytes free
```

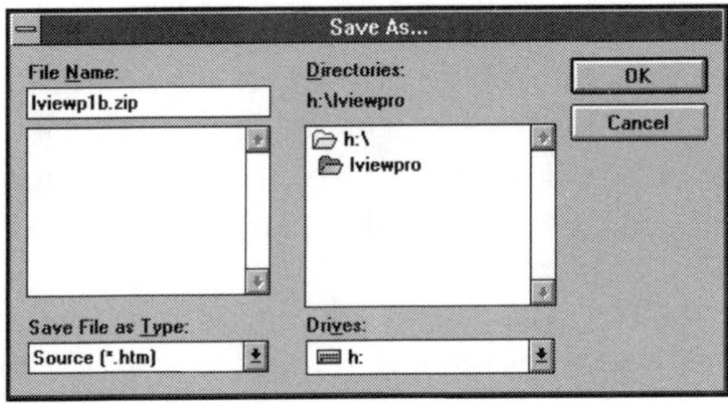

Figure 23.3 *Downloading lviewp1b.zip to h:\lviewpro.*

Step 4 Install the program as a Windows program item. Make the Windows program group that will hold the Lview Pro icon the selected group. Select the menu item File | New. Check Program Item and then click on OK. Enter the Description, Command Line, and Working Directory entries in the Program Item Properties box as shown in Figure 23.4. Click on Change Icon and select the Lview Pro icon, again as shown in Figure 23.4. Click on OK to complete the Windows installation.

Step 5 Configure Netscape to use the program. Execute the sequence Options | Preferences | Helper Applications. This will bring up the Helper Applications dialog box as shown in Figure 23.5. Use the scroll bars in the large text box to bring the line containing the File type image/gif into view. Click on the item to highlight the line. The items in the Extension Column will appear in the Extensions: text box in the middle of the screen. The radio button in the Action frame is set to correspond to the entry in the Action column.

Next, click on the Browse button located in the lower-right corner of the Action frame. This will bring up the Select an appropriate viewer dialog box as shown in Figure 23.6. This is a typical Windows File Open dialog box. Adjust the Drives and File Name fields until you get to the path holding the recently installed Lview Pro. In this example, the path is h:\lviewpro\lviewp1b.exe. Highlight the file lviewp1b.exe and then click on OK to accept the entry.

Program Item Properties

Description:	LView Pro 1.B	OK
Command Line:	lviewp1b	Cancel
Working Directory:	H:\LVIEWPRO	
Shortcut Key:	None	Browse...
	☐ Run Minimized	Change Icon...
		Help

Figure 23.4 *Creating a new program item for Lview Pro.*

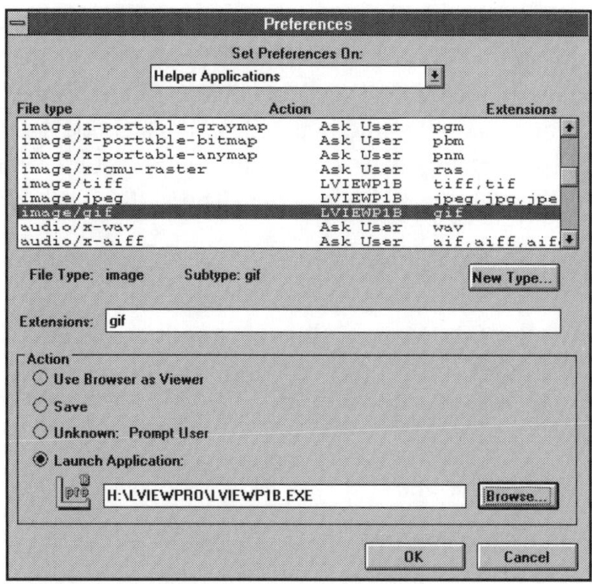

Figure 23.5 Netscape's Helper Application Preferences dialog box.

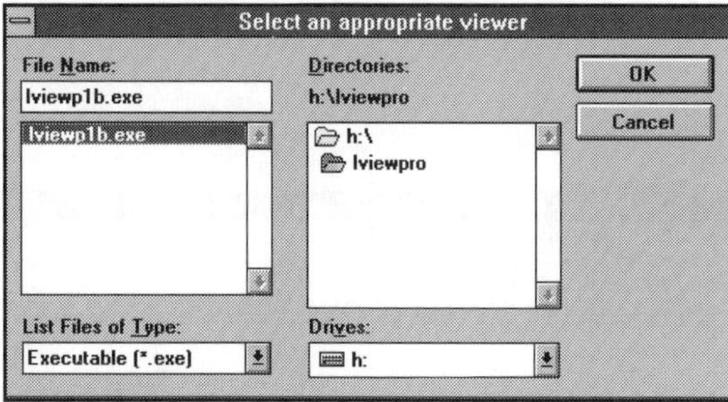

Figure 23.6 Selecting a viewer.

The helper program's icon (if it has one) should appear in the lower-left corner of the Action frame when you get back to the Helper Applications Preferences. Repeat the process described above for JPEG and TIFF file types. Click on OK to complete the configuration of Lview Pro.

Even after installing Lview Pro, Netscape displays JIF files. However, if you click on the image with the right mouse button and then select View This Image, the image displays from within Lview Pro. You can then do any of the wonderful image manipulations Lview supports.

Step 6 Test the program. You can't be sure your helper installation is complete until you go on the Web, download a file, and see (or hear) it presented correctly by the new helper. Two excellent sources of test files exist. The first is "Multimedia File Formats on the Internet: A Beginner's Guide for PC Users." This was created by Allison Zhang, azhang@admin.stmarys.ca, a graduate student at Dalhousie University in Halifax, Nova Scotia. The URL for this document is:

```
http://ac.dal.ca/~dong/contents.htm
```

Figure 23.7 shows the first page of this outstanding document while Figure 23.8 shows the first page of the Table of Contents. The categories covered are:

- Introduction
- How to Download the Files
- How to Use the Files
- Text Files
- Compressed Files
- Software
- Games

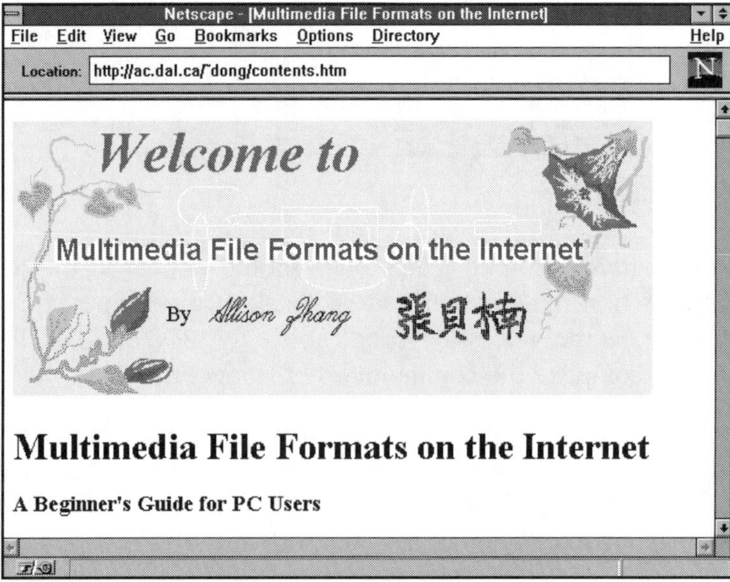

Figure 23.7 The home page of Allison Zhang's Multimedia Guide.

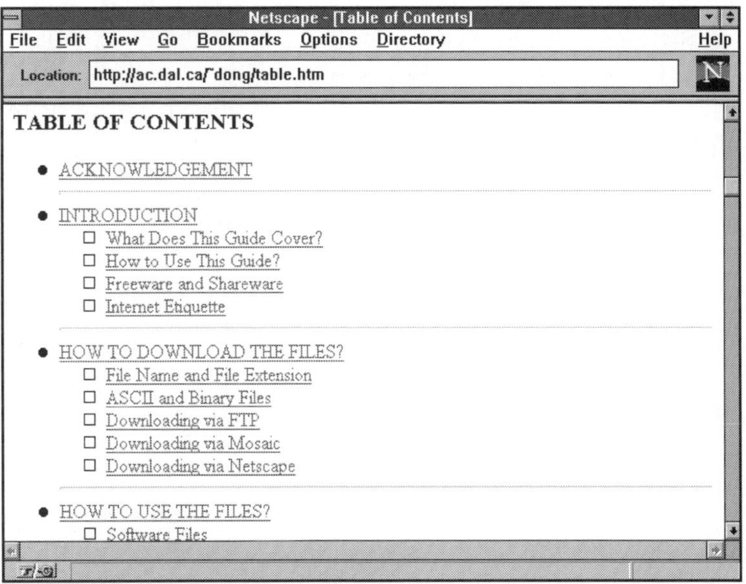

***Figure 23.8** The Multimedia Guide's Table of Contents.*

- Pictures
- Sound and Music
- Foreign Languages
- Movies
- Appendix - List of File Extensions

If you want to learn more about multimedia documents, this is *the* place to be. I consider it one of the most outstanding resources on the Web.

The second excellent test site is reachable at:

```
http://www-dsed.llnl.gov/documents/WWWtest.html
```

The home page for this document is entitled, "WWW Viewer Test Page." The first page of this test suite is shown in Figure 23.9. There are 19 types of file formats testable using this document, which is maintained by the Lawrence Livermore National Laboratory.

Step 7 Delete any unnecessary files. If the program works correctly, the last step in the installation process is the "Action after Installation" section of the table. In this case, delete h:\lviewpro\lviewp1b.zip, the original ZIP file.

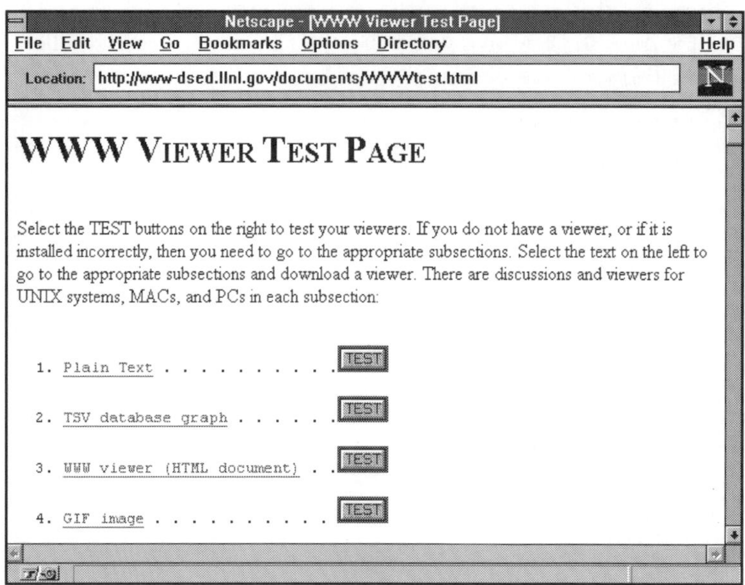

Figure 23.9 Lawrence Livermore Lab's WWW Viewer Test Page.

If you downloaded the program from a remote site, you might archive the ZIP file onto diskette for safekeeping.

ONE-STOP SHOPPING FOR VIEWERS AT NCSA

NCSA maintains an FTP directory containing some external viewers tested with Mosaic, which should all work with Netscape. The URL for this viewer site is:

```
ftp://ftp.ncsa.uiuc.edu/Web/Mosaic/Windows/viewers
```

Figure 23.10 shows the contents of this directory.

A synopsis of the Netscape helpers available at NCSA follows.

Lview Pro (lviewp1b.zip), a shareware image viewer for GIF and JPEG graphics images.

MPEGPLAY (mpegw32h.zip), a shareware mpeg viewer. MPEG is designed for viewing animated image or movie files. Netscape uses this viewer when you bring back an MPEG file. At present the MPEG file format doesn't support audio.

QuickTime (qtw11.zip), the necessary files that will allow you to run QuickTime movies (a format owned by Apple Computer) with the Windows Media Player.

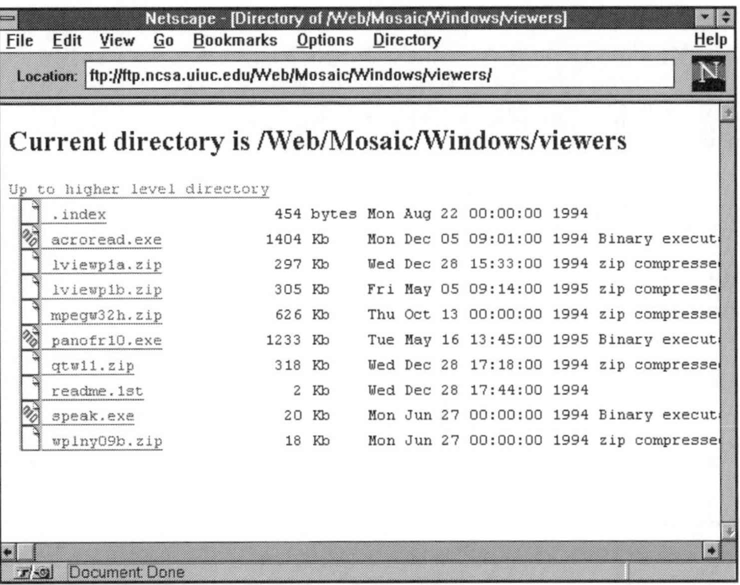

Figure 23.10 *The FTPable viewers Directory at NCSA.*

Wplany (wplny11.zip), a freeware audio player that works well with Netscape. Think of this one as Windows Play-Any. When Netscape passes an audio file to this application, you hear the file without having any control over the playback. If you want control over the playback, you will need WHAM (described below).

Speaker (speak.exe), a PC speaker driver produced by Microsoft, free to licensed users of Windows 3.1. This driver helps you get more than simple tones and beeps from the standard PC speaker, although it cannot rival even a minimal sound board.

Adobe Acrobat Reader (acroread.exe), a freely available PDF (Portable Document Format) file reader.

Three other helper files of interest, available on CICA, are shown below.

WHAM (wham131.zip), a freeware audio player that plays AU and AIF sound files for users with Windows-supported sound cards. Netscape allows full control over the audio file; a user can start and stop it through a small control window.

GhostScript (gs261exe.zip), a public domain PostScript document interpreter for Microsoft Windows. An enclosed use.doc file supplies installation instructions.

Ghostview (gsview11.zip), a public domain PostScript interpreter based on the original X11 interpreter for the X Windows System.

Installation Tables for Other Helper Programs

MPEG Viewer MpegPlay

Program Name: mpegw32h.zip
Version: Version 1.61
Path on CD-ROM: x:\helpers/mpegpla/setup.exe
FTP URL:
`ftp://ftp.ncsa.uiuc.edu/Web/Mosaic/Windows/viewers/mpegw32h.zip`
Status: Shareware, $25
Download To: h:\temp
Installation Action: Run h:\temp\setup. Select h:\mpeg as the directory to hold the program.

Netscape Preferences	**File Type:**	**Extensions:**
	video/mpeg	mpeg, mpg, mpe

Action After Installation: Delete all files in directory h:\temp and then delete directory h:\temp.

Note: This is a 32-bit application. Win32s must be installed before running the program.

QuickTime Video Player

Program Name: qtw111.zip
Version: Version 1.1.1
Path on CD-ROM: x:\helpers\quiktime\qtnotify.exe
FTP URL:
`ftp://bitsy.mit.edu/pub/dos/web/helperapps/qtw111.zip`
Status: No charge for personal use
Download To: h:\quick-tm
Installation Action: Select program group to hold icon, enter File|New, fill out dialog box, and select icon.

Netscape Preferences	**File Type:**	**Extensions:**
	video/quicktime	qt, mov

WHAM Sound Player

Program Name:	wham131.zip
Version:	Version 1.31
Path on CD-ROM:	x:\helpers\wham\wham.exe
FTP URL:	

`ftp://ftp.cica.indiana.edu/pub/pc/win3/sounds/wham131.zip`

Status:	Shareware; $20 registration	
Download To:	h:\wham	
Installation Action:	Select program group to hold icon, select File | New, fill out dialog box, and select icon.	
Netscape Preferences	**File Type:**	**Extensions:**
	audio/x-wav	wav
	audio/x-aiff	aiff, aif, aifc
	audio/basic	au, snd
Action After Installation:	Delete h:\wham\wham131.zip.	

Note: WHAM requires the presence of a hardware sound card.

EXPLORER TIP

Poor Man's Sound Blaster

Can I get sound from the PC speaker with Netscape? Subscribe to a list even remotely associated with Netscape, and you'll hear this question on almost a daily basis. Yes, you can direct multimedia sound to your PC speaker. However, be forewarned, the results will *not* have people trading in their stereos.

Getting Netscape to produce sound from your PC speaker requires a driver for the speaker. You can get the Microsoft speaker driver without charge at the following URL:

```
ftp://ftp.microsoft.com/Softlib/MSLFILES/SPEAK.EXE
```

First, create a new directory to hold the downloaded file; let's assume g:\speaker. Download speak.exe, which is a self-extracting archive. To uncompress the file, simply execute it from the DOS command line:

```
G:\SPEAKER\>SPEAK
```

speaker.drv and oemsetup.inf, which are created when speak.exe is expanded, must remain in the same directory.

The driver must next be installed—and, being a driver, the process is *not* the same as the install process for typical Windows applications. From Program Manager select the menu item Main|Control Panel|Drivers|Add. Select Unlisted or Updated Drivers from the Add dialog box. Enter the path of speaker.drv in the Install Drive dialog box; in this example g:\speaker.exe. Select Add Driver for PC-Speaker from the Add Unlisted or Update Drivers dialog box. Click on OK, and strange sounds will begin coming from your speaker as the driver is initialized. Change the settings in the PC-Speaker Setup dialog box to improve the sound quality. Click on OK when you are finished and choose the Restart Windows option.

Having installed the speaker driver, you now get sounds whenever you start Windows, make a mistake, or exit Windows. If these sounds become jarring to your ears, you can turn them off. Making Windows mute requires selecting Main|Control|Panel|Sounds, and simply making sure that there is no X in the check box Enable System Sounds.

speaker.drv makes your PC multimedia ready, after a (somewhat shabby) fashion. However, you still need a sound viewer program that Netscape executes to present sounds. WHAM, I've found, does not work well with a PC speaker; use the program Wplany instead. You can find a copy at the NCSA helper's page mentioned earlier as wplny11.zip. If you have trouble getting into NCSA (it's a very busy place), another FTP URL for this program is:

```
ftp://ftp.cica.indiana.edul/pub/pcwin3/sounds/wplny11.zip
```

Download the file to a new directory \wplan and uncompress the file. Configure Netscape's audio helpers as shown above for WHAM. Try the Lawrence Livemore Lab's demo page for some AU sounds. LLNL's WWW Viewer Tester lives at:

```
http://www-dsed.llnl.gov/documents/WWWtest.html
```

If you're lucky, your speaker may actually produce something recognizable.

Future MIME Types

Netscape has the ability to support MIME types not currently in use, or even currently in existence. In the unlikely event a new document type is developed—and a helper application is available—prior to the release of a new version of Netscape, it can be configured quickly.

In the more likely event that a new extension is added to an existing MIME type, take the following actions:

1. Execute the sequence Options | Preferences | Helper Applications.
2. Highlight the MIME type from the File Type column.
3. Add the new extension immediately after the current extensions in the Extensions text box.
4. Click on OK.

To add an entry that is a completely new MIME type, follow these steps:

1. Execute the sequence Options | Preferences | Helper Applications.
2. Click on the New Type button, which will bring up the Configure New Mime Type dialog box as shown in Figure 23.11.
3. Enter the new MIME type into the Mime Type text box. Text and Audio are MIME types.
4. Enter the MIME subtype into the Mime SubType text box. HTML is a subtype of Text and x-wav is subtype of Audio.
5. Enter the new extension in the Extensions text box.
6. Click on OK.
7. Configure the helper application for the new MIME type exactly as you did previously.

LET'S REVIEW

To accommodate new data types that will invariably emerge as the Web evolves, Netscape and most browsers support a system that allows new data types to be presented to the user through a *helper program* or external viewer. When a file comes down from a Web server, the browser looks up the file extension in a table, and if a helper is available to support that file extension, launches the helper application with the name of the file as the first parameter.

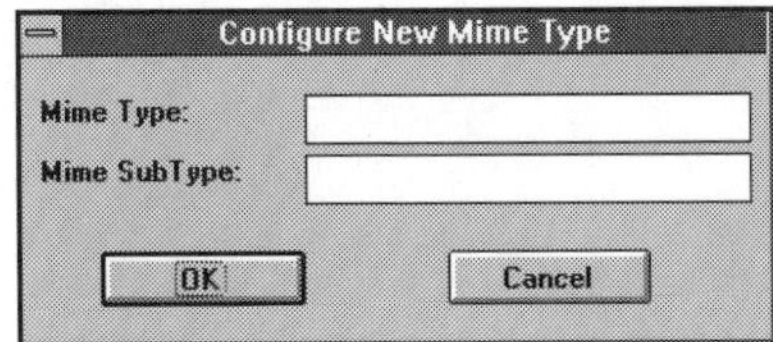

Figure 23.11 *Configuring a new MIME type.*

Newer Web servers type a file using the MIME (Multipurpose Internet Mail Extensions) system.

Netscape has tested a number of helper programs with its browser, and publishes links to information about the helper programs and the helper program archive files themselves. The main page for this information is at

```
http://home.netscape.com/eng/mozilla/1.1/relnotes/windows-1.1.html
```

Netscape allows helpers to be set up from its Preferences dialog box.

Installing a viewer for Netscape is a seven-part process:

1. Create a new directory to hold the program files.
2. Copy the file from the CD-ROM or FTP the file to the new directory.
3. Uncompress the file if necessary (which is typically inside a ZIP archive).
4. Create a Windows Program Manager icon for the program.
5. Enter the help information in Netscape's Preferences dialog box.
6. Test the helper application.
7. Delete any unneeded files.

Helper applications canbe configured for any MIME type, both currently defined types and types that may be developed in the future.

Advanced Netscape Features

In addition to being a powerful browser, Netscape provides features to allow you to subscribe to newsgroups and send and receive messages. Let's put these useful features to work.

In any race, sooner or later the leaders break away from the pack. So has it been with Web browsers in the last year or so. Mosaic kept its lead for a surprisingly long time, until what seems like only a few months ago. Then, a challenger named Netscape came out of nowhere and grabbed the crown of King Browser in a crowded field. In countless tests, Netscape users make about 75 percent of the connections to major Web sites. (A server can determine the connecting browser's brand and version.)

(Well, not exactly out of nowhere. The guy who wrote Netscape is the same guy who wrote Mosaic. Not many people have the opportunity to do something that important...*twice*.)

The speed of the transition is what makes this revolution surprising. In Web circles technological half-life is being measured in months, not years. There has never been a time in the history of the world when a technology has increased at the speed of Web utilization. Television and the telephone were snails by comparison.

In this chapter we'll take a look at some of the advanced features that Netscape provides. One of the more useful features is a powerful Usenet newsgroup reader. If you are not reading Usenet News, you're missing out on a lot of fun and information.

NETSCAPE'S USENET NEWSREADER

Even in its very first release, the Netscape browser went Mosaic one better by incorporating a powerful Usenet newsgroup reader. Such utilities, in the generic, are called *newsreaders*. Before looking at the specifics of this newsreader, a little background is in order. Usenet newsgroups have a long history on the Internet that goes back to the very early days and Bitnet. There are currently about 10,000 newsgroups, and new ones are being added at a rate of several a week. Newsgroups are much like electronic bulletin boards, and are very similar to the popular public forums on CompuServe. You can post a message to the group (that is, on the "board") and others who peruse the newsgroup can read your message at their leisure. Readers of your message can, in turn, reply to your posting, and their messages are logically associated with yours so that people reading the newsgroup understand that one is a follow-on to another. A series of such postings cascaded after one another is called a *thread*.

When you decide you want to read a newsgroup regularly, you tell your newsreader the name of the group, and it *subscribes* to the group for you. This means that the name of the group is held by the newsreader, and when you want to read the group, you need only click on the newsgroup's name. As some of the names of the groups are long and complex (how many "die"s are in alt.barney.dinosaur.die.die.die?), subscribing is simpler than typing the whole name every time you want to read a group.

Using Netscape to read postings to newsgroups is much like browsing a series of related Web documents. Click on a link while viewing the "table of contents" of a newsgroup, and the cited posting appears on your screen. Compared to other documents, newsgroup offerings have advantages and disadvantages. Messages are organized by topics into threads, which is a major advantage. You have the ability to post your own contributions to either the individual originating the message or to the entire group, another advantage. You may of course begin what you hope might become your own thread. No graphics, poor formatting, and limited linking abilities are some of the disadvantages of newsgroups.

Netscape has many newsreader features; however, the program doesn't help you to get started other than subscribing you to three groups: news.announce.newusers; news.newusers.questions; and news.answers. Unless you're content to participate in these three newsgroups, you have to find other groups that intrigue you.

Newsgroup Hierarchy

The names of Usenet newsgroups are built on a hierarchical structure. The top level comes first, followed by a period and the name of the next level, and so on. The major categories of newsgroups are shown in Table 24.1.

There are also a host of national and regional top level groups. Australian newsgroups begin with "aus" while German ones begin with "de" (Deutsch); "ba" is the San Francisco bay area and "nj" is New Jersey.

A brute force approach to selecting newsgroups is simply to subscribe to all groups in a given category and then unsubscribe to those of no interest after

Table 24.1 *Major Categories in the Usenet Newsgroup Hierarchy*

Category	Description
alt	Alternative newsgroups, not moderated, very frequently off-the-wall
binet	Biology
bit	Varied topics from Bitnet mail
biz	Gems from the business world
comp	Computers—software, hardware, and programming
ddn	Defense Data Network
gnu	Free Software Foundation
ieee	Institute of Electrical and Electronic Engineers
info	Varied topics from University of Illinois mailing list
k12	Of interest to pre-college students and teachers
misc	If it doesn't fit anywhere else, it's here
rec	Recreation, hobbies, pets, and such
sci	The sciences
soc	Social topics
talk	Controversial topic discussion
u3b	AT&T 3B computers
vmsnet	DEC VAX/VMS and DECNET computer stuff

you've spent a few hours scanning them all. Word-of-mouth works well, too—ask those with similar interests what *they've* read.

Searching for Newsgroups on the World Wide Web

Surprisingly, there is no truly general newsgroup search capability online using Web browser forms, at least not to my knowledge. For that you have to go to Unix shell utilities. The closest thing to newsgroup searching is the Usenet FAQ machine at Ohio State University. See Chapter 21 for more details on this site and how to use it to locate newsgroups. The majority of newsgroups do not have a FAQ document; however, those that do probably represent about 95 percent of all newsgroup subscriptions. To access the Ohio State server, point your favorite browser to:

```
http://www.cis.ohio-state.edu/hypertext/faq/usenet/FAQ-List.html
```

Another Web source requires going directly to the FAQ directory on the MIT FTP machine. I discussed this site as well in Chapter 21. The URL for this site is:

```
ftp://rtfm.mit.edu/pub/usenet/news.answers
```

Netscape as Newsreader

Usenet News has its own protocol, and Netscape must be told where to obtain news. Figure 24.1 shows the Netscape Preferences dialog box that contains the News panel. Select Options|Preferences to activate the Preferences dialog box. If Mail and News is not displayed in the top field, click on the down arrow and make that selection. Enter the News (NNTP) Server address obtained from your Internet provider or system administrator.

You should also select a path for your News RC File. The "RC" stands for "read command." These files are much like Windows INI configuration files. When Netscape is initially installed, the file newsrc is placed in c:\. I prefer keeping all related files in the same path as the executable program. If you specified a path for your news RC file in this step, copy newsrc from c:\ to the specified directory. Click on OK to accept your entries.

Let's Get the News

If your directory buttons have been hidden, as mine have, put Netscape in newsreader mode by selecting Directory|Go to Newsgroups; otherwise, click on the Newsgroups button. There will be a short delay while the news is

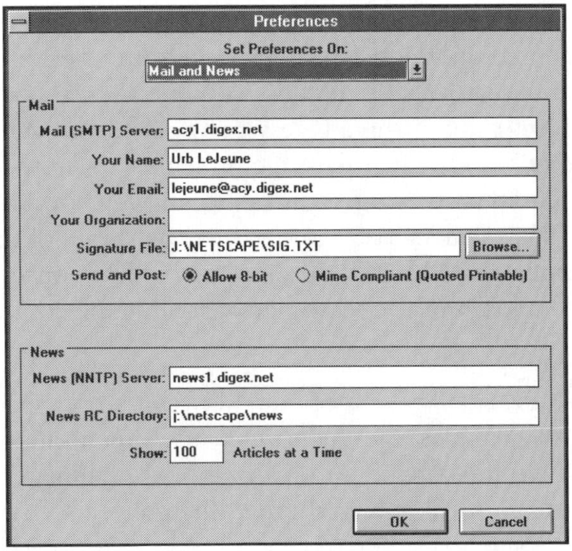

Figure 24.1 *The Netscape Mail and News Preferences dialog box.*

fetched from your news server. The first screen will look something like Figure 24.2. The three default subscribed newsgroups are shown, along with the number of unread messages in each. (After a period of time unread message will "scroll off" the newsgroup and be unobtainable.)

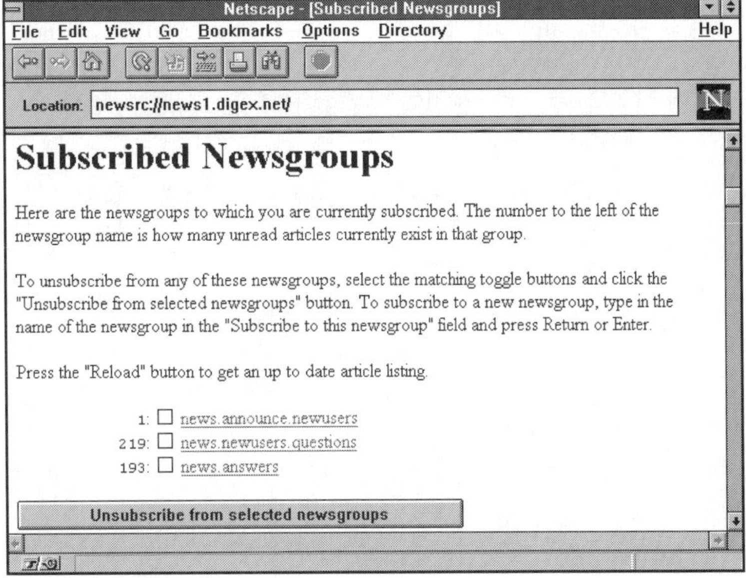

Figure 24.2 *Netscape's opening newsgroup window.*

Netscape presents newsgroups with two identical rows of buttons, one at the top of each page and an identical set at the bottom of each page. Netscape organizes newsgroup articles by threads. The first person posting a message with a new subject starts a thread. Any answers to this new message are presented together with the first message, indented to show the hierarchical relationship to the initial posting. Answers to answers are indented still further, and so on. This characteristic of newsgroups is one of the primary reasons for their popularity. Grouping postings with all responses to the original subject offers the opportunity to view a group within the context of a running idea or subject.

There may be a substantial period of time between an original posting and a response to the original message. A *chronological* organization of newsgroup contributions would thus create an organizational nightmare. If you are accustomed to reading e-mail in arrival order, the concept of subject organization may require some adjustment.

Let's click on the news.newusers.questions anchor shown in Figure 24.2. After a delay, which may be considerable if many messages are unread, the group's messages (which Netscape calls *articles*) display as shown in Figure 24.3.

It's easier to see in color (which we obviously can't reproduce here) but some articles are anchors and in blue (as well as being underlined) while other

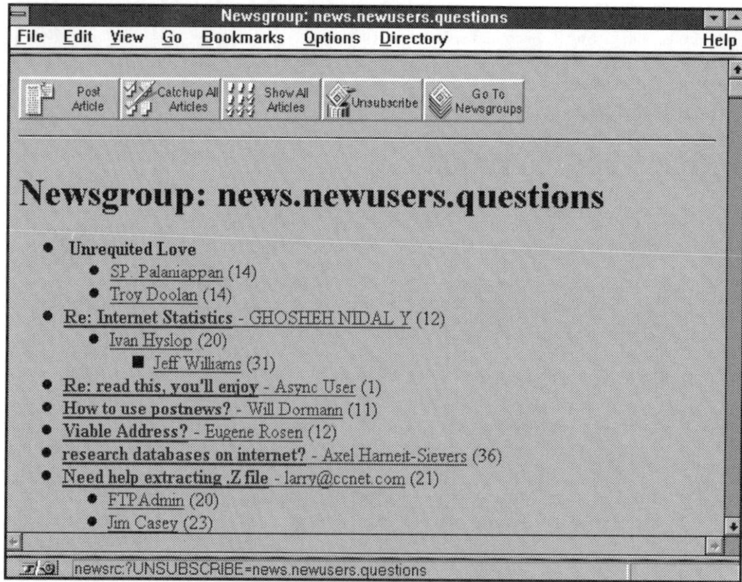

Figure 24.3 *The first page of newsgroup news.newusers.questions.*

articles are not anchors and displayed in black. An article that is not an anchor (no underline or color) has expired and is no longer available, but remains shown because it has responses, and knowing the name of the original article helps you put the whole thread in context. Unrequited Love on the first line would be an example. Any article whose title begins with "Re:" ("regarding:") is a response. Original articles and replies to original articles have round bullets; replies to replies have square bullets.

Look at the second thread in Figure 24.3. The subject is "Internet Statistics" and the oldest available posting on this subject was submitted by Ghosheh Nidaly. The indentation of the next line indicates that Ivan Hyslop responded to Ghosheh. The indentation of the next line shows that Jeff Williams responded to Ivan, not Ghosheh. If Jeff had responded directly to Ghosheh, there would be no indentation. Notice the square bullet, indicating that Jeff's article was a reply to Ivan's reply.

Responding to a Posted Message

A little further down the news.newusers.questions group (though not shown in Figure 24.3) is an intriguing subject, "HELP!!! I NEED HELP!!" (Capital letters on newsgroups traffic indicate urgency or loudness.) Clicking on the anchor brings up the message, as shown in Figure 24.4. Apparently, Mike Harman is having a problem locating additional newsgroups from within Netscape.

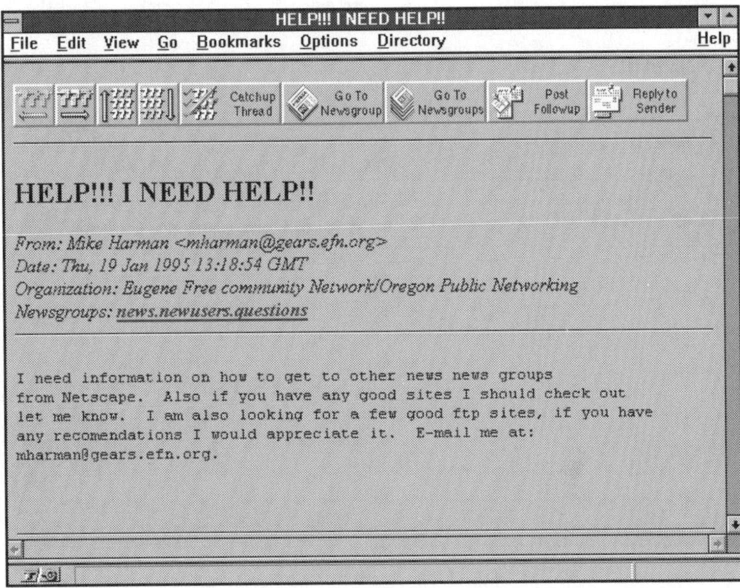

***Figure 24.4** Reading a message in a newsgroup.*

When viewing an individual message, the button bars at the top and bottom are different from those shown on the newsgroup page. Clicking on Reply to Sender will send a private e-mail message to Mike Harman, allowing you to reply to his request without your reply being seen by any of the subscribers to the group. On the other hand, clicking on Post Followup will post a response message to the newsgroup that all subscribers can read. Figure 24.5 shows the mail dialog box executed after clicking on Post Followup. The subject and newsgroup fields are both automatically completed.

Most significantly, Mike's original posting is also included in "quoted" format. In both Internet e-mail and newsgroup postings, anything on a line following a ">" is quoted from the original message. You can edit out any portions of the original message not pertinent to your reply. Having something of the original message in your reply can be very handy in placing your reply in context, both for the poster of the original message and those people who are reading the thread.

To enter an answer to Mike's dilemma shown in Figure 24.6, click on Post Message. The reply will appear in the newsgroup, faithfully linked in a thread with the original posting. Had you clicked on Reply to Sender instead, the dialog box would have been much the same, only without the subject field automatically completed.

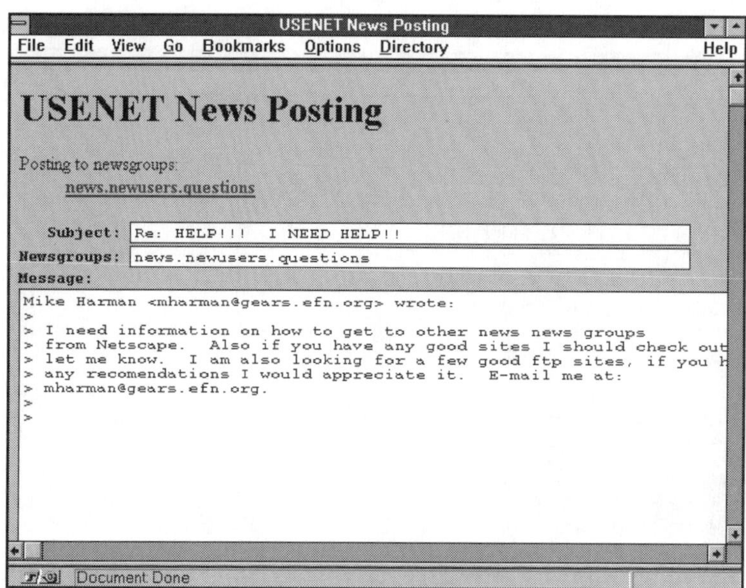

Figure 24.5 *The initial dialog box after clicking on Post Followup.*

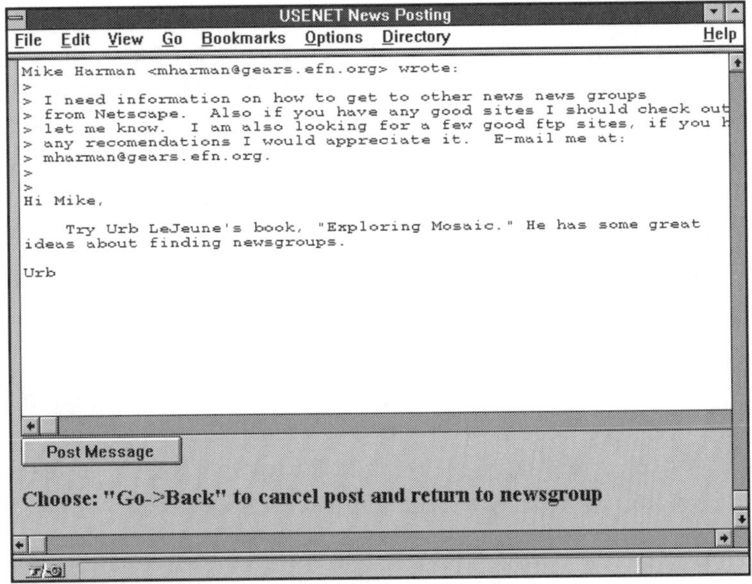

Figure 24.6 *The Post Followup Newsgroup dialog box with reply.*

Referring back to Figure 24.4, the buttons at the top of a displayed message are, from left to right:

- **Left arrow** Displays the previous article in the current thread.
- **Right arrow** Displays the next article in the current thread.
- **Up arrow** Displays the first article in the thread of the previous topic.
- **Down arrow** Displays the first article in the thread of the next topic.
- **Catchup Thread** Marks all messages in the current thread as having been viewed.
- **Go To Newsgroup** Brings up the newsgroup list page.
- **Go To Newsgroups** Brings up the Subscribe/Unsubscribe form that displays your current newsgroup subscriptions. You can click on the name of any listed newsgroup (each one is a link) to display the newsgroup's first page.
- **Post Followup** Displays the Post Article dialog box into which you enter and send your article as a response to the current article in the thread. The Message field "quotes" the text of the current article, with each line pre-

ceded by an angle bracket (<). You should delete all lines not directly pertaining to your response, to avoid needless repetition. Enter your own text conveying your response. You can enter a short summary of your response in the Subject field. The newsgroup's field shows the name of the newsgroup to receive your posting. (This is automatically filled in with the name of the newsgroup you were reading.) After filling in the fields of the form, click on the Post Message button to post the response to the newsgroup.

- **Reply to Sender** Produces the Mail Document dialog box for you to enter and send a private e-mail message to the author of the current article. Your message is *not* posted to the newsgroup. A personal e-mail message does not become part of the thread. You should use private e-mail whenever your response is intended for the current article's author rather than the newsgroup readership as a whole.

The Catchup Thread button requires a little further explanation. Once you read a newsgroup message, it will *not* appear on the newsgroup listing page the next time you enter the newsgroup. If you decide that the current thread is of no interest to you, clicking on the Catchup Thread button will, in effect, hide *all* messages in the thread so that you will not see them in the listing the next time you read the group.

Buttons on the Listing Page

Go back to Figure 24.3 and take a look at the buttons at the top and bottom of the newsgroup page. Here's what they mean and what they do:

- **Post Article** Displays the Post Article form into which you enter your article. Type the contents of the article in the Message field and a title in the Subject field. The name of the newsgroup to receive your posting is automatically filled in the newsgroups field. After completing the form, click on the Post Message button to post the article to the newsgroup.

- **Catchup All Articles** Marks all articles as having been viewed, so that they will not be displayed the next time you read the newsgroup.

- **Show New Articles/Show All Articles** If you're viewing all articles, the Show New Articles button limits the display to *only* those articles marked as unread. If you're viewing only articles marked as unread, the Show All Articles button returns to the display of both read and unread articles.

- **Subscribe/Unsubscribe** When you subscribe to a newsgroup, the name and location of the newsgroup is added to your News RC file (newsrc). If you are not currently subscribed to the newsgroup, clicking on Subscribe logs your subscription in newsrc. If you are currently subscribed, Unsubscribe pulls your subscription from Nnewsrc. Pressing either button changes your subscription status and produces a form that allows you to subscribe or unsubscribe from additional newsgroups if you so choose. This form displays the names of any newsgroups to which you currently subscribe and, next to each newsgroup name, a check box. Each newsgroup name is a link to the newsgroup, allowing you to jump in and check out the newsgroup while you're trying to decide whether or not to subscribe. To terminate your subscription from any of the displayed newsgroups, click its check box and press the long button labeled Unsubscribe from selected newsgroups. To log a subscription to a new newsgroup, enter a newsgroup name in the Subscribe to this newsgroup field and press Enter. Check the **View All Newsgroups** button to bring up a page that lists all available newsgroups. This listing is *huge*—keep that in mind before you click!

- **Go to Newsgroups** Displays a form that offers the same choices as the Subscribe or Unsubscribe button (without changing your subscription status to the current newsgroup). You can click on the name of any listed newsgroup (each one is a link) to display the newsgroup page. The leftmost button, Post Article, does exactly that. Click on the Post Article button if you wish to start a new thread.

Subscribing and Unsubscribing to Newsgroups

And now the details, plus a real-world runthrough. Return to the Subscribed Newsgroups page. If you're reading a newsgroup, click on Go To Newsgroups. If you're not in the newsgroup environment, click on Directory | Go to Newsgroups or the Newsgroups button. Let's unsubscribe to the group news.announce.newusers. Click on the check box to the left of the name of the group. Figure 24.7 shows the group news.announce.newusers about to become history. Any number of groups can be marked for unsubscription at one time. Click on the Unsubscribe from selected newsgroups button and they're gone.

I heard that the group alt.humor.puns is fun, so let's give it a try. Figure 24.8 shows the name of the group entered in the Subscribe to this Newsgroup edit box. Press Enter and we're subscribed.

You can subscribe to several groups in one shot. The "*" character may be used as a wild card when subscribing to newsgroups. I know there is a top

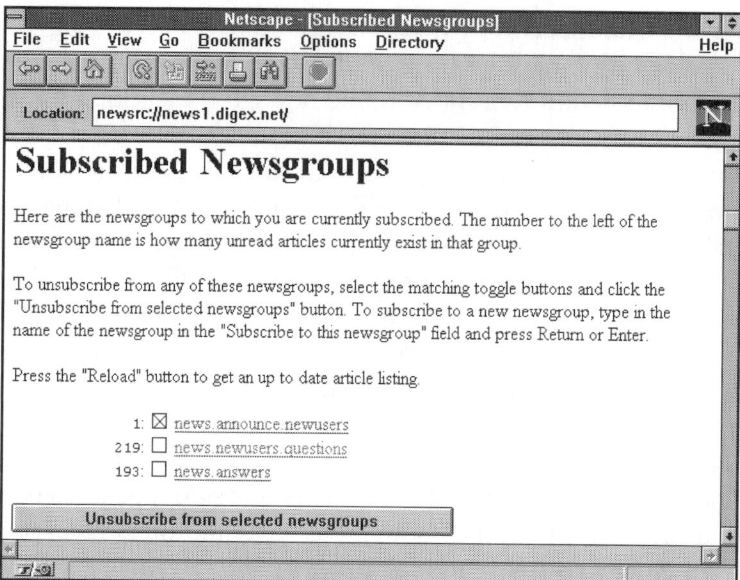

Figure 24.7 *Unsubscribing from news.announce.newusers.*

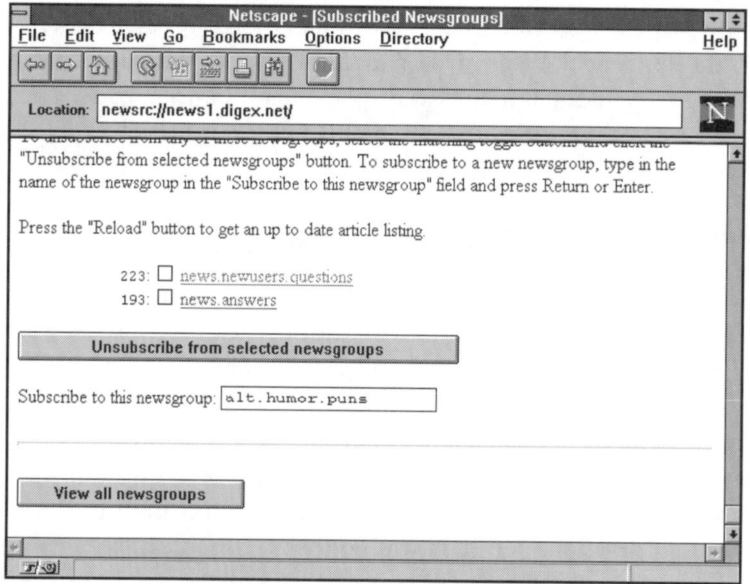

Figure 24.8 *Subscribing to alt.humor.puns.*

level geographic hierarchy of newsgroups beginning with "nj", so subscribing to the entire list of New Jersey newsgroups with "nj.*" will let me know what's there and I can prune the list down to size at my leisure.

Editing Netscape Bookmark Files

Way back in Chapter 4, I mentioned we would explore how Netscape bookmark files can be edited manually in this chapter. True to my word, here we go.

Here are a few suggestions before we take the big plunge. First, *never edit a bookmark file while Netscape is running.* Netscape reads a specified bookmark file when it loads and it overwrites the file when it terminates. Any changes you make to the bookmark file during an active session disappear when Netscape replaces the file. Second, always make a backup copy of a bookmark file before editing. If anything goes wrong, you can always go back to the original. Finally, start small. Begin your bookmark editing odyssey using a file with only a few entries.

Netscape's default bookmark file is bookmark.htm. You can specify a file name and path by selecting the Options | Preferences | Applications and Directories option. Let's select book.htm as a new bookmark file. Unfortunately, you must exit Netscape and restart for the new file to be used. When the bookmark file specified in the Applications and Directories preferences dialog box is empty or doesn't exit, only two entries will be listed when you open the Bookmarks menu: Add Bookmark and Edit Bookmarks.

For our project, let's add a few bookmarks to get the process started. Exit Netscape and bring up book.htm in your favorite text or HTML editor. The file looks something like:

```
<!DOCTYPE NETSCAPE-Bookmark-file-1>
<!-- This is an automatically generated file.
    It will be read and overwritten.
    Do Not Edit! -->
<TITLE>Urb LeJeune's Bookmarks</TITLE>
<H1>Urb LeJeune's Bookmarks</H1>
<DL><P>
    <DT><A HREF="http://www.yahoo.com/" ADD_DATE="799290570"
        LAST_VISIT="799289836">Yahoo</A>
    <DT><A HREF="http://www.charm.net:80/~lejeune/" ADD_DATE="799291529"
        LAST_VISIT="800475183">Urb's Home Page</A>
    <DT><A HREF="http://www.unipress.com/weblint/index.html#form"
        ADD_DATE="800557252" LAST_VISIT="800557207">Weblint</A>
</DL><P>
```

Don't be put off by the foreboding "Do Not Edit!" statement.

All the entries beginning with **<DT>** in the above listing originally appeared on one line. Do these tags look familiar? The .HTM file extension probably tipped you off; this file is an HTML file with a few Netscape "enhancements." Netscape uses the name you supplied in the Mail and News preferences dialog box when the document's title and heading were created. The heart of a Netscape bookmark document is the HTML definition list, which is enclosed between the **<DT> ... </DT>** tag pair. Individual bookmarks in the list are definition terms indicated by the **<DT>** tag at the start of a bookmark line. Each term is a link in the form of:

```
<A HREF="URL">Title</A>
```

The Netscape enhancements are the ADD_DATE and LAST_VISIT items, which are used as modifiers with the **<A>** tag. The number enclosed between the quotation marks represents the number of elapsed seconds since January 1, 1970. This is the system MS-DOS uses to keep time. It is also the scheme used in the Netscape history file.

Editing a Netscape Bookmark File

In this project we'll take a small bookmark file and manually edit the file using a text editor. We'll add some items and create and delete menu items. We'll move things around and generally put to rest the commonly held belief that Netscape bookmark files are mysterious and should not be edited by mere human beings.

Let's try a little editing experiment. First, save the file as book.org as a backup. Close the file and reopen the original book.htm file. Now for a little editing. Delete one of **<DT>** items and remove the ADD_DATE and LAST_VISIT information from the other two items. The revised **<DL>** portion of the file now looks like:

```
<DL><p>
    <DT><A HREF="http://www.yahoo.com/">Yahoo</A>
    <DT><A HREF="http://www.charm.net:80/~lejeune/">Urb's Home Page</A>
</DL><p>
```

Save the file and restart Netscape. When you open the Bookmarks menu, you'll see the two bookmarks. If you select View Bookmarks, you'll see that the Added On date has been updated to the current date. A question mark is in front of each bookmark and the Last Visited field is blank. After you visit both sites and exit Netscape, both date fields will be reinstated.

Building a Hierarchical Bookmark System

A hierarchical menu system is organized into levels of importance. The top level is very general. Each top level menu item may have multiple subordinate submenus, which may in turn have submenus, and so on. To illustrate, Computers as a top level item could have submenus of broad categories of PC, Mac, and so on. PC might have submenus named Programs, Documentation, and Hardware.

For the next part of the project we'll build a hierarchical system containing a three topic menu, namely Business, Computers, and Resources. Start by specifying a new bookmark file, or simply delete the book.htm items to start with a clean slate. Next, select the Bookmarks | View Bookmarks item from within Netscape. This brings up the Bookmark List dialog box. Click on the Edit button and the full Bookmark List will be displayed.

The important items for us right now are the three buttons in the right middle of the screen. New Bookmark allows us to add a bookmark. As a refresher, a bookmark is a URL and its associated title. A New Header is a menu or submenu title, while a New Separator is simply a line separating two logical groups of information.

Click on New Header and the words New Header appear. Go to the Name text box and enter "Computers". Next, click on New Header again and once more the title "New Header" appears in the Name text box as well as in the bookmark window. When you click on any "New" button, the item is inserted immediately under the currently highlighted item in the "big" bookmark window. This time enter Business as the header. With Business highlighted, click on New Header once again and enter Resources.

Business is now number two on the list but it should be the first item. Click on Business to make it the highlighted item. Click twice on the Up button to move this header to its proper position. When the headers for Business, Computers, and Resources are in their proper order, add a bookmark item to each header item. To refresh your memory, go to bookmark editing and highlight the menu item that will host your bookmark. Click on New Bookmark and enter a bookmark location such as http://www.yahoo.com and a name like Yahoo. Enter an item in each of the three groups. The leftmost window of the Bookmark List should look something like:

```
-Business
   Census Bureau Home Page
-Computers
   The Online Handbook
-Resources
   Yahoo
```

Click on the Close button and you're back to the main Netscape window. Exit Netscape and bring up the bookmark file in your trusty editor. It should structurally look like:

```
<DL><p>
</DL><p>
    <DT><H3 ADD_DATE="800992384">Business</H3>
    <DL><p>
        <DT><A HREF="http://gateway.census.gov/" ADD_DATE="800993083"
                  LAST_VISIT="800993073">Census Bureau Home Page</A>
    </DL><p>
    <DT><H3 ADD_DATE="800992390">Computers</H3>
    <DL><p>
        <DT><A HREF="http://home.netscape.com/home/online-manual.html"
                 ADD_DATE="800993030"
                 LAST_VISIT="800993020">The Online Handbook</A>
    <DT><H3 ADD_DATE="800992395">Resources</H3>
    <DL><p>
        <DT><A HREF="http://www.yahoo.com/" ADD_DATE="800993003"
            LAST_VISIT="800992996">Yahoo</A>
    </DL><p>
</DL><p>
```

Let's take another look with the non-essentials stripped away:

```
<DL><p>
<DT><H3>Business</H3>
    <DL><p>
        <DT><A HREF="http://gateway.census.gov/">Census Bureau Home Page</A>
    </DL><p>
    <DT><H3>Computers</H3>
    <DL><p>
        <DT><A HREF="http://home.netscape.com/home/online-manual.html"The Online
            Handbook</A>
    </DL><p>
    <DT><H3>Resources</H3>
    <DL><p>
        <DT><A HREF="http://www.yahoo.com/">Yahoo</A>
    </DL><P>
</DL><P>
```

So, what do we have? The entire structure, excluding the title and main heading, is a definition list. Each main menu is a **<DT>** definition term, like the main bookmark items were originally. The term (**<DT>**) in a menu item is an H3 heading. The items subordinate to a menu item are enclosed in a nested definition list. One other construct is a **<P>** paragraph tag following each **<DL>** or **</DL>** tag.

Add a new menu (header) item called Home Pages. Put it in alphabetic order. In the menu group put a link to my home page: http://www.charm.net/

~lejeune. If you're lazy like me, you'll want to know the easiest way to do this; highlight an existing menu group, copy (not cut) it to the Windows clipboard, move the cursor to the desired insertion spot, and add the new menu group.

Start highlighting at the **<DT>** tag beginning with the Computers header. Drag the pointer down to the **<P>** following the closing **</DL>** for the Computers group. Copy it to the clipboard. Then, place the cursor at the start of the **<DT>** menu item, which will follow the group about to be added, Resources in this case. Press Enter to create a blank line, place the cursor at the start of the blank line, and copy the contents of the clipboard. Edit the new group, taking out the date stuff if you're a purist. It should now look like this:

```
<DT><H3>Home Pages</H3>
    <DL><P>
        <DT><A HREF="http://www.charm.net/~lejeunel">Urb's Home Page</A>
    </DL><p>
```

Just to demonstrate we're not put off by the warning that editing can be hazardous to our health, let's add the Cool Site of the Day as a top-level item and have it appear first on the list. Add,

```
<DT><A HREF="http://www.infi.net/cool.html">Cool Site of the Day</A>
```

just under the first **<DL>**. Save the file and reload Netscape. Open the Bookmarks menu and you'll see four menu items with The Cool Site of the Day bookmark on top. Click on Home Pages and you'll have the link to Urb's home page.

How can we merge two menu groups and keep all of the individual bookmarks? Think about it for a minute and then recall what was involved in inserting a menu group. The bookmark items are enclosed by the **<DL></DL>** tags. If we were to just delete the leading and trailing **<DL>** tags and also delete the menu title line, the individual items would become orphans, not belonging to any group. (In this case they would become top-level items.) The easiest way to edit a menu group for removal is to highlight the bookmark items to be moved, cut them to the clipboard, and copy them to the new group. Finally, delete the three lines defining the group to be removed, namely, the title line and the two **<DL>** tags. Try putting Urb's home page into the Computers group.

The stripped-down version of the revised Computers section would be:

```
<DT><H3>Computers</H3>
    <DL><p>
        <DT><A HREF="http://home.netscape.com/home/online-manual.html"">The
Online Handbook</A>
        <DT><A HREF="http://www.charm.net/~lejeunel"">Urb's Home Page</A>
    </DL><p>
```

The old Home Pages skeleton, as shown below, would be deleted.

```
<DT><H3>Home Pages</H3>
    <DL><p>
    </DL><p>
```

One last exercise. Let's split a menu group, making the lower half a subordinate menu group. The modified Computers menu now has two items: the Online Handbook and Urb's Home Page. Let's make Home Pages a submenu that is immediately subordinate to the Computers menu group. Let's additionally keep the link to my page in the Home Pages submenu. The current menu group (with dates removed for clarity) should look something like:

```
<DT><H3 >Computers</H3>
    <DL><p>
        <DT><A HREF="http://home.netscape.com/home/online-manual.html">The
            Online Handbook</A>
        <DT><A HREF="http://www.charm.net/~lejeunel">Urb's Home Page</A>
    </DL><p>
```

When revised, it becomes:

```
<DT><H3>Computers</H3>
    <DL><p>
        <DT><A HREF="http://home.netscape.com/home/online-manual.html">The
            Online Handbook</A>
        <DT><H3> Home Pages</H3>
         <DL>
           <DT><A HREF="http://www.charm.net/~lejeunel">Urb's Home Page</A>
         </DL>
    </DL><p>
```

Maintaining large Netscape bookmark files is much easier with an HTML or text editor than using Netscape's bookmark editor. After you've edited Netscape's bookmarks for a spell, you'll have a much better appreciation and understanding of lists in general. Remember you're an explorer. Don't forget to back up first and be very careful that your HTML constructs contain both opening and closing tag pairs.

LET'S REVIEW

Netscape contains a powerful newsreader feature for subscribing to and reading Usenet newsgroups. Newsgroups are a distinctive Internet protocol, similar in concept to CompuServe's public forums. Articles are posted to a newsgroup, where they may be read by anyone who reads the newsgroup. Followup articles may be posted to the newsgroup, such that they are logically connected to the articles that they follow, and are displayed hierarchically by Netscape. Followups may be posted to followups, and the logical progression of associated articles is called a thread.

Subscribing to a newsgroup means logging its name into a local disk file named newsrc. This allows you to read a newsgroup by clicking on an anchor rather than entering the full name of a newsgroup, which may be complex and difficult to remember. Netscape contains button controls supporting the subscribing and unsubscribing to newsgroups, either by one at a time or (via wild cards) by entire related groups of newsgroups at one time.

PART 4

The Internet Connection Kit

The Fastest Road to the Web

There's no faster way to get out onto the Web than with NetManage's Automatic Internet!

Perhaps the finest thing ever published by the *National Lampoon* in its heyday (25 years ago or so, yikes!) was a cartoon depicting a hot dog standing at its mailbox, holding a piece of junk mail reading, "You may already be a wiener!" You may already be an Internet user. You may, in fact, already be a Web surfer. You may have come through the battle to get connected to the Internet without a scratch. If that's the case, the rest of this book probably won't help you too much.

But from my conversations with people here locally and on non-Internet online services, I get the feeling that a lot of people would sure like to be Webheads if they could only see the way there.

This chapter, and in fact the rest of Part 4, is my attempt to see you the rest of the way there.

ALL ROADS LEAD TO THE WEB

You can get to the Web a lot of different ways. Some cost more than others, some are easier than others, and some are available only in certain parts of the country. Ultimately, you're the one who has to decide how you're going to approach the process of connecting to the Internet and getting onto the Web. Part of the decision will turn on how much you want to know about the underlying technology. Are you curious at all about TCP/IP stacks? WinSock? IP addresses? This is useful information, especially when those inevitable Weird Things happen and you're left trying to figure out where the smoke is coming from. But today's software is good enough so that you don't really have to know anything about TCP/IP stacks to use the Web. (When Weird Things happen, reboot.) The choice is yours.

In putting this book together, I've arranged for several approaches to getting on the Web. The easiest is using NetManage's Automatic Internet system contained on the companion CD-ROM. This may not be the least expensive system, but it's certainly hands-down the least hassle of any system I've ever seen. If you don't already have an Internet account or a provider, I heartily recommend it. The rest of this chapter explains, with abundant screen shots, how to connect via Automatic Internet.

Many providers will simply hand you (or mail you) a diskette full of software when you sign up for an account. Run the install program on the diskette, and most of the work is done for you. Needless to say, I can't explain how to do this, because there are as many ways to go about it as there are providers in this country, and they are (as they say) legion. Knowledge never hurts—so I recommend reading Chapter 26, *SLIP/PPP and the Chameleon Sampler*, on the fundamentals of SLIP and PPP connections, even if your provider hands you software. Knowing what's going on helps a lot when you do it yourself.

You may encounter a provider who doesn't provide software—or your school or company may simply have a dial-in line allowing you Internet access—but setting up the client-side software is left up to you. In that case, go right to Chapter 26, where we'll discuss SLIP and PPP—and the Chameleon Sampler, which is also contained on the companion CD-ROM. Once you've installed the Sampler, you can run right up on Internet and surf the Web without additional delay.

Finally, you may be the independent type, and want to scout out everything on your own. That's fine—and Chapters 27 and 28 will explain how to find a provider on your own, and how to install Netscape and Win32s, which 32-bit Netscape requires. Looking for the right provider may take some time, but it can shave some monthly costs, and you'll learn a lot in the process.

NetManage's Automatic Internet

When I first saw the announcement about "Automatic Internet," I was skeptical, to put it mildly. Color me a cynic (is that one of the 64 Crayola colors?), but I've spent many hours helping people connect to the Internet using "Internet in One Damn Container Or Another" type software. It reminds me of the toys I used to put together at Christmas time: "Any ten year old can assemble this product," the label would proclaim. Sure, any ten-year-old with a Ph.D. in Mechanical Engineering from MIT. Maybe this time things will be different.

Automatic InternetInstant Internet is both a software product and a connection service. It helps you find a provider, and it configures your software automatically. There are three, basic steps in the process:

1. Install the Automatic Internet software.
2. Register the product with NetManage, which includes getting an Internet account from one of the providers involved with Automatic Internet.
3. Surf the Internet.

Don't let me keep you in suspense: Automatic Internet works like a charm. I installed the software in 12 minutes, all the while taking notes and doing screen shots for this book. I filled out an application for an Internet account with IBM, pressed dial, read and accepted the terms, and had my account, configuration, and demo software authorization in another 13 minutes. This time, additionally, I even took the time to get a cup of coffee. I had a friend—who had never installed a Windows application—read the instructions I wrote (which follow) and repeat the installation process. Again, under a half hour, not counting reading time. (He, however, was too nervous to get a cup of coffee.)

What you pay for this convenience and lack of hassle is that the package must be purchased after the 30-day free trial period (it is a commercial-quality application suite, not freeware or shareware) and the choice of providers does not provide a lot of price competition. But if what you mostly want is a turnkey, click-and-go onramp to the Web, this is definitely the way to go.

Note: Keep in mind the important differences between the Automatic Internet software presented in this chapter and the Chameleon Sampler presented in the next chapter.

The Chameleon Sampler is free but it is an older version and it does not provide as many Internet applications as the Automatic Internet software. It is also limited to 19.2 modem speeds.

The Internet Chameleon included with Automatic Internet includes all of the latest Internet utilities, but requires an average activation fee of $50 for permanent usage after the initial trial period. The fee is set by the Internet Service provider you select. Availability of free trial periods and connect time will vary by provider, as will monthly access charges for permanent accounts.

You can install Automatic Internet or the Chameleon Sampler but not both! If you try to install one of them on top of the other, the first one installed will be invalidated.

Installing Automatic Internet

Before you begin, make sure that you have at least 8 MB of free space on your hard disk (ten or twelve is even better) to hold the files for installation.

Installing Automatic Internet is a simple process. In fact, you can install it right from the companion CD-ROM. Normally, Automatic Internet comes on three disks, but we've included all of the files in the main directory \instinet, in the subdirectories\instinet\disk1, \instinet\disk2, and \instinet\disk3.

A preinstallation note: Do not install Automatic Internet on a computer with an existing version of Chameleon, ChameleonNFS, Chameleon32NFS, ChameleonNFS/X, Chameleon/X, or the Internet Chameleon that you wish to retain and use. Installing the Automatic Internet software will render these other products unusable.

Also, this system is for Windows and will not run on Windows NT.

Note: If you don't have a CD-ROM, you'll need to have someone copy the files in the \instinet directory to three disks. Copy the files from subdirectory \disk1 to the first disk, copy the files from \disk2 to the second disk, and from \disk3 to the third disk.

The files may also be FTPed directly from NetManage. The URL is:

```
ftp://ftp.netmanage.com/pub/demos/inet_cham/
```

Copy the disk1.exe, disk2.exe, and disk3.exe files to the \disk1, \disk2, and \disk3 directories, respectively. All three files are self-extracting compressed files. After the files have been copied and expanded, they can be treated exactly as those supplied on the CD-ROM.

The best part is that you can do everything in this process right from Windows, using the File Manager.

The Installation Process

Step 1 Use the File Manager and open the \instinet\disk1 directory on the companion CD-ROM. The directory structure is shown in Figure 25.1.

Step 2 Run setup.exe by double-clicking on it.

Next, you'll be prompted for a directory that Automatic Internet will use to permanently install the package. The default directory is c:\netmanag. You can change this as you see fit; I selected i:\netmanag, as shown in Figure 25.2. Click on Continue.

You will then see a series of progress messages as the setup program copies and expands the file from the source (companion CD-ROM) to your hard drive. Figure 25.3 shows the installation in progress.

After copying the files from the \disk subdirectory, you'll be prompted to insert disk 2. Change the name of the path from \disk1 to \disk2 as shown in

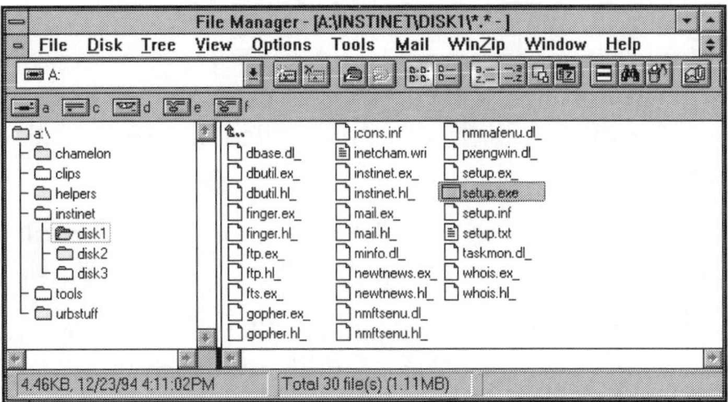

Figure 25.1 *Locating the setup.exe program for Automatic Internet.*

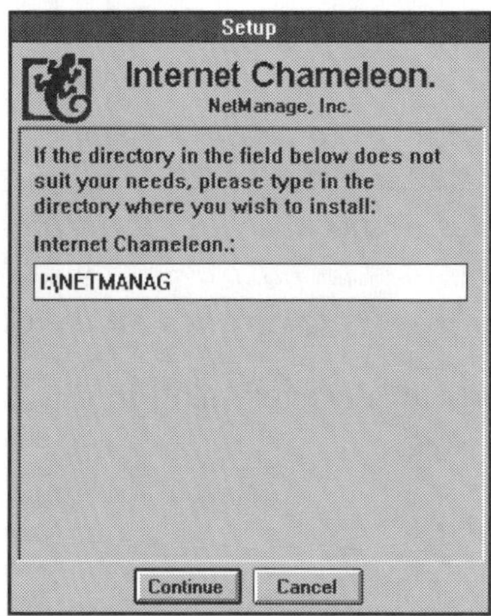

***Figure 25.2** Selecting a permanent directory for the Automatic Internet software.*

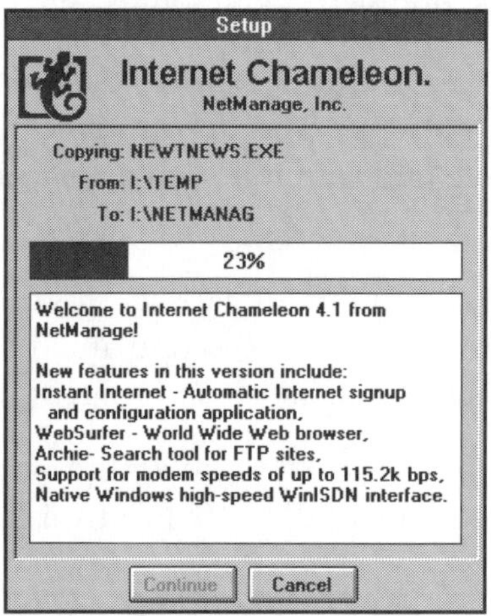

***Figure 25.3** Installation progress reporting.*

Figure 25.4. After these files have been installed, the setup dialog box will appear and you'll need to specify \disk3.

Finally, the two words bringing joy to all nervous installers: "Installation Complete." Click on OK and you're back to the Windows Program Manager.

Step 3 Run Automatic Internet. The Internet Chameleon group window will appear as shown in Figure 25.5. This figure shows the group before configuration. The icons for the package's other applications are added to the group when you have set up your account or registered for the free 30 day demonstration.

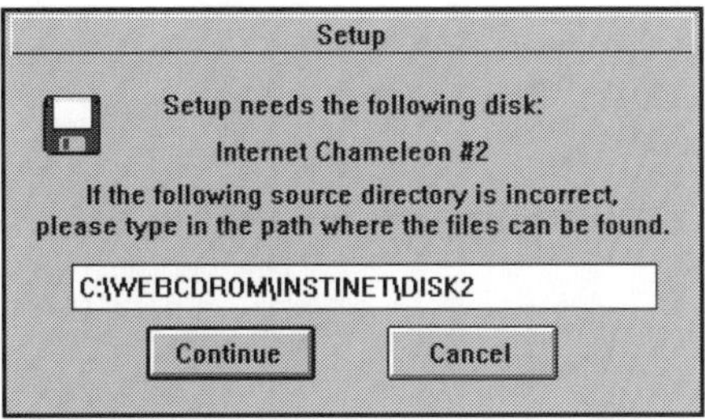

Figure 25.4 Selecting the second disk.

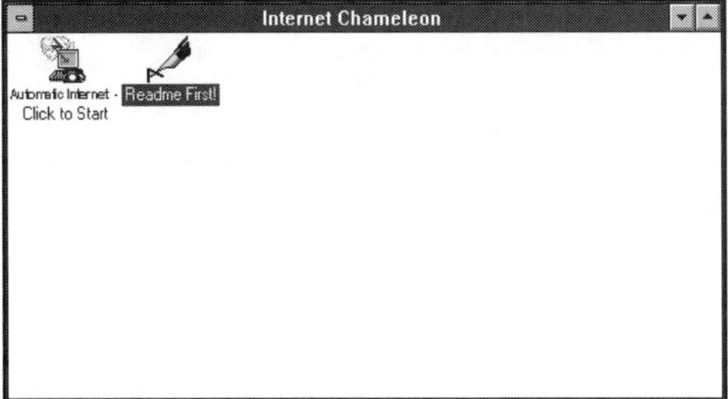

Figure 25.5 The initial Internet Chameleon group.

At this point you need to run Automatic Internet—and that will require several pages to describe.

Getting Connected with a Service Provider

Signing up for a new Internet account with a provider associated with the Automatic Internet package is an incredibly easy process. To start, double-click on the Automatic Internet icon in the Internet Chameleon group. (This group is shown in Figure 25.5.) This will run the Automatic Internet application, which will appear as shown in Figure 25.6.

There are six folders viewable in the Select Internet Provider window. Go to the folder for each of the five providers. (NetManage has a folder but they are not themselves providers of Internet connectivity.) You can get general help and more information about any specific provider. Click on More Info to obtain information about provider rates and account conditions. Check each very carefully before signing up with a specific provider. Account pricing may vary widely among the providers. Clicking the "Signup" button has become the Internet equivalent of signing on the dotted line.

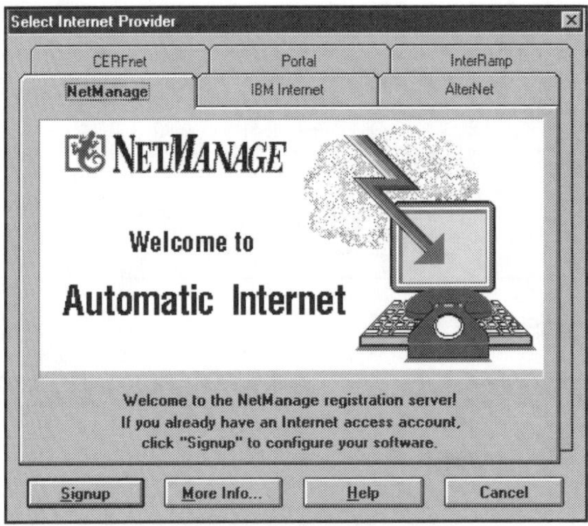

Figure 25.6 *The Automatic Internet Select Internet Provider window.*

I picked IBM as a provider since they have a local access number that is only a few dial zones away. Figure 25.7 shows the initial IBM screen. IBM offered a free trial before turning on the meter. The demo period is three hours of connect time or thirty days—whichever comes first. So what's to lose?

Before signing up, check the Phone List as shown in Figure 25.8. You can get there by first clicking on the Signup button and then clicking the Phone List button. Next, click on the Advanced button to verify your modem parameters, as

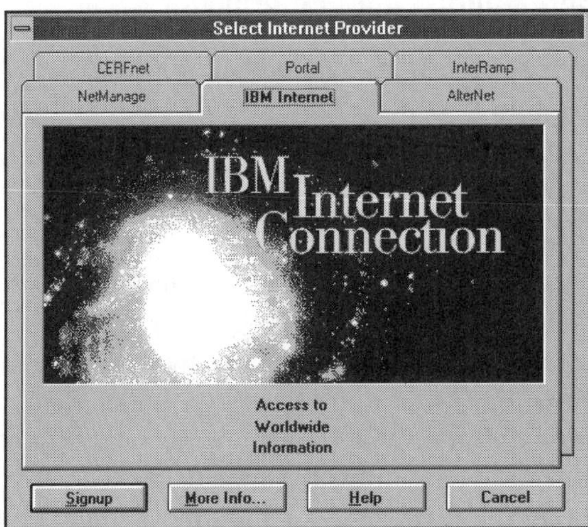

Figure 25.7 *The IBM Internet Connection folder.*

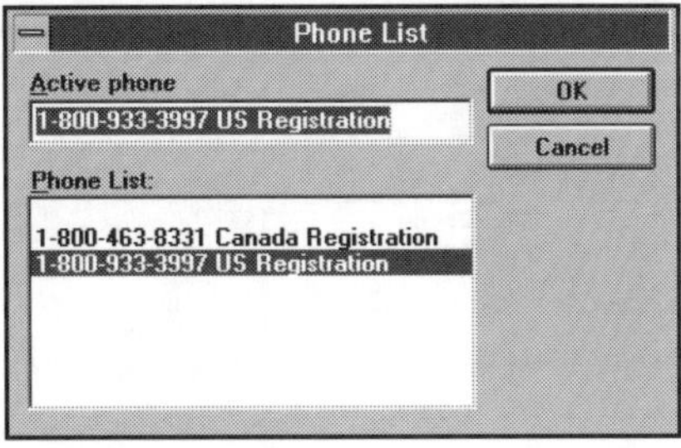

Figure 25.8 *IBM's signup phone numbers.*

shown in Figure 25.9. I tried the Automatic Internet application on five different computers and the program automatically produced the correct communication parameters each time—which is an amazing feat in itself.

After checking out all the providers, take the plunge with the provider of your choice. Click on the folder for your selected provider and click on Signup. You'll be greeted with an account application, which you should fill out, as I did (Figure 25.10).

> *Note: When you connect with one of the providers or with NetManage, you are making a direct connection, thus your credit card information is not going out over the Internet.*

The application has a second part, which I've shown in Figure 25.11. You must fill in your first, second, and third preferences for a user account identification. Not everyone has as unique a name as "urban lejeune." If your name is Jack Jones, you may find that "jackj" and "jjones" are both already taken; my suggestion is to make up something truly unique, like "fnord" or "wheezer." As a last ditch effort for me, I chose my ham radio callsign, which is guaranteed to be unique by the Federal Government, and nobody ever argues with *them*.

After entering the required information, click on Send. Your modem dials the selected number. There will be much flashing of traffic lights in the right hand

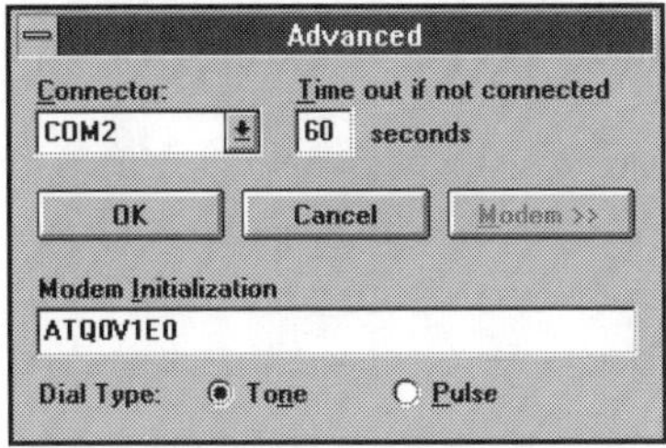

Figure 25.9 *Checking the modem configuration in the Advanced window.*

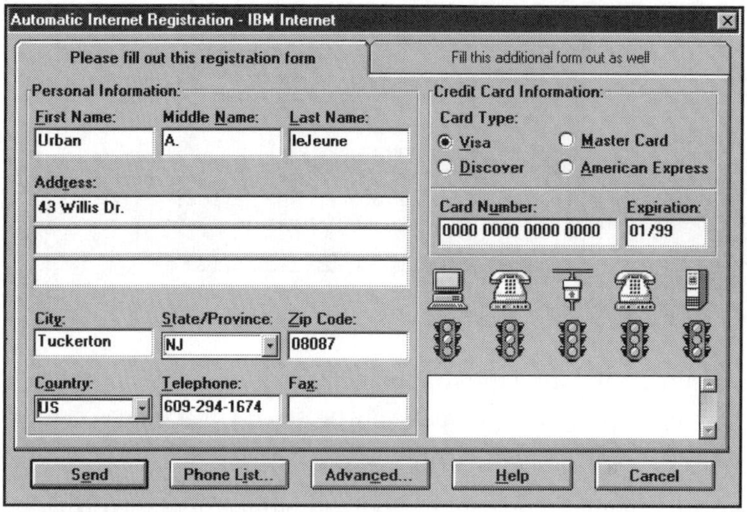

Figure 25.10 The first page of the account application.

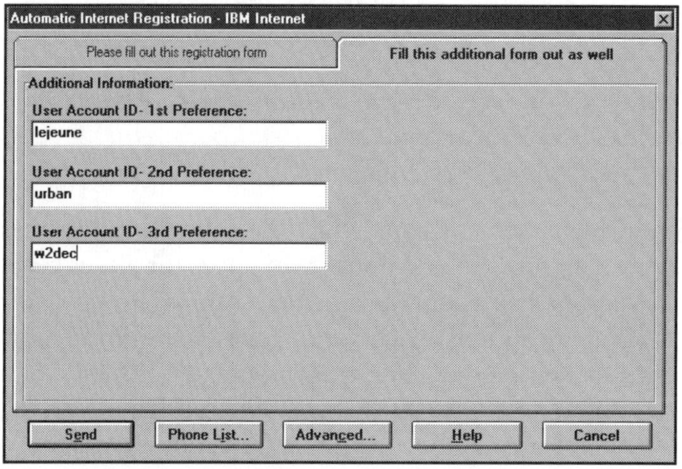

Figure 25.11 Entering the possible user IDs.

side of the Sign-Up window. Within a few minutes a message with account information and rates appears. If they are agreeable, or at least not too objectionable, click on Yes at the SERVICE ENROLL? prompt to accept the account.

Then, as if by magic, the program icons will start appearing in the Internet Chameleon group window. A screen will appear with your account information, including user ID and password. Your software is automatically configured, including the phone number of your closest dialup. Your mail and news servers are also configured. You have the option of saving your account information to a file—and if you are as forgetful as I am, accept the option graciously.

At this point you must exit and restart Windows to put the configuration options in force. After restarting Windows, open the Internet Chameleon group to see the display shown in Figure 25.12.

Logging In with Custom

Chameleon's Custom program is your gateway to the Internet. Double-click on the Custom icon to bring up the Custom window, as shown in Figure 25.13. This program handles dialing up your provider through your modem. You enter all configuration information from within this window. The line in the lower portion of the Custom window is your interface description. It is possible that you have more than one Internet account, and you can be configured for more than one connection. (But one is enough for me.) Each provider and different phone number for a given provider requires a unique interface description.

The first time you run Automatic Internet, verify the settings for port, modem, and dial under Custom's Setup menu. For more information on configuring Chameleon using Custom, see Chapter 26. Theoretically, Automatic Internet did all the configuring for you, and I encourage you not to change anything unless you're quite sure it needs to be changed. However, if you do change any configuration information, make sure you select File|Save to save the data.

Finally, click on the menu item Connect—and your modem dials your provider. I had a small problem the first time I tried to connect. My interface description was built with 1-609-987-9155 as the Dial number. I'm already in area code 609—if I dial 1-609 in front of any number, I get a recording saying

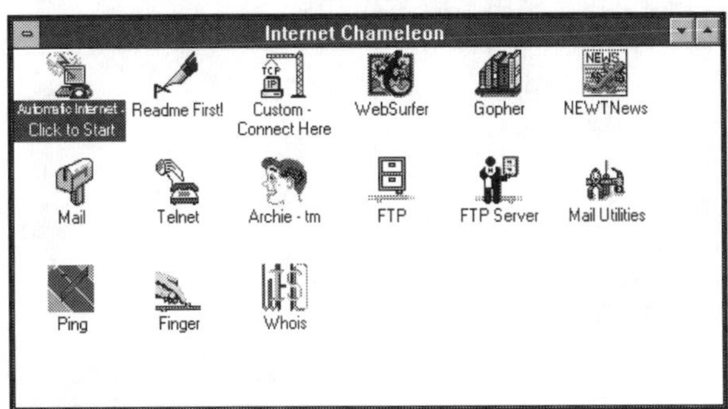

***Figure 25.12** The Internet Chameleon group with all icons.*

Custom - i:\netmanag\tcpip.cfg

File Interface Setup Services Connect Help

Interface:	IBM Internet1 - COM2, 19200 baud
Dial:	1-609-987-9155
IP Address:	1.1.1.1
Subnet Mask:	255.0.0.0
Host Name:	
Domain Name:	ibm.net

Name	Type	IP	Domain
IBM Internet1	SLIP	1.1.1.1	ibm.net

***Figure 25.13** The Custom window.*

nasty things. After taking out the 1-609 from the Setup | Dial entry, everything worked fine. The system will beep after a successful connection.

You are now on the Internet. And now the *coup de grâce*: Double-click on the WebSurfer icon in the Internet Chameleon group (see Figure 25.12), and you are on the Web! The next thing you see will be the home page of your chosen provider. In my case that's the IBM Internet Connection, as shown in Figure 25.14. If you have any problems, log your session. Click on the sequence Setup | Log before clicking on Connect.

There you have it, from CD-ROM to surfing the Internet using a full-featured graphical browser in just a few minutes! I don't think we can make it any easier than that without reading your mind.

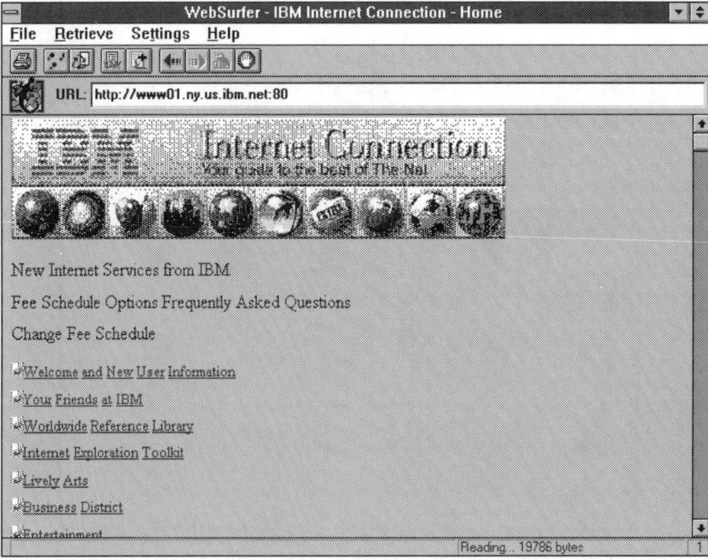

***Figure 25.14** IBM's home page displayed using WebSurfer.*

Traveling to the Post Office

Automatic Internet configures your mail reader. Each time you open a new account, it makes sense to read your mail almost immediately... sometimes the provider will send you a "Welcome!" note with information that may in fact be useful.

To read your mail, double click on the Mail icon in the Internet Chameleon group. Next, your Mail - Login dialog becomes active, as shown in Figure 25.15. Your mail Username will initially be the same as your Internet user ID. Click on OK and your mailbox appears next, as shown in Figure 25.16.

When you point to the icons on the toolbar and leave the mouse pointer still for a second, the description of the icon appears on the status bar—nice usability touch. Additional information on the Chameleon Mail program is contained in Chapter 26.

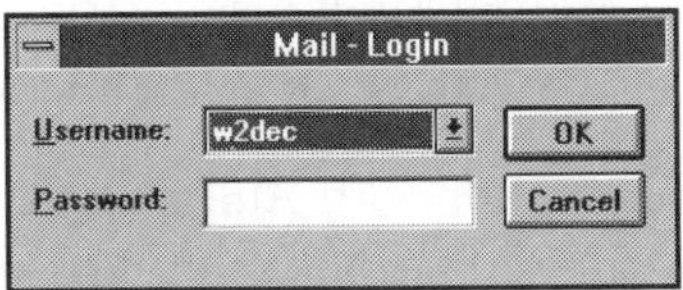

Figure 25.15 *Chameleon's Mail dialog.*

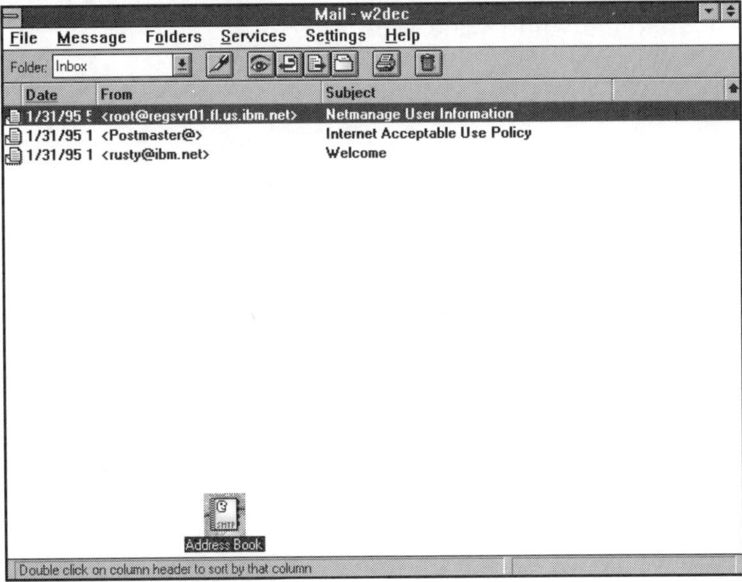

Figure 25.16 *A mailbox with the Inbox folder icon.*

LET'S REVIEW

It's been a long time coming; Automatic Internet is the closest thing I have seen to Instant Web Surfing. If you don't already have an Internet account and would like to obtain one with the least trouble possible, this is the way to go.

Once you install the three Automatic Internet file sets from the CD-ROM and perform a Windows setup of the resulting files, you'll have a single Windows application called Automatic Internet. Running this application shows you a form containing descriptions of five national Internet providers from whom you may choose. Look carefully at their terms and conditions, compare their costs (which will vary), and even call them with any questions you might have.

Once you choose a provider, one mouse click will dial NetManage's registration server and sign you up for an account with your chosen provider. Once you have provided credit card information (it is done over a secure, non-Internet dialup), Automatic Internet will install icons for all of the other Internet client applications that are part of the Chameleon Internet product suite.

As soon as you set up an account with Automatic Internet, check your new mailbox with the Chameleon Mail application. You'll probably have mail!

If you don't want to use the Automatic Internet road to Internet access, see the next several chapters for the tougher—if more interesting and probably cheaper—road to the World Wide Web.

SLIP/PPP and the Chameleon Sampler

Getting connected to the Internet with your own SLIP account may not be as hard as you think. Here's the Chameleon Sampler and how to use it.

Well, there's easy—and there's not so easy. We covered "easy" in Chapter 25, which explained how to use Automatic Internet to obtain an Internet account and configure your machine with all the necessary software with the least amount of time and hassle. You may not have any desire to learn more about the ugly details of Internet connection than you absolutely must—and if that's the case, you might as well skim past this chapter.

Because what we're going to do here is explain how to set up your own SLIP or PPP link to an Internet provider. Much of what you need is right on the CD-ROM bound into this book.

By definition, the Internet is composed of cooperating networks that communicate using a protocol called *TCP/IP*. TCP/IP is an acronym for Transmission Control Protocol/Internet Protocol. It's the method by which Internet data traffic is divided into little nuggets called *packets* and sent on their way.

Connecting our PCs directly to the Internet first requires a working knowledge of the fundamentals of TCP/IP. Next, we'll set up our PCs to communicate over a serial line with the TCP/IP protocol. Once our PCs become fluent in TCP/IP, we can use Netscape, and any of the other wonderful Windows Internet client programs. (*Client*, here, simply means the programs by which you as a desktop PC user request information or other services from the "big" machines on the Net, which we call *servers*.)

LET'S SPEAK TCP/IP

Directly connecting your PC to the Internet requires giving it the ability to communicate using TCP/IP. There are two general (and related) ways to accomplish this goal:

- A Serial Line Internet Protocol (SLIP) or Compressed SLIP (CSLIP) account
- A Point to Point Protocol (PPP) account

What is this wondrous thing called a protocol? A protocol is simply an agreement to do certain things in a certain way, in a certain order. The users on both ends of the connection must understand and follow the same set of rules (that is, the protocol) in order for meaningful communication to take place. This truism holds whether it's computers or humans doing the communicating.

SLIP is a communications protocol that supports TCP/IP Internet connection using a dialup telephone line. There is also a variant called Compressed SLIP. CSLIP is somewhat faster than SLIP since information is compressed before being sent over our relatively slow-speed telephone lines. The compressed information is subsequently expanded to its original size at the receiving site.

PPP is a newer protocol that functionally does what SLIP and CSLIP do. PPP is billed as a "cleaner" version of SLIP, and is supposedly more robust and even a little faster. (In truth, they're pretty much equivalent.) PPP access was uncommon until recently, but is becoming increasingly more available. All other things being equal (such as price and availability) choose PPP, if your provider offers both PPP and SLIP access. For the remainder of this chapter I'll use the generic term SLIP/PPP to refer to a SLIP, PPP, or CSLIP connection.

Getting directly connected to the Internet requires PPP, SLIP, or CSLIP access from your provider and a TCP/IP stack on your PC.

Static and Dynamic IP Addressing

When you access the Internet using a SLIP/PPP connection on your provider's side and a TCP/IP stack on your PC, you are directly connected to the Internet. Your PC has a unique and identifiable "home:" its own IP address. Each node on the Internet has its own distinctive address. Each unique address has two components, a Fully Qualified Domain Name (FQDN) and an associated IP address. My own individual FQDN is ITACOM.DIGEX.NET; the IP address associated with my FQDN is 199.125.129.17. There can be only one ITACOM.DIGEX.NET on the Internet at any given time. There is a one-to-one correspondence between FQDNs and IP addresses. IP addresses make life easy for computers, while FQDNs make life easy for us mere mortals.

There are two conceptual approaches used in the allocation of the unique IP addresses required for a SLIP or PPP access. One method, called *static addressing*, requires a unique and dedicated IP address for your PC. An FQDN is registered in your name, or in the name of your business. It is your personal IP address and no one will ever have your address as long as you keep it active.

This system worked well—until the Internet grew to have millions of users, many of whom wanted the convenience of SLIP and its attendant unique IP address. IP addresses soon came to be seen as a limited resource. However, an IP address for your PC needs to be unique only while the PC is connected to the Internet. As a consequence, many providers have registered a bank of several IP addresses and assign one to your PC whenever you log onto their system. You have exclusive use of the assigned IP address during the time that you're connected. You may in fact have a different IP address each time you log on. The process of assigning an IP address during the logon process is *dynamic address allocation* or simply *dynamic addressing*.

The big disadvantage of dynamic addressing is that you cannot run a server on a dynamically-addressed account. Running a server requires that your address resolve to a single IP address, now and always. (Otherwise, no one could find your server to log into it.) If you don't choose to run an Internet server (and very few individuals have the need or the ability), dynamic addressing is a big win, since it is often cheaper and generally easier for your provider to set up.

THE SHAPE OF A SLIP/PPP CONNECTION

The exact details of setting up a SLIP/PPP connection will vary depending on the TCP/IP stack software that you use and the connection software employed by your Internet access provider on the host side. Your provider may have a separate number for SLIP/PPP access and shell access. More and more, however, as the host software improves, all access comes into the provider through the same number.

A major difference in SLIP/PPP access is that you will no longer be using your familiar communications software. Your TCP/IP stack and related software will dial the number and communicate with your account using a script file—which (as its name implies) is a prearranged conversation between your PC and the provider's host system. Basically, the TCP/IP stack becomes the "modem program" that you use while you connect to the Internet, and the script file drives the connection process. The process departs from what you're used to in dialing into BBSes; for example, once you are connected, the TCP/IP stack goes into the background, managing the connection but no longer dominating the screen. You launch a client program—like Netscape or Mosaic—and the client program takes over the screen but communicates with the Internet through your TCP/IP stack still resident in memory, as shown in the icon space at the bottom of your screen.

The TCP/IP stack runs "underneath" your client applications. The TCP/IP stack, in turn, runs "on top" of Windows. When your PC communicates with the Internet using TCP/IP, your provider merely provides a pass-through connection. You will not be using any of the dreaded Unix programs, and you will not be using any disk space on your provider's host computer. All the action goes directly from the Net down to your PC.

A SLIP/PPP connection allows more than one of your Internet client programs to communicate with the Net over the same dialup link at the same time. This is possible because SLIP/PPP communicates via a stream of relatively independent packets, and two or more client programs can "interlace" their packet streams onto a single serial line. You can be FTPing a multi-megabyte file while you read your mail or surf the Net using Netscape. Since you only have one dialup line, throughput will be slower than with any single client acting alone. But at least you can continue to interact with the Net while the big file is coming across. This is a good reason to buy the fastest modem you can!

What Does WinSock Mean?

You're going to hear the term *WinSock* a lot as you forge your direct connection to the Internet. WinSock is the portmanteau jargon for Windows Sockets. Windows Sockets, in turn, is the Microsoft Windows version of something called Berkeley Sockets. Both Windows Sockets and Berkeley Sockets are specifications defining software libraries that allow programs to communicate with the Internet via TCP/IP. Berkeley Sockets was created for use with Unix systems, and when converted for Windows became Windows Sockets, or WinSock.

It's helpful to think of WinSock as a specification to which software can adhere. The WinSock library must exist as a Windows DLL called winsock.dll. Anyone can write a winsock.dll library, as long as it adheres to the Windows Sockets specification. Furthermore, anyone can write an Internet client application that knows how to "talk to" winsock.dll. Netscape and Mosaic are both WinSock-compatible client programs, in that they are both written to communicate with the Internet through the winsock.dll software library. There are a great many other WinSock compatible client programs, and more are being released every day. If you buy or acquire client software to run on your PC, make sure it is WinSock-compatible.

There are two major winsock.dll products in use today. One is Peter Tattam's Trumpet WinSock, a shareware product from Australia. The other is NetManage's Chameleon, which is present in two forms on the companion CD-ROM. Both Chameleon packages provide a winsock.dll Windows library, which furnishes WinSock-compatible communications.

IBM's OS/2 Warp, while not a clone of Windows, also supports the standard WinSock interface and Windows-based Internet client programs. Windows 95 also supports WinSock, by having its own built-in TCP/IP stack.

Let There Be Help

If I haven't shed sufficient light on the topic of TCP/IPing, don't despair. There is excellent reference material available. Frank Hecker, hecker@access.digex.net, has created a masterpiece called *Personal Internet Access Using SLIP or PPP: How You Use It, How It Works.* This massive work is over 110,000 bytes and takes about 40 pages to print. It's called slip-ppp.txt and may be FTPed from

```
ftp.digex.net
```

in the directory:

```
/pub/access/hecker/internet
```

Or point your browser to:

```
ftp://ftp.digex.net/pub/access/hecker/internet/slip-ppp.txt
```

You can also get to this document from Frank's interesting home page (he actually works for Netscape), which is:

```
http://access.digex.net/~hecker/
```

The document has also been "HTMLized" with hotlinks to other resources and references; its URL is:

```
http://www.access.digex.net/~hecker/papers/slip-ppp.html
```

Baltimore's Charm Net has a complete Web page devoted to Internet connectivity. The URL for their Personal IP page is:

```
http://www.charm.net/pip.html
```

All tolled, this gold mine page has links to about 50 SLIP/PPP/TCP/IP related resources and, additionally, pointers to 25 related Usenet Newsgroups. If you cannot find the answer to any personal IP question using either the Hecker document or the Charm Net Web page, that question doesn't have an answer.

What You Need and Where to Get It

In order to connect you to the Internet, your Internet provider supplies at least these three things:

- a dialup SLIP/PPP access phone number
- a SLIP/PPP user ID
- a password to go with the SLIP/PPP user ID. In addition, your provider will also supply an IP address for your use, via either static or dynamic addressing. More and more providers are moving to dynamic addressing, which does *not* require you to have your own individual IP address. Your provider may not stop there. You may receive a TCP/IP stack and other Internet utilities (including a Web browser) when you sign up. If so, so much the better! You can probably skip this chapter.

What we provide on the companion CD-ROM is the software that implements the TCP/IP stack that you'll need to communicate via SLIP or PPP. The package is called the Chameleon Sampler, and it's the "little brother" of the complete Automatic Internet package described in Chapter 25. In the rest of this chapter we'll explain how to install, configure, and use the Chameleon Sampler. In the next chapter we'll explain how to download and install the Netscape browser.

THE CHAMELEON SAMPLER

NetManage, the creator of the Chameleon Sampler, is one of the largest TCP/IP software vendors. The Chameleon Sampler package is a subset of their "big" Internet product, and actually was their "big" product some time back. They have allowed us to distribute the Sampler with this book in the hope that you will upgrade your copy of the Sampler to their top-of-the-line Internet Chameleon product, which I strongly encourage you to do.

The Chameleon Sampler is only configurable for serial connection. If your Internet connection is via a LAN, you will need the full commercial version of the Chameleon package. If your PC is connected to a LAN, you will have other considerations as well—do consult your system administrator for guidance.

Installing Chameleon

The installation of Chameleon Sampler is a three-part process:

1. Run the Chameleon setup program from the companion CD-ROM. (This program is setup.exe in the \chamelon directory.)
2. Configure the program.
3. Test the program and debug the configuration, if necessary.

The files included on the companion CD-ROM were the latest when this book went to press. Like most Internet software, they may change monthly or even weekly. If you would like to download the latest Sampler from the NetManage FTP server, you would FTP to:

```
ftp.netmanage.com
```

Once at the NetManage FTP site, file sampler.exe resides in directory:

```
/pub/demos/sampler
```

If you are downloading the package using a Web client, the URL is:

```
ftp://ftp.netmanage.com/pub/demos/sampler/sampler.exe
```

While you're connected to the NetManage's FTP machine, you might want to download a manual the NetManage folks have prepared for their product called "Internet Chameleon." Although the manual is for the Internet Chameleon product, many of the applications are very similar to those contained on the Sampler package. The manual, which is in Word for Windows 6.0 format, may be downloaded at:

```
ftp://ftp.netmanage.com/pub/demos/inet_cham/manual.zip
```

The file sampler.exe is a self-extracting archive file that contains all the files and programs required for the Chameleon Sampler installation. Since the file is self-extracting, there are no additional program requirements for file expansion. Start the installation process by creating a temporary directory on your hard disk to receive the file—let's assume the directory is c:\temp. You may use any disk drive or directory name that you choose.

From the Windows Program Manager, select File|Run and enter c:\temp\setup.exe in the Run dialog box, and click on OK. The SAMPLER expansion process will place slightly over 80 files in directory c:\temp. The Sampler consumes about 1.6 MB of disk space. Many of these individual files are compressed and are expanded in the setup process about to be described.

The next step installs the Chameleon Sampler as a Windows group. The Chameleon Sampler group contains icons for the individual programs bundled with the package. From within the Windows Program Manager select File|Run and enter c:\temp\setup.exe in the Run dialog box, and click on OK. The setup program will next display a message advising you that the Sampler is not a network aware program. If you are attempting to install a TCP/IP stack on a network, consult your system administrator for assistance.

The installation program next asks for the name of the directory in which you wish to install the Chameleon Sampler package, as shown in Figure 26.1. Although c:\netmanag is the path suggested by the installation program, you may of course substitute the drive and directory of your choice.

The setup.exe program transfers the Chameleon Sampler files to the directory you specified. You'll see a series of progress messages, as shown in Figure 26.2.

The installation program confirms the completion of the process in a message box. The installation program also adds the Chameleon Sampler's group icon to the Program Manager's main window. As the final step in the installation process, you can delete the contents of c:\temp and remove the directory itself.

Chameleon Sampler Setup

If the directory in the field below does not suit your needs, please type in the directory where you wish to install NetManage Chameleon Sampler

C:\NETMANAG

Continue Cancel

Figure 26.1 *Selecting a directory to contain the Chameleon Sampler.*

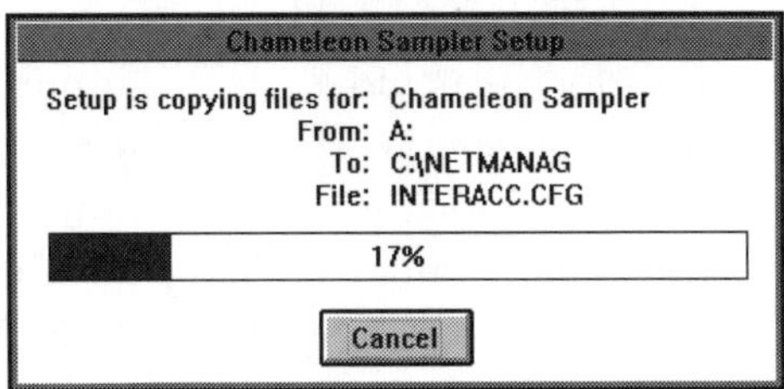

Figure 26.2 *Chameleon Sampler installation progress message.*

Configuring the Chameleon Sampler

Before starting the installation process, double-click on the README icon. Windows Write will execute and open readme.wri, Sampler's installation guide. Print it and have it available to complement the explanation that follows.

Start the configuration process by double-clicking on the Custom icon. If this is the first time you have used the Sampler, a blank Custom dialog box, as shown in Figure 26.3, will appear.

The Chameleon Sampler package comes with a group of predefined configuration files. A configuration file contains the logon sequence and configuration information for a specific provider. All Sampler configuration files use a .CFG extension. The configuration files are in the form:

Custom

File Interface Setup Services Connect Help

Interface:
Dial:
IP Address:
Subnet Mask:
Host Name:
Domain Name:

Name Type IP Domain

Figure 26.3 *Custom's configuration screen.*

```
provider.CFG
```

As an example, there is netcom.cfg for NetCom, psinet.cfg for PSI net, and so on.

If you're lucky, there may be a configuration file present for your provider. (Before you despair, however, ask your provider if they have a configuration file for Chameleon that they could send you. Many of the smaller providers do.) Predefined configuration files only require entry of a few items that are specific to you, such as your user ID and password.

To determine if your provider is included in the group bundled with the Chameleon Sampler, select Chameleon's File|Open menu item, which will display files with the .CFG extension. The configuration files are located in the path you specified during the Chameleon Sampler installation (by default, c:\netmanag). Figure 26.4 shows the Open Configuration File dialog box. For example, if you already have an account on CerfNet, select cerfnet.cfg as your configuration file. Click on OK and you'll go to the Port Settings dialog box. We'll get to port setting shortly; for now, click on OK to go back to the Custom window. Now, CerfNet-specific information will be displayed, as shown in Figure 26.5. You need only fill in the remaining blanks.

If your provider is not included as a Sampler preconfigured file, you'll have to create one the hard way. The purpose of the Custom dialog box is to create a configuration file (it will by default have a .CFG extension) containing one or more records. I would suggest that you use one configuration file for each of your Internet service providers, and one record in a file for each different account accessed on that file's provider. Most likely, you will have only one file with one record in it, unless you're configuring a group of accounts for your school or company.

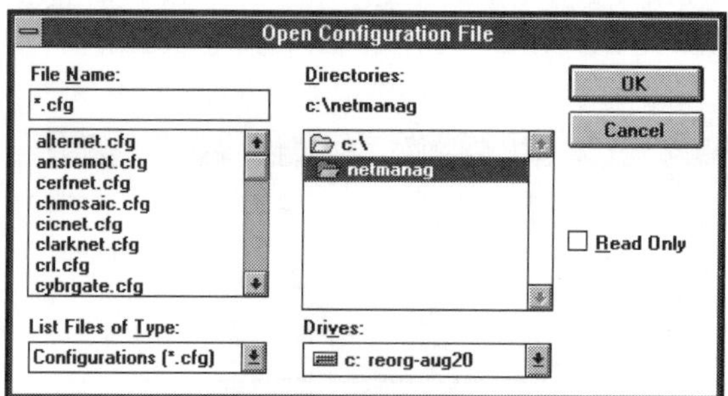

***Figure 26.4** Chameleon's predefined configuration files.*

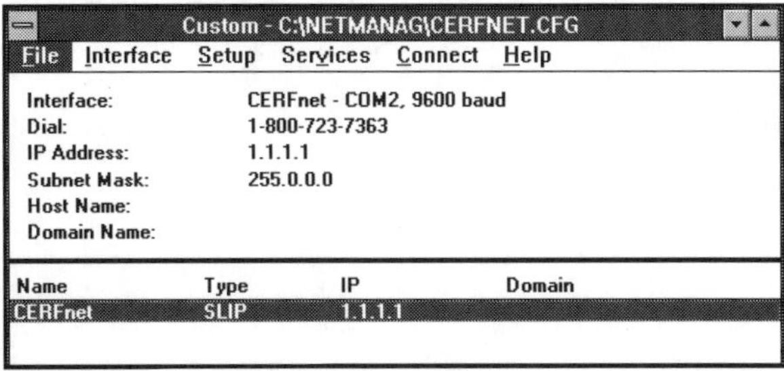

Figure 26.5 *Custom interface being configured for CerfNet.*

You may duplicate a Custom interface. If you are going to have multiple records, first configure and debug one record and then duplicate that record for other accounts. Much of the information, such as DNS servers and access telephone numbers, will remain the same. More on interface duplication shortly.

Custom Configuration

Create a custom configuration by selecting File | New. Next, select Interface | Add. The Add Interface dialog box, as shown in Figure 26.6, permits the entry of a name for the new record being created.

The Add Interface dialog box also requires the selection of an account type; your choices are PPP, SLIP, or CSLIP. Select the protocol supported by your access provider. Click on OK and you return to the main Custom dialog box with the newly entered information displayed, along with certain data that Custom fills in "by assumption." Figure 26.7 shows the partially complete entry. Don't be concerned if any of Custom's assumptions are incorrect—all the entries are changeable.

At this point the configuration has not been saved to a file, so let's create one and save the newly entered information. Enter File | Save As, and save your file via the Save Configuration File As dialog box. I would suggest that you name the file with either your IP name or your provider's name. For the sake of consistency, I also recommend keeping the file in the same directory as the

Add Interface
Name: ITACOM
Type: SLIP
OK Cancel

Figure 26.6 *Chameleon's Add Interface dialog box.*

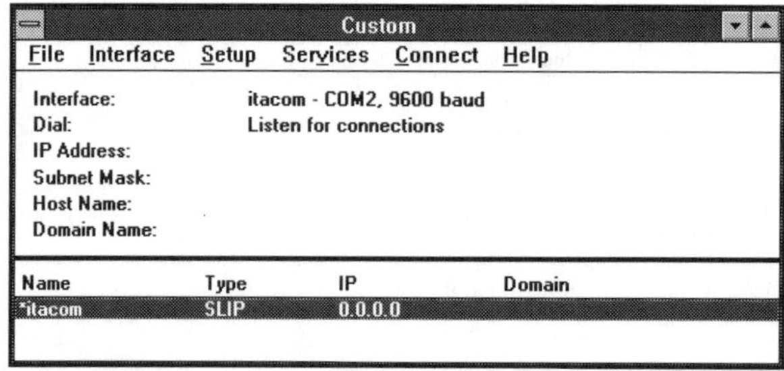

Figure 26.7 *A partially configured record.*

other Sampler files, and retaining the .CFG extension. In this example, we'll save the file as c:\netmanag\itacom.cfg.

Configuration Parameter Entry

We now enter the details of configuration. This is the only aspect of Chameleon that I dislike. The configuration process forces you to wade through what seems like a never-ending series of the same old sequence: Click on a menu bar item, enter data, and then click on OK. Why this process wasn't implemented as one data entry screen totally escapes me.

Chameleon's menu bar contains two entries that will take us through the required steps—namely, Setup and Services. Figure 26.8 shows Setup's drop-down menu. Let's start at the top and enter the necessary entries.

IP Address

Every *active* Internet node must have a unique IP address, a set of four number groups separated by periods. Active is the operative word in the previous sentence. You may have a unique IP address that belongs to you whether

Figure 26.8 *The Setup drop-down menu.*

you're logged into the Internet or not, or you may use an IP address selected from a pool of IP addresses when you log on to your provider's system. We described the nature of IP addresses earlier in this chapter. Enter your unique IP address, if you have one, in the IP Address field. If your IP address is dynamically assigned to you from an address pool, your provider will give you the correct address to insert into this field; it's typically 1.1.1.1.

Again, my unique IP address for ITACOM.DIGEX.NET is 199.125.129.17.

Subnet Mask

In what may be the gross oversimplification of the year, we can consider the subnet mask as a mechanism for determining if a network address is "on the local computer" or "not on the local computer." This parameter, which is a local area network thing, is not normally used for SLIP/PPP and it is "grayed out" and not accessible from the Chameleon Sampler's menu. As I mentioned earlier in this chapter, if you're accessing the Internet through a Local Area Network, you cannot use the Chameleon Sampler package.

Host Name

SLIP/PPP connections using a unique IP address do not normally need a host name. If you are accessing the Internet using a dynamically assigned IP, your provider will supply the required host name. This is frequently your user ID.

Domain Name

The domain name is the part of an Internet address uniquely identifying a particular company or organization. Most Internet domains are in the form:

```
organization.type
```

An example of a domain name is netmanage.com—the domain of the people who created Chameleon. The type portion is typically com (commercial), edu (educational), net (network provider), or org (organization, for nonprofits and other bodies). There are other special-purpose types as well, but those four are the bulk of the ones you'll see.

My unique Internet address is:

```
itacom.digex.net
```

My host name would be considered:

```
itacom
```

My domain name would therefore be:

```
digex.net
```

Let's check our progress. Figure 26.9 shows the result of entering all the above parameters. Again, don't be concerned with mistakes; everything is modifiable.

Communications Parameters

Collectively, Setup's drop-down menu items Port, Modem, Dial, and Login are the Chameleon's communications parameters. Let's look at each of these in turn.

Port Settings

Figure 26.10 shows the parameters available in the Port Settings dialog box. The Baud Rate and Connector parameters are a function of the modem your PC is using and the serial port associated with the modem. The other parameters are furnished by your Internet provider. If you have a 14.4 Kbps modem, check the 19200 radio button—this may seem counterintuitive, but it's the way it works.

If you're not sure of the port on which your modem works, use the Microsoft MSD program. Check the mouse setting from within MSD, and if the mouse is on COM1, your modem most likely connects to COM2. If your mouse is on COM2,

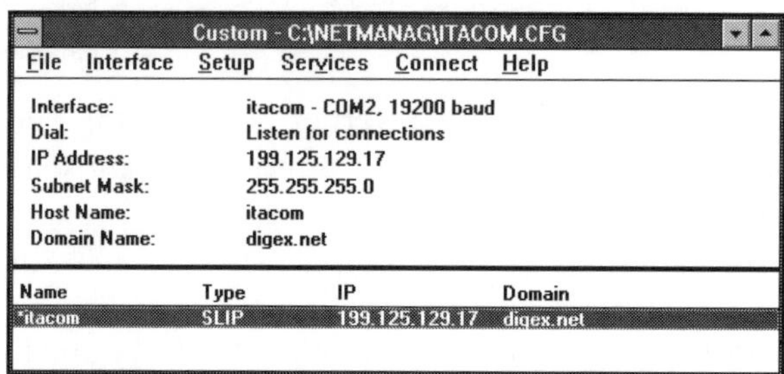

Figure 26.9 *Setup's drop-down menu.*

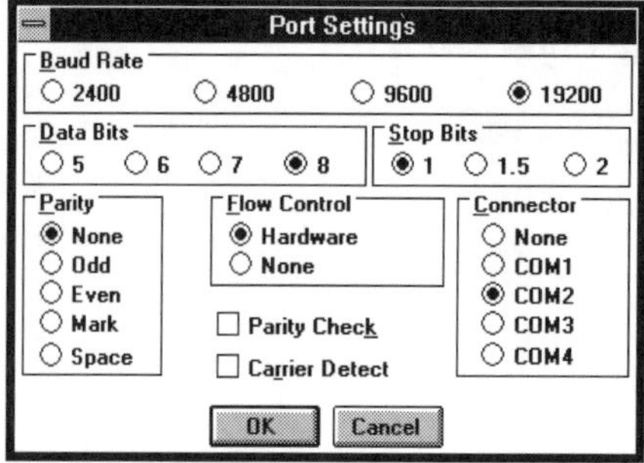

Figure 26.10 *Chameleon's Port Settings dialog box.*

your modem probably connects to COM1. You may also (though it is less common) have your modem on COM3 or COM4. Check any documentation that came with your machine for clues. If all else fails, you may have to simply try a port setting and see if you can hear the modem dial when you attempt to connect. You can usually go with the default values for the other Port settings, unless your provider specifically tells you otherwise. SLIP, PPP, and CSLIP are all 8-bit protocols and must have settings of 8 data bits, 1 stop bit, and no parity.

Modem Settings

Figure 26.11 shows the Modem Settings dialog box. The data in the Modem Settings dialog box are totally dependent on the characteristics of your individual modem. That's good news. If you have a Telebit or MultiTech modem (not likely if you're using a PC), check the appropriate radio button; otherwise, check the Hayes button. Hayes is the 800-pound gorilla of modem manufacturers; almost all other modem manufacturers comply with the Hayes standard. If you're not sure if your modem is Hayes compatible, leave the default setting as is and say a short prayer. Leave everything else as it is.

Dial Settings

Figure 26.12 shows the Dial Settings dialog box. Enter your provider's primary data telephone number. You may want to create duplicate records if your provider has multiple numbers that do not automatically roll over to each other. The standard Hayes modem dial string conventions can be used in this field. A comma indicates a delay. The characters "(", ")", and "-" are ignored

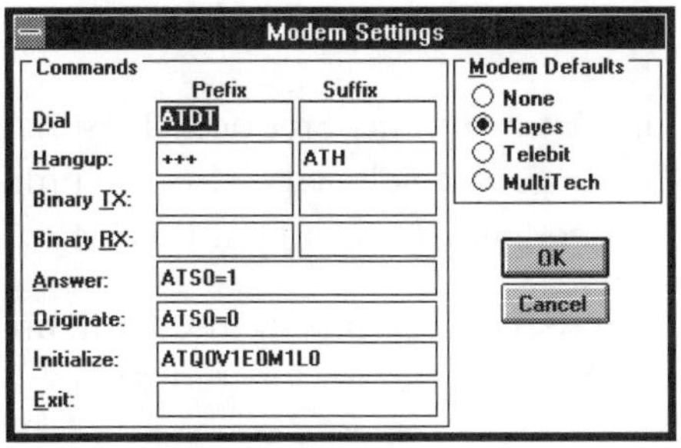

Figure 26.11 *Chameleon's Modem Settings dialog box.*

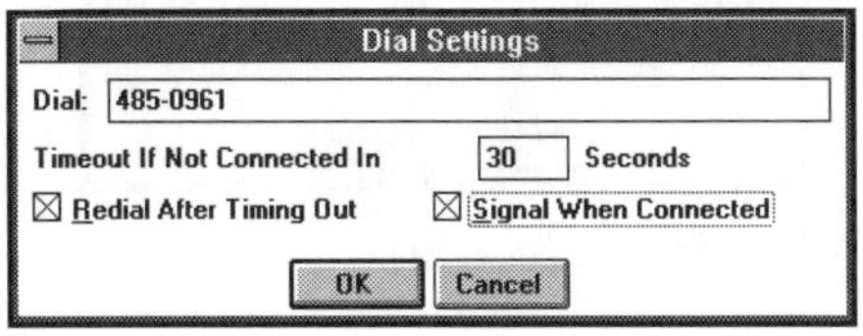

Figure 26.12 *Chameleon's Dial Settings dialog box.*

but may be used for readability. If you must dial 9 for an outside connection, wait for a new dial tone, then dial the number 444-5555 and enter the string 9,444-5555. Additional commas generate additional delay if needed. For example: 9,1(609)294-0320 would instruct the modem to first dial 9 and pause for a dial tone, then 1 and area code 609, and finally, the number 294-0320.

Chameleon considers you successfully connected when the script associated with this entry runs to completion. The Timeout If Not Connected In field is typically set to about 30 seconds—no need to listen to a busy signal.

Login Settings

Figure 21.13 shows the Login dialog box. Your Internet provider provides the entries for User Name and User Password. The entry for the Startup Command field is the command entered to start SLIP or PPP after getting to a shell account's system prompt. Since my account is a dedicated SLIP account (not a shell account) the field is left blank. In many cases the command is simply "SLIP" or "PPP" but to be sure you will have to ask your provider.

This completes the entry of Chameleon's communications parameters. There are only two more dialog boxes. There is light at the end of this particular tunnel, unless you're a pessimist and assume that that's a train heading our way.

Domain Name Servers

We now move to the Services menu in the Custom program. If you have trouble getting a SLIP/PPP connection up and going, there's a reasonably good chance the trouble lies within this section. Double check all entries, and then go back and double check again.

The menu items Default Gateway and Frequent Destinations don't apply to SLIP/PPP connections and are not selectable from within the Sampler package. The only entry that needs keyboarding at this point is Domain Servers.

Selecting Services | Domain Servers brings up the Domain Servers dialog box. A Domain Name Server (DNS) is a server located somewhere on the Internet,

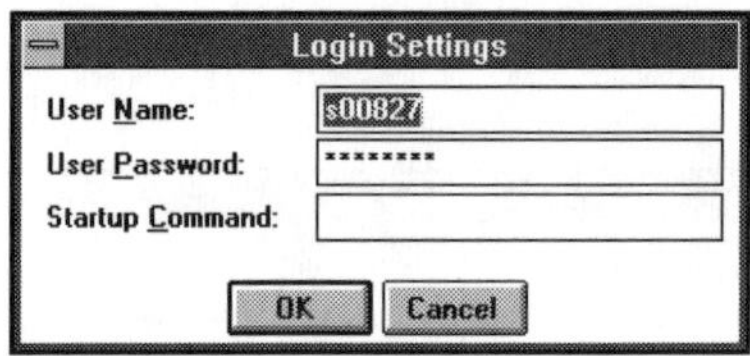

***Figure 26.13** Chameleon's Login Settings dialog box.*

whose job it is to take an Internet address in the form of ITACOM.DIGEX.NET and return a numeric IP address in a form often called a *quad*, such as 199.125.129.17. This quad is attached to packets sent out on the Internet. Your Internet provider will give you the IP address for at least one DNS; get three if your provider can provide more than one. In case Chameleon tries a domain server and finds it busy, it will try the other two addresses if it has them. Enter any DNS addresses you have in the Domain Servers dialog box, as shown in Figure 26.14.

After entering the DNS information, don't forget to go back and double check every item very carefully. One digit out of place will render an address completely worthless.

Interface Name

The last item in this phase of configuration is the Interface Name, and for that we have to return to the Setup menu. The Interface Name is the name of a set of parameters that taken together define one distinct "road into the Internet" via Chameleon. Chameleon allows you to define more than one interface to allow you to dial into more than one Internet account from the same machine. This may not be useful to you as a private individual, but if you ever have to set up a departmental Internet presence, it can be *very* handy.

Bring up the Interface Name dialog box by selecting Setup | Interface Name. This entry ties two things together, the Name as shown on the bottom line of the Custom window and an entry in the slip.ini file, which we'll get to in a minute. In this example we'll stick with the name "itacom". Enter it in the edit field; it's the only field in the dialog box.

The configuration file entry parameters are finally completed. Select File | Save to save the file as itacom.cfg.

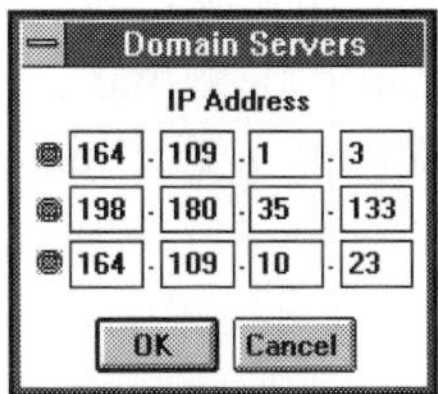

Figure 26.14 *Chameleon's Domain Servers dialog box.*

Chameleon's Scripts and slip.ini

If you have never worked with a script file, be prepared to age about two years in an evening. You should probably take a laugh break every once in a while—humor is my antidote to aging.

The Chameleon scripting feature permits the creation of unique dialogs between Chameleon and your provider's network. If you are fortunate to have a provider with a preconfigured script for Chameleon, your Chameleon installation is completed. If not, carry on.

In the directory where you installed your Chameleon files is a file called slip.ini. In the fashion of most Windows-style .INI files, it is divided into a series of sections, each of which has its name enclosed in square brackets. Each section name line is followed by a line beginning with "SCRIPT=" that contains the description of the dialog between Chameleon and your provider's system. The last line in each section (starting with "TYPE=") tells Chameleon the protocol type, typically SLIP or PPP. Let's start by taking a look at an example section of slip.ini:

```
[DEFAULT]
SCRIPT=login: $u$r word: $p$r
TYPE=SLIP

[AlterNet]
SCRIPT=login: $u$r word: $p$r enabled $2$r
TYPE=PPP

[itacom]
SCRIPT=login: $u$r word: $p$r
TYPE=SLIP
```

As you can see here, each configuration entry in slip.ini begins with a section name enclosed in square brackets. There is one section for each preconfigured entry and one section for each Interface Name item entered during the setup sequence that we've just been through. The first entry in an unmodified slip.ini file is called DEFAULT:

```
[DEFAULT]
```

DEFAULT assumes a very simple dialog between Chameleon and the host, and is the entry used when creating a new entry to correspond with a new Interface Name that you enter. If all of your new entries are identical, but different from the DEFAULT section, you might want to manually edit the DEFAULT section before "cloning" DEFAULT to those new entries. The second entry in the portion of slip.ini shown above is the preconfigured entry if your provider is AlterNet. The third section in the example listing was the one added when we entered the Interface Name "itacom", as discussed earlier in this chapter.

Script Syntax

Each section in slip.ini has the same basic form:

```
[section-name]
SCRIPT=<dialog>
TYPE=<SLIP or PPP or CSLIP>
```

The syntax of Chameleon's script language is fairly simple. In my description here, an item appearing in upper-case letters indicates that you enter the capitalized item *exactly* as shown. You must substitute your own entries between any "<>" pair. (Your substitution does not include the "<>" characters.) The syntax descriptor

```
SCRIPT=<dialog>
```

indicates that you must enter "SCRIPT=" exactly as shown. The "<dialog>" entry indicates that you will be filling in your installation-specific information within the "<>" pair. (More on this in just a minute.)

The entry

```
TYPE=<SLIP | PPP | CSLIP>
```

indicates a new line must begin with "TYPE=" and be followed by one (but only one) of the three choices, which must also be entered exactly as shown since they are capitalized. The character " | " indicates "or," and is *not* included when you enter the item.

Chameleon scripting language instructions take the form of:

```
SCRIPT=<provider-send>  <you-answer> ... more of the same.
```

Individual items are separated by at least one space or tab character. Let's look at an example:

```
SCRIPT=login: $u$r word: $p$r
```

First, the line must begin with "SCRIPT=". There is no space allowed either before or after the "=". What follows is a series of some number of "<provider-send> <you-answer>" pairs. (Only one such pair is shown in the example above.) The "<provider-send> <you-answer>" pair must be separated by at least one space or tab. The gist of it is that when Chameleon detects a <provider-send> string, it immediately transmits the corresponding <you-answer> string. Note that the strings are *not* enclosed in quotes.

In the example above, "login:" is a <provider-send> string that Chameleon expects to see during the dialog with your provider. The next item, ur, is the corresponding <you-answer> string. It contains two "replacement parameters" into which Chameleon substitutes an appropriate value. "$u" tells Chameleon to send the user ID. This is what you entered into the User Name field in the Login Settings dialog box. "$r" tells Chameleon to send a carriage return, which is the equivalent of pressing the Enter (or Return, hence the "r") key.

Think of it as robotic typing: If you were manually entering your user ID, you would enter a string containing your user ID and then press Enter, indicating the completion of the entry.

In the same example, the next entry

```
word: $p$r
```

indicates that Chameleon next looks for "word:", as in the last portion of "Password:", and replies by substituting the User Password value you entered in the Login Settings dialog box in place of the "$p" item. The $r once again instructs Chameleon to send a carriage return after the password.

If your account is a dedicated SLIP/PPP account, that (thankfully) may be all there is to a Chameleon script. The line that follows the SCRIPT line is simply the communications protocol used when Chameleon and your provider's network talk to one another. The entry is in the form of:

```
TYPE=SLIP
```

Again, no spaces on either side of the equal sign.

Here is the complete listing of Chameleon script symbols, which are sometimes called *escapes*:

Symbol	Description
$b	Cause a short "break" on the line
$c	Send the SLIP command
$d	Send the phone number
$f	Define a prompt
$n	Send a new line
$p	Send the password
$r	Send a carriage return
$s	Send a space
$t	Send a tab
$u	Send the user ID
$$	Send the "$" character
$1 - $9	Pause the indicated number of seconds

A Script Example

Let's take a look at a slightly more complicated script example, the [CTS] section contained in slip.ini:

```
[CTS]
SCRIPT=login: $u$r word: $p$r enabled $1$r
TYPE=PPP
```

Put as a table of <provider-send> <you-answer> exchanges, the script would translate as follows:

CTS Sends	Chameleon Replies with
login:	Your user ID and a return
word:	Your password and a return
enabled	A one-second pause and then a return

Building a Script for Charm Net

Our example is all well and good, but it sticks to your ribs better when you cook your own. As an exercise, let's build a script section for slip.ini based upon our experience with a login dialog. We'll take a "captured" login session from my own Charm Net account, and turn it into an actual working Chameleon script.

At Charm Net, my initial login places me in shell account mode. From the Unix shell, issuing the command PPP_ME activates my PPP account. The following is my actual Charm Net shell account login sequence with the PPP_ME command issued at the prompt:

```
                              Charm Net Entrance

Visiting?

     Login as "guest" and press the ENTER key when prompted for Password.

Problems?   Give us a call at (410) 558-3900

Arrival: Emerald on the Matrix

login: lejeune
Password:
Last login: Sat Jan  7 19:44:21 on pts002

Looking For Something?   Try "menu" or "help", Use "pine" for e-mail!

STATUS: GREEN
You have mail
lejeune@CHARM.NET:/home/lejeune> PPP_ME
```

Let's break out the important prompts and replies in script account format.

Charm Net Sends	Chameleon Replies with
login:	My user ID and a return
word:	My password and a return
lejeune>	The command PPP_ME and a return

The slip.ini entry corresponding to this dialog is:

```
[Charm.Net]
SCRIPT=login: $u$r word: $p$r lejeune> PPP_ME$r
TYPE=PPP
```

To verify the correctness of this script, look back to the table of Chameleon symbols and make sure you understand exactly what each portion of the script stands for. If you can do that, you can probably create a script on your own for any conceivable dialog that might occur between your system and your provider while you log in to the Net.

Duplication of Records

The last configuration issue needing discussion is the duplication of a Chameleon interface. There are times when I want to dial into my access provider from another phone number. Everything about my configuration remains the same—with the sole exception of the phone number dialed. I can easily duplicate the interface "itacom" as "call-ac" and make it a separate line on the Custom window. (I use "call-ac" since it's a local call from Atlantic City.)

This involves still another of Custom's main menu items. First, select menu item Interface|Duplicate from the Interface menu. This will bring up the Interface Name dialog box, as shown in Figure 26.15. Enter the new interface name (here, "call-ac") in the Name field. Click on OK.

Once you click on OK, you have two interface records with two names: "itacom" and "call-ac". They are, however, identical in terms of their data fields. Next, modify the fields in the new record that differ from their values in the old record. In this example, only the telephone number requires changing. Select Setup|Dial and enter the new phone number. Figure 26.16 shows the modified interface. Finally, save the modified configuration file by selecting the menu item File|Save.

After duplicating an interface, a new section using the interface name is created in slip.ini.

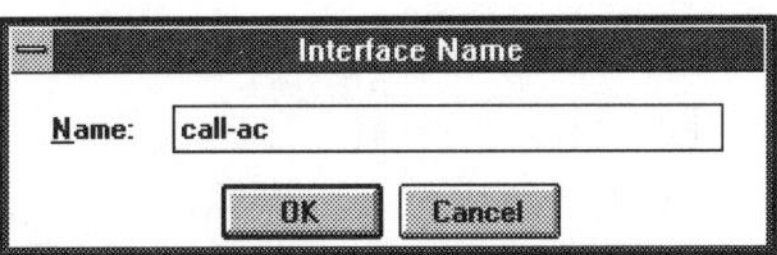

Figure 26.15 *Entering a new interface name.*

Custom - C:\NETMANAG\ITACOM.CFG

File Interface Setup Services Connect Help

Interface:	call-ac - COM2, 19200 baud
Dial:	348-6203
IP Address:	199.125.129.17
Subnet Mask:	255.255.255.0
Host Name:	itacom
Domain Name:	digex.net

Name	Type	IP	Domain
*itacom	SLIP	199.125.129.17	digex.net
call-ac	SLIP	199.125.129.17	digex.net

Figure 26.16 *Custom displaying two interfaces.*

Here's one additional example of how Chameleon's system of multiple interfaces may be used. Assume two people share the same computer. However, they have different accounts with the same Internet provider. Enter the configuration information for one user and save the file containing that interface. Next, duplicate the interface you initially created, and change the user ID and Password fields. Or, assume you have accounts with two different providers. Duplicate an interface and in the copied interface, change those fields containing data specific to your second provider. Interface fields not pertinent to your second provider remain unchanged—your modem information, for example.

Connecting with a Chameleon Interface

Once you get an interface fully configured, including its script, using it to connect is pretty simple. Bring up the Custom program showing the available interfaces as lines in the bottom pane of the window. (Look at Figure 26.16 for a Custom window with two interfaces in it.) Highlight the interface that you want to connect through by single-clicking on its line. The highlight bar should move to that line. Make sure the line you want is highlighted!

Then select the Connect item on the main menu. Chameleon will take it from there! You should hear your modem dial the phone, and at some point you may see (this varies with providers) portions of your login sequence on your screen.

How to Do It Yourself

I've described all you need to know to configure your own Chameleon script. Yes, it's a hairy business, but that's sometimes what it takes in these admittedly "wild frontier" days of the Internet. (In another few years, Internet access will be almost as boring as accounting software.) Here are some pointers for going about the process yourself.

First, log into your provider using a plain communications package like Microsoft Terminal. Try to "capture" the session, so that you can print an actual display of characters both coming and going. If you can't capture the session, take notes on a pad of every character you see come down from your provider's system, and every character you type in response. That will be the basis of your script.

Translate the dialog you recorded into a Chameleon script by perusing the table of script symbols shown earlier in this chapter and creating a series of <provider-send> <you-answer> pairs in the SCRIPT= line in slip.ini. Save the file to disk—and then try it by connecting to your provider using the interface you just created.

If your script can't establish a connection, usually the script will "freeze" partway through. You can determine where it freezes if you use Chameleon's session log feature. Select Setup | Log. This will open a session log. The entire dialog between Chameleon and your provider's computer will be saved in the log—and displayed in the log window while you watch. Next, click on Connect.

The sequence will begin, and you can observe what happens in the log window. When the system freezes, click on the Save button in the log window, give a name to your session file, and close the window. Then manually shut down the modem (the power switch does a good job here) and print your log file. Carefully check the interchange in the last portion recorded in the log.

Some common configuration problems include spaces where there shouldn't be any, and no space where there should be one. A missing $r carriage return is also a common omission. If everything stops after your user ID is transmitted, it's a good bet there is no $r following the $u. A space between two symbols that belong together (that is, $u $r rather than ur) will cause the same problem, since a space initiates a new command. In this instance, Chameleon sends the user ID and then begins waiting for a prompt ending in $r. (Can you tell why?) The remote system is still waiting for the user ID; it doesn't recognize the characters already sent as the user ID string until the string is terminated with a carriage return. If the last component of your script file activates a command, such as "PPP", a log session should show the cursor advancing to the next line if the command sent by Chameleon was in fact received by your provider. If the cursor doesn't advance, look for a missing $r. If there is in fact a $r where it should be, you may be having a timing problem. Try adding another $r.

Debugging is mostly a matter of trial and error, but it's a simple enough process that it shouldn't take more than a few tries to pin down what's gone wrong. In a pinch, your provider may be able to help you—and in fact, it's a rare provider these days who doesn't have a "canned" slip.ini file containing an interface to their system. With all the copies of Chameleon out there, it would be insanely bad business not to.

LET'S REVIEW

Netscape and most good Web browsers communicate directly with the Internet through a protocol called TCP/IP (Transmission Control Protocol/Internet Protocol). A system connected to the Internet through TCP/IP is actually a part of the Internet, albeit a small and intermittently connected part.

TCP/IP connections to the Internet are handled by Internet providers through accounts known as SLIP (Serial Line Internet Protocol) and PPP (Point to Point Protocol), which are similar and basically interchangeable. Both work equally well with Netscape.

When you obtain a SLIP or PPP account, your provider will either give you a unique set of numbers called an IP address, or a "dummy" number that allows you to draw an IP address from a pool of free addresses when you log in. If you have your own unique IP address, you access the Internet through static addressing; drawing an address from an address pool is called dynamic addressing. For people who connect to the Internet intermittently, dynamic addressing makes a lot of sense and is becoming much more common.

Windows applications that connect to the Internet via TCP/IP are usually WinSock-compatible. WinSock is a specification for Windows communication through TCP/IP. The Chameleon Sampler (which is included on this book's companion CD-ROM) is an implementation of the WinSock specification.

Your provider will probably be able to hand you a configuration file that will enable Chameleon to communicate with their remote system. If not, you will have to configure a file manually. This may be done using the instructions in this chapter. Such a configuration may have to be debugged by trial and error. Get a configuration from your provider (or from someone else who's already done the job successfully) if you can!

Last, but certainly not least, don't even think of going it alone without Frank Hecker's wonderful document, *Personal Internet Access Using SLIP or PPP: How You Use It, How It Works.* It's available at:

```
ftp://ftp.digex.net/pub/access/hecker/internet/slip-ppp.txt
```

The HTML version is at:

```
http://www.access.digex.net/~hecker/papers/slip-ppp.html
```

As Karl Malden would say, "Don't leave home without" Charm Net's Web page devoted to Internet connectivity. The URL for their Personal IP page is:

```
http://www.charm.net/pip.html
```

One last tip, when working on a project as complicated as configuring a TCP/IP stack, copious amount of coffee—or Jolt—may not truly help but they sure keep you awake.

Installing Netscape and Win32s

There are some common steps involved in installing Windows software from the Internet. Netscape and Win32s are two good examples of this truism. But, there are also some major differences....

The amount of work you'll have to do to get up on the Web depends heavily on what your provider offers you in addition to a dialup line. Many providers will give you an install diskette with a TCP/IP stack and a Web browser right on it, ready to install. That certainly makes your installation easier, but you can't always count on such technological generosity. In many cases, you'll just have to hunt down a browser on your own.

There's an additional wrinkle: The newer versions of Netscape may require prior installation of the latest version of Win32s. Netscape comes in 16- and 32-bit versions. However, the 16-bit version, n16e11n.exe, doesn't require Win32s. Here's a word of caution concerning Netscape and Win32s. If you want to run the 16-bit version of Netscape without Win32s, and Win32s is already installed on your system, double check to insure no other applications are using Win32s before you attempt to delete it from your system.

To run one of the 32-bit versions of Netscape with 16-bit Windows 3.1, you must first install Microsoft's Win32s compatibility module. So before I explain how to install Netscape, I should explain more about Win32s, including where to find it and how to "mount" it.

DO YOU NEED WIN32S?

If you intend to run Netscape on a system that needs Win32s for other applications, you must install Win32s. There is no charge for the software if you are a licensed Windows or WFW user. If you are going to run Netscape on a system where other applications don't require Win32s, or if you are running Windows NT or Windows 95, you will not need to install Win32s.

Bear with me, at this point, because some of the details of Win32s tend to get confusing. For instance, there are several different versions of Win32s floating around. As an added complication, it's often difficult to distinguish among the different versions of Win32s just by looking at them on a name-by-name basis. On many FTP sites, the same name represents different versions of Win32s. There are basically three different versions worthy of note. All versions have many mutations. The latest version of Win32s contains the Microsoft Object Linking and Embedding (OLE) 2.0 extension. You will need Win32s version 1.20 or later installed on your system.

First, verify that Win32s is already installed on your system. See if there is a win32s.ini file in your Windows system directory. (Try looking in the c:\windows\system directory.) If Win32s is not installed, you will need to install it. If you find a win32s.ini file, check its contents. The first three lines should look something like this:

```
[Win32s]
Setup=1
Version=1.20.123.0
```

The third line specifies the version—in this case, 1.20.

If you have version 1.20 or later installed, you're home free. You can actually use an earlier version of Win32s with some earlier versions of Netscape, but I'm assuming you want the latest and, hopefully, best of everything.

Installing Win32s

A later version of Win32s is provided on the companion CD-ROM so that you can install it on your computer. You can use the software provided on the CD-ROM or download a copy of Win32s from the Internet. Here is one reliable FTP site where you can get a copy of Win32s:

```
ftp.ncsa.uiuc.edu:/Web/Mosiac/Windows
```

Once you have the Win32s software, follow these steps to install it:

1. Run the program setup.exe. (This program is stored on the comapnion CD-ROM in the directory \tools\win32s.)
2. The installation program then tries to determine the location of your Windows system files. Setup displays the c:\windows\system path, as shown in Figure 27.1, and informs you that it will create a subdirectory named WIN32S subordinate to the c:\windows\system path. If you click on Continue, a series of progress messages is displayed as the Setup program uncompresses the files and places these files in the appropriate places.

After the installation runs to its conclusion you'll receive a completion message. After those kind words, click on OK. The next dialog box asks if you want to install Freecell. Click on Continue to install this game. There are two reasons to install Freecell: It's a great game and you can use it to verify the successful installation of Win32s.

After the installation of Win32s and Freecell are complete, Setup asks you to allow it to exit and restart Windows. After Windows restarts, take a few minutes to play Freecell. A brief aside: Freecell is a solitaire game that involves both luck and strategy. Strategy is more important than luck when playing Freecell, as opposed to regular Solitaire.

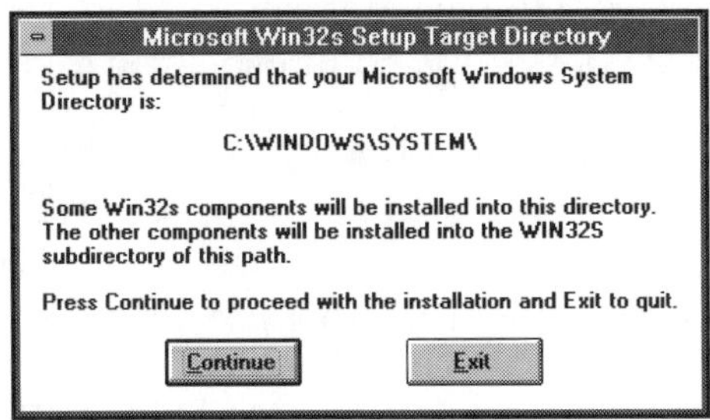

Figure 27.1 *Win32s Target Directory dialog box.*

Before you install Netscape or any other WinSock-compliant Web browser, you need to ensure that both you and your system meet a few requirements:

- Microsoft Windows, version 3.1 or later, must be installed on your computer and properly configured.
- You need to know how to use FTP to transfer files from a remote location, unless you have a Web browsing client already installed on your PC.
- It would be nice if you know how to use an ASCII editor, such as DOS EDIT or Windows Notepad.
- A TCP/IP stack, such as the Internet Chameleon or Trumpet WinSock, needs to be installed on you PC and must be properly configured.
- You must have an Internet connection that supports transmissions to a TCP/IP stack.
- You may also need the prior installation of Win32s for some browsers.

INSTALLING NETSCAPE

After you review the steps for one or more of these installations, you'll have a good instructional template that you can use to install other browsers.

Most Web browsers, including Netscape, are WinSock-compliant applications. This means that your computer must speak the language of networks—Transmission Control Protocol/Internet Protocol (TCP/IP). A TCP/IP stack is essentially a piece of "middleware" that allows your system to communicate with the Net. If you already have a TCP/IP stack installed, such as Trumpet or Chameleon, you're in good shape. Here's a good check to determine whether a TCP/IP stack is already installed on your system: Check your system for a file named WINSOCK.DLL. If you don't find this file, you're not yet ready to install a Web browser. First, read and work through Chapter 26, *SLIP/PPP and the Chameleon Sampler*. If your TCP/IP stack is up and running, you're ready to forge ahead.

Before you begin the installation of any browser, you must have available your full e-mail address, the domain name of your SMTP mail server, and the domain name of your NNTP news server. The domain names are available from your system administrator or Internet provider.

There are some common steps involved in obtaining and installing all Windows software from the Internet. To provide you with a conceptual model, I'll begin by using the procedures for locating and installing Netscape. In general, the installation process involves the following six steps:

1. Locate the Internet site that contains the desired program.
2. Download the file (FTP it) to a dedicated directory on your PC.
3. Uncompress the file, if necessary.
4. Add the program's parameters and icon to an existing Windows group.
5. Configure the program.
6. Test the program and, if necessary, debug the configuration.

Step 1 - Locate the Internet Site

To make this step as simple as possible, I'll provide you with the site where the desired browser package is stored. (I'll do this in Step 2.) By the way, the CD-ROM supplied with this book contains a file named urb-menu.html. This file is a Netscape bookmark list containing URLs for a large variety of interesting Web sites, including FTP URLs for connecting to all the sites mentioned in this chapter. The URLs point to the specific directory containing the target files. This file is a standard HTML file and may be viewed by any Web browser. If you're relatively new at downloading files, you might want to review Chapter 16, *Finding and Retrieving Files*, before proceeding. Chapter 16 is a complete tutorial for developing the skills necessary to locate information and programs on the Internet.

Step 2 - Download the Desired File to Your PC

I've made this point elsewhere in this chapter and in other chapters, but it bears repeating before we continue: Since FTPed files are typically obtained from Unix-based computers, be precise in your use of upper-case and lower-case letters in specifying file and directory names. In this demo example, version information is embedded in the file name, which helps in determining whether you're downloading the most current version of a file. The latest version of Netscape , as we go to press, is named n16e11n.exe, telling us that it's alpha version 1.1n. Netscape frequently has beta versions of the browser available. The naming convention previously used by Netscape is n16eVVbN.exe, where VV is the version number and N is the beta number. n16e11b3 was the last beta before the alpha version of version 1.1 was released. I would suspect the next beta would be n16e12b1. Beta versions tend to have more features but also more bugs. Should you use a beta or alpha version? This depends on if you like to live dangerously. I keep both versions on my system. Unfortunately, there is an abundance of obsolete software on the Internet. Try to download your browser of choice from the sites listed in this chapter because they are known for providing the most up-to-date versions.

The FTP domain name for downloading Netscape is ftp.netscape.com. The directory path to the software is /netscape/windows. The URL for downloading the file for the 16-bit version is:

```
ftp://ftp.netscape.com/netscape/windows/n16e11n.exe
```

The URL for the 32-bit version is:

```
ftp://ftp.netscape.com/netscape/windows/n32e11n.exe
```

If you are downloading the Mac or Unix version of Netscape, back up one directory level by clicking on:

```
Up to higher level directory
```

Then, the Unix and Mac files will be listed.

I would suggest you enter the URL without the filename since it may have changed before you read this. Netscape is a very busy site, especially after a new release of the software. I have built a menu with the latest version information as well as a listing of world-wide Netscape mirror sites. The URL for this document is:

```
http://www.charm.net/~lejeune/get-net.html
```

Prior to downloading a new package, create a temporary directory to hold the compressed file. Let's assume we create a directory temp on our g: drive.

If you are already cruising with Netscape or another Web browser and just want to get a different browser or an updated one, enter the URL shown above and press Enter. When arriving at the directory listing, click on the latest version of Netscape. Since this file has an .EXE extension, Netscape realizes it cannot process the file and displays the Unknown File Type dialog box as shown in Figure 27.2. Select the Save to Disk option. Next, you are prompted with a dialog box requesting the parameters for the PC end of the

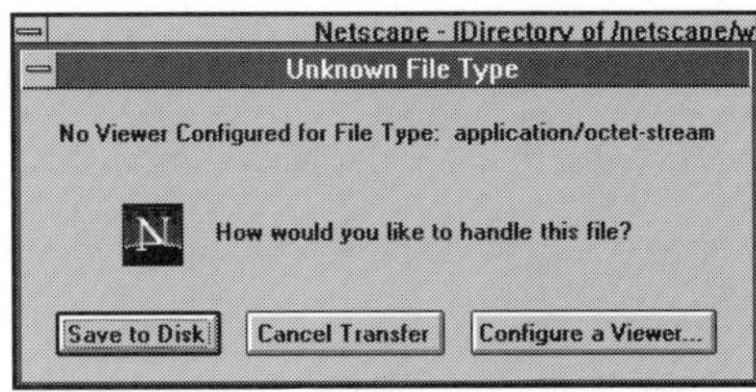

***Figure 27.2** Netscape displays the "Unknown" dialog box when it doesn't recognize an extension.*

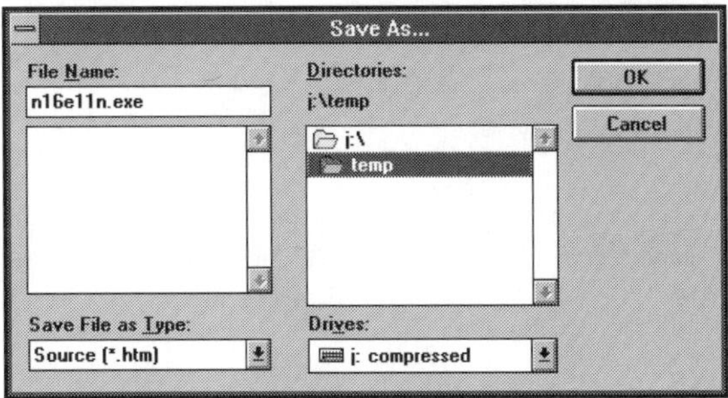

***Figure 27.3** The Save As dialog box.*

transfer. Figure 27.3 shows the Save As dialog box. The file name defaults to the same name as the remote file, if it is in a legal DOS format. You select a target file name and directory path just as you would in any other Windows application. Click on OK and the transfer starts.

If you do not yet have a Web browser, or if you prefer using FTP to transfer files, here's the approach. The following is the actual transcription of the FTP session used to download n16e11n.exe. In the first line, the "unix%" is a generic Unix prompt; your prompt will probably be different.

```
unix1% ftp ftp.netscape.com
Connected to ftp1.netscape.com.
220 ftp1.netscape.com FTP server (Version wu-2.4(3) Tue Dec 27 17:53:56 PST 1994
) ready.
500 'AUTH KERBEROS_V4': command not understood.
KERBEROS_V4 rejected as an authentication type
Name (ftp.netscape.com:lejeune): anonymous
331 Guest login ok, send your complete e-mail address as password.
Password:
230-Welcome to the Netscape Communications Corporation FTP server.
```

```
230-
230-If you have any odd problems, try logging in with a minus sign (-)
230-as the first character of your password.  This will turn off a feature
230-that may be confusing your ftp client program.
230-
230-Please send any questions, comments, or problem reports about
230-this server to ftp@netscape.com.
230-
230 Guest login ok, access restrictions apply.
Remote system type is UNIX.
Using binary mode to transfer files.
ftp> cd /netscape/windows
******  Much Licensing Information Deleted to Save Space ******
250-
250 CWD command successful.
ftp> binary
200 Type set to I.
ftp> get n16e11n.exe
227 Entering Passive Mode (198,95,249,66,40,38)
150 Opening BINARY mode data connection for n16e11n.exe (1599738 bytes).
226 Transfer complete.
1599738 bytes received in 81 seconds (19 Kbytes/s)
ftp> quit
221 Goodbye.
```

If you have FTPed this file to your Internet provider's system, you must next get it to your PC. There are many variations for doing this, so it's impossible to enumerate specific steps. Basically, you need to make sure your PC and your service provider's computer speak the same protocol language. Most Internet providers support the Zmodem protocol, as do most communications packages such as ProComm. In a basic sense, you typically start a transfer by entering

```
unix% sz file-name
```

at your Unix prompt, where *file-name* is the name of the file to be transferred, in this case n16e11n.exe. You may then receive a message to "Start your transfer." The next step is to have your communications program recognize that a Zmodem transfer has been started. Most Windows communications programs have an icon with a down arrow pointing to a file folder. When you have transferred the file to your PC, put it into a temporary directory as described above. To recap, I'll assume that you have successfully transferred n16e11n.exe to your PC and that it's domiciled as g:\temp\n16e11n.exe. Next, make g:\temp your default path and we're ready for the next step.

Step 3 - Uncompress the File

Almost without exception, large FTPable files are stored in compressed format to save disk space and transfer time. A compressed file is about 50 percent the size of its uncompressed version. In this case, the .EXE extension indicates that n16e11n.exe is in self-extracting form. From the command line, enter

```
G:\TEMP>N16E11N
```

and the extraction process will begin. Most of the other programs mentioned in this chapter have a .ZIP extension. To uncompress these browsers, you will need a program named PKUNZIP, WinZip, or a PKZIP-compatible uncompression utility. If you don't have PKUNZIP, or if you're unsure of how to use it, read Chapter 16, *Finding and Retrieving Files.*

Step 4 - Add the Program's Icon to Windows

This step explains the Windows installation component. The details in this step generally apply to installing any Windows programs, not just Web browsers. There are two possible paths for this step:

- The program may install into its own Windows group, which it creates during installation.
- The program may allow itself to be copied into an existing Windows group.

Before proceeding with this step, play it safe and look for a file named readme.txt or install.txt. There could be some variation on these naming themes. Look for one of these instructional files in the directory where the uncompressed program components are stored. We're in luck! The directory holding the expanded Netscape files contains a file named readme.txt. (The expansion of Mosaic produces a file named readme.wri. The .WRI extension tells us the file is in Windows Write format.) We will not always be so lucky; many times there will be no readme.txt, install.txt, or any other installation or setup help file.

If the program creates its own Windows group, you almost always will find a file named setup.exe or install.exe in the directory listing. For our example, there is a setup.exe accompanying this collection of files. If you don't find either of these files, look for a file having an .EXE extension with the basic program name, such as netscape.exe. If there are multiple files with .EXE extensions, the main one should be fairly large.

Make a note of the major file's name and the current directory. Start Windows. If Windows is already running, it's usually a good idea to terminate all other programs before installing a new application.

Since we do have a setup.exe for our example, we will start by selecting the sequence File | Run. Enter the path and name of the program that will start the installation process and click on OK.

Next, a notice appears stating the "Netscape Setup" has started, followed by an instruction to press Continue to install. The installation program will next ask for the path name to install Netscape, as shown in Figure 27.4.

After some disk activity, the setup's next interaction is a request for a Program Group to hold the Netscape icon, as shown in Figure 27.5. I selected my Internet Group, which is the group installed by the Internet Chameleon. I prefer to have all my Internet-related icons in the same program group.

Next, you're asked if you want to read the readme.txt file—a good idea if this is your first fling with Netscape. Finally, the ubiquitous license agreement and then your Netscape icon is displayed in the group you selected, as shown in Figure 27.6.

You can actually start to surf the Web at this point. Assuming that your TCP/IP stack is configured and tested, activate the stack. If you're using the Internet Chameleon or the Chameleon Sampler, activate Custom and click on Connect. After your SLIP/PPP connection has been established, click on Netscape and start surfing. If you have not installed a TCP/IP stack, you will want to read Chapters 25 and 26, *The Fastest Road to the Web* and *SLIP/PPP and the Chameleon Sampler.*

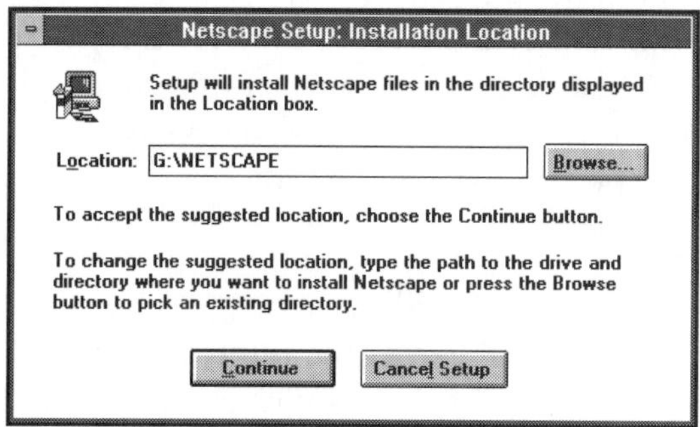

Figure 27.4 *Selecting a location to hold Netscape.*

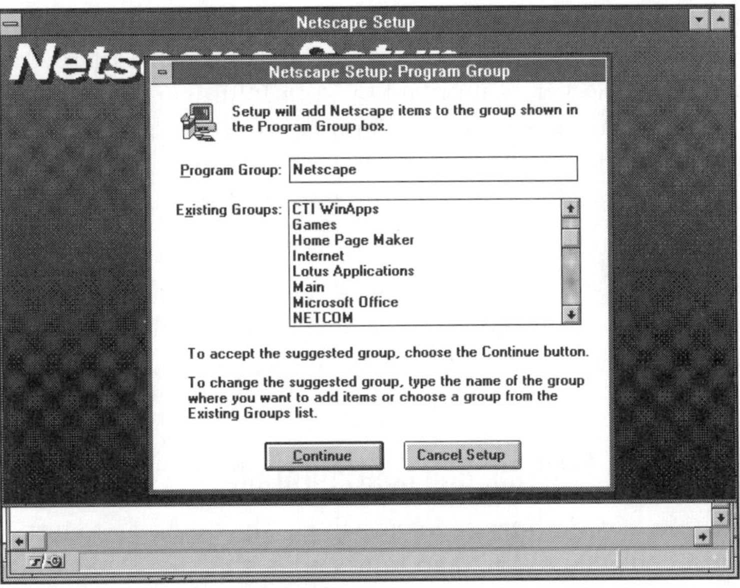

Figure 27.5 Selecting a program group to hold Netscape.

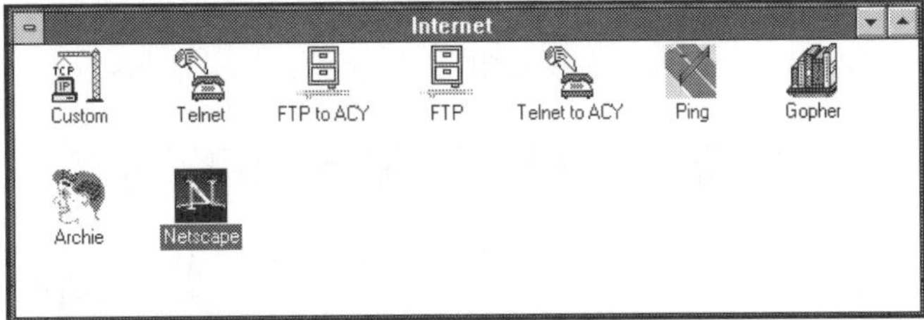

Figure 27.6 The Netscape icon in the program group of your choice.

Step 5 - Configure the Program

Netscape is highly customizable. Read Chapter 22, *Setting Your Netscape Preferences*, to get the inside scoop on configuring Netscape. Most configuration options can wait until you get an idea of how you want the browser to look and act. However, it's a good idea to configure your mail and Usenet news server right away so you can send mail from within Netscape and access Usenet newsgroups.

Execute the sequence Options | Preferences. There are eight different preference dialogs. The menu bar below the title Set Preferences On is a drop-down menu. If the Mail and News dialog box is not the one displayed, click on the down arrow button to the right of the text window and click on Mail and News. Figure 27.7 shows the Mail and News dialog box. Enter your Mail (SMTP) Server as supplied by your Internet provider. Your Name and Your Email entries are obvious entries. If you would like a signature block appended to all your mail messages, use any editor to create one in your Netscape directory, and enter the path and signature filename in the Signature File text box.

The News (NNTP) Server domain name is also furnished by your Internet service provider. Netscape keeps track of your Newsgroups preferences in a directory, the installation default being x:\netscape\news with x: being your Netscape drive.

Step 6 - Test the Program and Configuration

Well, there you have it, Netscape is installed. The best way to test Netscape and its initial configuration is to go forth and surf.

LET'S REVIEW

The Netscape browsers described in this chapter represent some of the major products available. I'm sure others will become available as time passes. The

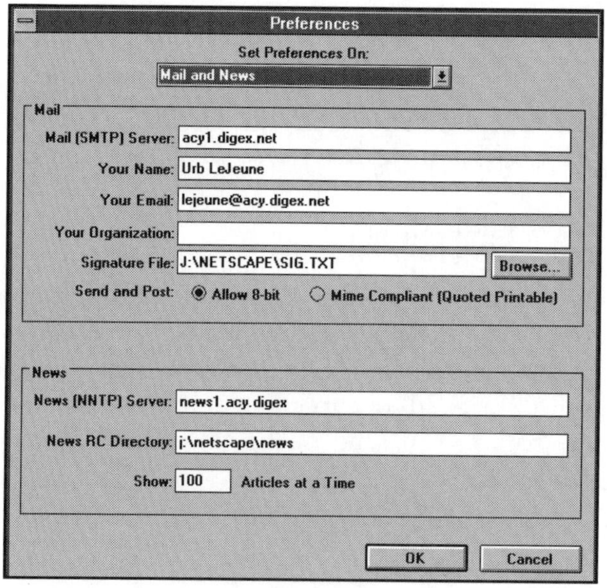

Figure 27.7 *The Mail and News preferences dialog box.*

procedures illustrated in this chapter should help you to install any newcomers, and should be of use in installing almost any Windows program.

I maintain two documents that may be of interest to you. The first, alternative Netscape download sites, may be accessed at:

```
http://www.charm.net/~lejeune/get-net.html
```

The second is actually part of a large menu. It contains the FTP site for all know browsers available for downloading. The menu is located at:

```
http://www.charm.net/~lejeune/urb-menu.html
```

If you find any additions or corrections to either list please let me know. My e-mail address is:

```
lejeune@acy.digex.net
```

Going Off on Your Own

If you're prepared to do a little research, you can find your own connection to the Internet, at the least cost, and in the process get a connection closely tailored to your specific needs.

In Chapter 25, I described Automatic Internet, which is perhaps the fastest and least difficult way ever devised for getting connected to the Internet. For the sake of simplicity, Automatic Internet requires that you choose one of a small group of national Internet service providers who have agreed to be a part of the program. You may not like any of the providers offered—and you may simply prefer to gain the experience of doing everything on your own. That's why this chapter is here: To help you find your own Internet service provider without signing up for Automatic Internet.

Until early 1992, it was very difficult to get access to the Internet unless you had an affiliation with an academic institution, research organization, or government agency. Since that time Internet service providers have begun appearing at an unbelievable rate, at both the national and local level. This is becoming increasingly common. The Atlantic City, NJ area—not exactly the technological capital of New Jersey—didn't have a local Internet provider until early 1994; fourteen months later there were three! Internet access, which was previously the private playground of a nebulous but very exclusive "in-crowd," has become commonplace. Almost anyone desiring an Internet account now has access to one, usually within the local calling area. (Some remote rural areas still must dial long-distance for Internet access—but this is not a problem unique to the Internet.)

Add to this equation the commercial online services. Within a period of six months in early 1995, Prodigy, Americia Online, and CompuServe all offered users access to the graphical wonders of the World Wide Web with their own browsers. This communicating troika potentially added an additional 8 million Web surfers to an already crowded beach front.

FINDING A SERVICE PROVIDER WITHOUT INTERNET ACCESS

In this section, and for the remainder of this chapter, I'll assume that you wish to obtain Internet access via a dialup modem connection. If you are going to need a high-speed direct connection to the Internet or a Local Area Network (LAN) connection, I would suggest you read a book dealing with those subjects. One such book is *Connecting to the Internet* by Susan Estrada (O'Reilly & Associates, 1994).

If you do not now have Internet access, or if you are going to upgrade your access to support Web browsing, you'll want a provider who can furnish the following:

- Dialup connection speeds of at least 14.4 Kbps. The provider should ideally offer 28.8 Kbps (also known as VFast) service even if you do not currently have a 28.8 modem. Modem prices are plunging—don't commit yourself to instant obsolescence.
- Sufficient lines into the server system or systems such that busy signals are rare or unknown. This can be a serious problem with small, cash-starved providers.
- PPP or SLIP accounts. These place you "on the Internet" and allow fast, graphic-oriented connections through Web browsers like Netscape.
- Voice (telephone) help available at least eight hours per day; 12 is better, but unusual.
- Requests for help by e-mail turned around in 24 hours or less. Most offer this, as it takes the heat off phone support to an extent.

Additional desirable factors would include:

- All services available for a local phone call. In larger cities, no problem.
- A SLIP or PPP account that includes Unix shell access for no additional charge. This is becoming frequently common, because it costs the provider so little—few who get addicted to SLIP/PPP accounts make much use of shell. However, if you ever really need to go after something with a shell type of account, it's nice to have one.
- Unlimited access hours for the basic charge (uncommon). Failing unlimited access, four to six hours per day of access at no additional charge. If you need more than that per day, you're either making your living on the Net or have a very serious newsgroup habit!
- There should be no additional charges beyond a flat monthly fee. This condition is becoming increasingly more difficult to find. At a minimum, the provider should offer unlimited access during non-peak hours.

  The capability to publish your own home page on the Web is highly desirable. If you don't think you want to publish now, you will after a few months of surfing.

  The ability to make files available for downloading using anonymous FTP is also desirable.

EXPLORER TIP

Checking Out Peak Times

Peak times for Internet providers are between 6 PM and midnight, local time. This is when the people log on who don't have work-related Internet access. Dial into your prospective provider's data lines during these hours to see if the lines are ever busy.

You do not even want to *think* about running a Web browser through a 2400 baud modem. It's possible with a 9.6 Kbps modem, but it isn't a pretty sight. Go for 28.8 now—the modems don't cost a great deal more than the common $80 14.4 Kbps jobs, and the difference is dramatic. Within a year or two, 14.4 Kbps modems will be doorstops and sold in piles at flea markets for $25. The Internet business has been bandwidth-driven—but now Internet is leading the drive toward more and more bandwidth for less cost.

Local Access Providers

Finding an Internet provider in your local area is easy, especially if you're not a lone wolf and have some connections in the local computer community. Ask at user group meetings, or just find where the local hackers hang out and ask them. If you don't know anyone locally who has an Internet account (and these days, Internet accounts are not the exotica they were even two years ago), call some of your local computer stores for information on providers. Companies providing LAN services are another good source of information. Look in your local Yellow Pages under computer related businesses. ("Online services" is not yet a universal Yellow Pages category.) Another good source of leads is a local university or community college. The MIS or computer services department in a school will certainly know who the local providers are.

ISPs by FAX or Phone

If you have fax access, call Wentworth Worldwide Media's fax system (717-393-2565) for a list of ISPs in your state. Once you're connected to the fax system, voice prompts direct you to your choices. If you or a friend already have e-mail access, you can receive the latest ISP information by sending e-mail to info-deli-server@netcom.comn. Put PDIAL in the subject line and leave the body of the message blank. InterNIC Information Services will also assist you in ferreting out a local ISP. Call them at 800-444-4345 or send an e-mail request to info@is.internic.net.

Locating a Service Provider When You Already Have Internet Access

You might justifiably ask, "If I have an Internet account, why would I want to find an access provider?" You may move—and can't take your account with you short of long-distance dialup. You may be a student leaving school for home and the thought of losing Internet access has you waking up screaming at night. You may think your current provider is a total loser. (Many, alas, are in over their heads on such "minor" issues as customer service and accurate billing.)

You can research local providers from within the Internet. From there, it's almost a sure thing. A comprehensive and well-maintained online guide to Internet access is maintained at Yahoo.com. Point a Web browser to:

```
http://akebono.stanford.edu/yahoo/Business/Corporations/nternet_Access_Providers
```

Figure 28.1 shows the first screen of the Internet Access Providers page. There are 38 pages of provider listings; there were only 24 pages of listings three

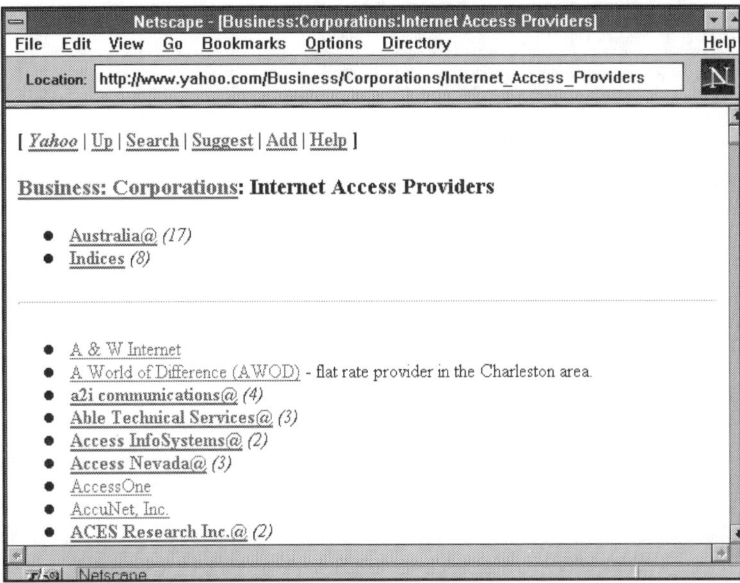

Figure 28.1 *The first page of the guide to Internet Access Providers.*

months ago. Each anchor is a link to additional and comprehensive information about the specific provider.

Figure 28.2 is the last page of the Internet Access Providers guide. Figure 28.3 shows the overall indexes. The link titled *Index-Internet Service Providers*

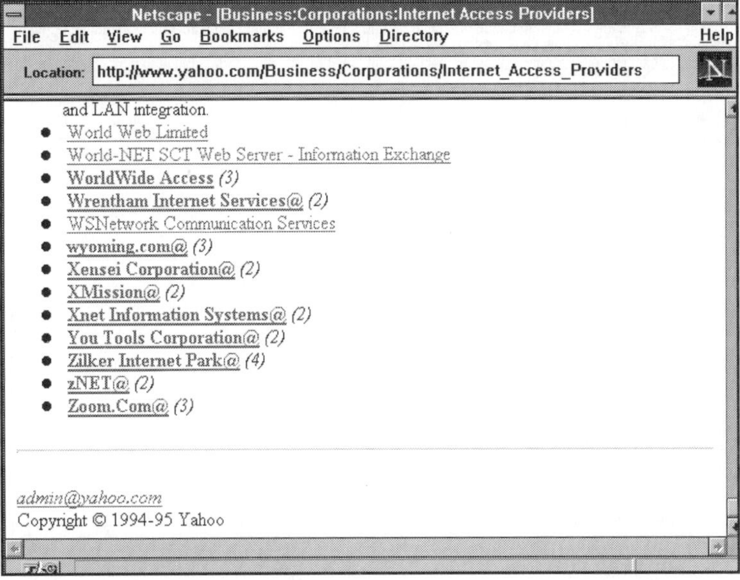

Figure 28.2 *The last page of the ISP page.*

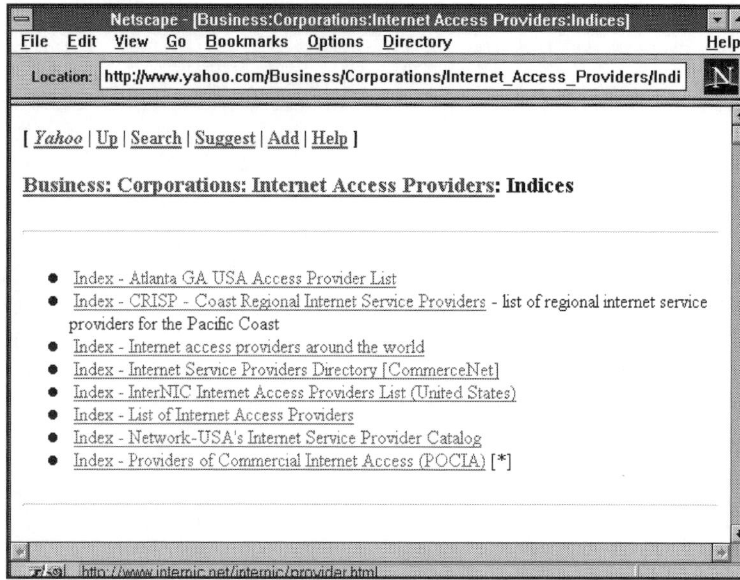

Figure 28.3 *The Index portion of Yahoo's ISP pages.*

Directory calls up the first page of the ISP Catalog. Click on *North America*, page down to the United States, and continue to the states. This produces listings like that shown in Figure 28.4, which includes my home area in New Jersey. The numbers in parentheses are area codes.

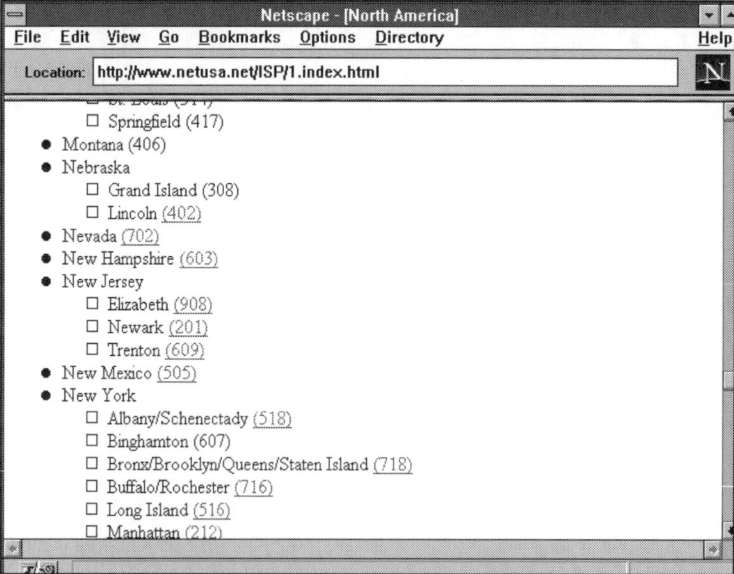

Figure 28.4 *The ISP page showing state entries, including New Jersey.*

Unlimited Message Units

It was inevitable: The more I used the Internet, the more people complained that my line was always busy. The solution was a second line. A second line is fairly inexpensive, provided both numbers get billed at the same time using a single billing statement. A "teen line" is the very appropriate term for this service in some areas. The second line's phone book listing can be different from the one assigned to the original line.

When arranging for the new line, the telephone company service representative asked, "How many monthly message units will you require?" Since I had no idea what a message unit was, I asked, "What would you suggest?" Big mistake! "Most people subscribe for 75 message units a month," the friendly voice at the other end of the phone replied.

When I received my first bill, which I expected to be about $12 since all my modem calls were to the same number in my local calling area, I was shocked to find my bill was $85. I called the billing representative and explained the situation. Surely this was a phone company mistake. Undaunted, she replied, "I'll check it and get back to you in a few minutes." You guessed it, no mistake! My multiple online hours per day had greatly exceeded my free 75 message units. That's the bad news. The good news is that unlimited message units are available for only a few dollars extra per month. It's the difference between making a lot of short calls or relatively few longer calls.

Make sure you have unlimited message units on your telephone service if you'll be using it to dial up the Internet. Betcha can't eat just one hour a day! As you might imagine, the account representative rarely tells you about the option unless you ask.

Narrowing Down the Field

Once you get the phone numbers of a local access provider or two, call them and start the check-out process. Use the form shown on the following pages to help with provider evaluation. Be aggressive, especially if there are several providers in your local area. Rates and services are rarely hammered in stone, except for the large national providers. Ask for a free month of access to check out their service. (Some already provide this.) Of course, ask the provider for references and call them. If an access provider is not willing to provide references, no matter what reason they give, they probably have something to hide. If you are subscribing to a PPP or SLIP account, will the ISP defer payment until the account is fully functional? Don't take this last aspect lightly. Configuring your PC for a TCP/IP type account is a non-trivial process. Will your prospective provider stick with you until everything is functioning normally?

Internet Service Provider Checklist

Use items 1 to 15 to evaluate different providers. After you've found a provider and have signed up, use items 16 through 29 to record information about your account.

Internet Service Provider's (ISP) Information

1 [ ] Business Person to Contact and Phone Number

____

____

2 [ ] Support Person to Contact and Phone Number

____

____

3 [ ] Hours of Normal Telephone Support

____

4 [ ] Emergency Phone Number

____

5 [ ] Data Phone Number and Alternates

____

____

____

6 [ ] Maximum Modem Speed Available Kbaud 9.6 14.4 28.8 56

7 [ ] Protocols Available PPP SLIP CSLIP TIA

8 [ ] Monthly Charge for Shell Account

____

9 [ ] Monthly Charge for SLIP/PPP Account

____

10 [ ] Does SLIP/PPP Charge also Include Shell Account? Yes No

11 [ ] Disk Storage Space at No Additional Charge (Megabytes)

____

12 [ ] Is a personal Web Home Page privilege included with a SLIP/PPP account at no cost? Yes No

13 [ ] If above is yes, what is disk space allotment in megabytes?

____

14 [ ] Can files be made available for anonymous FTP access as part of a basic shell account? Yes No

15 [ ] If above is yes, what is disk space allotment in megabytes?

____

16 [ ] Your Login Name

____

17 [ ] Your Password

____

18 [ ] Your e-mail address

____

19 [ ]	Data Bits	8	7	6	5
20 [ ]	Parity	None	Odd	Even	
21 [ ]	Stop Bits	1	1.5	2	

22 [ ] Your PC's IP Numeric Address

____

23 [ ] Your PC's Fully Qualified Domain Name (FQDN)

____

24 [ ] ISP Gateway IP Numeric Address and FQDN

____

____

25 [ ] ISP Domain Name Server (DNS) Primary IP Address

____

26 [ ] ISP Domain Name Server (DNS) Secondary IP Address

____

27 [ ] ISP Domain Name Server (DNS) Tertiary IP Address

____

28 [ ] SMTP Gateway (mail) FQDN

____

29 [ ] NNTP Gate (Usenet News) FQDN

____

AFTER YOU SELECT A PROVIDER

Now that you've scientifically evaluated your provider alternatives—or simply flipped a coin—take the plunge and sign up. In some cases the provider can activate an account within a few minutes of an online request or phone call in which you've given credit card information. Some providers may take a day or two to activate your account. It depends a lot on how organized they are, and perhaps how many times they've been burned on bad credit cards.

Let's assume for now that initially you are getting a standard shell account, not a SLIP/PPP account. I'm also assuming you have a modem up and going and know how to connect to an outside data service. If you are completely new to modem science, I would suggest you get a copy of *Modems for Dummies*, by Tina Rathbone (IDG Books, 1994). You may receive your account information online or, more typically, from a telephone call. In either case, fill in items 16 through 21 in the previous tip to make sure you have it all straight. This is especially true of passwords; your password may be dictated to you by your provider, and it may be a random sequence of characters that is devilishly hard to recall. You don't have to tape it to your office wall, but it should be on paper in some non-obvious place where you can find it.

Selecting an Account Name

Most Internet providers allow users to choose an account name. The size limitation, on Unix systems, is typically eight characters, although on some systems it's seven. The first part of your e-mail address is your user identification (user ID) so make it easy for other people to remember your account name. An e-mail address contains two components using the form your-user-name@your-domain-name. Your user-name must be unique on your-domain-name. Because domain names are also required to be unique across all of the Internet, the combination of the two names identifies a specific user. There is not another person in the world who will have your full e-mail address.

An obvious user name choice (at least to me since it's what I use) is your last name. If you're a lejeune, there is no problem; if you're a smith, well, sorry about that. (Keep in mind that case counts when you type your user ID during system login but *not* when sending e-mail.) If your selected name is already in use, you might want to try your-first-initial-your-last-name or just the other way around. Many people with common names choose a pseudonym for a user ID, so that Mike Smith might be wombat@foonet.com. It's not that he's hiding from anybody; it's just that every conceivable combination of Mike and Smith has already been taken on his domain. Most e-mail clients like Eudora allow a "real name" field for a full name (which doesn't have to be unique), so that people getting e-mail from wombat@foonet.com will see that, oh, yeah, that's Mike Smith's nickname. Genuinely concealing your identity on the Internet is not easy, and you should always assume that people who really want to find out who you are will almost certainly do so.

The initial password provided by your provider is temporary in most cases. You may in fact be automatically required to change your password the first time you connect to your new account—even if you aren't, change it anyway. If you are on a Unix system, the command to change your password is "passwd". Again, keep a paper copy (like the previous checklist) somewhere, but nowhere obvious—and ideally, nowhere in the same room with your computer or terminal. A former student of mine had a job with a computer security firm. She would go into someone's empty office, turn on the terminal, and about half the time, would be connected to their network account within 30 minutes. One of the main reasons was that about one quarter of the people had their password written on a piece of paper in one of their desk drawers. The rest used the names of their spouses, dogs, cats, or children as passwords. If you need to be safe, be at least a little subtle.

The next step in our configuration process is understanding your login process. When you attempt to log on to a system, the computer will ask a question such as "login:" and you respond with your account name and usually other information, such as the type of connection required. (Many providers allow you to select shell, SLIP, or PPP from a single login rather than having a distinct phone line for each.) You'll probably have to have a login script for establishing a SLIP or PPP connection. Such scripts are heavily dependent on the TCP/IP software you're using and, to a lesser extent, on the machinery your provider has set up for servicing connection requests. The good news is that most providers will hand you a script that requires little or no modification beyond your user ID.

However, things don't always work as planned, and when a login fails for some reason, it really helps to understand what's going on, as opposed to being clueless and simply along for the ride. Learn by doing. Use your communications program to manually connect to your provider's machine, change your password, and exit the system. Reconnect and exit a few times to ensure everything is normal and there are no surprises. If your shell-access modem program supports session capture (that is, writing everything appearing on the screen to a disk file), start it going and log on. When you're done, review the captured session and try to see the sense in it.

Here's an example. The following is my shell account login sequence, with a couple of annotations written in after the fact (by me) in square brackets:

```
Express Access (tm) Online Communications Service 800-969-9090
   Communications settings are eight bits no parity.
   Don't have an account? Login as new (no password).   [Billboard Stuff]

login: lejeune              [Prompt | Reply]
Password:                   [Prompt | Reply]
Last login: Fri Jan  6 10:53:38 from itacom.digex.net
SunOS Release 4.1.3 (ACY) #1: Mon Jan 31 19:11:16 EST 1994 [Billboard Stuff]

!  Send mail to "help" for customer support and assistance.
!  Do a 'help digex-contacts' for a list of Digex mail addresses.

o  The Express Access User's Guide is available online.  Type
   "help users-guide" to access it.
You have mail.              [Billboard Stuff]
Enter your terminal type, RETURN for vt100, ? for list:    [Prompt | Reply]

setting terminal type to vt100.
acy1%                       [System Prompt]
```

There are three typical components in a connection sequence:

- billboard information, which is of little or no interest
- dialog between the network and user
- the operating system prompt

The important ingredients in the above sequence are the required keyword prompts and the replies to those prompts. As an example from the above login sequence, the prompt "login:" requires my reply "lejeune". I did type a reply after the "Password:" prompt, but the space is blank because passwords are not "echoed" to the screen, or else are echoed as asterisks or periods. I pressed Enter following the "list:" prompt.

The first three lines of the captured session are simply a bulletin from the provider. My provider is pretty spare; some will send you whole screens full. Assuming you get the dialog correct, you'll reach the operating system prompt, which in my case is "acy1%".

It might be handy to make up a checklist form like the one below, substituting your login sequence for mine:

```
[ ]  Initial Login Sequence:
          Provider says: login:
          PC replies: lejeune
          Provider says: word:
          PC replies: help4me
          Provider says: list:
          PC replies: press Return key
          Operating system prompt: acy1%
[ ]  If your SLIP/PPP account is combined with your
     shell account, what is the command line entry required
     to start SLIP/PPP?____________________
```

A dedicated SLIP/PPP account starts using TCP/IP immediately upon login, so all you'll need are the prompt/reply pairs for your user ID and password. On the other hand, if you have a single account that functions for both shell and SLIP/PPP access, you will additionally need the command to initiate SLIP/PPP access. Enter this command in the blank on the form shown above.

You will also need the Domain Names and IP address for your SLIP or PPP account. Your provider will have to provide you with these. (A new mechanism called dynamic IP addressing may eliminate the need for your entry of an IP address. More and more providers are moving to this, as it makes their technical support challenge much easier. I spoke of dynamic IP addressing briefly in Chapter 21.)

If you made provisions for a SLIP/PPP account, enter the appropriate information in items 22 through 29 on the checklist provided earlier.

I know this has been tedious to the threshold of pain. However, it's the lack of attention to detail at this phase of the process that causes so much consternation and generates the horror stories that one hears about configuring TCP/IP stacks.

Call Forwarding Can Save You a Bundle

Here's a truly devious trick that may be able to save you a great deal of money if you're in the all-too-common situation of not having a local dialup for your Internet provider. Assume that you are in zone A and your provider is in zone C. It's a toll call from zone A to zone C. However, you have a friend in zone B, which is between you and your provider. It may be that from your friend's location, it is a local call for you and, additionally, a local call to your provider in zone C.

Have your friend install another phone line, which you agree to pay for. (Yes, this may require a fairly trusting friend. So what are friends for?) Most phone company hookups connect to a box outside the house, so the line usually doesn't have to run into your friend's house. You do not even need a phone on the new line. Temporarily connect a phone to the line and set the codes that will automatically forward the call to the Internet provider. Call forwarding information is stored in the phone company's central office, so there is no need to keep a phone connected to the line. Presto, unlimited access to your Internet provider for a flat monthly fee of about $14! Surf 'til you drop.

It gets even better. Once a call is placed and forwarded, you are switched off the newly installed line and it becomes available for another call. Any reasonable number of people can have their calls forwarded in this fashion without anyone ever getting a busy signal. Many people can connect to the same number simultaneously. Get four people to share the service and it costs each of you under $4 per month.

A small but enterprising Internet provider in my neck of the woods knows a good thing when he sees one. This provider pays the installation fee and the monthly charges for a call forwarding number that extends the local-call range of his Internet service. The user who "hosts" the phantom phone line receives a free Internet account. So far the phone company has not objected.

LET'S REVIEW

Finding an Internet service provider (ISP) on your own is largely a matter of research and networking within your local computing community. Ask fellow user group members or people who hang out at local computer stores which provider they use and which they recommend.

If you have access to a fax machine, there is a faxback index of providers sorted by state. Call Wentworth Worldwide Media at FAX number 717-393-2565.

If you have an associate with an Internet account, even if he or she is not local to you, there are online directories of Internet service providers that may provide pointers to the providers serving your community. The Yahoo database, as we have seen, maintains an excellent index of providers at the following URL:

```
http://www.yahoo.com/Business/Corporations/Internet_Access_Providers
```

The listings are alphabetical by provider name, but at the start of the HTML page a link to indexes is listed.

Make sure you request "unlimited message units" for the phone line on which you will be dialing into the Internet—even if the dialup is a local call. Otherwise, phone charges may turn out to be *much* higher on a monthly basis than they should be.

Once you've selected a provider, take the time to understand the log-in protocol required. Use a standard communications package like ProComm to log in, and take notes at every step of the way to be sure that you understand what's going on. An even more sure-proof method—providing your communications software supports this feature—is to capture the login sequence to a file. You can then print the file and have a hard copy for future reference.

Appendix A: Writing Great HTML

Underneath the slick point-and-click user interface of a Web browser such as Netscape or Mosaic lies an ASCII "markup language" that can easily be composed and edited with any Windows or DOS editor.

As you probably know, the language used by the Web is called *HTML*, which stands for *Hyper Text Markup Language*. The *hyper text* part means that a Web page can contain references to other Web pages or to various net resources such as Gophers and FTP sites. The *markup* part comes from the days when book and magazine publishing people made special marks on their authors' manuscripts to tell typesetters how to format the text. This process was called *markup*, and the term was adopted when people started inserting formatting instructions into their computer files.

Although we covered many of the basic features of creating Web pages with HTML in Part 2 of this book, this appendix provides a useful guide to most of the HTML features supported by leading Web browsers such as Netscape and Mosaic. As you spend more time creating Web pages, you'll find that this appendix will help you use the HTML tags.

In the Beginning There Was SGML

Many different markup languages have been developed over the past few decades. Each has provided a solution to the common problem of differentiating text to be formatted from descriptions of how to format it. One of the more widely used ones is called *SGML* or *Standard Generalized Markup Language*.

SGML markup contains *meta-information*, or information *about* text. This information doesn't have to be presentation commands. As in HTML and the Web, it can be coded as tags to represent hyper text links. Tags can describe things like "what follows is an author's name" or "here is a quote from *this* source."

This type of formatting brings a division between content and presentation. This division should be quite familiar to anyone who has used a word processor (like Microsoft Word) with *style sheets*. Of course, where a style sheet or a document file format is often specific to a particular program running under a particular operating system, SGML provides a way to encode meta-information in ASCII so it can be used by different programs on different systems from PCs to mainframes.

However, SGML is not a markup language *per se*; rather, SGML is a format that markup languages can follow. You certainly don't need to know all this about the nature of SGML to write Web pages, but as you wander the Web, you're bound to run into references to SGML from time to time.

HTML—The Language of the Web

The HTML that you'll use to create Web documents is actually a subset of the full SGML. HTML commands are enclosed in angle brackets, like <this>. Most commands come in pairs that mark the beginning and end of a part of text. The end command is often a repetition of the start command, except that it includes a forward slash between the opening bracket and the command name. For example, the title of an HTML document called "Habanero-Mango Chutney" would look like this:

```
<TITLE>Habanero-Mango Chutney</TITLE>
```

Similarly, a word or phrase that Netscape shows in **bold** type, would look like this:

```
<B>bold</B> type.
```

It's not too hard to mark up your text, but all the bracketed tags can make your source text hard to read and proofread. No one has created a true "Web processor," a WYSIWYG word processor that happens to read and write HTML files, but we're bound to see one soon. For now we have to use word processors, text editors, or simple "HTML editors" that display the tags, not their effects.

Using an HTML Editor

Many people do prefer using an HTML editor over a word processor like Microsoft Word or a simple text editor like Windows Notepad. In fact, we've included some handy HTML editors on the companion CD-ROM, including

Web Spinner and HTMLAssistant. It is easier to *start* writing HTML with an HTML editor than with a basic text editor because most HTML editors typically offer some sort of menu of tags. This can help you get acquainted with the HTML tag set.

The other advantage of an HTML editor is that when it inserts tags for you, it inserts both the start and the end tags. This feature greatly reduces the chance that your whole document will end up in the **<H1>** (first level header) style, or that a bold word will become three bold paragraphs.

You Still Have to Read HTML

No matter how you create HTML documents, you'll still need to learn how to read them. While an HTML editor may make it easier to insert tags such as **<B>** and **<OL>**, it can't help you decipher a document once it's created. Because an HTML editor lets you start writing without knowing all that much HTML, you might find yourself in a position where you can't even read your own work!

Using "Piggyback" Editors

Another approach to WYSIWYG Web document editing is to piggyback off an existing word processor. This involves creating a document with your favorite word processor and then converting the document to an HTML file.

Unfortunately, this approach has two disadvantages. First, converting a file from your word processor's format to HTML can be slow. Even if conversion is relatively fast, inserting an extra step between editing and previewing can slow you down. Second, HTML formats that don't correspond directly to your word processor's formats are either not supported or only supported in a roundabout way.

One example of a WYSIWYG piggyback is an RTF to HTML translation program. (We've included a program like this, called RTFTOHTM, on the companion CD-ROM.) This sort of program takes an RTF (or Rich Text Format) file generated by a word processing program and converts it to an HTML file.

Given that the best available Web editors don't support all of HTML, or are slow and awkward to use, you should expect to have to do manual touchup—or even to write HTML by hand.

The bottom line here is *you'll have to learn to read and write HTML* if you want to be a Web spinner. HTML tools will improve, but I suspect that you'll need to be familiar with the basics of HTML to publish on the Web.

HTML BASICS

All HTML files consist of a mixture of text to be displayed and HTML tags that describe how the text should be displayed. Normally, extra *whitespace* (spaces, tabs, and line breaks) is ignored, and text is displayed with a single space between each word. Text is always wrapped to fit within a browser's window in the reader's choice of fonts. Line breaks in the HTML source are treated as any other whitespace, and a *paragraph break* must be marked with a **<P>** tag.

Tags are always set off from the surrounding text by *angle brackets*, or the less-than and greater-than signs. Most tags come in "begin" and "end" pairs: for example, **<I>** ... **</I>**. The end tag includes a slash between the opening bracket and the tag name. There are a few tags that require only a start tag; I'll take particular care to point out these tags as they come up.

HTML is *case insensitive*: **<HTML>** is the same as **<html>** or **<hTmL>**. However, many Web servers run on Unix systems, which *are* case sensitive. This will never affect HTML interpretation, but will affect your hyperlinks: My.gif is not the same file as my.gif or MY.GIF.

Some begin tags can take *parameters*, which come between the tag name and the closing bracket like this: **<DL COMPACT>**. Others, like description lists, have optional parameters that will alter their appearance, if your reader's browser supports that option. Still others, such as anchors and images, require certain parameters and can also take optional parameters.

THE STRUCTURE OF AN HTML DOCUMENT

All HTML documents have a certain standard structure but Netscape and most other Web browsers will treat any file that ends in .HTML—.HTM on PCs—as an HTML file, even if it contains *no* HTML tags. All HTML text and tags should be contained within this tag pair:

```
<HTML> ... </HTML>
```

<HEAD> ... </HEAD> Tag

All HTML documents are divided into a *header* that contains the title and other information about the document, and a *body* that contains the actual document text.

While you should not place display text outside the body section, this is currently optional since Netscape will format and display any text that's not in a tag. Also, while you can get away with not using the **<HEAD>** tag pair, it's strongly recommended.

<BODY> ... </BODY> Tag

The body of the document should contain the actual contents of the Web page. The tags that appear within the body do not separate the document into sections. Rather, they're either special parts of the text, like images or forms, or they're tags that *say something* about the text they enclose, like character attributes or paragraph styles.

Headings and Paragraphs

In some ways, HTML text is a series of paragraphs. Within a paragraph, the text will be wrapped to fit upon the reader's screen. In most cases, any line breaks that appear in the source file are totally ignored.

Paragraphs are separated either by a explicit paragraph break tag, **<P>**, or by paragraph style commands. The paragraph style determines both the font used for the paragraph and any special indenting. Paragraph styles include several levels of section headers, five types of lists, three different "block formats," and the normal, or default paragraph style. Any text outside of an explicit paragraph style command will be displayed in the normal style.

<ADDRESS> ... </ADDRESS> Tag

The last part of the document body should be an **<ADDRESS>** tag pair, which contains information about the author and, often, the document's copyright date and revision history. While the address block is not a required part of the document in the same way that the header or the body is, official style guides urge that all documents have one. In current practice, while most documents use the **<HTML>**, **<HEAD>**, and **<BODY>** tag pairs, almost all documents have address blocks—perhaps because the address block is visible.

The format for using the **<ADDRESS>** tag is as follows:

```
<ADDRESS>Address text goes here</ADDRESS>
```

Comments

Comments can be placed in your HTML documents using a special tag as shown:

```
<!--Comment text goes here-->
```

Everything between the "<>" will be ignored by a browser when the document is displayed.

HEADER ELEMENTS

The elements used in the header of an HTML document include a title section and internal indexing information.

<TITLE> ... </TITLE> Tag

Every document should have a *title*. The manner in which a title is displayed varies from system to system and browser to browser. The title could be displayed as a window title, or it may appear in a pane within the window. The title should be short—64 characters or less—and should contain just text.

The title should appear in the header section, marked off with a **<TITLE>** tag pair; for example, **<TITLE>**Lime-Jerked Chicken**</TITLE>**. Netscape is actually such an "easy-going" browser that the title can appear anywhere in the document, even after the **</HTML>** tag, but future browsers might not be quite so clever and accommodating. Including a title is important because many Web search engines will use the title to locate a document.

The format for using the **<TITLE>** tag is as follows:

```
<TITLE>Title text goes here</TITLE>
```

Other <HEAD> Elements

There are a few HTML optional elements that may only appear in the document's header (**<HEAD>** tag pair). The header elements that browsers use are the **<BASE>** and **<ISINDEX>** tags. Both are *empty* or *solitary* tags that do not have a closing **</...>** tag and thus do not enclose any text.

The **BASE** tag contains the current document's URL, or *Uniform Resource Locator;* browsers can use it to find "local URLs."

The **ISINDEX** tag tells browsers that this document is an index document, which means that the server can support keyword searches based on the document's URL. Searches are passed back to the Web server by concatenating a question mark and one or more keywords to the document URL and then requesting this extended URL. This is very similar to one of the ways that forms data is returned. (See the section *Form Action and Method Attributes* for more information.)

Other header elements are provided, such as **<NEXTID>** and **<LINK>**, which are included in HTML for the benefit of editing and cataloging software. They have no visible effect; browsers simply ignore them.

NORMAL TEXT

Most Web pages are composed of plain, or *normal* text. Any text not appearing between format tag pairs is displayed as normal text.

Normal text, like every other type of paragraph style except the *preformatted* style, is wrapped at display time to fit in the reader's window. A larger or smaller font or window size will result in a totally different number of words on each line, so don't try to change the wording of a sentence to make the line breaks come at appropriate places. You'll be in for a big surprise!

 Tag

If line breaks *are* important, as in postal addresses or poetry, you can use the **
** command to insert a line break. Subsequent text will appear one line down, on the left margin.

The general format for this tag is:

```
<BR CLEAR=[Left|Right]>
```

The section listed between the "[]" is optional. This is a feature introduced as an HTML enhancement and supported by newer versions of Netscape.

Let's look at an example of how **
** is used. To keep

```
Coriolis Group Books
7339 East Acoma Drive, Suite 7
Scottsdale, Arizona 85260-6912
```

from coming out as

```
Coriolis Group Books 7339 East Acoma Drive, Suite 7 Scottsdale, Arizona
85260-6912
```

you would write:

```
Coriolis Group Books<BR>
7339 East Acoma Drive, Suite 7<BR>
Scottsdale, Arizona 85260-6912<BR>
```

The extended form of the **
** tag allows you to control how text is wrapped. The **CLEAR** argument allows text to be broken so that it can flow around an image to the right or to the left. For example, this tag shows how text can be broken to flow to the left:

```
This text will be broken here.<BR CLEAR=Left>
This line will flow around to the right of an image that can be displayed with
the IMG tag.
```

<NOBR> Tag

This tag stands for **NO BR**eak. This is another HTML extension supported by Netscape. To keep text from breaking, you can include the **<NOBR>** tag at the beginning of the text you want to keep together.

<WBR> Tag

This tag stands for **W**ord **BR**eak. If you use the **<NOBR>** tag to define a section of text without breaks, you can force a line break at any location by inserting the **<WBR>** tag followed by the **
** tag.

<P> Tag

The **
** command causes a line break within a paragraph, but more often we want to separate one paragraph from another. We can do this by enclosing each paragraph in a **<P>** tag pair, starting the paragraph with **<P>** and ending it with **</P>**. The actual appearance of the paragraphs will depend on your reader's Web browser: Paragraph breaks may be shown with an extra line or half line of spacing, a leading indent, or both.

The **</P>** tag is optional; most people include a single **<P>** at the beginning of each paragraph, at the end, or alone on a line between two paragraphs.

Logical and Physical Attributes

Character attribute tags let you emphasize words or phrases within a paragraph. HTML supports two different types of character attributes: *physical* and *logical*. Physical attributes include the familiar bold, italic, and underline, as well as a *tty* attribute for monospaced text.

Logical attributes are different. In keeping with the SGML philosophy of using tags to describe content and not the actual formatting, logical attributes let you describe what sort of emphasis you want to put on a word or phrase, but leave the actual formatting up to the browser. That is, where a word marked with a physical attribute like **<B>**bold**</B>** will always appear in **bold** type, an **<EM>**emphasized**</EM>** word may be *italicized*, underlined, **bolded**, or displayed in color.

Web style guides suggest that you use logical attributes whenever you can, but there's a slight problem: Some current browsers only support some physical attributes, and few or no logical attributes. Since Web browsers simply ignore any HTML tag that they don't "understand," you run the risk that your readers will not see any formatting at all if you use logical tags!

The standard format for using any of the physical attributes tags is as follows:

```
<tag>text goes here</tag>
```

You can nest attributes, although the results will vary from browser to browser. For example, some browsers can display ***bold italic*** text, while others will only display the innermost attribute. (That is, **<B><I>**bold italic**</I></B>** may show up as *bold italic*.) If you use nested attributes, be sure to place the end tags in reverse order of the start tags; don't write something like **<B><I>**bold italic**</B></I>**! This may work with some Web browsers but it may cause problems with others.

Keep in mind that even if current browsers arbitrarily decide that **<EM>** text will be displayed as italic and **<KBD>** text will be displayed as Courier, future browsers will probably defer these attributes to a setting controlled by the user. So don't conclude that citations, definitions, and variables all look alike and that you should ignore them and use italic.

<BLINK> ... </BLINK>

This is a new enhanced tag supported by Netscape. Text placed between this pair will blink on the screen. This feature is useful for getting someone's

Table A.1 *List of Physical Attributes*

Attribute	Tag	Sample	Effect
Bold	<B>	Some <B>bold</B> text	Some **bold** text
Italic	<I>	Some <I>italicized</I> text	Some *italicized* text
Underline	<U>	Some <U>underlined</U> text	Some underlined text
TTY	<TT>	Some <TT>monospaced (tty)</TT> text	Some monospaced (tty) text

Table A.2 *List of Logical Attributes*

Attribute	Tag	Use or Interpretation	Typical Rendering
Citation	<CITE>	Titles of books and films	Italic
Code	<CODE>	Source code fragments	Monospaced
Definition	<DFN>	A word being defined	Italic
Emphasis	<EM>	Emphasize a word or phrase	Italic
PRE	<PRE>	Used for tables and text	Preformatted text
Keyboard	<KBD>	Something the user should type, word-for-word	Bold monospaced
Sample	<SAMP>	Computer status messages	Monospaced
Strong	<STRONG>	Strong emphasis	Bold
Variable	<VAR>	A description of something the user should type, like <filename>	Italic

attention but if you use it too much, it could get rather annoying. The format for this tag is:

```
<BLINK>This text will blink</BLINK>
```

<CENTER> ... </CENTER>

This HTML enhancement makes some Web page authors feel like they've died and gone to heaven. Any text (or images) placed between this pair is centered between the left and right margins of a page. The format for this tag is:

```
<CENTER>This text will be centered between the left and right margins</CENTER>
```

<FONT> ... </FONT>

This HTML enhancement allows you to control the sizes of the fonts displayed in your documents. The format for this tag is:

```
<FONT SIZE=font-size>text goes here</FONT>
```

where *font-size* must be a number from 1 to 7. A size of 1 produces the smallest font. The default font size is 3. Once the font size has been changed, it will remain in effect until the font size is changed by using another tag.

<BASEFONT>

To give you even greater control over font sizing, a new HTML tag has been added so that you can set the base font for all text displayed in a document.

The format for this tag is:

```
<BASEFONT SIZE=font-size>
```

Again, *font-size* must be a number from 1 to 7. A size of 1 produces the smallest font. The default font size is 3. Once the base font size has been defined, you can display text in larger or smaller fonts using the "+" or "-" sign with the **<FONT>** tag. Here's an example of how this works:

```
<BASEFONT SIZE=4>
This text will be displayed as size 4 text.
<FONT SIZE=+2>
This text will be displayed as size 6.
</FONT>
This text will return to the base font size--size 4.
```

HEADINGS

HTML provides six levels of section headers, **<H1>** through **<H6>**. While these are typically short phrases that fit on a line or two, the various headers are actually full-fledged paragraph types. They can even contain line and paragraph break commands.

You are not required to use a **<H1>** before you use a **<H2>**, or to make sure that a **<H4>** follows a **<H3>** or another **<H4>**.

Standard format for using one of the six heading tags is illustrated by this sample:

```
<H1>Text Goes Here</H1>
```

LISTS

HTML supports five different list types. All five types can be thought of as a sort of paragraph type. The first four list types share a common syntax, and differ only in how they format their list elements. The fifth type, the "description" list, is unique in that each list element has two parts—a tag and a description of the tag.

All five list types display an element marker—whether it be a number, a bullet, or a few words—on the left margin. The marker is followed by the actual list elements, which appear indented. List elements do not have to fit on a single line or consist of a single paragraph—they may contain **<P>** and **
** tags.

Lists can be nested, but the appearance of a nested list depends on the browser. For example, some browsers use different bullets for inner lists than for outer lists, and some browsers do not indent nested lists. However, Netscape and Lynx, which are probably the most common graphical and text mode browsers, *do* indent nested lists; the tags of a nested list align with the elements of the outer list, and the elements of the nested list are further indented. For example,

- This is the first element of the main bulleted list.
    - This is the first element of a nested list
    - This is the second element of the nested list
- This is the second element of the main bulleted list.

The four list types that provide simple list elements use the *list item* tag, **<LI>**, to mark the start of each list element. The **<LI>** tag always appears at the *start* of a list element, not at the end.

Thus, all simple lists look something like this:

```
<ListType>

<LI>
There isn't really any ListType list, however the OL, UL, DIR, and
MENU lists all follow this format.

<LI>
Since whitespace is ignored, you can keep your source legible by
putting blank lines between your list elements. Sometimes, I like to put the
&lt;li&gt; tags on their own lines, too.

<LI>
(If I hadn't used the ampersand quotes in the previous list element,
the "&lt;li&gt;" would have been interpreted as the start of a new
list element.)

</ListType>
```

Numbered List

In HTML, numbered lists are referred to as *ordered lists*. The list type tag is **<OL>**. Numbered lists can be nested, but some browsers get confused by the close of a nested list, and start numbering the subsequent elements of the outer list from 1.

Bulleted List

If a numbered list is an ordered list, what could an unnumbered, bulleted list be but an *unordered list?* The tag for an unordered (bulleted) list is **<UL>**. While bulleted lists can be nested, you should keep in mind that the list nesting *may* not be visible: Some browsers indent nested lists; some don't. Some use multiple bullet types; others don't.

Netscape List Extensions

Netscape has added a useful feature called **TYPE** that can be included with unordered and ordered lists. This feature allows you to specify the type of bullet or number that you use for the different levels of indentation in a list.

Unordered List with Extensions

When Netscape displays the different levels of indentation in an unordered list, it uses a solid disk (level 1) followed by a bullet (level 2) followed by a square (level 3). You can use the **TYPE** feature with the **<UL>** tag to override this sequence of bullets. Here's the format:

```
<UL TYPE=Disc|Circle|Square>
```

For example, here's a list defined to use circles as the bullet symbol:

```
<UL TYPE=Circle>
<LI>This is item 1
<LI>This is item 2
<LI>This is item 3
</UL>
```

Ordered List with Extensions

When Netscape displays ordered (numbered) lists, it numbers each list item using a numeric sequence—1, 2, 3, and so on. You can change this setting by using the **TYPE** modifier with the **<OL>** tag. Here's how this feature is used with numbered lists:

```
<OL TYPE=A|a|I|i|1>
```

where **TYPE** can be assigned to any one of these values:

A	Mark list items with capital letters
a	Mark list items with lowercase letters

I Mark list items with large roman numerals
i Mark list items with small roman numerals
1 Mark list items with numbers (default)

Wait, there's more. You can also start numbering list items with a number other than 1. To do this, you use the **START** modifier as shown:

```
<OL START=starting-number>
```

where *starting-number* specifies the first number used. You can use the feature with the **TYPE** tag. For example, the tag

```
<OL TYPE=A START=4>
```

would start the numbered list with the roman numeral IV.

Using Modifiers with List Elements

In addition to supporting the **TYPE** modifier with the **<UL>** and **<OL>** tags, Netscape allows you to use this modifier with the **<LI>** tag to define list elements for ordered and unordered lists. Here's an example of how it can be used with an unordered list:

```
<H2>Useful Publishing Resources</H2>
<UL TYPE=Disc>
<LI>HTML Tips
<LI>Web Page Samples
<LI TYPE=Square>Images
<LI TYPE=Disc>Templates
</UL>
```

In this case, all of the list items will be displayed with a disc symbol as the bullet except the third item, "Images," which will be displayed with a square bullet.

The **TYPE** modifier can be assigned the same values as those used to define lists with the **<UL>** and **<OL>** tags. Once it is used to define a style for a list item, all subsequent items in the list will be changed unless another **TYPE** modifier is used.

If you are defining **<LI>** list elements for ordered lists **<OL>**, you can also use a new modifier named **VALUE** to change the numeric value of a list item. Here's an example:

```
<H2>Useful Publishing Resources</H2>
<OL>
<LI>HTML Tips
```

```
<LI>Web Page Samples
<LI VALUE=4>Images
<LI>Templates
</UL>
```

In this list, the third item would be assigned the number 4 and the fourth item would be assigned the number 5.

Directory and Menu Lists

The directory and menu lists are special types of unordered lists. The menu list, **<MENU>**, is meant to be visually more compact than a standard unordered list: Menu list items should all fit on a single line. The directory list, **<DIR>**, is supposed to be even more compact: All list items should be less than 20 characters long, so that the list can be displayed in three (or more) columns.

I'm not sure if I've ever actually seen these lists in use, and their implementation is still spotty: Current versions of Netscape do not create multiple columns for a **<DIR>** list, and while they let you choose a directory list font and a menu list font, they do not actually use these fonts.

Description List

The description list, or **<DL>**, does not use the **<LI>** tag the way other lists do. Each description list element has two parts, a *tag* and its *description*. Each tag begins with a **<DT>** tag, and each description with a **<DD>** tag. These appear at the start of the list element, and are *not* paired with **</DT>** or **</DD>** tags.

The description list looks a lot like any other list, except that instead of a bullet or a number, the list tag consists of your text. Description lists are *intended* to be used for creating formats like a glossary entry, where a short tag is followed by an indented definition, but the format is fairly flexible. For example, a long tag will wrap, just like any other paragraph, although it should not contain line or paragraph breaks. (Netscape will indent any **<DT>** text after a line or paragraph, as if it were the **<DD>** text.) Further, you needn't actually supply any tag text: **<DT><DD>** will produce an indented paragraph.

Compact and Standard Lists

Normally, a description list puts the tags on one line, and starts the indented descriptions on the next:

```
Tag 1
Description 1.
Tag 2
Description 2.
```

If you'd like a tighter look, you can use a **<DL COMPACT>**. If the tags are very short, some browsers will start the descriptions on the same line as the tags:

```
Tag 1  Description 1
Tag 2  Description 2
```

However, most browsers do not support the compact attribute, and will simply ignore it. For example, with current versions of Windows Netscape, a **<DL COMPACT>** will always look like a **<DL>**, even if the tags are very short.

INLINE IMAGES

Using only text attributes, section headers, and lists, you can build attractive looking documents. The next step is to add pictures.

<IMG ...> Tag

The **<IMG>** tag is a very useful HTML feature. It lets you insert *inline images* into your text. This tag is rather different from the tags we've seen so far. Not only is it an empty tag that always appears alone, it has a number of *parameters* between the opening **<IMG** and the closing >. Some of the parameters include the image file name and some optional modifiers. The basic format for this tag is:

```
<IMG SRC="URL" ALT="text"
     ALIGN=top|middle|bottom
     ISMAP>
```

Since HTML+ has emerged and additional Netscape extensions have been added, this tag has expanded more than any other HTML feature. Here is the complete format for the latest and greatest version of the **<IMG>** tag:

```
<IMG SRC="URL" ALT="text"
     ALIGN=left|right|top|texttop|middle|absmiddle|
           baseline|bottom|absbottom
     WIDTH=pixels
     HEIGHT=pixels
     BORDER=pixels
     VSPACE=pixels
     HSPACE=pixels
     ISMAP>
```

The extended version allows you to specify the size of an image, better control image and text alignment, and specify the size of an image's border.

Every **<IMG>** tag *must* have a **SRC=** parameter. This specifies a *URL*, or Uniform Resource Locator, which points to a GIF or JPEG bitmap file. When the bitmap file is in the same directory as the HTML document, the file name is an adequate URL. For example, **<IMG SRC=**MySmilingFace.gif**>** would insert a picture of my smiling face.

Some people turn off inline images because they have a slow connection to the Web. This replaces all images, no matter what size, with a standard graphic. This isn't so bad if the picture is essentially ancillary to your text, but if you've used small inline images as "bullets" in a list or as section dividers, the placeholder graphic will usually make your page look rather strange. Some people avoid using graphics as structural elements for this reason; others simply don't worry about people with slow connections; still others include a note at the top of the page saying that all the images on the page are small, and inviting people with inline images off to turn them on and reload the page.

Keep in mind that some people use text-only browsers, like Lynx, to navigate the Web. If you include a short description of your image with the **ALT=** parameter, text-only browsers can show *something* in place of your graphic. For example, **<IMG SRC=**MySmilingFace.gif **ALT=**"A picture of the author"**>**.

Since the **ALT** parameter has spaces in it, we have to put it within quotation marks. In general, you can put any parameter value in quotation marks, but you only need to do so if it includes spaces.

Mixing Images and Text

You can mix text and images within a paragraph; an image does not constitute a paragraph break. However, Web browsers like earlier versions of Netscape did *not* wrap paragraphs around images; they displayed a single line of text to the left or right of an image. Normally, any text in the same paragraph as an image would be lined up with the bottom of the image, and would wrap normally below the image. This works well if the text is essentially a caption for the image, or if the image is a decoration at the start of a paragraph. However, when the image is a part of a header, you may want the text to be centered vertically in the image, or to be lined up with the top of the image. In these cases, you can use the optional **ALIGN=** parameter to specify **ALIGN=top**, **ALIGN=middle**, or **ALIGN=bottom**.

Using "Floating" Images

With the extended version of the **<IMG>** tag, you can now create "floating" images that will align to the left or right margin of a Web page. Text that is displayed following the image will either wrap around the right-hand or left-hand side of the image. Here's an example of how an image can be displayed at the left margin with text that wraps to the right of the image:

```
<IMG SRC="limage.gif" ALIGN=left>
This text will be displayed to the right of the image
```

Specifying Spacing for Floating Images

When you use floating images with wrap-around text, you can specify the spacing between the text and the image by using the **VSPACE** and **HSPACE** modifiers. **VSPACE** defines the amount of spacing in units of pixels between the top and bottom of the image and the text that is displayed. **HSPACE** defines the spacing between the left or right edge of the image and the text that wraps.

Sizing Images

Another useful feature that has been added to the **<IMG>** tag is image sizing. The **WIDTH** and **HEIGHT** modifiers are used to specify the width and height for an image in pixels. Here's an example:

```
<IMG SRC="logo.gif" WIDTH=250 HEIGHT=310>
```

When a browser like Netscape displays an image, it needs to determine the size of the image before it can display a placeholder or *bounding box* for the image. If you include the image's size using **WIDTH** and **HEIGHT**, a Web page can be built much faster. If the values you specify for **WIDTH** and **HEIGHT** differ from the image's actual width and height, the image will be scaled to fit.

Using Multiple Images per Line

Since an image is treated like a single (rather large) character, you can have more than one image on a single line. In fact, you can have as many images on a line as will fit in your reader's window! If you put too many images on a line, the browser will wrap the line and your images will appear on multiple lines. If you don't want images to appear on the same line, be sure to place a **
** or **<P>** between them.

Defining an Image's Border

Typically, an image is displayed with a border around it. This is the border that is set to the color blue when the image is part of an anchor. Using the

BORDER modifier, you can specify a border width for any image you display. Here's an example that displays an image with a five pixel border:

```
<IMG SRC="logo.gif" BORDER=5>
```

IsMap Parameter

The optional **ISMAP** parameter allows you to place hyperlinks to other documents "in" a bitmapped image. This technique is used to turn an image into a clickable map. (See the section *Using Many Anchors in an Image* for more detail.)

HORIZONTAL RULES

The **<HR>** tag draws a *horizontal rule*, or line, across the screen to separate parts of your text. It's fairly common to put a rule before and after a form, to help set off the user entry areas from the normal text.

Many people use small inline images for decoration and separation, instead of rules. While using images in this manner lets you customize how your pages look, it also makes them take longer to load—and it makes them look horrible with inline images turned off.

The original **<HR>** tag simply displayed an engraved rule across a Web page. A newer version of the tag has been extended to add additional fea-

Table A.3 *Summary of <IMG> Parameters*

Parameter	Required?	Settings
SRC	Yes	URL
ALT	No	A text string
ALIGN	No	top, middle, bottom, left, right, texttop, absmiddle, baseline, absbottom
HEIGHT	No	Pixel setting
WIDTH	No	Pixel setting
BORDER	No	Pixel setting
VSPACE	No	Pixel setting
HSPACE	No	Pixel setting
ISMAP	No	None

tures including sizing, alignment, and shading. The format for the extended version of **<HR>** is:

```
<HR SIZE=pixels
    WIDTH=pixels|percent
    ALIGN=left|right|center
    NOSHADE>
```

The **SIZE** modifier sets the width (thickness) of the line in pixel units. The **WIDTH** modifier specifies the length of the line in actual pixel units or a percentage of the width of the page. The **ALIGN** modifier specifies the alignment for the line (the default is center) and the **NOSHADE** modifier allows you to display a solid line.

As an example of how some of these new features are used, the following tag displays a solid line, five pixels thick. The line is left justified and spans 80 percent of the width of the page:

```
<HR SIZE=5 WIDTH=80% ALIGN="left" NOSHADE>
```

HYPERMEDIA LINKS

The ability to add links to other Web pages or to entirely different sorts of documents is what makes the Web a *hypermedia* system. The special sort of highlight that your reader clicks on to traverse a hypermedia link is called an *anchor*, and all links are created with the anchor tag, **<A>**. The basic format for this tag is:

```
<A HREF="URL"
   NAME="text"
   REL=next|previous|parent|made
   REV=next|previous|parent|made
   TITLE="text">

text</A>
```

Links to Other Documents

While you can define a link to another point within the current page, most links are to other documents. Links to points within a document are very similar to links to other documents, but they are slightly more complicated, so we will talk about them later. (See the section, *Links to Anchors*.)

Each link has two parts: The visible part, or *anchor*, which the user clicks on, and the invisible part, which tells the browser where to go. The anchor is the text between the **<A>** and **</A>** tags of the **<A>** tag pair, while the actual link data appears in the **<A>** tag.

Just as the **<IMG>** tag has a **SRC=** parameter that specifies an image file, so does the **<A>** tag have an **HREF=** parameter that specifies the hypermedia reference. Thus, "**<A HREF=**SomeFile.Type>click here**</A>**" is a link to "somefile.type" with the visible anchor "click here".

Browsers will generally use the linked document's file name extension to decide how to display the linked document. For example, HTML or HTM files will be interpreted and displayed as HTML, whether they come from an http server, an FTP server, or a gopher site. Conversely, a link can be to any sort of file—a large bitmap, sound file, or movie.

Images as Hotspots

Since inline images are in many ways just big characters, there's no problem with using an image in an anchor. The anchor can include text on either side of the image, or the image can be an anchor by itself. Most browsers show an image anchor by drawing a blue border around the image (or around the placeholder graphic). The image anchor can somehow be a picture of what is being linked to, or it can just point to another copy of itself: **<A HREF=**image.gif>**<IMG SRC=**image.gif>**</A>**.

Thumbnail Images

One sort of "picture of the link" is called a *thumbnail* image. This is a tiny image, perhaps 100 pixels in the smaller dimension, which is either a condensed version of a larger image or a section of the image. Thumbnail images can be transmitted quickly, even over slow lines, leaving it up to the reader to decide which larger images to request. A secondary issue is aesthetic: Large images take up a lot of screen space, smaller images don't.

Linking an Image to Itself

Many people turn off inline images to improve performance over a slow network link. If the inline image is an anchor for itself, these people can then click on the placeholder graphic to see what they missed.

Using Many Anchors in an Image

The **<IMG>** tag's optional **ISMAP** parameter allows you to turn rectangular regions of a bitmap image into clickable anchors. Clicking on these parts of the image will activate an appropriate URL. (A default URL is also usually provided for when the user clicks on an area outside of one of the predefined regions.) While forms let you do this a bit more flexibly, the **ISMAP** approach doesn't require any custom programming—just a simple text file that defines the rectangles and their URLs—and this technique may work with browsers that do not support forms. An example of how to do this is on the Web site at:

```
http://wintermute.ncsc.uiuc.edu:8080/map-tutorial/image-maps.html
```

Links to Anchors

When an **HREF** parameter specifies a file name, the link is to the whole document. If the document is an HTML file, it will replace the current document and the reader will be placed at the top of the new document. Often this is just what you want. But sometimes you'd rather have a link take the reader to a specific section of a document. Doing this requires two anchor tags: one that defines an *anchor name* for a location, and one that points to that name. These two tags can be in the same document or in different documents.

Defining an Anchor Name To define an anchor name, you need to use the **NAME** parameter: **<A NAME=**AnchorName**>**. You can attach this name to a phrase, not just a single point, by following the **<A>** tag with a **</A>** tag.

Linking to an Anchor in the Current Document To then use this name, you simply insert an **<A HREF=**...**>** tag as usual, except that instead of a file name, you use a **#** followed by an anchor name. For example, **<A HREF=#**AnchorName**>** refers to the example in the last paragraph.

Names do not have to be defined before they are used; it's actually fairly common for lengthy documents to have a table of contents with links to names defined later in the document. It's also worth noting that while tag and parameter names are not case sensitive, anchor names *are*; **<A HREF=#**anchorname**>** will not take you to the AnchorName example.

Linking to an Anchor in a Different Document You can also link to specific places in any other HTML document, anywhere in the world—provided, of course, that it contains named anchors. To do this, you simply add the **#** and the anchor name after the URL that tells where the document can be found. For example, to plant a link to the anchor named "Section 1" in a file named complex.html in the same directory as the current file, you could use **<A HREF=**"Complex.html**#**Section 1"**>**. Similarly, if the named anchor was in http://www.another.org/Complex.html, you'd use **<A HREF=**"http://www.another.org/Complex.html**#**Section 1"**>**.

Table A.4 Summary of the <A> Tag Syntax

To:	Use:
Link to another document	<A HREF="URL">highlighted anchor text</A>
Name an anchor	<A NAME="Anchor Name">normal text</A>
Link to a named anchor in this document	<A href="#Anchor Name">highlighted anchor text</A>
Link to a named anchor in another document	<A href="URL#Anchor Name">highlighted anchor text</A>

USING URLS

Just as a complete DOS file name starts with a drive letter followed by a colon, so a full URL starts with a resource type—HTTP, FTP, GOPHER, and so on—followed by a colon. If the name doesn't have a colon in it, it's assumed to be a local *reference*, which is a file name on the same file system as the current document. Thus, **<A HREF=**Another.html**>** refers to the file "Another.html" in the same directory as the current file, while **<A HREF=**/html/File.html**>** refers to the file "File.html" in the top-level directory "html". One thing to note here is that a URL always uses "/", the Unix-style *forward* slash, as a directory separator even when the files are on a Windows machine, which normally uses "\", the DOS-style backslash.

Local URLs can be very convenient when you have several HTML files with links to each other, or when you have a large number of inline images. If you ever have to move them all to another directory, or to another machine, you don't have to change all the URLs.

<BASE> Tag

One drawback of local URLs is that if someone makes a copy of your document, the local URLs will no longer work. Adding the optional **<BASE>** tag to the **<HEAD>** section of your document will help eliminate this problem. While many browsers do not yet support it, the intent of the **<BASE>** tag is precisely to provide a context for local URLs.

The **<BASE>** tag is like the **<IMG>** tag in that it's a so-called empty tag. It requires an **HREF** parameter—for example, **<BASE HREF=**http://www.imaginary.org/index.html**>**—which should contain the URL of the document itself. When a browser that supports the **<BASE>** tag encounters a URL that doesn't contain a protocol and path, it will look for it relative to the base URL, instead of relative to the location from which it actually loaded the document. The format for the **<BASE>** tag is:

```
<BASE> HREF="URL">
```

Reading and Constructing URLs

Where a local URL is just a file name, a global URL specifies an instance of one of several resource types, which may be located on any Internet machine in the world. The wide variety of resources is reflected in a complex URL syntax. For example, while most URLs consist of a resource type followed by a colon, *two* forward slashes, a machine name, another forward slash, and a resource name, others consist only of a resource type, a colon, and the resource name.

The resource-type://machine-name/resource-name URL form is used with centralized resources, where there's a single server that supplies the document to the rest of the net, using a particular protocol. Thus, "http://www.another.org/Complex.html" means 'use the Hyper text Transfer Protocol to get file complex.html from the main www directory on the machine www.another.org', while "ftp://foo.bar.net/pub/www/editors/README" means 'use the File Transfer Protocol to get the file /pub/www/editors/README from the machine foo.bar.net'.

Conversely, many resource types are distributed. We don't all get our news or mail from the same central server, but from the nearest one of many news and mail servers. URLs for distributed resources use the simpler form resource-type:resource-name. For example, "news:comp.infosystems.www.providers" refers to the Usenet newsgroup comp.infosystems.www.providers, which is a good place to look for further information about writing HTML.

Using www and Actual Machine Names

In the HTTP domain, you'll often see "machine names" like "www.coriolis.com". This usually does *not* mean there's a machine named www.coriolis.com that you can FTP or Telnet to; "www" is an alias that a Webmaster can set up when he or she registers the server. Using the www alias makes sense, because machines come and go, but sites (and, we hope, the Web) last for quite a while. If URLs refer to www at the site and not to a specific machine, the server and all the HTML files can be moved to a new machine simply by changing the www alias, without having to update all the URLs.

Table A.5 A Partial Table of URL Resource Types

Resource	Interpretation	Format
HTTP	Hypertext Transfer Protocol	http://machine-name/file-name
FTP	File Transfer Protocol	ftp://machine-name/file-name
GOPHER	Gopher	gopher://machine-name/file-name
NEWS	Internet News	news:group-name
TELNET	Log on to a remote system	telnet://machine-name
MAILTO	Normal Internet e-mail	mailto:user-name@machine-name

USING SPECIAL CHARACTERS

Since < and > have special meanings in HTML, there must be a way to represent characters like these as part of text. While the default character set for the Web is ISO Latin-1, which includes European language characters like é and ß in the range from 128 to 255, it's not uncommon to pass around snippets of HTML in 7-bit e-mail, or to edit them on dumb terminals, so the escape mechanism also has to include a way to specify high-bit characters using only 7-bit characters.

Two Forms: Numeric and Symbolic

There are two ways to specify an arbitrary character: numeric and symbolic. To include the copyright symbol, ©, which is character number 169, you can use ©. That is, &#, then the number of the character you want to include, and a closing semicolon. The numeric method is very general, but not easy to read.

The symbolic form is much easier to read, but its use is restricted to the four low-bit characters with special meaning in HTML. To use the other symbols in the ISO Latin-1 character set, like ® and the various currency symbols, you have to use the numeric form. The symbolic escape is like the numeric escape, except there's no #. For example, to insert é, you would use é, or &, the character name, and a closing semicolon. You should be aware that symbol names are *case sensitive:* É is É, not é, while &EAcute; is no character at all, and will show up as &EAcute;!

PREFORMATTED AND OTHER SPECIAL PARAGRAPH TYPES

HTML supports three special "block" formats. Any normal text within a block format is supposed to appear in a distinctive font.

<BLOCKQUOTE> ... </BLOCKQUOTE> Tag

The block quote sets an extended quotation off from normal text. That is, a **<BLOCKQUOTE>** tag pair does *not* imply indented, single-spaced, and italicized; rather, it's just meant to change the default, plain text font. The format for this tag is:

```
<BLOCKQUOTE>text</BLOCKQUOTE>
```

<PRE> ... </PRE> Tag

Everything in a *preformatted* block will appear in a monospaced font. The **<PRE>** tag pair is also the only HTML element that pays any attention to the line breaks in the source file: Any line break in a preformatted block will be treated just as a **
** elsewhere. HTML tags can be used within a preformatted block, thus you can have anchors as well as bold or italic monospaced text. The format for this tag is:

```
<PRE WIDTH=value>text</PRE>
```

The initial **<PRE>** tag has an optional **WIDTH=** parameter. Browsers won't trim lines to this length; the intent is to allow the browser to select a monospaced font that will allow the maximum line length to fit in the browser window.

<ADDRESS> ... </ADDRESS> Tag

The third block format is the address format: **<ADDRESS>**. This is generally displayed in italics, and is intended for displaying information about a document, such as creation date, revision history, and how to contact the author. Official style guides say that every document should provide an address block. The format for this tag is:

```
<ADDRESS>text</ADDRESS>
```

Many people put a horizontal rule, **<HR>**, between the body of the document and the address block. If you include a link to your home page or to a page that lets the reader send mail to you, you don't have to include a lot of information on each individual page.

USING TABLES

Features like lists are great for organizing data; however, sometimes you need a more compact way of grouping related data. Fortunately, some of the newer browsers like Netscape have implemented the proposed HTML 3.0 specification for tables. Tables can contain a heading and row and column data. Each unit of a table is called a *cell* and cell data can be text and images.

<TABLE> ... </TABLE> Tag

This tag is used to define a new table. All of the table specific tags must be placed within the pair **<TABLE> ... </TABLE>**, otherwise they will be ignored. The format for the **<TABLE>** tag is:

```
<TABLE BORDER>table text</TABLE>
```

Leaving out the **BORDER** modifier will display the table without a border.

Creating a Table Title

Creating a title or caption for a table is easy using the **<CAPTION>** tag. This tag must be placed within the **<TABLE> ... </TABLE>** tags. Here is its general format:

```
<CAPTION ALIGN=top|bottom>caption text</CAPTION>
```

Notice that you can display the caption at the top or bottom of the table. By default, the caption will be displayed at the top of the table.

Creating Table Rows

Every table you create will have one or more rows (otherwise it won't be much of a table!). The simple tag for creating a row is:

```
<TR>text</TR>
```

For each row that you want to add, you must place the **<TR>** tag inside the body of the table (between the **<TABLE> ... </TABLE>** tags).

Defining Table Data Cells

Within each **<TR> ... </TR>** tag pair come one or more **<TD>** tags to define the table cell data. You can think of the cell data as the column definitions for the table. Here is the format for a **<TD>** tag:

```
<TD ALIGN=left|center|right
    VALIGN=top|middle|bottom|baseline
    NOWRAP
    COLSPAN=number
    ROWSPAN=number>
text</TD>
```

The size for each cell is determined by the width or height of the data that is displayed. The **ALIGN** parameter can be used to center or left or right justify the data displayed in the cell. The **VALIGN** parameter, on the other hand, specifies how the data will align vertically. If you don't want the text to wrap within the cell, you can include the **NOWRAP** modifier.

When defining a cell, you can manually override the width and height of the cell by using the **COLSPAN** and **ROWSPAN** parameters. **COLSPAN** specifies the number of columns the table cell will span and **ROWSPAN** specifies the number of rows to span. The default setting for each of these parameters is 1.

Defining Headings for Cells

In addition to displaying a table caption, you can include headings for a table's data cells. The tag for defining a heading looks very similar to the **<TD>** tag:

```
<TH ALIGN=left|center|right
    VALIGN=top|middle|bottom|baseline
    NOWRAP
    COLSPAN=number
    ROWSPAN=number>
text</TH>
```

USING FORMS

The HTML features presented so far correspond with traditional publishing practices: You create a hypermedia document, and others read it. With HTML forms, however, you can do much more. You can create a form that lets your readers search a database using any criteria *they* like. Or you can create a form that lets them critique your Web pages. Or—and this is what excites business people—you can use forms to *sell* things over the Internet.

Forms are easy to create. However, to *use* them you'll need a program that runs on your Web server to process the information that the user's client sends back to you. For simple things like a "comments page," you can probably use an existing program. For anything more complex, you'll probably need a custom program. While I will briefly describe the way form data looks to the receiving program, any discussion of forms programming is beyond this book's scope.

<FORM> ... </FORM> TAG

All input widgets—text boxes, check boxes, and radio buttons—must appear within a **<FORM>** tag pair. When a user clicks on a submit button or an image map, the contents of all the widgets in the form will be sent to the program that you specify in the **<FORM>** tag. HTML widgets include single and multi-line text boxes, radio buttons and check boxes, pull down lists, image maps, a couple of standard buttons, and a *hidden* widget that might be used to identify the form to a program that can process several forms.

Within your form, you can use any other HTML elements, including headers, images, rules, and lists. This gives you a fair amount of control over your form's appearance, but you should always remember that the user's screen size and font choices will affect the actual appearance of your form.

While you can have more than one form on a page, you cannot nest one form within another.

The basic format for the **<FORM>** tag is as follows:

```
<FORM ACTION="URL"
      METHOD=get|post>
text</FORM>
```

Notice that text can be included as part of the form definition.

Form Action and Method Attributes

Nothing gets sent to your Web server until the user presses a Submit button or clicks on an image map. What happens then depends on the **ACTION**, **METHOD**, and **ENCTYPE** parameters of the **<FORM>** tag.

The **ACTION** parameter specifies which URL the form data should be sent to for further processing. This is most commonly in the cgi-bin directory of a Web server. If you do not specify an action parameter, the contents will be sent to the current document's URL.

The **METHOD** parameter tells how to send the form's contents. There are two possibilities here: Get and Post. If you do not specify a method, Get will be used. Get and Post both format the form's data identically; they differ only in how they pass the forms data to the program that uses that data.

Get and Post both send the forms contents as a single long text vector consisting of a list of WidgetName=WidgetValue pairs, each separated from its successor by an ampersand. For example:

```
"NAME=Jon Shemitz&Address=jon@armory.com"
```

(Any & or = sign in a widget name or value will be quoted using the standard ampersand escape; any bare "&" and any "=" sign can therefore be taken as a separator.) You will not necessarily get a name and value for every widget in the form; while empty text is explicitly sent as a WidgetName= with an empty value, unselected radio buttons and check boxes don't send even their name.

Where Get and Post differ is that the Get method creates a "query URL," which consists of the action URL, a question mark, and the formatted form data. The Post method, on the other hand, sends the formatted form data to the action URL in a special data block. The Web server parses the query URL that a Get method creates and passes the form data to the form processing program as a command line parameter. This creates a limitation on form data length that the Post method does not.

Currently, all form data is sent in plain text. This creates a security problem. The optional **ENCTYPE** parameter offers a possible solution: Although currently this only allows you to ratify the plain text default, in the future, values may be provided that call for an encrypted transmission.

Widgets

From a users' point of view, there are seven types of Web widgets; all of them are generated by one of three HTML tags. Except for the standard buttons, all widgets must be given a name.

<INPUT> Tag

The **<INPUT>** tag is the most versatile, and the most complex. It can create single-line text boxes, radio buttons, check boxes, image maps, the two standard buttons, and the hidden widget. It's somewhat like the **<IMG>** tag in that it appears by itself, not as part of a tag pair, and has some optional parameters. Of these, the **TYPE=** parameter determines both the widget type and the meaning of the other parameters. If no other parameters are provided, the **<INPUT>** tag generates a text box.

The format for the **<INPUT>** tag is:

```
<INPUT
TYPE="text"|"password"|"checkbox"|"radio"|"submit"|"reset"|"hidden"|"image"
       NAME="name"
       VALUE="value"
       SIZE="number"
       MAXLENGTH="number"
       CHECKED>
```

The **TYPE** parameter can be set to one of eight values. We'll look at each of these options shortly. Each input must contain a unique name defined with **NAME**. The **VALUE** parameter specifies the initial value of the input. This value is optional. The **SIZE** parameter defines the size of a text line and **MAXLENGTH** is the maximum size allowed for the returned text.

Text Boxes

If the **TYPE=** parameter is set to **text** (or no parameter is used), the input widget will be a text box. The **password** input type is just like the text type, except that the value shows only as a series of asterisks. All text areas must have a name. Text areas *always* report their value, even if it is empty.

Check Boxes and Radio Buttons

Check boxes and radio buttons are created by an **<INPUT>** tag with a **checkbox** or **radio** type. Both must have a name and a value parameter, and may be initially checked. The name parameter is the widget's *symbolic name*, used in returning a value to your Web server, not its onscreen tag. For that, you use normal HTML text next to the **<INPUT>** tag. Since the display tag is not part of the **<INPUT>** tag, Netscape check boxes and radio buttons operate differently from their dialog box kin; you cannot toggle a widget by clicking on its text; you have to click on the widget itself.

A group of radio buttons is associated by having identical names. Only one (or none) of the group can be checked at any one time; clicking a radio button will turn off whichever button in the name group was already on.

Table A.6 *Syntax of the Text and Password Input Types*

Attribute	Required?	Format	Meaning
TYPE	No	TYPE="text" *or* TYPE="password"	Determines what type of widget this will be. Default is "text".
NAME	Yes	NAME="WidgetName"	Identifies the widget.
VALUE	No	VALUE="Default text"	You supply default value. Cannot contain HTML commands.
SIZE	No	SIZE=*Cols*	Width (in characters) of a single line text area. Default is 20.
SIZE	No	SIZE=*Cols,Rows*	Height and width (in characters) of a multi-line text area.
MAXLENGTH	No	MAXLENGTH=*Chars*	Longest value a single line text area can return. Default unlimited.

Table A.7 Syntax of the Check Box and Radio Types

Attribute	Required?	Format	Meaning
TYPE	Yes	TYPE=checkbox *or* TYPE=radio	Determines what type of widget this will be. Default is "text".
NAME	Yes	NAME="WidgetName"	A unique identifier for a checkbox; a group identifier for radio buttons.
VALUE	Yes	VALUE="WidgetValue"	The value is sent if the widget is checked.
CHECKED	No	CHECKED	If this attribute is present, the widget starts out checked.

Check boxes and radio buttons return their value if and only if they are checked.

Image Maps

Image maps are created with the **TYPE="image"** code. They return their name and a pair of numbers that represents the position that the user clicked on: The form handling program is responsible for interpreting this pair of numbers. Since this program can do anything you want with the click position, you are not restricted to rectangular anchors as with **<IMG ISMAP>**.

Clicking on an image map, like clicking on a Submit button, will send all form data to the Web server.

Submit/Reset Buttons

The **submit** and **reset** types let you create one of the two standard buttons. Clicking on a Submit button, like clicking on an image map, will send all form data to the Web server. Clicking on a Reset button resets all widgets in the form to their default values. These buttons are the only widgets that don't need to have names. By default, they will be labeled Submit and Reset; you can specify the button text by supplying a **VALUE** parameter.

Table A.8 Syntax of the Image Type

Attribute	Required?	Format	Meaning
TYPE	Yes	TYPE=image	Determines what type of widget this will be. Default is "text".
NAME	Yes	NAME="WidgetName"	Identifies the widget.
SRC	Yes	SRC="URL"	The URL of a bitmapped image to display.

Table A.9 Syntax of the Submit and Reset Types

Attribute	Required?	Format	Meaning
TYPE	Yes	TYPE=submit *or* TYPE=reset	Determines what type of widget this will be. Default is "text".
NAME	No	NAME="WidgetName"	The buttons never return their values, so a name will never be used.
VALUE	No	VALUE="WidgetValue"	The button text. Default is Submit or Reset, respectively.

Hidden Fields

A **hidden** type creates an invisible widget. This widget won't appear onscreen, but its name and value are included in the form's contents when the user presses the Submit button or clicks on an image map. This feature might be used to identify the form to a program that processes several different forms.

<TEXTAREA> ... </TEXTAREA> Tag

The **<TEXTAREA>** tag pair is similar to a multi-line text input widget. The primary difference is that you always use a **<TEXTAREA>** tag pair and put any default text between the **<TEXTAREA>** and **</TEXTAREA>** tags. As with **<PRE>** blocks, any line breaks in the source file are honored, which lets you include line breaks in the default text. The ability to have a long, multi-line default text is the *only* functional difference between a **TEXTAREA** and a multi-line input widget.

The format for the **<TEXTAREA>** tag is:

```
<TEXTAREA NAME="name"
          ROWS="rows"
          COLS="cols"> </TEXTAREA>
```

Table A.10 Syntax of the Hidden Type

Attribute	Required?	Format	Meaning
TYPE	Yes	TYPE=hidden	Determines what type of widget this will be. Default is "text".
NAME	Yes	NAME="WidgetName"	Identifies the widget.
VALUE	Yes	VALUE="WidgetValue"	Whatever constant data you might want to include with the form.

Table A.11 *Syntax of the <TEXTAREA> tag*

Attribute	Required?	Format	Meaning
NAME	Yes	NAME="WidgetName"	Identifies the widget.
ROWS	No	ROWS=*Rows*	TextArea height, in characters.
COLS	No	COLS=*Cols*	TextArea width, in characters. Default is 20.

<SELECT> ... </SELECT> Tag

The **<SELECT>** tag pair allows you to present your users with a set of choices. This is not unlike a set of check boxes, yet it takes less room on the screen.

Just as you can use check boxes for 0 to *N* selections, or radio buttons for 0 or 1 selection, you can specify the cardinality of selection behavior. Normally, select widgets act like a set of radio buttons: Your users can only select zero or one of the options. However, if you specify the **MULTIPLE** option, the select widget will act like a set of check boxes: Your users may select any or all of the options.

The format for the **<SELECT>** tag is:

```
<SELECT NAME="name"
        SIZE="rows"
        MULTIPLE>text/option list</SELECT>
```

Within the **<SELECT>** tag pair is a series of **<OPTION>** statements, followed by the option text. These are similar to **<LI>** list items, except that **<OPTION>** text *may not include any HTML markup.* The **<OPTION>** tag may include an optional selected attribute; more than one option may be selected if and only if the **<SELECT>** tag includes the **MULTIPLE** option.

Table A.12 *Syntax of the <SELECT> tag*

Attribute	Required?	Format	Meaning
NAME	Yes	NAME="WidgetName"	Identifies the widget.
SIZE	No	SIZE=*Rows*	This is the widget height, in character rows. If the size is 1, you get a pull-down list. If the size is greater than 1, you get a scrolling list. Default is 1.
MULTIPLE	No	MULTIPLE	Allows more than one option to be selected.

For example:

```
Which Web browsers do you use?
<SELECT NAME="Web Browsers" MULTIPLE>
<OPTION>Netscape
<OPTION>Lynx
<OPTION>WinWeb
<OPTION>Cello
</SELECT>
```

THE CGI

The CGI, or *Common Gateway Interface,* defines how a form handling program on a Web server should act. This includes the name1=value1&name2=value2 format of the form data vector, as well as how these programs interact with remote Web clients. A CGI program can be any sort of executable code, but on Unix servers, the most common executable seems to be a *Perl* script.

SECURITY

You should be aware that it's always possible for people to intercept forms data bound for your Web server. This means that until forms with encrypted **ENCTYPES** are widely supported, forms data cannot be considered 100 percent reliable—or 100 percent confidential.

The problem is that anyone who loads your form can read the HTML source to see where the forms data goes. If that data includes any tempting information like a credit card number, a thief may be tempted to watch traffic to your server for credit card numbers to steal. Since it can be relatively easy to intercept TCP/IP packets, this is a problem that you shouldn't ignore!

Basically, if you want to do online sales, *don't* use a plain text form to ask for a credit card number. Instead, use a service that lets customers create accounts over the Web but will only accept credit card numbers and expiration dates via a voice phone call or through snail (physical letter) mail. When your customers want to place an order, they don't run the risk of having their credit card number stolen; they would only have to supply a name and address to let the order taking system look up their credit card number.

Appendix B: A Survivor's Guide to Unix

The overwhelming majority of Internet accounts are set up on the Unix operating system. Unix is a system that is functionally similar to DOS, or System 7 on a Mac. But even if you are using a graphical interface like Netscape, there will be times when you'll need to confront Unix head on. For example, if you plan to write your own CGI scripts, you'll need to know how to at least fake your way around Unix.

Unix aficionados say Unix is more complex than DOS; however, it's less complex than operating systems found on IBM mainframes. Unix is also tough to learn and counter-intuitive. Therefore, I've put this appendix together to help you learn the basics. You can think of it as a crash course to get you through some of the more common commands once you come face-to-face with the dreaded Unix command line prompt.

Unix Commands

Unix will likely make you feel like you're traveling around in a foreign country because you're probably more familiar with a visual operating systems like Windows than a text-based command-line one. Basically, Unix is a system that requires you to enter commands manually. The difficult part, the part that tends to drive people crazy, is the exactness of the format of Unix commands. This means that if you make a mistake in typing in a command, you won't get any help from Unix. Fortunately, there are some general principles I can give you to help you get around in Unix.

Are Unix commands like DOS commands? You bet. In fact, both have highly structured component parts. You can think of a command as if it were a verb in English. Some examples include DOS's **copy, erase**, and **print** commands. The verb is the action part of the command—it tells the computer what to do. The action verb *always* comes first. But many commands require additional information. For example, if you want to delete a file, you must provide the following:

- The name of the command to delete a file.
- The name of the file to delete.

Let's assume that we want to erase a DOS file named urb.txt. At the DOS prompt we enter:

```
C:> del urb.txt
```

This action or "verb" tells DOS what to do. In some cases the command all by itself is enough information. For example, the DOS **cls** (clear screen) tells DOS to clear everything currently on the screen. To delete a file, we need to provide an object for our verb—the name of the file to be deleted. In the world of commands, this object is called a *parameter*. If more than one parameter is required, the information following the verb is called a *parameter list*. One such operation requiring multiple parameters is that of copying a file. To do this, we need to tell the operating system the following three things: the fact that we want to copy (*action*), the name of the original file (*from-where*), and the name of the new file (*to-where*):

```
command from-where to-where
```

The Unix equivalent of the DOS **copy** command is **cp**. (Remember, you were forewarned—the designers of Unix did not go out of their way to make life easier for users.) If we want to copy a file named urb.txt to a new file having the name pat.txt, the command would be:

```
unix% cp urb.txt pat.txt
```

Here, the portion of the command that you enter is shown in bold. The prompt, which is not in bold, precedes the part that you enter. (Your actual Unix prompt most likely will not be unix%.) The copy command (**cp**) used in this example requires three things:

- The name of the command to perform—**cp**.
- The name of the file to copy—urb.txt.
- The name of the new file—pat.txt.

One last and extremely important rule is that *each distinctive piece of information in a command must be separated by at least one space.* If a command contains a verb and one parameter, the parameter and the verb must be separated by one or more spaces. Likewise, if there are multiple parameters, each must be separated by at least one space. In the example **copy** command

```
unix% cp urb.txt  pat.txt
```

there must be at least one space between the **cp** and the filename urb.txt. Likewise, there must be at least one space between urb.txt and pat.txt. In computer jargon, *delimiter* is the technical term for these separators. Always remember, the computer is not nearly as smart as you are, so do all you can to help the poor thing do its task.

In summary, the key points for writing Unix commands include:

- The prompt, followed by a blinking cursor, is what greets you on the command line.
- A command instructs Unix to perform a specific action.
- The first component part of a command is always the action verb.
- The format of a command must be exact.
- Commands typically require additional information, which is specified using *parameters.*
- Each component of a command must be separated by at least one space.
- Unix commands are case sensitive.

CONVENTIONS YOU CANNOT IGNORE!

In this appendix, I'll use the following notation for our command-line prompt:

```
unix%
```

The prompt on your system will probably look different; it may be displayed with just the "%" character. Following the prompt is a command. Now the only catch is that *you must type a command exactly as you see it printed here.*

One of the biggest problems new Unix users have is that they forget that Unix is case sensitive. **LS**, **ls**, and **Ls** are all different to Unix, and only **ls** represents a command. (I spent an agonizing five minutes trying to figure out why I was getting an "invalid command" message when trying to change directories by entering CD in caps.) Command parameters are shown enclosed between the "< >" or "[ ]" pairs. The parameter list enclosed between the "< >" pair must be supplied while the parameter list enclosed between the "[ ]" pair is optional. The ellipsis (...) is used to indicate that the parameter may be repeated any number of times. The "!" character is used to indicate mutually exclusive parameters. To illustrate,

```
unix% cd [directory-path]
```

indicates that the command **cd** may be entered all by itself (to return to your home directory from any working directory) or a directory path name may be entered. The parameter enclosed within the square brackets is optional. However, if optional parameters are used, they must be in exactly the form shown. Since *directory-path* is enclosed between the "[ ]" pair, you supply the desired path name. Multiple directory names may be entered at the same time such as:

```
unix% cd /pub/ftp/Urb
```

Entering the **cd** command for each directory, although requiring fewer key strokes, is less error prone. The sequence

```
unix% cd /pub
unix% cd ftp
unix% cd Urb
```

accomplishes the same function as the multiple directory names used in the previous example. This command

```
unix% rm <file-name> [...file-name]
```

illustrates that the **rm** (remove) command requires at least one filename, although any number may be entered, such as **rm temp.001 temp.002**. The command

```
unix% cd [ .. ! <[directory-path]subdirectory-directory-name>]
```

indicates that the **cd** command doesn't require any parameters. **cd** entered without a parameter will change your current working directory from whatever it may be to your home directory. If a parameter is used, it must have one of two forms, either **cd ..** (cd and at least one space followed by two consecutive periods), or a subdirectory name optionally preceded by a directory path.

What's a File?

Unix stores information in terms of files. A file may be empty, or it may contain a collection of data. Text files primarily contain characters that may be entered from a keyboard. Binary files may contain characters that are not keyboard characters. Files are grouped together inside directories in much the same fashion as documents are grouped in a hanging folder. From a system standpoint, directories are also treated as files. (The same is true for DOS.) A directory may also contain one, or more, directories, which become subdirectories of the parent directory.

Files are stored within directories. The entire structure may be conceptualized as a file cabinet. The individual directories are drawers in the cabinet, with individual files like documents stored within the drawers. Executable programs and Unix scripts are also considered files. Unix considers nearly everything that stores or generates data a file.

DIRECTORIES

A directory structure is much like a family tree, with a specially designated directory, called the *root*, at the top of the structure. All references begin with the root directory. The root is designated as "/" (without the quotations). Directories subordinate to the root directory, also called child directories, may be added. The subdirectory may also have subdirectories. The entire structure is called a directory tree. See an example in Figure B.1.

In this illustration, Pat and Urb are subdirectories of the root. Karen and Joe are subdirectories of Pat, while Ben is a subdirectory of Urb. The subdirectory process may propagate for any number of levels, or until you run out of disk space. A directory without a child is a *leaf.*

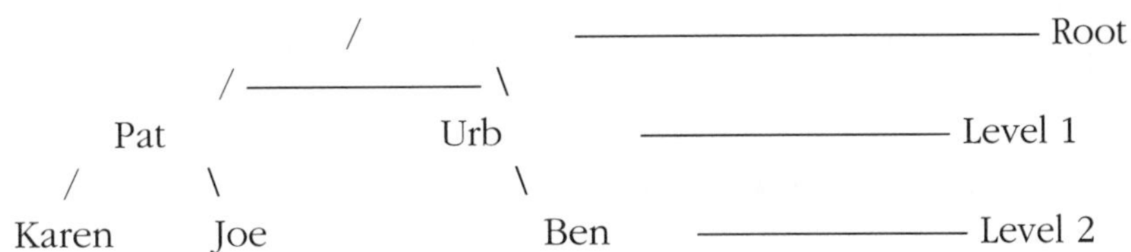

***Figure B.1** A sample Unix tree structure.*

When you log on to your system, you are automatically placed into what Unix calls your *home directory*. Typically your home directory has the same name as your logon name. Although your directory is certainly not the root directory of the system, it is convenient to conceptualize it as your personal root directory. You will rarely need to access a directory that is closer to the system root directory than your personal directory.

Your Home Directory

Your *home directory* is where you are placed when you first log on to a Unix system. It may be referenced by the tilde character "~" or by the standard system variable $HOME. (Because not all Unix shells recognize $home, the uppercase version is safer.)

Your Working Directory

Your *working*, or *current, directory* is the one that is currently accessed. If you change directories (**cd**), your working directory changes. To find the complete directory path (from the root) of your working directory, you need only enter:

```
unix% pwd
```

The output will be in the form of:

```
/user/local/LeJeune
```

The leftmost "/" indicates the root directory. The directory user is a subdirectory of the root; the directory local is a subdirectory of user; and lastly, LeJeune is a subdirectory of local. Notice that the last subdirectory, LeJeune, has two capital letters. Entering the name without the capitals will produce the dreaded "/user/local/lejeune: No such file or directory" message. Keep an eye out for this—it's bound to happen to you now and then.

Moving Around the Directory Structure

You may create a subdirectory using the **mkdir** (make directory) command. The syntax is:

```
unix% mkdir <[directory-path]new-directory-name>
```

If you omit the optional *directory-path* component, a subdirectory—using the name supplied as the new-directory-name parameter—is created immediately under the current working directory. If your working directory is /abc/def and you enter **mkdir** xxx, you will then have a path /abc/def/xxx. If you enter **mkdir** /abc/xxx, you will have path /abc/xxx.

The **rmdir** (remove directory) command is the complement of **mkdir**. The syntax is:

```
unix% rmdir <[directory-path]directory-name-to-delete>
```

Unix will not remove a directory unless it is empty, which means it doesn't contain any files or subdirectories.

The **cd** (change directory) comes in three flavors:

```
unix% cd [ .. ! <[directory-path]subdirectory-directory-name>]
```

The syntax shown here indicates that the **cd** command may be entered without a parameter since everything else is optional. If a parameter is entered, the "!" indicates that it must take the form of either:

```
unix% cd ..
```

or

```
unix% cd [directory-path]subdirectory-directory-name
```

If you enter **cd** with no parameters, you will be returned to your home directory. **cd ..** (cd followed by at least one space followed by two consecutive periods) will back up your working directory one level toward the root. If you don't use the **cd** option or the **cd ..** option, you must use the following option:

```
unix% cd [directory-path]subdirectory-directory-name
```

Remember the syntax conventions, everything between the "[" and the "]" is optional. However, if a parameter is specified, it must take either of the two forms within the square brackets. The "!" indicates one or the other. **cd** (without a parameter), **cd $HOME**, and **cd ~** are all functionally the same thing.

FILE MANIPULATION COMMANDS

The terms *command* and *program* are used interchangeably in Unix parlance. Generally, issuing a command causes execution of the named program. The **ls** (list) command will provide a directory listing. The syntax is:

```
unix% ls <[switches] [directory-path]filename>
```

If *directory-path* is omitted, the working directory is assumed. The most common switch is in the form

```
unix% ls -l
```

which provides a detailed listing. There must be at least one space between the command name and the start of any switches. Entering **ls** without any parameters produces a listing containing only filenames. The following is an example of an **ls** listing:

```
absent          mother-boards
acm.dat         musthave.txt
acy-bill        n
ad              ncsa
advertising     netinfo
amipro          nets
```

The use of the **-l** switch will produce a detailed listing similar to the following:

```
-rw-     1 lejeune users   33154   Jun23   12:16   1liners
-rw-     1 lejeune users   4559    Apr12   17:27   486
-rw-     1 lejeune users   29845   Jun20   19:24   Archie-Reference-Manual
-rw-     1 lejeune users   1387    Jun10   13:07   Internet-primer
drwx-    2 lejeune users   512     Mar28   17:46   Mail
drwx-    2 lejeune users   512     May12   11:17   News
-rw-     1 lejeune users   314     May12   14:01   blond
-rwx-    1 lejeune users   20      Jun22   07:15   borland
-rwx-    1 lejeune users   139     May13   13:57   garbo
drwx-    2 lejeune users   512     Jun23   14:55   gopher
```

The leftmost group of 10 columns deserves special attention. A "d" in the first position denotes a subdirectory. Mail, News, and gopher are directories in this listing. (Remember that case counts. If you want to change to directory Mail, you must enter **cd Mail**.) The remaining nine columns represent the Unix protection scheme. These nine columns are partitioned into logical sets of three each. The three sets, from left to right, are user (you), group, and others (the remainder of the world.) Unix is a multi-user network. Groups, which can be ignored for our purposes, represent work groups. Each set has the three components read, write, and execute. If you create a file, the protection scheme might initially be set to:

```
rw-           - - -   - - -
     User     Group   Others
```

The actual initial file creation protection scheme is determined by your system administrator. The groupings shown above would indicate that you have read and write privileges for this file but it cannot be executed. No one in your workgroup, or any others, have any access to the file. A dash in the listing simply means no privilege. If this file is to be an executable script, your executable privilege must be turned on. (More on this in a minute.) The listing would then be:

```
rwx            - - -         - - -
```

If you turn off the write protection for a specific file, you cannot accidentally delete that file. You may read a write-protected file but you will not be able to change or delete the file. If you give execution privilege to people in your group, and anyone else in the universe, your listing would be:

```
rwx            - - x         - - x
```

One caveat: A file must have read privilege as well as execute privilege before the system allows execution. A file listing with:

```
rwx            rwx           rwx
```

would give everyone everything.

You may ignore the next column. The next item is the owner of the file followed by the group. Next comes the file size, followed by the file's creation or modification date and time. The last entry is the file name.

CHANGING FILE AND DIRECTORY PROTECTION

The command used to change the protection for a file, or directory, is **chmod** (change mode.) The syntax is:

```
unix% chmod <[a][u][g][o]> <<-!+>[r][w][x]> file-name
```

u, g, and o indicate the three major categories of user, group, and other. The letter "a" indicates all three groups, which is also the default. The "+'" parameter enables and the "-" parameter disables. The r, w, and x parameters indicate read, write, and execute. Assume that you have recently created a file named garbo. Immediately after the creation of file garbo, it would probably have the following listing:

```
rw-   - - [stuff removed] garbo
```

The user has read and write privileges but no execute privilege. The group and the world have no privileges at all for file garbo. Let's assume first that the file garbo is to be an executable script; additionally, you want to get everyone (user, group, and others) to have the ability to execute the script. Execution requires both read and execute privileges. The command enabling file garbo to be executed by everyone would be:

```
unix% chmod ugo+rx garbo
```

or

```
unix% chmod a+rx garbo
```

Either of these commands would change the user, group, and others modes to executable and readable. The new listing would be:

```
rwx    r-x    r-x   [stuff  removed]    garbo
```

People in your workgroup, and anyone else in the universe, could execute this file, but only you could display, modify, or erase the file. The directory holding the file must also allow execution. The directory protection need only be changed once. Assuming that garbo is in your home directory, you could enter

```
unix% chmod a+rx ~
```

or

```
unix% chmod a+rx $HOME
```

That is, the enabled directory will now allow execution, for files that have been execute enabled, for all three groups.

Let's assume that file big-dummy has protection that gives everyone everything. The listing would be:

```
rwx  rwx  rwx  [stuff removed]  big-dummy
```

Also assume that you want to take away all privileges for the group "others." You would enter:

```
unix% chmod o-rwx dummy
```

The "-" parameter removes privileges. A listing for big-dummy would now be:

```
rwx  rwx  —  [stuff removed]  big-dummy
```

Copying and Moving Files

The Unix commands for copying and moving files are **cp** and **mv**. Here are the general formats for these commands:

```
unix% cp [source-path]source-filename [destination-path]destination-filename
unix% mv [source-path]source-filename [destination-path]destination-filename
```

The source and destination file names don't need to be the same. Actually, the move command (**mv**) is frequently used to rename a file. To move a file named urb from your home directory to path /abc/def and change the name to pat in the process, you'd enter:

```
unix% mv $HOME/Urb /abc/def/Pat
```

Deleting Files

Unix files are removed using the **rm** command. Here's the syntax required:

```
unix% rm [-i] [path-name]file-name
```

The **-i** (interactive switch) tells the command to prompt the user to approve the operation before a file is deleted. I think it's a good idea to use this switch if you use wild cards as part of your file name. Unix wild cards tend to be more inclusive than DOS wild cards. The command

```
unix% rm -i temp*
```

deletes all file names beginning with the string "temp". However, the use of the **-i** switch causes the system to prompt for approval before deleting each file matching the mask .You are prompted with:

```
rm: remove 'temp001'?
```

Unless your reply is "y" or "yes" the system will not delete the file.

Unix Globs, aka Wild Cards

The "*" and "?" characters are called *glob constructs* in Unix. There once was a program named glob that functionally expanded names containing wild cards. However, no one seems to really know where the name originated. The asterisk "*" is a glob construct that expands to any string of zero or more characters. For example, the command

```
unix% ls g*
```

lists all files that begin with g. The file gaaa.xxx would be included in Unix but not in DOS, so be careful. Unix uses of globs tend to be more inclusive than their DOS counterparts. The "?" glob stands for any character in the same position. For example,

```
unix% ls ?abc
```

lists all files and directories that have any first letter and abc as the second, third, and fourth characters, respectively. Unix provides an additional glob that is lacking in DOS. The "[]" pair can match any one of the characters inside the brackets. As an example,

```
unix% ls [123]xyz
```

lists any file that has a 1, 2, or 3 in the first character position and xyz as the second through fourth characters. Thus, files with names like, 1xyz, 2xyz, and 3xyz would be listed. You may indicate a range of characters within the brackets by enclosing the first character and the last character between the character "-". The glob [a-z] would expand to any lowercase letter. Globs may be combined. For example, the command

```
unix% ls [a-z]*
```

lists all files in the current directory and all subdirectories having a lowercase first letter.

GET ME SOME 'MORE' 'CAT'

Two commands that may be used for viewing text files are **cat** (concatenate) and **more**. **cat** will display the entire contents of a file on your terminal without pausing. Unfortunately, the file will scroll merrily out of sight if it has more lines that you have lines on your terminal. On the other hand, when more is used, it will pause every time the screen is filled. Pressing Enter will advance one line while pressing the space bar will refill the screen. The syntax is:

```
unix% cat [path]file-name [...[path]file-name]
unix% more [path]file-name [...[path]file-name]
```

PIPING

Using the command **more** in conjunction with other commands will produce listings on the terminal that would otherwise scroll off the screen. Piping is the technical term for taking the output from one command and passing it to another command. The vertical bar (|) indicates piping. The command:

```
unix% ls -l | more
```

takes the output from the **ls** command and passes it to the command **more**.

MISDIRECTION AND REDIRECTION

The character < is used to redirect input to a command; the character > is employed to redirect output from a command. **echo** is a command that normally displays everything following the command on the terminal. Let's use the **echo** command, coupled with the > redirection symbol, to create a new command. In the following example

```
unix% echo "Now is the time" > text.tmp
```

the **echo** command's parameter "Now is the time" would normally be displayed on the screen. Adding the redirection symbol > will direct the parameter to the file text.tmp. The file is created if it does not exist; if the file already exists, it replaces and erases the old version. If you want the output appended to an existing file, use two consecutive >> symbols. The sequence

```
unix% echo  "Now is the time">text.tmp
unix%  echo  "for everyone to party">> text.tmp
```

```
unix% more text.tmp
unix% rm text.tmp
```

would first create a file text.tmp with a line of text "Now is the time". Next, the line "for everyone to party" is appended to file text.tmp. File text.tmp will then be displayed as follows:

```
Now is the time
for everyone to party
```

and finally, the file text.tmp will be removed.

GETTING HELP

There are two Unix commands that will give you more help than you ever wanted. The **man** (manual) command will display documentation for a command. The form is:

```
unix% man <command>
```

The commands listed in this guide are short form. Use **man** to get all the options. The **man** command uses the **more** command without being told. Great people, these Unix programmers. Using redirection, you could get the online documentation for program mail and write it to a file, mail.doc. You could then transfer it to your home computer and subsequently print the file. Here's how to use the command **man** with redirection to file mail.doc:

```
unix% man mail > mail.doc
```

If you don't know the name of a command, but you have an idea of what it does, use the **apropos** command. (The use of the **apropos** command requires that the "whatis" database be installed on your system.) For example, if you don't know the specific command but you're sure that there must be a command that does what the DOS copy does, you would enter

```
unix% apropos copy
```

and you will be greeted with a flock of commands that have copy in their description. This list would include cp - copy files. You could then do a **man** **cp** to get the lowdown on the **cp** command.

ALIASES AND SCRIPTS

An *alias*, which is frequently called a macro, is typically a name substitution. One of the major uses of an alias allows substitution of familiar names for the frequently abstruse Unix command names. As an example, you could create an alias "dir" that would actually evoke the **ls** command.

Almost all operating systems contain the ability to create an executable file. A *script*, which is an executable file in Unix parlance, permits the entry and execution of a repetitive command series that might otherwise be entered, one at a time, at the command line prompt. The series of commands, contained within a script file, may then be executed by entering only a few keystrokes. Within DOS these executable files are called batch files and must have an extension of .BAT. Scripts are created using an editor and subsequently made executable script by using the **chmod** command. Scripts and DOS batch files are frequently used to reduce an extended command line sequence to a few keystrokes.

SUMMARY

So there you have it, DOS and Windows fans, not exactly everything that you wanted to know about Unix but were afraid to ask (sounds like a great name for a book), but a good start. If you are more comfortable with DOS than you are with Unix commands, you may want to create a series of aliases and scripts so you can use the names of the DOS commands you are familiar with. For example, you could create an alias "dir" that would actually evoke the **ls** command. Scripts, which are much like DOS batch files, are Unix executable files. A series of repetitive commands may be included in a script and executed by simply entering the name of the script. Many of the tips contained in this book are shortcut Unix scripts.

The next appendix, Appendix C, details the design, creation, and use of aliases and scripts.

Appendix C: Unix Aliases and Scripts

I have a love/hate relationship with my computer. I love what I can do with it but I hate what I have to go through to make the darn thing work. If it's so smart, why doesn't it recognize I mean "dir" when I type "dur"? "What's all this got to do with Unix?" you might ask.

Even the most dedicated Netscape fans typically spend more time than they would like at the dreaded Unix prompt. After you make the decision to include CGI Scripts in your bag of tricks, you will be spending more time than you want to at the Unix prompt. Fortunately, aliases and scripts can simplify Unix life. This appendix is designed to make your life easier—and if you don't get to know and love Unix by the time you've finished reading it, at least you'll have learned enough to make Unix act like DOS.

THE UNIX ALIAS

I hate unnecessary keystrokes! The most frequent command I issue from the Unix prompt invokes "pine", which is my favorite mail program. If I enter just "pine", it puts me in the program's menu and then I have to press "i" to get to the index of my mail. This may not seem like a big deal to you, but why should I have to enter:

```
unix% pine -i
```

and not just enter "p"? This is where aliases come to the rescue. A Unix alias takes the form:

```
alias  <new-name> <command>
```

For example, here's the alias that automates my pine program startup:

```
unix% alias p pine -i
```

Then, any time I type "p" during the current session, I'll be in pine with the mail index displayed. Is this progress, or what?

But what can you do if you want to create an alias that will be around not for only just the current session? When you first log onto your system, Unix checks the two files, .login and .cshrc, and executes all the commands contained in these files. We could place our alias definition in the .chsrc file as shown here:

```
alias  p  pine -i
```

The next time we log on, the alias would take effect.

Redefining Commands

Aliases can also be used to redefine existing Unix commands. Let's create an alias for the Unix copy (**cp**) command. Recall that the format for this command is:

```
cp <old-file> <new-file>
```

If the file specified with the *new-file* parameter already exists, it will be erased when the command executes! Fortunately, the **cp** command supports switch "-i", which prompts the user to approve the copy operation. This could save you from accidentally deleting an important file. Here's how this "safety" feature can be incorporated by adding this alias to the .cshrc file:

```
alias  cp  cp -i   #  Prompt for approval before overwriting.
```

Anything following the "#" character is treaded as a comment in .cshrc.
If you issue the command

```
unix% cp abc.txt xyz.txt
```

and xyz.txt already exists, you will be prompted with:

```
cp: overwrite 'xyz.txt'?
```

Let's take the alias feature one step further. If you're a DOS user, you'll appreciate this alias. We'll set up the Unix **cp** command to work when "copy" is entered. Here's the alias you'll need:

```
alias copy   cp  #  DOS simulation
```

The Unix delete command (**rm**) is equally as dangerous as the **cp** command, since Unix doesn't provide an undelete command to bail us out. So, here are two aliases that you'll find useful:

```
alias rm     rm  -i  # Prompt before overwriting
alias del    rm      # DOS simulation
```

Combining Commands

An alias becomes more powerful when you combine two or more commands. For example, let's assume you want to send me a talk request. If I'm not currently logged on, the request falls on deaf ears. The Unix finger command, in the form @acy.digex.net, will produce a listing of the people currently logged onto my system. This list may be long. We can fine-tune what we see by using the Unix **grep** command. This command searches an input stream for a target string and displays any line containing the search key. The command:

```
unix% finger @acy.digex.net | grep lejeune
```

does the job. If I'm logged on, the following line is displayed:

```
lejeune  Urb LeJeune           p0      Mon 09:23  itacom.digex.net
```

If I'm not logged on, nothing will be displayed. The only problem with a command like this is that it is awkward to type. So let's use an alias to bail us out. Without going into the gory details, an alias containing multiple commands requires that the command portion be enclosed within single quotation marks. An "Urb checkup" alias would therefore be:

```
alias urbon 'finger @acy.digex.net | grep lejeune'
```

Now just type "urbon" at the prompt, and the alias does its magic.

Multiple commands separated by semicolons can be in a single alias. Let's create an alias named "change" that will make all files in directory $home/www readable and executable by everyone. After changing the mode of all files, it displays a directory listing to show that the changes worked. Here's the alias definition:

```
alias  change  'chmod +rx $HOME/www/*; ls -la  $HOME/www'
```

$HOME is a Unix variable that contains your home directory path. The +rx parameter for the **chmod** command is the equivalent of entering 755.

Creating Your Own Set of Aliases

Now that you know the basics of writing aliases, you'll probably want to create your own .cshrc file that will be loaded when you log into your Unix account. Here's a snippet from my .cshrc file to give you an idea of some of the aliases I use:

```
#
#  Aliases to make UNIX less dangerous.
#
alias  compress                             compress -v
alias  cp      cp -i   # Prompt for approval before overwriting
alias  mv      mv -i   # Prompt for approval before overwriting
alias  rm      rm -i   # Prompt for approval before overwriting
alias  finger  'finger \!* | more' # Pause finger when screen fills
#
# Aliases to make UNIX commands more MSDOS-like.
#
alias  copy   cp
alias  del    rm
alias  dir    "ls -la \!* | more" # Pause listing when screen fills
alias  move   mv
alias  type   more
#
#  Aliases to make UNIX more useful.
#
alias  course  'lynx /homeb/sjiug/help/index.html' # Roadmap course
alias  menu    'lynx /etc/webmenu/menu.html'       # Startup menu
alias  h       history   # Shortcut key for history command
alias  last    'last | more'
alias  p       pine -i
```

Unix Scripts

A Unix script is like a DOS batch file. However, Unix scripts are much more powerful. You execute the commands contained within a script by entering the name of the script at the Unix prompt. Scripts are easy to create if you follow these three simple steps:

1. Create the script file using a Unix text file editor such as pico or emacs.
2. Convert the text file to an executable script using the command **chmod**.
3. Test the script. (Go to step 1 if this step fails.)

Let's go over these steps by creating a simple script named "ask" that will prompt the user for a name and display the user's input.

Step 1: Creating a Script. First, create (or edit) a text file by invoking your favorite Unix editor. As with DOS BAT files, scripts can receive passed parameters and can also have variables. A variable can be any user-defined string. Placing a "$" in front of a variable causes the variable to be expanded. Here are the lines you should enter in the editor for our simple "ask" script:

```
echo what is your name?
read name
echo "hello"  $name
```

When you finish typing these lines, save the file and exit the editor.

Step 2: Making the Script Executable. Use the change mode command (**chmod**) to make the file executable:

```
unix% chmod +x ask
```

Step 3: Executing the File. At the command line, enter the name of the script:

```
unix% ask
```

The "read" command takes input from the keyboard and places it in the variable "name". The "echo" command first displays the constant "hello" followed by the contents of the variable "name".

Parameters passed from the command line take the form $1, $2 .. $n, where $1 is the first command line parameter, $2 the second, and so on. Let's modify "ask" to take a first name as a command line parameter and prompt for a last name:

```
echo what is your last name?
read name
echo "hello"  $1  $name
```

Execute the script with a command line parameter:

```
unix% ask Urb
```

For example, if you enter "LeJeune" in reply to the prompt, the output would be:

```
hello Urb LeJeune
```

Redirection can be effectively used with a Unix script. The > symbol indicates the result of the left side if the arrow is passed to what is on the right. For example, the command

```
unix% echo "Well Done" > done.txt
```

would create a file done.txt and place the line, Well Done, into the file. If the file done.txt already exists, it will be deleted. The double arrows >> indicate that the text from the left side will be appended to the file specified on the right side. The commands

```
unix% echo "Well Done" > done.txt
unix% echo "The End" >> done.txt
```

first create file done.txt and then add the line "Well Done". The next command appends the line "The End" to the file done.txt.

The symbol < takes what is on the right side of the < and directs it to what is on the left side. Let's make a mailing list for a group of people who frequently get mailed identical messages. We want each one to think he or she is getting an original e-mail message. First, create a file named mail.txt containing the body of the mail message. Next, create a script mail2list containing one line for each recipient in the form of:

```
mail -s  "$1"  <address> < $2
```

The first few lines might be:

```
mail -s "$1"   acme@hardware.com   < $2
mail -s "$1"   chicken@little.org  < $2
```

Next, make mail2list executable:

```
unix% chmod +x mail2list
```

Mail the group the message that you previously entered in mail.txt, with a subject of Wednesday's Meeting:

```
unix% mail2list "Wednesday's Meeting" mail.txt
```

Command-line parameters are usually delimited by a space; therefore, a parameter containing a space must be enclosed within quotation marks.

A script can also perform tests. A condition starts with an "if" and ends with a "fi". (Too cute for words, right?) Let's build a script that will do one thing if a command-line parameter is present and something else if there is no command-line parameter. The following line checks if there was a command-line parameter:

```
if test -z "$1"
```

The test is true if there is no passed parameter. Whenever I start Gopher, I first change to a directory "gopher" so any Gopher-associated files appear in the same directory. When I finish borrowing, I want my default directory to be my home directory. I also want to be able to enter "go" and have Gopher start at the University of Minnesota. However, if I enter a Gopher site after "go", Gopher should start at the specified site. Here is the complete "go" script:

```
# Script "go" to start a gopher session
#
# The syntax is:
#              go [domain-name]
# If a domain name is specified, the gopher session will start at that site;
# otherwise, the gopher session will start at the University of Minnesota.
#
cd /$HOME/gopher  # change to subdirectory gopher
if test -z "$1"
    then # There is no passed parameter
        gopher gopher.tc.umn.edu
    else  # There is a passed parameter
       gopher $1
fi      # end if
cd $HOME   # change back to home directory
```

If you have created a bookmark file, enter

```
unix% go -b
```

to start Gopher with your bookmark as the top level menu.

Archie is frequently busy. Even if I get connected right away, there is a wait while Archie searches. I find it convenient to mail Archie a request and have the old boy mail me back the results when he gets around to it. It usually doesn't take very long. The following script accomplishes this task, demonstrating redirection in both directions. Here's "findfile":

```
# Script "findfile" to send an email search request to an archie server
#
# The syntax is:
#              findfile string
```

```
 # Replace string with the file name (or substring) to find.
 #
 # Test to see if there is a passed parameter.
 #
if test -z "$1"
  then # There is no passed parameter
    echo
    echo "The syntax for this script is:"
    echo "     find <search-string>"
    echo "replacing <search-string> (without the <>) with"
    echo "a string, or substring, that is the name of the"
    echo "file you are trying to locate"
    echo
  else  # There is a passed parameter
    # Create a file archie.tmp and write the following five strings.
    echo "set search sub" > archie.tmp
    echo "set output_format terse" >> archie.tmp
    echo "set sortby rfilename" >> archie.tmp
    echo "set maxhits 200" >> archie.tmp
    echo 'find' $1 >> archie.tmp       # Write string with passed parameter
    echo "quit" >> archie.tmp
    # Mail file archie.tmp to archie server
    # Substitute your favorite archie server below
    #
    mail archie@archie.rutgers.edu < archie.tmp
    rm archie.tmp  # Delete file archie.tmp
fi # end if
```

This script is a little more robust since it checks for a passed parameter and furnishes the user with instructions if not found. The script also creates the temporary file archie.tmp and erases the file after sending it.

If I want to find the latest version of Netscape for Windows and, additionally, where it is available for downloading, I would perform an Archie search on "n16e11n". I would enter:

```
unix% findfile n16e11n
```

In short order, Archie sends back my requested information, all nicely formatted and sorted.

Creating and Adding to Small Unix Files without Using an Editor

Invoking an editor to create a one-line script is overkill. It is also a waste of time to use an editor to perform a task like appending a line to an existing file. A way around this is to use the Unix **echo** command coupled with command redirection. Let's assume that you have discovered that the Law Library at the Washington and Lee University is one of the great Internet Telnet sites. (It is.)

You want to create an executable script named wl. The script is to contain the single line "telnet liberty.uc.wlu.edu". Once you have created the script, you no longer have to remember the domain name. You will also be able to Telnet to the W&L Law Library by entering "wl" at the command-line prompt.

The **echo** command normally displays the command's parameter on the terminal. However, the output of echo may be redirected to a file in the following fashion:

```
unix% echo telnet liberty.uc.wlu.edu>wl
```

Make the file executable with this command:

```
unix% chmod +x wl
```

Be a little careful. If the file "wl" already exists, it will be erased when the new one-line file is created. If you want to add additional lines to the end of a file, use the ">>" redirection symbol. If the file does not already exist, it will be created.

Appendix D: Web Publishing Resources

The collection of Web sites, HTML tools and utilities, and electronic and hardcopy books and magazines in this chapter gives you a varied and fairly extensive education with which to venture forth into the world of Web publishing.

When using the resources listed here, remember that Web sites can change location, or vanish altogether, literally overnight. Similarly, new ones are constantly being added. Don't be surprised, then, if you type the URL for one of these sites and get an error message or something totally different from what's described here.

If a really great HTML converter, Netscape helper, or other Web resource seems to be missing from those discussed here, it's probably because it's already included on the CD-ROM. To find out, review highlights of the CD-ROM Appendix E. Still, I've inevitably left out someone's favorite, absolutely indispensable source of Web and HTML wisdom. I'm eager for you to tell me where that great site is, or to provide any other additions or corrections. Please e-mail them to us via The Coriolis Group home page:

`http://www.coriolis.com/coriolis`

How This Guide Is Organized

Each item in this chapter was selected for its relevance to Web publishing and HTML. To specify which items you'll probably find most helpful, I've used a five-star rating system. Stars indicate *usefulness specifically for creating and managing Web pages*, not judgment of any other criteria.

General resources for creating Web pages are listed first here, followed by Web-based HTML guides and documents, then sites for specific HTML tools and related utilities. Resources for specific issues related to Web publishing follow: CGI and VRML, sights and sounds, and legalities. Lastly, magazines and books are reviewed. Note that resources are listed alphabetically within sections.

Your guide to the stars

☆☆☆☆☆	Don't miss these if you have even a passing interest in creating your own Web pages.
☆☆☆☆	Lots of information useful to many Web publishers.
☆☆☆	Also useful, but not as extensive, well-organized, or well-maintained as higher-rated sites.
☆☆	Of some use for specific purposes.
☆	Not the worst you can find, but of such narrow scope as to be of little use to the average Web publisher.

Sites for HTML Stuff

The sites listed in this section are those with extensive links to Web publishing and HTML resources throughout the Web. Several of these make excellent launching points for developing your own hotlist of Web pages.

☆☆☆☆ Best of the Web

`http://wings.buffalo.edu/contest/`

Want to see how HTML should be done—or at least how the poll's respondents think it should be done? Surf on over here and save a few pages to disk. Be sure to look especially carefully at the entrants for "Best Document Design." As for the design of this site itself, it's not fancy, but it is fast and easy to use.

☆☆ Building Internet Servers

`http://www.charm.net/~cyber`

Although devoted to the broader topic of building Net servers for DOS, Windows, and Mac environments, this page from CyberGroup, Inc. includes links to several HTML-specific sites, as well as book and software reviews.

☆☆ Hypermedia and the Internet

`http://life.anu.edu.au/education/hypermedia.html`

This site contains dozens of loosely organized links, generally relating to using and understanding the Web. It's a pretty standard list of resources, better organized at other sites, although it might be worth a look if you happen to be in Australia, where this site originates.

☆☆ Index of /computing/information-systems/www/tools

`http://src.doc.ic.ac.uk/computing/information-systems/www/tools/translators/`

Not a site for casual browsing; this is a no-frills archive of HTML tools. No explanations are given, just directory listings. Some directories are empty, while others have dozens of files that can be FTPd (downloaded) from here. If you know exactly what you're looking for, you can get it here without a lot of fuss, as long as you're comfortable with navigating through directory trees.

☆☆☆ Interesting Business Sites on the Web

`http://www.rpi/edu/~okeefe/business.html`

You won't learn how to write HTML directly from this site by Bob O'Keefe at Rensselaer Polytechnic Institute, but you will learn what it can do for you and your business. The relatively small number of carefully selected links, updated frequently, provide excellent examples of how organizations large and small are creating a presence on the Web. Save a few that you particularly like (or dislike) to disk and study their use of HTML.

☆☆☆☆ PC Week Navigator's World Wide Web Tools

`http://www.pcweek.ziff.com/~pcweek/WebTools.html`

A good site with links to all the essential HTML documents and products. Not as extensive as the Virtual Library site, but a good place for beginners looking to build a basic HTML library.

☆☆☆ Subjective Electronic Information Repository

`http://cbl.leeds.ac.uk/nikos/doc/repository.html`

Although you'd never be able to tell from the name, if it has to do with WWW or HTML, it's probably listed among the hundreds of links here. Finding a particular tool, site, or document could take some time and effort, however. This site can be slow, and there's little in the way of explanation, so you'll probably have to rely on trial and error. Also, some sections, particularly "Manuals and FAQs," are too Unix-oriented. If you decide to check this site out, be sure to peruse the links at "How to Do Fancy Stuff" and "About HTML."

☆☆☆ TECFLA WWW and Internet Manuals, Demos, and Guides

http://tecfa.unige.ch/info-www.html

TECFLA stands for "Technologies de Formation et Apprentissage," part of the University of Geneva, which explains why some of the links from this site are to French articles and software. Ignore the icons at the top of the page; it's hard to tell what they do, anyway. (For example, clicking on the icon of a bottle and trashcan takes you to the "ftp dump," an archive of mostly French files.) In fact, skip everything and go directly to "Help for WWW Information Providers" (currently page 4). Here you'll find well-organized and helpfully annotated links, although the page could use some pruning to remove dead sites and revise changed ones. Links to icon archives, image-processing programs, and Netscape-specific sites are particularly helpful.

☆☆☆☆☆ Virtual Library: WWW Development Section

http://www.stars.com/Vlib/

This extremely useful site, part of the Virtual Library by Alan Richmond at NASA's Goddard Space Flight Center, contains hundreds of links to interesting resources for Web publishers, organized by topic. From *annotation* to *forms* to *VR*, if it has to do with Web development, you'll find it here. If you've been Web surfing for a while, you'll especially appreciate the nonglamorous but highly usable format, which minimizes scrolling. This is one for your hotlist.

☆☆☆☆ Web Communications Home Page

http://www.webcom.com

Unnapologetically a marketing vehicle for Web Communications, a "WWW presence provider," it still provides lots of good information. Unlike many broader sites that devote only part of their space to Web publishing, this one is targeted strictly at those who want to set up a full-blown Web site. It's especially useful if you're interested in doing business on the Web, since it covers advanced Web topics like security, forms creation, and clickable image maps. You can also get a short manual from here, "Web Communication's Comprehensive Guide to Publishing on the Web." While I might not call this manual "comprehensive," it does have a few special sections that set it apart from similar guides, notably "How to Widely Publicize Your Site."

☆☆☆ The Web Developer's Virtual Library

http://www.charm.net/~web/

This is not a particularly big or well-organized site, but it's got some great links, including job banks for Web developers (for when you're ready to cash in on all the time you've invested learning HTML), tutorials, and "Ask Dr. Web," a help desk staffed by volunteers.

☆☆☆☆☆ The World Wide Web—Tools for Aspiring Web Weavers

http://www.nas.nasa.gov/NAS/WebWeavers/

Starting with just this extremely helpful, well-organized site, you could get everything you'd need to learn HTML, and then design, publish, and manage your own Web pages. You'll find links to news, tools, tutorials, technical standards, documentation, and more. Fast and uncluttered, WebWeavers is a good example of efficient HTML design in its own right. Definitely one to add to your hotlist.

☆☆☆☆ The WWW and HTML Developers' Jumpstation

http://oneworld.wa.com/htmldev/devpage/dev-page.html

If you spend much time at all Web-surfing for HTML-related areas, you're sure to see lots of references to this one. Links to sites for art and graphics are particularly helpful. Note, though, that it deals more with the Mosaic Web browser than with Netscape.

Web and HTML FAQs and Docs

The following sites provide information about the history and use of HTML in varying degrees of detail and readability.

☆☆☆ Beginner's Guide to HTML

http://www.ncsa.uiuc.edu/demoweb/html-primer.html

This classic introductory guide from NCSA is quite well done, especially the section on troubleshooting. The site itself, however, can be very slow. Also, the material is geared toward NCSA's own Mosaic browser rather than Netscape, although this isn't too much of a problem in a basic text.

☆☆☆☆☆ Composing Good HTML

http://ww.williamette.edu/html-composition/strict-html.html

Despite its Unix orientation, this document should be required reading for would-be Web publishers. To make this as easy as possible, it's available online or can be downloaded as either a hyper text document or a standard text file. "Composing Good HTML" picks up where other style guides and primers leave off, with practical advice on good Web publishing practices, common errors, and things to avoid.

☆☆☆☆ Entering the World Wide Web: A Guide to Cyberspace

http://www.eit.com:80/web/www.guide/guide.toc.html

This attractive, introductory text by Kevin Hughes contains, among other things, a wonderfully concise and readable explanation of HTML and URLs. If you're just beginning to wonder what you can do with the Web—or better yet, if you're trying to impress your boss with what it can do—this site, with its strong "gee whiz" quotient, is the place to go. Note, though, that you'll need to overlook some Unix terminology—or you might as well start getting used to it, since you'll see it everywhere on the Net.

☆☆☆ How to Write HTML Files

http://kcgl1.eng.ohio-state.edu/www/doc/htmldoc.html

A little outdated (we're actually talking a few months, but that can be a long time in cyberspace), this document is still a good place to get started figuring out what HTML is and how to use it. The bulk of this site is divided into sections for beginning, intermediate, and advanced users, so you can dive in at the appropriate place. The writing is straightforward. Note that this can be a slow site.

☆☆☆ HTML Documentation Table of Contents

http://www.utirc.utoronto.ca/HTMLdocs/NewHTML/htmlindex.html

Just like it says, this is the home page for an introductory HTML guide by Ian Graham, a professor at the University of Toronto. A good, solid introduction.

☆ Hyper Text MarkUp Language

http://www.w3.org/hypertext/WWW/MarkUp/MarkUp.html

From CERN, the developers of the Web itself, this one is *the* technical paper describing the history and current status of existing and upcoming versions of

HTML. If you're a Web historian or researcher, this is great; if you just want to put up a few Web pages as quickly and painlessly as possible, this is more than you need to know.

☆ W3 Server Software

`http://www.w3.org/hypertext/WWW/Daemon/Overview.html`

Another CERN site, this document is pretty heavy going. Try this introductory sentence, "A W3 server, like the ftp daemon, is a program which responds to an incoming tcp connection and provides a service to the caller." If that piques your interest, have fun; otherwise, leave it for the really seriously Web-minded.

HTML Tools and Related Stuff

Here are the sites that are jam-packed with goodies to help you create HTML documents using a word processor such as Ami Pro or Word for Windows. Tools are also featured to help you write better HTML documents.

☆☆ Amiweb12.zip

`ftp://oak.oakland.edu/SimTel/win3/amipro/`

Are you an Ami Pro aficionado feeling left out by all the Word-to-HTML converters available for the downloading? Get this freeware Ami Pro add-on, similar to the popular Word-based HTML Assistant, and join in the fun!

☆☆☆☆ HaL Software Systems

`http://www.halsoft.com/html-val-svc/index.html`

Once you've written a few HTML documents, go to this site by Mark Gaither to have them validated (checked to see whether they're in proper syntax). Just enter the URL of the page you want to check or type text in manually, select the level of standards that you want, and instantly see how well you've done.

☆☆ HTML Author

`http://www.salford.ac.uk/docs/depts/iti/staff/gsc/htmlauth/summary.html`

HTML Author provides a Word for Windows 6.0 template and macros for writing HTML pages in Word. In addition to basic features, it supports simple tables, as well as non-English versions of Word. It also formats pages based on Netscape displays. That's the good news. The bad news: This site can be painfully slow.

☆☆☆ HTML Converters

http://union.ncsa.uiuc.edu:80/HyperNews/get/www/html/converters.html

You'll find links to dozens of sites for news, utilities, word processing macros, and conversion programs for HTML here. DOS/Windows, Mac, and Unix sites are included. Not very well organized, but lots of good links.

☆☆ HTML Writer home page

http://lal.cs.byu.edu/people/nosack/index.html

Under construction and not updated as often as it should be, this site is primarily for downloading HTML Writer, a "donationware" Windows HTML editor. The software has several useful features, including a Test function that supports all major Web browsers and a Remove Tags function. Even if you're not interested in HTML Writer, this site is worth a look for its "WWW and HTML Information and Resources" links, including some relatively hard-to-find sites.

☆☆ Internet Assistant

http://www.microsoft.com/pages/deskapps/word/ia/default.htm

This Word-to-HTML toolkit from Microsoft is available for English, French, and German versions of Word 6.0a and later. It automatically turns Word documents into simple Web pages, with *simple* being the operative word. If you want to do fancy stuff, you'll still have to write HTML code. It also allows Word to be used as a somewhat limited Web browser—but with Netscape around, why bother? Be warned: It can be a slow download.

☆☆☆☆☆ Net Software for Windows PCs

http://www.utirc.utoronto.ca/HTMLdocs/pc_tools.html

Unlike other HTML-related sites, this one concentrates strictly on DOS and Windows. (Yes, there are a few DOS links, despite the name.) Frank explanations and reviews of its links are extremely helpful and can save a lot of online time. I have only one complaint: It's too short!

☆☆☆☆ Tools for World Wide Web Providers

http://www.w3.org/hypertext/WWW/Tools/

This popular, well-maintained Web space from CERN contains a large list of links to HTML filters, editors, validators, converters, and more.

☆☆☆ Word Viewer

http://www.microsoft.com/pages/deskapps/word/ia/default.htm

Part of Microsoft's vision to make Word the lingua franca of the Web, this program enables non-Word users to view and print Word documents exactly as they would appear in native format. If everyone had a copy of this, we wouldn't need anything else to use Word-based online sites, or so the marketers from Microsoft suggest. Word Viewer is freeware; in fact, Microsoft encourages its distribution. (Hmmm....wonder why?)

CGI and VRML

You say you've completely mastered HTML and are looking for a new challenge? Check out the next generation of HTML, called *CGI* (the Common Gateway Interface)—and the generation beyond that, called *VRML* (Virtual Reality Modeling Language)—at these sites.

☆☆☆☆ The Common Gateway Interface

http://hoohoo.ncsa.uiuc.edu/cgi/overview.html

If you're curious about CGI, which can serve as a way to allow greater interactivity between your Web site and its users, check out this page. With the help of the CGI programs and information archived here, visitors to your Web pages can fill out forms, take surveys, play games, and more. This NCSA site is not for beginners, but then, neither is CGI.

☆☆☆ WebSpace home page

http://www-sgi.com/Products/WebFORCE/WebSpace/

Silicon Graphic's WebSpace is a 3D browser for sites designed with VRML, possible heir to HTML. Presently, you'll only be able to use WebSpace if you're running Windows NT, but it's supposed to be available soon for the rest of the Windows family, as well as the Power Mac. Get the FAQs on VRML and WebSpace, download the software, and then sample some Doom-like VRML sites from here. Note, though, that the links at this site are definitely not for slow modems or computers, and are best explored during non-peak hours.

☆☆ *Wired*'s VRML Forum

http://vrml.wired.com/

An "open forum" from *Wired* magazine, this site contains a loose collection of VRML papers, proposals, and projects. If you're interested in the cutting edge of Web design and can follow the techno-jargon, this is the place to hang out with VRML researchers and programmers.

Adding Sights (and Sounds) to Your Site

To get in on the emerging multimedia Web publishing frontier, here are some useful tools, icons, art, and music.

☆☆☆☆ Graphics Viewers, Editors, Utilities, and Information

`http://www2.ncsu.edu:80/bae/people/faculty/walker/hotlist/graphics.html`

Yes, it's a long and clumsy URL to type in, but you'll probably only type it in once because you'll want to add it to your hotlist. You'll find over 100 links to great sources of help for working with graphics, video, and animation.

☆☆☆ Icons from Rutgers University

`http://www.ns.rutgers.edu/doc-images/`

You'll find dozens of GIF icons, buttons, and logos here. Unless you can handle Unix-based tar compression, you'll have to download them individually; they're small though, so it's not much of a problem. (Mac and PC-compressed archives are said to be coming soon.)

☆☆☆☆ Images, Icons, and Flags

`http://www/nosc.mil/planet_earth/images.html`

Most of the photographs and illustrations cataloged at this site have to do with nature and space, not surprisingly, since this page is part of the Planet Earth Web site. You can use a few GIFs directly from here, but you'll probably use it most for its comprehensive system of links to sources of art all over the Web. There's a lot to dig through here, but if you need images that can be processed into attractive icons and logos, it's worthwhile.

☆☆☆ Music Resources on the Net

`http://www.music.indiana.edu/misc/music_resources.html`

Interested in adding some sounds to your sites? You'll find nearly 800 links to all kinds of music here, from accordions to ZZ Top. Many of the files here are in AU format, rather than the more commonly used WAV or MIDI formats, so you'll need to make your selections carefully. You'll also need to make sure you're not stepping on any musical toes: Much of the stuff here is copyrighted, so be sure to read those readme files thoroughly. (Also check out the resources listed in the "Legalities" section of this chapter.)

☆☆☆ The Transparent/Interlaced GIF Resource

`http://dragon.jpl.nasa.gov/~adam/transparent.html`

Download these tools and supporting documentation to create particularly cool-looking GIFs for any environment: DOS/Windows, Mac, or Unix.

☆ WWW Icon Collection

`http://www.bsdi/com/icons/`

This short page has only three links, but these links contain hundreds of icons, most in the public domain. However, almost all of them are in XPM or XBM format instead of GIF, making them of limited use for DOS/Windows.

☆☆☆☆ Yahoo's Music List

`http://www.yahoo.com/Entertainment/Music`

Links to thousands of sound and music resources, organized by type, are found here. If you can hear it and get it on the Net, you can get it from this site.

Free Art

If you're not an artist, you'll want to have a ready supply of free art that you can use. Here are some of the better stocked sites to help you spice up your Web pages.

☆☆☆☆ Sandra's Clip Art Server

`http://www.cs.yale.edu/HTML/YALE/CS/HyPlans/loosemore-sandra/clipart.html`

This is the place to go if you are looking for great clip art. Here you'll find useful clip art collections from other archive sites on the Internet. The pictures were collected from a variety of sources, including various public-domain Amiga, Atari, PC, and Macintosh clip art collections. Many useful color clip art images are also available.

☆☆☆ Department of Computer Science Icon Browser

`http://www.di.unipi.it/iconbrowser/icons.html`

This site features a collection of useful icons that you can use to create your own Web pages. All of the icons are displayed in tables so that you can view all of them and find the one you want.

☆☆☆☆☆ Public Domain Web Art by Poppe-Tyson Advertising

`http://www.poppe.com`

This is the home page of the company that designed Web art and pages for Netscape. If you are looking for some useful free art and some great design ideas, this is one of the better places to hang out.

Legalities

Confused about who has the legal right to do what in cyberspace? You're not alone; law on the Net frontier is complicated and still being defined. If you're going to publish there or use what others have published, you'd better keep an eye on its evolving status, starting with these sites.

☆☆ Copyright Act of 1976, as amended (1994)

`http://www.law.cornell.edu:80/usc/17/overview.html`

A hyper text version of the basic U.S. copyright law. It's surely not much fun, but you should browse through it anyway for a basic understanding of how to protect what you put on the Web, as well as legal use of what others have put there.

☆☆☆ Copyrights in Cyberspace

`http://www.digital.com/gnn/bus/nolo/copy.html`

This brief and readable article from Nolo Press's Web space explains how copyright law affects you as a user and publisher of online material. It also includes a link to an order form for the author's book, *The Copyright Handbook*.

☆ Law on the Internet

`ftp://midnight.com/pub/LegalList/`

Download this shareware file (you're supposed to pay if you actually print it) for 429K worth of legal resources all over the Net. Note, however, that many of the sites listed here are newsgroups or e-mail lists, not Web sites.

☆☆ Villanova Law School Legal Automation Papers

`gopher://ming.law.vill.edu/11/.efl/`

This gopher menu contains reports and articles related to intellectual property rights in cyberspace. Most of this stuff is not exactly light reading (surprise!), but it's good to know it's there if you—or your lawyer—needs it.

Periodicals (Online and on Paper) Related to Web Publishing

You'll only find one magazine in this section that rated more than three stars (and that one is actually an online one, or *ezine*). It's not that there aren't good Net-related magazines—in fact, there's a glut of them, with a new one appearing almost every month. However, none is aimed directly and exclusively at Web publishers; most concentrate on articles that are variations of "Wow, check out this cool site I found" instead of "Wow, check out this cool site I made."

The magazines discussed in this section, therefore, vary from issue to issue in their attention to Web and HTML topics—great one month, negligible the next. Unless some enterprising publisher steps in to fill the gap, keep an eye on these at the newsstand (real or virtual), and buy or download them in the good months.

☆☆☆ *Boardwatch* (ISSN 1054-2760)

This magazine represents the opposite end of the design spectrum from other popular Net-related magazines, especially *Wired*, with their wild color and type combinations. In fact, it's downright plain, reminiscent of the *Commodore User* era of computer periodicals. But don't buy it for the pictures, buy it for the articles. *Boardwatch* is the only widely distributed magazine for the creators rather than the users of bulletin board systems and, by extension, Web sites. As such, you'll find it a good source for instruction, problem-solving ideas, and as a forum to share the experiences of running a site.

☆☆☆☆ *GNN NetNews*

`http://nearnet.gnn.com/gnn/gnn.html`

This weekly ezine is part of The Global Network Navigator, which won honorable mention for Most Important Service Concept from Best of the Web '94. *GNN NetNews* is small, but full of interesting and well-written articles. (It's also sponsored by a recruiting firm, so expect a low-key ad or two in each issue.)

☆☆ *Interactivity* (ISSN 1077-8047)

This new magazine is geared toward interactive publishing, including, but not limited to, the Web. You'll have to pick and choose among the articles in any given issue. In a recent issue, for example, instructions on CD-ROM mastering are of little use to the average Web publisher, while other articles like "Guide to File Formats" and "How to Put Together a Web Site" are great.

☆☆ *Internet World* (ISSN 1064-3923)

An interesting and fun magazine, *Internet World* covers all of the Net, with side-trips into commercial online services. General emphasis is on the Web most months, but topics that specifically affect Web publishers are discussed only occasionally. Most articles include source lists with Web sites to explore.

☆☆☆ *The Net* (ISSN 1080-2681)

This new monthly has just begun to define itself. At the moment, it's all over the place, in both style and content. It's less hyper-designed than *Wired*, but still desperately seeking hipness—the premiere June 1995 issue, for example, has the page numbers "scrawled" in someone's not-too-readable handwriting. Yes, it looks cool, but it takes a moment to figure out what page you're on. On the other hand, the articles themselves are (thankfully) readable, basic-black text on white paper. Much of the magazine is devoted to new and casual users, but the pull-no-punches evaluations of books, software, and Web sites make *The Net* worthwhile browsing for Web publishers. Also in its favor, HTML tools and Web utilities, including shareware and freeware that you can get online, are reviewed candidly and concisely.

☆☆☆ The *Netsurfer Digest* home page

`http://www.netsurf.com/nsd/index.html`

Here you can subscribe to free ezines, get back issues, and link to a few related sites. You'll want to browse through the weekly *Netsurfer Digest*, but the (more or less) monthly *Netsurfer Focus* is where the real value is for Web publishers.

☆☆☆ *PC Magazine* (ISSN 0888-8507)

Don't overlook this venerable font of computer knowledge and (especially) opinion. Make sure, however, to get the network edition for coverage of Web-related news and reviews beyond what's in the regular newsstand version, as well as special features on the state of the Net.

☆ *Publish* (ISSN 0897-6007)

A monthly that bills itself as "the magazine for electronic publishing professionals" should be just what the Web weaver ordered, right? Unfortunately not in this case, where "electronic publishing" means "high-end desktop publishing." There are a few Web-related reviews and news items, but even these don't include URLs. Save your money.

☆☆ *Wired* (ISSN 1059-1028)

You've probably seen this, um, attention-getting magazine if you've been following the evolution of the Net for any amount of time. Among the articles warning about government censorship, reviewing alternative music, and so on, you'll find reviews of Web-related products and the occasional helpful article for Web publishers. Unlike some other magazines about the Net, *Wired*'s articles include plenty of Web sites for more information. You can also check out the corresponding Web site, *HotWired*, at http://www.wired.com. It's free (right now, anyway), but you have to register.

Books

By the time you read this, there will probably be many more books on HTML and Web publishing than are currently available; publishers seem to be preparing an avalanche of them. (*Warning: shameless self-congratulation follows.*) Of course, the best books are the ones you already got when you bought this bundle, but here are some others to be aware of. (*End shameless self-congratulation.*)

☆☆☆☆ *HTML Manual of Style*

by Larry Aronson (ZD Press, ISBN 1-56276-300-8)

Dry, text-heavy, and relatively short, this book is nevertheless a classic, and a good complement to *Teach Yourself Web Publishing*.

☆☆ *Managing Internet Information Services*

by Cricket Liu et al. (O'Reilly & Associates, ISBN 1-56592-062-7)

Geared too much toward Unix in its discussion of HTML tools and converters, this book nevertheless contains some helpful information on running a Net site, including a good (but too brief) discussion of legal issues and extensive sections on security.

☆☆☆☆ *Teach Yourself Web Publishing with HTML in a Week*

by Laura Lemay (Sams, ISBN 0-672-30667-0)

`http://slack.lne.com/lemay/theBook/index.html`

You *could* probably do all of this in a week, but it would be like cramming for college finals. If you take your time with this guide, you'll be richly rewarded by a thorough understanding of HTML. The extensive appendices are particularly good sources of reference material.

☆☆☆ *World Wide Web Bible*

by Bryan Pfaffenberger (MIS:Press, ISBN 1-55828-410-9)

A thorough general Web text, this book is generally well-written, with over 100 pages specifically on HTML. But hey, who drew the thumbs-down icon that shows up about every 10 pages? It's a good concept, but surely they could have found a better-looking piece of public-domain clip art on the Net!

☆ *The World Wide Web Unleashed*

by John December and Neil Randall (Sams, ISBN 0-672-30617-4)

A massive tome (over 1,000 pages), this book is already outdated, with no discussion of Netscape and only the briefest mention of CGI. Many of the URLs given here have changed or disappeared; such is the peril of publishing about the Web! It devotes only 67 pages to HTML.

Appendix E: Using the Web Surfing and Publishing CD-ROM

The companion CD-ROM contains over 130M of the best programs and clips for getting the most out of the Web, especially if you're interested in HTML and Web publishing. A few of these shareware and freeware programs and resources are described here, but see the CD-ROM directory for the complete list.

You've probably heard of shareware described as "software on the honor system." Basically, if you try it and decide to keep it, you should register and pay for it. Basic registration instructions are given for each of the shareware programs discussed here, but more details can be found in the programs themselves, usually in the form of a readme file or screen.

Freeware is fully functional software that the author has generously made available to whomever wants it, no strings attached (although commercial versions, with more features, are sometimes available). Note, however, that the author almost always retains full rights to the program, and distribution policies vary, so read any copyright information carefully before you sell your favorite freeware program to a hundred of your closest friends.

The audio and visual clips and art, images, and icons on the CD-ROM are in the public domain, which means that no single person or organization claims copyright. That means you can do whatever you want with them and to them—except, of course, claim copyright.

Enjoy!

AUDIO, VIDEO, ANIMATION, AND CLIP ART

What: Hundreds of audio and visual clips to dress up your Web pages
Where on the CD-ROM: \clips branch
Where on the Net: Various sites

You'll find over 40M worth of audio, video, animation, and image files on the CD. All the clips can be run directly from the CD as long as the appropriate player or viewer program is installed on your PC. They provide examples, inspirations, and the beginning of your own collection of multimedia goodies to add to your Web pages.

Audio

The audio files in WAV format provide sound effects for every conceivable situation, while the MIDI files provide pieces of music in styles ranging from classical to country. One especially nice thing about the MIDI files here is that they're not tiny pieces that seem to be over before they've begun—some play as long as 10 minutes! You can play the audio files with Windows' own Sound Recorder and Media Player accessories, or, for cooler-looking control panels and more playback options, use the Wham and Wplay programs in the \helper branch of the CD.

Images

If you've been looking longingly at all the nifty buttons, bullets, lines, and icons on other people's Web pages, check out the files in \clips\images and \clips\art. They're public domain and ready to use in GIF, BMP, and PCX formats. If one of these clips is almost, but not quite, right for your purpose, just install Paint Shop Pro from the CD (discussed later in this chapter) and change it!

Video and Animation

The animation and video files in \clips\animatio and \clips\video will provide examples and inspiration when you're ready to add movement to your Web site. To run the FLC and FLI files, use the AAplayer program in \helpers\waaplay. You can play it right from the CD, or, if you prefer, copy it to the hard disk. In either case, run aawin.exe, choose File|Open Animation, select the one you want to watch, click the >> (play) button, and watch it go. You can even add WAV or MIDI sound effects if you like, using File|Get Sound. The Truespace animations can be run by the ViewSpace program, discussed later in this chapter.

Two types of video clips are included on the CD: AVI and MPEG. AVI videos can be run by Windows' Media Player accessory, but MPEG requires the MPEGplayer program discussed later in this chapter.

HomePage Creator

What: Visual home page designer tool
Where on the CD-ROM: \tools\hpc

HomePage Creator is a brand new tool that is included with this book to help you automatically create your own page. It's not just another HTML editor. It allows you to insert a picture, text, and links to your favorite sites on the Web and then it does the dirty work of generating HTML tags for you. This program is covered in more detail in Chapter 9.

The installation procedure for HomePage Creator is easy: Just run the SETUP.EXE program in the directory \tools\hpc. You'll need to specify the directory where you want to install the HomePage Creator program. The developer of this program, Demetris Kafas, is currently developing a more feature-rich version of HomePage Creator that you'll be able to purchase in the future.

HotMetal

What: HTML editor
Where on the CD-ROM: \tools\hotmetal
Where on the Net: ftp://ftp.ncsa.uiuc.edu/Web/html/hotmetal/

HotMetal is a Windows-based, freeware HTML editor from SoftQuad. An HTML editor is a stand-alond program; it's used by itself to write Web pages, not added on to a word porcessor or other program.

HotMetal has several elements that make it a good choice for beginning HTML publishers. It sticks to the basic, standard features of HTML, so you won't be overwhelmed by dozens of different tags. In fact, selecting Hide Tags from the View menu lets you ignore the tags altogether, so you can read just the text on the page that, for example, you saved to disk from someone else's Web site. Also from the View menu, the Structure function creates an "outline" of your document, so you can keep track of its links without driving yourself crazy.

Best of all, HotMetal comes with 14 templates for typical documents like home pages, customer registration forms, and hotlists. Just choose File | Open Template, pick the appropriate one from the list, type your text in between the tags, save it as an HTM file, and voila!—instant HTML. Be sure to start with readme3.htm, a template that describes the other templates.

It is possible to run HotMetal straight from the CD, but installing it on your hard disk is more practical. It's not self-installing, so you'll have to copy the entire \hotmetal branch from the CD to the root directory of your hard drive, and then make an icon for it as follows:

1. In Program Manager, open the group in which you want HotMetal to belong.
2. Choose File|New. The Program Item option should be selected. Click OK, and the Program Item Properties dialog box should appear.
3. Type *Hot Metal* in the Description box.
4. Click Browse and navigate through your hard disk until you find sqhm.exe. Click on that file to select it, then click OK.
5. Click OK again, and the HotMetal icon should appear in your group.

HotMetal takes up only about 5M of hard disk space, but is fairly greedy for memory, so unless you have plenty of RAM to spare, it's a good idea to shut down other programs when you run it.

HTML Assistant

What: HTML editor
Where on the CD-ROM: \tools\htmlasst
Where on the Net: http://fox.nstn.ca/~harawitz/htmlpro1.html

HTML Assistant is an extremely popular, freeware HTML editor for Windows. Like HotMetal, it's a stand-alone program for creating Web pages. The two differ, however, in their approach and specific set of features. HTML doesn't come with a wide variety of prewritten templates like HotMetal does, but makes up for it with an elegant interface and, especially, an easy-to-use Test function that lets you see how your page will actually look on the Web.

The installation procedure for HTML Assistant is basically the same as for Hot Metal: Copy the directory and create a program icon. The file that runs HTML Assistant (step 4 in the installation instructions listed for HotMetal) is different from the one for HotMetal, of course; the one to browse for here is htmlasst.exe.

To create a page with HTML Assistant, start by choosing Command\Display Standard Document Template. This will bring up a skeleton Web page with basic codes. Add your text, and then add other elements by clicking on them from the toolbars or selecting them from the menus. When your page looks ready, choose Save and type in the filename, including the HTM extension. **Important:** You have to explicitly type *.htm*; it won't be added for you, and without it, your pages won't display properly.

The real fun starts after you've saved a document. Click the Test button. The first time you do this, you'll be asked for the test program name—the file name of the browser program you use. HTML Assistant will then run the browser, and your pages will appear just as they would on the Web! Note, however, that you have to end the browser yourself so HTML Assistant can restart it the next time you want to test a page. Once you've gotten the hang of basic HTML, dive into HTML Assistant's extensive support for URLs and start linking things up.

MPEGplay version 1.65

What: Player for MPEG videos
Where on the CD-ROM: \helpers\mpegpla
Where on the Net: ftp://ftp.cica.indiana.edu
ftp://gatekeeper.dec.com/pub/micro/msdos/win3/desktop/

MPEGplay is a very fast video player for Win32s and WinG. If you don't already have either of these Windows extensions, Win32s is available as freeware on the CD-ROM. Install it on your hard disk by running \win32s\disk1\setup.exe before installing MPEGplay.

MPEGplay's interface looks like a VCR, with the standard rewind, stop, and play buttons, plus an extra one that allows a video clip to be played frame-by-frame. To get the most out of any machine, MPEGplay gives the user control over the number of colors displayed in the clip and the size of the window. If you have a fast machine, you can set these options high for the best detail; if you have a slower machine, you can sacrifice a little detail for less jerky motion. You can even choose Movie|Time Play to find out how fast your PC is playing the video, in frames per second.

MPEGplay is shareware. If you find it useful, support it by sending $25 (U.S.) for a single-user license to

Michael Simmons
P.O. Box 506
Nedlands WA 6009
Australia

The included register.txt file has more details.

Paint Shop Pro version 3.0

What: Image conversion and enhancement program
Where on the CD-ROM: \helpers\psp
Where on the Net: http://www.internet.com:80/~jasc/

Paint Shop Pro, from JASC Corporation, is a shareware program that gives you control of your graphics. You might use it, for example, to open a PCX file, copy a small part of it to a new window, resize and flip the new image, put a red border all around it, and save it as a GIF file. It would then be ready to use as an icon for your Web pages.

Paint Shop Pro has several features that have made it the standard shareware graphics-conversion program for several years:

- Screen capture
- Multiple document windows
- Filters for special effects
- Support for over file formats
- TWAIN scanner support
- Batch conversion, so you can, for example, turn ten WMF images into GIFs with a single click

Paint Shop Pro is self-installing; just run setup.exe from the CD. If you use the program for more than 30 days, buy it by sending $69 to

JASC, Inc.
10901 Red Circle Drive, Suite 340
Minnetonka, MN 55343

ViewSpace

What: 3D animation program
Where on the CD-ROM: \helpers\viewspace\disk1

ViewSpace is a freeware 3D animation and rendering program from Caligari Corporation. You can use it with objects that have been created separately by a CAD program, or with Truespace animations. ViewSpace is relatively easy to use, but at first you'll probably want to make use of its online help. (You might need to resize the program window to see the Help menu. Unlike most Windows programs, ViewSpace's menu bar is at the bottom of the window.)

To run an animation, you simply choose File | Animation. To create an animation, you first position your wireframe objects in the 3D space by choosing File | Load Object. Then, using the tools at the bottom of the window, you can move, rotate, render (add surfaces and depth), and ultimately animate them.

ViewSpace is self-installing; just run vsetup.exe. Note, however, that ViewSpace is not for slower computers. To really use it, you'll need a fast 486 or a Pentium with plenty of RAM and a fast video card.

Web Spinner

What: HTML editor
Where on the CD-ROM: \tools\webspin

Web Spinner is the new kid on the block of HTML editors. It is a very powerful but easy-to-use editor for creating HTML documents. Web Spinner is a snap to install and get started with. You just need to make sure that you have Win32s installed on your computer if you are running Windows 3.1. If you are running Windows 95, you won't need Win32s to run Web Spinner. To learn more about how to use Web Spinner, see Chapter 10 where we use it to create a home page and a complete HTML style guide.

Epilogue

Well, it looks like we both made it to the end of the book! In some ways, the book's completion makes me sad. If you want, you can send me a note at LeJeune@acy.digex.net to cheer me up.

It seems like yesterday when my publisher at The Coriolis Group, Keith Weiskamp said, "How would you like to turn the Mosaic book into a World Class Netscape book?" The road hasn't always been smooth, but Keith didn't just help me over the rough spots, he cleared them away.

One of the frustrating aspects of writing a book on the World Wide Web and its associated products is the rate of change. The day after the CD-ROM went out for stamping, a new version of an included program was released. How can we best cope with the dynamic entity we lovingly call the Internet? How best to update a book committed to paper and ink? Perhaps "the Internet taketh away and the Internet shall giveth back...."

I have added a pointer to my home page called, "Late Breaking News." It lists things that have changed since the publication of this book. (The book had to stop somewhere and I had lots more material than we could reasonably include.) I conceptualize the Late Breaking News page as a sort of "ongoing epilogue" to this book. The URL for my home page is

```
http://www.charm.net/~lejeune/
```

and the URL for Late Breaking News is:

```
http://www.charm.net/~lejeune/latenews.html
```

I've also added a pointer to good things that fell to the editors' scissors; the URL to these gems is:

```
http://www.charm.net/~lejeune/net-cut.html
```

You should also check out the cool Web site belonging to The Coriolis Group, the publisher of this book. You'll find additional material about this book and other Internet titles including a handy *Mosaic EXplorer Pocket Companion* for exploring Netscape and the Web. You'll even find a complete online guide to getting hundreds of free goodies from the Internet. To get there, point your browser to:

```
http://www.coriolis.com/coriolis
```

As a branch off my home page, I've added a menu of all the URLs contained in this book, listed by chapter and page number. The idea behind this menu is two-fold; it will save you the trouble of typing in long URLs and it will keep the list current. If a URL changes, I'll make sure to change it on the menu. The URL to this list is:

```
http://www.charm.net/~lejeune/net-url.html
```

If you're considering creating a home page of your own, and your Internet provider doesn't offer a way for you to place you page on the Web, drop me a note. I have an very inexpensive way for you to get published.

I would truly appreciate any and all input and feedback. If you find anything in the book needing correction or addition, please let me know. If you have any questions, I'll try to help.

Most of all, enjoy your status as a certified Webspace Explorer. I think Jeff would call you a Webhead; I wouldn't be quite so crass. Paraphrasing what they tell you when you graduate from just about anything, "You are awarded the title, Professional HTML Devotee, Ph.D.—with all the rights and privileges appertaining thereto." If I only knew Latin, I would really lay it on you.

Thanks for reading the book and, as Jeff always says, "Keep in touch."

Urb LeJeune lejeune@acy.digex.net
43 Willis Dr.
Tuckerton, NJ 08087

INDEX

—A—

—B—

—C—

—D—

—E—

—F—

—G—

—H—

—J—

—K—

—L—

—S—

—T—

—V—

—W—

The Coriolis Group Home Page!

You'll be able to browse our wide selection of books and order them directly online, get a sneak preview of upcoming titles, and check out the latest issue of ***PC TECHNIQUES*** Magazine. Just set your Web browser to:
http://www.coriolis.com/coriolis

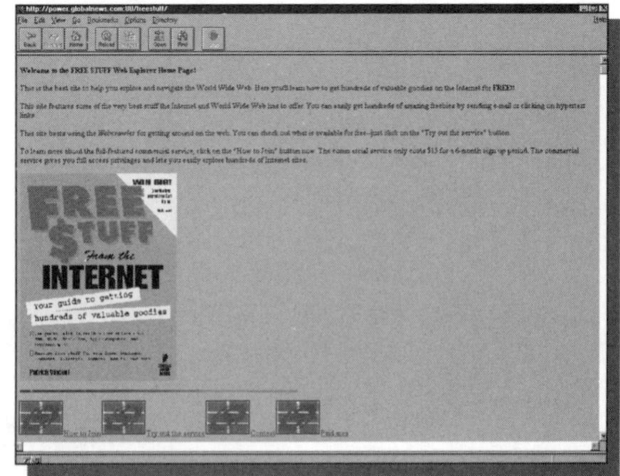

And don't forget to stop by the FREE $TUFF Web site where you'll get access to the bestselling ***FREE $TUFF from the Internet***—absolutely free. And if you want to cruise on over into the paid area, you'll get the hypertext links that will take you directly to all the FREE $TUFF you could ever want!! Set your Web browser to:
http://power.globalnews.com/freestuff

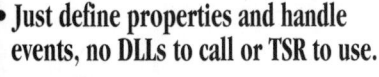